Reconstruction
in the United States

Recent Titles in
Bibliographies and Indexes in American History

Reconstruction in the United States

An Annotated Bibliography

Compiled and Annotated by
David A. Lincove

Foreword by Eric Foner

Bibliographies and Indexes in American History, Number 43

GREENWOOD PRESS
Westport, Connecticut • London

Library of Congress Cataloging-in-Publication Data

Lincove, David A.
  Reconstruction in the United States : an annotated bibliography / compiled and
annotated by David A. Lincove ; foreword by Eric Foner.
      p.   cm.—(Bibliographies and indexes in American history, ISSN 0742–6828 ; no. 43)
  Includes indexes.
  ISBN 0–313–29199–3 (alk. paper)
  1. Reconstruction—Bibliography.   I. Title.   II. Series.

  Z1242.8.L56   2000
  [E668]
  016.9738—dc21   99–053148

British Library Cataloguing in Publication Data is available.

Library of Congress Catalog Card Number: 99–053148
ISBN: 0–313–29199–3
ISSN: 0742–6828

First published in 2000

Greenwood Press, 88 Post Road West, Westport, CT 06881
An imprint of Greenwood Publishing Group, Inc.
www.greenwood.com

Printed in the United States of America

The paper used in this book complies with the
Permanent Paper Standard issued by the National
Information Standards Organization (Z39.48–1984).

10 9 8 7 6 5 4 3 2 1

For My Parents

Dan and Barbara Lincove

Contents

State and Local Reconstruction in the South

Acknowledgments

I would like to extend my gratitude to Ohio State University Libraries, directed by William Studer, for providing me with research leaves and travel funds that were vital in the preparation of this book. The O.S.U. Libraries is a rich source for published literature on Reconstruction, and what the library does not own was partially made up through the exceptional services of the Interlibrary Loan Department, led by Jennifer Kuehn, and the lending services provided by the OhioLink libraries and many other libraries throughout the United States. Other institutions that I visited provided additional resources, particularly the libraries at the Ohio Historical Society, University of Kentucky, Vanderbilt University, Tulane University, and the Methodist Theological School in Ohio.

Many thanks go to individuals who gave me assistance. I would like to thank John David Smith (North Carolina State University Department of History) for taking the time while teaching in Germany to read a draft of the manuscript and offer valuable suggestions and comments. Jose Diaz (O.S.U. Libraries) also read the manuscript and offered me important help with editing the work. I appreciate the discussions that we had about the bibliography and his words of encouragement. Thanks are due to Eric Foner (Columbia University Department of History) for writing the "Foreword" and examining a portion of the book. Additional assistance and encouragement were provided by Michael Les Benedict (O.S.U. Department of History), and O.S.U. library colleagues Steve Rogers, James Bracken, and Jean Ives. At Greenwood Press, Cynthia Harris, history reference editor, was always ready to answer my questions, and Frank Saunders, production editor, provided valuable editorial assistance. My wife, Merry Lynne, had to endure the years of work that I put into this book, and I am most grateful for her patience and support.

Foreword

A century and a quarter after it came to a close, Reconstruction remains perhaps the most controversial and least understood era of American history. The term itself applies both to a specific period of the nation's past and to a prolonged and difficult process by which Americans sought to reunite a nation sundered by the Civil War, and come to terms with the destruction of slavery. As a chronological period, Reconstruction is usually said to have begun in 1865, with the Union's victory in the Civil War, although in reality steps toward reuniting the nation and recasting Southern life began during the war itself. The era of Reconstruction ended in 1877, when the federal government irrevocably abandoned the idea of intervening in the South to protect the rights of black citizens. As a historical process through which sectional reconciliation was achieved and a new system of labor and race relations devised to replace the shattered world of slavery, Reconstruction lasted at least to the end of the nineteenth century.

Historical writing on Reconstruction began during the era itself, and continues to the present day. Reconstruction scholarship, one historian has written, is a "dark and bloody ground," a vast body of writing marked by sharp differences of opinion and radical changes in interpretation, especially in the last two generations. It is remarkable that the work that follows, by David Lincove, is the first comprehensive annotated bibliography of Reconstruction scholarship. It is indeed a daunting achievement not simply to compile this extensive listing of scholarly writings on Reconstruction, including selected scholarship on fiction, but to offer the prospective researcher a well-considered introduction to each and every item selected except for dissertations. Because of the range of subjects covered from national and local politics to law, economics, religion, education, gender relations, violence, and numerous other aspects of the period and the extremely valuable brief comments on each entry, *Reconstruction in the United States* will undoubtedly prove indispensable to scholars for many years to come.

Readers who peruse this volume will quickly get a sense of the remarkable creativity of scholars of Reconstruction in the past thirty years. Until then, the prevailing interpretation viewed the period as one of unrelieved sordidness in political and social life. The villains of the piece were vindictive Radical Republicans, who sabotaged Andrew Johnson's lenient plan for bringing the South back into the Union, and instead fastened black supremacy upon the defeated Confederacy. An orgy of corruption and misgovernment allegedly followed, only brought to a close when the South's white communities banded together to restore "home rule" (a polite euphemism for white supremacy). Resting on the assumption that black suffrage was the gravest error of the entire Civil War period, this interpretation survived for decades because it accorded with and legitimated firmly entrenched political and social realities, including radical segregation and the disenfranchisement of southern black voters (which lasted from around 1900 to 1965).

Although some scholars had already challenged elements of this point of view, it was not until the 1960s, the decade of the civil rights revolution or "second Reconstruction," that the traditional interpretation was entirely dismantled. Once they discarded the assumption of black incapacity, historians came to view Reconstruction as a praiseworthy effort to build an interracial democracy from the ashes of slavery. The era was portrayed as a time of extraordinary progress in the South; indeed, if Reconstruction was "tragic," it was because change did not go far enough, especially in the failure to distribute land to the former slaves. But in the federal civil rights laws and Fourteenth and Fifteenth Amendments enacted during the period, Reconstruction laid the groundwork for future struggles for racial equality.

As Lincove's bibliography shows, the overthrow of the traditional interpretation of Reconstruction not only produced new scholarship on familiar issues -- the conflict between Andrew Johnson and Congress, for example -- but unleashed a flood of writing on previously neglected aspects of the period. Blacks themselves emerged as major historical actors, rather than victims manipulated by others. Their political and religious organizations, economic aspirations, and the social divisions among them attracted a great deal of scholarly attention. The economic transformation of the South and the complex process by which various modes of free labor replaced the labor system of slavery, became the focal point of numerous studies, especially in the 1970s and 1980s. Other historians sought to place this country's adjustment to emancipation in an international context, comparing Reconstruction in the United States with the aftermath of slavery in the Caribbean, Brazil, and elsewhere. Most recently, Reconstruction scholars, like those studying many other periods of American history, have devoted close attention to the role of gender in Reconstruction, the reconstitution òf black families, how the Civil War affected ideologies of manhood, and how freedom may have had different meanings for freed women than for their brothers and husbands.

If any single impression emerges from this volume, it is the continued vitality of Reconstruction scholarship. So long as the issues central to Reconstruction remain unresolved - the balance of power in the federal system, the place of black Americans in national life, and the relationship between economic and political democracy - the era seems certain to attract the attention of new generations of historians.

Eric Foner
DeWitt Clinton Professor of History
Columbia University

Preface

The massive and still growing collection of literature on Reconstruction illustrates the continuing interest in a crucial period in American history. Modern race relations and civil rights law can be traced from Reconstruction, and many of the themes of post-Civil War America still exist today, including racism, civil rights, states' rights, and the powers of the executive, legislative, and judicial branches of government at the federal and state levels. This bibliography is intended to enhance the access to historical writing on Reconstruction that not only sheds light on a dynamic and complicated period, but also promotes greater understanding of contemporary American society.

Defining the bounds of a bibliography of writings on Reconstruction is not clear cut. As Eric Foner notes in the Foreword, the period can be defined as a chronological period or the process of reuniting the nation and reforming the South after the Civil War. At its broadest focus, Reconstruction could begin early in the Civil War and extend beyond the 19th century based on the continuing impact of wartime and postwar reforms. In this bibliography Reconstruction begins with the wartime activities in Congress, attempts by President Abraham Lincoln to garner political support among Southern Unionists, and the initial transition of many slaves to freedom. Most of the book covers the period from 1865 to 1877 when Congress, the president, and Southerners, both black and white, struggled to reunite the nation and set a path for the future of the freedmen and the South in general. The conclusion of the period came with the controversial national elections of 1876 that led to the presidency of Rutherford B. Hayes and an end to what was left of the federal government's Reconstruction program in the South. Relevant U.S. Supreme Court decisions through the early 1880s are also included. Within this chronological context, the topics include national and Southern politics, race relations, law, labor, agriculture, education, religion, economics, business, family, and gender.

This bibliography provides students and researchers with a systematic, comprehensive tool for finding historical writing and published primary sources on Reconstruction that appeared from 1877 to 1998. The publications include books, essays in books, journal articles, doctoral dissertations, and a few masters theses that appeared as long journal articles.   Access to many of the large number of masters theses on Reconstruction is available in the footnotes and bibliographies of relevant sources, union catalogs such as O.C.L.C. *Worldcat* and R.L.I.N. (Research Libraries Information Network), *Masters' Abstracts International* (online via *Dissertation Abstracts International*), and individual library catalogs.   Users of this book should understand that extensive published and unpublished sources on Reconstruction originated from the years 1861 to 1876.   These sources serve as the basis for most research projects, but they have been left for a different compilation.   The intention in this bibliography is to focus on post-Reconstruction historical writing - literature produced by historians, critics, and participants looking back on the period or their experiences - and the first-time publication of primary materials such as diaries, memoirs, and letters.   Reprints of books published during the Civil War and Reconstruction are excluded. For the convenience of researchers, a chronology of events in Reconstruction precedes the main text, and in the Appendix there are the texts of the 13th, 14th, and 15th Amendments to the U.S. constitution and citations to federal acts and U.S. Supreme Court cases cited in the bibliography.

References are cited once and arranged topically or geographically as illustrated in the Contents.   The bibliography begins with relevant Reconstruction document collections, reference sources, pedagogical literature, and general historiography and surveys.   National politics of Reconstruction follows with emphasis on political biography, presidential administrations and policies, congressional activities, and constitutional law.   The largest part of the book focuses on the core of Reconstruction literature - the political, social, and economic life of the South after the Civil War.   The literature specifically on the South is divided geographically, beginning with regional studies presented topically followed by research on state and local issues.   The literature not only covers Reconstruction in the former states of the Confederacy - Alabama, Arkansas, Florida, Georgia, Louisiana, Mississippi, North Carolina, South Carolina, Tennessee, Texas, and Virginia - but also the changes and disruptions of life that occurred in Washington, D.C., Indian territories, and the former slaveholding border states that did not secede - Delaware, Kentucky, Maryland, Missouri, and West Virginia.

The chapter entitled "Regional Reconstruction in the South" provides a topical arrangement offering comparative literature with examinations of more than one state or a region of the South.   This literature gives a broad geographic approach for appreciating the common threads and the differences between different parts of the South on issues such as urban race relations, the Ku Klux Klan, sharecropping, and black participation in politics.   "State and Local Reconstruction in the South" is arranged by state and then topics based on the idea that while there were many similarities in the processes and activities of Reconstruction across the South, each state and locality was different.   There were variations in population, wartime experiences, and political, social, and cultural traditions. Geographic variations led to different experiences among black freedmen, levels of violence, and attitudes of whites toward black freedom.   There were also varied responses to the implementation of political reform, the work of the Freedmen's Bureau and Northern missionary organizations, and changes in education, agriculture, and economic development. The last chapter illustrates how national debates, constitutional changes, and race relations affected Reconstruction reforms in the Northern and Western states.

All references were examined and annotated by the compiler, except for doctoral dissertations. Many citations to dissertations appear as separate references, but when dissertations are closely related to books that were published in later years, they are noted in annotations. Abstracts of most of the dissertations may be found in *Dissertation Abstracts International*. The descriptive annotations in this bibliography provide information related to an author's thesis or purpose along with key names and topics of particular importance. Many annotations also include "see" and "see also" references to other items in the bibliography and to additional publications that do not appear as separately numbered items. The additional references were judged to be closely related material. As a result there are more sources cited in this book than the 2,904 numbered references. The additional items cited in annotations are indexed in the author index with an "a" following the item number (e.g. 804a) unless they are written by the same author as the main reference.

Author and subject indexes conclude the book. Users of the subject index should look up all terms or names relevant to their research and take note of "see" and "see also" references to other subject headings.

David Lincove
Ohio State University Libraries

Chronology of Major Events in Reconstruction

1861

August 6	First **Confiscation Act** authorized federal seizure of slaves employed in arms or labor against the U.S. The 2nd Confiscation Act of *July 17, 1862* proclaimed freedom for slaves held by Confederates who continued to commit treason or support the rebellion after a 60 day deadline.

1862

April 16	Congress ordered **emancipation of slaves in Washington, D.C.** and plans for the compensation of slave holders.
June 19	Congress **banned slavery from the territories.**
	Appointment of provisional military governors for Louisiana, Tennessee, and North Carolina.

1863

January 1	President Lincoln issued **Emancipation Proclamation** following his preliminary proclamation of *September 22, 1862*. All slaves are permanently emancipated in areas still controlled by the Confederacy.
March 3	**Captured and Abandoned Property Act** provided for confiscation and sale of abandoned land.
April 20	**West Virginia** admitted as new state.

July 2 — Morrill Land Grant College Act.

December 8 — President Lincoln announced **Proclamation of Amnesty and Reconstruction** to return Southern states to Union based on amnesty and finding 10% of 1860 electorate to take loyalty oath. He attempts to establish Unionist governments in Louisiana, Arkansas, Virginia, and North Carolina.

1864

July 2 — **Wade-Davis Bill** for the future Reconstruction of the South passed Congress. President Lincoln announced his pocket veto of the bill on *July 8*. The bill required a majority of the electorate to take a loyalty oath. The veto represented the growing differences between Lincoln and Congress regarding which branch of government was responsible for Reconstruction. Angered by Lincoln's veto, Senator Benjamin F. Wade and Rep. Henry Winter Davis attack the president for overstepping his authority. The **Wade-Davis Manifesto** appeared in the *New York Times* on August 5.

November 8 — **Abraham Lincoln reelected** president of the U.S.

December 6 — **Salmon P. Chase** became chief justice of the U.S. Supreme Court.

1865

February 13 — **Virginia** constitutional convention met according to Lincoln's Reconstruction plan.

March 3 — **Freedmen's Bureau** established. Congress renewed the Freedmen's Bureau on *July 16, 1866* after President Johnson vetoed the bill on constitutional grounds. Another extension passed on *July 6, 1868*.
Charter of **Freedmen's Savings and Trust Co.** issued.

April 5 — Unionist William G. Brownlow elected governor of **Tennessee**.

April 14 — President **Lincoln assassinated** in Washington, D.C. He died April 15. Andrew Johnson becomes president.

May 29 — President **Johnson announced his Reconstruction policies** to restore the former Confederate states to the Union and grant amnesty to most Confederates who took an oath of allegiance. On *December 6* the President announced that all former Confederate states have been restored to the Union.

November 24   Mississippi is the first Southern state to pass **Black Code** legislation restricting the freedom of black citizens.

December 4   **Congress refused to endorse Johnson's actions** and denied recognition to the elected governments in the South and their representatives to Congress.

December 13   **Joint Committee of Fifteen** formed by Congressional Republicans to examine the issues of suffrage and Southern representation in Congress.

December 18   **13th Amendment** abolished slavery effective after ratification by 27 states.

1866

February 8   **Southern Homestead Act** passed Congress.

April 9   Congress passed the first **Civil Rights Act** over President Johnson's veto. The act provides blacks with citizenship and equal civil rights (no mention of suffrage) for all persons born in the U.S. (except Indians). Johnson believed the bill was a violation of states' rights.

May   **Ku Klux Klan** founded in Pulaski, Tennessee.

May 1-3   **Memphis race riot** left many blacks dead and their property destroyed.

June 16   Congress submitted the **14th Amendment** to the states for ratification after passing the bill on *June 13*. Ratification by former Confederate states became a requirement for them to be restored to the Union. It was an important issue in the November Congressional elections. Ratification was achieved on *July 28, 1868*. The guarantee of federal protection of civil rights of black citizens was weakened by the **Slaughter-House Cases** decided by the U.S. Supreme Court in *1873*.

June 20   **Joint Committee of Fifteen** recommended that authority for Reconstruction lay with Congress instead of the President.

July 24   **Tennessee restored** to the Union after it ratifies 14th Amendment.

July 30   **New Orleans race riot**, set off by Republican meeting to reconsider state constitution, leaves many black and white Republican casualties. Along with the **Memphis riot** on

May 1-3, there was evidence for Congressional Republicans that Johnson's Reconstruction plan was not working to safeguard the rights and security of the freedmen and to ensure loyal governments in the South. The riots contributed to the ground swell of opinion in the North against Johnson's Reconstruction.

August 14   **National Union Party** meeting in Philadelphia was supported by President Johnson as a way to empower moderate Republicans and Democrats before the November congressional election.

August 28   **President Johnson began speaking tour,** his "Swing 'Round the Circle," designed to gain support for his Reconstruction policies. The tour ended *September 15*.

November   **Republican victories in congressional elections** empowered the Radicals to move forward with their own program for the South.

December 17   U.S. Supreme Court ruled in *ex parte Milligan* against suspension of civil courts in favor of military courts.

1867

January 14   Loyalty oath cases decided by U.S. Supreme Court in *ex parte Garland* and *Cummings v. Missouri.*

March 2   **Reconstruction Act** passed over President's veto begins Congressional (Radical) Reconstruction. Additional Reconstruction acts passed on *March 23, July 19, and March 11, 1868* to increase the powers of regional commanders to carry out the congressional program.

March 11   President appointed commanders of military districts.

1868

February 24   **President Johnson impeached** by House of Representatives (124-47) on 11 charges, including violating the Tenure of Office Act and Command of the Army Act. Both passed Congress on *March 2, 1867*.

March 30   **Senate begins trial** of the President and concluded with an acquittal on *May 16* due to lack of 2/3 majority (35 for v. 19 against).

June 22-25	Omnibus Act in **Congress readmitted Arkansas (*6/22*); Alabama, Florida, Georgia, Louisiana, North Carolina, and South Carolina (*6/25*)** to the Union. Georgia was expelled on *December 1* and readmitted on *July 15, 1870*.
October 4	Democrats defeated Republicans in **Tennessee**.
October 5	Democrats defeated Republicans in **Virginia** prior to readmission to Union.
November 3	Presidential **election resulted in victory of Republican Ulysses S. Grant** over Democrat Horatio Seymour. The black vote provided the margin of victory.

1870

January 26	**Virginia** readmitted to Union.
February 23	**Mississippi** readmitted to Union.
February 25	**Hiram Revels** became the first black U.S. senator when he replaced Jefferson Davis.
March 30	**15th Amendment** ratified. It prohibits discrimination of voting rights based on "race, color, or previous condition of servitude."
March 31	**Texas** readmitted to Union.
May 31	**Enforcement Act** passed (second and third acts pass *February 28* and *April 20, 1871*) in response to Ku Klux Klan violence against blacks in the South. Congress seeks to enforce the 14th and 15th Amendments.
August 4	Democrats defeated Republicans for control of legislature in **North Carolina**.

1871

March 3	Congress enacted **Southern Claims Commission** to reimburse Southerners who maintained loyalty to the Union for loss of property during the war.
November 1	Democrats defeated Republicans in **Georgia**.

1872

May 1   **Liberal Republicans** met at Cincinnati and **nominated Andrew Greeley for president.** Democratic Party also backed Greeley who supported economic and civil service reforms and sought an end to Reconstruction.

May 22   **Amnesty Act** removed political disabilities of all former Confederates except for about 500 former political and military leaders.

November 5   **Grant won a second term** in presidential election. Greeley died on November 29th.

1873

January 14   Democrats regained power in **Texas**.

April 14   Supreme Court decision in **Slaughter-House Cases** commenced the weakening of federal ability to enforce the 14th Amendment.

September 13   Banks owned by Jay Cooke and Co. failed, leading to the **Panic of 1873**. The economic depression was national and severely effected the South's recovery from the Civil War.

1874

November 10   Democrats defeated Republicans in **Arkansas**.

November 14   Democrats defeated Republicans in **Alabama**.

1875

March 1   **Civil Rights Act** passed to guarantee equal rights in public places without regard to race and forbids exclusion of blacks from jury duty. The act was declared unconstitutional in the **Civil Rights Cases** decided by the U.S. Supreme Court in decision of *October 15, 1883*.

November 2   **Democrats won majority in U.S. House** of Representatives.

                 Democrats defeated Republicans in **Mississippi**.

1876

March 27   U.S. Supreme Court decision in *United States v. Cruikshank* and *United States v. Reese* weakened

Enforcement Acts. ***United States v. Harris*** on *January 22, 1882* likewise.

November 7	**Presidential election** between Republican Rutherford B. Hayes and Democrat Samuel J. Tilden resulted in a controversy over who won based on disputed election returns on December 6 from Louisiana, South Carolina, Florida, and Oregon.

1877

January 2	**Democrats defeated Republican regime in Florida** state elections.
January 29	Congress established **Electoral Commission** to decide which election returns from 4 states to accept. On *February 8* it concluded by awarding electoral votes from disputed states to Hayes. The decision was made along straight party lines. On *March 2* Hayes was declared the victor by one vote in the House, but he won based on promises to Southern Democrats, including the removal of Federal troops from the South. The South promised to follow civil rights laws. The **"Compromise of 1877"** thus brings Reconstruction to an end.
April	The loss of military support led to the **end of Republican regimes in South Carolina (4/10) and Louisiana (4/24)**.

1883

October 15	Civil Rights Cases. *See under* Civil Rights Acts (March 1, 1875).

1896

May 18	U.S. Supreme Court ruled in ***Plessy v. Ferguson*** that "separate but equal" public accommodations for races is lawful under 14th Amendment.

1899

December 18	U.S. Supreme Court ruled in ***Cummings v. Georgia*** that "separate but equal" education of races is lawful under 14th Amendment.

Document Collections, Reference Sources, and Teaching Aids

1.   Adonis, James F. "Using Local History, Primary Source Material, and Comparative History to Teach Reconstruction." *Magazine of History* [OAH] 4 (Winter, 1989): 9-10.   This is the first of four articles in the winter, 1989 issue that offers ideas about teaching Reconstruction to students. Other articles include Brian C. Gunn, "Reconstruction Through Role Playing," 71-73; Lys A. Schaeffer, "Reconstruction: From the Students' Perspective," 74-77; and David M. Seiter, "Reconstruction Era: Resouces For a Balanced Approach," 78-80.

2.   *American Historical Association's Guide to Historical Literature.* 3rd Edition. Edited by Mary Beth Norton. 2 Vols. New York: Oxford University Press, 1995. Pp. 1407-1411.   Includes a very selected list of books and journal articles with annotations. See references 42.782 to 42.851.

3.   Aptheker, Herbert (ed.). *A Documentary History of the Negro People in the United States.* 2 Vols. Secaucus, NJ: Citadel Press, 1951. 942p.   Documents related to Reconstruction appear at the beginning of volume 2. Documents are taken from federal and state government publications, newspapers, books, and periodicals.

4.   Arnold, Louise. "Reconstruction." In *The Era of the Civil War--1820-1876. Special Bibliography 11.* Carlisle Barracks, Pa.: U.S. Army Military History Institute, 1982. Pp. 522-534.   Lists selected books, U.S. government documents, and theses from the period of Reconstruction to the 1970s.

5.   Baker, Gary G. *Andrew Johnson and the Struggle for Presidential Reconstruction 1865-1868.* Boston: D. C. Heath and Co., 1966. 178p. App. Tbls. This resource for high school students includes excerpts from articles, speeches, books, and other contemporary documents. Discussion questions are included.

6.   Benedict, Michael Les. *The Fruits of Victory: Alternatives in Restoring the Union, 1865-1877.* Rev. Ed. Lantham: University Press of America, 1986. 159p. Bibl. (Rpt. of J. B. Lippincott, 1975)   This book is a teaching aid for

students studying how decisions were made leading to the implementation of Reconstruction policies. The emphasis is on analyzing contemporary perspectives and issues that influenced Republicans.

7.   Bailey, Thomas Brantley, Jr.   "Historical Interpretation of the Reconstruction Era in United States History as Reflected in Southern State Required Secondary School Level Textbooks of State Histories." Ed.D. University of New Mexico, 1967. 476p.

8.   Berlin, Ira et. al.   *Freedom, A Documentary History of Emancipation, 1861-1867.*   Cambridge: Cambridge University Press, 1982-1993.   Ills. Ports. This series of letters and documents, chosen from the collection at the National Archives of the United States, illustrate the experience of black slaves as they were emancipated during the Civil War and experienced freedom for the first two years after the war.   These volumes, complied by the Freedmen and Southern Society Project, include: Series 1, vol. 1: *The Destruction of Slavery* (1985), 852p; Series 1, vol. 2: *The Wartime Genesis of Free Labor: The Upper South* (1993), 775p.; Series 1, vol. 3: *The Wartime Genesis of the Lower South* (1990), 937p.; Series 2: *The Black Military Experience* (1992), 852p. (For related volumes see # 1126, 1127. Also see *Slaves No More: Three Essays on Emancipation and the Civil War.* Ed. by Ira Berlin et. al. New York: Cambridge University Press, 1992. The essays are based principally on the documents from the above series.)

9.   Bink, Dean C. "What Did Freedom Mean?: The Aftermath of Slavery as Seen by Former Slaves and Former Masters in Three Societies." *Magazine of History* (OAH) 4 (Winter 1989): 35-46. Ills.   Bink provides extended quotations taken from the writings of former slaveowners in the U.S. and Africa, former slaves in the U.S., and from interviews with former slaves in Cuba and the U.S. to illustrate how such documents can be used to teach the immediate problems associated with emancipation.

10.   *A Compilation of the Messages and Papers of the Presidents.* 20 Vols. New York: Bureau of National Literature, Inc., [1917].   For public papers produced by Presidents Lincoln, Johnson, Grant, and Hayes, see vols. 7-9 (Lincoln), vol. 9 (Johnson, Grant), and vol. 10 (Grant, Hayes). An index was published in 1929.

11.   Cox, LaWanda and John H. (eds.). *Reconstruction, the Negro, and the New South.* Columbia: University of South Carolina, 1973. 425p.   Included are a wide range of documents related to the struggle for civil rights from Reconstruction to the 1890s. The documents mainly include presidential veto messages, interviews, legislative acts, political party platforms, and letters.

12.   Crowe, Charles (ed.). *The Age of Civil War and Reconstruction, 1830-1900: A Book of Interpretative Essays.* Homewood, Il.: Dorsey Press, 1966. 479p. This study guide includes 161 pages of reprinted articles and portions of books on

various aspects of Reconstruction.　　Each section has an introduction and bibliography.

13.　　Current, Richard N. (ed.). *Reconstruction, 1865-1877.* Englewood Cliffs: Printice-Hall, 1965. 183p.　　Includes selected reprints of eyewitness accounts. (See also # 70)

14.　　Davis, Robert Scott, Jr.　"Documentation for Afro-American Families: Records of the Freedmen's Savings and Trust Company." *National Genealogical Society Quarterly* 76 (June 1988): 134-146. Ills. Tbl.　　Davis provides examples of how the records of the Freedmen's Bank can be used for genealogical research.

15.　　Davis, Robert Scott, Jr.　"Freedmen's Bureau and Other Reconstruction Sources For Research in African-American Families, 1865-1874." *Journal of Afro-American Historical and Genealogical Society* 9, 4 (1988): 171-176.　　Davis briefly describes key sources of documentary sources on blacks in Reconstruction, such as the National Archives' holdings of papers from the Freedmen's Bureau and the Freedmen's Savings and Trust Co.　He also discusses sources of records on Georgia blacks produced at the state and county levels that are held by the Georgia Department of Archives and History.

16.　　Donald, David. *The Nation in Crisis, 1861-1877.* New York: Appleton-Century Crofts, 1969. 92p.　　Offers a basic, selected bibliography of resources on the Civil War and Reconstruction.

17.　　Emanuel, Gary Lynn.　"An Analysis of the Textbook Treatment of the Reconstruction Period:　Changes That Occurred Between Editions of College Level Survey Textbooks." Ph.D. University of Northern Colorado, 1979.

18.　　Festle, Mary Jo.　"Reading Reconstruction With Students." *Journal of American History* 83 (March 1997): 1353-1356.　　Festle discusses how to do textual analysis in teaching Reconstruction.

19.　　Fleming, Walter L.　*Documentary History of Reconstruction - Political, Military, Social, Religious, Educational, and Industrial, 1865 to the Present Time.* 2 Vols. Cleveland:　Arthur D. Clark Co., 1906. Vol. 1: 493p. Vol. 2: 480p. Facim. Ills.　　Fleming provides the largest published collection of original sources on Reconstruction.　Most of the documents are federal and state government publications, political platforms, and excerpts from contemporary and historical accounts published by both Northern and Southern writers.　The documents are arranged topically and each one includes a reference to its date and source. (See also Fleming's *Documents Relating to Reconstruction.* Morgantown, W.V., 1904.)

20.　　Green, Robert P. J.　"Reconstruction Historiography: A Source of Teaching Ideas." *Social Studies* 82 (July/August 1991): 153-157.　　Historical writing on Reconstruction is used as the basis for teaching high school students the value of inductive and critical reasoning in the study of how history is interpreted by historians.

21.   Hart, Albert Bushnell. *The Reconstruction Era: Eyewitness Accounts.* Westwood, Ma.: PaperBook Press, 1992. 15p. Ills. Ports.   This tabloid size publication provides a collection of documents from the postwar years that give various perspectives on the social and political conditions in the South and legal reforms that would effect the entire nation. It is intended for secondary school students.

22.   Hesseltine, William B. *The Tragic Conflict: The Civil War and Reconstruction.* New York: George Braziller, 1962. 528p.   This book includes 10 selections mainly from contemporary periodicals and newspapers and excerpts from monographs.

23.   Hofstadter, Richard and Beatrice K. Hofstadter (eds.). *Great Issues in American History: From Reconstruction to the Present Day, 1864-1981.* 602p. Note on Sources.   Part one includes a collection of speeches, court decisions, government documents, and individual opinions from President Lincoln, Thaddeus Stevens, Wade Hampton, and President Johnson.

24.   Holt, Thomas C. "Reconstruction in United States History Textbooks." *Journal of American History* 81 (March 1995): 1641-1651.   Holt analyses seven American history textbooks published between 1989 and 1993 with a focus on the authors' presentation of Reconstruction.   Whether they offer a conventional narrative or conceptual framework, all have the same weakness in common, the failure to adequately explain the collapse of Reconstruction and the aspirations of freedmen.

25.   Hummell, Ray O., Jr. *Southeastern Broadsides Before 1877: A Bibliography.* Richmond: Virginia State Library, 1971. 501p. Ills.   This bibliography represents the holdings of 53 libraries throughout the Southern states. All broadsides were produced in those states prior to 1877. The book is organized by state and each reference includes a portion of the broadside text and the holding library.

26.   Hyman, Harold M. (ed.). *The Radical Republicans and Reconstruction, 1861-1870.* Indianapolis: Bobbs-Merrill, 1967. 538p. Bibl.   In this collection of 68 documents, Hyman includes many documents from prewar and wartime years that reflect Radical Republican philosophy about the purpose of government and the nation. The documents reveal that activities to reconstruct the South began much earlier than the day after the war ended. In his long introduction, Hyman proposes that historians ought to recognize wartime Reconstruction issues much more than they have shown in their publications. He also reviews Reconstruction writing and historians' changing interpretations of the period.

27.   Johannsen, Robert W. (ed.). *Reconstruction 1865-1877*. New York: Free Press, 1970. 215p.   Seventeen documents are reprinted that illustrate the divergent contemporary opinions about the direction of Reconstruction. The documents were taken from executive and congressional publications as well as articles from periodicals and books. They provide a chronological review of key issues including Republican politics, black codes, the Freedmen's Bureau, the election of 1872, civil rights, the Mississippi Plan, and the future of the South.

28.   Krug, Mark M. "On Rewriting of the Story of Reconstruction in the U.S. History Textbooks." *Journal of Negro History* 46 (April 1961): 133-153.   Krug reviews the approach of U.S. history textbooks and concludes that writers need to consult a broader array of sources to avoid traditional interpretations that are very critical of Radical Reconstruction and the importance of black civil rights, and express sympathy with the Ku Klux Klan. The studies of the last 20 years should be incorporated into textbooks to reflect new research on the topic.

29.   Lynd, Staughton (ed.). *Reconstruction*. New York: Harper and Row, 1967. 181p. Bibl.   This book provides excerpts from published historical accounts on various aspects of Reconstruction. The selections give an indication of the divisions among interpreters of the period.

30.   McWhiney, Grady (ed.). *Reconstruction and the Freedmen*. Chicago: Rand McNally and Co., 1963. 53p. Bibl.   This study guide for students uses excerpts from a variety of primary sources for a better understanding of what contemporaries thought about equal rights, emancipation, and freedom.

31.   Moebs, Thomas Truxtun. *Black Soldiers - Black Sailors - Black Ink: Research Guide on African-Americans in U.S. Military History, 1526-1900*. Chesapeake Bay: Moebs Publishing Co., 1994. 1654p. Facim. Ills. Port. Tbls. The portion from 1865 to 1876 is on pages 710-801. Each entry is mainly to a person, with information about where, when, and in which unit they served. Other entries include black troop strength in the Southern states and references to the Indian wars and regiments. A bibliography to works about black soldiers and sailors includes a section on Reconstruction (p. 1012-1013). (Also see *Blacks in the United States Armed Forces: Basic Documents*, edited by M. J. MacGregor and N. Bernard, Wilmington, De.: Scholarly Resources, Inc., 1977.)

32.   Morgan, David Earl. "The Treatment of the Reconstruction Period in United States History as Reflected in Selected American High School History Textbooks: 1890-1983." Ph.D. Loyola University of Chicago, 1985.

33.   Perman, Michael (ed.). *Major Problems in the Civil War and Reconstruction: Documents and Essays*. Lexington: D. C. Heath and Co., 1991. 598p.   The book reprints selected documents and scholarly essays from books and journals to serve as a teaching aid. The documents on Reconstruction include parts of speeches and writings, mostly by Republicans from the North and South and Southern black leaders. Brief bibliographies follow each chapter.

34.   Reidy, Joseph P. "Slave Emancipation Through the Prism of Archives Records." *Prologue* 29 (Summer 1997): 105-111. Ills.   Reidy briefly surveys various document collections at the National Archives that are essential tools for understanding the transition of blacks form slavery to freedom. He comments on the records of the War Department's bureau of Colored Troops, the U.S. Army commands, the Freedmen's Bureau, The Adjutant General of the Army, the Department of Justice, the Comptroller of the Currency, the U.S. Senate, the U.S. House of Representatives, and the pension records of black Civil War veterans and eligible dependents.

35.   Richter, William L.   *The ABC-CLIO Companion to American Reconstruction, 1862-1877.* Santa Barbarta: ABC-CLIO, 1996. 505p. Bibl. Chron. Ills.   This reference book consists of encyclopedic articles ranging from a few paragraphs to several pages on people, institutions, and topics. Richter introduces the book with a discussion of historiography. He includes a 12 page chronology, beginning with the Morrill Tariff (April 12, 1861) and ending with the U.S. Supreme Courts decision in Cummings v. Georgia (December 18, 1899). The book also includes a 47 page bibliography of books and articles and a detailed subject index.

36.   Rozwenc, Edwin Charles (ed.). *Reconstruction in the South.* 2nd Ed. Lexington, Ma.: Heath and Co., 1972. 308p. Ill. Bibl. (First edition published 1952)   Includes 14 reprints of previously published journal articles or parts of books on a wide range of issues related to Reconstruction. The selections, published from the 1940s through the 1960s, are mainly revisionist interpretations of congressional policy; carpetbaggers, scalawags, and freedmen in politics; redeemers; and racism in the South.

37.   Sheiner, Seth M. *Reconstruction: A Tragic Era?* New York: Holt Reinhart & Winston, 1968. 122p. Bibl.   Includes selected readings on Reconstruction written by historians during the 20th century.

38.   Shenton, James P. (ed.). *The Reconstruction: A Documentary History of the South After the War: 1865-1877.* New York Putnam, 1963. 314p.   Includes a selection of excerpts from periodical articles, books, newspapers, government documents, and a few manuscripts published either during or after Reconstruction up to the early 20th century.

39.   Stalcup, Brenda (ed.). *Reconstruction: Opposing Viewpoints.* San Diego: Greenhaven Press, Inc., 1995. 310p. App. Bibl. Chron.   This book is an aid for students who seek an understanding of various opinions on Reconstruction based on contemporary sources.

40.   Sterling, Dorothy (ed.). *The Trouble They Seen: Black People Tell the Story of Reconstruction.* Garden City, N.Y.: Doubleday and Co., 1976. 491p. Ills. Ports.   Sterling uses portions of manuscripts, speeches, government documents, and oral histories to illustrate how blacks viewed their lives during Reconstruction.

41.   Stiles, T. J. (ed.). *Robber Barons and Radicals: Reconstruction and the Origins of Civil Rights*. New York: Perigee Press, 1997. 438p. (In Their Own Words)   Stiles provides insight into Reconstruction through a chronological narrative from 1865 to 1877 that includes the words of participants in the South and the North. There is particular focus on politics in Yazoo County, Mississippi through the eyes of Northerner Albert T. Morgan and former slave John R. Lynch. Other eyewitness accounts from contemporaries are from Gen. O. O. Howard, Rep. George Boutwell of Massachusetts, Elizabeth Cady Stanton, Andrew Carnegie, Sen. John Sherman of Ohio, Gov. Jacob Cox of Ohio, L. Q. C. Lamar of Mississippi, and Gov. Daniel Chamberlain of South Carolina.

42.   Thornbrough, Emma Lou (ed.). *Black Reconstructionists*. Englewood Cliffs, NJ: Prentice Hall, 1972. 182p. App. Bibl.   Included are selected texts revealing the black leaders in the period of Reconstruction. Documents illustrating Southern, Northern, and British views toward blacks and the writings of selected historians also appear. Many of the documents are taken from congressional hearings and documents, convention proceedings, newspapers, and historical monographs. The black leaders covered include James T. White, William H. Grey, Jonathan C. Gibbs, Emmanuel Fortune, Henry McNeal Turner, John Roy Lynch, Beverly Nash, Robert C. DeLarge, Frances L. Cardozo, Richard H. Cain, Oscar Dunn, Jonathan Jaspers White, James T. Rapier, Blanche Kelso Bruce, Hiram Rhodes Revels, Mumford McCoy, Solomon White, P. B. S. Pinchback, Robert Gleed, and Robert Brown Elliott. British commentators mentioned are Robert Somers, Wiliam Hepworth Dixon, and George Campbell.

43.   Trefousse, Hans L. (ed). *Background for Radical Reconstruction. Testimony Taken from the Hearings of the Joint Committee on Reconstruction, the Select Committee on the Memphis Riot and Massacres, and the Select Committee on the New Orleans Riots-1866-1867*. Boston: Little Brown and Co., 1970. 182p. Selections from congressional hearings are intended to provide a broad, coherent view of the conditions of blacks and white in the South, effects of President Johnson's plan of Reconstruction, black suffrage, and the need for congressional interference. The testimony of a variety of Northerners and Southerners provide insights into congressional leaders who participated and why presidential Reconstruction failed.

44.   Trefousse, Hans. *Historical Dictionary of Reconstruction*. Westport: Greenwood Press, 1991. 284p. Bibl. Chron.   This reference work includes explanatory entries on persons, events, legislation and legal cases, principles, and issues significant in Reconstruction history. Entries for each state that seceded and border states are also included. Includes bibliographic references, an index, and chronology.

45.   Trefousse, Hans L. *Reconstruction: America's First Effort at Racial Democracy*. Huntington, NY: Krieger Publishing Co., 1979. 225p. Bibl. (Rpt of 1955 edition).   Trefousse writes a brief account of Reconstruction followed by the text of 26 documents that make up most of the book. The documents include the

Reconstruction Acts, the black code of Mississippi, Supreme Court case decisions, and portions of books written about the period.

46.   Unger, Irwin (ed.). *Essays on the Civil War and Reconstruction.* New York: Holt, Rinehart and Winston, 1970. 434p. Portions of previously published articles and books are reprinted as a study guide for students.

47.   Wish, Harvey (ed.). *Reconstruction in the South, 1865-1877, First-Hand Accounts of the American Southland After the Civil War By Northerners and Southerners.* New York: Noonday Press, 1966. 318p. Bibl. Wish selected 32 individual perspectives on Reconstruction from a wide variety of contemporary sources including government documents, periodicals and books. The reprinted accounts are from foreign travelers, presidents and congressmen, Supreme Court justices, Southern klansmen, carpetbaggers, and freedmen.

48.   Woodworth, Steven E. (ed.). *American Civil War: A Handbook of Literature and Research.* Westport: Greenwood Press, 1996. 754p. App. This book lists selected publications on Reconstruction, mainly from the past 50 years. The portions relevant to Reconstruction include sections on "Southern Occupation" by Richard M. Zuczek (pp. 547-560), "Economics" by Howard Bodenhorn (pp. 561-575), "Emancipation, Freedmen, and the Freedmen's Bureau" by James Alex Bagget (pp. 576-585), and fiction about Reconstruction in "Novels and Other Fictional Accounts" by Sharon L. Gravett (pp. 607-608). Each section begins with a bibliographic essay on historiography and research directions.

General Historiography and Surveys of Reconstruction

49.   Alexander, Roberta Sue. "Presidential Reconstruction: Ideology and Change." In *The Facts of Reconstruction: Essays in Honor of John Hope Franklin*. Baton Rouge: Louisiana State University Press, 1991. Pp. 29-51.   Alexander provides an historiographic analysis of writing on Reconstruction since the mid-1970s and compares it with the work of conservatives during the first half of the 20th century and early revisionists in the 1960s and 1970s. She describes the diversity of recent research and calls for more regional studies on social, economic, and cultural developments of both blacks and whites.

50.   Allen, James S. *Reconstruction: The Battle for Democracy (1865-1876)*. New York: International Publishers, 1937. 256p. App. Bibl. Ills.   Allen's Marxist interpretation emphasizes the replacement of the slave oligarchy by a bourgeois-democratic dictatorship supported by oppressed classes of the South, including the freedmen. The period is viewed as a glorious time of accomplishment of democratic reforms that ultimately failed to provide lasting change. Reactionary forces eroded the revolutionary movement. Former slaveholders who retained their landed estates overpowered the budding union of farmers and laborers.   Allen hopes that revolutionary forces in the 1930s will deliver new reforms.

51.   Anderson, Eric and Alfred A. Moss, Jr. (eds.).   *The Facts of Reconstruction: Essays in Honor of John Hope Franklin*. Baton Rouge: Louisiana State University Press, 1991. 239p.   As a tribute to the contributions of Franklin to Reconstruction scholarship, this work offers 9 original essays that deal with a variety of issues. An afterward on Reconstruction historiography summarizes and compares the arguments made by each author. The point of departure for all essays is Franklin's *Reconstruction: After the Civil War* (see # 91). (For individual references see # 49, 527, 634, 681; also see John R. Lynch, *The Facts of Reconstruction*, # 2055.)

52.   Beale, Howard K. "The Decision of Reconstruction." Ph.D. Harvard University, 1927.

53.   Beale, Howard K. "On Rewriting Reconstruction History." *American Historical Review* 45 (July 1940): 807-827.   Beale calls for a reevaluation, fresh approaches, less bias, and more intensive research on Reconstruction. He wants more focus on economics, labor, government corruption, the role of black Americans, and attempts to establish more democratic governments in the Southern states.

54.   Belz, Herman. *Abraham Lincoln, Constitutionalism, and Equal Rights in the Civil War Era.* New York: Fordham University Press, 1998. 265p.   Belz revises articles previously published (see # 178, 634) In his introduction Belz discusses the historiography and issues regarding the Civil War and Reconstruction as a revolutionary period. He believes that it was not revolutionary, mainly because revolution was not intended. (See also # 636.)

55.   Belz, Herman. *Reconstructing the Union: Theory and Policy During the Civil War.* Ithaca: Cornell University Press, 1969. 336p. Bibl.   Belz emphasizes wartime Reconstruction more than many other historians have done. The central issue was the status of the states that seceded and how to bring the states together again within the Union. Belz discusses the constitutional issues and the power struggle between Congress and President Lincoln over Reconstruction policy. He believes that before Lincoln's death, the president and Congress had achieved sufficient consensus on Reconstruction to design a formula for dealing with postwar reunification.   (See also Belz's Ph.D. dissertation with the same title from Washington University, 1966.)

56.   Bernstein, Harry.   "South America Looks at North American Reconstruction." In *New Frontiers of the American Reconstruction.* Edited by Harold M. Hyman. Urbana: University of Illinois Press, 1966. Pp. 87-104. Bernstein explains how intellectuals and writers in South America and Latin America viewed American slavery and its abolition as well as the victory of federalism over states rights. They viewed these events in the context of their own experience of slavery and civil wars, although the points of comparison are few.

57.   Binkley, William C. "The Contribution of Walter Lynwood Fleming to Southern Scholarship." *Journal of Southern History* 5 (May 1939): 143-154. Brinkley survey's Fleming's career and his major publications. Fleming's main influences on historical scholarship were his publications and his impact on the development of graduate programs and scholarship in Southern history in the South. More time is needed to evaluate Fleming's long term influence. (See also # 98)

58.   Bowers, Claude G. *The Tragic Era: The Reconstruction After Lincoln.* Cambridge, Ma.: Literary Guild of America, Inc., (Riverside Press), 1929. 567p. Bibl. Ports.   Bowers writes that Reconstruction was a time of terrible corruption, violence, and destruction against the South, and it represented the desecration of the American constitution. He depicts President Johnson as the embodiment of good and the Radicals as the embodiment of evil in their approaches to the South during the postwar years. He views the black codes as benign and necessary for order,

while the Ku Klux Klan represents a savior of civilization. Bowers' theme is typical among the books on Reconstruction that were written in his time.

59.   Bratcher, John V.   trans. and ed.   "A Soviet Historian Looks at Reconstruction." *Civil War History* 15 (September 1969): 257-264.   Russian historian A. V. Efimov comments about R. F. Ivanov's *The Negroes' Struggle for Land and Freedom in the South, USA 1865-1877* (Moscow, 1959). Efimov reflects the Soviet perspective on Reconstruction, and he admires the work of Marxist historians in the U.S., such as W. E. B. DuBois and James Allen. He is highly critical of the reactionary bourgeois writings of William Dunning and the racial themes in works by E. M. Coulter and Carter G. Woodson. Efimov believes that Ivanov's book is the most complete study of the black masses in the Civil War era.

60.   Brooks, Albert N. D.   "Negro History Evaluates Emancipation." *Negro History Bulletin* 26 (January 1963):   back page, 153.   The successes of Reconstruction are recalled in Brooks' support for continued struggle for the full emancipation of African Americans in the 20th century. The criticism and biased accounts of Reconstruction are compared with those of the New Deal.

61.   Buck, Paul H. *The Road to Reunion, 1865-1900.* Boston: Little Brown and Co., 1937. 320p.   Buck takes a topical approach to what he believes is a period of national consolidation and integration.   With the defeat of the Confederacy, sectional antipathy and distrust substantially dissolved and true peace prevailed within a generation. Buck views Reconstruction as a time of Northern vindictiveness driven by radical elements in the Republican Party. He views blacks as helpless pawns who were better off in the peace of the post-Reconstruction years. (See also Buck's "Reconciliation of North and South." Ph.D. Harvard, 1935.)

62.   Buckmaster, Henrietta. *Freedom Bound.* New York: Macmillan Co., 1965. 185p. Bibl. Chron.   Buckmaster provides a brief history of Reconstruction from the perspective of both the reformers who tried to make revolutionary changes in postwar society and the freedmen who yearned for and vigorously sought freedom, equality of civil rights, and an independent life. Reconstruction was just the beginning of a long road to true freedom for blacks in America.

63.   Burgess, John W. *Reconstruction and the Constitution, 1866-1876.* New York: Charles Scribner's Sons, 1902. 342p.   Burgess writes a political history of Reconstruction with particular emphasis on the constitutional conflict between the president and Congress. He also includes chapters on the impeachment of Andrew Johnson, the election of 1876, and international relations between 1867 and 1877. Burgess supported the attempt to ensure both the loyalty of the South and the civil rights for freedmen, but he strongly rejected black suffrage and racial equality based on his belief in the natural domination and leadership of the white race.

64.   Camejo, Peter. *Racism, Revolution, Reaction, 1861-1877: The Rise and Fall of Radical Reconstruction.* New York: Monad Press, 1976. 269p. Bibl. Camejo explains Reconstruction with a Marxist interpretation. His starting point is

the economic determinism of Charles and Mary Beard and Howard K. Beale. He is highly critical of the white revisionist historians of the 1950s and 1960s who were either not dedicated to racial equality or whose interpretations of Reconstruction were weakened by a rejection of a materialist approach, a superficial explanation for the failure of Reconstruction and the persistence of racism in American society. Camejo views the Republican Party as succumbing to industrial capitalists who turned their interests away from civil rights for all races toward class oppression.

65.   Carter, Hodding. *The Angry Scare: The Story of Reconstruction*. Garden City: Doubleday and Co., 1959. Bibl.   Resistance to racial equality brought unity among white Southerners and thus guaranteed that Radical Reconstruction would fail.   The resulting legacy of racial tension and provincialism intruded into the moral, economic, political, and cultural life of the South from that time to the present day.   Reconstruction did not solve the problems of the Union victory in the Civil War because of Radical Republican policies and Southern whites' determined rejection of racial reform.   Carter relies on secondary sources.

66.   Clemenceau, Georges. *American Reconstruction 1865-1870, and the Impeachment of President Johnson*. Ed. with an Introduction by Fernand Baldensperger. Trans. by Margaret MacVeagh. New York: Lincoln MacVeagh - The Dial Press, 1928. 300p. Ports.   The author and future French Prime Minister visited the U.S. as American correspondent of the Paris *Temps*.   His communications, arranged chronologically, reflect a liberal French belief in democracy and the equality of men.   He favored the principles of the Republican Party in Reconstruction and supported the ideas of equal rights and economic opportunities for freedmen.   (See also Clemenceau's "Notes on America and Americans." *Independent* (December 27, 1906): 1537-1540; and # 329)

67.   Cox, Samuel S. *Three Decades of Federal Legislation 1855-1885*. Providence, R. I.: S. A. and R. A. Reid, Publ., 1885. 726p. Map. Ports.   Cox was a Democratic congressman from Ohio from 1857 to 1865 and a congressman from New York mainly from 1869 to 1885. Although a Democrat, he states that he has written an unbiased account of federal political history from the mid1850s until the decade following Reconstruction.   He believes that too much Republican power is mainly responsible for the war and allowing a dark period of Reconstruction to rule the South.   Cox is critical of President Johnson, the Southerners who sought a virtual return to slavery, Ku Klux Klan violence, the corrupt state governments in the South, and the unneccesary extension and expenditure of the Freedmen's Bureau.

68.   Craven, Avery. *Reconstruction: The Ending of the Civil War*. New York: Holt, Rinehart & Winston, 1969. 330p. Bibl.   This survey approaches Reconstruction as the last phase of the Civil War.   Reconstruction formed a continuum in the struggle over the degree of freedom and equality that may coexist in a democratic society.   Craven grants the Republicans sincerity in their efforts to provide the freedmen with equality of rights and true freedom, but in the end the the revolution failed because it was unrealistic.   In the 1870s Republican ideology on

individual freedom put responsibility for success on the shoulders of each individual rather than the government, even in an environment of hostility to the black citizens.

69.   Crowe, Charles (ed.). The Age of Civil War and Reconstruction, 1830-1900: A Book of Interpretive Essays. Homewood, Il.: Dorsey Press, 1966. 479p. Crowe provides brief historiographic essays and bibliographies followed by readings taken from published articles and books on various issues related to the period. With regard to Reconstruction the readings deal with politics, the constitution, racial discrimination, and equality. See pages 239-258, 315-476.

70.   Current, Richard N. (ed.). *Reconstruction in Retrospect: Views From the Turn of the Century.* Baton Rouge: Louisiana State University Press, 1969. 165p. Current reprints 7 articles of the 9 articles that appeared in the *Atlantic Monthly* in 1901 on Reconstruction that reflect early 20th century opinions about political and racial attitudes. (See # 81, 164, 476, 951, 1049, 2351; For the articles not reprinted see # 870, 1911) The seventh article is Bliss Perry's "Concluding Comments" that summarizes the preceding articles.

71.   Curry, Richard O. "The Abolitionists and Reconstruction: A Critical Appraisal." *Journal of Southern History* 34 (November 1968): 527-545.   Curry focuses on what historians have written about the attitude of abolitionists toward Reconstruction, particularly equal rights for freedmen. Through the works of others, he offers evidence supporting contradictory interpretations of the abolitionist spirit. Some abolitionists continued to support civil and political rights for all races, but others took a more conservative stance or simply believed that the passage of the constitutional amendments eliminated barriers to equality.

72.   Curry, Richard O. "The Civil War and Reconstruction, 1861-1877: A Critical Overview of Recent Trends and Interpretations." *Civil War History* 20 (September 1974): 215-238.   Curry explains that the entire period from 1861 to 1877 ought to be approached as a unified period. With regard to the postwar period he examines research related to the ideology of congressional Republicans, the impeachment of President Johnson, the role of the Supreme Court, the election compromise of 1877, and the role of blacks and scalawags.

73.   Daniel, W. Harrison. "The Response of the Church of England to the Civil War and Reconstruction in America." *Historical Magazine of the Protestant Episcopal Church* 47 (March 1978): 51-72.   Anglican opinions expressed mainly in newspapers and religious periodicals reflect a pronounced bias towards the South in the Civil War, but did not necessarily favor slavery. In Reconstruction opinions continued to favor the South in the political struggle between President Johnson and the Republican Congress. Johnson seemed to have the most appropriate policy that emphasized gradual change. Anglican writers generally disapproved of immediately bestowing equal civil rights on the freedmen.

74.   Dante, Harris L. "Reconstruction History: Recent Interpretations." *Social Education* 18 (February 1954): 59-62.   Dante reviews how interpretations of

Reconstruction have changed since the early 20th century, and he emphasizes that recent historians show less bias in their interpretations.

75.   Degler, Carl N. "Dawn Without Noon: The Myths of Reconstruction." In *Myth and Southern History.* Edited by Patrick Gerster and Nicholas Cords. Chicago: Rand McNally, 1974. Pp. 155-169.   In this chapter from Degler's *Out of Our Past* (1970) he argues that many traditional ideas about the nature of Reconstruction are either partially true or totally false. He refers to the mythical scenario of the vengeful Congress, military despotic rule in the South, the wholesale corruption of the Radical state regimes that left most whites with no voice whatsoever, and the dramatic reversal to prosperity and good government after Reconstruction. Degler offers a more balanced perspective on the period.

76.   Degler, Carl N. "Rethinking Post-Civil War History." *Virginia Quarterly Review* 57 (Spring 1981): 250-267.   Degler refers to various recent (1970s) interpretations of the postwar Southern economy and society to make the point that historians periodically rewrite history based on the viewpoints and concerns of their generation. In so doing they apply new theories or perspectives that enrich historical interpretation of the past.

77.   DuBois, W. E. Burghardt. *Black Reconstruction in America: An Essay Toward a History of the Part Which Black Folk Played in the Attempt to Reconstruct Democracy in America, 1860-1880.* New York: Atheneum, 1975. 746p. Bibl. (Rpt. of Russell and Russell, 1935)   DuBois's writes an early revisionist work emphasizing the role of blacks in Reconstruction, particularly in the context of a revolutionary worker force and the struggle against racial prejudice. He interprets Reconstruction in economic terms with both black and white labor facing Southern capitalists (i.e. landowners and merchants) as well as carpetbaggers and Northern abolitionist-capitalists. In different ways Northern and Southern capitalists sought to manipulate labor. DuBois surveys political and economic events throughout the South and seeks to reveal truth rather than long held myths and prejudices. He explains the reaction of white landowners against blacks and reforms (i.e. counterrevolution) that doomed Reconstruction and darkened the future of the freedmen. But DuBois recognizes the progress that Reconstruction brought to the live of ex-slaves, particularly in educational opportunities, and greater freedom and independence. In the last chapter he reviews Reconstruction historiography.

78.   DuBois, W. E. Burghardt. "Reconstruction and its Benefits." *American Historical Review* 15 (July 1910): 781-799.   DuBois defends the Southern Reconstruction governments against charges of corruption, malfeasance, and hypertaxation. Critics exaggerated and ignored positive, long lasting contributions in public education, social welfare, and constitutional or statutory reform. These reforms were influenced by black enfranchisement because it gave blacks the political strength to influence Southern politics.

79.   Dunning, William Archibald. *Essays on the Civil War and Reconstruction and Related Topics.* New York: Peter Smith, 1931. 397p. (Rpt. and partial

revision of Macmillan, 1897)   This book collects previously published articles by Dunning. (See # 81, 233, 523, 672) Taken together they provide a history of Reconstruction and Dunning's views on the course of Reconstruction and the constitutional issues related to the Civil War, military government, black suffrage, civil rights, and states' rights. He also discusses the impeachment of President Johnson and the collapse of Reconstruction in the South. The book became an important statement of white, conservative scholarship that set the tone for a generation of historians writing local and national histories of Reconstruction and the American public's negative perception of the period.

80.   Dunning, William A. *Reconstruction, Political and Economic*. New York: Harper Torchbook, 1982. 378p. Bibl. Maps. Port. (Rpt. of Harper and Broth, 1907)   Dunning's book is a history of postwar America with emphasis on political Reconstruction as formulated in Congress and institutions in the South.   His interpretation focuses on the mistakes and the disastrous consequences of Reconstruction and their devastating impact on the South. There is very limited discussion of the freedmen except for their general demoralization by the consequences of their freedom and the congressional program. The social and economic vibrancy of the North and West is contrasted with the ruin in the South.

81.   Dunning, William A. "The Undoing of Reconstruction." *Atlantic Monthly* 88 (October 1901): 437-449.   Dunning describes how Reconstruction was weakening even before all of the former Confederate states had returned to the Union. After the passage of the Reconstruction Acts of 1867, the Republican Party in the South began to disintegrate due to internal quarrels, the loss of competent white leadership, and the influence of black leaders who were usually ignorant or dishonest.   Also, the South vigorously opposed legislated change during Reconstruction and in the decades that followed conservatives circumvented the constitution in order to eliminate blacks form political influence.

82.   Finzsch, Norbert and Jürgen Martschukat.   *Different Restorations: Reconstruction and 'Wiederaufbau' in Germany and the United States: 1865, 1945 and 1989*. Providence: Berghahn Books, 1996. 422p. Bibl.   This book is the result of the Krefeld Historical Symposium on German and American history. The ten essays seek to compare periods of reconstruction and reunification to discover insights into rebuilding following conflict. Issues considered include the lost cause and remembrance in national sections or regions, racism, political decisions, party politics, identities, and the impact on culture and society among defeated peoples.

83.   Fleming, Walter Lynwood. *The Sequel to Appomatox: A Chronicle of the Reunion of the States. Part 2 of The Confederacy and Reconstruction*. New Haven: Yale University Press, 1919. 322p. Bibl.   In this history of Reconstruction Fleming touches on Southern and national politics, religion, and education. His perspective is a conservative one that reflects his dislike of the Radicals and their policies, while showing sympathy with the plight of Southern whites.

84.   Foner, Eric and Olivia Mahoney. *America's Reconstruction: People and Politics After the Civil War*. New York: Harper Perennial, 1995. 151p. Bibl. Ills. This brief illustrated history of Reconstruction was written to accompany an exhibit that first appeared at the Valentine Museum in Richmond, Virginia in 1995. One of the purposes of the exhibit and the text is to disseminate a more realistic picture of Reconstruction than the old stereotypes and misconceptions that have lingered despite the major reinterpretations by historians.

85.   Foner, Eric. "The Continuing Evolution of Reconstruction History." *Magazine of History* [OAH] 4, 1 (1989): 11-13.   Foner reviews the changing course of Reconstruction interpretations and describes his *Reconstruction: America's Unfinished Revolution* (see # 87) as a new synthesis of modern scholarship.

86.   Foner, Eric. "The New View of Reconstruction." *American Heritage* 34 (October/November 1983): 10-15. Ills.   Foner explains how historical research since the 1960s has significantly revised the standard interpretations of Reconstruction.   The evidence and new interpretations, some of which echoed earlier accounts that were disregarded, illustrate the central roll of blacks in Reconstruction, the meaning of freedom in American society, the true contribution of Reconstruction governments, and the long term consequences that made possible legal and social reform.

87.   Foner, Eric. *Reconstruction: America's Unfinished Revolution, 1863-1877*. New York: Harper and Row, 1988. 690p. Bibl. Ills. Ports.   Foner offers a new synthesis of contemporary scholarship and a general, multidimensional study of Reconstruction.   He combines political, social, and economic issues within a national context of the expanding authority of the federal government, the reforming impulse of the postwar era, and the breadth of changes going on in both the North and the South.   He highlights the black experience in Reconstruction, the class and labor changes in the South for blacks and whites, and the evolving nature of racial attitudes.   Foner recognizes the positive aspects of the postwar years, but he concludes that Reconstruction failed to complete the changes to ensure equality and freedom in American society.

88.   Foner, Eric. "Writing About Reconstruction: A Personal Reflective." In *Looking South: Chapters in the Story of an American Region*. Edited by Winfred B. Moore, Jr. and Joseph F. Tripp. New York: Greenwood Press, 1989. Pp. 3-16. Foner's essay is about his personal perspective on the writing of Reconstruction history, particularly in light of his research for the book *Reconstruction: America's Unfinished Revolution* (see # 87). He discusses key themes in Reconstruction historiography and the influence of American society on Reconstruction history. (See also Foner's "The Continuing Evolution of Reconstruction History," *Magazine of History* [OAH] 4 (Winter, 1989): 14-33.

89.   Foster, William Z. *The Negro People in American History*. New York: International Publications, 1970. 608p. Bibl.   Foster, who ran for president as the

nominee of The Workers (Communist) Party (1928, 1932), provides a history of black Americans from a Marxist-Leninist perspective. The period of the Civil War and Reconstruction is considered to be a time of revolution against the capitalist exploitation of the Southern planters by forces for free labor, but it was also the culmination of a longstanding struggle between the planters and the Northern industrialists. Because of racial discrimination the exploitation of blacks by planters and merchants continued during Reconstruction due to government weakness and compromise. Foster also discusses the interaction of the Marxist International Workers' Association with black organizations, although there were few black Marxists during Reconstruction.

90. Franklin, John Hope. "Mirror for Americans: A Century of Reconstruction History." *American Historical Review* 85 (February 1980): 1-14. Franklin broadly reviews the main currents in Reconstruction historiography to demonstrate that historians have had great difficulty separating their own biases or contemporary agendas from the study of Reconstruction. Like Howard K. Beale 40 years before (see # 53), Franklin calls for the separation of Reconstruction research from stereotypes and contemporary concerns or needs, and for more thorough explanations of issues in order to focus on the truth about the postwar years.

91. Franklin, John Hope. *Reconstruction: After the Civil War.* Chicago: University of Chicago Press, 1961. 258p. Bibl. Chron. Ill. In this key revisionist study Franklin views Reconstruction as a time of hope for the development of civil rights and democracy in the South. But the Southern oligarchy combined with waning Republican enthusiasm for forcing equal rights for freedmen to produce a failed program for change. The achievements of the war, national union and emancipation, were not adequately reinforced in the postwar years. The Northern political elite was more concerned with creating an environment for economic and industrial expansion than with establishing a solid foundation for the future prosperity of all Americans. (See also Franklin's *From Slavery to Freedom: A History of American Negroes*, New York: Alfred A. Knopf, 1994. 7th ed.)

92. Franklin, John Hope. "Reconstruction and the Negro." In *New Frontiers of the American Reconstruction.* Edited by Harold M. Hyman. Urbana: University of Illinois Press, 1966. Pp. 59-76. This brief review of the historiography of blacks in Reconstruction establishes the basis for Franklin's argument about revisionist writing. Revisionist history shows that the freedmen were not in control of state governments and that they avidly sought education and opportunities to improve themselves and make themselves good citizens of the country. Despite the 14th and 15th Amendments, the U.S. denied blacks equal rights and opportunities to improve. The challenge of the post-Reconstruction century was to fulfill the promise of Reconstruction. August Meier comments (pp. 77-86) on Franklin's paper, but instead of focusing on what Franklin actually wrote, he sets out to explain where the research is heading on the role of blacks in Reconstruction. In general, Meier emphasizes that research should focus on what blacks thought and did in Reconstruction instead of the traditional approach that has concentrated on what whites thought and did about blacks.

93.   Franklin, John Hope. "Wither Reconstruction Historiography?" *Journal of Negro Education* 17 (Fall 1948): 446-461.   In this review essay of E. Merton Coulter's The South During Reconstruction, 1865-1877 (see), Franklin offers a highly critical assessment based on Coulter's biased approach to sources and presentation of evidence.   Coulter's flawed methodology led to his summary rejection of revisionist writing, his negative view of Reconstruction, and his disregard for other perspectives, including those written by contemporary blacks.

94.   Freeman, Patricia A. "'The *Times* of London and Reconstruction of the Southern States: 1865-1877." Ph.D. University of Washington, 1977. 226p.

95.   Gallaway, B. P.   "Economic Determinism in Reconstruction Historiography." *Southwestern Social Science Quarterly* 46 (December 1965): 244-254.   Gallaway summarizes the views of historians of Reconstruction who emphasized economic determinism as the cause of Radical Republican policies. He focuses on Charles and Mary Beard's *The Rise of American Civilization* (1927); Vernon L. Parrington's *Main Currents in American Thought* (1927-1930); and Howard K. Beale's *The Critical Year* (see # 439).   Although the economic determinists have been discredited, Gallaway credits them with the growth and greater respectability of Reconstruction scholarship since the 1930s.

96.   German, John. "Mulattoes and Race Mixture: American Attitudes and Images From Reconstruction to World War I." Ph.D. University of North Carolina, 1976. 420p.

97.   Gray, Daniel Savage.   "Bibliographic Essay: Black Views on Reconstruction." *Journal of Negro History* 58 (January 1973): 73-85.   Gray surveys the historical writing of black participants and historians.   He emphasizes the value of contemporary black commentators compared with white writers.   He clarifies that black historians since the late 19th century blazed a path of revisionism that is only now accepted by many white historians.   The writers stressed the positive role of the freedmen, black politicians, and progress made by blacks to lift themselves up from slavery despite the opposition of whites.

98.   Green, Fletcher.   "Walter Lynwood Fleming: Historian of Reconstruction." *Journal of Southern History* 2 (November 1936): 497-521. Green briefly discusses Fleming's life, comments on several works, and provides a partially annotated bibliography of Fleming's writings.   Green places Fleming within a new, contemporary group of Reconstruction historians who have revised the old, negative view of President Johnson by emphasizing his wise statesmanship and stressing the social and economic significance of Reconstruction, particularly the economic domination of the North and East to the detriment of the South and West.

99.   Gutman, Herbert   (ed.).   "English Labor Views the American Reconstruction: An Editorial in the *Bee Hive* (London), September 22, 1874." *Labor History* 9 (Winter 1968): 110-112.   In the reprinted editorial from a labor

weekly newspaper the editor urges the white South to accept the Reconstruction reforms and the participation of the freedmen in the social, political, and economic life of the nation.

100.   Hall, Esther Marguerite. "A Critique of the New York Daily Press During Reconstruction, 1865-1869." Ph.D. University of Wisconsin, Madison, 1925.

101.   Hall, Stephen Gilroy. "'Research as Opportunity': Alrutheus Ambush Taylor, Black Intellectualism, and the Remaking of Reconstruction Historiography, 1893-1954." *UCLA Historical Journal* 16 (1996): 39-60.   In this essay on the contributions of Taylor to the growth and development of African-American history and education, Hall examines Taylor's pioneering research and publishing efforts that illustrate the role of blacks in Reconstruction, particularly in South Carolina, Virginia, and Tennessee (see).   Taylor sought objectivity in his research, and he revealed positive outcomes of Reconstruction that contradicted the widely accepted interpretation of William A. Dunning. His works were early contributions to a more balanced view of the postwar years, and they helped promote the field of African-American history.

102.   Hamilton, Holman. "Before 'The Tragic Era': Claude Bowers's Earlier Attitudes Toward Reconstruction." *Mid-America* 55 (October 1973); 235-244. Bowers has been criticized for his history of Reconstruction in *The Tragic Era* (see # 58) because of his partisanship and racism.   Hamilton searches in Bowers' background to explain his Democratic pro-Southern stance in a positive light, although Bowers was not always consistent.   His attitude towards blacks was not characterized by racism.

103.   Hamilton, Peter Joseph. *The History of North America. Volume Sixteen: The Reconstruction Period.* Philadelphia: George Barrie & Sons, 1905.   567p. Chron. Ills. Ports.   Hamilton approaches Reconstruction from a sectional and national perspective. He includes chapters on the border states and Northern states. Also, there is an additional chapter on churches in Reconstruction. Although civil rights, justice, and freedom for blacks were critical themes of Reconstruction, Radical Reconstruction resulted only in dictatorial government, corruption, and a backlash from Southern whites.

104.   Harper, Alan D. "William A. Dunning: the Historians Nemesis." *Civil War History* 10 (March 1964): 54-66.   Harper provides a highly critical assessment of Dunning's work on Reconstruction with an emphasis on the prejudice and racism revealed in *Reconstruction, Political and Economic* (see # 80). Dunning completely supported Johnson's Reconstruction policies and his fight against congressional Republicans.   His themes became the foundation for many other scholarly works which offered negative stereotypes of freedmen, scalawags, carpetbaggers, and Radical Republicans.

105.   Harris, Alexander. *A Review of the Political Conflict in America, From the Commencement of the Anti-Slavery Agitation to the Close of Southern*

Reconstruction, Comprising also a Resume of the Career of Thaddeus Stevens.
Westport: Negro Universities Press, 1970. (Rpt of Oxford: Clarendon Press, 1919)
Harris is highly critical of the Republican Party for its fanaticism and
unconstitutional behavior in subjugating the South in war and peace. He compares
Reconstruction with the Reign of Terror in the French Revolution and Republicans
with European communists of his own day. Thaddeus Stevens is viewed as a
participant in the subversion of republicanism and freedom.

106.   Henry, Robert Selph. *The Story of Reconstruction.* Indianapolis: Bobbs-
Merrill Co., 1938. 633p. Ills.   This narrative history focuses mainly on politics
but also discusses Southern agriculture, education, transportation, and society.
Henry writes a moderate interpretation for the 1930s. He believes that Lincoln's
Reconstruction plan would have been best, but he also recognizes that the
Reconstruction that occurred was less extreme than the white South's view of it and
that it led to positive developments for black Americans.

107.   Hermann, Janet Sharp. "Reconstruction." In *Encyclopedia of American
Political History: Studies of the Principle Movements and Ideas.* Vol. III. New
York: Charles Scribner's Sons, 1984. Pp. 1082-1096. Bibl.   Hermann provides a
brief narrative of political developments with cross references to related sections in
the encyclopedia.

108.   Holliday, Carl. "The Reconstruction - Its Actual Workings." *Methodist
Quarterly Review* 72 (April 1923): 297-311.   Holliday offers a narrative of
Reconstruction history mainly focusing on political and legal highlights at the
national level. He expresses a negative view of congressional Reconstruction and
the idea that there can be any real equality between blacks and whites.

109.   Howorth, Paul Leland. *Reconstruction and Union, 1865-1912.* New
York: AMS Press, 1975. 255p. Bibl. (Rpt. of New York: Henry Holt and Co., 1912)
Howorth wrote during a period of harsh condemnation of Reconstruction, but he
takes a somewhat moderate approach. He clearly shows the racial biases and
stereotypes typical of his age and he refers to Reconstruction as a "dark period", but
he also believes that the South was not harshly treated and that Reconstruction was
inevitable in order to preserve the Union. Reconstruction was a time of hope for the
freedmen, but the resistance to radical policies of the Republicans doomed it to
failure. See pages 57-85.

110.   Hyman, Harold M.   "Reconstruction and Political-Constitutional
Institutions: The Popular Expression." In *New Frontiers of the American
Reconstruction.* Edited by Harold M. Hyman. Urbana: University of Illinois Press,
1966. Pp. 1-33.   Hyman begins by reviewing the political and constitutional
issues regarding Southern secession and the overall impact of the Civil War on the
future authority of the federal government relative to the authority of the states. The
war provided an opportunity to reconstruct weak institutions, and Reconstruction
was part of the whole process that was clearly needed. Alfred H. Kelley comments
(pp. 40-58) on Hyman's paper by pointing to Hyman's thesis that Reconstruction

was a revolutionary process. Kelley explains why he believes that Reconstruction was part of a continuum of nationalism in constitutional authority illustrated by its explicit federal direction. The tradition of nationalism weakened states' rights and dual federalism.

111.   Ignatiev, Noel. "'The American Blind Spot': Reconstruction According to Eric Foner and W. E. B. DuBois." *Labour/Le Travail* 31 (Spring 1993): 243-251. Ignatiev compares Foner's *Reconstruction: America's Unfinished Revolution* (see # 87) and DuBois' *Black Reconstruction in America* (see # 77) and differentiates their ideological approaches. DuBois wrote in the context of the labor struggle and was influenced by the labor movement of the 1920s and 1930s. Foner concentrates on class differences but not in the context of revolutionary class struggle.

112.   Jones, Robert H. *Disrupted Decades: The Civil War and Reconstruction Years*. New York: Charles Scribner's Sons, 1973. 543p. Bibl. Ills. Maps.   Jones believes that Reconstruction was unsuccessful because it failed to secure a promising future for American blacks.   Politics, compromise, business, white opposition, and judicial decisions broke down the promise of emancipation and reform. (See also Jones' *Fields of Conflict: The Civil War and Reconstruction in America*, Krieger, 1998.)

113.   Kennedy, Stetson. *After Appomatox: How the South Won the War*. Gainesville: University Press of Florida, 1995. 321p. Bibl. Ills.   Although the South was defeated in war, it won the peace by vigorously refusing to change its racist attitudes and successfully convincing the North that the two regions could get along fine based on their mutually accepted notions of white supremacy. The result of the white South's violent opposition to Reconstruction was the virutal restoration of the antebellum South as far as blacks were concerned. Kennedy describes the true nature of Reconstruction and the "Big Lie" taught by white Americans about the era.

114.   Johnson, Ludwell H. *Division and Reunion: America 1848-1877*. New York: John Wiley and Sons, 1978. 301p. Bibl.   In his coverage of both wartime and postwar Reconstruction, Johnson is partial to the restrained, pragmatic approach of Lincoln, and he is critical of the Republican governments in the South due to their corruption and manipulation of black voters. He explains that the forced changes implemented in the South by congressional Radicals were responsible for violence and contributed to postwar sectional animosity that remained for decades.

115.   Killian, Lewis M. "The Ambivalent Position of the Negro in the South 1867-1900." *Negro History Bulletin* 23 (January 1960): 81-86.   The struggle of the freedmen for racial equality in Reconstruction is compared without he same struggle in the mid-20th century. He hopes that the U.S. Supreme Court's rejection of the Civil Rights Act of 1875, a symbol of the federal governments turn away focusing on equality, will not be repeated.

116.   Kolchin, Peter. *American Slavery 1619-1877*. New York: Hill and Wang, 1993. Bibl. 304p.   In the last chapter Kolchin provides a brief review of the course of Reconstruction with emphasis on its revolutionary nature and positive progress despite the disappointment that reforms did not go far enough or were reversed by Southern whites.

117.   Koussar, J. Morgan and James M. McPherson (eds.). *Region, Race, and Reconstruction: Essays in Honor of C. Vann Woodward*. New York: Oxford University Press, 1982. 463p.   The third section of this festschrift includes 5 articles on Reconstruction written by former students of Woodward. (See # 593, 751, 953, 983, 1010) In the introduction the editors' discuss Woodward's tremendous influence, style of writing, and major themes of research in Southern history and race relations. The book includes a bibliography of Woodward's writings.

118.   Lindley, Lester G. "Restoration v. Reconstruction: Eliminating Slavery Through Contract Reform in Post-Civil War America." In *Contract, Economic Change, and the Search For Order in Industrializing America*. By Lester G. Lindley. New York: Garland Publishing, 1993. Pp. 265-280.   Lindley discusses the different approaches of President Johnson and the congressional Republicans to the restoration of peace. Johnson viewed slavery as an institution that could be eliminated without also changing attitudes and practices. Republicans tried to effect changes in racial attitudes and behaviors. Johnson sought to control blacks through social contracts while Republicans wanted to offer them opportunities. His philosophy led to Jim Crow and persevered until the second half of the twentieth century.

119.   Lynch, John R. "More About the Historical Errors of James Ford Rhodes." *Journal of Negro History* 3 (April 1918): 139-157.   Lynch responds to an essay that is critical of his comments about Rhodes writing on Reconstruction. The source of the essay is not cited. The unnamed writer describes Lynch's narrow, unscholarly approach, his inaccuracies, and lack of judgment. Lynch defends himself on each point and concludes with an appeal for Americans to eliminate race as a political issue.

120.   Lynch, John R. "Some Historical Errors of James Ford Rhodes." *Journal of Negro History* 2 (October 1917): 345-368.   Lynch is highly critical of Rhodes' interpretation of Reconstruction (see # 141). Rhodes' work was biased in favor of white Southern Democrats, and he showed racial prejudice. Lynch offers several examples of inaccuracies and distortions relating to events in Mississippi, and he points out positive aspects of Reconstruction.

121.   Lynch, John R. *Some Historical Errors of James Ford Rhodes*. Boston: Cornhill Publishing Co., 1922. 115p. Ports.   Lynch offers a strongly worded critique of Rhodes' treatment of Reconstruction in his history of the U.S. (see # 141). He calls attention to Rhodes' racial and political biases, his misuse of sources that led to a description of Reconstruction that wholly distorted the truth about

Republican politics and leadership, particularly in Mississippi. In defense of Rhodes a chapter written by "an expert" describes Lynch's own biases and his reliance on memory and experience in Mississippi rather than impartial evidence. Lynch concludes with comments on the politics of race and states' rights during the late 19th and early 20th centuries.

122.   Lynd, Staughton. "Rethinking Slavery and Reconstruction." *Journal of Negro History* 50 (July 1965): 198-209. Lynd examines interpretations of 20th century historians on the nature of slavery and abolitionism, the issue of the necessity for war, and the revolutionary nature of Reconstruction. He contends that the major failure of the federal government in Reconstruction was not providing an economic foundation for the freedmen to succeed. Lynd gives particular emphasis to the Reconstruction writings of Eric McKitrick, Kenneth Stampp, and W. E. B. DuBois.

123.   McKitrick, Eric. "Reconstruction: Ultraconservative Revolution." In *The Comparative Approach to American History*. Edited by C. Vann Woodward. New York: Basic Books, 1968. Pp. 146-159. Bibl.   McKitrick argues that the Civil War and Reconstruction were generally conservative events. The only revolutionary events that occurred resulted from the struggle between the executive and legislative branches of government over the course of Reconstruction. Significant change, such as black enfranchisement, lasted only for a short time before white conservatives regained power and began to systematically reverse the legal rights of the freedmen. The federal system restricted revolutionary tendencies.

124.   McPherson, James M. *The Abolitionist Legacy: From Reconstruction to the NAACP*. Princeton: Princeton University Press, 1975. 438p. App. Bibl.   A portion of this book examines the activities and influence of white, mostly male, abolitionists in the struggle for civil rights for blacks during the last years of Reconstruction. McPherson believes that the 1870s were years when most abolitionists did not turn away from the freedmen toward other interests as suggested by other historians (eg. Woodward, Meier). He focuses on the 284 abolitionists who sought ways to make blacks more equal with whites in American society. Many individuals continued their efforts after Reconstruction. The names of the abolitionists are listed in the appendices. (See also # 753)

125.   McPherson, James M. *Ordeal by Fire: The Civil War and Reconstruction*. New York: Alfred A. Knopf, 1982. 694p. Bibl. Glossary. Ills. Maps. Ports. McPherson provides a thorough, yet succinct, account of Reconstruction issues as they existed during and after the war. He addresses the long held myths about the period and explains why Reconstruction ended after just a few years. McPherson examines the political, social, and economic developments in postwar America and how they contributed to the demise of Republican rule in the South.

126.   McPherson, James M. "Some Thoughts on the Civil War as the Second Revolution." *Hayes Historical Journal* 3 (Spring 1982): 5-20. Ill.   McPherson interprets the Civil War and Reconstruction as a partially successful and unfinished

revolution. Dramatic changes were made in the lives of American blacks and in Southern society that were not completely eliminated by the Democratic backlash after Reconstruction.

127.   McPherson, James M. *The Struggle For Equality: Abolitionists and The Negro in the Civil War and Reconstruction.* Princeton: Princeton University Press, 1964. 474p. Bibl.   Abolitionists, such as members of William Lloyd Garrison's Massachusetts Antislavery Society, church antislavery societies, and many unorganized supporters of abolitionism, did not fade away with the beginning of the Civil War. McPherson demonstrates that they were active throughout the war and during Reconstruction with efforts to secure the absolute end to slavery and equal rights for the freedmen. In the 1870s the achievements of abolitionism were crushed by Republican compromise and political expediency. (See also McPherson's "The Abolitionists and the Negro During the Civil War and Reconstruction." Ph.D. Johns Hopkins University, 1962.)

128.   McWhiney, Grady. "Reconstruction: Index of Americanism." In *The Southerner as American.* Chapel Hill: University of North Carolina Press, 1960. Pp. 89-103.   Before and after the Civil War, both Northerners and Southerners were alike in many ways, particularly in their belief in progress, material advancement, and democratic equalitarianism in the context of the white race. Reconstruction failed because the nation denied economic power to blacks based on race, and by the end of the period Northerners and Southerners were more alike than ever. McWhinney optimistically views the decades from the 1870s to the 1950s as a period of continued Americanization of the nation and that race became less important than status and material accumulation.

129.   Moore, Robert Joseph. "Historians' Interpretations of the Reconstruction Period in American History." Ph.D. Boston University, 1961.

130.   Morton, W. L. "Canada and Reconstruction, 1863-1879." In *New Frontiers of the American Reconstruction.* Edited by Harold M. Hyman. Urbana: University of Illinois Press, 1966. Pp. 105-124.   Morton, a Canadian historian, explains that the Union victory in the Civil War and the Reconstruction that followed were factors that led to the Confederation in Canada in 1867.

131.   Muller, Philip R. "Look Back Without Anger: A Reappraisal of William A. Dunning." *Journal of American History* 61 (September 1974): 325-338. Muller summarizes Dunning's career as a historian by emphasizing on his contributions to Civil War and Reconstruction historiography. Muller is highly complimentary of *Essays on the Civil War and Reconstruction* (see # 79) but critical of *Reconstruction: Political and Economic* (see # 80) because it lacked sufficient research and care. The problems in the latter book led to accusations that Dunning was a racist and an apologist for the South. Such accusations do not match his true perspective or intentions.

132.   Murphy, Richard W. *The Nation Reunited - War's Aftermath.* Alexandria, Va.: Time-Life, 1987. 176p. Bibl. Ills. Map.   Murphy offers lavish illustrations along with a survey of Reconstruction history. He emphasizes that while the reform movement failed to achieve its immediate goals, it established a legal basis for future reforms to ensure equality of civil rights, and it had a greater impact in the North than was expected.

133.   Oberholtzer, Ellis Paxson. *A History of the United States Since the Civil War.* 5 Vols. New York: Macmillan Co., 1922-1926.   Reconstruction is given extensive coverage in volumes 1-3. Oberholtzer offers a chronological narrative from 1865 to 1878. His approach to the period and to racial issues was consistent with the conservative criticism of Radical Republican reforms written in the early 20th century.

134.   Patrick, Rembert W. *The Reconstruction of the Nation.* New York: Oxford University Press, 1967. 324p. Ills. Maps. Ports. Tbls.   Patrick writes a general history of the Reconstruction period, including chapters on foreign affairs and American social life. He believes that Reconstruction was a failure, because whatever gains appeared to be made in bringing black people into the mainstream of American society were mostly destroyed when Northern Republicans finally gave in to the demands of Southern whites. This resulted in a victory for white supremacy and the relegation of blacks to a new type of servitude.

135.   Patton, Jacob Harris. "Reconstruction." *Magazine of American History* 20 (September 1888): 204-218.   Patton believes that the American people do not understand the issues and events of Reconstruction. He surveys the major issues, focusing principally on why Congress insisted on rejecting President Johnson's program, the Northern reaction to the black codes, and black suffrage. He recognizes significant positive results in Reconstruction, particularly in the realm of education.

136.   Perman, Michael. *Emancipation and Reconstruction 1862-1879.* Arlington, Va.: Harlan Davidson, 1987. 150p. Bibl.   Perman believes that Reconstruction was too complex to pin failure on specific issues or persons. His approach is to explore whether Reconstruction ever had a chance of success and to avoid being judgmental. He concludes that there was little chance of success because there were too many contradictions in federal government policies, too much reliance on law and not enough on enforcement, and, in particular, federal hesitancy to take action when needed.

137.   Perman, Michael. *Reunion Without Compromise: The South and Reconstruction, 1865-1868.* Cambridge: Cambridge University Press, 1973. 376p. Bibl. Tbl.   Perman argues that only by understanding the perspectives and needs of Southern leaders in 1865 can a realistic analysis of Reconstruction be made. The revisionist historians of the 1950s and 1960s, such as Eric L. McKitrick, Kenneth Stampp, Lawanda and John Cox, and David Donald, believed that Southerners were willing to accept change in 1865 had a program of reconciliation been administered

competently. Perman believes that the idea that there was a basis for reconciliation was unrealistic. In fact, Southern leaders prior to 1868 resisted any sort of reconstruction that ran counter to their interests. The problem with Reconstruction is that it was controlled by moderates who allowed too many ways to interpret or avoid the reforms.

138.   Potter, David. *Division and the Stress of Reunion, 1845-1876.* Glenview, Ill.: Scott, Foresman, and Co., 1973. 237p. Ills. Ports.   Potter offers a survey of the period of prewar sectional division, the Civil War, and Reconstruction. He emphasizes that contemporaries of the Civil War era did not clearly understand the racial and political issues raised by the war and emancipation. He seems to suggest that better understanding and appreciation of reality might have contributed to finding better solutions to postwar Reconstruction. Each chapter is followed by suggested readings.

139.   Potter, Jacob Harris. "Reconstruction." *Magazine of American History* 20 (September 1888): 204-218.   Potter argues that Reconstruction by Congress, including the enfranchisement of the freedmen, was necessary as a way to protect the freedmen and promote their improvement. Their freedom, education, and labor will improve the nation.

140.   Randall, James G. and David Donald. *The Civil War and Reconstruction.* 2nd ed., Revised With Enlarged Bibliography. Lexington, Ma.: D. C. Heath, 1969. 866p. Ill. Maps. Ports. (2nd ed. originally published in 1961; 1st ed. by Randall, Boston: D.C. Heath, 1937)   The last nine chapters of this book provide a survey of political, social and economic development during the Reconstruction period. The authors' approach is consistent with the revisionists of the 1960s, and they frequently cite other revisionist accounts written since the 1930s to reinforce the evidence showing that economic life in the South was active and growing quickly, that blacks made significant and important economic and social progress after emancipation, and that political and social life was not marked by shame. An extensive, mostly annotated bibliography is divided by periods and includes a section of biographical references.

141.   Rhodes, James Ford. *History of the United States From the Compromise of 1850...*[title varies]. 9 Vols. New York: Macmillan Co., 1893-1928. Ill. Maps. Ports.   Volume 4-7 cover the period of the Civil War and Reconstruction (vol. 4: 1862-1864; vol. 5: 1864-1866; vol. 6: 1866-1872; vol. 7: 1872-1877).   Rhodes' treatment of Reconstruction focuses on political developments at the national and state levels. His work interprets American history from 1850 to 1877 as one of revolutionary change ending in a stronger, more unified nation and a nationalism that would strengthen in the decades after Reconstruction. Rhodes criticized President Johnson's political tactics and ineptness, and he supported federal power to ensure a loyal, reformed South as well as protection of the freedmen, but he strongly opposed the vengeful behavior of the Radicals. His racist views underpin his interpretation of Reconstruction as resulting in black rule, Republican coercion, and political corruption.

142.   Roark, James L.   "'So Much for the Civil War':   Cash and Continuity in Southern History." In *The Mind of the South: Fifty Years Later*. Edited by Charles W. Eagles.   Jackson: University Press of Mississippi, 1992.   Pp. 85-112. Commentary by Lacy K. Ford, Jr., pp. 101-112.   In his examination of Wilbur J. Cash's *Mind of the South* (New York: A. A. Knopf, 1941).   Roark disputes Cash's view that there was social, political, and cultural continuity from antebellum South to postwar South.   Roark explains that the South changed greatly and that Reconstruction was an attempt to reinforce and deepen the changes to race and class relations, political freedom, and the economy of the South.   In his commentary Ford agrees that Cash exaggerated the theme of continuity, but Cash clearly understood Southern symbols and myths that can be traced from the 1980s back to the mid-19th century.

143.   Schoonover, Thomas   (ed. & trans.).   *A Mexican View of America in the 1860s: A Foreign Diplomat Describes the Civil War and Reconstruction*. Rutherford, N. J.:   Fairleigh Dickison University Press, 1991.   271p.   Bibl. Port. Matías Romero was Mexican Chargé and minister in Washington from 1860 to 1867.   He wrote voluminous correspondence   (*Correspondencia de la Legación Mexicana Imprenta del Gobcerno, 1870-1892*) that were published in ten large volumes.   Romero offers a narrative of American affairs to help formulate effective policies in Mexican-American relations.   Schoonover translated a portion of Romero's summations of his dispatches   (*Resenas Políticas*). That focus on the American Civil War and Reconstruction based on popular and U.S. government publications.

144.   Schouler, James.   *History of the United States of America Under the Constitution. Vol. VII, 1865-1877*.   New York: Dodd, Mead and Co., 1913.   398p. App. Tbls.   Schouler's seventh and final volume of his history of the U.S. focuses almost entirely on the issues of Reconstruction.   He offers a very sympathetic view of Andrew Johnson who he believes has been mistreated by historical writers, particularly James Ford Rhodes [see # 141).   Schouler bases his views mainly on Johnson's papers and the diary of Gideon Welles, Secretary of the Navy.   His assessment of the Grant administration is quite critical based on the weakness of Grant as a political leader.

145.   Scott, Eben Greenough.   *Reconstruction During the Civil War in the United States of America*.   Boston: Houghton, Mifflin & Co., 1895.   432p.   App. Scott reviews the history of national and state power in America as a basis for his discussion of wartime efforts by the president and Congress to devise a plan for restoring the Union.   He is critical of those Radical Republicans who claimed that the Southern states had no constitutional basis to secede but then refused to recognize them as existing states after the end of hostilities.   For this reason Scott argues that the Republican Party was not a party that gave much sanctity to the Constitution unless it was to their advantage.

146.   Shaffer, Donald Robert. "Marching On: African-American Civil War Veterans in Postbellum America, 1865-1951." Ph.D. University of Maryland, 1996. 336p.

147.   Sharkey, Robert L. *Money, Class, and Party: An Economic Study of Civil War and Reconstruction.* Baltimore: Johns Hopkins Press, 1967, 1959. 346p. Bibl. Tbls.   The idea that the Radical Republicans, though not united on Reconstruction politics, can be viewed as holding a united economic philosophy is flawed. Sharkey believes that Charles and Mary Beard's emphasis on economics in their interpretation of the Civil War and Reconstruction (*Rise of American Civilization*, 4 vols., New York: Macmillan, 1927-1942) must be corrected after taking a close look at the divergent views within the Republican Party. The party not tied to Northern big business and finance, and actually fractured over issues such as currency, tariffs, and inflationary, and monetary policies. The most radical of the Radicals, such as Rep. Thaddeus Stevens of Pennsylvania, supported soft money and protective tariff policies, both of which were opposed by New York banking interests. Sharkey offers both an analysis of economic policy of the Republican and Democratic parties and a review of historical interpretations from the late 19th century to the 1950s. (Revision of Sharkey's Ph.D. disseration, Johns Hopkins University, 1958.)

148.   Sheehan, Donald. "Radical Reconstruction." In *Essays in American Historiography: Papers Presented in Honor of Allan Nevins.* Edited by Donald Sheehan and Harold C. Syrett. New York: Columbua University Press, 1960. Pp. 37-49.   Sheehan briefly reviews Reconstruction historiography up to the mid-twentieth century. His emphasis, however, is on the inability of mid-century historians to take sides in the same way that earlier historians did. He explains this situation by pointing to the way professional historians are trained to be objective and to consider all sides of an issue. This has resulted in either indecision or ambivalence regarding the motives of Radical Republicans, the distinctiveness of Southern politics, the efforts of Southern whites to regain control of their states, the basis for the black codes, and the price paid by blacks for the restoration of democracy in the South.

149.   Simkins, Francis B. "New Viewpoints of Southern Reconstruction." *Journal of Southern History* 5 (February 1939): 49-61.   Partisan condemnations of Reconstruction usually center on the political aspirations of blacks and the Reconstruction governments that were accused of corruption and radicalism. Simkins emphasizes unbiased moderation in analyzing the period. He suggests that there were positive activities in the social, religious, educational, and commercial realms for both freedmen and whites. It was, in fact, a period of increased optimism that ought to be studied for a better understanding of Southern race relations today.

150.   Smith, John David. *Black Voices From Reconstruction 1865-1877.* Brookfield, Conn.: Millbrook Press, 1997. 174p. Bibl. Ills.   Smith cites primary and secondary sources in his survey of Reconstruction written for young readers.

151.   Stampp, Kenneth M. *The Era of Reconstruction, 1865-1877*. New York: Alfred A. Knopf, 1966. 229p. Bibl.   Stampp examines the main issues of contention between revisionist historians and the long established views of William Dunning who depicted Reconstruction as disgraceful, scandalous, and a complete failure. Stampp emphasizes that when the period is studied closely without preconceived notions and biases, a more realistic picture of events emerges. While agreeing with some of the traditional criticism of Republican motives and federal and state government corruption, Stampp reveals that Southerners were not treated brutally, and many Republicans sincerely cared about helping freedmen and encouraged aid and assistance through the Freedmen's Bureau. The passage of the 14th and 15th Amendments legally ensured civil rights for blacks and made Reconstruction a long term success.

152.   Stampp, Kenneth M. and Leon Litwack. *Reconstruction: An Anthology of Revisionist Writings*. Baton Rouge: Louisiana State University Press, 1969. 531p. This book of 23 previously published journal articles and book chapters provides views of Lincoln, Johnson and the Radical Republicans, the response of the freedmen to emancipation, local Republican politics in the South, and the basis for the collapse of Reconstruction in national and local governments.

153.   Taylor, A. A. "Historians of the Reconstruction." *Journal of Negro History* 23 (January 1938); 16-34.   In this address delivered at the annual meeting of the Association for the Study of Negro Life and History on November 2, 1937 Taylor offers a survey of the historiography of Reconstruction. He focuses on major monographs written from the 19th century until the 1930s.

154.   Taylor, Joe Gray. "The White South From Succession to Redemption." In *Interpreting Southern History: Historiographical Essays in Honor of Sanford W. Higgenbotham*. Edited by John B. Boles and Evelyn Thomas Nolen. Baton Rouge: Louisiana State University Press, 1987. Pp. 162-198.   Approximatley half of Taylor's article is devoted to a brief discussion of books on Reconstruction that have been published between 1960 and 1980. The footnotes cite additional books and articles.

155.   Tilley, John Shipley. *The Coming of the Glory*. New York: Stratford House, 1949. 290p.   This book is an impressionistic survey of the institutions of slavery, secession and state sovereignty, and Reconstruction. While he does not favor slavery, Tilley presents a decidedly sympathetic account of the South's perspective on states' rights, the hypocrisy of the North, and the ravages of Reconstruction.

156.   Trent, W. P. "New South View of Reconstruction." *Sewanee Review* 9 (January 1901): 13-29.   Looking back to the period of Reconstruction Trent believes that the period was disastrous and tragic for the South and the nation as a whole. The major problems were the indiscretions of President Johnson and Radical Republicans who disregarded moderate and conservative proposals to inflict punishing legislation on the South. The South's refusal to change and Ku Klux

Klan violence cannot be excused, but they were caused by the radical policies of the Republicans. Ironically, the existing Republican government of 1901 does nothing in the face of increasing disregard for the civil rights of blacks.

157.   Ulrich, William J.   "The Northern Military Mind in Regard to Reconstruction, 1865-1872: The Attitudes of Ten Leading Union Generals." Ohio State University, 1959.

158.   Walden, Daniel. "W. E. B. DuBois: Pioneer Reconstruction Historian." *Negro History Bulletin* 26 (February 1963):159-160, 164.   DuBois' work on Reconstruction, particularly in his *Black Reconstruction* (see # 77), represents an ambitious attempt to redirect historians toward the positive aspects of the period and the contributions of blacks to building a better society.

159.   Weisberger, Bernard A. "The Dark and Bloody Ground of Reconstruction Historiography." *Journal of Southern History* 25 (November 1959): 427-447.   In Weisberger's survey of historical writing, he emphasizes the need for continued research on nearly all significant aspects of the period. Traditional interpretations grounded in works of Rhodes, Burgess, and Dunning have been in revision for more than 20 years, but they are still widely prevalent in textbooks and historical research. In light of the great contemporary changes in black-white relations in America, it is vital to dig deeper into the history of Reconstruction to understand why and how race relations exist as they do and how they may proceed in the future. To this end Weisberger calls on historians to grapple with the "tragedies, paradoxes, [and] tidal forces in the culture" (p. 447) of America during the Reconstruction period and to shed their professional biases in order to arrive at a clearer understanding of the period. Also, he calls for the updating of American history textbooks and for a new synthesis of the entire Reconstruction period.

160.   Werstein, Irving. *This Wounded Land: The Era of Reconstruction 1865-1877.* New York: Delacorte Press, 1968. 176p. Bibl.   Werstein's survey of Reconstruction is intended for young readers. The period is viewed from a broader, more positive perspective than traditional interpretations of the postwar years as a time of total tragedy for the South.

161.   Wharton, Vernon. "Reconstruction." In *Writing Southern History: Essays in Historiography in Honor of Fletcher M. Green.* Edited by Arthur S. Link and Rembert W. Patrick. Baton Rouge: Louisiana State University Press, 1965. Pp. 295-315.   Wharton traces the course of historical writing on Reconstruction up to the 1960s by systematically discussing the approach or ideology of key monographs and articles. He is particularly critical of the orthodox school of James Ford Rhodes, John Burgess, William Dunning, and several of Dunning's disciples, such as E. Merton Coulter, who are consistently racist and biased in favor of the South. He describes the revisionist works of John Lynch, W. E. B. DuBois, David Donald, John Hope Franklin, Frances Simkins, Robert Woody and others who seek to provide more balanced accounts that show more interest and sympathy with

blacks and clearer perspectives on Republicans in the South. Wharton warns revisionist historians against simplistic accounts of evil versus goodness.

162. White, James B. "Changing Interpretations of the Negro in the Reconstruction Governments." *Negro History Bulletin* 22 (November 1958): 31-32. Early trends among white historians (e.g. John Reynolds, Allan Nevins, and E. M. Coulter) to interpret Reconstruction with biases and an incomplete perspective began to reverse in the 1920s (e.g. A. A. Taylor, John Hope Franklin) and continues as more documentary evidence becomes available and writers have greater insight into the postwar period.

163. Williams, T. Harry. "An Analysis of Some Reconstruction Attitudes." *Journal of Southern History* 12 (November 1946): 469-486. (Rpt. in *The Selected Essays of T. Harry Williams.* Baton Rouge: Louisiana State University, 1983.) Williams compares the traditional negative stereotypes of Reconstruction expressed by historians who followed the interpretations of William Dunning with the revisionists who noted the positive aspects of Reconstruction. Williams believes that both approaches offer little explanation of the motives of people in Reconstruction, and he also rejects Marxist economic explanations. Such theories are too simple to explain the complexity of Reconstruction. He considers Howard K. Beale's economic thesis as probably the best explanation of what motivated Northern capitalists, Southern white planters, and even the lower class, Southern white yeoman farmers. Williams examines the various factions in Reconstruction using Louisiana as a test case.

164. Wilson, Woodrow. "The Reconstruction of the Southern States." *Atlantic Monthly* 87 (January 1901): 1-15. Wilson proposes to illuminate the revolutionary impact of the Civil War and Reconstruction. He points to the changed constitution and the strengthened federal power in relations with the states. As the power of the federal government grew, the result was the melding of a national consciousness and experience that would have permanent consequences for the future of the nation. The passions of Reconstruction still exist, and the period should be studied by historians with a dispassionate quest for truth.

165. Woodward, C. Vann. "Reconstruction: A Counterfactual Playback." In *The Future of the Past.* By C. Vann Woodward. New York: Oxford University Press, 1989. Pp. 183-200. Woodward explains the reasons for the failure of Reconstruction by questioning the concept that success was never realistic. His comparisons with emancipation in other countries and his speculation about how Reconstruction might have been conducted does not lead him to a definitive conclusion other than to urge historians to approach the period openly in its own context and with the recognition of the complex nature of human relations.

166. Woody, Robert H. "A History of the South." *South Atlantic Quarterly* 48 (January 1949): 119-130. In this essay Woody comments mainly on E. Merton Coulter's book *The South During Reconstruction, 1865-1877* (see # 831) and sets it within the historiography of the Reconstruction period. Coulter shows that he is not

a revisionist, and he finds little of benefit from the Reconstruction experience. Woody mentions other historical works as comparisons, particularly the work of W. E. B. DuBois (see # 77).

167.   Wood, Forrest G. *The Era of Reconstruction, 1863-1877.* New York: Thomas Y. Crowell, 1975. 113p. Bibl.   Wood writes a brief guide to the key issues of Reconstruction beginning during the Civil War. He views Reconstruction as a revolutionary movement that was the culmination of abolitionism. Due to the prevalence of racism in the U.S. and the changing leadership in Congress, Reconstruction had little chance of success.

National Politics of Reconstruction

General Studies and Biographies

168.   Abbott, Richard H. *Cobbler in Congress: The Life of Henry Wilson, 1812-1875.* Lexington: University of Kentucky Press, 1972. 289p. Bibl. Ports. Before becoming vice-president in Grant's second term (1873-1877), Wilson (born Jeremiah Jonas Colbath) had been a Massachusetts state legislator and U.S. senator. He was known for his antislavery convictions, his support for equal rights for blacks, and his desire for a quick nonvindictive Reconstruction of the South. He was often criticized by conservatives for his liberal views, by the Radicals for posing as a moderate, and by both sides as too much the politician. (See also of Abbott's Ph.D. dissertation, University of Wisconsin, 1965.)

169.   Andrews, Matthew Page. "American Responsibility for 'Reconstruction' Debts." *Landmark* 8 (November 1926): 698-702.   Andrews argues that the federal government should take responsibility for the large debts incurred by the corrupt, unrepresentative Reconstruction governments in the Southern states.

170.   Arcanti, Steven J. "To Secure the Party: Henry L. Dawes and the Politics of Reconstruction." *Historical Journal of Western Massachusetts* 5 (Spring 1977): 33-45.   Dawes was a Republican Massachusetts congressman who opposed the methods of the Radicals in the struggle with President Johnson to control Reconstruction. His concern for preserving a strong Union led to his rejection of Johnson when the president showed inflexibility by vetoing key legislation and attempted to organize a new political party.

171.   Ashby, Paul F. *The Federal Administration, 1865-1877.* Ph.D. University of Chicago, 1950.

172.   Auchampaugh, Phillip G. "Charles O'Connor's View of the Prosecution of Jefferson Davis, 1867." *Tyler's Quarterly Historical and Genealogical Magazine*

29 (January 1948): 181-183.   In a letter dated October 19, 1867 Davis's attorney, O'Connor, suggests that President Johnson and other government officials, including many Republican members of Congress, oppose putting Davis on trial, but refuse to do anything to avoid it for political reasons.

173.   Avillo, Philip J., Jr. "Property and Race: The Dilemma of Slave State Republican Congressmen and the Origins of Reconstruction, 1863-1867." *Southern Studies* 23 (Summer 1984): 125-144.   Avillo examines the voting records of Republican congressmen from slaveowning border states to test Howard K. Beale's assertion (see # 439) that they slavishly followed the national party on its core issues of tariffs, currency, and property. Their voting patterns reflected local economic concerns, and even though they helped pass Reconstruction legislation, they frequently did not agree with the party's racial policies that were opposed in their districts. The Republican ascendancy in the border states was short-lived, because racial issues and opposition to white disenfranchisement brought Democrats back to power.

174.   Avillo, Philip J., Jr. *Slave State Republicans in Congress 1861-1877.* Ph.D. University of Arizona, 1975.

175.   Bancroft, Frederic. "Seward's Part in Reconstruction, 1865-1869." In *The Life of William H. Seward. Vol. II.* New York: Harper & Brothers, 1900. Ports. Pp. 443-469.   Seward is described as a man of moderation with regard to Reconstruction.   He supported President Johnson's policy favoring a quick, nonantagonistic Reconstruction in order to bring the nation together. Indeed, Seward designed the original policy, but he strongly opposed Johnson's methods of carrying it out. He disagreed with the Radical Republican proposals, but he was not belligerent towards them and did not become a leader in Johnson's campaign to defeat his opponents. Seward has been judged too harshly by past historians for his role in Reconstruction.

176.   Beale, Howard K. "The Tariff and Reconstruction." *American Historical Review* 35 (January 1930): 276-294.   Beale departs from constitutional issues emphasized by historians Dunning and Rhodes to focus on the protective tariff. The tariff was a device used by the Radicals to ensure the political and economic strength of Northern industries before the South could return to Congress and team up with antiprotectionist Western states as they did prior to the Civil War. The Radicals deemphasized the tariff in the West and emphasized it in the North as a way to placate Western farmers and gain a clear victory in the congressional elections of 1866.

177.   Belden, Thomas Graham. *The Salmon P. Chase Family in the Civil War and Reconstruction: A Study in Ambition and Corruption.* Ph.D. University of Chicago, 1952.

178.   Belz, Herman. "The Freedmen's Bureau Act of 1865 and the Principle of No Discrimination According to Color." *Civil War History* 21 (September 1975):

197-217.   The congressional debate on the Freedmen's Bureau bill was based on the need for government assistance after the war and the ideology of legal equality of the races. The philosophy of *laissez faire* could be used as an argument against special treatment for blacks, but in this case, it was used to make the bill technically color blind by including white refugees as one of the groups needing assistance.

179.   Belz, Herman. "Henry Winter Davis and the Origins of Congressional Reconstruction." *Maryland Historical Magazine* 67 (Summer 1972): 129-143. Belz considers the origins of congressional Reconstruction to be a bill written in 1862-1863 by Davis, a Unionist congressman from Maryland. The bill became the Wade-Davis bill that President Lincoln killed with a pocket veto. Belz emphasizes that the bill was not a departure from constitutional traditions because Republicans recognized the constitutional system that allowed the states, even the rebellious ones, to reform themselves within a framework supervised at the national level.

180.   Benedict, Michael Les. *A Compromise of Principle: Congressional Republicans and Reconstruction, 1863-1869.* New York: W. W. Norton, 1974. 493p. Bibl. Graphs. Ills. Ports.   Benedict argues against the notion that there was solid Radical Republican opposition to the Reconstruction policies of both Lincoln and Johnson. He classifies Republicans by radical, centrist, and conservative factions in the House and the Senate and traces their activities and votes on critical issues. The results show that congressional Reconstruction legislation was based on compromise. Even though events in the South and Johnson's policies pushed conservatives and centrists into the ranks of the Radicals, they moderated the Radicals' program in the Civil Rights Bill of 1866 and the Reconstruction Acts of 1867. Benedict points to compromises in 1867 as more pivotal for Republicans than the 1866 congressional victory.   (See also Benedict's *The Right Way: Congressional Republicans and Reconstruction, 1863-1869.* Ph.D. Rice University, 1971.)

181.   Benedict, Michael Les. "Equality and Expediency in the Reconstruction Era: A Review Essay." *Civil War History* 23 (December 1977): 322-335.   The essays in *Radical Republicans in the North: State Politics During Reconstruction* (see # 2835, 2849, 2895) consistently show that national issues, particularly equal rights for black Americans, were important at the local level. Benedict explains that the theme of values conflict is clearly evident in the support of congressional Republicans for equal rights while the majority of Northern Republican voters were inherently racist.

182.   Benedict, Michael Les. "The Rout of Radicalism: Republicans and the Elections of 1867." *Civil War History* 18 (December 1972): 334-344.   Benedict emphasizes the importance of state elections in 1867 to the future of both Reconstruction legislation and the Republican Party. The elections proved to be a defining event because voters swung power away from the Radicals toward the conservative Republicans who had already played an important role in moderating Radical legislation on Reconstruction. Conservatives would henceforth be in

control of Reconstruction legislation, the impeachment of Johnson in 1867-1868, and the Republican Party's choice of a presidential candidate in the 1868.

183.   Benedict, Michael Les. "Salmon P. Chase and Constitutional Politics." *Law and Social Inquiry* 22 (Spring 1997): 459-496.   Includes an extended analysis of Niven's book on Chase (see # 325) and an assessment of Chase's career. Benedict emphasizes Chase's greatness not only as an antislavery proponent, treasury secretary under Lincoln, and his concern for individual rights as chief justice of the U.S. Supreme Court, but also for his conservatism toward revolutionary change in American government.   Chase reflects the ambiguity and divided nature of the American people during the Civil War and Reconstruction.

184.   Bensel, Richard Franklin. *Yankee Leviathan: The Origins of Central State Authority in America, 1859-1877.* Cambridge: Cambridge University Press, 1990. 452p. Diagr. Maps. Tbls.   The founding of the Republican Party and the victory of the North in the Civil War led to a dramatic increase in federal authority in the U.S. Further centralization during Reconstruction failed and then stalled for the rest of the 19th century.   The expansion of federal authority combined with sectional animosity and wartime destruction to stunt economic growth in the South during Reconstruction.   Ultimately the Southern economy grew by integrating into the national economy, but Southern separatism continued to stymie further centralization of national power.

185.   Black, Ernest Patrick. *The Reconstruction Dilemma: Northern Theory and Southern Tragedy.* Ph.D. State University of New York at Buffalo, 1983. 392p.

186.   Blaine, James G. et al. "Ought the Negro to Be Disfranchised? Ought He to Have Been Enfranchised?" *North American Review* 128 (1879): 225-283.   Nine essays comprise this forum. Blaine's defense of black suffrage is followed by 7 responders: L. Q. C. Lamar, Wade Hampton, James G. Garfield, Alexander H. Stephens, Wendell Phillips, Montgomery Blair, and Thomas A. Hendricks. Blaine also provides a conclusion. Among the writers, Blaine, Phillips, and Garfield were prominent Republicans and the rest were prominent Democrats.

187.   Blaine, James G. *Twenty Years of Congress: From Lincoln to Garfield.* 2 Vols. Norwich, Conn.: Henry Bill Publishing Co., 1893. 723p. App. Index of Names. Ports.   Blaine, Republican Speaker of the House from Maine (1869-1876), provides his perspective on the issues before the Congress and nation. Volume 2 of the two volume set begins with the installation of Andrew Johnson as president and proceeds in chronological fashion with the major issue of Reconstruction taking up a significant portion of the volume.   Blaine clearly favored congressional Reconstruction as a necessary program for the readmission of the Southern states and the protection of the freedmen. Blaine recognizes that the Republicans made mistakes in the conduct of Reconstruction, but he places the blame for the turmoil in the South during Reconstruction in the lap of white Southerners who rejected the 14th Amendment when acceptance would have brought about gradual change. He

also bemoans the weakness of the Republican Party in the South and its abandonment by Southern Unionists who refused to accept black suffrage.

188.   Blassingame, John W. and John R. McKivigan (eds.). *The Frederick Douglass Papers. Series One: Speeches, Debates, and Interviews. Vol. 4: 1864-1880.* New Haven: Yale University Press, 1991. 663p. App.   Douglass was the best known black American of the 19th century. Volume 4 of his papers is arranged chronologically with the text of speeches and conversations taken from among different sources that are cited in the text. The documents illustrate Douglass's work for equal rights and opportunities for blacks following the Civil War. The book includes a partial speaking itinerary and a detailed subject index.

189.   Blight, David W. *Frederick Douglass' Civil War: Keeping Faith in Jubilee.* Baton Rouge: Louisiana State University Press, 1989. 270p. Bibl. Port. Blight discusses Douglass's perspective on abolitionism, the Civil War and Reconstruction.   Douglass clearly supported and pushed for radical reforms, particularly black suffrage, and he strongly backed the Republican Party as the only organization that had the power and willingness to make changes. He viewed Reconstruction as the government's opportunity to eliminate racial discrimination and bring blacks into the American mainstream, but he also knew the process took time and that white supremacy throughout the nation had to be overcome.

190.   Blue, Frederick J. *Salmon P. Chase: A Life in Politics.* Kent, Oh.: Kent State University Press, 1987. 420p. Bibl. Port.   Bluse examines Chase's career as an Ohio abolitionist senator (1850-1856, 1860), Ohio governor (1856-1859), wartime secretary of state in Lincoln's cabinet, and chief justice of the U.S. Supreme Court (1865-1873). Chase worked closely with President Johnson to formulate a Reconstruction, but Chase consistently supported black civil rights, including suffrage.   As Chief Justice his court made several decisions relevant to Reconstruction issues, such as *Ex parte* Milligan on the jurisdiction of military courts in the South; Cummings v. Missouri on the use of oaths; *Ex parte* McCardle on the Supreme Court's jurisdiction in *habeas corpus* cases; and the Slaughter-House Cases on the constitutionality of the 14th Amendment. In his role as presider at the trial of President Johnson, he affirmed the neutrality of the Court in impeachments.

191.   Boney, F. N. "Grassroots Reconstruction and Continuity in the South." *Southern Studies* 19 (Fall 1980): 286-290.   Boney criticizes the failure of the first Reconstruction and the weakness of efforts at civil rights reforms in later years. He expresses optimism about the future with the existing presidential administration of a white Southerner, Jimmy Carter. Yet he states that blacks have always put too much reliance on the power of the federal government to effect real change.

192.   Boutwell, George S. Reminiscences of Sixty Years in Public Affairs. Vol. 2. New York: McClure, Phillips & Co., 1902.   Boutwell was a Massachusetts Republican congressman from 1863 to 1869, Secretary of the Treasury from 1869 to 1873, and U.S. senator from 1873 ot 1877. A portion of this volume includes his

thoughts on postwar issues related to the South, the impeachment of President Johnson, and the administration of President Grant.

193.   Boyd, William K. "Gideon Welles on War, Politics, and Reconstruction." *South Atlantic Quarterly* 11 (April 1912): 180-186.   Boyd briefly comments on Welles' diary published in 1910-1911 (see # 403) in which Welles expresses his opposition to Radical Reconstruction policies and his support for President Johnson.

194.   Bradley, Bert. "Negro Speeches in Congress: 1869-1875." *Southern Speech Journal* 18 (May 1953): 216-225.   Bradley examines the speeches of 11 black congressmen on the civil rights bills that were debated during the 1870s until a bill finally passed in 1875. He finds that their speakers mainly defended the bill against critics or declared that blacks had earned the rights described in the bill.

195.   Bridges, Roger D. *The Constitutional World of Senator John Sherman, 1861-1869.* Ph.D. University of Illinois, 1970. 464p.

196.   Briggs, Emily Edson. *The Olivia Letters: Being Some History of Washington City for Forty Years as Told by the Letters of a Newspaper Correspondent.* New York: Neale Pub. Co., 1906. 445p. Port.   Briggs wrote for the *Philadelphia Press* and used the pseudonym Olivia. These "letters" which are more like impressionistic editorials, offer her perspective on a wide range of persons and events in Washington from January, 1866 to January, 1882, including pieces on women, President Johnson's impeachment trial, Benjamin F. Wade, John Bingham, Ulysses S. Grant, Phil Sheridan, Thaddeus Stevens, John Sherman, Zachariah C. Chandler, Oliver P. Morton, and Charles Sumner.

197.   Brock, William R. *An American Crisis: Congress and Reconstruction, 1865-1867.* New York: Harper Torchbooks, 1966. 312p. Bibl. (Orig. published by St. Martin's Press, 1967)   Brock explores the behavior and goals of Congress, particularly the Radical Republicans, in its quest to fashion a new order in the democracy of the U.S. following the Civil War. He is concerned with the ideas and motives of Congress, and emphasizes the reformist goals of the Radicals. Although the Radicals failed to change Southern society, their efforts are noteworthy because they introduced new laws in the form of constitutional amendments that were never repealed and gave the freedmen hope for the future. Ironically it was the constitution that stymied the reformers in their day.

198.   Brock, William R. "Reconstruction and the American Party System." In *A Nation Divided: Problems and Issues of the Civil War and Reconstruction.* Edited by George M. Fredrickson. Minneapolis: Burgess Publishing Co., 1975. pp. 81-112.   Strong party unity evaded both Democrats and Republicans in Reconstruction because neither party could build widespread appeal for their political ideologies in both the North and the South. The two party system failed in the South, and the dominance of class and race over national issues lasted for decades.

199.   Brodie, Fawn M. *Thaddeus Stevens: Scourge of the South.* New York: W. W. Norton, 1959. 448p. Bibl. Ports.   Rep. Stevens of Pennsylvania was the subject of both vilification and high admiration from his contemporaries and historians.   Brodie depicts him as a man of contradictions who acted with both extreme ruthlessness and caring for his fellow man.   He was an eternal pessimist who was never satisfied with his achievements.   Stevens' personality faults, combined with his insistence on justice, generated the energy and support necessary to produce at least the legal basis for equal rights for blacks.

200.   Brown, Ira V.   "William D. Kelley and Radical Reconstruction." *Pennsylvania Magazine of History and Biography* 85 (July 1961): 316-329. Kelley, a Republican congressman from Pennsylvania   (1861-1890), is widely known for his support for the protective tariff, but Brown explains that he was also a strong Radical who supported the party's Reconstruction program, including black suffrage.

201.   Brownlow, Paul C.   "The Northern Protestant Pulplit on Reconstruction, 1865-1877." Ph.D. Purdue University, 1970. 291p.

202.   Brownlow, Paul C.   "The Pulpit and Black America, 1865-1877." *Quarterly Journal of Speech* 58 (December 1972): 431-440.   This study of Northern Protestant opinion of blacks and civil rights during Reconstruction is based on 91 sermons delivered by ministers from 10 Protestant denominations in 18 Northern states and the District of Columbia. The sermons reveal that from 1865 through 1868 Northern preachers enthusiastically supported the Republican program for equal rights, black suffrage, and economic aid to the freedmen. Beginning in 1869 support for these goals diminished, possibly because the goals appeared to be met or because blacks were no longer needed as a tool to control the South and enhance the power of the Republican Party.

203.   Burgess-Jackson, Keith.   "Democracy Versus Republicanism: Detroit Press Reaction to the Reconstruction Act of 1867.*" Southern Studies* N.S. 1 (Winter 1990): 305-330.   The Detroit press reflected the national split between the Republican and Democratic parties.   The author examines editorial opinions expressed in the *Advertiser and Tribune* (Republican critic of Johnson) and the *Free Press* (Democratic).

204.   Butler, Benjamin F.   *Private and Official Correspondence of General Benjamin F. Butler.* 5 vols. Norwood, Ma.: Plumpton Press [privately published], 1917.   The letters published in these volumes were either written by or to Butler from April, 1861 to March, 1868. They include correspondence while he was in command of New Orleans from May 1 - December 2, 1862 and from the first three years of Reconstruction.   Butler was an ardent Radical who supported the congressional program of Reconstruction and the right of blacks to civil rights, including manhood suffrage.

205.   Callender, E. B. *Thaddeus Stevens: Commoner.* Boston: A. Williams & Co., 1882. 210p. App.   This book offers a very positive account of Stevens that is written in a eulogistic tone.

206.   Cate, Wirt Armistead. *Lucius Q. C. Lamar: Secession and Reunion.* Chapel Hill: University of North Carolina Press, 1935. 594p. Bibl. Ills. Ports. Cates provides a highly complimentary biography of Lamar, a respected Mississippi and congressional statesman, orator, U.S. Secretary of the Interior (1885-1887), and U.S. Supreme Court Justice (1888-1893). Lamar favored secession, and at the end of the war he did not participate in public life until his election to Congress in 1872. As a Democrat Lamar opposed Radical Reconstruction and worked to educate the Congress about the South and sectional reconciliation. This was evident in his famous eulogy to Charles Sumner in April 27, 1874 and his influence in the settlement of the Hayes-Tilden presidential election controversy in 1876/77. Cate reveals his own bias against Radicals that influences his entire presentation of Reconstruction period. (See also a similar evaluation of Lamar in Frank E. Shanahan, Jr., "L. Q. C. Lamar: An Evalaution," *Journal of Mississippi History* 26 (May 1964): 91-122.)

207.   Chase, Salmon P. *Diary and Correspondence of Salmon P. Chase.* In *Annual Report of the American Historical Association for the Year 1902.* Vol. II. Washington: G.P.O., 1903. 527p.   This book includes a few letters relevant to Reconstruction, and a larger portion related to Civil War issues, particularly Louisiana. The Louisiana letters were written by George S. Dennsion. Letters written by Chase were written between February, 1846 and May, 1861. The diary covers only July-October, 1862. The letters to Chase written between May, 1865 and June, 1870 were written by Horace Greeley, William G. Brownlow, Wager Swayne, John Jay, William Cullen Bryant, Samuel Ward, Murat Halstead, and Johns Hopkins. Also included is a Calendar of Letters printed in other publications with a brief reference to the source.

208.   Chase, Salmon P. *The Salmon P. Chase Papers.* 5 Vols. Edited by John Niven. Kent, Oh.: Kent State University Press, 1993-   Volumes 1 includes Chase's journals from 1829 to 1872. There are many journal entries revealing his views on black suffrage, the Wade-Davis bill, the 13th and 14th Amendments, Andrew Johnson's policies and impeachment, Republican politics and Reconstruction in general. The correspondence in volumes 2-5 cover 1823 to 1873. (For more complete correspondence see the *Salmon P. Chase Papers* on microfilm published by University Publications of America in 43 reels.)

209.   Cheek, William and Aimee Lee Cheek. "John Mercer Langston: Principle and Politics." In *Black Leaders of the Nineteenth Century.* Edited by Leon Litwack and August Meier. Urbana: University of Illinois Press, 1988. Pp. 102-126. Port. The authors emphasize that Langston represented the ideal of black self reliance and self assertion in the struggle for equality in a racist nation. The authors examine Langston's entire career. With regard to Reconstruction his activities thrust him into national prominence as the leader of the National Equal Rights League from 1864 to

1868 that encouraged the formation of local leagues in Southern states and pushed for equality of civil rights and justice in courts. In this role and as an inspector for the Freedmen's Bureau, he gained the respect of both blacks and whites by his moderate, yet insistent, tone for black rights. His strong oratorical skills contributed to his popularity that led to conflict with other black leaders, including Frederick Douglass. (See also Langston's autobiography: *From the Virginia Plantation to the National Capital or the First and Only Negro Representative in Congress from the Old Dominion.* New York: Kraus Reprint Co., 1969. [Rpt. of Hartford: American Publishing Co., 1894.])

210.   Christopher, Maurine. *America's Black Congressmen.* New York: Thomas Y. Crowell, 1971. 283p. Bibl. Ills. Ports.   Brief biographies are provided on all blacks who served in the U.S. House of Representatives and the Senate between 1870 and 1971. The following persons from the Reconstruction period are covered: Hiram R. Revels, Blanche K. Bruce, and John R. Lynch from Mississippi, Joseph H. Rainey, Robert Smalls, Robert Brown Elliott, Richard H. Cain, Alonzo J. Ransier, Robert DeLarge from South Carolina, Jefferson F. Long from Georgia, Josiah T. Walls from Florida, and Charles E. Nash and P. B. S. Pinchback from Louisiana. The chapters provide biographical information, but the focus is on congressional careers.

211.   Clark, John G. "Historians and the Joint Committee on Reconstruction." *Historian* 23 (May 1961): 348-361.   Clark reviews interpretations of the Joint Committee of Fifteen, particularly the work of Benjamin Kendrick (# 281) and Howard K. Beale (# 439). He calls for additional research on the role of business interests in Congress immediately after the Civil War, and a closer look at Committee members and the attitudes of Northern Republicans and the Republican Party regarding the freedmen.

212.   Clark, John G. "Radicals and Moderates on the Joint Committee on Reconstruction." *Mid-America* 45 (April 1963): 79-98.   It is difficult to clearly define "radicals" and "moderates" regarding Republican Reconstruction policymaking in 1865 and 1866. Rigid classification of these two groups provides an inaccurate guide to political attitudes in Congress. Clark criticizes traditional definitions of these two groups based on generalizations regarding Northeastern capitalist hegemony, Republican Party power in the South, black suffrage, and defining the appropriate way to bring the Southern states back into the Union. Clark focuses on several representatives of the Radicals and Moderates, including Radical congressmen Thaddeus Stevens of Pennsylvania and Elihu Washburne of Illinois and moderates Senator William P. Fessenden and Congressman John Bingham, both of Ohio.

213.   Clontz, William Harold. "An Analysis of the Political Career of Frederick Douglass, 1865-1895." Ph.D. University of Idaho, 1976. 435p.

214.   Coben, Stanley. "Northeastern Business and Radical Reconstruction: A Re-examination." *Journal of American History* 46 (June 1959): 67-90.   Coben

challenges the interpretation that Northeastern business influenced congressional Republicans to design Radical Reconstruction in order to further their economic interests.   The business interests promoted protective tariffs, national banks, noninflationary hard currency, and political and economic exploitation of the South. He explains that the various business interests disagreed among themselves about the best economic policies and the course of Reconstruction.   Congressional decision making cannot be explained by referring to the influence of business.

215.   Cohen, Nancy.   "The Problem of Democracy in the Age of Capital: Reconstructing American Liberalism, 1865-1890." Ph.D.   Columbia University, 1996. 380p.

216.   Coulter, E. Merton.   "Amnesty For All Except Jefferson Davis: The Hill-Blaine Debate of 1876." *Georgia Historical Quarterly* 56 (Winter 1972): 453-494. Ills.   Congressmen Benjamin H. Hill of Georgia and James G. Blaine of Maine were the principle debaters regarding a bill that proposed amnesty to all former Confederates who had not yet received it.   Blaine insisted on amending the bill so that Jefferson Davis would be excluded.   The emotion charged debate that ensued recalled the horrors of the war.   The bill did not pass and the debate rankled many Southern observers who remembered it for many years.

217.   Coulter, E. Merton.   "Sherman and the South." *North Carolina Historical Review* 8 (January 1931): 41-54.   Gen. William T. Sherman was a postwar friend of the South based on his opposition to protracted Reconstruction and emphasis on the quick restoration of peace and normalcy.   He opposed abolitionism and cared little for the civil rights of blacks.   Coulter explains Sherman's personality and his actions during and after the war.   (See also # 337)

218.   Cox, LaWanda.   "From Emancipation to Segregation: National Policy and Southern Blacks."   In *Interpreting Southern History: Historiographical Essays in Honor of Sanford W. Higginbotham.*   Edited by John B. Boles and Evelyn Thomas Nolen.   Baton Rouge: Louisiana State University Press, 1987. Pp. 199-253.   This is an extensive survey of Reconstruction historiography that focuses primarily on writing since the early 1960s.   Cox relates the writing to the social and political developments of the period, particularly the movements for civil rights and black power.   Cox discusses the various issues that historians have researched during the past 25 years and also points to the increasing use of statistical methodologies as a tool to provide fresh insights into Reconstruction.   She suggests that Reconstruction as a period or a concept has lost meaning in light of the complex issues of post Civil War America.

219.   Cox, LaWanda and John H.   "Negro Suffrage and Republican Politics: The Problems of Motivation in Reconstruction Historiography." *Journal of Southern History* 33 (August 1967): 303-330.   The authors examine 20th century interpretations of Republican motives for supporting the 15th Amendment. Historians who wrote during the first 30 years emphasized that Republicans intended to use the black vote for political advantage and were hypocrites for

allowing racial discrimination in the North.   New documentation and the contemporary civil rights movement produced more favorable views of the Republicans that emphasized their idealism and genuine interest in equal political rights for black Americans.   The authors believe that the Republicans were less concerned with winning elections than establishing a principle of equality in a crisis situation.

220.   Cox, LaWanda and John H. *Politics, Principle and Prejudice, 1865-1866*. New York: Collier-Macmillan, 1963. 294p. Bibl.   The authors seek a fresh examination of the political struggle in the national government over the shape and direction of Reconstruction.   They examine the conservative movement led by Secretary of State William Seward and Thurlow Weed to form a new moderate political party with Johnson as its leader.   But Johnson's decision to oppose federal protection of civil rights for freedmen and the Freedmen's Bureau bill brought to the fore the issue of congressional power and the right of the freedmen to fair treatment. Johnson's unbending principles and his political mistakes caused moderate Republicans to distrust him and to swing their support to the Radicals.

221.   Cox, LaWanda. "The Promise of Land for the Freedmen." *Mississippi Valley Historical Review*   45 (December 1958): 413-440.   Cox analyses the legislative process during 1863-1865 that led to the passage of the Freedmen's Bureau bill in March, 1865 with provisions for the sale or rent of land to the freedmen. The bill changed from a war measure to a search for long term solutions to the problem of providing assistance to millions of freedmen in need of security. Cox deemphasizes the impact of Northern business interests on the final outcome. Republicans wanted land distribution to break up large plantations and to provide freedmen independence from abuse from both Southern employers and Northern land speculators.

222.   Crenshaw, William Vanderclock. "Benjamin F. Butler: Philosophy and Politics, 1866-1879." Ph.D. University of Georgia, 1976. 363p.

223.   Current, Richard N. "Love, Hate, and Thaddeus Stevens." *Pennsylvania History* 14 (October 1947): 259-272. (Rpt. in *Arguing With Historians: Essays on the Historical and Unhistorical*. Middletown: Wesylean University Press, 1987. Pp. 83-96)   Some historians and Stevens' contemporaries may have thought that the Pennsylvania congressman was motivated by love of the black man or hate for the Southern white man, but Current explains that neither was the key motivating factor for Stevens. More powerful factors were political expediency and a desire to maintain Republican power in his state and the North.

224.   Current, Richard Nelson. *Old Thad Stevens: A Story of Ambition*. Madison: University of Wisconsin Press, 1942. 344p. Bibl. Ills. Port.   Current seeks a new, balanced interpretation of Stevens.   He depicts the Pennsylvania congressman and Speaker of the House as an ambitious, Republican politician whose main interests were the enhancement of his own power and the power of the Republican Party, the needs of big business, including iron-making and railroads,

and the subjugation of the South for as long as possible. Stevens' reputation for supporting the common man and equality among all men of any race is contradicted by his contribution to the growing power of big business. For Stevens, avid Republicanism was a means to power. (See also Current's "Thaddeus Stevens: The Man and the Politician." Ph.D. University of Wisconsin, 1940.)

225.   Davis, Van M. "Individualism on Trial: The Ideology of the Northern Democracy During the Civil War and Reconstruction." Ph.D. University of Virginia, 1972.

226.   Dinunzio, Mario R. "Lyman Trumbull, United States Senator." Ph.D. Clark University, 1964. 215p.

227.   Dodd, Dorothy. "Henry J. Raymond and the *New York Times* During Reconstruction." Ph.D. University of Chicago, 1933.

228.   Donald, David. *Charles Sumner and the Rights of Man.* New York: Alfred A. Knopf, 1970. 595p. Bibl. Ports.   Donald offers a narrative of Sumner's public and private life from 1850 until his death in 1874. He describes Sumner as a leader of ideas rather than of practical politics. Sumner advanced the cause of equality for all citizens, and he supported suffrage for blacks and the importance of offering them a realistic chance to succeed as free people in the South. But Sumner's Republican colleagues usually disregarded his ideas and proposals. Even though he withdrew his support from President Grant over civil service and foreign relations issues, he also could not accept the reactionary politics of the Liberal Republicans who opposed the use of federal power to enforce Reconstruction legislation. When he died Sumner was revered mainly for his sincerity and the moral principles that he expressed.

229.   Donald, David H.. *The Politics of Reconstruction.* Baton Rouge: Louisiana State University Press, 1965. 105p. App. Tbls. (Walter Lynwood Fleming Lectures in Southern History)   In an effort to revitalize Reconstruction scholarship Donald uses a statistical approach to analyzing congressional votes on Reconstruction legislation between 1864 and 1867. In three essays he identifies factions within the Republican Party and how those factions shaped responses to Lincoln's and Johnson's approaches toward reconstructing the South and the formulation of legislation culminating in the first Reconstruction Act of 1867. He includes three appendices with tabulated voting data and groups of congressmen by faction.

230.   Dorris, Jonathan T. *Pardon and Amnesty Under Lincoln and Johnson: The Restoration of the Confederates to Their Rights and Privileges, 1861-1898.* Chapel Hill: University of North Carolina, 1953. 459p. Bibl.   The issues of pardon and amnesty were intertwined with the debate about the status of the Confederacy during the Civil War and the years of Reconstruction, as well as the issue of property confiscation and disenfranchisement. Presidential policies of both Lincoln and Johnson were marked by leniency, even in the case of most

Confederate leaders. Dorris discusses many individual pardon cases, particularly in North Carolina. (See also Dorris's "Pardon and Amnesty During the Civil War and Reconstruction." Ph.D. University of Illinois, 1926.)

231.   Dorris, Jonathan T. "Pardoning John Cabell Breckinridge." *Register of the Kentucky Historical Society* 56 (October 1958): 319-324.   Breckinridge ran for president as a Democrat in 1860 and represented Kentucky in the U.S. Senate in 1861 prior to his decision to join the Confederate Army. After the war he fled the country until he was sure that he could return without being arrested and that he would be included in President Johnson's universal amnesty of December, 1868.

232.   DuBois, Ellen Carol. "A New Life: The Development of An American Woman Suffrage Movement 1860-1869." Ph.D. Northwestern University, 1975. 397p. (See also DuBois' *Feminism and Suffrage.* Ithaca: Cornell University Press, 1978)

233.   Dunning, William A.   "The Second Birth of the Republican Party." *American Historical Review* 16 (October 1910): 56-63.   Dunning seeks to correct the idea that the Republican Party existed as the same political party from its founding in 1854 to his own day. The Union Party that emerged from the national convention in Baltimore in 1864 fragmented into conservatives who backed Johnson's Reconstruction plan and a coalition of moderates and radicals who sought to introduce fundamental change in the South. The latter group actually represents the reborn Republican Party that emerged from the November, 1866 election to legislate its own Reconstruction.

234.   Dyer, Brainerd. *The Public Career of William M. Evarts.* Berkeley: University of California Press, 1933. 297p. Bibl. (*Publications of the University of California at Los Angeles in Social Sciences*, Vol. 2, 1933).   Dyer discusses Evarts entire career as a lawyer, Republican congressman and Senator from New York, and attorney general under Andrew Johnson and secretary of state under Rutherford Hayes.   Although Evarts disagreed with Johnson's Reconstruction policies, he served as one of the president's attorneys during the impeachment trial and served in his cabinet during the last few months of 1868. Dyer suggests that Evarts accepted the role of Johnson's attorney simply in the course of his professional duties as an attorney irrespective of his politics. Evarts also played a role in the resolution of the controversial electoral returns from the South in the 1876 presidential election.

235.   Ellingsworth, Huber W. "The Confederate Invasion of Boston." *Southern Speech Journal* 35 (Fall 1969): 54-60.   On the occasion of the centennial of the American Revolution during the summer of 1875, several prominent Southerners were invited to participate in the celebration. Their warm reception and their positive words about North-South relations were early indications of sectional reconciliation.

236.   Everett, Lloyd T. "The 'Case of Jefferson Davis': Why No Trial." *Tyler's Quarterly Historical and Genealogical Magazine* 29 (October 1947): 94-116.

Everett quotes extensively from the Davis case reports from the 4th U.S. Circuit Court to argue that Davis was denied his constitutional right to a speedy trial and to *habeas corpus*. He blames both Lincoln and Johnson for this error. Chief Justice Salmon P. Chase was a key player in upholding the constitution, particularly the 14th Amendment that was the basis for freeing Davis form custody after being held without trial for 3 1/2 years.

237.   Ezell, John S. "The Civil Rights Act of 1875." *Mid-America* 50 (October 1968): 251-271.   Ezell reviews the tortuous track in the 1870s of Charles Sumner's proposal to extend federal protection to blacks by providing a statutory basis for equal access to public accommodations, transportation and other facilities. The law was considered more of a symbol than practical legislation. Parts of the law were found unconstitutional by the U.S. Supreme Court in the "Civil Rights Cases" (1883).

238.   Fessenden, Francis. *Life and Public Services of William Pitt Fessenden United States Senator From Maine 1854-1864; Secretary of the Treasury 1864-1865; U.S. Senator From Maine 1865-1869.* 2 Vols. Boston: Houghton Mifflin, 1907. 374p., 365p. Ills. Ports.   In volume 2 Fessenden's son describes his father's work as chair of the Joint Committee of Fifteen on Reconstruction following the war.   The committee made recommendations regarding congressional Reconstruction policies.   He also describes his father's courageous vote against convicting Johnson at the president's impeachment trial. He quotes liberally from letters and documents written by or to Fessenden as evidence in this highly complimentary biography of a moderate Republican.

239.   Folmar, John Kent.   "The Erosion of Congressional Support for Republican Congressional Reconstruction in the House of Representatives, 1871-1877: A Roll-Call Analysis." Ph.D. University of Alabama, 1968. 456p.

240.   Foner, Eric. "Thaddeus Stevens, Confiscation, and Reconstruction." In *Politics and Ideology in the Age of the Civil War.* By Eric Foner. New York: Oxford University Press, 1980. Pp. 128-149.   Rep. Stevens of Pennsylvania symbolized radicalism in the Republican Party when he sought the confiscation of lands owned by leading plantation owners. He wanted a way to provide land to the freedmen and poor whites, to gain their support for the Republican Party, and to destroy the planter class. Most of Stevens' Republican colleagues could not support his proposal, because they opposed taking private property and going beyond the concept of reforming Southern society through the influx of Northern ideology and Northern settlers. They also opposed building a black yeoman class.

241.   Foner, Philip S. *The Life and Writings of Frederick Douglass. Vol. IV. Reconstruction and After.* New York: International Publications, 1955. 574p. Chron.   Foner discusses Douglass's contributions to the freedmen's struggle for civil rights after the war until his death in 1895. While his political acumen waned in the postwar years, the documents printed in this book illustrate Douglass' courage and drive for true freedom and civil rights. Part one of the documentary section

covers Reconstruction. Included are selected letters, speeches, interviews, and articles.

242.   Foner, Philip S. and George E. Walker (eds.). *Proceedings of the Black National and State Conventions, 1865-1900. Vol. I.* Philadelphia: Temple University Press, 1986. 441p. App.   The text of the proceedings of various black conventions throughout the country are arranged chronologically. The editors provide introductory comments before each proceeding and reference notes which further explain details about people and topics appearing in the text.

243.   Frederick, Duke. "The Second Confiscation Act: A Chapter of Civil War Politics." Ph.D. University of Chicago, 1966.

244.   Gambill, Edward L. *Conservative Ordeal, Northern Democrats and Reconstruction, 1865-1868.* Ames: Iowa State University, 1981. 188p. Bibl. North Democrats designed an unsuccessful strategy to defeat the Republicans by bringing President Johnson into their party and emphasizing the Northern public's disapproval of black suffrage. They also expected public support for a lenient Reconstruction policy. This strategy led to divisions among Democrats, but mainly it weakened their political and moral position by making them subject to accusations of disloyalty to the Union and creating the need for a strong Republican Reconstruction policy. Republicans effectively sidestepped the black suffrage issue until public opinion shifted to their favor. (See also Gambill's "Northern Democrats and Reconstruction, 1865-1868." Ph.D. University of Iowa, 1969. 379p.)

245.   Gambill, Edward L. "Who Were the Senate Radicals?" *Civil War History* 11 (September 1965): 237-244. Tbls.   Gambill investigates what the Radical Republicans stood for and who they were in 1866. Using roll call votes of 47 Republican and Democratic Senators during the 39th Congress on bills related to Reconstruction, Gambill identifies the strength of support of each Senator for Radical causes. He rates the support of each Senator and identifies them according to categories of support and cohesiveness.

246.   Gayarre, Charles. "William H. Seward on Reconstruction." *Southern Bivouc* 4 (February 1886): 521-523.   Gayarre, a member of the Louisiana Union Democratic delegation at the National Philadelphia Convention in 1866, describes a conversation he had with Secretary of State William H. Seward regarding Northern misunderstanding of the South.

247.   George, James Z. *The Political History of Slavery in the United States - Book II: Legislative History of Reconstruction.* New York: Mnemosyne, 1969. 342p. (Rpt. of Neale Publishing Co., 1915)   George examines mainly on how the Republican Congress abused the South by forcing it to accept dishonorable and unacceptable federal laws and black domination in order to return to the Union. The Northern Radicals are depicted as hypocrites who expected more from the South than they did from their home states. George was Chief Justice of the Supreme Court in Mississippi and later a U.S. senator.

248.   George, Mary Karl, Sister.   "Zachariah Chandler: Radical Revisited."
RSMPh.D. St. Louis University, 1965. 392p.

249.   Gibbs, Thomas V. "John Willis Menard, The First Colored Congressman
Elect." *A.M.E. Church Review* 3 (April 1887): 426-432.   Menard, a native of
Illinois, moved to New Orleans in 1865, became involved in politics and publishing,
and won election to Congress in 1868. Gibbs reprints the text of Menard's first
speech in Congress and the comments on the speech in the *Cincinnati Commercial,
New York Herald, Washington (D.C.) Daily Chronicle*, and *Washington (D.C.)
Union*.

250.   Gillette, William. *Retreat from Reconstruction, 1869-1879*. Baton Rouge:
Louisiana State University Press, 1979. 463p. Bibl.   Gillette believes that the
decade beginning in 1869 was the key period when Reconstruction had a chance for
success but instead failed to achieve what its framers hoped for. From the national
perspective, the Republican Party and Northern whites generally lacked the
necessary unity and dedication to ensure that policies would work. The Grant
administration acted ineffectively and racism in the North ensured both a lack of
identification and sympathy for the needs of blacks and the defeat of laws that did
not and could not change public attitudes. By 1874 reconciliation with the South
and disillusionment with Reconstruction indicated a national retreat from the intent
of the Reconstruction laws.

251.   Gorham, George C. *Life and Public Services of Edwin M. Stanton*. 2
Vols.   Boston: Houghton, Mifflin and Co., 1899.   Ills. Facim. Maps. Ports.
Gorham writes a highly complimentary account of Stanton's work as secretary of
war during the Civil War, his contributions to defeating President Johnson's
Reconstruction plan, and his courage when he refused Johnson's request to resign
from his cabinet office. (For a similar perspective on Stanton, see also Frank Abial
Flower's *Edwin McMaster Stanton: The Autocrat of Rebellion, Emancipation, and
Reconstruction*. Akron: Saalfield Publishing Co., 1905.)

252.   Grimes, Alan P. "Negro Suffrage and Nineteenth Century Liberalism:
Views of the New York *Nation* During Reconstruction." *Negro History Bulletin* 14
(December 1950): 55-57, 67-68. Ills.   The *Nation*, founded in 1865 by Edwin L.
Godkin, opposed universal manhood suffrage in favor of applying qualifications to
ensure knowledgeable voting. After 1868 the *Nation* took an even stronger view
against black suffrage because of the influence of corrupt politicians and
carpetbagger regimes in the South. Godkin feared that a mass of uneducated voters
would ruin the country. This attitude carried over to the paper's opposition to
populism and suspicion of majority rule until after Godkin's death and the beginning
of the Progressive Era.

253.   Grossman, Lawrence. *The Democratic Party and the Negro: Northern
and National Politics 1868-1892*. Urbana: University of Illinois, 1976. 212p.
Bibl.   In the first three chapters of this book Grossman examines the Democratic
Party's policy towards race and Reconstruction. The Democrats emerged from the

Civil War just as they entered it, split into factions politically, but they were united against federal race reform. The party's policy was not a foundation on which it could defeat the Republicans, but their insistence on states' rights allowed the Party to appeal to a broader audience. The New Departure tactic was designed to suppress the issue of race in the North and generate political support among voters with other traditional issues.

254.   Hanchette, William. "Reconstruction and the Rehabilitation of Jefferson Davis: Charles G. Halpine's Prison Life." *Journal of American History* 56 (September 1969): 280-289.   Halpine published an account of Davis' treatment in prison during 1865 and his own ideas about the recent war. He used a diary written by Davis' doctor, John R. Craven, as a principle source. The book was intended as a political tract designed to generate sympathy for Davis and royalties for Halpine and Craven. President Johnson approved of the book and waited until it was published in June, 1866 before allowing Davis to leave prison. Davis opposed the book because it was filled with false statements attributed to him. Despite criticism of the book it has been used and praised by Davis biographers, including Douglas Southall Freeman, E. Merton Coulter, and Burton J. Hendrick.

255.   Harris, Wilmer C. *The Public Life of Zachariah Chandler, 1851-1875.* Lansing: Michigan Historical Commission, 1917. 152p. Bibl. Ports.   Chandler became a Republican Senator from Michigan in 1857 and kept his seat until 1875 and briefly in 1879. He became a Radical and strongly supported congressional Reconstruction in the South and the impeachment of President Johnson.   He attacked Liberal Republicans and sought to maintain pressure on the South. Harris's biography is largely adulatory of Chandler's political strength and abilities, but he is mildly critical of his methods.

256.   Harrison, John M. "David Ross Locke and the Fight on Reconstruction." *Northwest Ohio Quarterly* 35 (Winter 1962-63): 18-31. Port.   Locke edited the Toledo *Blade* during the struggle between Congress and President Johnson over Reconstruction during 1865 and 1866. He wrote editorials under his own name and a pseudonym, Petroleum Vesuvius Nasby. Harrison examines Locke's opinions in light of the editor's reputation as a Radical sympathizer. Locke's writings reveal that he was a moderate who supported conciliation between the mainstream Republicans and Johnson so that the Radicals would not gain so much power that the president would be pushed into the Democratic camp.

257.   Hart, Albert Bushnell. *Salmon P. Chase.* Boston: Houghton, Mifflin, 1899. 465p.   Hart provides a generally positive biography of Chase in this volume of the American Statesman Series.

258.   Haskins, William Anthony.   "The Rhetoric of Black Congressmen, 1870-1877: An Analysis of the Rhetorical Strategies Used to Discuss Congressional Issues." Ph.D. University of Oregon 1977. 295p.

259.   Henry, George Seldon, Jr.   "Radical Republican Race Policy Toward the Negro During Reconstruction, 1862-1872." Ph.D. Yale University, 1963. 386p.

260.   Hogan, Horace Henry.   "United States vs. Jefferson Davis." *Sewanee Review* 25 (April 1917): 220-225.   The emotions of the immediate postwar years might have proved fatal to the life of the imprisoned Jefferson Davis, but Hogan credits the U.S. constitution for ensuring that justice was done. Even so, it was President Johnson's general amnesty proclamation at Christmas in 1868 that actually brought Davis' prosecution to an end.

261.   Hollister, O. J. *Life of Schuyler Colfax*. New York: Funk and Wagnalls, 1886. 535p. Ports.   This book is a sympathetic biography of the Indiana Republican who served as Speaker of the House of Representatives in three consecutive Congresses (1863-1869) and as vice president with President Grant from 1869 to 1873 before being stained by the Credit Mobilier scandal. Colfax was a strong supporter of congressional Reconstruction in the South.

262.   Holzman, Robert S. "Benjamin F. Butler: His Public Career." Ph.D. New York University, 1953. 392p.

263.   Hood, Janice Carol. "Brotherly Hate: A Quantitative Study of Southern Reconstruction Congressmen, 1867-1877." Ph.D. Washington State University, 1974. 373p.

264.   Horowitz, Robert F. *The Great Impeacher: A Political Biography of James M. Ashley*. New York: Brooklyn College Press, 1979. 227p. Bibl. Port. (Studies in Social Change, 9)   Ashley was one of the most influential Republican congressmen during his service from 1859 to 1869. The Ohio politician was an ardent abolitionist and builder of the state Republican Party who consistently supported emancipation of the slaves and the full extension of civil rights, including suffrage. He was involved in writing Reconstruction legislation beginning in 1862 and leading the first Radical efforts to impeach President Johnson in 1867. Ashley's reputation suffered at the hands of early 20th century historians, but Horowitz presents a positive view of the man without forgetting his personality weaknesses that tended to increase the controversy around him and helped to shorten his congressional career.

265.   Horowitz, Robert F. "Seward and Reconstruction: A Reconsideration." *Historian* 47 (May 1985): 382-401.   Horowitz proposes to give a complete explanation of Seward's support for Johnson's Reconstruction policies. The key to Seward's support was a plan that would result in a calm, stable environment in domestic affairs so that his foreign policy objectives would have a better chance of success. Seward held a grandiose plan for the expansion of American interests and power to Asia and other regions of the world. This was more important to him than the rights of the freedmen that he believed were the responsibility of the states. By examining Seward's speeches, letters, and interviews, it becomes clear that he was not a moderating force in Johnson's cabinet, nor was he simply trying to hold on to

his cabinet post. His differences with Johnson related to tactics, not substance, in Reconstruction policy.

266.   House, Albert V., Jr. "Northern Congressional Democrats as Defenders of the South During Reconstruction." *Journal of Southern History* 6 (February 1940): 46-71.   Northern Democrats provided a weak and generally ineffective defense of the South in the face of Republican majorities in both houses of Congress from 1865 to 1873. Democrats, led by Rep. Samuel J. Randall of Pennsylvania, Sen. Thomas F. Bayard of Delaware, and Sen. Allen G. Thurman of Ohio, offered little help to the South on economic issues and usually failed on political and civil rights issues because the Democratic leadership lacked skill and they refused to compromise with moderate Republicans. House believes that Democrats were also too influenced by home constituencies to take independent positions on national issues.

267.   House, Albert V., Jr. "The Speakership Contest of 1875: Democratic Response to Power." *Journal of American History* 52 (September 1965): 252-274. In the congressional elections of 1874 the Democratic Party captured control of the House of Representatives. This victory gave them an opportunity to effect national policies and build a strong party for the next presidential election in 1876. The Democrats' selection of Michael C. Kerr of Indiana as Speaker of the House turned into a tremendous mistake, because he could not provide strong leadership in the House or in the party. The result was the weakening of the Democrats' position in the next election.

268.   Houston, G. David. "A Negro Senator." *Journal of Negro History* 7 (July 1922): 243-256.   Houston elaborates on the achievements of Blanche K. Bruce, the first black U.S. senator who served from 1875 to 1881. He emphasizes Bruce's courage and persistence to uphold the rights and dignity of black citizens, but Bruce also participated in a variety of Senate affairs. House quotes liberally from Bruce's senate speeches.

269.   Howard, Victor B. *Religion and the Radical Republican Movement 1860-1870.* Lexington: University of Kentucky Press, 1990. 297p. Bibl. since the mid-1820s Radical Christians in the North were a major force behind the antislavery movement and the emancipation of the slaves during the Civil War. The movement was not unified but its social action agenda contributed to the ideological basis for the Republican Party, particularly the Radical Republicans. These Christians supported Radical Reconstruction based on their view of reforming the world, eliminating sin, and creating an society of equality among all citizens. The strength of Radical Christian support for Reconstruction waned by the mid-1870s. Among the radical churches were the Congregation Church, the Methodist Episcopal Church North, the Baptists, and the New School Presbyterians.

270.   Hughes, David F. "Salmon P. Chase: Chief Justice." Ph.D. Princeton University, 1963. 386p.

271.   Hughes, David F. "Salmon P. Chase: Chief Justice." *Vanderbilt Law Review* 18 (March 1965): 569-614.   Hughes discusses the politics behind Chase's appointment to the U.S. Supreme Court in 1864 and the significant influence that he had over the court during Reconstruction. Chase is depicted as a complex man who was an independent, controversial, hardworking justice who safeguarded judicial power and infuriated Radicals in Congress.

272.   Isaacs, A. Joakim. "The Presidents and the Press in the Reconstruction Era." Ph.D. University of Wisconsin, 1966. 243p.

273.   Jellison, Charles A. *Fessenden of Maine: Civil War Senator*. Syracuse: Syracuse University Press, 1962. 294p. Bibl. Ills. Ports.   Fessenden was chair of the Joint Committee on Reconstruction that recommended the 14th Amendment to restrict former Confederates and to enfranchise the freedmen. As a moderate in the Republican Party, he was reluctant to coerce the South beyond the 14th Amendment. His role was otherwise limited by the Radicals, and despite his dislike for President Johnson's leadership, he voted against conviction in the impeachment trial. Jellison provides a complimentary perspective of the Maine senator (1855-1869).

274.   Johnson, Kenneth R. "Legrand Winfield Perce: A Mississippi Carpetbagger and the Fight For Federal Aid to Education." *Journal of Mississippi History* 34 (November 1972): 331-356.   Perce served in the Union Army during the war and settled in Natchez in 1865. In 1869 he won election to the U.S. Congress as a Republican. He is best known for his work to place the federal government in a more influential position to assist the states with public education. In 1872 he sponsored a bill (HR802) that sought to establish a national education fund from proceeds of public land sales, but the bill never passed because of political opposition.

275.   Jolly, James A. "The Historical Reputation of Thaddeus Stevens." *Journal of the Lancaster County Historical Society* 74 (Easter 1970): 33-71. Ills. Port.   Jolly surveys the course of historical interpretation on Stevens' career in Congress and writes his own analysis of Stevens' style and contributions to postwar Reconstruction. Stevens was truly dedicated to the equality of men and the power of Congress in government affairs. He could act with stern principles but also with pragmatism. Historians' interpretations of him have followed their biases regarding Reconstruction, but many assessments have simplified a very complicated character.

276.   Jones, James P. *John A Logan: Stalwart Republican From Illinois*. Tallahassee: University of Florida Press, 1982. 291p. Bibl. Ports.   Jones examines Logan's career from 1866 until his death in 1886. The war turned his prewar Democratic sympathies into Republicanism as expressed in his opposition to President Johnson's Reconstruction policies, his support for impeachment, and his strong advocacy of civil rights for freedmen. Jones emphasizes Logan's pragmatism and idealism as a congressman to counter accusations of corrupt, opportunism that came from Logan's critics. (See also Jones' "John A. Logan: Politician and Soldier." Ph.D. University of Florida, 1960. 555p.)

277.   Jones, James P. "Radical Reinforcement: John A. Logan Returns to Congress." *Journal of the Illinois State Historical Society* 68 (September 1975): 324-336. Ports.   Jones describes Logan's transformation from a staunch Democratic congressman from Illinois prior to joining the Union Army to a Radical Republican by the end of the war and the early years of Reconstruction. Logan won reelection to Congress as a Republican in 1866, and he became a leader and a highly vocal member in opposition to President Johnson's Reconstruction policies and the South's attempts to avoid reforms. Logan publicly supported suffrage for black citizens.

278.   Julian, George. "The Death-Struggle of the Republican Party." *North American Review* 124 (1878): 262-292.   In Julian's examination of Republican Party history, he explains that the party mishandled the postwar period through its persistent cultivation of sectional animosity and political corruption. This led to its weakness by 1878.

279.   Julian, George. *Political Recollections, 1840-1872.* Chicago: Jansen, McClurg, 1884. 384p.   In his memoir Julian, a congressman from Indiana, provides his perspective of the reaction of his state to Reconstruction, black suffrage, the impeachment of President Johnson, and the Liberal Republican movement. He supported the Radical movement, including black suffrage and disenfranchisement of former rebels, but he wrote critically of the impeachment and turned away from President Grant by joining the Liberals. He provides comments on many individuals in Congress.

280.   Kahn, Maxine Baker. "Congressman Ashley in the Post-Civil War Years." *Northwest Ohio Quarterly* 36 (Summer 1964): 116-133.   Kahn depicts Republican Congressman James M. Ashley of Ohio as a sincere proponent of emancipation of the slaves. She briefly reviews Ashley's contributions to emancipation during the war and to the writing of the 13th Amendment. Ashley has not received enough credit for his role in the writing of the amendment.

281.   Kendrick, Benjamin B. "The Journal of the Joint Committee of Fifteen on Reconstruction, Thirty-Ninth Congress, 1865-1877." Ph.D. Columbia University, 1914. (Rpt. in New York: Columbia Univesity Press, 1914, 1915; Negro University Press, 1969)

282.   Kincaid, Larry. "The Legislative Origins of the Military Reconstruction Act, 1865-1867." Ph.D. Johns Hopkins University, 1968. 377p.

283.   Kincaid, Larry. "Victims of Circumstances: An Interpretation of Changing Attitudes Toward Republican Party Policy Makers and Reconstruction." *Journal of American History* 57 (June 1970): 48-66.   Kincaid outlines the historiography of Reconstruction and calls on historians to focus attention on the origins of congressional Reconstruction and why it failed. He proposes that historians dig deeper into the socioeconomic and political background of Republican Party members; the political ideas and activities of Northern interest groups; the way

legislative decisions were made; and the implementation of Reconstruction legislation.

284.   Kirkwood, Robert. "Horace Greeley and Reconstruction 1865." *New York History* 40 (July 1959): 270-280.   Greeley was editor of the New York *Tribune*. Kirkwood examines his editorial opinion about Reconstruction immediately after the war. Greeley's slogan, "Universal Amnesty-Universal Suffrage," expressed his desire for a quick, magnanimous peace, but one that would do justice to the freed slaves. He was concerned about the conservative policies of the new Southern governments, but he was not a Radical.

285.   Kitson, James T. "The Congressional Career of James G. Blaine, 1862-1876." Ph.D. Case Western Reserve University, 1971. 354p.

286.   Klingberg, Frank W. "Operation Reconstruction: A Report on Southern Unionist Planters." *North Carolina Historical Review* 25 (October 1948): 466-484. Klingberg criticizes the Southern Claims Commission's practice of rejecting the claims of many loyal Southern Unionists. It was the rejection of many legitimate Unionist claims that symbolized the failure to fulfill promises to this group and the difficulty encountered by the North in bringing about a warm peace with the South.

287.   Klingberg, Frank W.   *The Southern Claims Commission*.   Berkeley: University of California Press, 1955. 261p.   App. Bibl. Tbls.   (University of California Publications in History, vol. 50)   On March 31, 1871 Congress approved the formation of the Southern Claims Commission to hear the claims of Southern unionists whose property was confiscated by the Union Army during the Civil War. Klingberg explains the political nature of the debate prior to the passage of the bill and the influence of the Radical dominated commission in determining what constituted loyalty and legitimate claims against the federal treasury. The Radicals disallowed many claims based on a narrow definition of loyalty, and this led to disillusionment with federal authority among individuals who were important to the future of national unity.   (For a composite directory of claims from 1871 to 1880 see also Gary B. Mills (ed.), *Southern Loyalists in the Civil War: The Southern Claims Commission*.   Baltimore: Genealogical Publishing Co., 1994. 666p.)

288.   Klingberg, Frank W.   "The Southern Claims Commission: A Postwar Agency in Operation." *Mississippi Valley Historical Review* 32 (September 1945): 195-214.   Klingman explores how the commission worked in the context of revealing the significant number of Southerners who remained loyal to the Union. The commission received a large number of claims from Southerners, but it was quite strict in its interpretation of loyalty and did not liberally distribute funds even to loyalists.

289.   Klingman, Peter D. and David T. Geithman. "Negro Dissidence and the Republican Party, 1864-1872." *Phylon* 40 (June, 1979): 172-182.   Black political leaders struggled to advance the cause of civil rights, but the Republicans never

gave serious consideration to the needs of blacks, despite organized efforts at the National Negro Convention in Syracuse in 1864 and later in Washington in 1866. Black leaders even doubted President Grant's dedication to their cause, and after his reelection in 1872 they gave up their political offensive to preserve the gains that they had achieved.

290.   Kolchin, Peter. "The Business Press and Reconstruction." *Journal of Southern History* 33 (May 1967): 183-196.   Kolchin criticizes Howard K. Beale's thesis that congressional Reconstruction was the way that Radical Republicans and Northern big business sought to dominate the economy by suppressing the South and eliminating any chance that it would combine with Western business interests to gain national power.   In fact, the Radicals and big business did not agree about economic and political policies.   Kolchin uses Northern business publications to illustrate the disagreements. Of the 34 journals consulted, only *Iron Age* supported Radicalism.

291.   Korngold, Ralph. *Thaddeus Stevens: A Being Darkly Wise and Rudely Great.* New York: Harcourt, Brace and Co., 1955. 460p. Bibl.   Korngold focuses on the Stevens' tremendous influence over the congressional response to secession, war, and Reconstruction.   He believes that Stevens was a moderate Republican, not the vindictive devil that Southerners described, and his approaches to Reconstruction were always reasoned and based on a just resolution to postwar political and social problems.

292.   Krug, Mark M. *Lyman Trumbull: Conservative Radical.* New York: A. S. Barnes and Co., 1965. 370p. Bibl. Ill.   Krug describes Sen. Trumbull, a Democrat from Illinois, as an important part of the moderate Republican-Democratic coalition in Congress that turned the Radical's proposals into moderate Reconstruction legislation. Trumbull chaired the Senate Judiciary Committee and was a major author of the 13th Amendment (1865), the 2 Confiscation Acts (1861 and 1862), the Freedmen's Bureau Bill (1865), and the Civil Rights Act (1866), but he later opposed the Enforcement (Ku Klux Klan) Bill of 1871 believing that Congress had no authority to guarantee political rights for the freedmen. In general, he sought reconciliation with the South and regretted denying many white Southerners access to the political power.

293.   Langston, John Mercer. *Freedom and Citizenship. Selected Lectures and addresses of Hon. John Mercer Langston, LL.D., U.S. Minister Resident at Haiti.* Intro. By Rev. J. E. Rankin, D.D., of Washington. Miami: Mnemosyne Publishing, 1969. 286p. (Rpt. of Washington: Rufus H. Darby, 1883)   Most of the lectures focus on issues relevant to the freedmen in Reconstruction, including citizenship, suffrage, equality, Charles Sumner, politics, black soldiers, migration, and the future of blacks in America.   The lectures, delivered between 1865 and 1879, were intended to inspire blacks to be strong, to maintain their rights, and to have hope for the future.

294.   Lawson, Elizabeth. *The Gentleman From Mississippi: Our First Negro Congressman, Hiram R. Revels.* New York: np, 1960. 63p. Bibl.   Lawson's brief biography of Revels focuses on his career as a U.S. senator from January, 1870 to March, 1871.   He spoke out for civil rights and an end to racial segregation, and he voted mainly with the Radicals.   Lawson criticizes Revel's moderate stand on the political rights of former Confederates, his vote for the annexation of Santo Domingo, and his rejection of the Republican Party based on its hypocrisy on racial issues.

295.   Lerche, Charles O., Jr. "Congressional Interpretations of the Guarantee of a Republican Form of Government During Reconstruction." *Journal of Southern History* 15 (May 1949): 192-211.   Before the Civil War abolitionists argued that only by eliminating slavery could true Republican government exist in all states, and they noted that it was the federal government's responsibility to guarantee Republican government.   Radicals, such as Sen. Charles Sumner, believed that a state had to guarantee universal manhood suffrage to all races in order to be declared Republican in accordance with the constitution.   Lerche believes the issue of Republican government was just a ploy to get Republican Party programs through the Congress.

296.   Lewis, Elsie M. "The Political Mind of the Negro, 1865-1900." *Journal of Southern History* 21 (May 1951): 189-202.   Lewis reviews the thoughts of mostly free, Northern blacks about the rights of all blacks in the postwar era.   The Northern victory in the war was a time when black leaders organized and produced a body of writing calling for the federal government to uphold and enforce the principles of democracy and equality.   Frederick Douglass, John M. Langston, and Robert R. Delaney were part of the leadership that organized a national effort in the form of the National Equal Rights League in October, 1864 and publicized their demands in public speeches and in newspapers, such the *New Orleans Tribune*, a black paper edited by Louis Charles Roudanez.

297.   Libby, Billy W. "Senator Hiram Revels of Mississippi Takes His Seat, January-February, 1970." *Journal of Mississippi History* 37 (November 1975): 381-394.   Libby describes the bitter reaction of the Southern press to Revels' election to the U.S. senate, the excitement in Washington, D. C. in anticipation of his arrival, and the extended debate in the senate over the acceptance of his credentials.   The senate debate and vote in favor of Revels split along party lines.

298.   Linden, Glenn M. "A Note on Negro Suffrage and Republican Politics." *Journal of Southern History* 36 (August 1970): 411-420. Tbls.   Linden analyses the voting behavior of U.S. senators and representatives between 1859 and 1869 on issues effecting blacks as a method of testing the idea that Republicans genuinely favored equal rights for the races in the U.S.   He compared votes for measures favorable to blacks with black suffrage measures and concludes that there is great consistency among the Republicans in favor of enhancing the position of blacks in American society.   While other factors may have also played a role in the votes, the

data indicates that a liberal notion of racial equality existed under the law. Linden's article was a response Lawanda and John Cox (see # 219).

299.   Linden, Glenn M.   "'Radicals and Economic Policies: The House of Representatives, 1861-1873." *Civil War History*   13 (March 1967):   51-65. Linden uses voting records on specific issues, including Reconstruction and economic legislation, to examine the debate among historians about the definition of radicalism.   He concludes that there was no relationship between political and economic voting behavior.   Voting on economic issues tended to follow geographical patterns instead of political party.   Linden uses 76 roll call votes to identify 130 radicals and 83 non-radical Republican congressmen.   (See also Linden's   "Congressmen, Radicalism and Economic Issues, 1861-1873."   Ph.D. University of Washington, 1963. 336p.)

300.   Linden, Glenn M.   "'Radicals and Economic Policies: The Senate, 1861-1873." *Journal of Southern History* 32 (May 1966): 189-199.   Linden tests the use of voting patterns to discover whether the Radicals were an identifiable group among Republicans in the U.S. Senate.   Based on 82 roll call votes, he concludes that from July, 1861 until March, 1873, there was an identifiable group that voted to support blacks and to restrict former Confederates.   On economic issues no such group can be identified from 95 votes during the same period.   Economic votes were split geographically and do not lead to generalizations about the Radicals. .   (See also Linden's "Congressmen, Radicalism and Economic Issues, 1861-1873." Ph.D. University of Washington, 1963. 336p.)

301.   Linden, Glenn M.   "'Radicals' Political and Economic Policies, 1873-1877." *Civil War History* 14 (September, 1968): 240-249.

302.   Litwack, Leon F.   "Trouble in Mind: The Bicentennial and the Afro-American Experience." *Journal of American History* 74 (September 1987): 314-337. Ports.   In the 200th anniversary year of the U.S. Constitution, Litwack refers to Reconstruction in the context of black American history since emancipation. The entire period has been marked by the long, difficult struggle for true freedom and respect in American society. Despite the progress made in Reconstruction, the time was marked by promises and advancements that were destroyed under the weight of white racism.

303.   Lowe, Richard.   "The Joint Committee on Reconstruction: Some Clarifications." *Southern Studies* N.S. 3 (Spring 1992): 55-65. Tbls.   Lowe examines the witnesses and proceedings at the hearings conducted during the winter and spring of 1866 by the Joint Committee. The hearings have not been adequately mined by historians as a source for understanding how the committee operated and the evidence used as a basis for future legislative action on Reconstruction. Lowe concludes that the membership of the committee was dominated by Radicals and this was reflected in their bias in witness selection, the questions asked, and their perspective on the meaning of the Northern victory. Radical domination on the committee represented a minority opinion among Republicans in Congress.

304.   Maye, Edward. *Lucius Q. C. Lamar: His Life, Times, and Speeches, 1825-1893*. 2nd Ed. Nashville: Publishing House of the Methodist Episcopal Church, South, Barbee and Smith, Agents, 1896. 820p. App. Bibl. Ports.   Maye, a close friend of Lamar, wrote this book shortly after Lamar's death. He covers all the events central to Lamar's life, including his role in Reconstruction in Mississippi and at the national level. While Maye states that he does not seek to show sectional bias or to write a panegyric account, he delivers a highly complimentary study that uses extensive quotations from Lamar's speeches and letters to illustrate the man's greatness as a moderate voice of Southern pride and a patriot of national unity. Appendices include the text of 24 speeches and letters by Lamar.

305.   Mayne, John A. "L. Q. C. Lamar's 'Eulogy' of Charles Sumner: A Reinterpretation." *Historian* 22 (May 1960): 296-311.   Lamar's eulogy in Congress on April 27, 1874 produced mostly good will in the North after he asked for greater understanding of the South. Mayne believes that Lamar's speech was more propaganda than eulogy because of his defense of the South in Reconstruction and his criticism of Sumner. Letters written after the speech confirmed his real purpose.

306.   McCall, Samuel W. *Thaddeus Stevens*. Boston: Houghton Mifflin and Co., 1899. 369p.   McCall expresses a positive attitude toward Stevens, Radical Reconstruction, and the impeachment of Andrew Johnson.

307.   McCarthy, John L. "Reconstruction Legislation and Voting Alignments in the House of Representatives, 1863-1869." Ph.D. Yale University, 1970. 498p.

308.   McClendon, R. Earl. "Status of the Ex-Confederate States as Seen in the Readmission of United States Senators." *American Historical Review* 41 (July 1936): 703-709.   McClendon explores the status of senators from former Confederate states in the context of the Radical Republican concept that ex-Confederate states were no longer part of the Union and required readmission according to special criteria. The senate readmitted the new senators to seats defined as vacant not new. This mode of operation lends strength to the argument that the Southern states were never technically out of the Union and should have avoided special criteria for readmission.

309.   McCrary, James Peyton. "The Party of Revolution: Republican Ideas About Politics and Social Change, 1862-1867." *Civil War History* 30 (December 1984): 330-350.   The Republican Party supported revolutionary change in politics and society. This was the case even among moderates. Following 19th century American liberalism, they claimed to also follow the revolutionary traditions of 1776, 1789, and 1848. Emancipation, black suffrage, and land redistribution were revolutionary for the time, and they were not only spoken but were also published in pamphlets. They became part of the Republican ideology that Northern voters considered at election time. The failure of the party program in the South was not a failure of ideas but of Republican will power.

310.   McDonald, James L.   "The Republican Revival: Revolutionary Republicanism's Relevance for Charles Sumner's Theory of Equality and Reconstruction." *Buffalo Law Review* 38 (Spring 1990): 465-514.   McDonald argues that Sumner and the Radicals did not develop theories of equality in the mid-19th century, because they were part of a tradition of "revolutionary republicanism" that existed since the American Revolution. While this tradition was used to bring moderate Republicans to the side of the Radicals so that Congress could control Reconstruction, Democrats and Conservative Republicans simply labeled their opponents as Radicals detached from tradition. This tradition served as the bedrock for Reconstruction and the modern civil rights movement.

311.   McFarlin, Annjennette Sophie.   *Black Congressional Reconstruction Orators and Their Orations, 1869-1879.* Metuchen, N. J.: Scarecrow Press, 1976. 333p. Bibl.   Includes brief biographical information and the text of several speeches delivered by the 16 black congressmen who serviced in the 41st through the 45th Congresses. The congressmen were Blanche Bruce, John Roy Lynch, and Hiram Revels of Mississippi; Richard Cain, Robert Carlos DeLarge, Robert Brown Elliott, Joseph Hayne Rainey, Alonzo Jacob Ransier, and Robert Smalls of South Carolina; Jeremiah Haralson, James Thomas Rapier, and Benjamin Sterling Turner of Alabama; John Adams Hyman of North Carolina; Jefferson Franklin Long of Georgia; John Willis Menard and Charles Edmund Nash of Louisiana   (never served); and Josiah Thomas Walls of Florida.

312.   McMahon, Adrian M.   "The Concept of Freedom and Radical Abolitionists, 1860-1870." Ph.D. University of Texas, 1970. 225p.

313.   McPherson, James M. "Abolitionists, Women Suffrage, and the Negro, 1865-1869." *Mid-America* 47 (January 1965): 40-47.   After the Civil War women's suffrage leaders, Elizabeth Cady Stanton, Susan B. Anthony, and Parker Pillsbury, sought to unite their effort for women's suffrage with that of blacks. This effort was not supported by most supporters of black suffrage. The disagreement led many women to publicly oppose the 15th Amendment because it did not include women.   The leaders of the National Women's Suffrage Association were so concerned about their own goals that they could not support broader objectives.

314.   Meier, August. "Negroes in the First and Second Reconstruction of the South."   *Civil War History* 13 (June 1967): 114-130.   The promise of revolutionary change for black Americans was not achieved after the Civil War, and except for a small group of Radicals, blacks were betrayed by the Republican Party and Northern whites in general. The constitutional and legislative reforms that occurred were marked by extensive compromise, the degredation of black labor, and the return of land to former rebels. The second Reconstruction in the 20th century partially counterbalances the lost opportunity after the war.

315.   Menard, Edith. "John Willis Menard: First Negro Elected to the U.S. Congress-First Negro to Speak in the U.S. Congress: A Documentary." *Negro History Bulletin* 28 (December 1964): 53-54.   Menard, an Illinois native, arrived in

New Orleans in 1865 and became a local official, publisher of *The Free South*, and U.S. congressman in November, 1868. Excerpts from his first Congressional speech in February, 1869 are included along with press notices from various newspapers.

316.   Merriam, George S. *The Negro and the Nation: A History of American Slavery and Enforcement*. New York: Henry Holt and Co., 1906. 436p.   A substantial portion of this book focuses on Reconstruction, but black participation is minimized in favor of national politics. Although Merriam is partial to the North and the congressional plan of Reconstruction, he believes that the disenfranchisement of Southern whites went too far.

317.   Merrill, Louis T. "General Benjamin F. Butler as a Radical Leader During the Administration of President Andrew Johnson." Ph.D. University of Chicago, 1936.

318.   Merrill, Louis T. "General Benjamin F. Butler in Washington." *Records of the Columbia Historical Society* 39 (1938): 71-100. Port.   Merrill's character analysis of Butler provides the spectrum of critical and complimentary opinions on the man and includes a description of his activities during the impeachment of President Johnson.

319.   Miller, Alphonse B. *Thaddeus Stevens* New York: Harper and Row, 1939. 440p. Bibl.   Miller takes a positive view of Stevens' contributions to Reconstruction.

320.   Mowry, Duane (ed.). "Letters of Edward Bates and the Blairs, Frank P. - Sr., and Jr. - and Montgomery, From the Private Papers and Correspondence of Senator James Rood Doolittle of Wisconsin." *Missouri Historical Review* 11 (January 1917): 123-146.   Five of the letters printed were written by Edward Bates between 1865 and 1868. Bates was Attorney General in the Lincoln administration and a Missouri Whig prior to joining the prewar Republican Party. Bates expresses great dissatisfaction with the extreme policies of the Radicals. Sen. Doolittle was a frequent correspondent with Bates. Of the four other letters from the Reconstruction period from Frank P. Blair, Sr. and Montgomery Blair, all but one to Doolittle, expressing opposition to the Republicans. (For additional Doolittle correspondence see also # 321, and Mowry's "Post-bellum Days: Selections From the Correspondence of the Late James R. Doolittle," *Magazine of History* 17 (July-August 1913): 1-10, 49-64; also *Southern Historical Association Publications* 9 (January 1907): 6-9; 9 (March 1907): 94-105.)

321.   Mowry, Duane. "Senator Doolittle and Reconstruction." *Sewanee Review* 14 (October 1906): 449-458.   Published here are seven letters written in 1866 and 1871 by Southern men during Reconstruction and sent to Wisconsin senator, James Rood Doolittle. Doolittle was known as one of the few sympathetic voices for the South in the North.   The letters explain Southern loyalty to the U.S. and communicate observations and concern about the Freedmen's Bureau and the use of the constitution in the time of political stress. All writers seek sympathy for the

Southern plight. One additional letter is a testimony to the value of Sen. Doolittle written by President Samson of Rutgers Female College. (See also # 320)

322.   "Negroes in Congress 1868-1895." *Negro History Bulletin* 31 (November 1968): 12-13.   Includes capsule portraits of 20 black congressmen.

323.   Nichols, Roy Franklin. "United States vs. Jefferson Davis, 1865-1869." *American Historical Review* 31 (January 1926): 266-284.   Nichols explains the legal and political events from Davis' imprisonment in May, 1865 until February, 1869 when Attorney General William Evarts dropped all charges against the former president of the Confederacy.

324.   Nicklas, F. William. "William D. Kelley: The Congressional Years, 1861-1890." Ph.D. Northern Illinois University, 1983.

325.   Niven, John. *Salmon P. Chase: A Biography*. New York: Oxford University Press, 1995. 546p.   Niven provides a personal history of Chase written in a critical tone that depicts the man as a tragic figure.

326.   Otten, James T. "Grand Old Partyman: William A. Wheeler and the Republican Party, 1850-1880." Ph.D. University of South Carolina, 1976.

327.   Painter, Beverly Wilson and Holly Byers Ochoa.   "'Reconstruction,' September 6, 1865." *Pennsylvania History* 60 (April 1993): 196-212.   The editors print the text of Thaddeus Stevens' address at a public meeting in Lancaster County on the subject of Reconstruction. The text was taken from what was printed in the Lancaster *Examiner and Herald*.   Stevens outlines his position that change is required in the South for there to be a just peace.

328.   Palmer, Beverly Wilson (ed.). *The Selected Letters of Charles Sumner*. 2 Vols. Boston: Northeastern University Press, 1990. (Vol. 1: 1830-1859, Vol. 2: 1860-1974.)   The second volume provides many letters relating to Reconstruction. The bulk of the letters on Reconstruction are about Congress's role and suffrage, but other topics include constitutional issues, apportionment, civil rights, the Ku Klux Klan, and the state suicide theory.

328b.   Palmer, Beverly Wilson and Holly Byers Ochoa. *The Selected Letters of Thaddeus Stevens*. 2 Vols. Pittsburgh: University of Pittsburgh Press, 1997-1998. Ills.   (Vol. 1: January, 1814-March, 1865, Vol. 2: April, 1865-August, 1868.) Volume 1 includes some correspondence on wartime Reconstruction and volume 2 focuses on postwar Reconstruction politics in Congress, the reform of the South, the Republican Party, and the impeachment of President Johnson.   (See also *The Thaddeus Stevens Papers,* Wilmington: Scholarly Resources, 1993 on 12 reels.)

329.   Pearce, Haywood J., Jr.   "Georges Clemenceau: Chronicle of American Politics." *South Atlantic Quarterly* 29 (October 1930): 394-401.   Pearce examines Clemenceau's book, *American Reconstruction 1865-1870* (see # 66), in which the

author published his letters written to the Paris *Temps* while he was residing in New York. Pearce believes that the letters show a flare of literary brilliance and empirical perception, but Clemenceau showed strong bias in favor of the Radicals and black civil rights, and he lacked understanding of the constitutional and economic issues of Reconstruction.

330.   Pickens, Donald K. "The Republican Synthesis and Thaddeus Stevens." *Civil War History* 31 (March 1985): 57-73.   Pickens' goal is to place Stevens' approach to Reconstruction within its philosophical foundations. In his Radical program Stevens sought to break down the aristocratic nature of Southern society and instill an appreciation for 19th century Republicanism and capitalism that embraced self improvement, improvement of society, distribution of land among citizens, and economic liberty for all.

331.   Pierce, Edward L. *Enfranchisement and Citizenship: Addresses and Papers.* Edited by A. W. Stevens. Boston: Roberts Brothers, 1896. 397p.   Two chapters (p. 54-131, 142-184) relate to Reconstruction. Pierce describes his visit to Port Royal, S.C. in early 1862 as an agent for Secretary of the Treasury Salmon P. Chase and offers a positive picture of free black labor. Also, in a speech delivered on October 31, 1868, he compared the Reconstruction plans of presidents Lincoln and Johnson. Pierce believed that Lincoln would have avoided the problems encountered by Johnson and quickly led the nation to reconciliation and prosperity.

332.   Pierce, Edward L. *Memoir and Letters of Charles Sumner.* 4 vols. Boston: Roberts Brothers, 1894.   This is not Sumner's memoir but a biographical work that extensively quotes from Sumner's correspondence with a wide variety of individuals in the U.S. and Britain.   Volume 4   (1860-1874) centers around Sumner's activities during the Civil War and Reconstruction.   Pierce provides a sympathetic image of Sumter's principles of equal civil rights and the necessity of a thorough Reconstruction in the South.

333.   Pietre, Merline. "Frederick Douglass: A Party Loyalist, 1870-1895." Ph.D. Temple University, 1976. 230p.

334.   Polakoff, Keith I. "The Disorganized Democracy: An Institutional Study of the Democratic Party, 1872-1880." Ph.D. Northwestern University, 1968. 360p.

335.   Powell, Lawrence N. "Rejecting Republican Incumbents in the 1866 Congressional Nominating Conventions: A Study in Reconstruction Politics." *Civil War History* 19 (September 1973): 219-237.   Powell questions the the supposedly critical nature attributed to the elections of 1866 in the future of the Reconstruction. He studies why some Republican incumbents were rejected by their party and finds that local issues were more important than national issues. The election did not radicalize the Republican Party. That had already occurred either through elections or the legislative process.

336.　Quill, James Michael. *Prelude to the Radicals: The North and Reconstruction*. Washington, D.C.: University Publications of America, 1980. 168p.　Quill is particularly concerned with expressions of Northern public opinion toward the beginning of Reconstruction from April to December, 1865 prior to the reconvening of Congress. He views 1865 as the key year in determining the course of Reconstruction because of the Northern public's initial magnanimity towards peace with the South, and the impact on opinion from Lincoln's assasination, Southerner's attitudes toward defeat and reform, and decisions made by Andrew Johnson to reconstruct the South. Among various sources, Quill makes extensive use of Northern newspapers.　(See also Quill's "Northern Pubic Opinion and Reconstruction, April-December, 1865." Ph.D. University of Notre Dame, 1973. 272p.)

337.　Rable, George C. "William T. Sherman and the Conservative Critique of Radical Reconstruction." *Ohio History* 93 (Summer-Autumn 1984): 147-163. Ills. Port.　Sherman, a native of Ohio, viewed Reconstruction with conservatism typical of many men from his region. As a professional soldier he rejected the notion that the military could some how play a major role in reshaping the character of the South, and he cared more about the speedy restoration of peace and Southern governments than the long range impact of the war on the freedom and civil rights for former slaves.　He viewed social and political reform in the South with skepticism.　Despite his reservations, Sherman remained an active supporter of President Grant through the end of Grant's administration.

338.　Randall, James G. "Captured and Abondoned Property During the Civil War." *American Historical Review* 19 (October 1913): 65-79.　Randall discusses the disposition of confiscated property during Reconstruction.

339.　Randall, James G. "John Sherman and Reconstruction." *Mississippi Valley Historical Review* 19 (December 1932): 382-393.　Randall compares the inconsistent behavior of Republican Sen. Sherman of Ohio with that of the entire Radical program of Reconstruction. Just as the Radicals insisted that the former Confederate states were outside the Union but were required to pass constitutional amendments before reentry, Sherman expressed support for Johnson's policies and then voted with the Radicals. Randall does not accept the idea that Sherman had a moderating effect on the Radicals.　He believes that Sherman sided with the Radicals after receiving a great many anti-Johnson letters from his constituents. Randall views Reconstruction as a disastrous episode that resulted in only one success - "perpetuating the benefits of Republican Rule." (p. 383)

340.　Ray, Jessie H. "Early Negro Congressmen." *Negro History Bulletin* 14 (December 1950): 59, 61.　In this brief survey Ray defends the qualifications and contributions of black congressmen.

341.　Reeves, Bennie Leronius. "Lucius Quintus Cincinnatus Lamar: Reluctant Secessionist and Spokesman for the South, 1860-1885." Ph.D. University of North Carolina, 1973. 154p.

342.   Riddleberger, Patrick W.   *George Washington Julian: Radical Republican: A Study in Nineteenth Century Politics and Reform.* n.p.: Indiana Historical bureau, 1966. 344p. Bibl. Port.   Julian, formerly an Indiana Whig and Free Soiler with a history of reform, was recognized as a Radical in the 1860s who favored black suffrage and the congressional program of Reconstruction.   This position led to a clash with Indiana governor Oliver P. Morton who opposed suffrage but later changed his mind. Julian also voted against President Johnson in the impeachment trial. But Julian's outlook changed, and he lost his radical passion in favor of the Liberal Republicans whose defeat in 1872 led to his ouster from the Republican Party and eventual switch to the Democrats. Riddleberger suggests that aging may have softened Julian's strong Republicanism.

343.   Rogers, William Warren, Jr. "Reconstruction Journalism: The Hays-Hawley Letter." *American Journalism* 6 (Fall 1989): 235-244.   Republican Rep. Joseph Hawley of Connecticut was both a congressman and an editor of the *Harford Courant*. He published a letter from Republican Rep. Charles Hays of Alabama on September 15, 1874 that described the violence against black and white Republicans in his state. Rogers reviews the heated responses in the press to Hays' letter and concludes that they illustrate the partisan journalism that existed during Reconstruction.

344.   Roske, Ralph J. "The Post Civil War Career of Lyman Trumbull." Ph.D. University of Illinois, 1949.

345.   Ross, Earle D. "Horace Greeley and the South, 1865-1872." *South Atlantic Quarterly* 16 (October 1917): 324-338.   Greeley was no friend of the South when he supported a strong antislavery stance prior to the war and a vigorous campaign against the Confederacy during the war. Ross explains, however, that Greeley found many friends in the South when he urged an early end to the war and a lenient Reconstruction after the Northern victory. Greeley expressed himself mainly through his writings in the New York *Tribune* that he edited. He called on the president and Congress to follow a policy of universal amnesty of all Southerners and impartial suffrage of all male freedmen. He opposed discrimination based on race and insisted on protecting the civil rights of all people in accordance with what was just and reasonable. When Greeley broke from the Republican Party to lead the Liberal Republicans in 1872, his main focus was bringing Reconstruction to an end, and it was this policy that generated support from many white Southerners.

346.   Ross, Edmund G.   "Political Leaders of the Reconstruction Period." *Forum* 20 (October 1895): 218-234.   Ross, a former Republican Senator from Kansas who voted against conviction of President Johnson, describes mostly Republican colleagues in the Senate and the House who were significant players in Reconstruction.

347.   Rozwenc, Edwin Charles (ed.). *Reconstruction in the South.* Boston: D.C. Heath, 1952. 109p. (2nd edition, D.C. Heath, 1972. 308p.)   Includes

reprints from articles and books written by several historians during the twentieth century. The readings reflect different viewpoints, from the traditional perspective of the Dunning school of historians (Woodrow Wilson, Walter Fleming) who describes Reconstruction as a total failure, and early revisionists (W. E. B. DuBois, Francis Simkins) who recognize some positive results and view the role of blacks in a less stereotyped way. The second edition includes additional excerpts from the revisionist literature of the 1960s.

348.   Ruchames, Louis.   "Charles Sumner and American Historiography." *Journal of Negro History* 38 (April 1953): 139-160.   Most Northern and Southern historians have tended to criticize Sumner's personality and leadership of the Radical Republicans, because they were influenced by the increasingly intense nature of scientific racism that appeared by the end of the 19th century. At a time when Reconstruction was subjected to greater criticism, Sumner's insistence of racial equality under the law appeared highly flawed and unrealistic. Some of his biographers have been kinder, and Ruchames hopes that as racial tensions lessen, historical interpretations will be revised.

349.   Ruchames, Louis.   "William Lloyd Garrison and the Negro Franchise." *Journal of Negro History* 50 (January 1965): 37-49.   Ruchames criticizes historians who have characterized Garrison, editor of *Liberator*, as an abolitionist who turned into an arch conservative regarding black suffrage. He traces Garrison's statements to illustrate that the abolitionist never expressed opposition to enfranchising freedmen. Garrison defended the policies of President Lincoln that did not include suffrage in Louisiana in 1863, but he sought to ensure Lincoln's reelection and hailed the Emancipation Proclamation as an achievement. Eventually Garrison spoke out in favor of enfranchisement as a tool for freedmen to protect themselves from white Southerners who opposed their freedom.

350.   Russ, William A., Jr. "Anti-Catholic Agitation During Reconstruction." *Records of the American Catholic Historical Society of Philadelphia* 45 (1934): 312-321.   Russ explains how Protestant leaders assailed American Catholics as disloyal to the Union during the Civil War and Reconstruction. He suggests that Radical Republicans used traditional anti-Catholic sentiment to win elections and to push for the enfranchisement of blacks who were mostly Protestant and could be counted on to vote for Republicans.

351.   Russ, William A., Jr. "Congressional Disfranchisment, 1866-1898." Ph.D. University of Chicago, 1934.

352.   Russell, Mattie (ed.). "Why Lamar Eulogized Sumner." *Journal of Southern History* 21 (August 1955): 374-378.   Congressman Lucius Q. C. Lamar, a Democrat from Mississippi, eulogized Sen. Charles Sumner of Massachusetts on April 27, 1874 in the House of Representatives. His speech led to his immediate condemnation by fellow Southerners. One complaint came from former U.S. and Confederate senator, Clement Claiborne Clay of Alabama. Russell provides the text of Clay's response.

353.   Schruben, Francis W. "Edwin M. Stanton and Reconstruction." *Tennessee Historical Quarterly* 23 (June 1964): 145-168.   Stanton's role in Reconstruction has been interpreted differently by historians, but Schruben concludes that Stanton clearly sided with the congressional Radicals' approach toward the South between 1865 and 1867.   He suggests that Stanton undermined President Johnson's Reconstruction plan, a plan that he favored prior to Lincoln's death.   Johnson hesitated to remove Stanton from his cabinet post as secretary of war prior to 1867 because of Stanton's political abilities and power.

354.   Schurz, Carl. *The Reminiscences of Carl Schurz. Vol. III 1863-1869.* New York: McClure Co., 1908.   486p.   Ports.   This third and last volume of Schurz's reminiscences was cut short by his death in 1906.   Schurz, a German immigrant who became a respected journalist and politician, offers his personal perspective regarding events and important people of the period up to the beginning of the Grant administration and his own election to the U.S. Senate as a Republican from Missouri.   He observed the postwar South as an investigator for President Johnson in 1865, but his report worked against Johnson's lenient Reconstruction policies.   Schurz initially supported the Grant administration and a vigorous Reconstruction policy, but he eventually rejected Grant for the Liberal Republicans. Also included in volume 3 is a favorable sketch of his political career from 1869 to 1906 written by Frederic Bancroft and William A Dunning.   Excerpts from this book were published in *McClure's*: "The South After the War," *McClures* 30 (April 1908): 651-661; "First Days of the Reconstruction," 31 (May 1908): 39-51; "President Johnson and His War on Congress," 31 (June 1908): 145-158; "The Repudiation of Johnson's Policy," 31 (July 1908): 297-1908.

355.   Schurz, Carl. *Speeches, Correspondence and Political Papers of Carl Schurz.* 6 Vols. (1852-1906).   Edited by Frederick Bancroft on Behalf of the Carl Schurz Memorial Committee.   New York: G. P. Putnam's Sons, 1913.   Port.   The first three volumes include complete and partial copies of selected letters and speeches written by Schurz and a few letters received by Schurz from 1852 to 1880. Most of the documents, beginning in 1865, relate to political activities in Reconstruction in the South, Republican politics, conflicts with President Johnson, and views of the Grant administration and the Liberal Republican movement.   Other letters relate to international affairs.   Frequent correspondents were Massachusetts Senator Charles Sumner, *Nation* editor E. L. Godkin, *New York Tribune* editor Horace Greeley, and *St. Louis Democrat* editor W. M. Grosvenor.   Other correspondents were Benjamin H. Bristow, Samuel Bowles, Charles Francis Adams, and Rutherford B. Hayes.

356.   Sefton, James E.   "Chief Justice Chase as an Advisor on Presidential Reconstruction." *Civil War History* 13 (September 1967): 242-264.   Sefton adds commentary to a selection of letters from Salmon P. Chase of the U.S. Supreme Court to President Johnson regarding Chase's tour of the South during May, 1865. Chase reports his impressions of public feelings in the South and urges Johnson to take specific actions to reconstruct the Southern states, including the implementation of universal manhood suffrage for blacks.   Chase's emphasis on black suffrage

showed how unaware he was about the lack of support for suffrage in the White House, among Northern voters, and Republicans in Congress.

357.   Seip, Terry L. *The South Returns to Congress: Men, Economic Measures, and Intersectional Relationships, 1868-1879.* Baton Rouge: Louisiana State University Press, 1983. 322p. Bibl. Tbls.   This book is a collective biography and political analysis of the 251 men who represented the South in Congress during Reconstruction. Seip examines their image in the eyes of Northern colleagues, their collective voting records by party on various issues, including Reconstruction legislation, but focusing mostly on legislation related to economics and internal improvements that were so important after the Civil War.   Seip reveals the cohesiveness of the Southern delegates in their responses to politics and economics at the national level.   Northern congressmen and senators generally rejected or held little respect for the Southerners in either party.   This attitude contributed to the weakness of the Southern Republican Party in the South and the quick loss of interest by Northern Republicans in the continuation of Reconstruction.   (See also Seip's "Southern Representatives and Economic Measures During Reconstruction: A Quantitative Analytical Study." Ph.D. Louisiana State University, 1974. 358p.)

358.   Seward, Frederick W. *Seward at Washington as Senator and Secretary of State.* 3 Vols. New York: Derby and Miller, 1891. 561p.   Volume III covers 1861 to 1872. The son of William H. Seward includes many letters and documents.

359.   Shapiro, Samuel. "A Black Senator From Mississippi: Blanche K. Bruce (1841-1898)." *Review of Politics* 44 (January 1982): 83-109.   Shapiro provides a narrative and discussion of Bruce's political career and his post-Reconstruction work for the Republican Party, Republican presidential candidates, and federal officials.   Bruce's achievements were modest by today's standards, but Shapiro believes that he did what he could in the context of the racist American society in the 19th century.

360.   Sherman, John. *John Sherman's Recollections of Forty Years in the House, Senate and Cabinet. An Autobiography.* 2 Vols. New York: Werner, 1895. 1239p. Ports.   Volume 1 includes Sherman's perspective on Reconstruction and his personal position on President Johnson's policies, impeachment, and President Grant's policies. The Senator from Ohio supported the Republican Reconstruction plan and black suffrage, and he voted for impeachment. The book includes some of Sherman's letters.

361.   Shortreed, Margaret. "The Antislavery Radicals: From Crusade to Revolution 1840-1868." *Past and Present* 16 (November 1959): 65-87.   Shortreed defines prewar antislavery Radicals and the Radical Republicans of wartime and Reconstruction as revolutionists who sought to eliminate their opponents as a means to destroy the Southern planter aristocracy and to make Northern ideology and industry preeminent in the nation. The destruction of slavery and the legislated reforms in the South illustrate the self conscious revolution led by the industrial bourgeoisie. Pennsylvania Rep. Thaddeus Stevens, a leader of the movement,

sought to reshape Southern society, even if it had to be done with violence and vindictiveness.

362.   Shottwell, Walter G. *Life of Charles Sumner.* New York: Thomas Y. Crowell, 1910. 733p.   Shottwell's book is a sympathetic account of Sumner's life and the political issues that he pursued in the U.S. Senate.   He believes that Sumner's role in the Republican Party during the Civil War and Reconstruction was great. Shotwell concludes that Sumner was a great statesman.

363.   Shovner, Kenneth B. "The Life of Benjamin F. Wade." Ph.D. University of California, Berkeley, 1962.

364.   Silber, Nina. "Intemperate Men, Spiteful Women, and Jefferson Davis." *American Quarterly* 41, 4 (1989): 614-635. Ills. (Rpt. in *Divided Houses: Gender and the Civil War*, ed. by Nina Silber and Catherine Clinton, New York: Oxford University Press, 1992, pp. 283-305.)   Silber examines the impact of gender on sectional relationships from the antebellum period through early Reconstruction. Particularly by the end of the Civil War, Republican Northern middle and upper classes defined the South in terms of its weak men and emotional women. Weak manhood translated into an effeminate image of the South based on Northern values of manly hard work and free labor versus the lazy and whiny image of plantation owners. The Northern victory in the war can be interpreted as the affirmation of Northern masculine power that colored Republican policies toward Reconstruction in the South. Illustrative of the relationship between gender and public affairs were exaggerated images and descriptions of Jefferson Davis' capture in women's clothing.

365.   Silber, Nina. *The Romance of Reunion: Northerners and the South, 1865-1900.* Chapel Hill: University of North Carolina Press, 1993. 257p. Bibl. Ills. The two chapters covering Reconstruction years describe the gradual transformation of Northern opinion from feelings of dominance and pity to sympathy and sentimentality. (See also Silber's "The Romance of Reunion: Northern Images Of The South, 1865-1900." Ph.D. University Of California, Berkeley, 1989. 427p.)

366.   Silbey, Joel H. *Respectable Minority: The Democratic Party in the Civil War Era, 1860-1868.* New York: W. W. Norton, 1977. 267p. Bibl. Tbls.   Silbey focuses on the efforts of the Northern Democratic Party to reconcile its internal divisions during the war years and take control of the public's perception of the party. He examines the party in the context of national politics in war and presidential Reconstruction. The Republicans dominated Northern, as well as Southern and border state politics, but the Democratic election losses were close and showed some promise for the future. The party's image as an opponent of Reconstruction continued to hamper efforts to win public support in the Northern states.

367.   Simpson, Brooks D. *The Reconstruction Presidents.*   Lawrence: University Press of Kansas, 1998. 276p. Bibl.   Simpson compares the

Reconstruction policies and leadership of Lincoln, Johnson, Grant, and Hayes and emphasizes the varied context and pressures in which each had to work and make decisions. Only by studying each man in the proper context and in light of their personal prejudices, goals, and sense of what could be achieved can their approaches to Reconstruction be understood. Advancing the civil rights of the freedmen and protecting them from violence was supported by all except Johnson, but achieving this end proved to be impossible, even if their determination was stronger and greater resources were employed.

368.   Singer, Donald L. "For Whites Only: The Seating of Hiram Revels in the United States Senate." *Negro History Bulletin* 35 (March 1972): 60-63.   Singer follows the Senate debate over seating Revels as printed in the *Congressional Globe* in 1870. The debate reveals profound racism present among many of the senators. Also mentioned is Revel's career as a state senator, minister in the African Methodist Episcopal Church, and president of Alcorn University (1871-1874).

369.   Smith, Craig. "The Radical Republicans." In *Silencing the Opposition: Government Strategies of Suppression*. Albany: State University of New York Press, 1996. Pp. 53-79. Notes.   The Radical Republicans successfully stifled free speech among their enemies through the skillful use of public rhetoric and evidence of disloyalty. It was through such means, and with the help of President Johnson himself, that the Radicals seized the initiative and controlled public opinion. Smith emphasizes the power of political rhetoric in a democratic society.

370.   Smith, George Winston. "Some Northern Wartime Attitudes Toward the Post-Civil War South." *Journal of Southern History* 10 (August 1944): 253-274. Smith examines the economic approach of Northern businessmen, industrialists, and Republican politicians regarding the South from the time that Union troops began to occupy the Confederacy until the early years of Reconstruction. He explains that the general attitude of the North was one of exploitation, self interest, and planning for economic domination. The carpetbaggers were actually an expression of a Northern expansionist, industrial society.

371.   Smith, Samuel Denny. *The Negro in Congress 1870-1901*. Chapel Hill: University of North Carolina, 1940. 160p. Bibl. Tbls.   Most of this book is about black U.S. congressmen and senators during Reconstruction. Smith believes that the blacks in Congress were a failure, partly because of inherent deficiencies and lack of experience. Whatever these men accomplished in Congress is due to the help they received from whites and the fact that many of them were racially mixed. Despite the positive interpretations of black congressmen written by black historians, the failure of these congressmen illustrate why their race needs time to develop.

372.   Smith, Samuel Denny. "The Negro in the United States Senate." In *Essays in Southern History*. Edited by Fletcher Melvin Green. Chapel Hill: University of North Carolina Press, 1949. Pp. 49-66. (*James Sprunt Studies in History and Political Science*, 31)   Smith focuses on the experiences of U.S. Senators Hiram R. Revels (1870-1871) and Blanche K. Bruce (1874-1880), from

Mississippi. He believes that Revels and Bruce were "minor and ineffective" (p. 65) senators merely tolerated by their white colleagues. They mainly worked on racial issues, but their service provided no benefits to blacks and only raised the hostility of whites.

373.   Smith, Willard H. *Schyler Colfax: The Changing Fortunes of a Political Idol.* Indianapolis: Indiana Historical bureau, 1952. 475p. Bibl. Ills.   Smith criticizes Colfax and the Radicals' for their extreme policies, but he also believes that Colfax acted sincerely. The Indiana congressman and Speaker of the House was genuinely concerned about helping the freedmen, a fact overlooked by historians who focus on Colfax's involvement in the Credit Mobilier scandal when he was vice-president.

374.   Sproat, John G. *'The Best Men': Liberal Reformers in the Gilded Age.* New York: Oxford University Press, 1968. 316p. Bibl.   Chapter two (pp. 11-44) of Sproat's examination of Liberal reformers, such as E. L. Godkin and Carl Schurz, shows how they started out as strong Republicans but quickly retreated from what they considered to be Radical extremism in Reconstruction policy. They opposed the impeachment of President Johnson, grew disgusted with reports of corruption in Southern Republican governments and in the Grant administration, and their attitude toward blacks was characterized by ambivalence. The liberal elites gave up their emphasis on humanitarianism toward blacks because of their rigid principles of *laissez-faire* and individualism. This attitude only encouraged a society that put limits on the lives of the weakest group in society.

375.   Sproat, John G. "Blueprint for Radical Reconstruction." *Journal of Southern History* 23 (February 1957): 25-44.   As Lincoln's Secretary of War, Edward M. Stanton focused on the vigorous prosecution of the war, including the use of both the Emancipation Proclamation and the establishment of black military units as war measures. His close relationship with the Radicals led to his help with the formation of the American Freedmen's Inquiry Commission on March 16, 1863. In its final reports the commission arrived at the Radical's future position on Reconstruction, including congressional control, black suffrage, land distribution, the disenfranchisement of Confederate leaders, and conditions for the reentry of Confederate states into the Union.

376.   St. Clair, Sadie D. "The National Career of Blanche Kelso Bruce." Ph.D. New York University, 1947. 332p.

377.   Steiner, Bernard C. *Life of Henry Winter Davis.* Baltimore: John Murphy Co., 1916. 416p. Bibl. Port.   Steiner praises Davis for his oratorical and political skills as well as his character and principled nature. Davis, a congressman from Maryland, is described as a nationalist and a fighter to maintain the powers of Congress in relation to the executive branch. As one of the authors of the Wade-Davis Bill in 1863, he sought a congressional plan for Reconstruction, but it was vetoed by Lincoln. Davis responded with a manifesto that illustrated how his anger

could flair in political debate. Steiner is somewhat critical of Davis' antagonism toward Lincoln.

378.   Steiner, Bernard C. *Life of Reverdy Johnson.* Baltimore: Norman, Remington, Co., 1914. 284p. Port.   Johnson was a skillful lawyer and U.S. senator from Maryland. As a strong Unionist Democrat during the war, he maintained conservative ideas about the federal government's power in relation with the states. He partially supported Lincoln's Reconstruction plans until the Emancipation Proclamation of 1863 caused Johnson to reject the president. Ultimately he agreed to the 13th Amendment, but beyond that he acted as either a moderator or opponent of Republican Reconstruction legislation, including the 14th Amendment. He opposed black suffrage and the literal interpretation of equality of men. Johnson was a minority member of the Joint Committee of Fifteen on Reconstruction. He took Johnson's side in the impeachment process.

379.   Sumner, Charles. *The Works of Charles Sumner.* 20 Vols. New York: Lea and Shephard, 1870-1883.   Includes the Massachusetts senator's speeches, congressional resolutions and remarks, letters to periodicals, and other writings. The documents range from July 4, 1845 to the last year of his life in 1874.

380.   Swift, Donald. "John Bingham and Reconstruction: the Dilemma of a Moderate." *Ohio History* 77 (1968): 76-94. Port.   Swift explains that Republican Rep. John Bingham of Ohio, played a prominent role as a moderator of Reconstruction legislation. He was a principle designer of Section 1 of the 14th Amendment, and he participated in eliminating extreme features in the Enforcement Acts of 1870 and 1871. His moderating influence was not based on political expediency, but on his principles. Yet Bingham's conservatism did not keep him from supporting a vigorous Reconstruction policy, including black suffrage and the impeachment of President Johnson. Moderate Republicans produced Reconstruction legislation that could pass through Congress.

381.   Swift, Donald P. "Midwest Congressmen Vote on the Issues, 1869-1870." *Illinois Quarterly* 34 (December 1971): 54-64. Tbls.   Swift analyses the voting patterns of Republican and Democratic congressmen from Ohio, Indiana, Illinois, Michigan, Wisconsin, Minnesota, Iowa, Kansas, and Nebraska in the 41st Congress. He selected votes given on Reconstruction, protective tariff, soft money, railroads, tighter naturalization laws, and suppression of polygamy. He measures the degree of cohesive voting within each party. Swift finds significant cohesion between Republican radicals and conservatives across all issues with the exception of polygamy and the tariff.

382.   Syrett, John. "The Confiscation Acts: Efforts of Reconstruction During the Civil War." Ph.D. University of Wisconsin, 1971. 493p.

383.   Taylor, Alrutheus A. "Negro Congressmen a Generation After." *Journal of Negro History* 7 (April 1922): 127-171.   Taylor examines the backgrounds of 22 Southern blacks elected to Congress. He looks at their fitness to serve, the way

that they conducted themselves, and the legislation that they proposed and supported. He concludes that the congressmen had the abilities to do their jobs well, but they were at a great disadvantage due to racial prejudice and their lack of power in Congress.

384.   Thomas, Benjamin P. and Harold Hyman. *Stanton: The Life and Times of Lincoln's Secretary of War.* New York: Alfred A. Knopf, 1962. 643p.   In this complimentary biography of Stanton the authors want to provide an unbiased account to redress the earlier one-sided or incorrect historical accounts. Stanton was a controversial figure as Secretary of War during the Civil War and the early years of Reconstruction until 1868. The authors laud his general performance during the war and emphasize that his quarrel with President Johnson over the course of Reconstruction unfairly marked him as an obstructionist and plotter against the president. His stalwart position against Johnson was based on the sincere belief that the President's policies would ruin the nation and call into question the North's great sacrifices and the heroism of its soldiers. (See also Fletcher Pratt, *Stanton: Lincoln's Secretary of War*, New York: Norton, 1953)

385.   Thompson, Julius Eric. "Hiram R. Revels, 1827-1901:   A Biography." Ph.D. Princeton University, 1973. 220p.

386.   Thorndike, Rachel Sherman (ed.). *The Sherman Letters: Correspondence Between General and Senator Sherman From 1837 to 1891.* New York: Charles Scribners' Sons, 1894.   398p.   Port.   The daughter of William T. Sherman arranged the letters he exchanged with his brother, Sen. John Sherman of Ohio. Sprinkled throughout the period of correspondence during the Civil War and Reconstruction are comments about Reconstruction in general, black suffrage, Southern and national politics, conditions in the South, Andrew Johnson, and Ulysses S. Grant. Senator Sherman was a strong Republican. His brother William refused to side with a political party but tended to take more conservative views on Reconstruction, such as his rejection of universal suffrage.

387.   Trefousse, Hans L. *Ben Butler: The South Called Him BEAST!* New York: Twayne, 1957. 365p. Bibl. Ports.   Trefousse acknowledges Butler's demagoguery and political manipulations to enhance his own power. These faults are counterbalanced by Butler's achievements in successfully controlling wartime New Orleans and seeking political and civil equality for blacks and greater rights for laborers. Butler displayed passion and leadership in the prosecution of Johnson's impeachment trial, as chairman of the Reconstruction Committee during Grant's first administration, and in his support for both the Enforcement Acts in 1870 and 1871 and the Amnesty Act in 1872.

388.   Trefousse, Hans. "Ben Wade and the Negro." *Ohio Historical Quarterly* 68 (April 1959): 161-176.   U.S. Sen. Wade of Ohio was an example of a sincere proponent of black emancipation and civil rights even though he held personal prejudices against the black race. Trefousse explains that Wade's letters to his wife

reveal his racist feelings, but he was able to put these prejudices aside in order to vigorously fight for the recognition of basic human rights for blacks.

389.   Trefousse, Hans L. *Benjamin Franklin Wade: Radial Republican From Ohio*. New York: Twayne Publishers, 1963. 404p. Bibl. Port.   Senator Wade was a leader among the Radicals who insisted that Congress had responsibility for Reconstruction. Trefouse emphasizes that Wade did not seek vengeance on the South, only justice and equal rights for blacks and political security for the nation. His response to Lincoln's veto of the Wade-Davis Bill illustrated his discontent with Lincoln's Reconstruction plan, but his proposals for a 14th amendment to the constitution were milder than the bill proposed by the Joint Committee of Fifteen on Reconstruction. As President Pro Tem of the Senate at a time when there was no vice president in 1867, Wade took the lead in Johnson's impeachment. Trefouse believes that Wade's contributions helped build a foundation for the future equal rights movements. (See also the biography by Albert Riddle, *Life of Benjamin F. Wade*, Cleveland: W. W. William, 1886)

390.   Trefousse, Hans Louis. *Carl Schurz: A Biography*.   Knoxville: University of Tennessee Press, 1982.   386p. Bibl. Port.   Schurz, a German immigrant, fought with the Union during the Civil War and was among those who strongly opposed President Johnson's Reconstruction policies. he sought fairness and civil rights for the freedmen and a policy that would lead to social and political change in the South. Schurz's report to the president following his trip to the South during the summer of 1865 was a strong indictment of Johnson's policies and it received support from many Republicans in Congress. But Schurz turned away from Radical Reconstruction as he gradually rejected the Grant administration and embraced Liberal Republicanism. Trefousse characterizes Schurz's change of attitude during his term as U.S. Senator from Missouri. The senator turned his back on the blacks after years of supporting them, and he decided that local rule in the South was best. His support for Liberal Republicanism, particularly in Missouri, strengthened Democrats and ultimately underminded his own political position.

391.   Trefousse, Hans. "Carl Schurz's 1865 Southern Tour: A Reassessment." *Prospects* 2 (1976): 292-308. Port.   Trefousse describes Schurz's tour and emphasizes his keen perception of conservative white reluctance to accept defeat and civil rights for blacks and the need for a slow transition to home rule. His report played an important role in strengthening the convictions of Radicals that Congress should intervene in the Reconstruction process. The report continues to have value for researchers.

392.   Trefousse, Hans L. "The Motivation of A Radical Republican: Benjamin F. Wade." *Ohio History* 73 (Spring 1964): 63-74. Port.   Trefousse explains that while historians have closely examined many of the Radical Republicans, Sen. Wade of Ohio has not been the subject of much study. Most of the references to Wade accuse him of being an overly ambitious and vindictive man who sought punishment for the South and favors for Northern capitalists. Trefousse reverses the

traditional view of Wade and emphasizes the senator's respect and tenderness toward his opponents and his sincerity in his fight for human freedom.

393.   Trefousse, Hans. "Old Thad Stevens." *American History Illustrated* 16 (January 1982): 16-23. Ports. Ill.   Trefousse describes Stevens' contributions during Reconstruction as ground breaking and in advance of public opinion. He was able to thwart President Johnson's lenient Reconstruction plan in order to institute vigorous reforms to protect and give power to the freedmen. This led to the constitutional foundation for racial democracy in America.

394.   Trefousse, Hans L. The Radical Republicans: Lincoln's Vanguard for Racial Justice. New York: Alfred A. Knopf, 1969. 492p. Bibl. Ports.   Trefousse explains how the Radicals rose from the ranks of abolitionists beginning in the 1840s, how they solidified power within the Republican Party, and how they used their power to influence President Lincoln and the course of the Civil War and Reconstruction. By the mid-1870s they had virtually disappeared. With a few exceptions, the Radicals could not be easily defined by ideology, motives or geographic origins, but their positive achievements had a lasting impact on the power of the federal government and equality of American citizens. They were the key force behind reforms that provided a legal basis for freedom and full civil rights for blacks in American society.

395.   Trefousse, Hans. *Thaddeus Stevens: Nineteenth-Century Egalitarian.* Chapel Hill: University of North Carolina, 1997.   312p.   Bibl. Ills. Ports. Trefousse wrote this book to provide a new biography of Stevens in light of research on Reconstruction during the past 30 years. He emphasizes that historians have exaggerated Stevens' power in Congress. This is evident from his inability to persuade most Republicans to take his radical perspective in legislative debates, but Stevens was a vital force keeping the Republicans strong and moving the country forward toward racial justice and equality.

396.   Urofsky, Melvin I. "Blanche K. Bruce: United States Senator, 1875-1881." *Journal of Mississippi History* 29 (May 1967): 118-141.   Urofsky surveys the life of Bruce, a former slave who received his freedom and earned an education prior to and during the war. Bruce arrived in Mississippi in 1868 and became a planter and active in local affairs. In various elected positions, including U.S. senator in 1874, he upheld the civil rights and fair treatment of blacks and generally voted judiciously on all matters. He later served in several posts in Republican federal administrations.

397.   Van Deusen, Glyndon G. *Horace Greeley: Nineteenth Century Crusader.* Philadelphia: University of Pennsylvania Press, 1953.   445p. Bibl. Ills. Ports. Greeley's conservative position on Reconstruction clashed with his often liberal, humanitarian views. He was a crusader who broke with President Grant and the Republican Party over issues related to corruption and placing responsibility for the future of the South in the hands of conservative whites instead of white, Southern Republicans and blacks. Van Deusen examines Greeley's personality and praises

his role in building the great and influential *New York Tribune*. (See also *Horace Greeley's Papers 1831-1873*, Wilmington: Scholarly Resources, 1997. 4 reels.)

398.   Van Deusen, Glyndon G. *William Henry Seward*. New York: Oxford University Press, 1967. 666p. With regard to Reconstruction, Seward is depicted as one who maintained his loyalty for President Johnson while continuing positive relations with the Radicals. He did not support black suffrage, despite early indications that he would accept it.

399.   Vaughn, William P. "Separate and Unequal: The Civil Rights Act of 1875 and Defeat of the School Integration Clause." *Southwestern Social Science Quarterly* 48 (September 1967): 146-154.   Vaughn writes a brief account of the political and legislative history of the Civil Rights Act. Charles Sumner was at the center of a movement among a small number of Republicans to outlaw racial segregation in schools, but strong opposition, particularly in the South, forced the elimination of the provision from the bill, thus delaying and making more difficult acceptance of school integration in the mid-20th century.

400.   Wang, Xi. "Black Suffrage and Northern Republicans, 1865-1891." Ph.D. Columbia University, 1993. 548p.

401.   Wang, Xi. "Black Suffrage and the Redefinition of American Freedom, 1860-1870." *Cardozo Law Review* 17 (May 1996): 2153-2223. Tbls.   Wang explains why and how Republicans changed their opposition to black suffrage in 1860 to support for the 15th Amendment in 1869-70. The amendment was a compromise document reflecting the reluctance of a majority of Republicans to acknowledge racial equality. The amendment provided blacks with equal status and rights as voters, not the right to vote itself. The amendment merely introduced a period of struggle to fully implement the right. The essay is followed by comments from Akhil Reed Amar (2225-2229).

402.   Wang, Xi. *The Trial of Democracy: Black Suffrage and Northern Republicans, 1860-1910*. Athens: University of Georgia Press, 1997. 411p. Bibl. Tbls.   Wang examines how Northern Republicans decided to grant and enforce suffrage for blacks through legislative and constitutional means. Republicans were both drawn to reforms by dedicated Radicals and forced to compromise by moderates. All supported furthering democratic government, but they were split on how far to go with enhancing federal enforcement powers and the concept of racial equality. He refers to this as the "faction-unity complex" (p. xxv) that also characterized Republican politics for the rest of the 19th century. (See also Wang's "The Making of Federal Enforcement Laws, 1870-1872." *Chicago-Kent Law Review* 70 (1995): 1013-1058 which is rpt. from Wang's *The Trial of Democracy*)

403.   Welles, Gideon. "A Diary of the Reconstruction Period." *Atlantic Monthly* 105 (February 1910): 165-176; (March 1910): 367-377; (April 1910): 511-520; (May 1910): 697-706; (June 1910): 805-815; 106 (July 1910): 78-89; (August 1910): 238-248; (September 1910): 388-400; (October 1910): 537-548;

(November 1910): 680-689; (December 1910): 818-828; 107 (January 1911): 118-130. (Rpt. in 3 vols. by Boston: Houghton Mifflin, 1911)   Welles was Secretary of the Navy in cabinets of Lincoln and Johnson. He was a strong supporter of Johnson through the president's administration. The diary begins on Friday, April 21, 1865 when Welles describes the cabinet's rejection of Gen. William T. Sherman's peace convention of April 18. The diary ends on Saturday, April 17, 1869, his last day in office. Welles provides observations and opinions about his activities, conversations, people and government policies. A large section focuses on issues surrounding the impeachment of President Johnson.

404.   Welles, Gideon. *Selected Essays of Gideon Welles. Vol. 1: Civil War and Reconstruction. Vol. 2: Lincoln Administration.* Edited by Albert Mordell. New York: Twayne Publishers, 1960. 279p.   Mordell selected essays that were originally published in *The Galaxy* during the 1870s. Two of these essays in volume 1 are on the Reconstruction plans of Lincoln and Johnson. Volume 2 has a series of essays from *The Galaxy* and the *Atlantic Monthly* on Lincoln's presidency.

405.   West, Richard S., Jr. *Lincoln's Scapegoat General: A Life of Benjamin F. Butler 1818-1893.* Boston: Houghton Mifflin, 1965. 462p. Port.   This is a highly complimentary biography that includes discussion of Butler's support for civil rights as a Radical congressman from Massachusetts, and his leadership for liberal reform, the Enforcement Acts of 1870 and 1871, his leading role in the impeachment trial. West seeks to explode the negative myths about the man.

406.   White, Horace. *The Life of Lyman Trumbull.* Boston: Houghton Mifflin, 1913. 458p. Ill.   Trumbull decided that President Johnson had betrayed the cause of the Civil War with the vetoes of the Freedmen's Bureau and civil rights bills, but he reluctantly gave his consent to the approach of the Radical Republicans. White, a friend of Trumbull's, believes that Trumbull erred in his support for the Radicals. He made up for it when he reversed his position in 1871 to vote against the Ku Klux Klan bill.

407.   Woodburn, James Albert. *The Life of Thaddeus Stevens.* Indianapolis: Bobbs-Merrill, 1913. 620p. Ports.   Woodburn criticizes Stevens' methods of leadership in the House of Representatives and his policy on confiscation, but still presents a sympathetic picture of the Pennsylvania congressman. Stevens was not hateful and vindictive, but he aggressively defended the Union, opposed the landed elite, and dedicated himself to civil and political justice for all races. His ideology was the basis for his support for the impeachment of President Johnson was based on his Republican ideology.

408.   Woodward, C. Vann. "Seeds of Failure in Radical Race Policy." In *Frontiers of the American Reconstruction.* Edited by Harold M. Hyman. Urbana: University of Illinois Press, 1966. Pp. 123-147.   Woodward's "seeds of failure" refers to the clear racism of Northern whites, including a majority of Republicans, and the persistent political motives of the Republicans in the passage of Reconstruction legislation including the 14th Amendment. Most Northerners

opposed significant reforms to increase black civil rights, and this was reflected in the half hearted legislation passed by Congress. Congressional Republicans cared more about controlling elections than protecting freedmen. (See also Russel B. Nye's "Comment on C. Vann Woodward's Paper," on pages 148-156. Nye agrees with Woodward's thesis and briefly explains the basis for racial views that existed in the North prior to and after the Civil War; and Woodward's "Seeds of Failure in Radical Race Policy." *Publications of the American Philosophical Society* 110 (February 18, 1966): 1-9.)

409.   Woody, Thomas Frederick. *Thaddeus Stevens*. Harrisburg, Pa.: The Telegraph Press, 1934. 664p. Bibl. Ill.   Woody describes Stevens as an egalitarian and a man of convictions who was not ideologically wedded to the Republican party in all his views. (Woody also published *Great Leveler: The Life of Thaddeus Stevens*, New York: Stackpole, 1937. 474p.)

410.   Zeigler, Paul George II. "The Politics and Philosophy of the Republican Rights, 1861-1866." Ph.D. University of Virginia, 1973. 384p.

Studies on Abraham Lincoln, 1860-1865

411.   Bell, Landon C. "The Lincoln Myths are Passing - But Slowly. Bowers' Tragic Era." *Tyler's Quarterly Historical and Genealogical Magazine* 11 (January 1930): 200-215.   Bell criticizes the continuation of uncritical, unobjective studies on Lincoln's role in Reconstruction of the South. Claude Bowers' book, *The Tragic Era: The Revolution After Lincoln* (see # 58), is the focus of this discussion.

412.   Berwanger, Eugene H. "Lincoln's Constitutional Dilemma: Emancipation and Black Suffrage." *Papers of the Abraham Lincoln Association* 5 (1983): 25-47. Ills.   Berwanger argues that Lincoln was not the "reluctant emancipator" and opponent of black suffrage described by many historians since World War II. In fact Lincoln held virtually the same views as the Radicals, but his methods to achieve results were different.

413.   Cox, Lawanda. *Lincoln and Black Freedom: A Study in Presidential Leadership*. Columbia: University of South Carolina, 1981. 254p. Bibl.   In this analyses of Lincoln's philosophy on emancipation and wartime Reconstruction, Cox devotes significant space to the president's policy in Louisiana that served as proof that he desired truly loyal govenments in the South to help end the war and institute reforms. She clarifies the wide differences between the policies of Lincoln and Johnson, and offers a positive interpretation of the Republican Party's dedication to civil rights for blacks.

414.   Harris, William C. "Abraham Lincoln and Southern White Unionism." In *Abraham Lincoln: Sources and Style of Leadership*. Edited by Frank J. Williams et. al.   Westport: Greenwood Press, 1994.   Pp. 125-142.   Southern white

Unionists were the backbone of Lincoln's plans to bring the Confederate states back into the Union. He encouraged Union supporters in East Tennessee, Virginia, Arkansas and Louisiana, but due to factions among local Unionists, wartime Unionist governments were weak and had little impact in their states.

415.   Harris, William C. *With Charity For All: Lincoln and the Restoration of the Union.* Lexington: University Press of Kentucky, 1997. 354p. Bibl. Maps. Ports.   Davis concentrates on Lincoln's Reconstruction policies from 1861 until after his death in 1865. He provides a comprehensive treatment of how Lincoln sought to implement reunion of the nation, and he emphasizes Lincoln's policies that adjusted to the changing political and military situation.   Lincoln never waivered from swift, non-vindictive restoration of the South. Davis believes that Lincoln did not give in to the Radicals by 1865 and that the President's policies would more likely have succeeded after the war under his own direction rather than under Andrew Johnson.

416.   Hesseltine, William B.   *Lincoln's Plan of Reconstruction.*   Bloucester, Ma.: Peter Smith, 1963. 154p. Bibl. (Rpt. of Tuscaloosa: Confederate Publishing Co., 1960)   The idea that Lincoln would have brought about a quick and just reconstruction of the Union had he lived is just a myth.   Lincoln tried various approaches to bringing the Confederate states back into the Union, but all failed due to opposition in Congress and problems with Southern unionist governments. Even though the president did not have a workable Reconstruction plan when he died, he left a legacy of emancipation and a new relationship between federal and state governments that would transform the South after the war.

417.   Hyman, Harold M.   "Lincoln and Equal Rights For Negroes: The Irrelevancy of the 'Wadsworth Letter'." *Civil War History* 12 (September 1966): 258-266.   Hyman refers to Ludwell Johnson's article (see # 418) that claims to show that crucial portions of the Wadsworth letter are not original. He explains that whether or not the letter is truly Lincoln's is irrelevant, because Lincoln demonstrated a progressive shift toward the idea of civil and political equality of the races.

418.   Johnson, Ludwell H.   "Lincoln and Equal Rights: The Authenticity of the Wadsworth Letter." *Journal of Southern History* 32 (February 1966): 82-87. Johnson prints a letter supposedly written by Lincoln to Maj. James S. Wadsworth in January, 1864 regarding equal rights for all races and amnesty for all in the Confederacy once the North prevailed in the war.   Johnson questions the authenticity of portions of the letter, because Lincoln did not believe in racial equality and would not have written such ideas. (See also # 417 for a critique of Johnson, and Johnson's "Lincoln and Equal Rights: A Reply," *Civil War History* 13 (March, 1967): 66-73 in which he responds to criticism of his thesis.)

419.   Keys, Thomas Bland.   "Profanation of the Constitution: Radical Rule, 1861-1877." *Lincoln Herald* 90 (Spring 1988): 10-16. Port.   Keys argues that Lincoln and the Radicals were revolutionaries who sought to overthrow the

constitution and make the federal government the dominant power.   This was Lincoln's goal rather than preserving the Union.

420.   Lincoln, Abraham. *The Collected Works of Abraham Lincoln.* Edited by Roy P. Basler. New Brunswick, NJ: Rutgers University Press, 1953, 1955. 9 Vols. [First Supplement, 1832-1865 by Rutgers University Press, 1974; Second Supplement, 1848-1865 by Rutgers University Press, 1990.]   Includes correspondence, proclamations and other documents produced by Lincoln prior to and during his presidency.   For Reconstruction documents see the index   (v. 9) under "Reconstruction", state names, and personal names.   For related collections see also *Complete Works of Abraham Lincoln,* new and enlarged edition, ed. by John G. Nicolay and John Hay, Lincoln Memorial University, 1894, in 12 volumes. (Rpt. by New York: Francis D. Tandy, Co., 1905 in 12 volumes)

421.   McCarthy, Charles H.   *Lincoln's Plan of Reconstruction.*   New York: McClure, Phillips and Co., 1901.   531p.   App.   McCarthy examines Lincoln's wartime Reconstruction policies in Tennessee, Louisiana, Arkansas and Virginia, and the competing theories and plans of Reconstruction in Congress.   He compares Lincoln and Johnson regarding their policies of Reconstruction and finds marked differences between the two.   (See also McCarthy's "Reconstruction Under President Lincoln." Ph.D. University of Pennsylvania, 1898.)

422.   McCrary, James Peyton.   *Abraham Lincoln and Reconstruction: The Louisiana Experiment.*   Princeton: Princeton University Press, 1978.   423p.   App. Bibl. Tbls.   McCrary examines wartime Reconstruction in Louisiana from the perspective of Lincoln's attempt to establish a loyal government by the time the war ended.   Within the context of a revolutionary era of war and reconstruction, Lincoln's policies in Louisiana take on an experimental character, but he did not consider his 10% plan to be a model for the other Southern states.   His policies illustrate his pragmatism and flexibility that led him toward the position of the congressional Radicals.   This study includes a statistical analysis of the 1864 state constitutional convention.

423.   Morris, Robert L.   "The Lincoln-Johnson Plan For Reconstruction and the Republican Convention of 1864."   *Lincoln Herald* 71 (Spring 1969): 33-39. Morris examines whether Lincoln intentionally chose Andrew Johnson as his running mate in 1864 because Johnson was partial to Lincoln's ideas about Reconstruction.   Historians have disagreed on this issue, but Morris believes that Johnson was, indeed, Lincoln's choice for this reason, and because Johnson had Southern Unionist roots that broadened the national ticket and suggested that Lincoln did not consider the Southern states to be truly outside of the Union.

424.   Nevins, Allan.   "Lincoln's Plans for Reunion."   *Abraham Lincoln Association Papers* (1931): 51-92.   Lincoln's Reconstruction plan shows that he intended to restore a true reunion and not just force certain policies down the throats of unwilling Southerners.   Nevins recognizes that Lincoln's thoughts were still evolving and that it will never be know whether he would have prevailed over the

Radicals in Congress, but Nevins had no doubt that Lincoln's plan would have been much better than the vindictive Reconstruction of the Radicals.

425.   Nicolay, John G. and John Hay. *Abraham Lincoln: A History*. 10 Vols. New York: Century Co., 1914. (Originally published 1886-1890)   In their narrative biography of Lincoln and the events of the Civil War, the authors discuss wartime Reconstruction issues, particularly Lincoln's efforts to cut short the war by creating new governments in captured states and by freeing slaves.   This multivolume work by two of Lincoln's close associates is still considered an important work of biography about the president.

426.   Oates, Stephen B. "Toward a New Birth of Freedom: Abraham Lincoln and Reconstruction, 1854-1865." *Lincoln Herald* 82 (Spring 1980): 287-296. Ports. Oates explains that Lincoln strove to reform the South and the nation as far back as the Kansas-Nebraska Act of 1854.   Lincoln opposed slavery and oligarchy in the South, and during the war he became convinced that emancipation was a central goal.   By the end of his life he had clearly agreed with the congressional Radicals that the South had to be reformed and that the freedmen deserved justice.

427.   Randall, James G. "Design For Peace." In *Lincoln and the South*. Baton Rouge: Louisiana State University Press, 1946.   Pp. 117-161.   Lincoln's benevolent, nonvindictive approach toward reunion was the object of Radical Republican criticism that proved successful by the time of Lincoln's death.   The Radicals' reactionary response ruined what would have been a just peace.   Randall compares the rejection of Lincoln's plan and his death with the reaction of Congress to Woodrow Wilson's design for peace following World War I.

428.   Randall, James G. and Richard B. Current. *Lincoln the President. Vol. 4: The Last Full Measure*. New York: Dodd, Mead & Co., 1955. 421p. Bibl. Port. The foundation of Lincoln's Reconstruction policies was reconciliation and avoidance of revenge and radical change.   It is likely that had he lived, Lincoln would have followed a policy similar to Johnson's, that he would have clashed with congressional Radicals, that he would have produced a better result for the freedmen than occurred, and that his political skills would have helped him to avoid Johnson's mistakes.   About half of this book was written by Randall prior to his death. Current completed the remainder.

429.   Randall, James G. "Lincoln's Peace and Wilson's."   *South Atlantic Quarterly* 42 (July 1943): 225-242.   Randall compares the efforts of Lincoln, Johnson, and Woodrow Wilson to resolve a war and make a just peace.   Conciliation and moderation were defeated by a reactionary Congress that led the nation into years of negativism and vindictiveness.   The "crucial year" of 1866 is compared with 1918 when congressional elections helped to defeat moderate peace plans.   In both cases the postwar reconstruction turned sour for the United States.

430.   Robertson, John B. "Lincoln and Congress."   Ph.D.   University of Wisconsin, 1966.

431.   Russ, William A., Jr.   "The Struggle Between President Lincoln and Congress Over Disfranchisement of Rebels." *Susquehanna University Studies* 2 (March 1947): 210-220; 3 (March 1948): 221-243.   Russ illustrates the precedence for the disenfranchisement of rebels in his review of contesting wartime Reconstruction measures put forth by Lincoln and the Republican Congress.   At state and national levels there were examples of restricting political participation through the taking of oaths or by restricting classes of individuals.   The Reconstruction Acts of 1867 incorporated disenfranchisement, an action Russ believes was unwise and encouraged Southern defiance against the federal government.

432.   Trefousse, Hans L.   "Abraham Lincoln versus Andrew Johnson: Two Approaches to Reconstruction."   In *Society and Change: Studies in Honor of Béla K. Király*.   Edited by Steven Bela Vardy and Agnes Huszar Vardy.   New York: Columbia University Press, 1983.   Pp. 251-270.   Notes.   Trefousse concludes that Lincoln and Johnson's Reconstruction plans were quite different and reflect the broad differences between the two men.   Lincoln showed flexibility and growth in his approach to political reality and in overcoming some of his racist views. Johnson did not have the wartime political experience as president, and he had a stubborn disposition that resisted change after his mind was made.   He also maintained the racism learned in his youth.   (See also Trefousse's "Lincoln and Johnson." *Topic* 5 (Spring 1965): 63-75.)

433.   Wilbur, Henry Watson.   *President Lincoln's Attitude Towards Slavery and Emancipation With a Review of Events Before and After the Civil War*. Philadelphia: W. H. Jenkins, 1914.   220p.   Wilbur compliments Lincoln's Reconstruction plan and his ability to work with Congress despite their differences of methodology.   Andrew Johnson is the subject of Wilbur's criticism.

434.   Williams, T. Harry.   *Lincoln and the Radicals*.   Madison: University of Wisconsin Press, 1941.   413p.   Bibl. Ports.   Williams focuses on the methods and temper of the Radical faction of the Republican Party in its struggle to overcome both political moderates and conservatives in order to control the war and its aftermath.   He refers to the Radicals as Jacobins who struggled against Lincoln's moderate inclinations toward eliminating slavery, using blacks in the Union Army, and the wartime Reconstruction of occupied states.   For Williams, Reconstruction symbolizes the struggle of principles between executive and congressional power and the struggle of ideology and political will.   Lincoln's flexibility with the Radicals' demands led to their feelings of power, their confidence to take on still another president, and their energy to lead the nation in "the savage years of the tragic era" (p. 384).

Studies on Andrew Johnson, 1864-1868

Biography, Postwar Policy, and Election of 1866

435.   Albjerb, Marguerite Hall. "The New York *Herald* as a Factor in Reconstruction." *South Atlantic Quarterly* 46 (April 1947): 204-211.   James Gordon Bennett edited the *Herald* during the years of the Civil War and Reconstruction. The *Herald* was a conservative, independent newspaper that always tried to please its readers and follow the majority opinion. After the Republicans swept the 1866 congressional election, Bennett dropped his support for Johnson's Reconstruction plan. The *Herald's* rejection of the president contributed to his steady decline.

436.   Albjerb, Marguerite Hall. "The New York Press and Andrew Johnson." *South Atlantic Quarterly* 26 (October 1927): 404-416.   New York City newspapers initially expressed wary optimism when Johnson became president. Johnson encouraged radical and conservative Republicans with his harsh words for the South and his desire to follow Lincoln's Reconstruction plan. His Southern-bred Unionism encouraged Democrats. Eventually Johnson's inability to compromise and his harsh, intolerant approach toward congressional proposals repelled the press. Since the New York press, such as The New York *Herald*, *The New York Tribune*, *The New York Times*, and *The World*, collectively formed the most influential newspapers in the Union, their rejection of Johnson by the late fall of 1866 forebode only ill for the President's future.

437.   Andrews, Rena Mazyck. "Johnson's Plan of Restoration in Relation to that of Lincoln." *Tennessee Historical Magazine 2nd Series* 1 (April 1931): 165-181.   Lincoln and Johnson are compared as to their approaches to Reconstruction. Andrews believes that the failure of the Presidential Reconstruction was not due to the plan or differences in personality or tactics. It is possible that Johnson encountered bad luck and circumstances that led to the defeat of his policies that he had inherited from Lincoln.

438.   Barber, George. "Johnson, Grant, Seward, and Sumner." *North American Review* 145 (1887): 81-85.   Barber publishes two letters written by Gideon Welles, Secretary of the Navy under Lincoln and Johnson, to Republican Sen. Joseph S. Fowler of Tennessee that defend President Johnson in his struggle with Republicans in Congress prior to and during the impeachment. Fowler was one of 7 Republicans who voted to acquit Johnson. The letters were written on September 4, 1875 and November 9, 1875 shortly after Johnson's death.

439.   Beale, Howard K. *The Critical Year: A Study of Andrew Johnson and Reconstruction.* New York: Harcourt Brace and Co., 1930. 454p. Bibl. Ill. Beale focuses on the period from April, 1865 through the congressional elections in November, 1866. This period is viewed as key to the direction that Reconstruction would take and would ultimately set a course for the country in the decades that

followed.   The Republican victory in the elections over Johnson's moderate Reconstruction policy was won primarily through propaganda and deception against the president, and it allowed northeastern Republicans to institute an economic program with emphasis on big business, high tariffs, and solid currency.   Beale emphasizes economic issues as well as Republican domination as the ultimate goals of the Radicals.   He views black suffrage and civil rights as vindictive, misguided policies against the South that were not really supported by the majority of the North and the Republican Party.

440.   Beecher, Henry Ward. "Conditions of a Restored Union." In *Patriotic Addresses*. By Henry Ward Beecher. Edited by John R. Howard. New York: Fords, Howard, and Hulbert, 1891. Pp. 713-735.   In Beecher's sermon, delivered at Plymouth Church on October 29, 1865, he sought to apply Christian morality and generosity to Reconstruction. While he complimented President Johnson and favored a quick return of the Southern states to the Union without heavy punishment, he also insisted that former Confederate leaders be denied leadership roles in postwar governments and that the evil of slavery should be recognized in the Southern state constitutions. Beecher spoke in favor of full civil rights for blacks. He rejected white supremacy, but he discouraged interracial marriage and believed in the separation of the black and white people based on education and refinement.

441.   Beecher, Henry Ward.   "Reconstruction of the Southern States."   In *Patriotic Addresses*. By Henry Ward Beecher. Edited by John R. Howard. New York: Fords, Howard, and Hulbert, 1891. Pp. 736-749.   Two letters written by Beecher are printed. The first, written on August 30, 1866 to the Soldiers' and Sailors' Convention held at Cleveland, Ohio, professes his dissatisfaction with the delay in bringing the former Confederate states back into the Union. His second letter to a parishioner on September 8, 1866 is a defense of his Reconstruction position that was criticized as being outside of the mainstream of the Republican Party.

442.   Blackburn, George M. "Radical Republican Motivation: A Case History." *Journal of Negro History* 54 (April 1969): 109-126.   Blackburn examines the opinions of politicians and the newspapers in Michigan during 1865 and 1866 regarding President Johnson's Reconstruction plan. In general opinions split along party lines with Democrats supporting Johnson and Republicans holding mixed views but mainly coming out against him. Republicans wanted significant political and social reforms in the South.   They did not care much about black enfranchisement and civil rights, but the issue symbolized the South's willingness to change.

443.   Boutwell, George S.   "Johnson's Plot and Motive."   *North American Review* 141 (December 1889): 570-579.   Boutwell suggests that Johnson never intended to begin a careful experiment in Reconstruction, but decided early to establish a speedy program. He describes the president's partiality toward the Democratic Party and his subsequent erratic behavior.

444.   Bowen, David W. *Andrew Johnson and the Negro*. Knoxville: University of Tennessee Press, 1989. 206p. Bibl.   Bowen examines the meaning of racism in the context of Johnson's life and career.   Race played a part in Johnson's decisions, even if racism was not explicitly and consciously intended.   Johnson's response to racial issues was based on his background and personality, as well as his interpretation of what the Northern victory in the Civil War meant to the nation. Bowen emphasizes that racism was an ideology of Johnson's time, even though its meaning differed among persons who agreed with the concept of white supremacy. (See also Bowen's *Andrew Johnson and the Negro*, Ph.D., University of Tennessee, 1977; and "Andrew Johnson and the Negro." *East Tennessee Historical Society's Publications* 40 (1968): 28-49. Port.)

445.   Brabson, Col. Fay Warrington. *Andrew Johnson: A Life in Pursuit of the Right Course 1808-1875*. Durham, N.C.: Seeman Printery, Inc., 1972. 306p. Port. Brabson became interested in Johnson as a young man growing up in Greenville, Tennessee, Johnson's former residence.   He writes an evenhanded, descriptive biography of the president who he admires for his skill at organizing men under his leadership and his ability to use them effectively in the political arena.   Brabson blames Johnson's lack of success in his struggle with the Radicals on his negative campaigning style in the 1866 election and the inept advice from his advisors.

446.   Brown, Wenzell. "Fearless Andrew Johnson." *American Mercury* 70 (May 1950): 608-617.   This is a highly favorable account of Johnson's life. Brown believes that Lincoln and Johnson were ideologically identical, and Johnson receives high marks for courage and determination in the face of political foes in Congress.

447.   Brown, William G. "The Tenth Decade of the United States: Andrew Johnson and 'My Policy'." *Atlantic Monthly* 96 (December 1905): 760-775. Brown sympathizes with Johnson's Reconstruction policies and the desire of the Southern states to rebuild their economies, but he criticizes the South's refusal to change in light of their defeat in war and the emancipation of the slaves.

448.   Brownlow, Paul C. "The Northern Protestant Pulpit and Andrew Johnson." *Southern Speech Communications Journal* 10 (Spring 1974): 248-259. Between 1865 and 1868 Northern Protestant ministers who spoke out on national politics projected conflicting signals regarding President Johnson's leadership of Reconstruction. There was broad support until 1866 when many clergy decided that Johnson's policies were not good for the country. Whether speaking out in support or in opposition to the president, the clergy contributed to public hysteria and an exaggerated image of the man.

449.   Cashdollar, Charles D. "Andrew Johnson and the Philadelphia Election of 1866." *Pennsylvania Magazine of History and Biography* 92 (July 1968): 365-383. Cashdollar downplays the idea that Johnson's campaign tour to promote his Reconstruction policies was a disaster because of the President's demeanor when meeting with the public. More important was Johnson's confusion about how to

present the issues and his failure to use the most effective trump card available, the issue of black equality. His visit to Philadelphia in late August, 1866 was to a city that would have been very receptive to Negrophobia, but Johnson produced ammunition for the Radicals by asking the public to forget the past, despite the huge war losses and the former Confederates in Southern state governments

450.   Castel, Albert. "Andrew Johnson: His Historiographical Rise and Fall." *Mid-America* 45 (July 1963): 175-184.   Castel charts the waves of historical opinion on President Johnson.   There were three main periods - writers who condemned Johnson's faults and methods, such as James Ford Rhodes; writers who elevated Johnson's stature, particularly William Dunning and Howard Beale; and recent critics, including Lawanda and John Cox, Eric McKitrick, and David Donald, who based their studies on Johnson's personality and his racism. Castel emphasizes that professional ambition, the availability of new evidence or the reinterpretation of old evidence, and the influence of contemporary social and political attitudes explain the rise and fall of Johnson. Racial attitudes of historians are a significant barometer of Johnson interpretations.

451.   Castel, Albert. *The Presidency of Andrew Johnson.* Lawrence: University of Kansas Press, 1979. 262p. Bibl.   Castel offers an interpretative history of Johnson's years in office.   He examines Johnson's Reconstruction policies, the confrontation between the president and Republicans in Congress, and the impeachment and trial. In each case Castel explains the interpretations of historians and provides his own opinions.   In his concluding chapter he reviews the historiography on Johnson's presidency and states that he is among those historians who classify themselves as conservative revisionists.   Castel is not critical of Johnson for thinking and acting as a man of mid-19th century America, and he is severely critical of the neo-Radical historians who do.   He recognizes the essential ideological (i.e. Jacksonian) approach that caused Johnson to act inflexibly and ineptly at a time when wise political leadership was essential.   With regard to impeachment, Castel clearly believes that the impeachment was an emotional, political action, and that there was no basis for for the charges against Johnson.

452.   Chadsey, Charles Ernest. "The Struggle Between President Johnson and Congress Over Reconstruction." Ph.D. Columbia University, 1896. 142p. (Rpt. by New York: AMS Press, 1967)

453.   Cimprich, John. "Military Governor Johnson and Tennessee Blacks, 1862-1865." *Tennessee Historical Quarterly* 39 (Winter 1980): 459-470.   As military governor, Andrew Johnson's view of slavery and blacks changed from support for slavery to enthusiastic support for emancipation.   His advocacy of civil rights for blacks, however, did not go beyond their personal liberty, education, compensation for labor, and choice of work.   After becoming president in 1865, Johnson maintained this attitude along with his Jacksonian ideals that led him to reject federal interference in local self government except for his limited efforts to reform the Southern governments in order to restore them to the Union.   Johnson's bias and

egotism contributed to his difficulties with his Reconstruction plan and the goals of congressional Republicans.

454.   Conklin, Forrest. "Wiping Out 'Andy' Johnson's Moccasin Tracks: the Canvass of Northern States By Southern Radicals, 1866." *Tennessee Historical Quarterly* 52 (Summer 1993): 122-133. Ills. Ports.   The Republican Party enlisted the support of Southern Radicals during the Congressional campaign of 1866. As President Johnson engaged in his ill fated tour of the Midwest to generate support for his Reconstruction policies and the candidates for Congress who supported him, Republicans met in Philadelphia and then fanned out across the North to gain supporters for a vigorous Reconstruction. Heading up the Southern delegation was Gov. William G. Brownlow of Tennessee who made a career of fighting against Johnson.

455.   Cox, John H. and LaWanda. "Andrew Johnson and the Ghost Writers: An Analysis of the Freedmen's Bureau and Civil Rights Veto Messages." *Mississippi Valley Historical Review* 48 (December 1961): 460-479.   The authors examine President Johnson's first two veto messages to discover who had assisted him and whether this assistance played a part in the final messages. Based on handwriting comparisons and a review of different drafts, the main contributor to both veto messages was determined to be Secretary of State William H. Seward, although Seward strongly urged Johnson to use much more conciliatory language than appeared in the final messages. The authors suggest that Johnson's decision to strongly reject both the Freedmen's Bureau and Civil Rights Bills directly effected his relationship with Congress and turned the moderate Republicans against him.

456.   Dorris, J. T. "Pardon Seekers and Brokers: A Sequel of Appomattox." *Journal of Southern History* 1 (August 1935): 276-292.   President Johnson's proclamation of amnesty of May 29, 1865 excluded 14 classes of former Confederates who would not receive a general pardon unless they applied and gained approval from the president in accordance with specific procedures. Beginning in August hundreds of persons were besieging Washington to request a quick pardon, and it appeared that Johnson had given up his restrictive grant of amnesty when large numbers of persons were successful. Pardon brokers and lawyers actively sought pardons for clients.

457.   Dunning, William A. "A Little More Light on Andrew Johnson." *Massachusetts Historical Society Proceedings*, Ser. 2, 19 (November 1905): 395-405.   In this address to the Massachusetts Historical Society Dunning explains that evidence and conjecture point to George Bancroft as the principle author of President Johnson's first annual message on December 4, 1865. Dunning surmises that Bancroft wrote the speech based on its moderate tone and the fact that Bancroft held ideas wedded to the Jacksonian Democratic Party that Johnson agreed with. Such ideas include the sanctity of the constitution, significant autonomy of the states, the perpetuity of the Union and the divine providence of American achievement and progress. (See also Dunning's "More Light on Andrew Johnson." *American Historical Review* 11 (April 1906): 574-594.)

458.   Foner, Eric (ed.). Andrew Johnson and Reconstruction: A British View."
Journal of Southern History 41 (August 1975): 381-390.   The British view of
Reconstruction is evident in the two letters printed here from the British Minister to
the U.S., Frederick W. A. Bruce, to the British Foreign Secretary, George William
Frederick Villiers, fourth Earl of Clarendon. The first letter, written on February 9,
1866, refers to Bruce's private meeting with Johnson about suffrage in the U.S. In
the letter of May 6, 1866 Bruce responded to the Earl's request for information about
Reconstruction, a phenomena being followed closely in Britain. Bruce comments
on the protection of the freedmen, Radicals in Congress, racism, and black labor.
Foner notes that Bruce personally sided with Johnson against the Radicals.

459.   Gerry, Margaret S. "The Real Andrew Johnson." *Century Magazine* 115,
ns93 (November 1927-April 1928): 54-64, 218-230.   Johnson's stand on
Reconstruction was based on the constitution, while the Radicals stand was based on
human emotions. Gerry views this as a quality of Johnson's, even though a more
prudent, diplomatic policy would have been to negotiate a significant weakening of
Republican policy. This would likely have been Lincoln's approach. The conflict
between the president and Congress led to his unjust impeachment and illustrates
Johnson's courageous, but inept, approach to Reconstruction.

460.   Gipson, Lawrence H. "The Statesmanship of President Johnson: A Study
of the Presidential Reconstruction Policy." *Mississippi Valley Historical Review* 2
(December 1915): 363-383.   Gipson offers a sympathetic account of Johnson in
his struggle to implement a Reconstruction policy that he says was entirely
consistent with the policy of President Lincoln. He believes that Johnson's policies
were generous and based solidly on the constitution. Johnson changed his initial
harsh Reconstruction policy to a lenient approach toward the South, a position that
was consistent with Northern public opinion. Gipson doubts very much whether
Lincoln could have done any better in the struggle with the Radicals in Congress.

461.   Graf, Leroy P. and Ralph W. Haskins (eds.). *The Papers of Andrew
Johnson*. Vol. 1- Knoxville: University of Tennessee Press, 1967- Ills. Ports.
The editors have gathered personal and public documents into this series from
document collections in various locations in the U.S. The largest collections are at
the Library of Congress and the National Archives in Washington, D. C. The
editors admit that a complete reprinting of all Johnson documents could never be
assured, but they seek to provide a comprehensive collection from 1822 until
Johnson's death in 1875. As of May, 1999 the set is complete up to April, 1869
(vol. 15). Brief annotations accompany most documents. Volume 1 includes a
genealogical chart of Johnson's family and a history of references to Johnson in the
Journals of the Tennessee House and Senate (1835-1837, 1839-1843) and the U.S.
House of Representatives (1843-1853). The completed volumes covering
Johnson's presidency include volumes 8-14. Many libraries own the microfilm
edition of the *Andrew Johnson Papers* kept at the Library of Congress Manuscript
Division and the related *Index to the Andrew Johnson Papers* (Government Printing
Office, 1963). (See also # 503)

462.   Halperin, Bernard S. "Andrew Johnson, the Radicals, and the Negro, 1865-1866." Ph.D. University of California, Berkeley, 1966. 227p.

463.   Hamilton, J. G. de Roulhac. *Life of Andrew Johnson: Seventeenth President of the United States.* 2nd Ed. Sponsored by The Andrew Johnson Woman's Club of Greenville, Tennessee. Greenville, Tn.: Brown Print Co., 1930. 33p.   This pamphlet offers a brief, sympathetic account of Johnson's life and presidency. Also included is a reprint of Col. John Trotwood Moore's (Tennessee State Librarian and Archivist) article on Johnson that appeared in the *Saturday Evening Post* on March 30, 1929 and other reflections on Johnson's career.

464.   Hamilton, J. G. de Roulhac. "The Southern Policy of Andrew Johnson." *Proceedings of the 16th Annual Session of the State Literary and Historical Association of North Carolina, Raleigh, November 8-9, 1915.* Raleigh: Edwards and Broughton, 1916. Pp. 65-80.   Hamilton reviews Johnson's Reconstruction policies and praises him as a friend of the South and a courageous patriot of the Union and the constitution.

465.   Hays, Williard. "Andrew Johnson's Reputation." *East Tennessee Historical Society's Publications* 31 (1959): 1-31; 32 (1960): 18-50. Port.   Hays analyses what historians have written about Johnson and the course of his reputation from Johnson's day until the early 1960s. Early historians were highly critical of Johnson, but after new sources appeared, more sympathetic works prevailed. Hays agrees with the recent historical accounts that favor Johnson's Reconstruction plan, that consider his impeachment to be purely a political move, and that cite his courageousness.

466.   Hyman, Harold M. "Johnson, Stanton, and Grant: A Reconsideration of the Army's Role in the Events Leading to Impeachment." *American Historical Review* 66 (October 1960): 85-100.   Secretary of War Edward M. Stanton and Gen. Ulysses S. Grant gradually objected to and actively opposed Johnson's Reconstruction policies because the return of unreconstructed rebels to public office throughout the South exposed the military to taunts and legal suits and showed that Johnson was not prepared to make major changes after a war that took the lives of so many Northern soldiers. The support of Stanton and Grant for the Republicans illustrates the important influence of military and political affairs on the events that led to Johnson's impeachment.

467.   Irelan, John Robert. *History of the Life, Administration, and Times of Andrew Johnson, Seventeenth President of the United States.* Chicago: Fairbanks and Palmer, 1888. 630p.   Irelan is mostly critical of Johnson's presidential abilities. He quotes extensively from government documents.

468.   Jones, Rev. James S. *Life of Andrew Johnson.* Greenville, Tn.: East Tennessee Publishing Co., 1901. 384p. Ill. Ports. (Rpt. by AMS Press, 1975) Jones' offers a sympathetic account of the President's term in office. The book

begins with a note from Johnson's daughter, Mrs. Martha Johnson Patterson, who recommends the work to the public.

469.   Kilar, Jeremy W.   "Andrew Johnson 'Swings' Through Michigan: Community Response to a Presidential Crusade." *Old Northwest* 3 (September 1977): 251-273.   Kilar describes Johnson's September, 1866 campaign trip through Southern Michigan and Detroit and the response of the local press. The President's reception varied from place to place, but most Michigan voters learned of the trip from newspapers. Most Republican papers were highly partisan against him. Newspaper accounts contributed to forming the negative impression of the trip.

470.   Kraut, John A. "Henry J. Raymond on the Republican Caucuses of July, 1866." *American Historical Review* 33 (July 1928): 835-842.   Both houses of Congress refused to adjourn during the summer of 1866 because of the intensifying struggle between Republicans and President Johnson over Reconstruction policy. Raymond, congressman from New York's 6th district and editor of the *New York Times*, recorded the proceedings of the Republican caucuses. His notes are reprinted. The notes reveal that Republicans believed that adjournment would allow the president to strengthen his power over Reconstruction policy.

471.   Lately, Thomas. *The First President Johnson: The Three Lives of the Seventeenth President of the United States of America.* New York: William Morrow, 1968. 678p. Bibl. Ills. Ports.   Lately offers a narrative of Johnson's life. Half of the book covers the period of Johnson's presidency, his "third life." Lately quotes frequently from source materials.

472.   Levstik, Frank R. "A View From Within: Reuben D. Mussey on Andrew Johnson and Reconstruction." *Historical New Hampshire* 27 (Fall 1972): 1676-171. Ills.   Mussey served as President Johnson's confidential secretary from April until November, 1865 when he resigned over his disagreements with Johnson's Reconstruction policies. Levstik provides a letter from Mussey to William Henry Smith, a Republican newspaper editor in Ohio, expressing Mussey's dissatisfaction.

473.   Lomask, Milton. *Andrew Johnson: President on Trial.* New York: Farrar, Straus, and Cudahy, 1960. 376p. Bibl.   Lomask depicts President Johnson's activities regarding Reconstruction as a courageous attempt to uphold the U.S. constitution in the face of radical measures attempted by Republicans. Johnson's victory in his impeachment trial is viewed as a vindication of his political principles.

474.   Majeske, Penelope K. "Johnson, Stanton, and Grant: A Reconsideration of the Events Leading to the First Reconstruction Act." *Southern Studies* 22 (Winter 1983): 340-350.   Majeske explore the role of Gen. Grant and the U.S. Army in the South in the relationship between President Johnson and Congress. Grant and the Republicans saw problems in Johnson's Reconstruction policies, and Grant quarreled with Secretary of State Edwin M. Stanton over control of the Army.

The first Reconstruction act of March 2, 1867 enhanced Grant's power and put him in direct conflict with the president.   Majeske wonders about the relationship between Grant's enhanced power and his eventual presidential candidacy in the Republican Party.

475.   Mantell, Martin E. *Johnson, Grant, and the Politics of Reconstruction.* New York: Columbia University Press, 1973. 209p. Bibl.   The political and military struggle in the federal government helps define the postwar years of 1867 and 1868. President Johnson and Gen. Grant struggled over the Army's control of the South, and this relationship was complicated by Grant's appointment as secretary of war in 1867. This took place within the context of hostility between the president and the Republican controlled Congress over the philosophy and course of Reconstruction and the political war that led to the impeachment of the president. The passage of the Reconstruction legislation and Grant's victory in the presidential election of 1868 seemed to resolve these conflicts.

476.   McCall, Samuel W. "Washington During Reconstruction." *Atlantic Monthly* 87 (June 1901): 817-826.   McCall discusses presidential leadership to reunite the states after the Civil War. Any attempt to leave Congress out of a Reconstruction plan was flawed, and Johnson's uncompromising stand against the Republican Party's initiatives caused his failure, although McCall acknowledges Johnson's patriotism and sincerity of purpose.   He believes that Johnson's impeachment was more the result of partisanship than legality, and he recognizes that the Republican Reconstruction plan led to a number of evil developments, but also peace, the maintenance of freedom, and progress for the black race in America.

477.   McCaslin, Richard B. *Andrew Johnson: A Bibliography.* Westport: Greenwood Press, 1992. 314p. Chron. Serial consulted. Indexes.   This bibliography lists 2,025 sources covering Johnson's life and career. McCaslin includes briefly annotated references to manuscript repositories and collections, newspapers and periodicals, articles in periodicals, published writing by and about Johnson, writings about associates in and out of government, historiographical writings, dissertations, and references to films, museum collections, and other iconography.

478.   McKitrick, Eric L. *Andrew Johnson and Reconstruction.* Chicago: University of Chicago, 1960. 534p. Bibl.   McKitrick's work is a partial reinterpretation of the historical writing on Johnson that appeared during the previous 30 years. The earlier writing went too far in venerating Johnson, partially in reaction to even earlier accounts that vilified him. McKitrick recognizes the qualities of Johnson's personality and initial approach to Reconstruction, but he blames Johnson for the political turmoil that resulted in the near complete dissolution of his influence and his defeat to the Radical Republicans in the struggle to determine how the South would be reformed. There was virtually no substance to indictments that led to his impeachment. The book offers an analytical approach and narrative to the events and controversies from 1865 to May, 1868 when Johnson

was tried by the Senate. (See also McKitrick's Ph.D. dissertation with the same title from Columbia University, 1959.)

479.   Milton, George F. "Andrew Johnson-Man of Courage." *East Tennessee Historical Society's Publications*, 3 (January 1931): 23-34.   Milton writes a brief biographical sketch of Johnson with emphasis on his positive character traits. He is critical of historians who have criticized Johnson and his record as president.

480.   Milton, George F. "Canonization of a Maligned President." *Independent* 121 (September 1, 1928): 200-202, 217.   Milton reviews the career of Andrew Johnson and explains how history has given him a bad mark when he deserves to be respected for his defense of democracy and his upholding of the traditions of farmers and laborers.

481.   Milton, George Fort. *The Age of Hate: Andrew Johnson and the Radicals.* New York: Coward-McCann, Inc., 1930. 787p. Bibl. Ills. Ports.   Milton's phrase, "age of hate", is intended to describe the attitude of the Radical Republicans toward both the South and Johnson's concept and program of Reconstruction. He offers a narrative of the period from the 1864 election of Lincoln and Johnson to the end of Johnson's presidency in March, 1869. Milton expresses support and sympathy for Johnson in his struggle with the Radicals to institute a plan of Reconstruction consistent with the U.S. constitution.

482.   Moore, Robert J. "Andrew Johnson: The Second Swing 'Round the Circle." *Proceedings of the South Carolina Historical Association* (1966): 40-48. Moore examines the changing perspectives on Johnson from historians of Reconstruction. The "second swing" refers to how opinions of Johnson have returned to the negative evaluations that were prevalent early in the 20th century when William Dunning and James Ford Rhodes were setting the pace of Reconstruction historiography. Moore surveys historical writing up to the mid-1960s.

483.   Nash, Jr., Howard P. *Andrew Johnson: Congress and Reconstruction.* Rutherford: Fairleigh Dickinson University Press, 1972. 170p. Bibl.   This volume covers the period from the beginning of Johnson's presidency in April, 1865 until his impeachment trial in 1868. Nash believes that Radical Reconstruction would have been avoided if Johnson had been more willing to cooperate with congressional Republicans in 1866, and the South had not insisted on returning to antebellum ways.

484.   Nettles, Curtis. "Andrew Johnson and the South." *South Atlantic Quarterly* 25 (January 1926): 55-64.   Johnson held a consistent philosophy toward to the South and the nation from the time he entered national politics until the demise of his presidency. He was always a strong Unionist, a defender of democracy, and a believer in the preservation of states' rights. Johnson was a nationalist who believed that a lenient postwar policy was best for the Union and the common Southerner.

485.   Notaro, Carmen Anthony. "History of the Biographical Treatment of Andrew Johnson in the Twentieth Century." *Tennessee Historical Quarterly* 24 (Summer 1965): 143-155.   Notaro reviews three historiographic perspectives on the performance of Johnson as president.   Prior to the late 1920s Johnson was depicted in demeaning terms (see works by Burgess, DeWitt, Rhodes, Schouler). From the late 1920s until 1960 he was generally complimented (see works by Winston, Stryker, Bowers, Milton, Beale).   Since the 1960s historians have accepted Johnson's good character but criticized him for his lack of flexibility (see works by LaWanda Cox).

486.   Ogg, Frederick Austin. "The Reconstruction Period." *Current History and Modern Culture* 12 (March 1902): 7-10.   Ogg reviews the response of congressional Republicans to Johnson's Reconstruction policy from 1865 to mid-1866.

487.   Ortiz-Garcia, Angel Luis.   "Andrew Johnson's Veto of the First Reconstruction Act." Ph.D. Carnegie-Mellon University, 1970. 201p.

488.   Phifer, Gregg. "Andrew Johnson Delivers His Argument." *Tennessee Historical Quarterly* 11 (September 1952): 212-234.   Phifer studies Johnson's 1866 campaign speeches as published by newspaper reporters.   He emphasizes Johnson's organization, despite the president's lack of formal preparation, and his natural public speaking abilities. Phifer believes that the Radical press exaggerated Johnson's speech problems that were due to hoarseness.

489.   Phifer, Gregg. "Andrew Johnson Loses His Battle." *Tennessee Historical Quarterly* 11 (June 1952): 148-170; 11 (December 1952): 291-328; 11 (March 1952):3-12.   President Johnson's 1866 campaign trip speeches are summarized. The study is based on 35 speech texts collected from 46 newspapers in 9 states and the District of Columbia.   The main themes were peace and reconciliation, the constitution, suppression of party partisanship, and the presidential versus congressional power. Johnson's critics exaggerated his faults, but the trip had little effect on the election compared with the disorganization of the Democrats, the Radical domination of the press, and Johnson's political mistakes during the campaign.

490.   Phifer, Gregg.   "Andrew Johnson Versus the Press in 1866." *East Tennessee Historical Society's Publications* 25 (1953): 3-23.   Phifer focuses on the response of the press to Johnson's campaign trip during August and September prior to the congressional election in November.   The Northern press covered the trip extensively.   Phifer cites the strong Republican bias of most Northern newspapers and magazines.   The press published filtered accounts of Johnson's speeches and how he responded to his detractors. Journalists were more influential in shaping opinion than Johnson himself.

491.   Phifer, Gregg [Lyndon G.]   "The Last Stand of Presidential Reconstruction: A Rhetorical Study of Andrew Johnson's Swing Around the Circle in 1866." Ph.D. University of Iowa, 1950.

492.   Ramage, Burr J.   "Andrew Johnson's Administration." *South Atlantic Quarterly* 1 (April 1902): 171-182; (July 1902): 256-265.   Ramage questions Johnson's competency as president and his behavior in dealing with Reconstruction. Johnson is to blame for the failure of his policies because he lacked a pragmatic view.   Congressional Reconstruction also failed politically, and it engendered bitterness and reinforced sectionalism.   The benefits included legal reforms, better local government, and advances in education and civil rights for blacks.

493.   Reece, B. Carroll. *The Courageous Commoner: A Biography of Andrew Johnson.* Charleston: Educational Foundation, Inc., 1962. 168p. Bibl.   Reece sympathizes with Johnson's Reconstruction policies and the president's courageous stand against the Radicals.   Reece strongly criticizes the Radicals for their politicization of Reconstruction for the purpose of maintaining power, their vindictiveness against the South, and their hypocrisy on the issue of racial equality.

494.   Riddleberger, Patrick W. *1866: The Critical Year Revisited.* Carbondale: Southern Illinois University Press, 1979. 287p. App. Bibl. Ports.   Riddleberger provides a narrative and analysis of political events and ideas that shaped the year that produced the key to the future of postwar reconstruction. The title of the book alludes to Howard K. Beale's earlier work [see # 439] that was revisionist in its day, but Riddleberger reviews revisionist criticism of Beale published in the 1950s and 1960s [see # 197, 214, 220, 478]. His review of 1866 defines the civil rights debates and the executive-legislative power struggle as the central themes in the disagreement over the 14th Amendment, the Freedmen's Bureau Bill, and the Civil Rights Bill of 1866.   The political battles of 1866 and 1867 between President Johnson, Southern whites, and congressional Radicals was a continuation of the Civil War in a different form.

495.   Royall, Margaret Shaw. *Andrew Johnson - Presidential Scapegoat: A Biographical Re-evaluation.* New York: Exposition Press, 1958. 175p. Bibl. Royall's brief biography of Johnson and his wife, Eliza, is intended as a rehabilitation of the president's reputation as a man of integrity.   She criticizes Johnson detractors for their selfishness and their desire to distort his personality and political record.

496.   Russell, J. F. S.   "Lincoln's Successor: President Andrew Johnson." *History Today* 4 (September 1954): 618-626. Ports.   Russell reviews Johnson's career and concludes that the unfortunate rejection by Congress of his Southern policies led to the tragedy of Radical Reconstruction. Most historians are critical of Johnson and believe that he has no place in the Jacksonian-Roosevelt Democratic tradition.

497.   Schlegel, Marvin W.   "Lincoln Versus Johnson: The Tragedy of Reconstruction."   *Virginia Social Science Journal* 2 (1967): 119-133.   Schlegel argues that divergent personalities and leadership styles between Lincoln and Johnson indicate why their approaches to Reconstruction and the Radicals also differed.   Despite the Radical defeat of Johnson, his policy of leniency and white supremacy in the South prevailed by the end of the 19th century.

498.   Schoonover, Thomas.   "The Mexican Minister Describes Andrew Johnson's 'Swing Around the Circle'."   *Civil War History* 19 (June 1973): 149-161. This book includes translations of dispatches from Matias Romero, Mexican Minister to the U.S., to Sebatian Lerdo de Tejada, Mexican Minister of Foreign Relations.   The dispatches and the text of a speech were written while Romero accompanied President Johnson on his campaign tour prior to the congressional elections of 1866.   The dispatches raise questions about the intended impact of the tour on foreign affairs   and broadens the President's otherwise narrow domestic perspective.   Romero offers his interpretation of Johnson, Secretary of State William Seward, Gen. Ulysses S. Grant, and U.S.-Mexican relations.

499.   Schouler, James.   "President Johnson and Negro Suffrage."   *Outlook* 82 (January 1906): 69-73.   Schouler writes approvingly of Johnson's opposition to a federal mandate for black suffrage, and he describes the early support in Congress for the president's policies.

500.   Schouler, James.   "President Johnson's Papers."   *Proceedings of the Massachusetts Historical Society*, Ser. 2, 20 (October 1906): 427-437.   In his address to the Massachusetts Historical Society, Schouler describes the conflict between Johnson and Congress over Reconstruction, including the impeachment. Schouler believes that Johnson meant well in his Reconstruction policy, but his inflexibility and temper destroyed his administration and hurt the South.

501.   Schouler, James.   "President Johnson's Policy."   *Outlook* 82 (February 1906): 264-268.   Schouler seems to agree with Johnson's approach toward Reconstruction that followed Lincoln's policy of moderation.   The president's political mistakes during 1866 were unfortunate given his sincerity and political abilities.

502.   Sefton, James E.   *Andrew Johnson and the Uses of Constitutional Power.* Boston: Little, Brown and Co., 1980. 212p. Bibl.   Sefton's book is partly a political biography and partly a narrative of Johnson's clash with Congress over constitutional principles of power.   Johnson lost in this competition between the executive and the legislative branches because he would not compromise what he thought was right about limitations to federal authority and the responsibilities of the states.

503.   Simpson, Brooks D., Leroy P. Graf, and John Muldowny (eds.).   *Advice After Appomatox: Letters to Andrew Johnson, 1865-1866. Special Vol. No. 1 of the Papers of Andrew Johnson.* Knoxville: University of Tennessee Press, 1987. 259p.

App.   The editors transcribed and published letters written by selected writers to President Johnson on the conditions in the South, the prospects for a transition from separation to reunion, and the problems encountered by blacks in their new state of freedom.   The writers, who were asked by Johnson to make the reports, provide suggestions regarding how he should deal with these issues.   Included are letters from Supreme Court Chief Justice Salmon P. Chase (May, 1865); former Tennessee congressman and close friend Harvey M. Watterson (June-July, September-October, 1865); Republican politician Carl Schurz (July-September, 1865); *New York Times* war correspondent Benjamin C. Truman (October, 1865-March, 1866); and Gen. Ulysses S. Grant (December, 1865).   The epilogue also includes observations of Gen. George G. Meade and George H. Thomas; Johnson's message to Congress (December 18, 1865), a list of Truman's reports in the *New York Times*, and 2 additional humorous observations. (See also # 461)

504.   Smith, Willard H. "Schuyler Colfax and Reconstruction Policy." *Indiana Magazine of History* 39 (December 1943): 323-344.   Colfax was the Republican Speaker of the House from 1863 until 1869 when he became vice-president under Grant.   Smith emphasizes Colfax's leadership role in the Radical opposition to President Johnson in the struggle over whether Congress or the president would control Reconstruction. The Speaker may have been somewhat moderate compared with Thaddeus Stevens, but he supported Reconstruction legislation and the impeachment of Johnson.

505.   Stampp, Kenneth M. *Andrew Johnson and the Failure of the Agrarian Dream*. Oxford: Clarendon Press, 1962. 25p.   In this lecture Stampp discusses the nature of the conflict between Johnson and Republicans in Congress. Johnson's attempt to reshape the character and goals of Lincoln's Reconstruction plan led to the return of power to the Southern elite and reflected his hidden admiration for them and a lack of concern for the freedmen.   His miscalculation of Southern intentions and attitudes and his narrow constitutional interpretations led to his defeat.

506.   Stryker, Lloyd Paul. *Andrew Johnson: A Study in Courage*. New York: Macmillan, 1929. 881p. App. Bibl. Ills. Ports.   Stryker is highly sympathetic with the president's character and judgment, and his approach to Reconstruction. He is strongly critical of the Radical Republicans and their vindictiveness against the South. Johnson was vindicated by historical events, but historians have abused him and not recognized his greatnes.

507.   Tappan, George L. *Andrew Johnson-Not Guilty*. New York: Comet Press Books, 1954. 139p.   In his sympathetic account of Johnson's life, Tappan defends the president in the struggle with the Radical Republicans in Congress.

508.   Trefousse, Hans L. "Andrew Johnson and the Failure of Reconstruction." In *Toward a New View of America: Essays in Honor of Arthur C. Cole*. Edited by H. L. Trefousse. New York: Burt Franklin Co., 1977. Pp. 135-150. Notes. Immediately after the Civil War most Southerners were willing to cooperate with a

reasonable plan of Reconstruction, but President Johnson's lenient plan for reunion reenergized Southern nationalism and resistance to broader proposals, particularly regarding black suffrage and restrictions on white suffrage. Trefousse believes that there was a good chance that Johnson could have forced the South to cooperate with moderate proposals.

509.   Wagstaff, Thomas. "Andrew Johnson and the National Union Movement, 1865-1866." Ph.D. University of Wisconsin, 1967. 373p.

510.   Wagstaff, Thomas. "The Arm-in-Arm Convention." *Civil War History* 14 (June 1968): 101-120.   The National Union Movement was organized by conservative Republican supporters of President Johnson's Reconstruction plan. The movement sought to reorient the Republican Party by attracting support from moderates and enough Democrats in the North and South to form an unbeatable alliance against the Radicals going into the elections of 1866. The Philadelphia convention in August, 1866 seemed to successfully focus attention on National Unionists, but the alliance failed, partly due to Johnson's behavior during his campaign trip in the fall.

511.   Winston, Robert W. *Andrew Johnson: Plebeian and Patriot.* New York: Henry Holt and Co., 1928. 549p. App. Bibl. Ill. Port.   Even though Johnson had character flaws, particularly his stubbornness and tactless style, he was a national hero for his determination to uphold the constitution and preserve a union of strong states. Winston agrees with the Presidents gentle approach toward the South after the war, because it could have led to gradual change, including black suffrage. Radical Reconstruction was actually "more wicked and more criminal" (p. 519) than the secession of 1860.

Impeachment

512.   Albright, Claude.   "Dixon, Doolittle, and Norton: The Forgotten Republican Votes." *Wisconsin Magazine of History* 59 (Winter 1975-1976): 91-100. Ills. Tbls.   Republican Senators James R. Doolittle of Wisconsin, James Dixon of Connecticut, and Daniel S. Norton of Minnesota voted for acquittal at President Johnson's impeachment trial, but historical accounts of the Senate vote have not counted them as Republicans. Albright explains that their long-standing support for Johnson and their generally conservative voting records on Reconstruction issues led the Radicals to disregard them as Republicans and count only the "renegade" Republicans who decided late to vote with the president. The three Senators are more typical of Republicans before and after the Radicals held power.

513.   Bayless, R. W.   "Peter G. Van Winkle and Waitman T. Willey in the Impeachment Trial of Andrew Johnson." *West Virginia History* 13 (January 1952): 75-89.   Senators Van Winkle and Willey of West Virginia were influenced by

different factors in their opposing votes to convict Johnson. Bayless also discusses the perspective of the West Virginia press. Van Winkle was accused of betraying his party after his vote against conviction. Willey also opposed conviction, but he voted with his party for political purposes.

514.   Beauregard, Erving E. "The Chief Prosecutor of President Andrew Johnson." *Midwest Quarterly* 31 (Spring 1990): 408-422.   Congressman John Bingham of Ohio was a moderate Republican who lost faith in the president and led the prosecution at the impeachment trial. Beauregard suggests that Bingham's religious, educational, and family background prepared him for the duty.

515.   Benedict, Michael Les. *The Impeachment and Trial of Andrew Johnson.* New York: W. W. Norton, 1973. 212p. App. Bibl. Tbls.   Benedict analyses why the impeachment took place and how Johnson was acquitted. He closely examines the composition of the Republican Party and its attitudes toward Johnson and other economic and political concerns. Republicans were not unified and their attitudes toward impeachment were at least partially tied to support for particular money and tariff policies. Benedict assesses the support of individual congressmen in relation to their economic perspective, their dedication to racial equality, and the establishment of loyal Southern governments.

516.   Benedict, Michael Les. "A New Look at the Impeachment of Andrew Johnson." *Political Science Quarterly* 88 (September 1973): 349-367.   Benedict alters the traditional view of the impeachment of Johnson that focuses on Congress's evil attempt to reshape the balance of power between the executive and legislative branches of government. A more accurate interpretation should emphasize the reluctance of moderate and conservative Republicans who deliberately delayed proposals for impeachment until the president pushed them into the Radical camp by his actions that appeared to be unlawful or to violate congressional authority.

517.   Berwanger, Eugene H. "Ross and the Impeachment: A New Look at a Critical Vote." *Kansas History* 1 (Winter 1978): 235-242. Ills. Port.   Republican Senator Edmund G. Ross voted against conviction in the impeachment trial of President Johnson. He immediately came under fire from colleagues and Republicans in Kansas for betraying the cause to enhance his influence with the president. Bewanger examines Ross's own defense against detractors and credits the June 13, 1868 letter of editor Henry C. Whitney in the Burlington Kansas *Patriot*. Whitney offered an insightful analysis of Ross's motives that give credence to the senator's defense, but in 1868 the letter was ignored.

518.   Boutwell, George S. "The Impeachment of Andrew Johnson." *McClure's* 14 (December 1899): 171-182. Ill.   Boutwell, who was chairman of the mangers of the impeachment trial, describes the events that led to the trail. He continued to believe that the impeachment of Johnson was appropriate and a just cause. (See also # 192)

519.   Bridges, Roger D.   "John Sherman and the Impeachment of Andrew Johnson."   *Ohio History* 82 (Summer-Autumn 1973): 176-191. Ill. Port.   Sen. Sherman of Ohio voted in favor of impeachment mainly to secure the proper balance of power between Congress and the president and to ensure that Reconstruction reforms would go forward. Although he was a principal author of the Tenure of Office Act of March 2, 1867, he had no problem with Johnson's right to remove Stanton as Secretary of War, but he wanted a replacement who would cooperate with the Republican Reconstruction program. Bridges believes that Sherman's expressed satisfaction with the acquittal was sincere.

520.   Dewitt, David Miller. *The Impeachment and Trial of Andrew Johnson Seventeenth President of the United States: A History.* New York: Russell and Russell, 1967. 646p. (Reissue of New York: Macmillan, 1903)   Dewitt offers a narrative of Johnson's difficulties with Congress followed by an extended description of the impeachment proceedings from preparation to acquittal. His approach is sympathetic towards Johnson and critical of the methods used by the Republican Party. He is in agreement with Johnson's Reconstruction policies.

521.   Donald, David. "Why They Impeached Andrew Johnson." *American Heritage* 8 (December 1956): 20-25, 102-103. Ills.   Donald does not focus on specific charges against Johnson but on the man himself and the decisions that he made from April, 1865 until his impeachment and trial in March, 1868. Blame for the radical course of Reconstruction can be distributed widely, but Johnson was ultimately responsible for creating and allowing an environment of confrontation to build. His faults of character, his lack of political leadership, and his lack of appreciation of Northern public's concern about Southern recalcitrance created an atmosphere in which support for impeachment could flourish.

522.   Dower, Thomas. "The Role of S. Boutwell in the Impeachment and Trial of Andrew Johnson." *New England Quarterly* 49 (December 1976): 596-617. Republican Rep. George Boutwell of Massachusetts was an instigator and manager of the trial. He vigorously pursued the removal of Johnson from the presidency out of concern for national security which he believed was threatened by Johnson's policies and use of power. Boutwell contributed to the development of the impeachment process and the precedent for impeachments when presidents misuse their authority.

523.   Dunning, William A. "The Impeachment of President Johnson." *Papers of the American Historical Association* 4 (October 1890); 143-177 [463-503]. Dunning writes a political and constitutional survey of the impeachment that focuses on the issues of Johnson's violation of the Tenure of Office Act and the constitutional power of the president to appoint and dismiss cabinet officials.

524.   Edmunds, George F.   "Ex-Senator Edmunds on Reconstruction and Impeachment." *Century Illustrated Monthly Magazine* 85 (1912-13): 863-864. Sen. Edmunds, a Republican from Vermont during Reconstruction, wrote a letter to the editor reacting to earlier articles by Otis (see # 536) and Henderson (see # 526)

regarding the impeachment of President Johnson. He proposed to correct their errors by emphasizing the correctness of congressional Reconstruction policies and the orderliness of the Senate during impeachment proceedings.

525.   Frierson, Hon. William L.   "The Impeachment and Trial of Andrew Johnson." *Proceedings of the 41st Annual Session of the Bar Association of Tennessee* (May 30-31 1922): 122-138.   Former solicitor general of the U.S. and Tennessean William Frierson summarizes the issues leading to and during Johnson's impeachment trial. He defends the president against those who would lead the nation into error.

526.   Henderson, Gen. Joseph B.   "Emancipation and Impeachment: Recollections of the Senator Who Proposed the Thirteenth Amendment, and Was One of the Seven Republicans Who Thwarted the Attempt to Impeach President Johnson." *Century Illustrated Monthly Magazine* 85 (1912-13): 196-209. Ill. Ports. Henderson, a Republican senator from Mississippi during Reconstruction, describes himself as a moderate who favored the general direction of Johnson's Reconstruction policies but opposed him on specific issues. He strongly opposed the impeachment because it was a purely political manuever with no legal basis. Personalities and personal ambitions were the driving forces behind the affair. Henderson provides some background to other Republican senators who voted against impeachment. (See # 524)

527.   Howard, Thomas W. "Peter G. Van Winkle's Vote In the Impeachment of President Johnson: A West Virginian As a Profile in Courage." *West Virginia History* 35 (July 1974): 290-295.   Howard comments on Van Winkle's decision to acquit the president. The senator is described as a "nominal Republican" who would eventually switch his party membership to the Democrats. His decision was likely based on conscience rather than political expediency.

528.   Hunt, Gaillard. "The President's Defense: His Side of the Case, As Told By His Correspondence." *Century Illustrated Monthly Magazine* 85 (1912-13): 420-434. Ill. Ports.   Hunt, head of the manuscripts division at the Library of Congress, focuses on the initial, conflicting support for Johnson during his impeachment from various Democratic and Republican factions. He describes the activities of Johnson's defenders, particularly Jeremiah S. Black, who resigned from the defense due to a supposed conflict of interest. He also writes about Johnson's personality and the president's defense against the specific charges made against him by Radical senators.

529.   Ilse, Louise.   "Changing Interpretation of Andrew Johnson's Impeachment." *Social Education* 11 (October 1947): 255-258.   Aside from the immediate political and personal issues that led to Johnson's impeachment, Ilse also discusses social, economic, and nationalist factors.

530.   Jellison, Charles A. "Ross Impeachment Vote - A Need for Reappraisal." *Southwestern Social Science Quarterly* 41 (September 1960): 150-155.   Jellison

questions the compliments bestowed on Kansas Senator Edmund G. Ross by some prominent historians based on Ross's courageous vote against the impeachment of President Johnson. It is not known why Ross, an avowed Radical, decided to vote in the negative, but he took successful advantage of his situation by asking Johnson to appoint friends to federal offices.

531.   Kilar, Jeremy W. "'The Blood-Rugged Issue is Impeachment or Anarchy': Michigan and the Impeachment and Trial of Andrew Johnson." *Old Northwest* 6 (Fall 1980): 245-269.   Public opinion in Michigan on the impeachment of President Johnson is measured using newspapers and contemporary writings. Kilar shows how the press was effective in leading opinion from opposition to Johnson's policies to emotional condemnation and calls for his removal.

532.   Kurtz, Henry I. "The Impeachment of Andrew Johnson." *History Today* 24 (May 1974): 299-305; 24 (June 1974): 396-405.   Kurtz reviews the events and issues of President Johnson's relations with Congress and his eventual impeachment and trial in 1868 in light of the possibility of a second impeachment of a president in 1974. He is critical of the way the Republicans conducted the impeachment and trial, particularly the weakness of the case against Johnson.

533.   Lewis, H. H. Walker. "The Impeachment of Andrew Johnson: A Political Tragedy." *American Bar Association Journal* 40 (January 1954): 15-18, 80-87. This is a review of the backgroud and proceedings of the impeachment.

534.   McDonough, James Lee and William T. Alderson (ed.). "Republican Politics and the Impeachment of Andrew Johnson." *Tennessee Historical Quarterly* 26 (Summer 1967): 177-183.   The memorandum reprinted was written by Gen. John M. Schofield. The memo refers to the possible impact of a conviction on the government and on Schofield's nomination to the cabinet. He would succeed Edwin M. Stanton as secretary of war in 1868.

535.   Mushkat, Jerome. "The Impeachment of Andrew Johnson: A Contemporary View." *New York History* 48 (July 1967): 275-286. Ill.   Portions of New York Congressman John V. L. Pruyn's journal are published covering congressional impeachment activities from February 21, 1868 to May 26, 1868.

536.   Otis, Harrison Gray. "The Impeachment of Andrew Johnson-The Cause of Impeachment." *Century Illustrated Monthly Magazine* 85 (1912-13): 186-195. Ill. Otis served in the Union Army and, at the time of writing this article, was editor of the *Los Angeles Times*. He focuses blame for the impeachment mainly on white Southerners who sought the virtual reenslavement of Southern blacks, the election of disloyal men to office, and the violent intimidation of black and white Republicans. (See also # 524)

537.   Parsons, R. C. "History of the Impeachment Trail of Andrew Johnson, President of the United States." *Western Reserve Law Journal* 2 (February 1896): 1-

7; 2 (March 1896): 35-49.   Parsons, who apparently was an eyewitness, describes the impeachment trial in an article reprinted from the *Cleveland Leader.*

538.   Patton, James W. "Tennessee's Attitude Toward the Impeachment and Trial of Andrew Johnson." *East Tennessee Historical Society's Publications* 9 (1931): 65-76.   Tennessee's congressional delegation, excluding Sen. Fowler, favored the conviction of President Johnson.   Gov. William Brownlow worked hard against Johnson because they were political enemies.   Patton compares the attitudes of state Republican leaders with the opinions appearing in the press, but concludes that opinions were inconsistent.

539.   Perdue, M. Kathleen. "Salmon P. Chase and the Impeachment of Andrew Johnson." *Historian* 27 (November 1964): 75-92.   As Chief Justice of the U.S. Supreme Court, Chase presided over the Senate impeachment of the president. Chase was not trusted by the Radicals managing the trial, because he opposed the the impeachment proceedings. He was blamed for the failure to convict Johnson based on the perception that he influenced several Republicans to vote against conviction.   Perdue does not believe Chase can be held accountable for such influence or power over the proceedings. She suggests that he was selected as a scapegoat by the Radicals.

540.   Rable, George C.   "Forces of Darkness, Forces of Light: The Impeachment of Andrew Johnson and the Paranoid Style." *Southern Studies* 17 (Summer 1978): 151-173.   Rable reviews the development of the case against Johnson as a way to reexamine how the case has been interpreted by historians. He views the impeachment as a struggle between two extremes that would not compromise. He refers to Richard Hofstadter's "paranoid style" thesis in American politics in which political struggles are characterized as between light and dark or good and evil. Rable believes that the Radicals pressed their case for this reason, not because there were firm grounds for conviction. He believes that it was necessary and proper to rid the government of an obstructer of congressional Reconstruction.

541.   Rehnquist, William H. *Grand Inquests: The Historic Impeachments of Justice Samuel Chase and President Andrew Johnson.* New York: William Morrow and Co., 1992. 303p. Bibl.   Supreme Court Chief Justice Rehnquist examines the impeachment of Chase (1801) and Johnson (1868) in the context of their extraordinary times and the threat to the balance of powers established by the U.S. constitution. Both impeachments are viewed as mainly political maneuvers by Congress that could have undermined the powers of the judiciary and the presidency if the trials had led to convictions.

542.   Roske, Ralph J. "Republican Newspaper Support For the Acquittal of President Johnson." *Tennessee Historical Quarterly* 11 (September 1952): 263-273. Northern newspapers that supported acquittal of the president at his impeachment trial comprised a minority based on Roske's study of 41 Republican newspapers in 13 states and the District of Columbia.

543.   Ross, Edmund G. *History of the Impeachment of Andrew Johnson.* New York: Burt Franklin, 1965. 180p. (Rpt. of Sante Fe: New Mexico Printing Co., 1896)   The story of the impeachment is told with extensive quotation from trial documents. Ross, a Republican who voted against conviction, believes that the affair was an act of Republican partisanship and that Johnson's victory was a vindication for him and the constitutional system. (See also "Historic Moments: The Impeachment Trial." *Scribner's Monthly* 11 (April 1892): 519-524 in which Ross describes the mood of Congress and the casting of votes on charges of impeachment on May 15, 1868.)

544.   Schoonover, Thomas. "Mexican Affairs and the Impeachment of President Andrew Johnson." *East Tennessee Historical Society's Publications* 46 (1974): 76-93.   Schoonover suggests that foreign affairs played a role in the decision of some Radical Republican congressmen to seek the impeachment of Johnson in January, 1867. The Radicals sought a more aggressive policy than the administration to force the French out of Mexico because the French presence threatened republican government and American power in the hemisphere. The unsuccessful attempt to pass an impeachment resolution was partly a tactic to remove Secretary of State Seward and alter American foreign policy.

545.   Sefton, James E. "The Impeachment of Andrew Johnson: A Century of Writing." *Civil War History* 14 (June 1968): 120-147.   In his survey of major monographs on impeachment, Sefton cites topics that need addressing: biographical works on contemporary senators and congressmen, details on legislative operations, statistical studies of voting, and the motivations of Johnson's supporters and detractors.

546.   Smith, Gene. *High Crimes and Misdemeanors: The Impeachment and Trial of Andrew Johnson.* New York: William Morrow, 1977. 320p. Bibl. Ills. Ports.   In his narrative account Smith emphasizes the importance of events in shaping the actions of the players in the impeachment proceedings. Neither the Radicals nor Johnson are whitewashed as saint or sinner.

547.   Stathis, Stephen W. "Impeachment and Trial of President Andrew Johnson: A View From the Iowa Congressional Delegation." *Presidential Studies Quarterly* 24 (Winter 1994): 29-47.   The 8 man Iowa delegation in the House of Representatives and the Senate was totally Republican, but they represented the differences of opinion that surrounded the issue of impeachment of the president. Stathis examines their views with particular emphasis on Sen. James W. Grimes, one of the seven Republicans who voted against a conviction, and Rep. James F. Wilson, chairman of the House Judiciary Committee, who originally opposed impeachment but ultimately served as one of the House managers arguing the case against Johnson.

548.   Tracy, John E. "The Impeachment and Trial of Andrew Johnson." *Michigan Alumnus Quarterly Review* 60 (December 5, 1953): 1-11. Port.   Tracy summarizes Johnson's life and his confrontation with the Republicans in Congress.

549.   Trefousse, Hans L. "The Acquital of Andrew Johnson and the Decline of the Radicals." *Civil War History* 14 (June 1968): 148-161.   The Radicals were in decline prior to the impeachment, and the failure to convict the president hastened the decline further.   The Radical movement gradually dissipated because of declining support in the North, loss of members, and the failure of Reconstruction in the 1870s.

550.   Trefousse, Hans L.   "Ben Wade and the Failure of Impeachment of Johnson." *Historical and Philosophical Society of Ohio* 18 (October 1960): 241-252. Port.   Trefousse explains that the possibility of Ohio's Sen. Wade becoming president in the event that Andrew Johnson was convicted was one of the key reasons for Johnson's survival.   Wade's Republican colleagues did not want to deal with his persistent, "old school" Radicalism and support for reforms at a time when the majority of the party sought stability.

551.   Trefousse, Hans L.   *Impeachment of a President: Andrew Johnson, The Blacks, and Reconstruction.*   Knoxville: University of Tennessee Press, 1975. 252p. Bibl. Port.   Johnson's aversion to civil rights for blacks because of their inherent inferiority to whites was the basis for his opposition to Radical Reconstruction and his condemnation of anyone who sought compromise.   This approach, and his support of moderate Republicans, led to his impeachment, even though the impeachment was based on weak evidence and Republicans disagreed about its political impact.   The president's acquittal energized Southern conservatives to resist Reconstruction and led to the eventual disintegration of Republican state governments in the South.

Studies on Ulysses S. Grant, 1865-1877

Biography, Postwar Policy, and Election of 1868

552.   Bedeau, Adam.   *Grant in Peace From Appomattox to Mount McGregor: A Personal Memoir.*   Hartford: S. S. Scranton and Co., 1887. 591p. Ills.   Bedeau, a former aid-de-camp to Grant during the Civil War, provides a personal history that includes letters from Grant and himself mainly after Reconstruction.   He discusses the period of Reconstruction and Grant's relations with President Johnson and his cabinet.

553.   Carpenter, John A.   *Ulysses S. Grant.*   New York: Twayne, 1970. 217p. Bibl. Chron. Notes.   Carpenter stresses the difficulties that Grant encountered in his efforts to reunite the nation, restrain Southern whites, and protect the freedmen in the postwar years.   He is clear that Grant was unsuccessful, but the president should not be blamed for the failure.   Grant's desire to shape events in the South was met with decreasing enthusiasm by other Republicans who sought stability over the tension and disruption of reforms and the weak Republican regimes in the Southern states.   Carpenter explains that in his second term   (1873-1877)   Grant did not

devote significant attention to the South. (See also Carpenter's "Ulysses S. Grant: Tarnished Hero." *Topic* 5 (Spring 1965): 76-82 in which he describes Grant's ever present image as a hero.)

554.   Church, William Conant. *Ulysses S. Grant and the Period of National Preservation and Reconstruction.* Garden City: G. C. Publishing Co., 1926. 473p. Port.   Provides a very positive description of Grant as president during Reconstruction.

555.   Coleman, Charles H. "The Election of 1868: The Democratic Effort to Regain Control." Ph.D. Columbia University, 1933. 407p. (Rpt. in Columbia University Studies, 392, Columbia University Press, 1933.)

556.   Current, Richard N. "President Grant and the Continuing Civil War." In *Ulysses S. Grant: Essays and Documents.* Edited by David L. Wilson and John Y. Simon. Carbondale: Southern Illinois University Press, 1981. Pp. 71-82. (Rpt. in *Arguing With Historians: Essays on the Historical and Unhistorical.* Middletown: Wesylean University Press, 1987. Pp. 71-82)   Current attempts to rescue Grant from the negative evaluations by historians since William Dunning by emphasizing Grant's intentions and attempts to enforce the constitution to bring about equal civil rights and security for the freedmen. Grant showed determination, but politics and violence impeded his efforts.

557.   Grant, Ullyses S. *The Papers of Ulysses S. Grant.* Vol. 1- Edited by John Y. Simon. Carbondale: Southern Illinois University Press, 1967-. Calendar. Chron. Ills. Port.   Personal and public documents are reprinted and annotated from various collections in the U.S. The documents begin with 1837 in volume 1 and run through January 31, 1872 in volume 22 (as of June, 1999). Volumes relating to the Civil War include vol. 2-14 (April, 1861-April, 1865). The Reconstruction period is covered by the remaining published volumes. Many research libraries own the microfilm edition of Grant's *Papers, 1844-1885* (32 reels) that are kept at the Library of Congress, Manuscript Division and *Index to Ulysses S. Grant Papers* (Washington: GPO, 1965).

558.   Hesseltine, William B. *Ulysses S. Grant - Politician.* New York: Frederick Ungar, 1957. 480p. Bibl. Ills. Ports. (Rpt. from Dodd, Mead, & Co., 1935)   Hesseltine believes that Grant was a well-meaning president, but he criticizes Grant's bland and weak performance and abilities as a political leader. He views the defeat of Reconstruction in the South as a repudiation and defeat of Grant's policies.   Grant lost substantial support for his policies within the Republican Party and the public throughout America. Hesseltine offers a generally negative view of the Republican program of Reconstruction.

559.   Mantell, Martin Eden. "The Election of 1868:   The Response to Congressional Reconstruction." Ph.D. Columbia University, 1969. 269p.

560.   McCartney, Ernest Ray. "The Crisis of 1873." Ph.D. University of Nebraska, Lincoln, 1932.

561.   McFeely, William S. *Grant: A Biography*. New York: W. W. Norton, 1981. 592p. Bibl. Ills. Ports.   McFeely characterizes Grant's personal and professional life as mainly a quest for recognition and high position rather than following deeply held principles and clear goals. His life found purpose only in war, but not necessarily to eliminate slavery, to preserve the Union, or to spread Republicanism. The achievements of his presidency were marred by scandal and his lack of enforcement of Reconstruction legislation. McFeely criticizes Grant for his unwillingness to take vigorous actions to prosecute white Southerners who sought to intimidate white Republicans and to crush the civil rights of blacks in the South. He believes that Grant's lack of will contributed to the breakdown of Reconstruction.

562.   Moran, Philip R. (ed.). *Ulysses S. Grant 1822-1885. Chronology-Documents-Bibliographic Aids*. Dobbs Ferry, N.Y.: Oceana Publications, 1968. 114p.   Moran provides a reference work to Grant's life and presidency. All of the documents are from Grant's two terms as president and include mostly items related to Reconstruction.

563.   Perret, Geoffrey. *Ulysses S. Grant: Soldier and President*. New York: Random House, 1997. 542p. Ill.   This popular biography includes brief attention to Grant's Reconstruction policies.

564.   Rawley, James A. "The General Amnesty Act of 1872: A Note." *Journal of American History* 47 (December 1960): 480-484.   Congress approved the act on May 22, 1872. It lifted the political disabilities from certain groups of white Southerners as stipulated in section 3 of the 14th Amendment. Rawley points out that the act restored the right of most of the restricted classes to hold public office. It said nothing about the right to vote because the 14th Amendment did not restrict suffrage for any white Southerners. Historians have mistakenly associated disenfranchisement with the 14th Amendment and reenfranchisement with the amnesty law.

565.   Scaturro, Frank J. *President Grant Reconsidered*. Lanham: University Press of America, 1998. 137p. Bibl. Graph. Port.   In his critical historiographical study, Scaturro argues against the traditional negative interpretations of Grant as president. He focuses on the issues that have made Grant a target for detractors, including civil service corruption and Reconstruction, and he explains how historians have distorted Grant's record and accomplishments. Scaturro calls on American historians to have the courage to break away from politicized, establishment interpretations of Grant and to seek a truly accurate view of a president who, in general, has not been judged fairly.

566.   Simpson, Brooks D.   "Another Look at the Grant Presidency." *Proceedings of the South Carolina Historical Association* (1990): 7-17.   Simpson calls for a reevaluation of Grant that does not focus mainly on what his critics said,

on political problems with Reconstruction, or on corruption. Historians need to recognize Grant's approach to the presidency and what he tried to accomplish in a very difficult environment marked by Republican Party transition and attempts to bring peace and justice to the South.

567.   Simpson, Brooks D. *Let us Have Peace: Ulysses S. Grant and the Politics of War and Reconstruction, 1861-1868.* Chapel Hill: University of North Carolina Press, 1991. 339p. Bibl. Port.   Grant's perspective on the relationship of politics, war, and the soldier form the basis of Simpson's work that spans the Civil War and Reconstruction up to Grant's election to the presidency in November, 1868. During war and peace Grant sought to carry out the policies of the political leadership and not attempt to create and influence policy through political intrigue or public pressure. As a soldier his goal was to win the war in accordance with policy goals. In his role associated with President Johnson's policy of Reconstruction, he sought sectional reconciliation and justice for the freedmen, but concluded that Johnson's policies were misguided and would not lead to the betterment of the nation. Despite his longstanding antipathy for politics and politicians, Grant decided that he had the stature and understanding to finally conclude a just peace. Simpson analyses these issues in the context of interpretations of Grant's leadership during the war and the years prior to his presidency. (See also Simpson's Ph.D. dissertation, University of Wisconsin, 1989.)

568.   Simpson, Brooks D. "Ullyses S. Grant and the Failure of Reconstruction." *Illinois Historical Journal* 81 (Winter 1988): 269-282. Ports.   Grant sought to reconcile both North and South and also blacks and whites. But sectional and racial reconciliation in the form of Reconstruction failed during his administration because the white South refused to accept blacks as equal citizens and acted out their opposition with violence. Simpson's examination of Grant's opinions and actions from 1865 to the end of his presidency clarifies that Grant sincerely wanted to heal the nation and preserve civil rights for blacks. The fact that he failed to resolve these postwar problems should not overshadow his intentions.

569.   Smith, Donnal V. *"Salmon P. Chase and the Nomination of 1868."* In *Essays in Honor of William E. Dodd By His Former Students at the University of Chicago.* Edited by Avery O. Craven. Chicago: University of Chicago Press, 1935. Pp. 291-319.   Smith explains how Chase pursued the nomination for president in 1868, first from the Republican Party and then from the Democrats. In 1865 he accepted Lincoln's nomination to be Chief Justice of the U.S. Supreme Court, but his dissatisfaction with the job led him into increasing involvement in politics. Chase was originally a Ohio Radical, but his moderate views on Reconstruction, his support for President Johnson at his impeachment trial, and the swelling support for Gen. Grant in 1867 eliminated him from contention among Republicans. Some Democrats seriously considered him, and he encouraged their interest, but the Democratic Party selected Horatio Seymour of New York who better represented the Party.

570.   Wilson, David L.   "Ulysses S. Grant and Reconstruction." *Magazine of History* [OAH] 4 (Winter 1989): 47-50. Ills.   Wilson discusses Grant's role in the Johnson administration mainly as the ranking general of the U.S. Army.   Grant gradually rejected Johnson's methods and policies in Reconstruction.   The general sympathized with the need to protect the freedmen from abuse and denial of civil rights.   Grant supported political reforms in the South, but he sought to avoid personal involvement in politics.

571.   Wooley, Edwin C.   "Grant's Southern Policy."   In *Studies in Southern History and Politics*. New York: Columbia University Press, 1914. Pp. 176-201. President Grant's policies were based on the need for peace and the acceptance of the law. He fully supported the Republican's legislative and constitutional reforms to protect and to guarantee political and civil rights to the freedmen.   Wooley describes Grant as mainly reactive, rigid, and lacking in leadership in his attempt to solve the problems of the South in Reconstruction.

572.   Zilversmit, Arthur.   "Grant and the Freedmen."   In *New Perspectives on Race and Slavery in America: Essays in Honor of Kenneth M. Stammp*. Edited by Robert H. Abzug and Stephen E. Maizlish.   Lexington: University Press of Kentucky, 1986. Pp. 128-145.   Grant was not an abolitionist, but he eventually supported emancipation and civil rights. During his presidency he maintained this position of support, even as members of his party turned toward compromise. By the end of his second term Grant's policies followed Northern public opinion. As public opinion shifted away from the constant problems of black rights in the South, so did Grant. Grant's changing policy reflects the bias of his time, but at least he pursued justice as long as he could. No one else in his position could have done much better.

Liberal Republicanism and the Election of 1872

573.   Ahern, Wilbert H.   *"Laissez Faire* vs. Equal Rights: Liberal Republicans and the Limits to Reconstruction." *Phylon* 40 (March 1979): 52-65.   Liberal Republicans, the breakaway group from the regular Republican Party, came together to support political equality among all citizens without the suppression of former Confederates, even though this would likely lead to a reduction of political power for the freedmen and the Republicans in the South. Ahern believes that historians have labeled the Liberal Republican stand as racist, but he asserts that historians have distorted the Liberal Republican movement and not recognized its emphasis on equal rights.   The party's approach toward equal rights grew in popularity after the election of 1872 and helped to limit the effectiveness of Reconstruction.

574.   Ahern, Wilbert H.   *Laissez Faire Versus Equal Rights: Liberal Republicans and the Negro, 1861-1877*. Ph.D. Northwestern University, 1968. 356p.

575.   Benedict, Michael Les.   "Reform Republicans and the Retreat From Reconstruction."   In *The Facts of Reconstruction: Essays in Honor of John Hope Franklin*.   Baton Rouge: Louisiana State University Press, 1991.   Pp. 33-77. Enthusiasm for Radical Republicanism declined in the late 1860s in favor of Liberal Republicanism as reformers, such as E. L. Godkin of *Nation* and Charles Eliot Norton of the *North American Review*, became enthralled with science and its application to society.   They expressed a *laissez-faire* philosophy of human development that contributed to running down radicalism and depriving the freedmen of active government intervention to guarantee equality with whites under the law.

576.   Downey, Matthew T.   "The Rebirth of Reform: A Study of the Liberal Reform Movement 1865-1872."   Ph.D.   Princeton University, 1963.   655p.

577.   Durden, Robert Franklin.   *James Shepherd Pike: Republicanism and the American Negro, 1850-1882*.   Durham: Duke University Press, 1957.   249p.   Bibl. Pike, a journalist originally from Maine, transformed himself from a Radical Republican to a Liberal Republican because he opposed the impeachment of Johnson, despised the Grant administration, and refused to support black suffrage. In 1873 he toured South Carolina for the New York *Tirbune* and published *The Prostrate State: South Carolina Under Negro Government* (New York: Appleton, 1873), a polemic against Grant, the failing policies of Reconstruction, and black equality. (See also # 2356)

578.   Gerber, Richard A.   "The Liberal Republican Alliance of 1872."   Ph.D. University of Michigan, 1967.   531p.

579.   Gerber, Richard A.   "Liberal Republicanism, Reconstruction, and Social Order: Samuel Bowles as a Test Case."   *New England Quarterly*   45 (September 1972): 393-407.   Based on the ideas of Samuel Bowles, the influential editor of the Springfield, Massachusetts *Daily Republican* who helped to formulate Liberal Republican policies, Gerber concludes that members of the Republican Party who rejected President Grant and Radical policies were actually counterrevolutionaries seeking the same thing that they had always wanted - national harmony and social order.   Bowles believed that Grant's policies would lead to the destruction of national harmony and must be opposed.

580.   Gerber, Richard A.   "The Liberal Republicans of 1872 in Historiographical Perspective."   *Journal of American History* 62 (June 1975): 40-73.   Gerber reviews historical writing on the nature of Liberal Republicanism from James Ford Rhodes in 1899 to recent works in the mid-1970s. Early interpreters of the break away party originally described it as reformist (e.g. anticorruption and civil service reform) or reunionist   (halt Reconstruction, deemphasize sectional differences). Revisionists redefined the argument in terms of racism and the fundamental conservatism of the Liberals. It was the issue of race that repelled the Liberals from the Radicals and made them seek a more orderly society.

581. McPherson, James M. "Grant, or Greeley? Abolitionist Dilemma in the Election of 1872." *American Historical Review* 71 (October 1965): 43-61. New York *Herald* editor Horace Greeley made reconciliation with the South as the key issue in his bid for the presidency in the 1872 election against President Grant. Abolitionists were disappointed with Grant's inconsistent policy of maintaining peace and protecting the freedmen, but they would not support Greeley because they believed that local whites would not uphold civil rights. Abolitionists believed that coercion of the South had to continue.

582. Mohamed, Ali N. "Civil Rights in the Nineteenth Century: Frederick Douglass vs. the Pro-Republican Press." *Proteus* 12, 1 (1995): 29-34. Douglass continued to work for equal rights for blacks, but his efforts were undermined when the *New York Times* criticized the Civil Rights Act of 1875 and the U.S. Supreme Court weakened its application in their rulings. Mohamed emphasizes the influence of the press on stifling race reforms in America.

583. Riddleberger, Patrick W. "The Break With Radical Ranks: Liberals vs. Stalwarts in the Election of 1872." *Journal of Negro History* 44 (April 1959): 136-157. Riddleberger's examination of several Liberal Republicans and Stalwart Republicans distinguishes between the parties and why key players either rejected the Liberal agenda or embraced it in the national election of 1872. He elaborates on Liberal Republicans Sen. Lyman Trumbull of Illinios, George W. Julian of Indiana, Sen. Charles Sumner of Massachusetts, and party leader Carl Schurz. The Stalwarts mentioned here who supported Grant included Sen. Benjamin Wade of Ohio and Sen. Zachariah Chandler of Michigan. Among other issues, the Stalwarts stood for continued government intervention in the South, while the Liberal Republicans supported a *laissez-faire* approach, including amnesty for former Confederates.

584. Riddleberger, Patrick W. "The Radicals' Abandonment of the Negro During Reconstruction." *Journal of Negro History* 45 (April 1960): 88-102. Riddleberger analyses the backgrounds of the men who led the Liberal faction of the Republican Party and how they decided to abandon the fight for civil rights for blacks in the South in 1872. Former abolitionist supporters of the freedmen, including Andrew Greeley, George Julian, Carl Schurz, Charles Sumner and Lyman Trumbull were among the Liberal Republican leaders who changed their perspective based partly on personal and political disenchantment with President Grant. Many Liberals were influenced by racial prejudice or support for the idea of institutional restraint in the lives of American citizens. Most Liberals believed in emphasizing national unity and allowing blacks to find their own path to civil rights.

585. Ross, Earle Dudley. "The Liberal Republican Movement." Ph.D. Cornell University, 1915. 267p.

586. Tusa, J. "Power, Priorities, and Political Insurgency: The Liberal Republican Movement, 1869-1872." Ph.D. Pennsylvania State University, 1970. 389p.

587.   Watterson, Henry. "The Humor and Tragedy of the Greeley Campaign." *Century Illustrated Monthly Magazine* 85 (1912-13): 27-45.   Ports.   Ill. Watterson, a Democrat and journalist for the Louisville *Courier-Journal*, provides a journalist's perspective on the Liberal Republican convention in Cincinnati in May, 1872 and the entire presidential election campaign. He provides descriptions and opinions on notable attendees to the convention, including fellow journalists Whitelaw Reid, Carl Schurz, David Davis, Horace Greeley, and others. Watterson believes that Greeley held out hope for the white South and probably represented the best chance for the Liberal Republicans to snare both Republican and Democratic voters. Following this article are critical comments from Whitelaw Reid and Horace White.

Election of 1876

588.   Beatty, Bess. "A Revolution Gone Backward: The Black Response to the Hayes Administration." *Hayes Historical Journal* 4 (Spring 1983): 5-25.   Ill. Blacks generally gave strong support to the Republican candidacy of Rutherford B. Hayes for president in 1876, but when President Hayes showed that he would not keep his promise to protect the civil rights of blacks, they withdrew their support in bitter disappointment.

589.   Benedict, Michael Les. "Southern Democrats and the Crisis of 1876-1877: A Reconsideration of *Reunion and Reaction*." *Journal of Southern History* 46 (November 1980): 489-524. App. Graphs. Tbls.   Benedict presents an opposing view to C. Vann Woodward's *Reunion and Reaction* (see # 615) on the Compromise of 1877 that concluded the controversial election of 1876. Benedict deemphasizes Woodward's economic interpretation as the basis for a solution to the election controversy and also says that no deal was made. There were two outstanding factors behind the Republican victory. Northern Democrats were in a poor political position to press their case for a Tilden victory, thus ensuring a victory for Hayes. Also, Hayes and other Republicans decided that they would join the reform wing of the Republican Party thus ensuring a new Southern policy. As further evidence for his thesis, Benedict includes an aggregate count of roll call votes between February 23 and March 3, 1877 and the percentage of various groups of Democrats who voted with the Republicans.

590.   Black, J. S. "The Electoral Conspiracy." *North American Review* 125 (1877): 1-34.   Black was a counsel for the Democratic presidential candidate, Samuel Tilden, in the Electoral Commission of 1877. He provides a strongly worded argument describing the fraud perpetrated by the Commission in the name of partisan politics. Black's article is countered by E. W. Staughton in "The 'Electoral Conspiracy' Bubble Exploded," *North American Review* 125 (1877): 193-234. Staughton criticizes Black for his biased account of the Commission's decision.

591.   Clark, James C. "The Fox Goes to France: Florida, Secret Codes, and the Election of 1876." *Florida Historical Quarterly* 69 (April 1991): 430-456.   In the disputed election of 1876 Florida's four electoral votes were awarded to Republican candidate Rutherford B. Hayes rather than Democrat Samuel J. Tilden.   Clark describes how this occurred and how confusion among Florida Democrats over secret coded messages from New York contributed to Tilden's defeat.   After the election Republicans broke the code and publicized Democratic Party attempts to buy the election.

592.   Clendenen, Clarence C. "President Hayes' 'Withdrawal' of the Troops-An Enduring Myth." *South Carolina Historical Magazine* 70 (October 1969): 240-250. There is a widespread notion that Hayes' agreement to pull troops out of the South meant that a large number of federal troops were still stationed there twelve years after the end of the Civil War. The truth is that only 3,230 troops of the entire U.S. Army of 28,000 nationwide were in the the Southern states, and they were mainly in Louisiana, South Carolina, and Florida in 1876. The troops stationed in the South did little more than protect revenue officers.

593.   DeSantis, Vincent P. "Rutherford B. Hayes and the Removal of the Troops and the End of Reconstruction." In *Region, Race, and Reconstruction: Essays in Honor of C. Vann Woodward.* New York: Oxford University Press, 1982. Pp. 417-451.   DeSantis explores the historiography of the so called "Compromise of 1877" that is viewed as officially bringing Reconstruction to an end when Hayes agreed to the removal of federal troops from Louisiana and South Carolina. In 1951 C. Vann Woodward (see # 615) changed the accepted view of the election agreements by explaining that there were really several meetings over a few months that involved various issues in addition to troop withdrawals, such as federal funding of Southern railroads and Democratic control of Southern patronage. More recent writing by Peskin (see # 605), Benedict (see # 589), Polakoff (see # 606), and Gillette (see # 250) have corrected errors in Woodward's thesis, but his interpretation continues to be accepted.

594.   Electoral Commission of 1877. *Proceedings of the Electoral Commission and of the Two Houses of Congress in Joint Meeting Relative to the Count of Electoral Votes Cast December 6, 1876, for the Presidential Term Commencing March 4, 1877.* Washington: GPO, 1877. 1087p.   Includes correspondence, hearings, and documents produced by the commission.

595.   Ewing, Elbert William R. *History and Law of the Hayes-Tilden Contest Before the Electoral Commission: The Florida Case 1876-77.* Washington, D.C.: Cobden Publishing Co., 1910. 194p.   Ewing, an attorney and counselor of the U.S. Supreme Court, examines how Rutherford B. Hayes became president as a result of the legal and extralegal workings of the Electoral Commission and supporters of both Hayes and Tilden. The focus is on the disputed Florida voter returns and both federal and state authority as the basis for the commission's decisions. Ewing concludes that there is no doubt that the case of the Florida returns and other issues show that Republicans committed both immoral and illegal acts that

resulted in a stolen or bought victory. Hayes may not have participated in the deal-making and frauds, but he assented to them.

596.   Fairman, Charles. *Five Justices and the Electoral Commission of 1877.* Suppl. to v. 7 of *History of the Supreme Court of the Unite States.* New York: Macmillan, 1988. 202p. Ports.   Fairman examines the role of 5 Supreme Court justices on the commission that decided who would be president following the contested election returns from November, 1876. He covers the history leading up to the commission's appointment on January 29, 1877, the proceedings of the commission, and the public response to the commission's decision. He also discusses the influence of Abram S. Hewitt's account of the commission as told by historian Allan Nevins and Justice Joseph P. Bradley.

597.   Gibson, A. M. A Political Crime: *The History of the Great Fraud.* New York: William S. Gottsberger, 1885. 402p. App.   Gibson believes that Republican fraud in the counting of votes for president in Louisiana, South Carolina, and Florida led to Hayes' victory. The appendix provides additional evidence to support this opinion.

598.   Haworth, Paul Leland. *The Hayes-Tilden Disputed Presidential Election of 1876.* Cleveland: Burrows Brothers, 1906. 365p. App.   Haworth takes a pragmatic approach in his history of the 1876 election controversy that was decided by the Electoral Commission in 1877. He believes that fraud did occur in the electoral process in South Carolina, Florida, and Louisiana and that both political parties were involved, particularly the local Democrats. Haworth accepts the decision of the Electoral Commission as a moderate one that avoided further sectional conflict. The appendix includes the text of the Electoral Commission Act.

599.   Kleber, Louis C. "The Presidential Election of 1876." *History Today* 20 (Novmeber 1970): 806-813. Ills. Ports.   Kleber describes the events of the 1876 election that led to a great scandal and threatened to bring on a new sectional war.

600.   Koenig, Louis W. "The Election That Got Away." *American Heritage* 11 (October 1960): 4-5, 99-104. Ills.   Koenig emphasizes that the U.S. constitution does not have provisions for resolving electoral conflicts such as those that emerged from the election of 1876. He claims that Republican Rutherford B. Hayes' victory over Democrat Samuel J. Tilden was achieved through connivance and fraud by Hayes' supporters. The victory was brokered by Southern leaders and Hayes who promised an end to Reconstruction.

601.   Kuntz, Norbert A. "The Electoral Commission of 1877." Ph.D. Michigan State University, 1969. 236p.

602.   Lewis, Walker. "The Hayes-Tilden Election Contest." *American Bar Association Journal* 47 (January 1961): 36-40; (February 1961): 163-167.   Lewis writes a brief history of the election dispute, and he points out the problem of involving the U.S. Supreme Court in a political dispute.

603.   Monroe, James. "The Hayes-Tilden Electoral Commission." *Atlantic Monthly* 73 (October 1893): 521-538.   Monroe reviews the activities of the electoral commission of 1877 and includes extensive quotations from the *Congressional Record.* He concludes that there was no fraud in the commission's decision that Hayes won the presidency, and he commends the nation for its ability to settle this difficult dispute.

604.   Northrup, Milton H. "A Grave Crisis in American History: The Inner History of the Origins and Formation of the Electoral Commission of 1877." *Century Magazine* 62 (1901): 923-934.   The Electoral Commission was formed to resolve the impasse over which candidate had won the presidential election of 1876. Northrup provides details on congressional deliberations to form the Commission. He includes extended quotations, presumably from his own notes and possibly the *Congressional Globe.* Northrup was secretary of the Special Committee of the House of Representatives charged with deciding the appropriate course of action.

605.   Peskin, Allan. "Was there a Compromise of 1877?" *Journal of American History* 60 (June 1973): 63-75.   Peskin critically examines C. Vann Woodward's thesis on the election controversy (see # 615). He asserts that the negotiation of a compromise between Republicans and Southern Democrats to end the disputed election between Rutherford B. Hayes and Samuel Tilden was less important than the withdrawal of David Davis from the Electoral Commission. Davis was biased toward Tilden, but his replacement with a Hayes sympathizer led to a Republican victory. The real decision occurred prior to negotiations. Peskin criticizes several parts of the compromise emphasized by Woodward, such as Republican promises of development aid and home rule for the South. The "deal" was not significant because it had no real influence on the election and led to very little results in future decades.   Woodward responded to Peskin in a letter   ("Yes, There Was a Compromise of 1877," *Journal of American History* 60 (June, 1967): 215-223) by first demonstrating that a compromise unfulfilled, such as the Compromise of 1850, does not mean that no compromise existed. The promises made by Hayes illustrate that Southern Democrats struck a great deal for themselves. They achieved home rule, received a Pacific railroad, and won other promises that made a lasting impression on the South.

606.   Polakoff, Keith Ian. *The Politics of Inertia: The Election of 1876 and the End of Reconstruction.*   Baton Rouge: Louisiana State University Press, 1973. 343p. Bibl.   Polakoff is mainly interested in the power structure of political parties as illustrated in the presidential campaign and election of 1876. Political power and influence within the Democratic and Republican parties was so fragmented and dispersed that the resolution of the election dispute could not be centralized. The result was a series of events that probably stripped the election from its rightful winner, Democrat Samuel J. Tilden, and handed it to Rutherford P. Hayes, who made promises to the South that were meaningless except for the recognition of Democratic victories in South Carolina and Louisiana. The resolution of the election was not a reflection of change in American politics but continued fragmentation and decentralization of power in the political system.

607.   Rable, George C. "Southern Interests and the Election of 1876: A Reappraisal." *Civil War History* 26 (December 1980): 347-361.   Rable investigates the election from the perspective of Democrats in South Carolina, Florida, and Louisiana, and Republican supporters of Rutherford B. Hayes who recognized that Reconstruction had failed and needed to be concluded. With Republicans in charge of counting votes in the three states, Southern Democrats knew that they had to compromise to achieve their goal of home rule. They negotiated for home rule and Hayes was ready to accept it.

608.   Severn, Bill. *Samuel J. Tilden and the Stolen Election.* New York: Ives Washington, Inc., 1968. 220p.   In this narrative biography of the New York Democrat who was denied the presidency in the 1876 election, Severn compliments Tilden for his integrity, political savvy, and service to his party and nation. Tilden denied Boss Tweed control of the state Democratic Party during the postwar years and put the country before his own ambition by accepting his defeat in an election that he, and most historians, believed was stolen by the Republicans.

609.   Simpson, Brooks D. "Ulysses S. Grant and the Electoral Crisis of 1876-77." *Hayes Historical Journal* 11 (Winter 1992): 5-22. Ills. Ports.   Simpson explains that Grant's political savvy and maintenance of the *status quo* between November, 1876 and March, 1877 maintained peace and helped preserve the presidency for the Republican Party. In so doing Grant served the nation and his party.

610.   Sternstein, Jerome L. (ed.). "The Sickles Memorandum: Another Look at the Hayes-Tilden Election-Night Conspiracy." *Journal of Southern History* 32 (May 1966): 342-357.   The reprinted memorandum was written by General Daniel E. Sickles, formerly of the Union Army. The memo seems to destroy the long accepted theory that the Republicans concocted a conspiracy to steal the 1876 election away from Democrat Samuel J. Tilden.

611.   Theisen, Lee Scott. "A 'Fair Count' in Florida: General Lew Wallace and the Contested Presidential Election of 1876." *Hayes Historical Journal* 2 (Spring 1978): 20-32. Ill. Port.   Wallace of Indiana participated in the Republican Party's efforts to ensure a fair vote in Florida that would result in a Republican victory in the presidential election. Afterwards he was bitter that his work did not lead to an appointment by President Hayes.

612.   Vazzano, Frank P. "The Louisiana Question Resurrected: The Potter Commission and the Election of 1876." *Louisiana History* 16 (Winter 1975): 39-57. Less than two years after the disputed election of 1876, Congress was embroiled in accusations against the Republican Party for stealing Democratic votes in Louisiana. New York Democrat Clarkson N. Potter sponsored a resolution requesting an investigation into the claims of vote stealing in East Feliciana Parish. The commission's findings reinforced beliefs already held about the election.

613.   Watterson, Henry. "The Hayes-Tilden Contest for the Presidency, Inside History of a Great Crisis." *Century Illustrated Monthly Magazine* 86 (1913): 3-20. Ill. Ports.   Watterson was a Democratic congressman from Kentucky at the time of the election. He was a partisan of Tilden and assisted with both the investigation of election returns in Louisiana and as a referee and agent for South Carolina at the Wormely Conference where, he says, a deal was struck to end military occupation in the South in exchange for Hayes' victory. He provides colorful descriptions of several persons, including both Hayes and Tilden.

614.   Williams, T. Harry (ed.). *Hayes: The Diary of a President 1875-1881. Covering the Disputed Election, the End of Reconstruction, and the Beginning of Civil Service.* New York: David McKay Co., 1964. 329p. Chron.   Hayes' diary chronicles the politics that led to the end of Reconstruction in the South. Also included are letters and comments that reveal Hayes' views on the dramatic events of the time.

615.   Woodward, C. Vann. *Reunion and Reaction: The Compromise of 1877 and the End of Reconstruction.* Boston: Little Brown and Co., 1966. 263p. Note on Sources. (Reprint of original edition, 1951; A revised edition appeared in 1956) Woodward revises the traditional interpretation of the resolution to the national election of 1876. He rejects the theory of a great compromise between Democrat Samuel Tilden and Republican Rutherford Hayes that handed the presidential election to Hayes in return for concessions to the South.   Instead, Woodward emphasizes that Hayes' partiality to the Whig perspective on internal improvements split the Democrats and his sympathy toward white Southerners made it easier for him to cut a deal with Southern Democrats to end Reconstruction where it still existed. Southerners promised to uphold the civil rights of blacks, but Woodward explains that the deal was a betrayal of Radical Republican goals and had a long lasting impact of race relations.

Legal and Constitutional Issues

616.   Amar, Akhil Reed. *The Bill of Rights: Creation and Reconstruction.* New Haven: Yale University Press, 1998. 411p. App.   Amar discusses the meaning of the Bill of Rights, particularly its application to the rights of citizens versus the rights of states. The 14th Amendment fundamentally changed the lexicon and meaning of the Bill of Rights from clauses describing the power structure of the government to a document defining the rights of citizens protected by both the federal and state governments.   Amar agrees that the amendment incorporates the Bill of Rights and defines it as protection for citizens, particularly minorities. He views Reconstruction as a defining period for the constitution, even if the U.S. Supreme Court rejected what Congress intended until the mid-20th century.

617.   Anderson, John Curtis. "The Attitude of the Southern States Toward the Fourteenth Amendment." *Negro History Bulletin* 12 (October 1948): 10-11, 15-18.

Anderson offers a state by state summary illustrating that, among the Southern states, only Tennessee eagerly accepted the 14th Amendment after it was proposed in 1866. All other states (Virginia was not discussed) rejected the amendment until new governments were formed as required by the Reconstruction Acts of 1867.

618.   Avins, Alfred.   "Anti-Miscegenation Laws and the Fourteenth Amendment: The Original Intent." *Virginia Law Review* 52 (October 1966): 1224-1255.   Avins argues that the 14th Amendment did not give the federal judiciary the power to strike down laws against miscegenation. After examining the origin of the amendment and other Reconstruction legislation, he concludes that Republicans did not consider miscegenation to be an issue. They did not believe in race mixing and never intended to eliminate state laws prohibiting it.

619.   Avins, Alfred. "The Civil Rights Act of 1866, the Civil Rights Bill of 1966, and the Right to Buy Property." *Southern California Law Review* 40 (1967): 274-306.   Avins explores the legal basis for the Civil Rights Act of 1866 and concludes that the framers intended to ensure freedmen the right to own property, but they did not intend for the law to require the seller to sell his property to anyone. Avins believes that those who base the housing law in the 1966 Civil Rights Bill on the 1866 act are making a fallacious argument.

620.   Avins, Alfred. "The Civil Rights Act of 1875: Some Reflected Light on the Fourteenth Amendment and Public Accommodation." *Columbia Law Review* 66 (May 1966): 873-915.   Avins criticizes broad interpretations of the 14th Amendment that include to protecting citizens against any form of discrimination, even forms not specifically stated in the Civil Rights Act of 1875. He examines congressional debates leading to the passage of the bill to show that a narrow interpretation was the intent of the framers of the 14th Amendment. Discrimination in private business was not banned in either the amendment or the act.

621.   Avins, Alfred. "*De Facto* and *De Jure* School Segregation: Some Reflected Light on the Fourteenth Amendment From the Civil Rights Act of 1875." *Mississippi Law Journal* 38 (March 1967): 179-247.   Avins believes that congressional debates schools from 1866 to the Civil Rights Act of 1875 reveal that the overwhelming majority of Republicans did not support the idea of integrated schools. Clearly any reliance on the 14th Amendment in Brown v. Board of Education (1954) is illegitimate because the amendment was never intended to force a person to go to school with another person if it is not their choice.

622.   Avins, Alfred. "The Fifteenth Amendment and Literacy Tests: the Original Intent." *Stanford Law Review* 18 (April 1966): 808-822.   Avins uses congressional debates as his main source to conclude that the framers of the amendment clearly supported the use of literacy tests as long as they are not administered in a discriminatory manner. There is no legal basis in the original intent of the law for Congress to consider elimiminating literacy tests in the 1965 Voting Rights Act based on the 15th Amendment.

623.   Avins, Alfred. "The Fourteenth Amendment and Jury Discrimination: The Original Understanding." *Federal Bar Journal* 27 (Summer 1967): 257-290. Jury selection is under state jurisdiction and is not protected as a civil right under the 14th Amendment. Radical Republican attempts during Reconstruction to base nondiscrimination in jury selection on the Civil Rights Act of 1866 and the 14th Amendment were unsuccessful and the framer of both laws never intended it to be so. In 1879 U.S. Supreme Court Justice Stephen J. Field explained that jury participation is a political right, not a civil right.

624.   Avins, Alfred. "Fourteenth Amendment Limitations on Banning Racial Discrimination: The Original Understanding." *Arizona Law Review* 8 (Spring 1967): 236-259.   Avins questions whether the clauses relating to the equal protection and the rights of citizenship in the 14th Amendment relate only to racial discrimination. In his examination of congressional documents and debates from war and postwar years, he suggests that there is no justification for focusing the law against racial discrimination when it ought to be for the protection of all groups in society. The law does not mention race and the framers did not intend for it to be specified.

625.   Avins, Alfred. "Literacy Tests and the Fourteenth Amendment: The Contemporary Understanding." *Albany Law Review* 30 (June 1966): 229-260. Avins argues that Congress did not intend to prohibit literacy tests in the 14th Amendment as a requirement for voting. Section 1 does not address the issue of voting because such rights reside with the states, and section 2 does not apply because the tests do not automatically deny anyone the vote. Modern efforts to eliminate literacy tests (Voting Rights Act of 1965) based on the 14th Amendment are therefore misguided. (See also the same argument in Avins' "Literacy Test, The Fourteenth Amendment, and the District of Columbia Voting: The Original Intent," *Washington University Law Quarterly* (1965): 429-462; and a similar argument in Avins' "Literacy Tests and the Fifteenth Amendment: The Original Understanding," *South Texas Law Journal* 12 (1970): 24-71 which indicates that literacy tests were debated and intentionally excluded from the 15th Amendment as an imposition on the states as long as the tests were applied equally among all potential voters.)

626.   Avins, Alfred. "Racial Segregation in Public Accommodations: Some Reflected Light on the Fourteenth Amendment From the Civil Rights Act of 1875." *Western Reserve Law Review* 18 (1967): 1251-1283.   Avins reviews the legislative history of the Civil Rights Act of 1875 to determine whether Congress intended to eliminate racial segregation based on the 14th Amendment or to ensure equal treatment. He excludes consideration of Democrats due to their strong biases. Avins focuses instead on moderate Republicans who almost unanimously opposed a legal requirement of racial integration and were mainly concerned with either the exclusion of or unequal segregation of blacks. Avins believes that the 14th Amendment does not prohibit segregation and that the majority opinion in Plessy v. Ferguson correctly interpreted the spirit of the law.

627.   Avins, Alfred.   "The Right to Bring Suit Under the Fourteenth Amendment: The Original Intent." *Oklahoma Law Review* 20 (August 1967): 284-300.   Avins does not believe that the equal protection clause of in the 14th Amendment applies to all rights of citizens.   Congress interpreted the right to sue as part of the rights of citizenship and not part of the equal protection clause.   (Avins' concern about inflated interpretations of the equal protection clause are also expressed in "The Right to Be a Witness and the Fourteenth Amendment," *Missouri Law Review* 31 (1966): 471-504.)

628.   Avins, Alfred.   "The Right to Hold Public Office and the Fourteenth and Fifteenth Amendments: The Original Understanding." *Kansas Law Review* 15 (1966-1967): 287-306.   With the *Congressional Globe* as the main source of evidence, Avins argues that Congress intentionally excluded from the amendments any federal protection over the right of an individual to be admitted to public office. Courts and other interpreters of the constitution should recognize Congressional intent as the fundamental basis for applying constitutional provisions to contemporary legal cases.   (Avins makes the same argument in "The Right to Hold Public Office and the Fourteenth and Fifteenth Amendments: The Original Intent," *Mercer Law Review* 18 (1966-1967): 367-397.)

629.   Avins, Alfred.   "School Segregation and History Revisited." *Catholic Lawyer* 15 (Autumn 1969): 308-355.   Avins believes that recent attempt to base school desegregation on the 14th Amendment (e.g. Brown v. Board of Education) is misguided based on the opinions of Reconstruction senators and congressmen on the issue.   He concludes that a majority in Congress opposed school integration and refused to include it in legislation and amendments.   (For a similar approach see Avins' "Federal Aid to Education Policies, 1865-1888:   Some Reflected Light on School Segregation and the Fourteenth Amendment," *Alabama Law Review* 21 (Fall 1968): 61-118.)

630.   Avins, Alfred.   "'State Action' and the Fourteenth Amendment." *Mercer Law Review* 17 (1965-1966): 352-265.   Avins argues that Congress intended for clauses in Section 1 of the 14th Amendment related to privileges and immunities, due process, and equal protection to be directed toward state actions, not private actions, that violate the civil rights of citizens.   Federal jurisdiction applies only when states do not or cannot uphold the law, and any attempt to expand federal authority over private actions is unconstitutional.   Courts maintained this interpretation until the 1940s when more expansive interpretations commenced. (Avis also argues the same point in "Federal Power to Punish Individual Crimes Under the Fourteenth Amendment: The Original Intent," *Notre Dame Lawyer* 43 (February 1968): 317-343.)

631.   Aynes, Richard L.   "Constricting the Law of Freedom: Justice Miller, the Fourteenth Amendment, and the Slaughter-House Cases." *Chicago-Kent Law Review* 70,2 (1994): 627-688.   Aynes criticizes Justice Miller's opinion for the majority in the Slaughter-House Cases in 1873. Apparently Miller followed his conservative bias against the amendment by deliberately ruling as he did.   The other

Justices with the majority also voted in accordance with their biases. The ruling weakened the privileges and immunities clause of the 14th Amendment and thereby weakened the intent of Congress to protect the rights of black citizens by applying the Bill of Rights to the states.

632.   Aynes, Richard L. "On Misreading John Bingham and the Fourteenth Amendment." *Yale Law Review* 103 (March 1993): 57-104.   Aynes argues that Sen. Bingham, the main author of Section 1 of the 14th Amendment, was not alone in his interpretation that the privileges and immunities clause extends the authority of the Bill of Rights to the states. He reviews the historical basis for incorporation and cites reactions from Bingham's contemporaries and newspapers to show that Bingham's approach was valid and that historian Charles Fairman's critique of incorporation is incorrect (see # 632).

633.   Beauregard, Erving E.   "John A. Bingham and the Fourteenth Amendment." *Historian* 50 (November 1987): 67-76.   Bingham, principal author of the 14th Amendment, did not intend for the law to protect the rights and property of corporations as suggested by economic historians Charles and Mary Beard in *Rise of American Civilization* (1927).   Bingham's Calvinist religious background, his education, and his conviction in the principles of equality and inalienable rights mentioned in the Declaration of Independence served as the foundation for his sincere proposal to protect and preserve equal rights for the freedmen and all other citizens.

634.   Belz, Herman. "The Constitution and Reconstruction." In *The Facts of Reconstruction: Essays in Honor of John Hope Franklin.* Baton Rouge: Louisiana State University Press, 1991. Pp. 189-217.   Belz compares three approaches to the relationship between the constitution and the Reconstruction amendments: the Dunning-Burgess interpretation emphasizing revolutionary constitutional change; the Revisionist interpretation that views the changes as completing the original constitutional principles of liberty and freedom; and the neoabolitionist view that change was revolutionary in favor of racial equality. Belz favors the approach of the Revisionists.   The framers of the amendments did not seek to overhaul the constitution, but to protect the rights of all citizens, including freedmen.

635.   Belz, Herman.   *Emancipation and Equal Rights: Politics and Constitutionalism in the Civil War Era.* New York: W. W. Norton, 1978. 171p. Bibl.   Belz examines the interplay of federalism, Republican government, and the definition of equal civil rights for all Americans. Most Northern Republicans sought to preserve a federal system that emphasized strong local powers, but unlike their political opponents, they interpreted Republicanism to include federal responsibility to ensure individual liberty. Historians who interpret the results of Reconstruction in terms of its failure to change racial attitudes or ensure equality are not recognizing the important advancement of black freedoms during and after Reconstruction. Belz makes a similar argument in *A New Birth of Freedom: The Republican Party and Freedmen's Rights, 1861-1866* (Westport: Greenwood Press, 1976) in which he emphasizes the legislative successes of the Republican Party that laid the legal

precedent for both black equality and civil rights for all Americans without betraying constitutional guarantees of state power.

636.   Belz, Herman. "Equality and the Fourteenth Amendment: The Original Understanding." In *Abraham Lincoln, Constitutionalism, and Equal Rights in the Civil War Era.* New York: Fordham University Press, 1998. Pp. 170-186. (Revised from *Benchmark* 4 (1990): 329-346.)   Belz discusses the meaning of equality as it originally applied to the 13th Amendment, the Civil Rights Act of 1866, and the 14th Amendment. He contrasts the narrow intent of the framers with the much more expansive interpretations of these acts at the end of the 20th century. Belz believes that the concept of equality in the Reconstruction amendments did not apply to racial discrimination and was consistent with the intent of the framers of the constitution. A social and political revolution was not intended.

637.   Benedict, Michael Les. "Preserving Federalism: Reconstruction and the Waite Court." *Supreme Court Review* (1978): 39-80.   Chief Justice Morrison R. Waite (1874-1888) had a reputation for tearing down the constitutional authority of the federal government that was constructed by Republicans in Reconstruction. Benedict examines the American tradition of federal-state powers before the Civil War and court actions afterwards. He concludes that the Waite court actually confirmed the ideology advanced in Reconstruction legislation and constitutional amendments that sought to increase federal power to protect the rights of citizens, but only within the context of dual federalism, a concept that recognized the continued power of the states.

638.   Benedict, Michael Les. "Preserving the Constitution: The Conservative Basis of Radical Reconstruction." *Journal of American History* 61 (June 1974): 65-90.   Benedict reviews the writings of revisionist historians (e.g. Eric McKitrick, Alfred H. Kelley, and William Brock) who emphasize the Republican Party's fundamental conservatism in Reconstruction, and he provides the theoretical framework to support the revisionist approach. The Republicans, including the Radical core, maintained a strong sense of "state-centeredness" (p. 89) in Reconstruction reform legislation and the 14th and 15th Amendments. Although the Republicans sought to make changes in the political and social relations in the South and to protect the rights and security of freedmen, they tried to do this within the context of states' rights. Reconstruction failed because Republican conservatism tempered the entire program.

639.   Benedict, Michael Les.   "The Problem of Constitutionalism and Constitutional Liberty in the Reconstruction South." In *An Uncertain Tradition: Constitutionalism and the History of the South.* Edited by Kermit L. Hall and James W. Ely, Jr. Athens: University of Georgia Press, 1989. Pp. 225-249.   The Reconstruction behavior of the governments in the South illustrates that a constitution does not have much meaning unless a large majority of the population is committed to it. Congressional Republicans and many Southern state Republicans sought to devise state governments to provide civil equality for black citizens, but most white Southerners felt left out of the system, either because they were legally

excluded or because the constitution did not represent their beliefs.   Benedict explains that Republican actions were clearly contradictory from the perspective of a majority of the population in most Southern states who were also struggling for liberty and democracy.   By the middle of the 1870s Southern whites had ideological allies in the North who helped to bring down Republican rule in the South.

640.   Benedict, Michael Les.   "Reconstruction: The Civil War Amendments." In *The Supreme Court and the Civil War*.   Edited by Jennifer Lowe.   Washington: Supreme Court Historical Society, 1996.   Pp. 89-97.   Ills.   The response of the U.S. Supreme Court to cases filed under the Reconstruction amendments was to preserve federalism at the expense of protecting individual civil rights.   This response was consistent with the court's decisions prior to the Civil War.   The court recognized federal power in protecting some basic rights, but it severely weakened federal powers provided by the 14th Amendment.   Although the language of the amendment is unclear, the intent of the Republicans in Congress was disallowed, thus establishing a precedent for future cases until the mid-20th century.

641.   Berger, Raoul.   "Constitutional Interpretation and Activist Fantasies." *Kentucky Law Journal* 82 (1993-94): 1-28.   Berger emphasizes that it is wrong for the Supreme Court to extend constitutional interpretations beyond the intent of the Congress.   In this case he refers to   the 14th Amendment and its use to extend federal powers and the Bill of Rights over the states.   He criticizes recent articles by Erwin Chemerinsky in "The Supreme Court and the Fourteenth Amendment: The Unfullfilled Promise," *Loyola of Los Angeles Law Review* 25 (June 1992): 1143-1157 and David A. J. Richards (see # 770).

642.   Berger, Raoul.   "The Fourteenth Amendment: Light From the Fifteenth." *Northwestern University Law Review* 74 (October 1979): 311-371.   Berger analyses the original intent of the Republican framers of the 14th Amendment.   In particular, he focuses on the issue of suffrage, a right that congressmen in 1869 denied was conferred in the 14th Amendment and was needed in the form of the 15th Amendment. Furthermore, Berger examines the meaning of due process, equal protection, privileges and immunities, and incorporation of the Bill of Rights in his investigation of the amendment.   He notes that modern application of the 14th Amendment has led to judicial reinterpretation without regard to the legislative intent of the framers.

643.   Berger, Raoul.   *Government by Judiciary: The Transformation of the Fourteenth Amendment*.   Cambridge: Harvard University Press, 1977. 483p. App. Bibl. Index of Cases.   An examination of contemporary documents reveals that the framers of the 14th Amendment sought conservative, limited goals and not the expansive interpretations attributed to them by many later commentators and courts of law. He focuses on section 1 to emphasize that Republicans intended to provide equal justice and natural rights to blacks, but they clearly did not intend for the amendment to incorporate the Bill of Rights, which restricts only the federal government and excludes racial integration and black suffrage that were the purview of the states.   Present day courts should recognize original intent, not social bias and

sensibilities. (See also a critical response to Berger's thesis in Michael Kent Curtis, "The Bill of Rights as a Limitation on State Authority: A Reply to Professor Berger," *Wake Forest Law Review* 16 (February 1980): 45-101. Curtis argues that Berger's thesis reflects a faulty reading of history by misinterpreting congressional intent and Republican ideology. Berger responded to Curtis in "Incorporation of the Bill of Rights in the Fourteenth Amendment: A Nine-Lived Cat." *Ohio State Law Journal* 42 (1981): 435-466. He reexamines the ideas of Congressman John Bingham of Ohio to reinforce his thesis and explains that activists, such as Curtis, seek to emphasize the tradition of destroying federalism so that the judiciary will have reasons to apply emotion rather than law to case decisions; also see Aviam Soifer's "Protecting Civil Rights: A Critique of Raoul Berger's History." *New York University Law Review* 54 (June 1979): 651-706.)

644.   Berry, Mary Frances. *Military Necessity and Civil Rights Policy: Black Citizenship and the Constitution, 1861-1868.* Port Washington, NY: Kennikat Press, 1977. 132p. Bibl.   Berry argues that it was military necessity that led the North to use blacks in the Union Army, and it was their vital contributions and participation in the victory over the Confederacy that created the appropriate mind set in Congress leading to the extension of citizenship and civil rights to blacks. Congress acted by passing the Civil Rights Act of 1866, the 14th and 15th Amendments, and the Reconstruction Acts of 1867. Civil rights for blacks became practically nonexistent as traditional prejudices and inadequate protection weakened black freedom.

645.   Beth, Loren P. "The Slaughter-House Cases-Revisited." *Louisiana Law Review* 23 (April 1963): 487-505.   The Slaughter House Cases decided by the Supreme Court in 1873 nullified the privileges and immunities clause of the 14th Amendment and seemed to strip the federal government of the power to protect the civil rights and liberties of American citizens. Political and legal bias contributed to the decision, because the justices were unconcerned with the intent of the framers of the amendment. Beth emphasizes the influence of Justice Samuel F. Miller's interpretation because it had the most impact on the amendment. Even though the decision was legally correct, it was skewed to the purposes of the court majority. Eventually the due process clause was used to bypass the limitations on federal power in civil rights cases established by this case.

646.   Bickel, Alexander M. "The Original Understanding of the Segregation Decision." *Harvard Law Review* 69 (November 19550: 1-65.   Bickel interprets the original understanding of the 14th Amendment in the context of the 1954 decision of the Supreme Court in Brown v. Board of Education. He believes that Congress intended to have an impact on the civil rights of blacks in the short term, but in the long term it wanted to protect the rights of all citizens. Congress did not spell out the full meaning of the law, but intentionally left this to future congressional discretion. The 1954 court could therefore explain its decision in the context of the nation in 1954 rather than 1866.

647.   Binder, Guyora. "The Slavery of Emancipation." *Cardozo Law Review* 17 (May 1996): 2063-2102.   Binder questions the definitions of slavery and freedom. She argues that the 13th Amendment did not truly eliminate slavery as a living institution. While the slave became technically free, postwar American society did not allow them true freedom and, in fact, bound them in slavery based on the "status of race." This reality existed simultaneously with Reconstruction reforms, thus revealing fundamental conflicts in American society. This article is followed by critical comments by Michael Les Benedict (p. 2103-2112) and Eric Foner (p. 2113-2114).

648.   Bishop, Timothy.   "The Privileges and Immunities Clause of the Fourteenth Amendment: The Original Intent." *Northwestern University Law Review* 79 (March 1984): 142-190.   Bishop explores what Congress intended in the 14th Amendment to determine whether the interpretation of the privileges and immunities clause should be revised. He uses legislative history and what Republicans said and wrote as evidence of intent. He highlights the thoughts of Senators John Bingham of Ohio and Jacob Howard of Michigan. Bishop concludes that there is no solid evidence for what the Republican majority intended because they were confused about the meaning of the privileges and immunities clause and they made compromises to pass the amendment through Congress.

649.   Bond, James E.   *No Easy Walk to Freedom: Reconstruction and the Ratification of the Fourteenth Amendment.* Westport: Praeger, 1997. 295p. Bibl. Bond examines the reception of the 14th Amendment in each former Confederate state as revealed in newspapers and secondary sources. The debate on the amendment reveals a common thread throughout the South, that Southerners did not suspect that any part of the amendment incorporated and made the states subject to the Bill of Rights. Even supporters of the amendment assumed that states would still have broad discretion over the definition of citizens' rights. It was generally understood that the proposal provided equal rights for blacks and federal guarantees when states failed to uphold the law. Historical analysis proves that the U.S. Supreme Court has misinterpreted the 14th Amendment from the beginning, particularly the concept of its incorporation of the Bill of Rights.

650.   Bond, James E.   "The Original Understanding of the Fourteenth Amendment in Illinois, Ohio, and Pennsylvania." *Akron Law Review* 18 (Winter 1985): 435-467.   In the state ratification debate, as revealed in newspapers in Illinois, Ohio, and Pennsylvania during the fall of 1866, Republicans and Democrats did not argue about the application of the proposed 14th Amendment to the Bill of Rights. Critics focused their objections to the grant of rights to blacks. But Congress intended to protect the rights of all citizens, and for many years the U.S. Supreme Court ruled in error by upholding the jurisdiction of the states over citizens' rights. Bond doubts whether the constitutional controversies over the amendment have been settled.

651.   Boudin, Louis B. "Truth and Fiction About the Fourteenth Amendment." *New York University Law Review* 16 (November 1938): 19-82.   Boudin examines

the idea that there was a congressional cabal promoting the 14th Amendment to protect corporate rights.

652.   Bradford, M. E. "'Changed Only a Little': The Reconstruction Amendments and the Nomocratic Constitution of 1787." *Wake Forest Law Review* 24 (1989): 573-598.   Constitutional change ought to be based on the political philosophy of the Constitution of 1787. The response of the courts and the public after 1875 to the Reconstruction amendments veered away from constitutional roots that Bradford refers to as nomocratic government based on a "mode of operation and devotion to a body of laws which codified that mode" (p. 573).

653.   Brandwein, Pamela Teal. *Reconstructing Reconstruction: The Supreme Court and the Production of Historical Knowledge.* Ph.D. Northwestern University, 1994. 336p.

654.   Braxton, A. Caperton. *The Fifteenth Amendment: An Account of the Enactment.* Address Delivered Before Virginia State Bar Association For the Year 1903. Lynchburg, Va.: J. P. Bell Co., n.d. 78p.   Braxton was born in West Virginia in 1862 but eventually practiced law in Virginia until his death in 1914. In his account of how the 15th Amendment came about, he argues that black suffrage was opposed by nearly all Americans before and after the Civil War and that the only reason it became part of the constitution was because it was forced on the American people. The Radical Republicans who sought the passage of the amendment wanted only to enhance the power of the party.

655.   Breslin, Timothy Michael. *The Civil Rights Act of 1871: The Judicial Determination of the Import of Section 1983 For Civil Rights in Public Education.* Ph.D. Duke Univesity, 1977. 297p.

656.   Buchanan, G. Sidney. *The Quest For Freedom: A Legal History of the Thirteenth Amendment.* Houston: *Houston Law Review*, 1976. 209p.   The importance of the 13th Amendment went beyond the freeing of the slaves. It had far ranging implications regarding federal authority over the states to influence individual rights. Buchanan examines what the authors of the amendment intended and how it was used to define the 14th and 15th Amendments, the Freedmen's Bureau Act of 1866, Civil Rights Acts from 1866 to 1875, and relevant legal cases. Many legislators and jurists of Reconstruction understood that the 13th Amendment ensured equality before the law and guaranteed that the "badges of slavery," such as denying suffrage, would be prohibited. This interpretation was not widely accepted during Reconstruction.

657.   Burton, Harold H. "Two Significant Decisions: *Ex Parte* Milligan and *Ex Parte* McCardle." *American Bar Association Journal* 41 (February 1955): 121-124, 176-177.   Burton, an associate justice of the U.S. Supreme Court, provides a narrative on the issue of military court jurisdiction in civil cases. Both cases were won by the defendants, and in the case of McCardle, which originated in Mississippi, the 1867 *Habeas Corpus* Act was amended by Congress to repeal the

Supreme Court's jurisdiction in such cases. The Radicals only sought to avoid a negative decision that would effect their entire Reconstruction program. The result of the McCardle case illustrated judicial weakness in relation to Congress.

658. Colbert, Douglas L. "Affirming the Thirteenth Amendment." *Annual Survey of American Law*, Book 2 (1995): 403-414. Colbert calls for a broad interpretation of the 13th Amendment that applied during Reconstruction and could apply today to remedy discrimination. Discrimination is equated with the "badges and incidents of slavery" that was recognized by the Supreme Court as being part of the 13th Amendment when it ruled in the Civil Rights Cases in 1883.

659. Collins, Charles Wallace, Jr. "The Failure of the Fourteenth Amendment as a Constitutional Ideal." *South Atlantic Quarterly* 11 (April 1912): 101-115. Collins explains that the 14th Amendment has failed in its objective to ensure equal treatment and equal rights for all races. The courts weakened the law by upholding the right of states to regulate individual rights, and Southern whites have simply ignored the law because they originally objected to it and were not allowed to vote on it due to widespread disenfranchisement. The amendment was forced on the nation by a Republican Party seeking to enhance its national power. Collins is highly critical of the law because it does not enhance democracy but diminishes state power and encourages litigation, particularly by corporations seeking to use the law to their advantage.

660. Collins, Charles Wallace, Jr. *The Fourteenth Amendment and the States*. Boston: Little, Brown, and Co., 1912. 220p. App. Collins reviews the intentions of the Republican Congress and the history of U.S. Supreme Court rulings related to the amendment. Court rulings have mainly reversed the intended effect of the law on federal power to protect the civil rights of blacks. Collins criticizes the amendment because it is unenforceable, unnecessary, and it attempted to take lawful power away from the states. The appendixes include a statistical summary of Supreme Court decisions from 1868 to 1910 and a chronological table of relevant cases.

661. Cottrol, Robert J. "The Thirteenth Amendment and the North's Overlooked Egalitarian Heritage." *National Black Law Journal* 11 (Summer 1989: 198-211. Cottrol criticizes the long held view that the Reconstruction reforms were never intended to revolutionize racial equality because nearly all of the framers and the Northern population were thoroughly racist. He argues that the egalitarian tradition in the North was applied to black citizens and that the enforcement clause of the 13th Amendment illustrated the sincerity of North to ensure freedom and equal civil rights for blacks.

662. Cresswell, Stephen E. "Resistance and Enforcement: The U.S. Department of Justice, 1870-1893." Ph.D. University of Viginia, 1986. 229p.

663. Currie, David P. "The Constitution in the Supreme Court: Civil War and Reconstruction, 1865-1873." *University of Chicago Law Review* 51 (Winter 1984):

131-186.   Currie offers a critical examination of landmark opinions made by the U.S. Supreme Court led by Chief Justice Salmon P. Chase. He discusses *Ex parte* Milligan that invalidated military trials of civilians; Cummings v. Missouri and *Ex parte* Garland that struck down state and federal test oaths; Mississippi v. Johnson, Georgia v. Stanton, *Ex parte* Milligan, and U.S. v. Klein on federal jurisdiction emanating from Reconstruction legislation; Texas v. White on the illegality of secession and validity of Reconstruction; and Hepburn v. Griswold on wartime financial measures. (See also Currie's "The Constitution in the Supreme Court: Limitation or State Power, 1865-1873," *University of Chicago Law Review* 51 (Spring 1984): 329-365 in which he focuses mainly on the Slaughter House Case and issues unrelated to Reconstruction. Currie discusses the influence of several Supreme Court justices, particularly Salmon P. Chase, Samuel F. Miller and Stephen J. Field.)

664.   Curtis, Michael Kent.   *No State Shall Abridge: The Fourteenth Amendment and the Bill of Rights.* Durham: Duke University Press, 1986. 279p. Curtis explores the debate about the applicability of the Bill of Rights to the states based on interpretations of the abridgment clause of the 14th Amendment. He provides an historical analysis of the origins of the amendment, the intentions of the Republicans in Congress who wrote it, and how interpretations have been applied in court. Curtis believes that the amendment extends the authority of the Bill of Rights to the states, but judges have made interpretations based on personal political ideology.

665.   Daniels, Winthrop M.   "Constitutional Growth Under the Fourteenth Amendment." *South Atlantic Quarterly* 29 (January 1930): 16-34.   Daniels reviews the historical events leading up to the passage of the 14th Amendment and suggests that it has had lasting impact on the civil rights of blacks.

666.   Davis, William Watson.   "The Federal Enforcement Acts." In *Studies in Southern History and Politics.* New York; Columbia University Press, 1914. Pp. 203-228.   Republicans intended to enforce the 14th and 15th Amendments by suppressing the Ku Klux Klan and extending Republican rule for a few more years, but they failed because many conservative whites simply ignored them or avoided prosecution and federal courts and agents were unable to carry out the law due to lack of resources. Davis believes that the acts were arbitrary and out of touch with public opinion in the North and the South.

667.   Dew, Lee A.   "The Racial Ideas of the Authors of the Fourteenth Amendment." Ph.D. Louisiana State University, 1960. 379p.

668.   Dew, Lee A.   "The Reluctant Radicals of 1866." *Midwest Quarterly* 8 (April 1967): 261-276.   The views of several radical and moderate Republicans are examined to determine their motives for supporting the 14th Amendment. Dew concludes that the Radicals certainly had a mission to help the black Americans by enacting reforms, but the Amendment was basically a conservative document that

maintained the balance of federal and state powers. The Radicals led a conservative revolution that led to disappointing results for black citizens.

669.   DuBois, Ellen Carol. "Outgrowing the Compact of the Fathers: Equal Rights, Woman Suffrage, and the United States Constitution, 1820-1878. *Journal of American History* 74 (December 1987): 836-862.   DuBois shows how women who led the movement for women's rights, including Susan B. Anthony and Elizabeth Cady Stanton, tried to use the 14th and 15th Amendments as a springboard to victory for equality of the sexes. Originally they supported equality for women and blacks, but they eventually focused only on women. The weakening of the amendments by the U.S. Supreme Court proved that women would need their own amendment to achieve success.

670.   Dunne, Gerald T. "The Reconstruction Amendments: A Bicentennial Remembrance." In *Our Peculiar Security: The Written Constitution and Limited Government*. Edited by Eugene W. Hickok, Jr. et. al. Lanham: Rowman and Littlefield Publishers, 1993. Pp. 179-186.   Dunne's examination of the Reconstruction amendments concentrates on the 14th Amendment. This amendment is depicted as a mysterious piece of metaphysical writing that even the brightest of Supreme Court Justices and clerks have yet to really understand. The lack of understanding extends to the intent of the Congress that approved it.

671.   Dunning, William A. "The Constitution of the United States in Civil War and Reconstruction, 1860-1867." Ph.D. Columbia, University, 1885.

672.   Dunning, William A.   "The Constitution of the United States in Reconstruction."   *Political Science Quarterly* 2 (December 1887): 558-602. Dunning examines the constitutional ramifications of the Reconstruction legislation with particular emphasis on states' rights versus federal power, granting and enforcement of civil rights, military rule, the Freedmen's Bureau, and the status of the states in secession and reunion. In this context Dunning surveys the major Reconstruction legislation and constitutional amendments. He believes that the constitution was stretched and twisted into a revolutionary form in order to strengthen the federal government in favor of Radical policies in the South.

673.   Edgington, T. B. "The Repeal of the Fifteenth Amendment." *North American Review* 188 (July 1908): 92-100.   Edgington proposes the repeal of the amendment because the framers did not foresee how it would promote race conflict and prejudice, lead to the destruction of local government, and fail to guarantee suffrage for blacks.

674.   "The End of the Civil Rights Bill." *The Nation* 37 (October 18,1883): 326. The editor of *The Nation* reports on the U.S. Supreme Court's ruling in the Civil Rights Cases (1883) that the Civil Rights Act of 1875 is largely unconstitutional. The ruling shows that the 14th Amendment did not restructure powers between the federal and state governments as defined in the original constitution.

675.   Eubank, Sever L.   "The McCardle Case: A Challenge to Radical
Reconstruction." Ph.D. Peabody College For Teachers of Vanderbilt University,
1954.

676.   Eubank, Sever L.   "The McCardle Case: A Challenge to Radical
Reconstruction." *Journal of Mississippi History* 18 (April 1956): 111-127.
Eubank examines the legal arguments in the U.S. government's prosecution of
Vicksburg *Times* editor William H. McCardle for libel and other crimes, and he
criticizes Republican tactics. The case involved the constitutionality of denying
McCardle a trial by jury in a military court. The case called into question the
constitutionality of congressional Reconstruction, because Republicans operated on
the premise that the former Confederate states were zones of occupation not legally
part of the Union. The case prompted Congress to amend the Judiciary Act of 1868
to deny *habeas corpus* appeals to the U.S. Supreme Court. Eubank criticizes
Republican tactics.

677.   Faber, Daniel A. and John E. Muench. "The Ideological Origins of the
Fourteenth Amendment." *Constitutional Commentary* 1 (Winter 1984): 235-279.
Bibl.   When the Republicans passed the 14th Amendment legislation it represented
their attempt to codify what they already agreed was part of the natural law of
human rights handed down from the 18th century Enlightenment. Even though
Congress did not clearly specify the full meaning of the rights guaranteed by the
amendment, they intended the law to serve as a positive act of confirmation of the
natural laws of men and the authority of the federal government to guarantee those
rights.

678.   Fairman, Charles. "Does the Fourteenth Amendment Incorporate the Bill
of Rights? The Original Understanding." *Stanford Law Review* 2 (December 1949):
5-139.   (Rpt. in *The Fourteenth Amendment and the Bill of Rights: The
Incorporation Theory.*   New York: DeCapo, 1970)   Fairman studies the
discussions in Congress and state legislatures on the proposed 14th Amendment. He
concludes that courts have interpreted the privileges and immunities clause and the
due process clause in different ways with regard to federal jurisdiction over state and
local laws, but there is no documentation illustrating congressional intent to change
the constitutional structure of power. Congress wanted to insure that blacks enjoyed
the same civil rights as whites, protection of rights inherent in U.S. citizenship, and
federal standards for state enforcement, but even this authority cannot be clearly
defined. There is no evidence to support the application of the 14th Amendment
generally to federal protection of rights in amendments I-VIII of the constitution.
(For a response to Fairman see William W. Crosskey, "Charles Fairman,
'Legislative history,' and the Constitutional Limitations on State Authority,"
University of Chicago Law Review 22 (Autumn 1954): 1-143 which argues that
legal history back to 1789 contradicts Fairman's thesis. For a related article on
judicial interpretations during the 19th and 20th centuries see Stanley Morrison,
"Does the Fourteenth Amendment Incorporate the Bill of Rights: The Judicial
Interpretation," *Stanford Law Review* 2 (December 1949): 140-173.)

679.   Fairman, Charles. *History of the Supreme Court of the Unite States. (Vol. VI, VII) Reconstruction and Reunion 1864-1888.* New York: Macmillan, 1971, 1984. 1540p. 836p. Case Index. Ports. Tbls.   Fairman demonstrates how deeply involved the Supreme Court was in the legislative and constitutional issues of Reconstruction.   In these two volumes he systematically reviews the court's response to cases involving federal-state relations, the test oath, Reconstruction Acts of 1867, federal court jurisdiction, the indestructibility of states, constitutional amendments, citizenship, the Civil Rights Acts (1866, 1875), Enforcement Acts, railroads, and bonds.   In so doing, the history of the members of the court is revealed, particularly the leadership of Chief Justice Salmon P. Chase (1864-1873) and Morrison R. Waite (1874-1888). The Reconstruction cases cited include *Ex parte* Milligan, *Ex parte* McCardle, Georgia v Grant, *Ex parte* Yerger, Texas v White, Slaughter-House Cases, Civil Rights Cases.

680.   Fernandez, Ferdinand F.   "The Constitutionality of the Fourteenth Amendment." *Southern California Law Review* 29 (1966): 378-407.   The arguments for and against the constitutionality of the 14th Amendment are discussed without regard to the content of the amendments.   Fernandez believes that constitutional procedures were followed and that events of the Civil War created a unique situation that allowed Congress to interpret their powers broadly.

681.   Finkelman, Paul. Rehearsal for Reconstruction: Antebellum Origins of the Fourteenth Amendment." In *The Facts of Reconstruction: Essays in Honor of John Hope Franklin.* Baton Rouge: Louisiana State University Press, 1991. Pp. 1-27.   Finkelman criticizes historians who emphasize how the rights of Northern blacks deteriorated during the antebellum period. He believes that for at least three decades prior to the Civil War the Northern states generally improved the lives of blacks at least from standpoint of opportunities for education and civil rights. The core of the Republican party was united in support of improving the legal status of blacks. Their work for the 14th Amendment was the culmination of prewar legal activities to free slaves and provide them with most of the rights and privileges of other citizens.

682.   Flack, Horace Edgar. *The Adoption of the Fourteenth Amendment.* Ph.D. Johns Hopkins University, 1906. (Published by Johns Hopkins Press in 1908)

683.   Flanigan, Daniel. "The Criminal Law of Slavery and Freedom, 1800-1868." Ph.D. Rice University, 1973. 518p.

684.   Foner, Eric. "Rights and the Constitution in Black Life During the Civil War and Reconstruction." *Journal of American History* 74 (December 1987): 863-883.   Foner discusses how emancipation transformed the slaves into a group that would insist on the rights due free men in America. Whether through military service, personal and economic independence, or political rights, the freedmen actively sought full rights and privileges as spelled out in the 13th, 14th, and 15th Amendments. Radical Reconstruction seemed to deliver much of what the freedmen sought, but they quickly learned that the promises could not be fulfilled, and that

even their own personal and economic security could not be guaranteed by the only power that they trusted, the federal government. Reliance on federal power conflicted with 19th century ideology favoring states rights in local affairs. The failure of Reconstruction led to the deepening and spreading of racism as an American institution.

685.   Frank, John P. and Robert F. Munro. "The Original Understanding of 'Equal Protection of the Laws'." *Columbia Law Review* 50 (February 1950): 131-160. The authors review the debates prior to the passage of the 14th Amendment in their investigation of the original understanding of Section 1. Even though interpretations may have changed during and after Reconstruction, at the time of passage the congressional supporters of the amendment intended to establish the legal basis for the elimination of racial discrimination and segregation in public life. Congress did not intend to grant suffrage or protect against discrimination in private situations. They sought to create free men of the ex-slaves, not a special class of freedmen.

686.   Franklin, John Hope. "Enforcement of the Civil Rights Act of 1875." *Prologue* 6 (Winter 1974): 225-235. Ills. The Civil Rights Act of 1875 sought to make unlawful the denial of equal and full access for all Americans to public accommodations and to service on grand or petit juries of all federal and state courts. The law stipulated specific punishment in the case of convictions or failure to enforce the law. Before the law was found unconstitutional in 1883, it was met by a barrage of criticism from white supremacists and those who believed it to be unenforceable or unconstitutional. Even backers of the law did not offer enthusiastic support. The law was tested on many occasions, but enforcement was usually lax or nonexistent in both the North and the South. White supremacy overruled equal rights.

687.   Frantz, Laurent B. "Congressional Power to Enforce the Fourteenth Amendment Against Private Acts." *Yale Law Journal* 73 (July 1964): 1354-1384. Frantz discusses the U.S. Supreme Court cases that weakened federal authority to enforce the 14th Amendment against private offenses. The main cases were U.S. v. Cruikshank, U.S. v. Harris, and the Civil Rights Cases. These court decisions and the intent of the framers of the amendment clearly conflict. Their application in recent times favor federal power over civil rights, but there continue to be disagreements.

688.   Frasure, Carl M. "Charles Sumner and the Rights of the Negro." *Journal of Negro History* 13 (April 1928): 126-149. Frasure surveys Sen. Sumner's contributions to the struggle to abolish slavery and to ensure the right of freedmen to equality in American society. Sumner was a major force behind congressional Reconstruction, particularly the 15th Amendment and the Civil Rights Act of 1875, although the final civil rights bill was a weakened version of the original proposal, and it passed the Senate after his death. He was a sincere champion of equal rights for all Americans.

689.   Fridlington, Robert. *The Reconstruction Court 1864-1888.* Millwood, NY: Associated Faculty Press, 1987. 244p. Bibl. Chron. Ports.   This book serves as a reference guide to the key events and decisions of the Supreme Court of Chief Justices Salmon P. Chase (1864-1873) and Morrison R. Waite (1873-1888). Part one is a detailed chronology of political and legal events; part two provides summaries and selected texts from key court decisions; and part three includes brief biographies of all justices who served during the period. Also, Fridlington provides summary information in a list of all justices who served on the court from 1789 to 1986.

690.   Gambone, Joseph G. "*Ex Parte* Milligan: The Restoration of Judicial Prestige." *Civil War History* 16 (September 1970): 246-259.   The Milligan decision in 1866 by the U.S. Supreme Court had a direct impact on the Republican plan for Reconstruction and resurrected the court from the depths it had fallen in its power relationship with Congress and the president. The court decided that military commissions could not serve as courts when local civil courts were functioning, at least when an emergency or war did not exist. Its action to uphold the civil liberties of individuals indicated that the court's prestige was on the rebound during Reconstruction.

691.   Garner, James Wilford.   "The Fourteenth Amendment and Southern Representation." *South Atlantic Quarterly* 4 (July 1985): 209-216. Tbl.   Garner discusses whether the 15th Amendment perfected and supplemented section 2 (abrogating the "three-fifths" clause for counting slaves to determine congressional representatives) of the 14th Amendment or completely invalidated it by introducing a new law to take its place. This debate about the intent of Congress refers to voting laws adapted by the Southern states in recent years (i.e. late nineteenth century to early twentieth century).

692.   Gerber, Richard Allan. "Civil Rights for Freed People: The Issue of Private Discrimination Revisited." *Connecticut Review* 15, 2 (1993): 25-33. Republican leaders in Congress intended for the Reconstruction constitutional amendments and civil rights legislation to secure equal civil rights and protections for black Americans and to protect them from both governmental and private acts of discrimination.   The legal basis for this interpretation begins with the 13th Amendment that not only eliminated slavery but the "badges of slavery" represented by private discrimination based on race. Congress enacted the Civil Rights Acts of 1866 and 1875, the 14th and 15th Amendments, and the Enforcement Acts of 1870-1871 to further clarify this protection.   The U.S. Supreme Court weakened protection against private discrimination in U.S. v. Cruikshank and the Civil Rights Cases.

693.   Gillette, William. *The Right to Vote: Politics and the Passage of the Fifteenth Amendment.* Baltimore: Johns Hopkins Press, 1969 (c1966). 206p. Bibl. The 15th Amendment was a moderate document written by moderate Republicans who intended to provide blacks with an equal opportunity to vote and, perhaps more importantly, to enfranchise blacks who lived in the North. Southern blacks would

definitely support the Republican Party, but it was in the North that their support was considered crucial. Gillette reviews congressional debates after the amendment was proposed in 1869 and its reception in each region of the country. He also discusses various perspectives of historians. (See also Gillette's "The Power of the Ballot: The Politics of Passage and Ratification of the Fifteenth Amendment." Ph.D. Princeton University, 1963. 283p.)

694.   Graham, Howard Jay. "The 'Conspiracy Theory' of the Fourteenth Amendment." *Yale Law Review* 47 (December 1937): 371-403; "The 'Conspiracy Theory' of the Fourteenth Amendment: 2." 48 (December 1938): 171-194. Graham explores whether Congress, particularly Ohio Senator John A. Bingham, intended for the 14th Amendment to protect the rights of corporations as "persons." After an examination of congressional documents and court decisions prior to 1866, he concludes that Congress did not intend to include corporations in its definition of "persons." But Graham also emphasizes that by 1866 there was already a precedent for the treatment of corporations as personal entities, and that the application of the 14th Amendment to the rights of corporations was unavoidable in the post Civil War legal environment.

695.   Graham, Howard Jay. "The Early Antislavery Backgrounds of the Fourteenth Amendment." *Wisconsin Law Review* 3 (May 1950): 479-507; 3 (July 1950): 610-661. (Rpt. in *Emancipation and Reconstruction.* Edited by Paul Finkelman. New York: Garland, 1992)   Graham investigates the influence of popular antislavery literature on the Republican ideology of members of the Joint Committee of Fifteen on Reconstruction that drafted the 14th Amendment in 1866. He hypothesizes that the moral and ethical foundations of antislavery arguments for the freedom and rights of blacks, as well as the equality and protection of American citizens as espoused in the 1830s, had either a direct or indirect influence on the Republicans. Congressmen were influenced by earlier propaganda literature, court decisions, and discussions on the issues. This may explain how the same phraseology used in the 1830s could appear in the amendment of the 1860s. Graham admits that he cannot absolutely prove the connection but suspects that it is there.

696.   Graham, Howard Jay. *Everyman's Constitution: Historical Essays on the Fourteenth Amendment, the 'Conspiracy Theory', and American Constitutionalism.* Madison: State Historical Society of Wisconsin, 1968. 631p. App.   In 14 essays Graham examines the intent of the framers of the 14th Amendment and its interpretation by courts, particularly regarding the antislavery background leading up to the amendment, the history of due process, the language of the amendment, and the extension of "person" to corporations.   All essays are reprints from previously published law review journals.

697.   Gressman, Eugene.   "The Unhappy History of the Civil Rights Legislation."   *Michigan Law Review* 50 (January 1952): 1323-1358. Constitutional amendments and civil rights legislation during Reconstruction established the basis for federal protection of civil rights for American citizens, but

beginning with the Slaughter-House Cases in 1873 the Supreme Court began to weaken federal authority in favor of state power in civil rights protection.

698.   Halbrook, Stephen P. *Freedmen, the Fourteenth Amendment, and the Right to Bear Arms, 1866-1876*. Westport: Praeger, 1998. 230p. Bibl. Tbl. of Cases.   Congressional and state documents and newspapers are the main sources in this examination of the theory of congressional intent to incorporate the Bill of Rights in the 14th Amendment. In his discussion of proceeding, debates, and public reaction to congressional legislation, Halbrook is particularly concerned with whether the 2nd Amendment which guarantees the right to bear arms was part of the congressional program to provide a legal basis for freedom and civil liberties for blacks.   He believes that Congress included the right to bear arms among the liberties protected in the 14th Amendment, but the U.S. Supreme Court did not support such incorporation as revealed in United States v. Cruikshank in 1876 that weakened federal jurisdiction in support of the Enforcement Acts intended to protect the rights of freedmen. Even though incorporation has been accepted by the courts in the 20th century, the issue of the public's right to bear arms remains controversial

699.   Hall, Kermit L. "Political Power and Constitutional Legitimacy: The South Carolina Ku Klux Klan Trials, 1871-1872." *Emory Law Journal* 33 (Fall 1984): 921-951.   (Rpt. in *Emancipation and Reconstruction*. Edited by Paul Finkelman, New York: Garland, 1992).   Hall calls on historians to interpret the trials from the perspective of the 1870s, not their own time.   Instead of whitewashing South Carolina whites as simply racist, historians need to understand the anxieties of the white community regarding the extension of federal authority at the local level, the attempt to prop up the Republican Party in the state, and the ingrained racial prejudice by those who had recently treated blacks as slaves. He questions historians who criticize President Grant for lack of enforcement by pointing out that federal action resulted in the arrest of hundreds of suspects and won several convictions.   The problem with the trials is that the constitutional basis for federal protection of civil rights was not satisfactorily proven.   With regard to constitutional interpretation, the trials were a victory for the white South.

700.   Hall, Kermit L. "The Reconstruction Era As a Crucible for Nationalizing the Lower Federal Courts." *Prologue* 7 (Fall 1975): 177-186.   The Civil War and Reconstruction placed pressure on the federal judiciary that had long sought relief from a backlog of cases.   Conflict arose with attempts to nationalize and expand district federal courts to take pressure off of the circuit duties of the U.S. Supreme Court justices and the tradition of local state court jurisdiction.   In addition to increasing litigation in Northern states, Reconstruction brought on a steady flow of cases from freedmen and Unionists in the South.   Attempts by Republicans to reform the federal judiciary in 1862 and again in 1869 maintained the traditional structure and balance of federal and state courts with only the creation of circuit judges to relieve the burden on Supreme Court justices.   Expanding federal jurisdiction in cases, such as civil rights, were as far as the Republicans could go to nationalize the court system.

701.   Hamilton, Howard Devon. "The Legislative and Judicial History of the Thirteenth Amendment." Ph.D. University of Illinois, 1950. 289p.

702.   Hamilton, J. G. de Roulhac. "The Removal of Legal and Political Disabilities, 1868-1898. *South Atlantic Quarterly* 2 (October 1903): 39-51. Hamilton focuses on the congressional debates about disabilities imposed by the 14th Amendment on Southerners who aided the Confederacy. He provides extensive quotations from journals, newspapers, and various government publications, including congressional proceedings. Most of the article covers the period of Reconstruction, but Congress's refusal to grant universal amnesty was delayed until 1898.

703.   Harris, Robert J. *The Quest For Equality: The Constitution, Congress and the Supreme Court.* Westport: Greenwood Press, 1977. 172p. Index of Cases. (Rpt. of Baton Rouge: Louisiana State University Press, 1960)   Harris is particularly concerned with the development of the 14th Amendment and its treatment by federal courts. The concept of equality as expressed in the 14th Amendment was consistent with American traditions, but extending equality and protection to blacks was the main difficulty. Harris discusses the struggle to pass the amendment in Congress, its application in courts compared with its original intent, and the court's weakening of the original purpose to ensure equal civil rights for blacks.

704.   Harrison, John C. "Reconstructing the Privileges and Immunities Clause." *Yale Law Journal* 101 (May 1992): 1385-1474.   Harrison analyses the meaning of section 1 of the 14th Amendment in a way that departs from the traditional focus on the equal protection clause. The usefulness of section 1 goes beyond equal protection and extends to the privileges and immunities clause that has baffled legislators and jurists since Congress voted on it in 1866. The clause may be defined by its grant of equality of rights or "entitlements" for all citizens. State abridgment of equal rights for specific groups would violate the law. This clause constitutionalized the rights of citizenship described in the Civil Rights Act of 1866. The meaning of the privileges and immunities clause can be found in the context of America in 1866.

705.   Hillard, Richard Leon. "The Origins and Development of Substantive Due Process to 1868." Ph.D. Ohio State University, 1978. 170p.

706.   Hoemann, George Henry. "What God Wrought: The Embodiment of Freedom in the Thirteenth Amendment." Ph.D. Rice University, 1982. 350p. (Rpt. in New York: Garland, 1987)

707.   Hoeveler, J. David, Jr. "Reconstruction and the Federal Courts: The Civil Rights Act of 1875." *Historian* 31 (August 1909): 604-617.   Hoeveler describes the historical background to the Civil Rights Act of 1875. The act extended federal court power beyond the provisions of the Civil Rights Act of 1866 by offering exclusive federal court jurisdiction on all cases arising from the new law. The denial

of civil rights in local courts was not a requirement for federal jurisdiction. The law was reinforced by the Jurisdiction (Judiciary) Act of 1875, but the Supreme Court ruled the Civil Rights Act unconstitutional in 1883.

708.   Holmes, Robert M. "The Fourteenth Amendment and the Bill of Rights - An Historical Interpretation." *South Carolina Law Quarterly* 7 (Summer 1955): 596-619.   Opinions expressed in 44 newspapers suggest that the framers of the 14th Amendment intended it to apply the Bill of Rights to the states. Holmes criticizes Charles Fairman who wrote that the first 8 amendments were not intended to be part of the 14th Amendment (see # 678).

709.   Hyman, Harold M. and William M. Wiecek. *Equal Justice Under Law: Constitutional Development 1835-1875.* New York: Harper and Row, 1982. 571p. Bibl. Ills. Maps. Ports.   The authors provide a survey that discusses the legal and constitutional issues of the Civil War and Reconstruction, particularly the legislation that extended federal authority over the states, and the federal courts that followed conservative public opinion rather than consider creative interpretations of the law. In its interpretations of the 14th Amendment, the Enforcement Acts of 1870-1871, and the Civil Rights Acts of 1865 and 1875, the U.S. Supreme Court of the 1870s and 1880s gave up its responsibility for ensuring equality of citizens before the law and reinforced traditional notions of state power over citizens' rights.

710.   Hyman, Harold M. *A More Perfect Union: The Impact of the Civil War and Reconstruction on the Constitution.* New York: Alfred A. Knopf, 1973. 562p. Bibl.   Hyman emphasizes that the popular belief that the Civil War and Reconstruction resulted in the concentration of power in the federal government at the expense of the states is clearly wrong. Even Radical Republicans were distinctly concerned with avoiding a constitutional revolution. The Reconstruction legislation and constitutional amendments brought changes, at least for a brief period, but they were the result of compromise and moderation that did not upset federal-state power relations in a significant way. In general, among American political leaders, there was the intention to preserve constitutional traditions and the legitimacy of court litigation to define legislative action relevant to the constitution. While this meant only limited real change for freedom and justice for blacks in the nineteenth century, the work of Reconstruction was revived in the mid-twentieth century to create at second more effective attempt to ensure the rights of black Americans within the context of the constitution.

711.   Hyman, Harold M. *The Reconstruction Justice of Salmon P. Chase: In Re Turner and Texas v. White.* Lawrence: University Press of Kansas, 1997. 184p. Bibl.   Hyman explores Chase's vision of social liberalism and conservative politics as illustrated by his decisions on issues of freedom under the 13th Amendment in *In Re Turner* and the legality of the Confederate state prewar bonds in *Texas v. White.* Chase, who was a strong antislavery activist and chief justice of the U.S. Supreme Court from 1864-1873, sought a free society in the postwar period that would preserve traditional federalism without racism.

712.   Jager, Ronald B. "Charles Sumner, the Constitution, and the Civil Rights Act of 1875." *New England Quarterly* 12 (September 1969): 350-372.   Sumner was the force behind the Civil Rights Act.   The idea that it ought to conform with precedence in accordance with Anglo-American law was irrelevant, because the tradition of precedence did not recognize the need for reform and innovation in constitutional interpretation.   When the act was ruled unconstitutional, it was based on a narrow interpretation of the 14th Amendment.   Sumner's pragmatic approach to political reforms reveal his complex personality and his sincere dedication to establishing equal civil rights for all citizens.

713.   James, Joseph B.   *The Framing of the Fourteenth Amendment*.   Urbana: University of Illinois Press, 1956. 220p. App. Bibl.   James examines the phases in the formulation of the amendment up to the congressional election of 1866.   He notes that earlier studies were based mainly on congressional documents and newspapers, and his study uses a broader array of sources.   A core of Radical Republicans, led by Rep. John Bingham of Ohio, Rep. Thaddeus Stevens of Pennsylvania, and Rep. William P. Fessenden of Maine, were forced to compromise on the issues of black suffrage and disenfranchising former rebels in order to reach an agreement.   The Republican Party was greatly concerned with the lack of support for black suffrage in the North.   A compromise bill would ensure a victory in the 1866 election and maintain Republican dominance.   The Radicals supported the amendment as a way to guarantee that the Bill of Rights protected all citizens of the nations, including blacks.   (See also James' Ph.D. dissertation with the same title from University of Illinois, 1939)

714.   James, Joseph B.   "The Immediate Purpose of the Fourteenth Amendment."   *Indiana Magazine of History* 39 (December 1943): 345-361.   Congressional Republicans, including the most radical members, compromised principles in the writing of the 14th Amendment because they did not want to increase the chances of losing in the congressional elections of 1866.   James emphasizes the disappointment of the Radicals with the final version of the amendment, but they acceded to it because they believed its original provisions to be out of line with Northern public opinion (i.e. voters) and certainly beyond any hope of a presidential signature.

715.   James, Joseph B. "Is the Fourteenth Amendment Constitutional?" *Social Science* 50 (Winter 1975): 3-9.   James briefly describes how the 14th Amendment was ratified by the states and adresses questions about whether the methods used in the ratification process were unconstitutional.

716.   James, Joseph B. *The Ratification of the Fourteenth Amendment*.   Macon, Ga.: Mercer University Press, 1984. 331p. Bibl.   James examines the intention of the framers and the response of the nation to the 14th Amendment passed on June 13, 1866.   He offers a state by state account and clarifies the problems that the amendment had in both the North and the South. Without the affirmative votes of Southern states, delivered under duress, the amendment would not have passed because of opposition in the North.   The framers succeeded in molding a

compromise that would give the Republican Party a platform or program for Reconstruction leading into the congressional elections of 1866. The amendment was intended to exact some measure of guarantee from the South about the future of the region, but otherwise there were many different motivating factors in support of the law. James acknowledges the unusual and extralegal nature of the ratification, but the long history of the amendment, since its enactment on July 28, 1868, has solidified it as an integral part of American law.

717.   James, Joseph B. "Southern Reaction to the Proposal of the Fourteenth Amendment." *Journal of Southern History* 22 (November 1956): 477-497. The Southern response to the 14th Amendment prior to the Reconstruction Acts of 1867 was total rejection with the exception of Tennessee. Particularly objectionable to the state legislatures were the provisions defining citizenship, disenfranchisement of classes of former rebels, and the hint of black suffrage. President Johnson encouraged this response by expressing strong objections to the proposal. Also, Southerners believed that the amendment was a Republican ploy to gain advantage prior to the 1866 congressional elections. Republican victories in 1866 and the South's rejection of the amendment gave Congress an excuse to implement a harsh reconstruction plan and to block the South from regaining national power.

718.   Kaczorowski, Robert J. "To Begin the Nation Anew: Congress, Citizenship, and Civil Rights After the Civil War." *American Historical Review* 92 (February 1987): 45-68. The moderate and radical Republicans who crafted and supported the 13th and 14th Amendments intended revolutionary change in the American constitution. They emphasized expanded federal powers to guarantee the civil rights of all citizens. The Civil Rights Act of 1866 and other legislation also supported federal authority. In the 1870s the U.S. Supreme Court decided that revolutionary interpretations of federal power were unconstitutional and that the 13th and 14th Amendments must be understood as supporting states' rights in the preservation of civil rights. The authority for ensuring black civil rights was left to Southern state governments.

719.   Kaczorowski, Robert J. "The Chase Court and Fundamental Rights: A Watershed in American Constitutionalism." *Northern Kentucky Law Review* 21 (1993): 151-191. In this examination of the historical basis for the Supreme Court's decision in the Slaughter-House Cases of 1873, Kaczorowski emphasizes that it represented a key event in bringing down the revolution in constitutional law attempted during Reconstruction. A healthy Chief Justice Chase, who was a dissenter in the case, might have been able to sway enough support to effect the court's decision. (See also responses to Kaczorowski in Harold M. Hyman, "Comment on Robert Kaczorowski's Paper, The Chase Court and Fundamental Rights," *Northern Kentucky Law Review* 21 (1993): 192-202; and Lowell F. Schechter, "A Comment in the Chase Court and Fundamental Rights," *Northern Kentucky Law Review* 21 (1993): 203-214.)

720.   Kaczorowski, Robert J. "Federal Enforcement of Civil Rights During the First Reconstruction." *Fordham Urban Law Journal* 23 (Fall 1995): 155-186.

The author describes how the Grant administration briefly, but successfully, defended the civil rights of blacks in the South and crushed the power of the Ku Klux Klan. Kaczorowski emphasizes that even with the prosecution of the Klansmen, many problems were encountered by the executive and judicial branches with carrying out the enforcement in accordance with the Enforcement Acts of 1870 and 1871. Lack of resources, intimidation of judges, case loads, public distrust and fatigue with Grant's Reconstruction policies were among the issues contributing to the elimination of civil rights enforcement and the end of Reconstruction.

721.   Kaczorowski, Robert J.   "The Nationalization of Civil Rights: Constitutional Theory and Practice in a Racist Society, 1866-1883." Ph.D. University of Minnesota, 1971. 336p. (Rpt. by New York: Garland, 1987)

722.   Kaczorowski, Robert J. *The Politics of Judicial Interpretation: The Federal Courts, Department of Justice and Civil Rights, 1866-1876.* New York: Oceana, 1985. 241p.   The author emphasizes the importance of the federal judiciary in the efforts made by the Republican Congress to establish federal authority over the civil rights of American citizens. Legislation and constitutional amendments gave federal courts, the Freedmen's Bureau, and the Justice Department the jurisdiction over rights that heretofore were the jurisdiction of state courts. In practice, however, federal courts mainly followed the political mood of the North and pulled back from full enforcement of civil rights.

723.   Kaczorowski, Robert J. "Revolving Constitutionalism in the Era of the Civil War and Reconstruction." *New York University Law Review* 61 (November 1986): 8634-940.   The 13th and 14th Amendments were the basis for the Republican approach to nationalize citizenship and authority to protect the rights of individuals. The framers of the amendments clearly intended a broad interpretation that enhanced federal powers over the states to ensure the rights of black citizens., There was general agreement on this issue among federal legal officials until the Supreme Court reversed the trend in favor of the state power in the Slaughter-House Cases of 1873. Blacks in the South suffered the consequences.

724.   Kausik, R. P. "The Issue of Political Rights for Blacks: The Formative Period, 1865-1877." *Indian Journal of American Studies* 10 (January 1980): 58-64. Kausik discusses the origins of the civil rights legislation and constitutional amendments as a way to find what the Republican Party intended for the civil rights of blacks citizens. He suggests that sincere support for black rights was lacking.

725.   Kelly, Alfred H.   "The Fourteenth Amendment: The Segregation Question." *Michigan Law Review* 54 (June 1956): 1049-1086.   Kelly explores the origins of the 14th Amendment and the intent of its framers as a way to determine whether the amendment was intended to guard against the establishment of a caste system. The framers did sought to establish the equality of all citizens based on radical antislavery ideology that developed during the prewar decades.

726. Klaus, Samuel (ed.). *The Milligan Case*. New York: Alfred A. Knopf, 1929. 476p. Bibl. Port. In the case of *Ex parte* Milligan the U.S. Supreme Court decided that Congress and the president had no powers beyond those indicated in the constitution and that the denial of *habeas corpus* to Lambdin P. Milligan during wartime and his trial by a military commission were unconstitutional. The decision, coming as it did in 1866, had serious implications for the conduct of military authority in the South during Reconstruction. Klaus provides a lengthy introduction outlining the issues and chronology of the case. Otherwise, the book consists of the text of the case as it was presented and argued before the Supreme Court. Appendixes include the Proceedings of A Military Commission and documents on the court's opinion in an earlier but related case, *Ex parte* Merryman in May, 1861.

727. Kohl, Robert. "The Civil Rights Act of 1866, Its Hour Come Round at Last: Jones v. Alfred H. Mayer Co." *Virginia Law Review* 65 (March 1969): 272-300. Kohl discusses the development of the Civil Rights Act of 1866 and its application to a housing discrimination case in 1968. He suggests that the act, for many years an obscure piece of legislation, could have been applied in a similar, broad fashion if the federal courts had investigated its legislative history. The idea that later legislation, such as the 14th Amendment and the Enforcement Act of 1870, narrowed the scope of the Civil Right Act is not supported by history.

728. Kull, Andrew. "The Enforcement After Emancipation of Debts Contracted For the Purchase of Slaves." *Chicago-Kent Law Review* 70 (1994): 493-538. Kull discusses the legal controversy during Reconstruction regarding debts incurred when slaves were purchased prior to emancipation. State and federal courts recognized the continuing legitimacy of these contracts and in most cases decided in favor of the sellers' right to the fulfillment of the purchase contract. To do otherwise would have made emancipation retroactive for the period when slavery was legal.

729. Kutler, Stanley I. "*Ex Parte* McCardle: Judicial Impotency? The Supreme Court and Reconstruction Reconsidered." *American Historical Review* 72 (April 1967): 835-851. Kutler explores the case of *Ex parte* McCardle (1868) in the context of critics who labeled the court's decision as symbolic of a shamefully weak Supreme Court bowing to an aggressive Congress. William McCardle, a Vicksburg, Mississippi editor, challenged the jurisdiction of military courts established by the Reconstruction Acts over local courts. Congress quickly revised legislation which would block the Supreme Court from finding in McCardle's favor. Kutler believes that the court's decision in favor of Congress reflected the exercise of power, not weakness. He further supports this position by citing the case of *Ex parte* Yerger.

730. Kutler, Stanley I. *Judicial Power and Reconstruction Politics*. Chicago: University of Chicago Press, 1968. 178p. Bibl. Port. Kutler's book is a collection of nine essays that collectively argue against the traditional view of the Supreme Court as a weak institution during Reconstruction. Many historians have long believed that the court lost power to the Republican Congress that insisted on its own concept of postwar policy. Kutler argues that the opposite is true, that the Supreme Court, chaired by Chief Justice Salmon P. Chase, acted with determination,

restraint, and activism in the decisions that came before the court on issues of *habeas corpus*, military and federal courts vs. state courts, civil rights, and the application of the 14th Amendment. A variety of cases are cited, particularly *Ex parte* Milligan, *Ex parte* McCardle, Georgia v. Stanton, Slaughter-House Cases and *Ex parte* Yerger. Also, Kutler emphasizes the importance of legal histories of Reconstruction instead of focusing entirely on civil rights and the issues of the freedmen.

731.   Kutler, Stanley I. "Reconstruction and the Supreme Court: The Numbers Game Reconsidered." *Journal of Southern History* 32 (February 1966): 42-58. Kutler rejects the traditional view that the Republican Party supported a reduction of Supreme Court justices from 9 to 7 because the Radicals were hostile toward the Court and were determined to gain more power against President Johnson's policies. In fact, there is evidence to show that there were operational reasons for reducing the number of justices in the judicial reform act of July 23, 1866, and that Johnson did not oppose the bill. There is no correlation between support or nonsupport for Presidential Reconstruction and the bill to reduce the number of justices, although the Republican Congress did want to adjust the Supreme Court to ensure Northern domination.

732.   Labbé, Ronald. "New Light on the Slaughterhouse Monopoly Act of 1869." In *Louisiana's Legal Heritage*. Edited by Edward F. Haas. Pensacola, Fl.: Perdido Bay Press, 1983. Pp. 143-161. Labbe explains the historical background to the Slaughter-House cases that attempted to apply the 14th Amendment's guarantee of due process to corporate persons and defined the separation of federal and state authority over the civil rights of citizens in such a way that federal authority was damaged. The case centered on the political and legal struggle in New Orleans between city officials and butchers over the government's power to regulate the slaughtehouse business. A struggle between supporters of government power to regulate and those who opposed it led to an interpretation of the amendment originally intended for securing the rights of black citizens under federal authority. The U.S. Supreme Court ruling in 1873 weakened federal jurisdiction and increased state jurisdiction in civil rights cases.

733.   Lado, Marianne L. Engelman. "A Question of Justice: African-American Legal Perspectives on the 1883 Civil Rights Cases." *Chicago-Kent Law Review* 10 (1995): 1123-1195. Lado analyses the published responses of black Americans to the Supreme Court's decision in the Civil Rights Cases in 1883. The ruling struck down provisions of the Civil Rights Act of 1875 barring discrimination in public accommodations. There were a wide variation of responses that Lado classifies by themes - democracy and natural law, the importance of the 13th, 14th, and 15th Amendments in defining civil rights, criticism of the ruling based on congressional intent, the need for broad interpretations of the constitution, and the willful intent of the court to arrive at a certain outcome.

734.   *Landmark Briefs and Arguments of the Supreme Court.* Washington: University Publications of America, 1975-   Volumes 4 - 8 include extensive

documentary evidence related to Supreme Court decisions during Reconstruction. Briefs and arguments were written by lawyers on both sides of cases. Among the cases included are in volume 4: *Ex parte* Milligan, Cummings v. Missouri, *Ex parte* Garland, Mississippi v. Johnson, *Ex parte* McCardle; volume 5: Georgia v. Stanton, *Ex parte* McCardle continued, Texas v. White; volume 6: Hepburn v. Griswold, Slaughter-House Cases ; volume 7: U.S. v. Cruikshank ; and volume 8, Civil Rights Cases.

735.   Larsen, Charles Edward. "Commentaries on the Constitution, 1865-1900." Ph.D. Columbia University, 1952. 305p.

736.   Lemmon, Sarah M. "Transportation Segregation in the Federal Courts since 1865." *Journal of Negro History* 38 (April 1953): 174-193.   The issue of segregation or restricting the use of common transportation carriers began during Reconstruction. Lemmon discusses the development of the issue after the Civil War and how the federal courts ruled on cases between 1873 and 1950.

737.   Lewis, Frederick P. *The Dilemma in its Congressional Power to Enforce the Fourteenth Amendment.* Washington, D.C.: University Press of America, 1980. 102p. App. Bibl.   Lewis reviews the history of the U.S. Supreme Court's interpretation of the 14th Amendment and explores the original intent of Congress. He is particularly concerned with whether the powers advanced in the law are rightfully and intentionally in the hands of Congress or the states. The struggle among radical and conservative Republicans in Congress did not lead to a cohesive majority that agreed on the content of the law. To search for congressional intent is fruitless because political factions struggled to complete a bill that could be passed. Lewis seems to agree that Congress probably intended the law to apply federal protection to the rights of persons who are wronged as a member of an identifiable group, thus leaving ordinary crimes to the states. Extracts from major congressional civil rights legislation are included.

738.   Linden, Glenn M. *Politics or Principle: Congressional Voting on the Civil War Amendments and Pro-Negro Measures, 1838-1869.* Seattle: University of Washington Press, 1976. 88p. App. Bibl. Tbls.   Linden compiled the voting records of U.S. senators and congressmen on the 13th, 14th, and 15th Amendments in order to reveal how consistent the legislators were in support of Republican reforms in favor of civil rights for blacks. He also compiled votes taken in the Congress on other pro-black measures between 1838 and 1864 for all persons who voted on the amendments and had been in the Congress in earlier years. The issue of consistency in support of legislation assisting blacks may illustrate motives for the votes that were cast. The voting records reveal patterns of consistent support or rejection of pro-black legislation among many legislators, but a larger number of them increased their support over the period compared with those who decreased their support. Republicans and Democrats took separate sides in the voting, with Republicans increasingly supporting reforms and Democrats increasingly opposing them.

739.   Maltz, Earl M.   "The Civil Rights Act and the Civil Rights Cases: Congress, Court and Constitution." *Florida Law Review* 44 (September 1992): 605-635.   The Civil Rights Act of 1875 interpreted and attempted to enforce Section 1 of the 14th Amendment regarding federal government jurisdiction over private acts as opposed to only government acts.   Maltz focuses on the legislative history of the act and the relevant rulings of the Supreme Court   (i.e. Slaughter-House Cases in 1873; *Ex parte* Virginia in 1879; Strauder v. West Virginia in 1879) prior to the landmark Civil Rights Cases in 1883.   He concludes that the act went beyond the conservative intentions of the Reconstruction amendments, and the Supreme Court took a moderate position between the two.   Maltz considers the Civil Rights Cases ruling as moderate and non-reactionary.

740.   Maltz, Earl M.   *Civil Rights, the Constitution, and Congress, 1863-1869.* Lawrence: University Press of Kansas, 1990. 198p. Bibl. Tbls.   Maltz uses a variety of sources but relies mainly on public documents, particularly debates published in the *Congressional Globe* and other congressional documents. He states that the public documents clearly reveal the intent of Congress when it passed the 13th, 14th, and 15th amendments to the constitution and the Civil Rights Act of 1866.   That the foundations for congressional action were legal decisions made about federal and state authority prior to the Civil War.   The moderate/conservative majority in the Republican Party did not support total racial equality and recognized the historical power of the states.   Maltz agrees that judicial adherence to the original intent of Congress is appropriate and that congressional intentions emphasized only limited enhancement of federal authority over the states.   The amendments and the Civil Rights Act were conservative documents approved through compromise.

741.   Maltz, Earl M.   "The Fourteenth Amendment as Political Compromise - Section One in the Joint Committee on Reconstruction." *Ohio State Law Journal* 45 (1984): 933-980. App. Tbls.   Section one includes phrases related to citizenship, privileges and immunities of citizens, due process and equal protection under the law. Maltz examines the voting patterns and the political ideology of members of the Joint Committee to determine whether this information sheds light on the committee's intent.   The votes on key issues do not reveal a conclusive pattern, except to show the domination of the moderate and conservative committee members.   There is evidence of intent to preserve the government power structure and avoid a federal mandate for black suffrage, but there is also evidence favorable to the concept that the Bill of Rights is encompassed by the amendment and applies to the states.

742.   Maltz, Earl M.   "Fourteenth Amendment Concepts in the Antebellum Era." *American Journal of Legal History* 32 (October 1988): 305-346.   Both proslavery and antislavery factions in the U.S. agreed on the equality of citizens before the law and the rights to equal protection of life, liberty and property.   This agreement was based on context of a white society.   The application of these principles to blacks became the fundamental issue in the debate over the interpretation of the 13th and 14th Amendments.   Antislavery proponents did not emphasize eliminating racial

discrimination. They focused on the concept of equality before the law for all citizens irrespective of race.

743.   Maltz, Earl M. "Reconstruction Without Revolution: Republican Civil Rights Theory in the Era of the Fourteenth Amendment." *Houston Law Review* 24 (March 1967): 221-279.   Maltz believes that some historians, such as Robert Kaczrowski, Harold Hyman, and William Wiecek have underestimated the influence of conservative Republicans on legislation that addressed civil rights during Reconstruction. From the 1850s to the debates on the 14th Amendment most Republicans would take only limited steps to expand federal authority at the state and local levels. Conservative Republicans moderated the Civil Rights Act of 1866 and section one of the 14th Amendment because they disagreed with extreme changes, and they did not think that the legislation would pass Congress in original form.

744.   Maltz, Earl M. "'Separate But Equal' and the Law of Common Carriers in the Era of the Fourteenth Amendment." *Rutgers Law Journal* 17 (Spring/Summer 1980): 553-568.   Legal cases involving "separate but equal" issues in public transportation by private carriers arose during the Civil War and may have influenced the framers of the 14th Amendment. The cases were more complex than simply federal versus state authority. Supporters of the amendment may have intended it to restrict private actions of discrimination that could be interpreted as governmental action.

745.   Maltz, Earl M. "The Waite Court and Federal Power to Enforce the Reconstruction Amendments." In *The Supreme Court and the Civil War*. Edited by Jennifer M. Lowe. Washington: Supreme Court Historical Society, 1996. Pp. 75-88. Ills. Ports.   Historians disagree whether the Supreme Court led by Chief Justice Morrison R. Waite (1874-1888) was a reactionary or a moderate force regarding civil rights of blacks and federal power to enforce the Reconstruction laws passed by Congress. Maltz examines the Court's response to cases on these issues and concludes that the decisions of the Waite court were generally consistent with "mainstream" Republican goals in Reconstruction. The court could have been a stronger voice for federal power to protect civil rights, but it left open opportunities for the effective use of Reconstruction legislation. The main cases cited are U.S. v. Cruikshank, U.S. v. Harris, the Civil Rights Cases, *Ex parte* Yarbrough, *Ex parte* Virginia, and Strauder v. West Virginia.

746.   Mancuso, Luke. "'Reconstruction is still in Abeyance?: Walt Whitman's *Democratic Vistas* and the Federalizing of National Identity." *ATQ* 8 (September 1994): 229-250.   In Whitman's lengthy essay published by *Galaxy Magazine* in 1871, he responded to Thomas Carlyle's criticism of mass democracy ("Shooting Niagra: and After?," *New York Times*, August 16, 1867) and to the expansion of democracy in the U.S. through the extension of voting rights to blacks in the 15th Amendment. Even though Whitman had doubts about black suffrage, he fully supported the amendment and mass democracy as a way to eliminate discrimination and make the Union stronger. A developing democracy would push Reconstruction

beyond racial and political factions toward the benefits of a revolutionary process in America.

747.   Matthews, John Mabry. *Legislative and Judicial History of the Fifteenth Amendment.* Baltimore: Johns Hopkins Press, 1909. 126p. List of Cases Cited. (*Johns Hopkins University Studies in Historical and Political Studies*, Ser. 27, no. 6-7.) Mathews characterizes the passage of the 15th Amendment in Congress as a compromise between humanitarians, nationalists, and states righters. Congress intended for the amendment to be based on national authority in all elections in the nation.   In his discussion of the passage, supporting legislation, and court interpretations, Mathews suggests that the strength of the amendment was whittled away by apathetic public opinion.

748.   Mawhinney, Eugene Alberto.   "The Development of the Concept of Liberty in the Fourteenth Amendment." Ph.D. University of Illinois, 1955. 314p.

749.   Mayers, Lewis. "The Habeas Corpus Act of 1867: The Supreme Court as Legal Historian." *University of Chicago Law Review* 33 (Autumn 1965): 31-59. Mayers argues that the Habeas Corpus Act was not intended to be expansive legislation validating Reconstruction, offering new remedies for state prisoners, and supporting the 14th Amendment. Historical examination indicates a more limited view that calls into question recent uses of the 1867 act in the Supreme Court to vacate state criminal convictions.

750.   McDonald, Forrest. "Was the Fourteenth Amendment Constitutionally Adopted?" *Georgia Journal of Southern Legal History* 1 (Spring/Summer 1991): 1-21.   McDonald reviews the history of the ratification of the 14th Amendment and concludes that it was passed by the Senate and ratified by the states in an irregular and unconstitutional manner.

751.   McFeely, William S. "Amos T. Akerman: The Lawyer and Racial Justice." In *Region, Race, and Reconstruction: Essays in Honor of C. Vann Woodward.* New York: Oxford University Press, 1982. Pp. 395-415.   Akerman was appointed Attorney General of the U.S. in June, 1870. Although originally from New Hampshire, he moved to Georgia in 1846.   He believed that the Reconstruction Acts and the 14th and 15th Amendments offered an opportunity to create a better society in the South based on equal opportunity and justice. He fought the Ku Klux Klan so diligently with civil rights suits that President Grant was forced to remove him in December, 1871 because Grant feared that his aggressive actions in favor of legal equality would be successful. Civil rights cases continued after his dismissal, but without the dedicated participation of the attorney general.

752.   McMahon, Edward. "Some Side-Lights on Reconstruction." *Pacific Review* 2 (June 1921): 58-68.   McMahon focuses on the actions of the Republican Congress to demonstrate its authority to strengthen federal court jurisdiction over appeals in cases which stemmed from violations of the Reconstruction Acts of 1867. In the case of *Ex parte* Milligan, handed down on February 17, 1868, Supreme

Courts Justice Salmon P. Chase ruled that the Court did not have jurisdiction in cases of *habeas corpus*, but before the ruling Congress had quickly repealed the questionable portions of the Judiciary Reform Act of 1867. The Republicans wanted to demonstrate that Congress had the power to decide jurisdiction of the Supreme Court, but when leaders believed that the Court would decide against them and possibly effect their entire Reconstruction program, they responded quickly when Supreme Court delayed its ruling to give Congress time to act.

753. McPherson, James M. "Abolitionists and the Civil Rights Act of 1875." *Journal of American History* 52 (December 1965): 493-510. Even after the 15th amendment was ratified in 1870, many abolitionists continued working for racial equality in the U.S. Northern abolitionists, led by Charles Sumner, favored reform legislation. McPherson explains how abolitionists pushed for legislation to outlaw discrimination, and he describes the political debates in the 1870s prior to the passage of the Civil Rights Act of 1875. The law had very little effect, but it represented an historical bridge between the 14th Amendment and the Civil Rights Act of 1964.

754. Mendelson, Wallace. "A Note on the Cause and Cure of the Fourteenth Amendment." *Journal of Politics* 43 (February 1981): 152-158. Mendelson explains that the confusion and disagreement within the Republican Congress on the words and the meaning of proposals for the 14th Amendment resulted in an amendment that cannot be clearly defined. This has allowed the Supreme Court to rule as it pleases. One should recognize the environment and events that led to the passage of the amendment, including the racist black codes. Taking note of the setting of the amendment offers meaning beyond the confusion in the words alone.

755. Meyer, Howard N. "Retrieving Self-Evident Truths: The Fourteenth Amendment." *This Constitution* 4 (Fall 1984): 11-16. Ills. Ports. The 14th Amendment expressed what was already in the U.S. constitution since 1787. Meyer explains this concept and briefly describes how the amendment was interpreted from its approval in 1868 up to the 1960s.

756. Meyer, Howard. *The Amendment That Refused to Die*. Radnor, Pa.: Chilton Book Co., 1973. 250p. App. Meyer examines the constitutional changes that took place during Reconstruction after the ratification of the 14th Amendment and how the intent of Congress was mangled and weakened by decisions of the Supreme Court. Despite the weakening and misinterpretations that the court allowed, particularly regarding the competition between federal and state jurisdiction over citizens, the true intent of the amendment never completely faded, and by the 1960s it became the foundation for insuring the rights of black citizens.

757. Miller, Kelley. "Have the Civil War Amendments Failed?" *South Atlantic Quarterly* 27 (April 1928): 117-129. Miller argues that the 13th, 14th, and 15th Amendments to the constitution have not completely failed, but are either completely enforced (13th) or enforced to some extent. Blacks have been able to

take advantage of much of what the amendments promised, but the fact that the laws have not been enforced to perfection is no reason to think that they are worthless.

758.   "Mississippi v. Johnson." *Dickinson Law Review* 16 (December 1911): 57-64. The editors criticize the U.S. Supreme Court's decision to deny a motion by Mississippi to stop President Johnson and the occupation Army in the state from enforcing the Reconstruction Acts of 1867.

759.   Morris, M. F. "The Fifteenth Amendment to the Federal Constitution." *North American Review* 189 (January 1909): 82-92.   Morris argues that the amendment is invalid because it was illegally adopted and was based on the fallacious concept of racial equality that is an outrage to "our Aryan civilization" (p. 83).   The illegality of the amendment is based on its passage by carpetbag legislatures that were compelled to pass it, and the fact that it was an addition, not an amendment, to the constitution. Additions require the unanimous consent of the states, a condition that was not met. (For criticsim of Morris see Albert Pillsbury's "The War Amendments," *North American Review* 189 (May 1909): 740-751. Pillsbury believes that appropriate procedures were followed and that the measure was necessary to suppress rebellion.)

760.   Mueller, Jean West and Wyrell Burroughs Schamel. "Reconstruction, the Fourteenth Amendment, and Personal Liberties." *Magazine of History* (OAH) 4 (Winter 1989): 60-66.   The authors suggest a lesson plan using the 14th Amendment and a petititon from black citizens of Cleveland, Tennessee to Congress regarding the need to enforce the amendment through legislative means.

761.   Nelson, William E. *The Fourteenth Amendment: From Political Principle to Judicial Doctrine.* Cambridge: Harvard University Press, 1988. 253p.   Nelson compares the understandings of the framers and ratifiers of the 14th Amendment with the way it was interpreted in the courts. During and after ratification there was no consensus about the exact meaning of the amendment in all respects, but the debate focused on whether the law guaranteed absolute rights or simply equality of rights in the context of antebellum traditions. The most important element defining the amendment was court interpretation. Lower courts made various applications of the law, but beginning with the Slaughter-House Cases in 1873. The Supreme Court decided that the law ensured equal rights. This preserved the power of state lawmaking and questioned the application of the Bill of Rights to the states. The court's interpretation was reversed in the 1930s.

762.   Palmer, Robert C. "The Parameters of Constitutional Reconstruction: Slaughter-House, Cruikshank, and the Fourteenth Amendment." *University of Illinois Law Review* (1984): 739-770.   Palmer analyses the majority and minority opinions of the Supreme Court in the Slaughter-House Cases and U.S. v. Cruikshank. Even though the former case decision weakened the 14th Amendment regarding federal power to safeguard the privileges and immunities of U.S. citizens, it was based on Justice Miller's interpretation of congressional intent and preserved some enhancements in federal power over liberties of citizens. The Cruikshank

ruling disregarded intent and cited Slaughter-House incorrectly. Cruikshank was more devastating to federal authority and the concept of the amendment's incorporation of the Bill of Rights and fundamental liberties.

763. Paluden, Phillip S. *Covenant With Death: The Constitution, Law, and Equality in the Civil War Era.* Urbana: University of Illinois Press, 1975. 309p. Bibl. Reconstruction offered the promise of freedom and equal civil rights to black Americans. There were Northern supporters of civil rights, but working against them was American legal tradition and perceptions of the government's role in society. Paluden examines the thoughts of Francis Lieber, Joel Parker, Sidney George Fisher, John Norton Pomeroy and Thomas M. Cooley to form a picture of the legal and social conflict in ideologies. These men represent the ideology of retreat from strong federal enforcement of civil rights and explaining that it was in the best interests of blacks. The result was a disaster for blacks and the failure of Reconstruction.

764. Paluden, Phillip S. "Law and the Failure of Reconstruction: The Case of Thomas Cooley." *Journal of the History of Ideas* 33 (October-December 1972): 597-614. Cooley was a legal thinker and jurist from Michigan whose publications and court decisions had an impact on the way many Americans interpreted the constitution, particularly regarding the 14th Amendment and Reconstruction. In his book, *Constitutional Limitations* (1868), and his essay in *Commentaries on the Constitution* (1873), Cooley reveals his Jacksonian foundation for individual liberty and freedom, respect for private property, and belief in restricted national power. While he fully supported the abolition of slavery and the importance of guaranteeing the rights of citizens, he also believed in the constitutional traditions of the antebellum period. His limited support for enhancing federal power to ensure equality of civil rights contributed to declining interest in pursuing civil rights reforms.

765. Pence, Charles R. "The Construction of the Fourteenth Amendment." *American Law Review* 25 (July-August 1891): 536-550. Pence examines the privileges and immunities clause with particular focus on its definition and its applicability to the Bill of Rights. He reviews cases from Reconstruction and afterwards, as well as the traditional application of the first 10 amendments to the federal government. Congress wanted the 14th Amendment to insure the rights of citizens with federal authority when states failed to do so.

766. Pierson, William Whately, Jr. "Texas Versus White." *Southwestern Historical Quarterly* 18 (April 1915): 341-367; 19 (July-October 1915): 1-36, 142-158. This case, decide by the U.S. Supreme Court on April 15, 1869, involved the validity of certain Texas indemnity bonds. In its decision the court seemed to validate congressional Reconstruction, but it hedged on the issue of the true status of the Confederate states after secession and once the war was finished. (See also Pierson's "Texas v. White: A Study in Legal History." Ph.D. Columbia University, 1916. 103p.)

767.   Pittman, R. Carter. "The Fourteenth Amendment: Its Intended Effect on Anti-Miscegenation Laws." *North Carolina Law Review* 43 (December 1964): 92-109.   Pittman argues that the framers of the Freedmen's Bureau Bill in 1866, the Civil Rights Act of 1866, and the 14th Amendment did not intend to strike down laws against miscegenation in the states.   The Reconstruction legislation did not have such an impact and should not be the basis for more recent attempts to strike anti-miscegenation laws.   Pittman includes a list of colonial anti-miscegenation laws from 5 states.

768.   Randle, E. H.   "The Three Last Amendments to the Constitution of the United States." *American Law Review* 44 (July-August 1910): 561-571.   Randle, an attorney from Mississippi, argues that the 13th, 14th, and 15th Amendments were all passed illegally.   Not only were Southern states forced to pass the amendments when they were not actually part of the U.S., but Congress followed illegal procedures, and the rights of many citizens were abused.

769.   "The Reconstruction Amendments: Then and Now."   *Rutgers Law Journal* 23 (Winter 1992): 231-303.   The text of a symposium at Rutgers University Law School includes papers delivered by Herman Belz, "Changing Perspectives on Reconstruction and the Constitution" - Eric Foner, "The Supreme Court's Legal History" - Robert J. Cottrol, "Reconstruction Amendment Historiography: The Quest For Racial and Intellectual Maturity" - William Wiecek, "The Constitutional Snipe Hunt" - Derrick Bell, "Reconstruction's Racial Realities" - Peter Charles Hoffer, "'Blind to History': The Use of History in Affirmative Action Suits: Another Look at City of Richmond v. J. A. Croson Co." - and James McClellan, "Commentary on the Papers Delivered by Professor Derrick Bell and Peter Charles Hoffer." Taken together these papers constitute an exploration of changing perceptions, interpretations, and applications of the 13th, 14th, and 15th Amendments in constitutional law.

770.   Richards, David A. J. *Conscience and the Constitution: History, Theory, and Law of the Reconstruction Amendments.* Princeton: Princeton University Press, 1993. 295p. App. Bibl.   Richards examines the 13th, 14th, and 15th Amendments in light of antebellum ethics and theory. He views the amendments as the theoretical culmination of the ethical and moral movement in abolitionism. They represent an expression of human rights practice and theory, and illustrate the legitimacy of political power. The amendments represent "revolutionary constitutionalism" (p. 258), a concept based on American traditions.   Richards believes that weak appreciation for the historical foundation of the Reconstruction amendments may render them ineffective.

771.   Riegel, Stephen J. "The Persistent Career of Jim Crow: Lower Federal Courts and the 'Separate but Equal' Doctrine, 1865-1896." *American Journal of Legal History* 28 (January 1984): 17-40.   The U.S. Supreme Court's decision in Plessy v. Ferguson in 1896 did not usher in a new period of legally sanctioned racial segregation. Riegel examines judicial decisions from 1865 to 1896 to show that segregation and the concept of "separate but equal" were not only *de facto* in the

South and the North prior to 1896, it was in fact *de jure*. A consistent pattern of Jim Crow segregation after the Civil War contradicts the interpretations of Woodward (see *Strange Career of Jim Crow*. New York: Oxford Unversity Press, 1955. Third ed., 1974) and Rabinowitz (see # 874-877) who focuses on the Plessy case as the beginning point of segregation cases in U.S. courts.

772.   Ross, Michael A. "Justice Miller's Reconstruction: The Slaughter-House Cases, Health Codes, and Civil Rights in New Orleans, 1861-1873." *Journal of Southern History* 64 (November 1998): 649-676.   One of the legacies of Justice Miller's majority opinion in the Slaughter-House Cases in 1873 was the weakening of the federal government's authority to enforce civil rights for blacks in accordance with the privileges and immunities clause of the 14th Amendment. Historians have criticized Miller for this decision and its negative impact on Reconstruction, but Miller and the majority of justices upheld federal authority to ensure the rights of citizens even as the court also sought to safeguard state authority to regulate business. Ross provides thorough coverage of the background to the cases that developed out of local public health controversies in New Orleans and were effected by local Reconstruction politics. He defends Miller's decision, but bemoans its application by future conservative courts and Southern lawmakers.

773.   Royall, William L. "Fourteenth Amendment: The Slaughterhouse Cases." *Southern Law Review* 4, n5 (October 1878): 558-584.   Royall favors the authority of the federal government to ensure the rights of U.S. citizens as proscribed by the 14th Amendment and the Civil Rights Act of 1866. He criticizes the Supreme Court's decision in the Slaughter-House Cases of 1873 in which the court weakened federal authority to enforce civil rights in the states.

774.   Russ, William A., Jr. "The Lawyer's Test Oath During Reconstruction." *Mississippi Law Journal* 10 (February 1938): 154-167.   Russ argues that the test oath requirement for lawyers in the border and former Confederate states was misguided because it caused many individuals to lose their ability to make a living and it could never work as a plan to improve the legal profession. Test oaths were struck down by the U.S. Supreme Court in *Ex parte* Garland in 1867.

775.   Schnapper, Eric. "Affirmative Action and the Legislative History of the Fourteenth Amendment." *Virginia Law Review* 71 (June 1985): 753-798.   The debate in the 1980s over the constitutionality of race based affirmative action legislation should take note of the historical use of such programs by Congress during and after the Civil War and the support provided by the 14th Amendment. Based on congressional debates from 1864 to 1870, there is adequate evidence to demonstrate the constitutionality of affirmative action programs and that the U.S. Supreme Court ought to recognize the original intent of Congress.

776.   Schwartz, Bernard. *From Confederation to Nation: The American Constitution, 1835-1877*. Baltimore: Johns Hopkins University Press, 1973. 243p. Index of cases.   The last three chapters deal with Reconstruction, particularly the constitutional issues of presidential and congressional power, the power of the states

versus the national government, and the role of military authority versus local civil authority. The Reconstruction amendments, particularly the 14th Amendment, and the Civil Rights legislation could not successfully change human behavior toward racial equality and civil rights, but they established the bases for future legislation in the 1950s and 1960s.

777.   Scott, John Anthony.   "Justice Bradley's Evolving Concept of the Fourteenth Amendment From the Slaughterhouse Cases to the Civil Rights Cases." *Rutgers Law Review* 25 (Summer 1971): 552-569.   Joseph P. Bradley was a U.S. Supreme Court justice from 1870 to 1892. Scott explains the change in Bradley's court opinions beginning with his dissent in the Slaughter-House Cases in 1873 and later rulings in U.S. v. Cruikshank in 1875. In both cases Bradley agreed that the Bill of Rights applies to the states and that the federal government had responsibilities to protect the rights of citizens, particularly the freedmen. But Bradley changed his position in 1883 when he stood with the majority in the Civil Rights Cases by rejecting the extension of federal authority over civil rights in the states.

778.   Sheffer, Martin S. "Did the Framers Intend Their Intentions? Civil Rights, the Fourteenth Amendment, and the Election Campaign of 1866." *Capital University Law Review* 12 (1982): 45-70. Sheffer examines the election campaign of 1866 to find out what the framers of the 14th Amendment said in their local campaigns and how voters responded to them. Congressional Republicans campaigned in support of civil rights, but most of them did not openly support the issue of black suffrage even if they actually favored it. They depicted the Democrats as opponents of basic civil rights and liberties for the freedmen. Republicans intended to legislate the rights of citizens on a broad basis and not just to effect specific identifiable rights.

779.   Sigler, Jay A. "The Rise and Fall of the Three-Fifths Clause." *Mid-America* 48 (October 1966): 271-277. In the original U.S. Constitution slaves were counted as three-fifths of a person for the purpose of population and representation in Congress. The 13th and 14th Amendments repealed the three-fifths clause and played a role in the redistribution of political power.

780.   Smith, Edward D.   "The Unfortunate History of America's First Comprehensive Civil Rights Bill, 1870-1883." *Negro History Bulletin* 47 (April-June 1984): 42-44. Smith briefly describes the difficult passage of the Civil Rights Act of 1875, its lax enforcement, and Supreme Court rulings that weakened it.

781.   Smith, George P. "Republican Reconstruction and Section Two of the Fourteenth Amendment." *Western Political Quarterly* 23 (December 1970): 829-853.   Section 2 of the 14th Amendment did not ensure suffrage for black males, but if they were denied the right to vote state representation in the House of Representatives would decline proportionately. Smith reviews the legislative history of section 2 and concludes that Republicans intended to deny the Southern states the benefit of counting former slaves to determine representation without also providing

former slaves with the franchise. The freedmen would certainly vote Republican and were needed if the Republicans had any hope of political success in the South.

782.   Smith, Jordan Marshall. "The Federal Courts and the Black Man in America, 1800-1883: A Study of Judicial Policy-Making." Ph.D. University of North Carolina, 1977. 362p.

783.   Spackman, S. G. F. "American Federalism and the Civil Rights Act of 1875." *Journal of American Studies* 10 (December 1976): 313-328.   Although the final bill that passed Congress was far weaker than the bills originally proposed by Charles Sumner, the act reinforced the trend set by the 13th, 14th, and 15th Amendments that reduced the federal system and enhanced the power of the national government in matters of citizenship. The framers of the amendments carefully left the states extensive leeway as long as equality existed. Spackman describes how the U.S. Supreme Court weakened the Republican drive toward enhanced national power and helped to establish a basis for the Civil Rights Cases (1883) that effectively killed the Civil Rights Act of 1875.

784.   Stephen, Gilbert Thomas. "The Separation of the Races in Public Conveyances." *American Political Science Review* 3 (May 1909): 180-204.   As an introduction to a discussion of the the the development of Jim Crow laws in the South, Stephen cites examples of legislation and judicial rulings on the separation of the races in public conveyances during and after Reconstruction. The Civil Rights Act of 1875 attempted to ensure equal access to various public institutions and conveyances, but court rulings tended to deny the authority of the federal government in such cases and emphasized separate-but-equal facilities because of the differences between the races.

785.   Stone, Alfred Holt. "Post Bellum Reconstruction: An American Experience." *Journal of Mississippi History* 3 (July 1941): 227-246.   Stone discusses the meaning and impact of the Reconstruction amendments on Southern whites.   Most whites did not support dramatic changes in the South, and they followed the political party that stood for as little change as possible.   Stone criticizes the forced, punitive nature of the amendments.

786.   Sullivan, Barry. "Historical Reconstruction, Reconstruction History, and the Proper Scope of Section 1981." *Yale Law Review* 98 (January 1989): 541-564. The author examines the congressional intent in the Civil Rights Act of 1866 with regard to its application to late 20th century cases.   History shows that Congress intended to protect citizens against public and private acts denying civil rights. (For a similar argument see Robert J. Kaczorowski, "The Enforcement Provisions of the Civil Rights Act of 1866: A Legislative History in Light of Runyon v. McCrary." *Yale Law Review* 98 (January 1989): 565-595.)

787.   Suthon, Walter J., Jr.   "The Dubious Origins of the Fourteenth Amendment." *Tulane Law Review* 28 (December 1953): 22-44.   Suthon argues that the 14th Amendment was forced on the Southern states in violation of the 5th

Amendment that gives procedures for amending the constitution. He raises the issue of whether the amendment can be ruled null and void. Suthon is particularly concerned with the use of the 14th Amendment as a basis for forced racial integration in the 1950s.

788.   Swinney, Everette. "Enforcing the Fifteenth Amendment, 1870-1877." *Journal of Southern History* 28 (May 1962): 202-218.   Congress sought to enforce the 15th Amendment by passing three bills to weaken the Ku Klux Klan. Swinney evaluates this legislation and revises the traditional negative view that it was ineffective and undemocratic. The laws had a strong impact during their first three years from 1870-1873, when the Justice Department's conviction rate ranged from 36%-49%, but beginning in 1874 federal interest in enforcing the laws declined under pressure of economic problems and strong opposition from Southern conservatives. The laws were difficult to enforce and local authorities and citizens refused to cooperate.

789.   Swinney, Everette. "Suppressing the Ku Klux Klan: The Enforcement of the Reconstruction Amendments, 1870-1874." Ph.D. University of Texas, 1966. 370p.

790.   "Symposium, One Hundred Twenty-Five Years of the Reconstruction Amendments Recognizing the Twenty-Fifth Anniversary of the *Loyola of Los Angeles Law Review*." *Loyola of Los Angeles Law Review* 25 (June 1992): 1135-1220.   Includes six brief articles mainly on the application of the constitutional reforms to American legal and judicial history after Reconstruction. David A. J. Richards ("Abolitionist Political and Constitutional Theory and the Reconstruction Amendments," 1187-1205) argues that the foundation for the amendments was specifically the Radical antislavery tradition that considered slavery to be a violation of the constitution. The constitutional tradition of equality should continue to impact present interpretations of the Reconstruction amendments. The amendments represent a tradition, not revolutionary change, in American constitutional history.

791.   Tarrant, Catherine W. "A Writ of Liberty or a Covenant With Hell? *Habeas Corpus* in the War Congresses, 1861-1867." Ph.D. Rice University, 1972.

792.   Taylor, Joseph H. "The Fourteenth Amendment, the Negro, and the Spirit of the Times." *Journal of Negro History* 45 (January 1960): 21-37.   Taylor briefly surveys how the 14th Amendment was interpreted by the judiciary and how this interpretation reflected contemporary ideas. One section deals with the period from 1865 to 1882. The Slaughter House Cases in 1873 are given to illustrate that the 14th Amendment was intended to protect black Americans.

793.   Ten Broek, Jocobus. *The Antislavery Origins of the Fourteenth Amendment*. Berkeley: University of California, 1951. 232p. Bibl. Tbl. of Cases. Ten Broek explains how the antislavery movement, beginning in the 1830s, laid the foundation for the Reconstruction amendments to the constitution. The Republican framers of the 14th amendment were closely familiar with or were themselves

abolitionists. The words and phrases that abolitionists used to argue the rights of all men were based on a philosophy of natural rights that applied to both the states and the federal government. The natural rights philosophy was expounded by abolitionists and became a part of the 13th and 14th amendments. Only by understanding the abolitionist roots of the amendments, in addition to contemporary debates, can historians recognize the intent of the framers. Ten Broek closely examines the background and definition of each section of the 14th Amendment. (See also the expanded edition published in 1965.)

794.   Ten Broek, Jocobus. "Thirteenth Amendment to the Constitution of the United States: Consummation to Abolition and Key to the Fourteenth Amendment." *California Law Review* 39 (June 1951): 171-203.   Ten Broek uses the congressional debates leading up to the passage of the 13th Amendment to argue that the amendment nationalized the natural right of freedom in the U.S. The law was supported by additional legislation that would give the federal government protection over the rights of free people. The 14th Amendment was intended, in part, to reenact the 13th Amendment with broad enforcement provisions.

795.   Thompson, Edwin B. "Benjamin Helm Bristow: Symbol of Reform." Ph.D. University of Wisconsin, 1940. 432p.

796.   Van Alstyne, William. "The Fourteenth Amendment, the 'Right' to Vote, and the Understanding of the Thirty-Ninth Congress." *Supreme Court Review* (1965): 33-86.   The author investigates the intent of Congress in the application of section 2 of the 14th Amendment to voting rights. Historical analysis seems to prove that malapportionment of a state legislature that results in the lack of voting power for a minority are not prohibited by the 14th Amendment. Apportionment is not related to equal protection in section 1 or to voting requirements in section 2.

797.   Vaughn, William P. "Separate and Unequal: The Civil Rights Act of 1875 and Defeat of the School Integration Clause." *Southwestern Social Science Quarterly* 48 (September 1967): 146-154.   Vaughn reviews the politics in Congress that led to the elimination of provisions for school integration in the Civil Rights Act. Charles Sumner was at the center of a movement among a small number of Republicans to outlaw racial segregation in schools.

798.   Wang, Robert. "The Conspiracy Theory of the Fourteenth Amendment." *Journal of Social Studies* 7 (Winter 1951): 43-46.   Wang believes that there was likely some understanding in Congress that corporations could be interpreted as persons under the due process clause of the 14th Amendment, but he disputes Roscoe Conkling's accusation that Sen. John Bingham of Ohio conspired for it to be so.

799.   Warsoff, Louis A. *Equality and the Law*. New York: Liveright Publishing Co., 1938. 324p. Bibl.   The intent of the framers of the 14th Amendment is compared with the actual use of the law in legal cases brought to court. Although the paramount reason for the amendment was to a build a strong

legal basis for providing and ensuring equal rights for black Americans, the courts have interpreted the due process and equal protection clauses so broadly as to make the law into something that was never intended. The protection of blacks was accomplished for the purpose of punishing the South, preserving the predominance of the Republican Party, and establishing congressional authority over the states. Warsoff agrees with the goals of the Republicans in Congress but believes that a constitutional amendment was the wrong way to achieve them.

800.   Weaver, Valeria W. "The Failure of Civil Rights 1875-1883 and its Repercussions." *Journal of Negro History* 54 (October 1969): 368-382.   The Civil Rights Act of 1875 did not succeed because it was ignored by citizens in both the North and the South, as well as being unenforced by the legal system. There was little commitment to the rights of blacks, and the concept of white supremacy was pervasive. The weak enforcement indicates that the courts followed public opinion instead of the law. The U.S. Supreme Court ruling in the Civil Rights Cases struck down the public accommodation sections of the law, thus eliminating legal impediments to racial discrimination.

801.   Webb, Ross A. "Benjamin H. Bristow: Civil Rights Champion, 1866-1872." *Civil War History* 15 (March 1969): 39-53.   Bristow, a Kentuckian who fought with the Union Army, was an active prosecutor of civil rights cases as assistant U.S. district attorney and later as U.S. attorney for Kentucky. He was particularly active in Kentucky where Ku Klux Klan violence and mob rule were pervasive. He successfully upheld federal authority to try offenders in federal court based on the Civil Rights Act of 1866, but in his most famous case, Blyew v. U.S., the Supreme Court ruled against federal authority in a local murder case and even questioned the right of black testimony. From 1870-1872 Bristow was U.S. Solicitor General in Washington, D.C.

802.   Weisberger, Bernard. "Dreams Deferred." *American Heritage* 41 (March 1990): 24, 26. Ill.   The election of Douglas Wilder as governor of Virginia and David Denkins as mayor of New York in 1989 prompts Weisberger to reflect on the great changes that have occurred in black political participation since Reconstruction. Even in Reconstruction black leadership in the politics of the Southern states was greatly exaggerated by detractors of equal rights and early twentieth century historians of the period. The 14th and 15th Amendments sought to extend equality of rights to American blacks, but disregard for the constitutional changes and court rulings made them almost lifeless provisions until the "Second Reconstruction" of the 1960s brought new strength to the the the constitution.

803.   Westin, Alan F. "John Marshall Harlan and the Constitutional Rights of Negroes: The Transformation of a Southerner." *Yale Law Review* 66 (April 1957): 637-710.   Westin explains how a former Kentucky slaveholder became a postwar Republican leader in his state and one who turned away from white supremacy towards total acceptance of equal justice and civil rights for all citizens. Harlan, an attorney and judge in Kentucky, was associate justice of the U.S. Supreme Court

(1877-1911). He became famous for his consistent defense of civil rights, most notably in the Civil Rights Cases (1883) and Plessy v. Ferguson (1896).

804.   White, G. Edward. "Reconstructing the Constitutional Jurisprudence of Salmon P. Chase." *Northern Kentucky Law Review* 21 (1993): 41-116.   White takes a broad view of the Chase Court (1864-1873) and depicts Chase as one whose rulings were based on antebellum traditions, not conventional Republican politics. (See also comments on White in Herman Belz, "Deep Conviction Jurisprudence and Texas v. White: A Comment on G. Edward White's Historicist Interpretation of Chief Justice Chase," *Northern Kentucky Law Review* 21 (1993): 117-131; and Michael Les Benedict, "Salmon P. Chase as Jurist and Politician: Comment on G. Edward White, Reconstructing Chase's Jurisprudence," *Northern Kentucky Law Review* 21 (1993): 133-150.)

805.   Whiteside, Ruth Ann. "Justice Joseph Bradley and the Reconstruction Amendments." Ph.D. Rice University, 1981. 355p.

806.   Wiecek, William M. "The Great Wit and Reconstruction: The *Habeas Corpus* Act of 1867." *Journal of Southern History* 36 (November 1970): 530-548. The *Habeas Corpus* Act increased federal court jurisdiction by allowing federal courts to review the actions of state courts and to overrule them on questions of individual liberty.   The law has been interpreted as a way for federal courts to provide freedmen better protection.   Wiecek provides a broad analysis of the impact of the act during the nineteenth and twentieth centuries.   He believes that the act is one example of how congressional Republicans enhanced the power of the federal judiciary during Reconstruction instead of weakening the courts as interpreted by most historians.

807.   Wilson, Kirt Hasketh. "Race, Rights, and Equality: A Rhetorical Analysis of the Congressional Debate Over the Civil Rights Act of 1875." Ph.D. Northwestern University, 1995.

808.   Woodward, C. Vann.   "Equality: America's Deferred Commitment." *American Scholar* 27 (Autumn 1958): 495-472.   Woodward reviews the war aims of the North (ie. Union and freedom) and the revolutionary intention of legislating equality.   The Republicans did all that they could do to establish the legal basis for racial equality, but the law outran reality.   The commitment made to equality could not be kept, not only because of great resistance among white Southerners, but also among white Northerners.   Historians should recognize the complexity of thought and emotion that existed during the Civil War era.

809.   Woodward, C. Vann. "The Political Legacy of Reconstruction." *Journal of Negro Education* 26 (Summer 1957): 241-248.   The political legacy of Reconstruction is the 15th Amendment that provided a constitutional basis for the enfranchisement of the freedmen.   Most Northerners, including abolitionists, had strong reservations about giving voting rights to the freedmen, but Congress overcame this feeling because they needed the political support of blacks so that the

Republican Party could dominate the South, and many congressmen agreed that blacks needed a way to defend themselves against a hostile, white South. Woodward compares black enfranchisement with the enfranchisement of millions of emigrants who came to American in the late 19th and early 20th centuries.

810.   Wyatt-Brown, Bertram. "The Civil Rights Act of 1875." *Western Political Quarterly* 18 (December 1965): 763-775.   Wyatt-Brown describes and criticizes the Republican Party's lack of enthusiastic dedication to the Civil Rights Act of 1875. It was a law that they did not intend to enforce and that represented more theory than reality.

811.   Zeigler, Donald H. "A Recommendation of the Younger Doctrine in Light of the Legislative History of Reconstruction." *Duke Law Journal* no. 5 (1983): 987-1044.   In the case of Younger v. Harris (401 US 37) in 1971 the Supreme Court began to reverse the legal doctrine laid down by Reconstruction legislation under the 14th Amendment that gave federal courts jurisdiction to guarantee due process and equal protection in state criminal and civil justice systems. Zeigler reviews the history of federal jurisdiction and concludes that the legislative and legal intent of the Reconstruction Congress should not be ignored any longer.

812.   Zuckert, Michael P. "Complete the Constitution: The Thirteenth Amendment." *Constitutional Commentary* 4 (Summer 1987): 259-283.   Zuckert believes that just examining the intent of the framers and the interpretations of historians do not adequately explain the process of Reconstruction. A better approach would be James Madison's concept of the incomplete constitution that requires amending to create the proper balance of power between federal and state governments. Although Congress did not anticipate additional legislation and constitutional amendments after it passed the 13th Amendment, except by giving itself the power of enforcement, the 14th and 15th Amendments were necessary to complete, not revolutionize, constitutional reform to ensure freedom and civil rights for all.

813.   Zuckert, Michael P. "Congressional Power Under the Fourteenth Amendment-The Original Understanding of Section Five." *Constitutional Commentary* 3 (Winter 1986): 123-156. Tbls.   The power of Congress to make laws effecting the private acts of individuals under Section 5 of the 14th Amendment was rejected by the U.S. Supreme Court in the Civil Rights Cases in 1883. The court also struck down federal powers established by the Enforcement Act of 1871. Zuckert discusses the debates leading to the amendment and the Klan act, and he also examines various theories of congressional intent by legal historians.

Regional Studies on Reconstruction in the South

General Studies on Postwar Transition

814.   Abbott, Martin (ed.). "The South as Seen by a Tennessee Unionist in 1865: Letters of H. M. Watterson." *Tennessee Historical Quarterly* 18 (June, 1959): 148-161.   Harvey M. Watterson traveled through the South in the fall of 1865 at the request of President Johnson. He was a close friend of the president, a fellow Tennessee Unionist, and a Democrat. Reprinted are six letters written by Watterson between September 26 and October 28, 1865. The letters were written from Alabama, Mississippi, and Louisiana. Abbott notes that the letters provide good political information, but Watterson showed Democratic biases and mentioned nothing about economic and social conditions.

815.   Abbott, Martin (ed.). "A Southerner Views the South, 1865: Letters of Harvey M. Watterson." *Virginia Magazine of History and Biography* 68 (October 1960): 478-489.   President Johnson sent Watterson to the South to report on conditions during the summer following the Civil War. The two men were longtime friends and fellow Tennesseans who agreed on many political issues. Abbott prints four of Watterson's letters to the president that were written in June and July, 1865 from Virginia and North Carolina. Watterson writes that Southerners have been utterly defeated, and that he agrees with Johnson's plan for Reconstruction.

816.   Abel, Emily K. "A Victorian Views Reconstruction: The American Diary of Samuel Augustus Burnett." *Civil War History* 20 (June 1974): 135-156. Excerpts from Barnett's diary, written during his tour of the South from April 22 to May 22, 1867, reveal the racial attitudes of a middle class Victorian from Bristol, England. He expressed skepticism of Radical reforms, but he would later become a leader for social reform in England.

817.   Avary, Myrta Lockett. *Dixie After the War: An Exposition of Social Conditions Existing in the South During the Twelve Years Succeeding the Fall of Richmond.* New York: Doubleday, Page & Co., 1906. 435p. Plates. Ports. Avary writes a highly sentimental account of the last days of slavery and the 12 years of Reconstruction, with particular focus on Virginia and South Carolina. The work is based on discussions and correspondence with family and friends as well as a tour of several Southern states. She offers a perspective on white, Southern woman, and believes that the attempt at racial equality during Reconstruction was a folly.

818.   Bennett, Aremona G.   "Phantom Freedom: Official Acceptance of Violence to Personal Security and Subversion of Proprietary Rights and Ambitions Following Emancipation, 1865-1910." *Chicago-Kent Law Review* 10,2 (1994): 439-491.   Bennett describes the coercive, discriminatory, and violent environment for black citizens in the Southern states after the Civil War. Whether the focus is on individual or group oppression of blacks or the action and inaction by state and federal courts, the legal freedom and right to own property was disregarded by state law and white tradition.

819.   Bhurtel, Shyam Krishna. *Alfred Eliab Buck: Carpetbagger in Alabama and Georgia.* Ph.D. Auburn University, 1981. 283p.

820.   Blackwell, Samuel M., Jr. *The Twelfth Illinois Cavalry and Cavalry Operations in the Civil War and Reconstruction.* Ph.D.   Northern Illinois University, 1995. 517p.

821.   Brewster, James. *Sketches of Southern Mystery, Treason, and Murder. The Secret Political Societies of the South, Their Methods and Manners.   The Phagedenic Cancer on Our National Life.* Milwaukee: Evening Wisconsin Co., 1903. 277p. (i.e. 316p.) (Rpt., New York: AMS Press, 1975)   Brewster served in the Union Army and lived in the South during Reconstruction. The stories about Reconstruction that comprise most of this book are based on his observations and experiences, as well as several published sources and Congressional committee reports. The result is several independent chapters relating to dishonesty and white violence against loyal Republicans and blacks.   The focus is on Louisiana, Mississippi, and South Carolina. Brewster is highly critical of the Ku Klux Klan and similar groups.

822.   Burger, Nash K. and John K. Bettersworth. *South of Appomattox.* New York: Harcourt, Brace and Co., 1959. 376p. Bibl. Ills. Ports.   The authors have written biographical sketches of 10 well known Southern men from diverse backgrounds who represent aspects of Southern unity and tradition. Among the ten men who participated in Reconstruction were Nathan Bedford Forrest, L. Q. C. Lamar, Wade Hampton, and James Longstreet. The other subjects were Robert E. Lee, Matthew Fontaine Maury, John C. Breckinridge, Alexander Stephens, "Old Joe" Johnston, and Jefferson Davis.

823.   Campbell, Sir George. *White and Black: The Outcome of a Visit to the United States.* New York: Negro University Press, 1969. 420p. (Rpt. from New York: R. Worthington, 1879)   Campbell traveled throughout a large portion of the U.S., including Virginia, North Carolina, South Carolina, and Georgia. He sought to understand race relations and the Southern economy for application to British colonies. Campbell's account is based on observations and interviews with many individuals.

824.   Carpenter, John A. "Atrocities in the Reconstruction Period." *Journal of Negro History* 47 (October 1962); 234-247.   Carpenter reviews contrary evidence regarding the truth of stories about atrocities perpetrated by whites against blacks. He concludes that the evidence illustrates that atrocities did occur and that widespread, gross exaggerations were uncommon. He points to the combination of evidence, including the violent tradition of the South, weight of evidence from Freedmen's Bureau agents, and the evidence gathered by Congress that led to legislation to protect freedmen.

825.   Carter, Dan. "Abolitionism and Reconstruction: The Case of Sidney Andrews." *Maryland Historian* 2 (Fall 1971): 93-102.   Carter follows Andrews' career as a journalist and commentator on the postwar South. As a capital correspondent for the Boston *Advertiser*, Andrews toured North and South Carolina, Georgia, and Alabama and made frequent reports to his editor. In 1866 he published his thoughts in *The South As It Was* (Tichnor & Fields, 1866). His perspective on Southern society became an important primary resource for future historians. Andrews moderate Republicanism turned radical in 1866, but by 1868-69 he rejected the Radicals and even the Freedmen's Bureau. Carter notes that Andrews' ideology was marked by individualism, *laissez faire*, racism, abolitionism and equal civil rights for all.

826.   Carter, Dan T. "The Anatomy of Fear: The Christmas Day Insurrection Scare of 1865." *Journal of Southern History* 42 (August 1976): 345-364.   Many white people in the Black Belt region feared a black uprising in 1865. As with many other rumors of insurrection in antebellum days, there was no evidence that freedmen were planning an uprising except in the imagination of fearful people in an unsettled period after the war. Carter believes the rumors of black insurrection helped to unite whites and to protect the region from "outsiders" who sought to change Southern traditions.

827.   Carter, Dan T. *When the War Was Over: The Failure of Self Reconstruction in the South, 1865-1867.* Baton Rouge: Louisiana State University Press, 1985. 285p.   The white leaders of the South attempted to bring about reunion on their own terms and with a defiant attitude that seemed to challenge their recent loss in the war. Carter explains that the leaders were a diverse and politically moderate group, but they refused to consider Northern attitudes about the needs and expectations of the freedmen and the changes wrought by war and emancipation. The plantation economy and prewar attitudes toward black labor dominated the

thinking of Southern leaders, caused the failure of self reconstruction, and led to Northern insistence on a more thorough transformation of the South.

828.   Carter, Hodding. *Their Words Were Bullets: The Southern Press in War, Reconstruction, and Peace*. Athens: University of Georgia Press, 1969. 78p. Bibl. In Chapter 3 Carter, a Southern newspaper editor, focuses on the difficulties of maintaining a reform perspective in the Southern press during Reconstruction. During Reconstruction and in the decades that followed, much of the white press automatically responded in a negative way to criticism of the South. Carter also writes about the Southern press during the Civil War and in the 20th century.

829.   Cimprich, John. "A Critical Moment and Its Aftermath for George H. Thomas." In *The Moment of Decision: Biographical Essays on American Character and Regional Identity*. Edited by Randall M. Miller and John R. McKivigan. Westport: Greenwood Press, 1994. Pp. 173-187.   The experience of seeing black soldiers fight and die with courage at the Battle of Nashville in 1864 changed Major Gen. Thomas's negative view of blacks and nurtured respect for them as soldiers and as men. Cimprich discusses the various issues and problems that Thomas faced as commander of the Military Division of the Tennessee during Reconstruction, particularly Thomas's attempt to protect the rights of freedmen, encourage nonviolence, and put down violence as it occurred. He was disappointed in many of his fellow, white Southerners who refused to abide by the law, because they believed that they were being persecuted by the North.

830.   Cooper, William, Jr. and Thomas E. Terrill. *The American South: A History*. 2nd Edition. New York: McGraw Hill, 1996. 824p. Bibl. Ills. Maps. (First edition - New York: McGraw Hill, 1991)   The authors explain the political, social, and economic issues of Reconstruction and review the persistent myths that have colored perceptions of the period.   One chapter is devoted to economic issues of agriculture, sharecropping and tenant farming, the lack of economic opportunity for the freedmen, country merchants, railroads, and urban and industrial growth. The authors include an extensive bibliographic essay on Southern history.

831.   Coulter, E. Merton. *The South During Reconstruction*, 1865-1877. Baton Rouge: Louisiana State University, 1947. 426p. Bibl. Ill. Maps.   Coulter shows great sympathy for the plight of the South in its struggle against the Radical Republican program of Reconstruction.   Reconstruction was doomed to failure, and when the South finally defeated Reconstruction, it carried forward Southern traditions from prewar days into the future.   Coulter includes chapters on race relations, economics, agriculture, transportation, urbanization and industrialization, culture, fashion, education, and religion. (See also Coulter's "To the Editor, Pacific Historical Review," *Pacific Historical Review* 23 (November 1954): 425-429 in which he responds to highly critical comments on his book made by Howard K. Beale in "The Professional Historian: His Theory and Practice," *Pacific Historical Review* 22 (August 1953): 227-255; and John Hope Franklin (see # 93).   Both historians criticize Coulter's methodology and his bias in favor of the South.

832.   Cox, LaWanda. "Reflections on the Limits of Possibility." In *Freedom, Racism, and Reconstruction: Collected Writings of LaWanda Cox.* Edited by Donald G. Nieman. Athens: University of Georgia Press, 1997. Pp. 243-280. (Rpt. from *Lincoln and Black Freedom: A Study in Presidential Leadership,* Columbia: University of South Carolina, 1981, 142-184.)   Cox examines the possibilities for a more positive outcome for the freedmen during Reconstruction had Lincoln lived, had Johnson been more flexible, had racism and sectional pride not been so prevalent, had greater federal coercion been used in the South, and had the Republicans maintained unity in favor of Reconstruction policies. These and other issues created obstacles that were too formidable to allow a successful transformation of the slaves into free people with equal civil and economic status with whites. The key event was Lincoln's death and Johnson ascendancy to power.

833.   Cruden, Robert. *The Negro in Reconstruction.* Englewood Cliffs, N. J.: Prentice Hall, 1969. 182p. Bibl.   Based on the revisionist histories of the 1950s and 1960s, this book is intended to educate the layman about the new interpretations of Reconstruction. Cruden emphasizes the struggle of blacks to find meaning in their new found freedom by striving for equality of rights and freedoms with white citizens. Reconstruction represents the beginning of the struggle and a belief that a national commitment to equality was made, even if it went unfulfilled until another time.

834.   Davis, William C. "Confederate Exiles." *American History Illustrated* 5 (June 1979): 30-43. Ills.   Approximately 10,000 Confederates left the U.S. for Europe, South America, and the Middle East from the end of the war until 1870. Many believed their lives depended on exile, while others rejected the idea of living under the rule of the U.S. or eventually decided the life in Reconstruction was too bitter to bear. Davis believes that the self exile was a tragedy for the South because it denied the region the benefit of accumulated knowledge and leadership when the South needed it the most.

835.   Davison, Charles C. "Race Friction in the South Since 1865." Ph.D. Southern Baptist Theological Seminary, 1922.

836.   Dodd, William E. "Robert E. Lee and Reconstruction." *South Atlantic Quarterly* 4 (January 1905): 63-70.   Lee's published letters and recollections (*Recollections and Letters of Robert E. Lee,* New York: Doubleday, 1904) are used to explain his position of Reconstruction policy. Lee supported Johnson's policies toward the South and the idea that the educated class of blacks should be enfranchised. When Congress took control of Reconstruction, Lee reacted disapprovingly, but he discouraged fellow Southerners from leaving the country, and hoped that they would work to restore the South to prosperity.

837.   Donald, David Herbert. "A Generation of Defeat." In *From the Old South to the New: Essays on the Transitional South.* Westport: Greenwood Press, 1981. Pp. 3-20.   Reconstruction is mentioned in the context of the defeat and humiliation felt by white Southerners, particularly the men who fought in the Civil War and

survived until the end of the century. The survivors who were alive in the 1890s acted against black civil rights by supporting Jim Crow laws.

838.   Donald, Henderson H. *The Negro Freedman: Life Conditions of the American Negro in the Early Years After Emancipation.* New York: Henry Schuman, 1952. 270p. Bibl.   Donald covers all aspects of black life including their response and adjustment to emancipation, social and family life, education, religion, crime, politics, and race relations. In general, Henderson's approach is based on the premise that the freedmen were totally unprepared for life as free people. He believes that they reacted to their environment based mainly on their experiences as slaves. A mature appreciation of free labor, living within the law, and showing individual initiative developed slowly.

839.   Ellingsworth, Huber W. "Ben Hill Speaks Out." *Southern Speech Journal* 22 (Summer 1957): 233-241.   Benjamin Hill, a popular politician and postwar public speaker from Georgia, offered an eloquent and direct explanation of the South's position toward Reconstruction in a speech in New York City in early October, 1868. Ellingsworth praises Hill's honest and bold insistence that the South would never accept racial equality even though it recognized military defeat and black emancipation.

840.   Ezell, John Samuel. *The South Since 1865.* New York: Macmillan, 1963. 511p. Bibl. Ill. Maps.   Ezell focuses on how Southern society and culture changed after the Civil War and how it returned to the "mainstream" of American life. He views Reconstruction as the beginning of a new South, not reconstructing or rebuilding the old. The war and the period of Reconstruction reinforced for white Southerners, in general, the uniqueness of their region and the rightness of white supremacy. Ezell includes survey chapters on agriculture, industrialization, labor, education, culture and society in the South.

841.   Fletcher, Marvin. "The Negro Volunteer in Reconstruction 1865-1866." *Military History* 32 (December 1968): 124-131.   Fletcher discusses the behavior of black U.S. Army troops participating in the occupation of the South and the conflict that occurred between the troops and white residents. He believes that neither the black troops nor Southern whites tried to adjust to the new postwar environment. The inevitable problems were not the fault of the federal government because troops were needed. Complaints against black troops led to their withdrawal.

842.   Fraser, Walter J, Jr. and Winfred B. Moore, Jr. (eds.). *From the Old South to the New: Essays on the Transitional South.* Westport: Greenwood Press, 1981. 286p. Map. Tbls.   Includes a collection of papers presented at The Citadel Conferences on the South in 1978 and 1979. The essays address whether change or continuity was the dominant theme in Southern society after 1850. The essays on Reconstruction include David Donald (see # 837) on Southern memories of defeat; W. L. Barney (see # 1429) on attitudes toward change in Dallas County, Alabama; J. P. Radford (see # 2462) on the social structure and architectural forms in Charleston,

South Carolina; and R. L. F. Davis (see # 1210a) on black labor after 1865 in the Natchez region of Mississippi and Louisiana.

843.   Fredrickson, George M.   "After Emancipation: A Comparative Study of White Responses to the New Order of Race Relations in the American South, Jamaica, and the Cape Colony of South Africa." In *What Was Freedom's Price?* Edited by David Sansing. Jackson: University Press of Mississippi, 1978. Pp. 71-92.   Reconstruction in the South is considered the most radical of attempts to bring about change between the races compared with other societies granting emancipation to slaves in the 19th century.   Not only did the freedmen receive freedom suddenly, but they were granted more civil rights than freed people of color in Jamaica or South Africa.   The near total defiance of Southern white society to the Reconstruction laws and the success at building a white supremacist society was unmatched in Jamaica and South Africa until the implementation of apartheid in the mid-20th century.

844.   Gerteis, Louis S.   *From Contraband to Freedman: Federal Policies Toward Southern Blacks 1861-1865.*   Westport: Greenwood Press, 1973.   255p. Bibl.   The treatment of blacks by federal authorities during the Civil War was often contradictory and not based on concepts of reform and racial equality.   Federal policies set the tone for postwar Reconstruction, and that meant that reforms would be limited.   In general, Reconstruction began as soon as slaves were freed by Union troops, but Gerteis defines this freedom as quite limited, whether it relates to service in the Army, labor programs, or the Freedmen's Bureau.   In reality Black freedom did not lead to great hope for the future.   Gerteis examines the course of federal policy and the people who participated in it.   (See also Gerteis' Ph.D. dissertation with the same title from University of Wisconsin, 1969.)

845.   Gibson, Betty.   "'Reconstruction' and 'Readjustment': Some Comparisons and Contrasts."   *Filson Club Historical Quarterly* 35 (April 1961): 167-173.   The border states that chose to remain loyal to the Union in Reconstruction faced many of the same issues as former Confederate states.   Gibson briefly discusses events in Maryland, Kentucky, Delaware, Missouri, and West Virginia.   Like the former Confederate states, they had to cope with changes brought about by the emancipation of slaves, demands for black civil rights, the local imposition of federal laws and agencies, and the rise of local Republicans.   Unlike the Confederate states, the Democratic Party did not face the same degree of difficulty in securing power.

846.   Green, Fletcher.   "The South in Reconstruction, 1865-1880." In *Travels in the New South: A Bibliography. Vol. I. The Postwar South, 1865-1900: An Era of Reconstruction and Readjustment.*   Edited by Thomas D. Clark.   Norman: University of Oklahoma Press, 1962.   Pp. 3-125.   This is a bibliography of travelers' accounts of the South during Reconstruction.   Green includes appraisals of 245 books most of which were published between 1865 and 1880.   Each reference includes the dates of travel and the library owning the copy that was reviewed. Some of the works listed are promotional materials from railroads, state bureaus of

agriculture and immigration, and business opportunities. The travelers were mainly from England, France, Germany, Scotland, and the U.S.

847.   Hammett, Hugh B.   "Reconstruction History Before Dunning: Hilary Herbert and the South's Victory of the Books." *Alabama Review* 27 (July 1974): 185-196.   In 1890 Alabama Congressman Hilary Herbert completed a book providing a Southern perspective on Reconstruction (see # 852). Although it was written as a propaganda piece to influence a congressional election, the book became highly influential among Northern readers and future historians. Herbert's defense of the South was particularly influential on the work of William A. Dunning, Walter Lynwood Fleming, James Ford Rhodes, and Howard K. Beale. These historians recognized the propaganda nature of Herbert's book, but they found his themes to be quite compelling, particularly the theme of sectional reconciliation.

848.   Hanchette, William.   "Reconstruction History--From Poetry." *Midwest Quarterly* 7 (April 19660: 253-268.   Poetic verse from the postwar years illustrate the varied emotions of blacks and whites. Hanchette used the Harris Collection of American Verse at Brown University as the basis for his research.

849.   Harris, Anne Barber. "The South As Seen By Travelers, 1865-1880." Ph.D. University of North Carolina, 1967. 287p.

850.   Harris, Robert L. "The South in Defeat, 1865." Ph.D. Duke University, 1956.

851.   Hennessey, Melinda Martin. "To Live and Die in Dixie: Reconstruction Race Riots in the South." Ph.D. Kent State University, 1978.

852.   Herbert, Hilary A. (ed.). *Why the Solid South? or Reconstruction and Its Results*. Baltimore: R. H. Woodward, 1890. 452p. App.   This book includes chapters on Reconstruction in each Confederate state and Missouri. The chapters are written by different authors and clearly present the white, conservative perspective with the idea of establishing the truth about Reconstruction and the wrongs of federal intervention in the states. Herbert believes that this book may aid in the encouragement of economic investment in the South by healing sectional differences.   (See also Herbert's "Reconstruction, Lincoln-Johnson Plan and Congressional," in his book, *The Abolition Crusade and Its Consequences, Four Period of American History*, New York: Charles Scribner's Sons, 1912. Pp. 208-228.)

853.   Hesseltine, William B. and David L. Smiley. *The South in American History*. 2nd Edition. Englewood Cliffs: Printice Hall, 1960. 630p. Bibl. Ills. (Originally published with the title *A History of the South 1607-1936*, New York: Printice Hall, 1936. The title changed with the 1943 edition.) This book provides a synthesis of Southern history and includes three chapters on Reconstruction that remained virtually unchanged from the 1936 edition to the 1960 edition. Hesseltine

views Reconstruction as having greater long term impact on the South than the war. He emphasizes Republican corruption and disunity, as well as white revolutionary reaction to Republican rule, as the basis for the failure of Reconstruction governments. He faults the Republicans for abandoning blacks to the white Southern ruling class.

854.   Hill, Lawrence F.   "The Confederate Exodus to Latin America, I." *Southwestern Historical Quarterly* 39 (October 1935): 100-134.   Part I of a three part article discusses the reasons that at least 8,000-10,000 Southerners left the U.S. for Mexico, Central America and South America during the first three to four years following the Civil War.   Hill emphasizes several factors, but the most important issues were the loss of personal property, the mass destruction throughout the South, the rising power of former slaves, and a total lack of trust and faith in a prosperous, happy future.   Parts II (January 1936, 161-199) and III (April 1936, 309-326) describe the life of Southern emigrants in their new homes and the communities that they built.

855.   Jacobson, Timothy Curtis.   "Tradition and Change in the New South, 1865-1910." Ph.D. Vanderbilt University, 1974. 476p.

856.   Little, Robert D.   "The Ideology of the New South: A Study in the Development of Ideas, 1865-1910." Ph.D. University of Chicago, 1950. 117p.

857.   Litwack, Leon.   *Been in the Storm So Long: The Aftermath of Slavery.* New York: Alfred A. Knopf, 1979. 651p. Bibl.   Litwack uses interviews with former slaves and a variety of contemporary sources, including letters, diaries, and newspapers in his examination of the response of blacks and whites to the end of slavery and the changes that it brought in the early postwar years.   Blacks sought to understand and express their freedoms, while Southern whites sought to maintain their traditional society as closely as possible. Litwack also illustrates the responses of Northern missionaries, teachers, and others in their interaction with Southern society.   He shows that for freedmen, wartime and postwar emancipation and the beginning of Reconstruction reforms were a time of confusion, elation, self discovery, feelings of betrayal, and hope for the future.

858.   Litwack, Leon.   "'Blues Falling Down Like Hail': The Ordeal of Black Freedom."   In *New Perspectives in Race and Slavery in America: Essays in Honor of Kenneth M. Stampp.*   Edited by Robert H. Abzug and Stephen E. Maizlish. Lexington: University Press of Kentucky, 1986. Pp. 109-127.   Freedom did not bring prosperity and justice to former slaves, but they often agreed that it was much better than slavery. Litwack emphasizes this point and the freedman's desire to meet the standards of white American society for social, economic and political acceptance. But blacks learned quickly that there were no standards of progress that would guarantee their acceptance and personal safety.   In general, whites would not tolerate success or opportunity for blacks.   White supremacy included suppression of black progress, physical and mental persecution, and public lynchings.

859.   Logue, Cal M.   "The Rhetorical Appeals of Whites to Blacks During Reconstruction."   *Communication Monographs* 44 (August 1977): 241-251. Logue examines how Southern whites tried to cope with the new status of the former slaves by attempting to persuade or control them through the force of their rhetoric as it appeared in newspapers and in public addresses.   Whites were generally resentful of black participation in public affairs, and they frequently attacked them openly or through veiled threats, paternalistic phrases, and the use of a black speaker in an antiblack campaign.   The rhetorical intimidation of blacks was mainly a monologue because blacks were no longer a captive audience as they were before the Civil War.

860.   Logue, Cal M.   "Rhetorical Ridicule of Reconstruction Blacks."   *Quarterly Journal of Speech* 62 (December 1976): 400-409.   Ills.   Many Southern newspapers, periodicals, and speeches consciously and systematically used rhetoric to create negative images of blacks.   The images were based on white perceptions of blacks from slavery and their resentment of Radical Reconstruction.   Logue explains that a linguistic tradition of racism developed from the Reconstruction period that persists to this day.

861.   Maddex, Jack P., Jr.   *The Reconstruction of Edward A. Pollard: A Rebel's Conversion to Postbellum Unionism.*   Chapel Hill: University of North Carolina Press, 1974. 110p. Bibl.   Pollard became known before the Civil War for his strong defense of slavery and the national ideals of the Confederacy.   After the war he gradually accepted Unionism and the Republican Party, but maintained support for white supremacy.   Maddex views Pollard's change in "worldview" as a "falsification of collective memory, smoothing over the transition from the Old South to the new America."   (p. 84)   Frequent references are made to Pollard's writings, including *The Lost Cause* (1866), *The Lost Cause Regained* (1868), and other histories of war, politics, and race.

862.   Mahen, Harold E.   "'We Feel to Bee a People':   Historiographical Perspectives on Blacks in Emancipation and Reconstruction."   *Maryland Historian* 26 (Spring-Summer 1985): 41-56.   Mahan discusses historical writing from the late 19th century to the 1990s that focuses on whether blacks actively asserted their freedom or were passive in their approach.   The trend has been toward emphasizing black assertiveness, particularly in the literature of the 1960s and 1970s.   Historical writing clearly reflects contemporary social and cultural ideas.

863.   McDonald, Archie P.   "Travel Notes of Reconstruction Days."   *Louisiana Studies* 8 (Fall 1869): 268-276.   McDonald offers a brief account of six travel accounts written about the South.   He covers works by Sidney Andrews, Whitelaw Reid, John T. Trowbrdige, Robert Somers, Charles Nordhoff, and Sir George Campbell.   These accounts are valuable for the insight of the outsider, even though they reflect personal prejudices.

864.   Moger, Allen W.   "Letters to General Lee After the War."   *Virginia Magazine of History and Biography* 64 (January 1956): 30-69.   Robert E. Lee

received thousands of letters from fellow white Southerners after the war expressing their anger and fears about the future, and they frequently asked for Lee's advise. Moger discusses these communications, including letters to Lee and letters that Lee's responses. Lee encouraged people to stay home and rebuild their lives as loyal Southerners and loyal Americans. He served as an enduring example of healing in his work as president of Washington College (later Washington and Lee) in Virginia, and he helped many people cope with the new postwar environment.

865. Newby, I. A. *The South: A History*. New York: Holt, Rinehart, and Winston, 1978. 559p. Newby's chapter on Reconstruction is mainly an analysis of the period rather than descriptive history. He views the period as having long lasting negative effects on the South due to the white over reaction to black freedom, civil rights reforms, political change, and the racial fears and hatreds that arose from desperation to maintain white supremacy.

866. Nieman, Donald G. (ed.) *African-American Life in the Post-Emancipation South*. 12 Vols. New York: Garland, 1994. The set includes articles previously published in a variety of journals and books. Each relevant article is included in this bibliography with a citation to the original source.

867. Nieman, Donald G. "From Slaves to Citizens: African-Americans Rights, Consciousness, and Reconstruction." *Cardozo Law Review* 17 (May 1996): 2115-2139. Nieman explains the development of black consciousness and action to demand and implement freedoms made legal by constitutional reforms. Freedmen learned from free blacks, the Freedmen's Bureau, Northern missionaries, and by actively participating in the politics and economy of the South. Even though Democratic regimes and violence reduced the equalitarian institutions that blacks struggled to maintain, the experience was not forgotten. This essay is followed by critical comments by Robert J. Kaczorowski (p. 2141-2147) and Randall Kennedy (p. 2149-2151).

868. Nolen, Claude H. *The Negro's Image in the South: The Anatomy of White Supremacy*. Lexington: University of Kentucky Press, 1967. 232p. Bibl. Nolen investigates the Southern white vision of blacks from the early days of American slavery until 1900. Many whites defended white supremacy based on scientific, scriptural, and historical bases. By the time of emancipation and Reconstruction, this historical inheritance was part of the Southern white culture and the reason for their opposition to black voting rights, and unlimited black aspirations in education, politics, and careers. Whites wanted to avoid any suggestion of racial equality. (See also Nolen's "Aftermath of Slavery: Southern Attitudes Towards Negroes, 1865-1900." Ph.D. University of Texas, 1963.)

869. Olsen, Otto H. "Southern Reconstruction and the Question of Self-Determination." In *A Nation Divided: Problems and Issues of the Civil War and Reconstruction*. Edited by George M. Fredrickson. Minneapolis: Burgess Publishing Co., 1975. pp. 113-141. Historians have not focused on the essential fact of Southern cultural independence as the main ingredient leading to the failure

of Radical Reconstruction. Northern attempts to coerce the South led to violence. Although the South did not practice moderation during the early postwar years, the congressional response to Southern attitudes did not recognize the reality of a distinctive South that focused on local power and resistance to change.

870.   Page, Thomas Nelson. "The Southern People During Reconstruction." *Atlantic Monthly* 88 (September 1901): 289-304.   This is a long lament over the deleterious impact of Reconstruction on the property and people in the South by the writer of novels set in Reconstruction. Page believes that Reconstruction actually cost the South more in most respects than the Civil War. He criticizes the attempt by Congress to legislate racial equality because it misled blacks and degraded their skills.

871.   Perman, Michael. "The South and Congress's Reconstruction Policy, 1866-1867." *Journal of American Studies* 4 (February 1871): 181-200.   Perman concentrates on the six months prior to the passage of the Reconstruction Acts in March, 1867 when the Southern states decided that they would not approve the 14th Amendment. The amendment was actually a chance for the South to accept a moderate plan of Reconstruction, but Southern leaders and journalists distrusted the Republican Party and believed that accepting the amendment would lead to demands for more concessions, including suffrage for the freedmen. Southern pride and refusal to voluntarily give away white Democratic power made the rejection of the 14th Amendment assured and led to harsher measures by Congress. Perman wonders why moderate Republicans expected the South to compromise.

872.   Pfanz, Harry Willcox. "Soldiering in the South During the Reconstruction Period, 1865-1877." 2 Vols. Ph.D. Ohio State University, 1958. 735p.

873.   Pressly, Thomas J. "Reconstruction in the Southern United States: A Comparative Perspective." *Magazine of History* [OAH] 4, 1 (1989): 14-33. Ills. Map. Tbl.   The impact of emancipation in the South is compared with emancipations in other nations, particularly Haiti, Jamaica, Russia, Cuba, Brazil and Zaria in northern Nigeria. The basis of the comparison is the ex-slave's success at gaining land, political power, education, and improved living conditions.

874.   Rabinowitz, Harold N. "From Exclusion to Segregation: Southern Race Relations, 1865-1890." *Journal of American History* 63 (September 1976): 325-350.   The immediate postwar years from 1865 to 1867 were a time when conservative, white governments continued the antebellum tradition of excluding blacks from public and private facilities. The Freedmen's Bureau and the Reconstruction policy of Congress changed the tradition from exclusion to segregation. Integration was rare, and despite the Civil Rights Acts of 1866 and 1875, customs were more powerful than laws. Blacks usually agreed to the segregation, because they believed it was the best that they could get in a hostile environment. Even though C. Vann Woodward emphasized the 1890s and early 20th century as the time when legal segregation first developed, the segregation laws simply affirmed a practice entrenched since Reconstruction. (See also Rabinowitz's

"From Exclusion to Segregation: Health and Welfare Services For Southern Blacks 1865-1890." *Social Services Review* 48 (September 1974): 327-354 that focuses on segregation in social and health services.)

875.   Rabinowitz, Howard N.   "More Than the Woodward Thesis: Assessing *The Strange Career of Jim Crow."* *Journal of American History* 75 (December 1988): 842-856; Woodward, C. Vann. "Strange Career Critics: Long May They Persevere." *Journal of American History* 75 (December 1988): 857-868. Port. Criticisms of Woodward's book about the history of race relations in America have included points relevant to the study of Reconstruction, because the debate involves the origins of racial segregation.   Critics have focused on the existence of segregation during and prior to Reconstruction.   Woodward put much more emphasis on the *de jure* segregation in the South of the late 19th and early 20th centuries. He responds to criticism by saying that his own focus on the timing of segregation was not appropriate and that more important considerations should be where and how segregation occurred.

876.   Rabinowitz, Howard N. *Race Relations in the Urban South, 1865-1890.* New York: Oxford University Press, 1978. 441p. Bibl. Tbls.   Rabinowitz examines race relations in Atlanta, Montgomery, Nashville, Raleigh and Richmond. He studies how blacks made the transition from slavery to freedom in urban settings; the relationship between large scale black migration to cities and the resulting conflict over civil rights and segregation; and the role of urban areas in Reconstruction.   Freedom and racism combined to increase the expectations and frustrations of freed slaves and their children, while the white community sought control of the black population through the creation of a caste society. (See also Rabinowitz's "The Search for Social Control: Race Relations in the Urban South, 1865-1890." 2 Vols. Ph.D. University of Chicago, 1973. 936p.)

877.   Rabinowitz, Howard N.   "Segregation and Reconstruction." In *The Facts of Reconstruction: Essays in Honor of John Hope Franklin.* Baton Rouge: Louisiana State University Press, 1991. Pp. 79-97.   Rabinowitz reviews the debate among historians about the origins of racial segregation in the U.S.   C. Vann Woodward and others focus on the 1890s, but some historians have documented segregation before the Civil War and during Reconstruction. The debate is confused by definitions and terms regarding the types and degrees of segregation, but Rabinowitz emphasizes that more research is necessary on *de facto* versus *de jure* segregation on one hand and how they relate to the commencement of institutional separation of the races. During Reconstruction "the real issue was not segregation as such, but equal treatment within a segregated society" (p. 97).

878.   Rable, George C.   "Bourbonism, Reconstruction and the Persistence of Southern Distinctiveness." *Civil War History* 29 (June 1983): 135-153.   Rable suggests that the military defeat of the South did not mark a turning point in Southern culture as many historians have suggested.   He examines the writings of newspaper editors and politicians to illustrate the essential continuity in Southern thought about the South from antebellum days through Reconstruction. Expressions

of longing for the culture of plantation slavery continued as did racist ideology, paternalism, persistent Southern nationalism, the "politics of personal honor" (p. 153), and a "rigid constitutionalism" (p. 153). These characteristics determined the white South's response to Reconstruction.

879.   Reagan, John. "Southern Political Views, 1865." *Publications of the Southern History Association* 6 (1902): 132-142; 210-219.   Includes Reagan's letter to President Johnson pleading the South's case against punishment and black suffrage.

880.   Reed, Spencer Harris. "British Travelers in the United States, 1835-1870." Ph.D. American University, 1931.

881.   Ritter, Charles Francis. "The Press in Florida, Louisiana, and South Carolina and the End of Reconstruction, 1865-1877." Ph.D. Catholic University of America, 1976. 321p.

882.   Roark, James L. *Masters Without Slaves: Southern Planters in the Civil War and Reconstruction.* New York: W. W. Norton, 1977. 273p. Bibl.   By relying on the letters, diaries, and notebooks from about 170 planter families throughout the Southern states, Roark describes the period from the perspective of the planter class as the institution of slavery disappeared. Slavery was the most important element holding together the plantation economy and culture. After emancipation many planters made adjustments to maintain their livelihood, but the loss of slavery brought down a way of life. Henceforth they relied on white supremacy, segregation, and labor controls, but their lives were transformed and their self identity was shattered forever. (See also Roark's Ph.D. dissertation with the same title from Stanford University, 1973.)

883.   Rose, Willie Lee. "Jubilee and Beyond: What Was Freedom?" In *What Was Freedom's Price?* Edited by David Sansing. Jackson: University Press of Mississippi, 1978. Pp. 3-20.   Rose discusses characteristics of emancipation and Reconstruction that historians use to explain why it was either a revolutionary period, an abortive revolution, or just one step beyond slavery. For the freedmen it certainly was a revolutionary time when dramatic changes occurred in their immediate condition and their was hope for a future that would broaden and confirm their freedom.

884.   Russ, William A., Jr. "Administrative Activities of the Union Army During and After the Civil War." *Mississippi Law Journal* 17 (May 1945): 71-89. Russ criticizes the use of the Union Army to assist the federal government with reconstructing the Southern states during and after the war. After the imposition of congressional Reconstruction in 1867, the use of the military to perform political work in the South was nothing short of declaring war once again.

885.   Rutherford, Miss. "Reconstruction Days-1865-76." *Confederate Veteran* 32 (August 1924): 305-307.   The author describes the very poor state of life during

the period and the resentments of white Southerners who felt persecuted, degraded, and that all was lost.

886.   Sansing,   David G.   (ed.).   *What Was Freedom's Price?*   Jackson: University Press of Mississippi, 1978. 126p.   This book includes six original essays reflecting current research on the transition from slavery to freedom in the South. The essays cover the meaning of freedom (see # 883); black identity and W. E. B. DuBois (see # 902); the economics of sharecropping (see # 1290); white responses to emancipation in various countries (see # 843); and international responses to emancipation (see # 907).

887.   Shaffer, Donald Robert. "Marching On: African-American Civil War Veterans In Postbellum America, 1865-1951." Ph.D. University of Maryland, 1996. 336p.

888.   Shapiro, Herbert. "Afro-American Responses to Race Violence During Reconstruction." *Science and Society* 36 (Summer 1972): 158-170.   Shapiro explains that blacks responded in various ways to white violence, including revenge, restraint, and retreat. Taken together they responded heroically when white allies refused to help them.

889.   Simkins, Francis Butler. *A History of the South*. 3rd Edition. New York: Alfred A. Knopf, 1963. 675p. Bibl. Ills. (Earlier editions, New York: Knopf, 1953; *The South Old and New: A History 1820-1947*, New York: Knopf, 1947) Simkins views Reconstruction as an experiment in social and political reform. He notes the positive developments of Reconstruction but judges it as a failure because black Americans emerged from the period weak and without equal rights. Despite the war and the social and economic changes of Reconstruction, the South's fundamental belief system from before the war remained intact. The persistence of antebellum values was evident from the bitterness generated by Republican reforms and black demands for equality.

890.   Smith, John David.   "The Old Arguments Anew: Proslavery and Antislavery Thought During Reconstruction." *Kentucky Review* 6 (Winter 1986): 3-23.   Using contemporary writing, Smith illustrates how important the issue of slavery was in the South after emancipation. Slavery defined sectional identification for most white Southerners, and they resisted treating blacks any differently than they did before the war. This attitude fueled Radical Reconstruction and generated nostalgic images in American literature of an institution characterized by contented slaves whose lives were ruined by freedom.

891.   Smith, John David. *An Old Creed For the New South: Proslavery Ideology and Historiography, 1865-1918*. Westport: Greenwood Press, 1985. 314p. Bibl.   Part one of Smith's book focuses on the postwar obsession of most white Southerners with the image of blacks as slaves and how this obsession was expressed in a wide variety of sources. The proslavery argument persisted during Reconstruction and beyond. The persistent proslavery attitude of Southern whites

was met by strong antislavery attitudes of most Northern whites, despite their deep seated racism. Smith examines the postwar clash of ideas about slavery and the place of blacks in American society. Part two of this book is a discussion of historical writing on the proslavery argument.

892.   Sowle, Patrick. "The Abolition of Slavery." *Georgia Historical Quarterly* 52 (September 1968): 237-255.   Sowle focuses mostly on the new relationship between Southern whites and blacks following emancipation. The new relationship is presented from the perspective of whites, particularly former slave owners and the ways devised to control the freedmen.

893.   Stover, John F. "The Ruined Railroads of the Confederacy." *Georgia Historical Quarterly* 42 (December 1958): 376-388.   More than half of the railroads in the South were either destroyed or in need of repair at the end of the Civil War. This condition made travel difficult. During the fall of 1865 four visitors to the South toured parts of the region and reported in published books about the conditions of rail travel. The travelers were Englishman John H. Kennaway, and Northerners Sidney Andrews, Whitelaw Reid, and John T. Trowbridge.

894.   Suggs, Henry Lewis (ed.). *The Black Press in the South, 1865-1979.* Westport: Greenwood Press, 1983. 468p. Bibl.   This book offers a state by state account of the development of the black press in Alabama, Arkansas, Florida, Georgia, Louisiana, Mississippi, North Carolina, South Carolina, Tennessee, Texas, and Virginia.   Each article, written by a different historian, provides brief information about the press during Reconstruction.

895.   Sutherland, Daniel E. "Former Confederates in the Post Civil War North: An Unexplained Aspect of Reconstruction History." *Journal of Southern History* 47 (August 1981): 393-410. Tbls.   Thousands of Southerners migrated out of the South to other countries and to the Northern states after the Civil War. Sutherland compiles characteristics of 198 emigrants in the North who were mostly under 40 years of age and professionals or students who had some connection to the North through friends, family, school, or prior residence. They tended to be a proud, often close knit group in urban areas. The migrants mingled with Northerners and influenced North-South reconciliation, or at least the views of some Northerners toward Southern people as distinct from the South. (See also Sutherland's "Exiles, Emigrants, and Sojourners: The Post-Civil War Confederate Exodus in Perspective." *Civil War History* 31 (September 1985): 237-256 in which he explains the main reasons for the exodus - land, jobs, education, adventure, a brighter future, emancipation and war bitterness.)

896.   Tate, William (ed.). "A Robert E. Lee Letter on Abandoning the South After the War." *Georgia Historical Quarterly* 37 (September 1953): 255-256. Lee wrote to a former Confederate soldier who asked for advice about emigrating to another country following the Civil War. Lee advised his as he advised others, to stay at home and help to "sustain and restore" (p. 255) the South.

897.   Toll, William. "Free Men, Freedmen, and Race: Black Social Theory in the Gilded Age." *Journal of Southern History* 44 (November 1976): 571-596. Toll discusses the developing relationship between free black intellectuals and writers and the freedmen from Reconstruction to the 1890s. During Reconstruction the writers depicted the freedmen as socially and culturally disabled and unfit for the responsibilities of citizenship, but they also wrote about how to reform the freedmen. Toll reviews the writings of men, such as John S. Fortune, Archibald Henry Grimké, George Washington Williams, and John Mercer Langston.

898.   Wagstaff, Thomas. "Call Your Old Master - 'Master': Southern Political Leaders and Negro Labor During Presidential Reconstruction." *Labor History* 10 (Summer 1969): 232-345.   During 1865-1866 Northern and Southern leaders discussed and debated the meaning of emancipation for black labor and race relations. Wagstaff examines what the leaders said, which generally included acceptance of black freedom and the need for black improvement, but they also insisted that blacks rely only on themselves, not the government. Underlying this view was the acceptance by blacks of an inferior status in American society.

899.   Wiggins, William H., Jr. "'Free at Last!': A Study of Afro-American Emancipation Day Celebrations." 2 vols. Ph.D. Indiana University, 1974. 509p.

900.   Wiley, Bell Irvin. *Southern Negroes 1861-1865*. New Haven: Yale University Press, 1965. 366p. Bibl. (Repr. of 1938 ed. by Yale)   Wiley focuses on the role of blacks in the Civil War, first under the Confederates and then under the Union military. In the second part of the book Wiley discusses the changes that occurred for the freedmen with regard to their labor for the Union Army and plantation owners, the education provided by the Army, and their participation in the war as soldiers. In general, the freedom that was the dream of many slaves did not materialize after emancipation. While some progress was made in education and military service, the treatment that the freedmen received by federal authorities was dreadful, whether they were soldiers, laborers, or contraband seeking protection. Early wartime signs of Reconstruction revealed that a vigorous struggle for real change would be necessary in the postwar years.

901.   Williamson, Joel. "Black Self-Assertion Before and After Emancipation." In *Key Issue in the Afro-American Experience*. Vol. 1. Edited by Nathan I. Huggins et. al. New York: Harcourt Brace Jovanovich, 1971. Pp. 213-239.   Black assertiveness was the basis for whatever progress they made in Reconstruction. This assertiveness in politics, church organization, labor and other affairs was consistent with the assertiveness that was exercised and suppressed during slavery. Emancipation revealed that many freedmen understood and sought to live a life equivalent with whites.

902.   Williamson, Joel.   "W. E. B. DuBois as a Hegelian." In *What Was Freedom's Price?*   Edited by David Sansing.   Jackson: University Press of Mississippi, 1978. Pp. 21-49.   Williamson views Reconstruction as a period when Northern whites attempted to eliminate a distinctive black culture and make the

freedmen more like the white race. It was also a period when blacks strove to integrate themselves culturally into the white race, but blacks were left with no cultural basis at all. Only in the late 19th century and the 20th century did blacks regroup under the leadership of DuBois to discover and redefine their black culture and black soul. DuBois used Hegelian philosophy to provide a foundation for his approach to racial identity.

903.   Wood, Forrest G. *Black Scare: The Racist Response to Emancipation and Reconstruction.* Berkeley: University of California Press, 1970, c1968.   219p. Bibl. Ills.   The emancipation of the slaves and the movement toward establishing racial equality in politics and society generated strong negative reactions from many whites. Racial prejudice based on white supremacy had a long history in the U.S., but it was the radical changes of the Civil War and its aftermath that caused a sudden violent response among some whites. The Northern white public sought justice, but they were apathetic and never seriously considered racial equality. Although Reconstruction offered black Americans the promise of freedom and equality, it was also a period when virulent racism took hold among many white Americans for a long time to come.

904.   Wood, Peter H. and Karen C. C. Dalton. *Winslow Homer's Images of Blacks: The Civil War and Reconstruction Years.* Austin: The Menil Collection. University of Texas Press, 1990. 144p. Chron. Ills.   This exhibit catalog of reproductions of mainly Homer paintings and sketches depicts Southern blacks during a time of national upheaval and change in their lives. The images are sympathetic and nonpolitical and show soldiers, children, women and men set in situations that have historical context. The authors interpret the social and cultural context of Homer's work in the context of the Civil War and the postwar years. In general, Homer's paintings of blacks represented a departure from other contemporary artistic work that reflect white stereotypes and prejudices. Included is an "Exhibit Checklist", a "Winslow Homer Chronology, 1850-79", and a chronology of "Images of Black Americans in Art, 1850-79."

905.   Woodward, C. Vann. *American Counterpoint: Slavery and Racism in the North-South Dialogue.* Boston: Little, Brown and Co., 1971, c1964. 301p.   The themes of revisionist historiography on Reconstruction are included in this survey of 19th century Southern history from both a national and international perspective. Woodward recognizes persistent themes of race relations, racial equality, white supremacy and sectional distinctiveness in Southern history. He believes that Reconstruction was not successful because it did not do justice to blacks. The Republicans and former abolitionists generally lost their fire for reform or enacted legislation that was only weakly enforced. The North-South agreement on white supremacy in America led to the weakening of a genuine, dedicated attempt to eliminate slavery and the racial attitudes that were its foundation. Woodward acknowledges that more enlightened racial attitudes would not be the result of war, legislation and half hearted force.

906.   Woodward, C. Vann. *The Burden of Southern History*. Baton Rouge: Louisiana State University Press, 1960. 205p.   Of the 8 essays in this book one focuses on Reconstruction. Taken together the 8 essays serve as an exploration into the place of the South in American history and key themes in Southern history. Woodward notes that the white South built a fence around supposedly sacred institutions and perceived ways of life that helped to form a peculiar, historical perspective. But the basis of this Southern perspective was transitory in the larger scheme of history.

907.   Woodward, C. Vann. "The Price of Freedom." In *What Was Freedom's Price?* Edited by David E. Sansing. Jackson: University Press of Mississippi, 1978. Pp. 93-113.   Woodward compares the emancipation and initial freedom of slaves and the response of their former masters and governing authorities in the the American South, West Indies, Spanish South America and Brazil. Of the societies that he explores, Woodward believes that in a comparative sense, the U.S. seemed to promise the most for its freedmen, but the result was the greatest of failures in the context of American society. The South united as never before in favor of white supremacy, and they were joined by the North.

908.   Wynes, Charles E. (ed.). *The Negro in the South Since 1865: Essays in American Negro History*. University, Ala.: University of Alabama Press, 1965. 263p.   The collection of previously published essays includes two that focus significantly on Reconstruction (see # 296, 1055).

909.   Wynes, Charles E. "The Race Question in the South as Viewed by British Travelers, 1865-1914." *Louisiana Studies* 8 (Fall 1974): 223-239.   Wynes reviews the comments written by several British travelers in the South on black labor and the opinions of whites about living with the freedmen. British travelers tended to analyze the black character and stereotype them positively or negatively. Some of the observers were John Edward Hillary Skinner, Charles Wentworth Dilke, David Macrae, Robert Somers, Sir George Campbell, and Francis Butler Leigh.

910.   Young, James Harvey. "A Woman Abolitionist Views the South in 1875." *Georgia Historical Quarterly* 32 (December 1948): 241-251.   Anna Elizabeth Dickenson, a dedicated abolitionist from Philadelphia, toured Virginia, North Carolina, South Carolina, Georgia, and Tennessee during the spring of 1875. She continued her earlier anti-Southern rhetoric in her speeches and visits to Union war memorials and sites of Confederate war prisons. Dickenson's views were tempered during her trip as she seemed to gain greater understanding for Southern problems

Postwar Politics

911.   Abbott, Martin. "Voices of Freedom: The Response of Southern Freedmen to Liberty." *Phylon* 34 (December 1973): 399-405.   Abbott surveys

public statements from several black conventions in the South between 1865 and 1869 to illustrate the tone and mood of blacks regarding their new freedom. They commonly called on federal and state governments and Southern white citizens in general to understand and respond to their desire for equal justice and treatment, particularly relating to the right to vote, labor contracts, and the criminal and civil justice system.

912.   Abbott, Richard H. "Black Ministers and the Organization of the Republican Party in the South in 1867: Letters From the Field." *Hayes Historical Journal* 6 (Fall 1976): 23-35. Ill. Ports.   After the passage of the Reconstruction Acts of March, 1867 the Republican Party organized an effort to gain the support of potential black voters in the South. Speakers were hired to spread the Republican message in a political and religious context and to ensure blacks did not drift to the Democrats. Letters written in the summer of 1867 are reprinted from four black speakers who participated in the effort, including Henry McNeal Turner, James Lynch, John Costin, and John Givens.

913.   Abbott, Richard H. "Civil War Origins of the Southern Republican Press." *Civil War History* 43 (March 1997): 38-58.   As Union forces moved into the South during the Civil War, Republican newspapers were established. Local Unionist newspapers were founded as well, either after the arrival of Union troops or behind Confederate lines. The federal government and the Army realized that promoting friendly sources of public information could help gather support for breaking down the Confederacy. Although Republican and Unionist newspapers proliferated where there were pockets of Unionist support, the ideas that they expressed varied significantly, and they usually closed within a couple of years.   Republican newspapers in the South did not flourish until the formation of Republican regimes after the passage of the Reconstruction Acts of 1867.

914.   Abbott, Richard H. *The Republican Party in the South, 1855-1877: The First Southern Strategy.* Chapel Hill: University of North Carolina Press, 1986. 303p.   Bibl.   Abbott mainly focuses on 1865 to 1868 when the national Republican Party had an opportunity to build a base of support in the South. But in their words and deeds, Northern Republicans usually showed very little interest in creating a strong Republican following.   Legislative actions and constitutional amendments were meant to either help the freedmen or secure Republican votes in the North. In reality, Northern Republican support of the Southern Republicans was weak and based more on appeasing white voters. A strong Republican Party in the South was unlikely anyway given the sectional animosity following the Civil War and the actions of the Radicals in Congress.

915.   Alexander, Thomas B. "Persistent Whiggery in the Confederate South 1860-1877." *Journal of Southern History* 27 (August 1961): 305-329.   Whig electoral candidates became more popular in the Confederacy than during antebellum days due to their antiwar position. A Whig-Unionist alliance took control of most Southern state governments after the war in 1865. Generally the Whigs were politically conservative. They agreed to the black codes and rejected

the 14th Amendment, but they played a prominent role in Republican state governments.   The fall of the Radical regimes beginning in 1870 represented victories for conservative Whigs, not Democrats.   By 1877 most Whigs reluctantly migrated to the Democratic Party.

916.   Allen, Ward. "A Note on the Origin of the Ku Klux Klan." *Tennessee Historical Quarterly* 23 (June 1964): 182.   The possible origin of the name of the Klan may be found in a passage from the travels of Pausanius written in Greek.

917.   Andrews, Norman A. "The Negro in Politics." *Journal of Negro History* 5 (October 1920): 420-436.   The traditional notion of black political domination and corruption in the South was either wrong or exaggerated.   Blacks relied on whites to take leadership positions and whites dominated state governments and committed most of the corruption.   Andrews views Reconstruction has a political success because it brought greater democracy to the South, poor whites were politically emancipated, and judicial and educational reforms were instituted for blacks.

918.   Aptheker, Herbert.   "Organizational Activities of Southern Negroes, 1865."   In *To Be Free: Studies in American Negro History.*   New York: International Publications, 1948.   Pp. 136-162.   Blacks throughout the South actively sought their rights as free citizens and to protest when their rights were being denied.   Conventions were held and petitions were sent to state constitutional conventions, state officials, and President Johnson.

919.   Avillo, Philip J., Jr.   "Ballots For the Faithful: The Oath and the Emergence of Slave State Republican Congressmen, 1861-1867." *Civil War History* 22 (June 1976): 164-174. Tbl.   The test oath was an important tool that eliminated many voters in the border states who were partial to the Confederacy.   The oath opened the way for Republicans in Missouri, Kentucky, West Virginia, and Maryland to gain political office and contribute to the Republican Reconstruction plan.   Avillo points out that Republican congressmen were more interested in placing restrictions on disloyal citizens than with equal rights for freedmen.

920.   Balk, Jacqueline and Ari Hoogenboom.   "The Origins of Border State Liberal Republicanism." *Radicalism, Racism, and Party Realignment, the Border States During Reconstruction.*   Edited by R. O. Curry.   Baltimore: Johns Hopkins Press, 1969.   Pp. 220-244.   Liberal Republicanism in Kentucky, Maryland, Missouri, and West Virginia was the result of years of progressive factionalism in the local Democratic and Republican parties.   Social and economic issues, as well as personal political gain, played an important role in bringing moderates in both parties together to seek new leadership and new solutions.   The authors view the movement as basically weak, opportunistic, and unable to produce success.   The shifting political factionalism and instability in the border states points to underlying reasons for the failure of the party.

921.   Bancroft, Frederic. *A Sketch of the Negro in Politics Especially in South Carolina and Mississippi.* Ph.D. Columbia University, 1885. (Published by New York: J. F. Pearson, 1885; New York: AMS Press, 1976.)

922.   Bell, John. "Constitutions and Politics: Constitutional Revision in the South Atlantic States, 1864-1902." Ph.D. University of North Carolina, 1970. 503p.

923.   Bennett, Lerone, Jr. *Black Power, U.S.A.: The Human Side of Reconstruction.* Chicago: Johnson Publishing Co., 1967. 401p. Bibl. Ill. Ports. Bennett emphasizes the real political power garnered by blacks and the positive things that they did during Reconstruction. He highlights the leadership of many black politicians and the enhancement of democratic government prior to the return of white Democratic Party regimes. Particular attention is directed to events in South Carolina, Louisiana, and Mississippi.

924.   Breese, Donald Hubert. "Politics in the Lower South During Presidential Reconstruction, April to November, 1865." Ph.D. University of California, Los Angeles, 1964. 438p.

925.   Brock, Euline W. *Black Political Leadership During Reconstruction.* Ph.D. University of North Texas, 1974. 375p.

926.   Brown, William G. "The Ku Klux Movement." *Atlantic Monthly* 87 (May 1901): 634-644.   Brown writes that the Klan and similar organizations, such as the Knights of the White Camellia, represented a popular movement of white Southerners against the evils of Reconstruction.   He cites the carpetbagger governments, Union Leagues, expansion of black political power, and the Freedmen's Bureau as evidence of Northern interference in the South.   The white reaction was normal, and even though the violence was unfortunate, Klan members had a goal worth fighting for.

927.   Chalmers, David. Rule of Terror: The History of the Ku Klux Klan. *American History Illustrated* 14, 9 (1980): 8-10; 14, 10 (1980): 44-48.   Chalmers depicts the Klan as a terrorist organization that used violence and intimidation against blacks and white Republicans.   Their motives were to crush Republican political power, put blacks in their "place", and punish suspects of petty thefts. Chalmers dispels traditional legends used to justify Klan activities.

928.   Chalmers, H. H. "The Effects of Negro Suffrage." *North American Review* 132 (1881): 239-248.   Chalmers believes that the enfranchisement of black Americans has not created political stability and, where their numbers are large, there has been and will be negative political effects throughout the U.S., particularly in the South. But he recognizes the permanence of black suffrage and calls on the white South to accept it as a fact for all time.

929.   Claude, Richard. "Constitutional Voting Rights and Early U.S. Supreme Court Doctrine." *Journal of Negro History* 51 (April 1966): 114-124.   Claude surveys the rulings of the Supreme Court to denials of voting privileges following the passage of the 14th and 15th Amendments. During Reconstruction the court found that the constitution does not guarantee citizens the right to vote because the amendments do not specifically define the rights of citizens. The court decided that qualifications for voting resided with the states, not with the federal government.

930.   Cook, Walter Henry. *Secret Political Societies in the South During the Period of Reconstruction: An Address Before the Faculty and Friends of Western Reserve University, Cleveland, Ohio.* 1914. 29p.   Cook delivers a thoroughly biased and racist account of Reconstruction from the white Southern perspective as a prelude to defending the activities of the Ku Klux Klan.

931.   Current, Richard N. "Reconstruction Without Regeneration, 1860-1870s." In *Northernizing the South.* Athens: University of Georgia, 1985. Pp. 50-82. Current emphasizes white Southern resistance and hostility to the attempted reform of their society by Northern Republicans.

932.   Current, Richard N. *Those Terrible Carpetbaggers.* New York: Oxford University Press, 1988. 475p. Ports.   Current provides a history of Reconstruction through the eyes of ten prominent carpetbaggers: Henry Clay Warmoth (Louisiana), Harrison Reed (Florida), George E. Spencer (Alabama), Willard Warner (Alabama), Albert T. Morgan (Mississippi), Robert K. Scott (South Carolina), Albion W. Tourgée (North Carolina), Daniel H. Chamberlain (South Carolina), Adelbert Ames (Mississippi), and Powell Clayton (Arkansas).   He examines their backgrounds and what they did and said in comparison with the propaganda of conservative whites who claimed that all carpetbaggers were, by definition, ignorant, illiterate, corrupt, and self seeking plunderers. He concludes that these ten men generally did not fit the negative stereotype, and even at their worst, they were no worse than their Southern detractors. The main reason for the low reputation of the carpetbaggers was their attempt to establish a new basis for race relations in the South.

933.   Current, Richard N. *Three Carpetbag Governors.* Baton Rouge: Louisiana State University, 1967. 108p. Bibl.   Current analyses the gubernatorial careers of Harrison Reed in Florida, Henry Clay Warmoth in Louisiana, and Adelbert Ames in Mississippi.   All three were stigmatized as corrupt, selfish outsiders who disrupted conservative Southern traditions. But they represent a more truthful image of carpetbaggers. They were well meaning, political moderates who performed well under the circumstances of Reconstruction. (See also Current's "Carpetbaggers Reconsidered." In *A Festschrift for Frederick B. Artz.* Edited by David H. Pinkney and Theodore Ropp. Durham: Duke University Press, 1964, pp. 139-157 [Rpt. in *Arguing with Historians: Essays in the Historical and Unhistorical,* Middletown: Wesleyan University Press, 1987, 115-131] for a similar argument that highlights Albion Tourgée, Albert T. Morgan, and Williard Warner.)

934.   Curry, Richard O. (ed.) *Radicalism, Racism, and Party Realignment, the Border States During Reconstruction.* Baltimore: Johns Hopkins University Press, 1969. 331p. Bibl essay.   In his introduction Curry summarizes the key issues of Reconstruction in Delaware, Maryland, West Virginia, Kentucky, Missouri, and Tennessee and comments on historical writing. Each of the 9 chapters have been cited separately. (See # 920, 948, 1077, 1567, 1838, 2024, 2191, 2482, 2809)

935.   Davis, Susan Lawrence. *Authentic History, Ku Klux Klan, 1865-1877.* New York: Susan L. Davis, 1924. 313p. Ports. Ills.   Davis dedicated her book to Southern women who helped the Klan, to Klansmen, and to the Klan itself. She offers a highly sympathetic account of the purpose and activities of the organization during Reconstruction. The information is based mainly on interviews with former Klansmen, the *Confederate Veteran*, and contemporary newspapers.

936.   Dawson, Joseph G., III. "Army Generals and Reconstruction: Mower and Hancock as Case Studies." *Southern Studies* 17 (Fall 1978): 255-272.   A comparison of commanders in the 5th Military District that included Louisiana and Texas reveals the influence of politics in military rule during Reconstruction. President Johnson removed Gen. Philip H. Sheridan after the general followed the Reconstruction Acts too enthusiastically. Before his replacement, Gen. Winfield S. Hancock, could arrive Gen. Joseph Anthony Mower actively removed many Democrats from office, further irritating the conservative white population. Hancock, a Democrat, reversed several orders and took a much more conciliatory approach toward the wishes of the local Democratic Party. Eventually Hancock was removed by President Grant after a dispute with the New Orleans city counsul.

937.   Degler, Carl N. *The Other South: Southern Dissenters in the Nineteenth Century.* New York: Harper and Row, 1974. 392p.   Degler refers to dissenters prior to 1900 as white people who stood for losing causes, whether it was slavery, Unionism in 1861, or the Republican Party in Reconstruction. He emphasizes diversity of thought in the South as opposed to the stereotype of a monolithic white ideology. On pages 191-263 he discusses the role of scalawags, carpetbaggers, and those who opposed black suffrage.

938.   Dorris, J. T. "Pardoning the Leaders of the Confederacy." *Mississippi Valley Historical Review* 15 (June 1928): 3-21.   Dorris discusses the content of amnesty petitions made by Confederate leaders in accordance with President Johnson's amnesty proclamation of May 29, 1865. He describes the petitions submitted by various leaders, such as Alexander Stephens (vice-president), John H. Reagan (Postmaster General), Robert E. Lee (Army general), and John A. Campbell (secretary of war and former associate justice of the U.S. Supreme Court). The pardon requests were notable for the requesters' frequent defense of the South and acceptance of defeat.

939.   Dunning, William A. "Military Government in the South During Reconstruction." *Political Science Quarterly* 12 (September 1897): 381-406. Dunning believes that the rule of the commanders of the five military districts in the

South was generally reasonable and effective, but he criticizes their broad authority. Commanders not only sought to protect life and property, but used their authority to appoint local civilians to offices, nullify local laws, and involve themselves in the local criminal justice system. Confusing government policies and one-man military rule led to the disaster of black enfranchisement.

940.   Drumm, Austin Marcus. "Union League in the Carolinas." Ph.D. University of North Carolina, 1955. 253p.

941.   Dyer, Brainerd. "One Hundred Years of Negro Suffrage." *Pacific Historical Review* 37 (February 1968): 1-20.   In his presidential address to the Pacific Coast Branch of the American Historical Association in 1967 Dyer explains how the issue of black suffrage evolved from the post-Civil War years to the mid-1960s.

942.   Editor. "Reconstruction and Disfranchisement." *Atlantic Monthly* 88 (October 1901): 433-437.   The enfranchisement of the freedmen was a serious mistake made by the Republican Party because Southern blacks were unprepared for it.   But the editor urges Southern governments of 1901 to stop systematically excluding black citizens from voting and apply voting qualifications equally to all races.

943.   Erskine, John. "The Decision of Judge John Erskine in the Case of *Ex Parte* William Law, Under the 'Attorney's Test Oath Act'." *Georgia Historical Quarterly* 3 (September 1919): 101-130.   After the Civil War attorneys in the South were told that they had to take an oath of loyalty prescribed by the test oath of July 2, 1862 in order to practice in U.S. courts. Southern whites considered the "Attorney's Test Oath Act" of January 24, 1865 as another humiliation for the Southern people. William Law, a South Carolina judge, contested the law in 1866. Erskine, U.S. District Court judge of the Southern District of Georgia, ruled in Law's favor based on the retrospective or *ex poste facto* nature of the test oath. The full decision of the court is reprinted.

944.   Fitzgerald, Michael W. *The Union League Movement in the Deep South: Politics and Agricultural Change During Reconstruction.* Baton Rouge: Louisiana State University Press, 1989. 283p. Bibl. Tbls.   Fitzgerald examines the growth of Union Leagues as they spread from the North to the South after the Civil War. White yeomen, the initial focus of the leagues, flocked to the organization in 1866. After the Reconstruction Acts of 1867 the leagues expanded greatly among the freedmen who viewed them as supporters of their civil rights. The leagues failed by 1870 after ideological divisions and attacks from the Ku Klux Klan. Fitzgerald focuses on the Union Leagues in Mississippi and Alabama where the leagues had very different experiences. (See also Fitzgerald's "The Union League Movement in Alabama and Mississippi: Politics and Agricultural Change in the Deep South During Reconstruction." Ph.D. University of California at Los Angeles, 1986. 397p.)

945.   Foner, Eric. "Black Reconstruction Leaders at the Grass Roots." In *Black Leaders of the Nineteenth Century.* Urbana: University of Illinois Press, 1988. Pp. 219-234.   Black political leaders were vital parts of black communities during Reconstruction because they served multiple roles in politics, advising freedmen, and in their own professional fields as clergy or artisans. The Reconstruction Acts of 1867 ushered in black political participation throughout the South and leaders rose within the Union Leagues and other organizations. Politics was an avenue for new careers for black leaders, but in general, it led to personal financial problems and threats of physical violence. The violent intimidation and murder of leaders badly hurt the black community and caused it to increase its reliance on the federal government to guarantee personal safety and civil rights.

946.   Foner, Eric. *Freedom's Lawmakers: A Directory of Black Officeholders During Reconstruction.* Revised Ed. Baton Rouge: Louisiana State University, 1996. 298p. Bibl. Ports. (Rev. from 1993 edition.)   Foner brought together biographical information on 1510 major state officials in the South including the District of Columbia and Missouri. Research during recent decades has brought many of these people out of total obscurity. All of the persons listed held office prior to the end of Reconstruction. Foner reviews the group collectively and includes a table illustrating its characteristics. Most of the biographical sketches include bibliographic references. There are indexes by state, occupation, office held, birth status, and topic.

947.   Foner, Eric. "Politics and Ideology in the Shaping of Reconstruction: The Constitutional Conventions of 1867-1869." In *The Evolution of Southern Culture.* Edited by Numan V. Bartley. Athens: University of Georgia Press, 1988. Pp. 28-46.   The state constitutional conventions that were held in accordance with the Reconstruction Acts of 1867 reveal both a common ideology among Republicans and the factions that would help destroy Republican power in the South. Foner describes the composition of convention delegations in various states that included country yeomen, former Whigs and Democrats (scalawags), Northerners (carpetbaggers), Northern and Southern blacks, and conservatives. Despite the factions, there was excessive optimism that a new day in Southern life was commencing.

948.   Gillette, William. "Anatomy of a Failure: Federal Enforcement of the Right to Vote in the Border States During Reconstruction." In *Radicalism, Racism, and Party Realignment, the Border States During Reconstruction.* Edited by R. O. Curry. Baltimore: Johns Hopkins Press, 1969. Pp. 265-304.   After the 15th Amendment became part of the constitution in March, 1870 Congress responded to the lax enforcement and intimidation of black voters throughout the South by passing five Enforcement Acts between May 31, 1870 and June 10, 1872, but the laws were too vaguely written and underfunded to effectively overcome the overwhelming opposition of whites throughout the region. Gillette detects a conflict of interest between national and local Republicans and believes that the symbolism of the enforcement powers in the hands of federal authorities lost the Republicans vital support, and led to congressional victories for the Democrats in the 1874

elections. The enforcement acts represent the failure of a promise to secure justice for American blacks.

949.   Gregory, Thomas W.   "Reconstruction and the Ku Klux Klan." *Confederate Veteran* 29 (August 1921): 292-296.   Gregory, who gave this address in 1906 several years prior to becoming President Woodrow Wilson's attorney general, explains why the Klan was necessary and a positive force for constitutional government and respect for the law.

950.   Hamilton, J. G. de Roulhac.   "Southern Legislation in Respect to Freedmen, 1865-1866." In *Studies in Southern History and Politics*. New York: Columbia University Press, 1914. Pp. 135-158.   Hamilton defends the legislation passed in several Southern states to control and provide rights to the freedmen. The black codes were misunderstood by the North because of the Northerners' misapprehension of Southern blacks and politics. Legislation similar to the black codes became necessary due to the white's fear of free blacks, the belief that the blacks would not work without the discipline of law, and the need for order in the community. Hamilton points to the existence of similar laws in the North, and the false, prejudicial statements that were spread regarding white attitudes toward the freedmen.

951.   Herbert, Hilary A.   "The Condition of the Reconstruction Problem." *Atlantic Monthly* 87 (February 1901): 145-157.   Hebert, an apologist for the position of the white conservative South during Reconstruction, sympathizes with the plight of whites and criticizes Northerners who expressed concern for the freedmen. He stands behind the South's attempt to regulate the freedmen after the war and deny them the right of suffrage based on their lack of education and experience. Congressional Republicans made no attempt to understand the needs and fears of the white South.

952.   Heyman, Jr., Max L.   "'The Great Reconstructor': General E. R. S. Canby and the Second Military District." *North Carolina Historical Review* 32 (January 1955): 52-80.   In accordance with the Reconstruction Acts of 1867 North and South Carolina were combined into the 2nd Military District. In early September, 1867 Canby became the commander until the two states were accepted back into the Union in June, 1868. Heyman's focuses on Canby's leadership style and the responses of Carolinians to him. Canby was viewed as paternalistic, stern, statesman-like, and a supporter of Radicalism, but it was always clear that he followed the stipulations of Congress.

953.   Holt, Thomas C.   "'An Empire Over the Mind': Emancipation, Race, and Ideology in the British West Indies and the American South." In *Region, Race, and Reconstruction: Essays in Honor of C. Vann Woodward*. New York: Oxford University Press, 1982. Pp. 283-313.   In this comparison of emancipation processes in Jamaica and the American South, Holt finds similarities in attitudes towards the ability of black freedmen to gain an education and develop as independent laborers. The lack of success by freedmen caused the British and

Americans to lose faith and interest in reconstructing the former slaves. The racial ideology of the mid-19th century led many whites to misunderstand the way the freedmen defined their own freedom. Holt emphasizes that historians should study ideas, such as racism, within historical context without broad generalizations and the imposition of contemporary biases.

954.   Horn, Stanley F. *Invisible Empire: The Story of the Ku Klux Klan, 1866-1871*. 2nd Ed. Montclair, N.J.: Patterson Smith, 1969. 452p. App. Bibl. Facim. Ills. (Originally published by Boston: Houghton Mifflin, 1939.)   Horn writes a comprehensive history of the Klan based mainly on congressional testimony from the Joint Select Committee to Inquire into the Condition of Affairs in the Late Insurrectionary States, interviews of contemporaries of Reconstruction, newspapers, and secondary sources. He discusses the growth of the Klan, its development in each Southern state, and its decline. Horn states that he seeks objectivity in his book, an issue which was controversial for reviewers when the book originally appeared in 1939. He does not condone the violence and intimidation perpetrated by Klan members, but he sympathizes with the concerns of the Klan which responded to an environment of corruption and oppression created by Radical regimes in the South. The appendices include the original and revised "Prescript" of the Klan, an interview of Gen. Nathan B. Forrest from the *Cincinnati Commercial* (August 8, 1868), and biographical sketches of the members of the Joint Select Committee.

955.   Hosmer, John H. and Joseph Fireman.   "Black Congressmen in Reconstruction Historiography." *Phylon* 39 (June 1978): 97-107.   The authors survey historical writing on black congressmen and conclude that the literature is almost always presented with bias.   The bias is either excessively negative, gratuitous, myth making, or condescending with little evidence to back up the perspectives.   This includes the writing of many revisionist historians.   The collective lack of evidence suggests that black congressmen did and said very little, thus offering incite into the failure of Reconstruction.

956.   Hume, Richard L.   "The Black and Tan Constitutional Conventions of 1867-1869 in Ten Former Confederate States: A History of Their Membership." Ph.D. University of Washington, 1969. 765p.

957.   Hume, Richard L.   "Carpetbaggers in the Reconstruction South: A Group Portrait of Outside Whites in the 'Black and Tan' Constitutional Conventions." *Journal of American History* 64 (September 1977): 313-330. Tbl.   Hume identifies white carpetbaggers who served as delegates to the constitutional conventions held between November, 1867 and February, 1869. The 159 "outside whites" were generally young and prosperous, and originally came South for commercial opportunity. They diverted to politics for idealistic reasons - to reform the South in the mold of the North, to push for industrialization, and to preserve their property and their lives. These Northerners made positive contributions at the conventions by voting as a bloc for various issues, including suffrage and education.

Their influence was out of proportion to their numbers, and as their influence declined in state politics, Republican rule weakened.

958.   Hume, Richard L.   "Negro Delegates to the State Constitutional Conventions of 1867-69." In *Southern Black Leaders of the Reconstruction Era.* Edited by Howard Rabinowitz. Urbana: University of Illinois Press, 1982. Pp. 129-153. Tbls. Illus.   Hume analyses black delegate's ages, racial backgrounds, prewar status, work backgrounds, and contributions to the state conventions. He concludes that the stereotype of the ignorant, illiterate, recently freed black politician is largely untrue. Most of them were literate, free persons prior to the war, and they came from a wide range of backgrounds. Black delegates contributed to writing progressive constitutions, but they were not able to build on this political base for future political power. Racism reversed progress in civil rights after Reconstruction, but at least Reconstruction provided a successful start to black participation in American society.

959.   Kirkland, John Robert.   "Federal Troops in the South Atlantic States During Reconstruction: 1865-1877." Ph.D. University of North Carolina at Chapel Hill, 1968. 367p.

960.   Kolchin, Peter.   "Scalawags, Carpetbaggers, and Reconstruction: A Quantitative Look at Southern Congressional Politics, 1868-1872." *Journal of Southern History* 45 (February 1979): 63-76. Tbls.   Kolchin examines the congressional delegations in the House of Representatives from the former Confederate states for the 40th through the 43rd Congresses (1867-1875). He looks mainly at carpetbagger versus scalawag strength and its correlation with black population and Democratic electoral wins. Kolchin recognizes variations from one state to another, but in general, he concludes that the strength within the state Republican parties rested with carpetbaggers. When scalawags predominated in congressional offices, it was a sign that the party was weakening and in trouble because they moderated party ideology.

961.   Ku Klux Klan, Prescript of the Order of the ***." *American Historical Magazine* 5 (January 1900): 3-26.   Reprinted is a copy of a pamphlet issued in 1868 entitled "Revised and Amended Prescript of the Order of the ***." An explanation of the document is included.   (See also Fleming, Walter L. "The Prescript of the Ku Klux Klan." *Publications of the Southern History Association* 9 (September 1903): 327-348.)

962.   Lester, John C. and Daniel L. Wilson. *Ku Klux Klan: Its Origins, Growth and Disbandment.* New York: DaCapo Press, 1973. 108p. App. Ills. (Rpt. of 1905 edition)   Lester claims that he was one of the original founders of the Klan before Nathan B. Forrest became its leader. He and Wilson depict the Klan as a nonpolitical group that sought order and honor for their states. They do not condone violence, but blame the violence mainly on persons who claimed to be Klan members but were not. The Klan organized because it was needed and then it

quickly disbanded. Walter Fleming's introduction provides historical background to the book.

963.   Litwack, Leon and August Meier (eds.). *Black Leaders of the Nineteenth Century.* Urbana: University of Illinois Press, 1988. 344p. Bibl. Ports.   Includes five essays on persons involved in Reconstruction: John Mercer Langston (see # 209); Martin Delaney (see # 2380); Blanche K. Bruce, Robert Brown Elliott, and Holland Thompson (see # 986); Henry McNeal Turner (see # 1702a), and an essay on leadership at the local level (see # 945).

964.   Lowry, Sharon K. "Portrait of an Age: The Political Career of Stephen W. Dorsey, 1868-1889." Ph.D. University of North Texas, 1980. 460p.

965.   Magdol, Edward. "Local Black Leaders in the South, 1867-1875: An Essay Toward the Reconstruction of Reconstruction History." *Societas* 2 (Spring 1974): 81-110. Tbls.   Magdol proposes to bring lower class black leaders out of obscurity to reveal their names and information about their lives and leadership roles. A better understanding of the activities of this group in postwar years sheds light on the black community throughout the South. Magdol's main source is the Ku Klux Klan hearings before a congressional committee in 1871 (*Condition of Affairs in the Late Insurrectionary States*, 42nd Congress, 2nd Session, Senate Report no. 41, 13 Vols., 1972)

966.   Marten, James. "The Making of a Carpetbagger: George S. Denison and the South, 1854-1866." *Louisiana Studies* 34 (Spring 1993): 133-160.   Denison, a native of Vermont, may be viewed as a typical carpetbagger who sought economic and political success in the prewar and postwar South. Conditions in the South created the right situation for what Marten refers to as the "carpetbagger impulse" or the urge to take a chance and seek adventure. Denison lived in Texas (1854-1862) and Louisiana (1862-1866), fought with the Union, and assisted with the occupation of New Orleans.

967.   McKelvey, Blake. "Penal Slavery and Southern Reconstruction." *Journal of Negro History* 20 (April 1935): 153-179.   Reconstruction governments sought to unburden their treasuries from the expense of convicts and crumbling prison systems. Instead of pursuing prison reform, Southern states created a system more cruel than slavery. McKelvey briefly describes conditions in each Southern state.

968.   McKinney, Gordon B. *Southern Mountain Republicans 1865-1900: Politics and the Appalachian Community.* Chapel Hill: University of North Carolina, 1978. 277p. Bibl. Tbls.   The introduction and the first two chapters are related to the Civil War and Reconstruction in the Appalachian regions of Kentucky, Virginia, North Carolina and Tennessee. The white, mountain people in this region did not identify themselves as a cohesive group until the Civil War, and the national Republican Party forced them to do so. By the end of the war strong Unionism and financial assistance from the Republicans generated local support. But the mountain people did not like Republican policies in favor of civil rights and suffrage for

blacks and the party's symbolism as an outside force attempting to direct the politics in the mountain region. Whites responded by leaving the party until race reforms were dropped, local issues were addressed, and the party was reorganized. (See also McKinney's "Southern Mountain Republicans and the Negro, 1865-1900," *Journal of Southern History* 41 (November 1975): 493-522 that elaborates on the reluctant acceptance of blacks by mountain whites.)

969.   McWhiney, H. Grady and Francis B. Simkins. "The Ghostly Legend of the Ku-Klux Klan." *Negro History Bulletin* 14 (February 1951): 109-112. Southern whites generally believed that black people were naturally frightened of the hooded, draped, ghostly figures in the Klan. Popular writers, such as Thomas Dixon (*The Clansman* [1905]), and historians, such as Claude Bowers and Walter Fleming, encouraged this belief. McWhiney and Simkins explain that this view was pure legend, and that the fears of blacks were due to threats of physical violence.

970.   Mecklin, John M. "The Black Codes." *South Atlantic Quarterly* 16 (July 1917): 248-259.   In the difficult political and economic environment at the end of the Civil War and with the emancipation of 3.5 million slaves, Southern state leaders wanted to ensure order, consistent labor, and the health and welfare of the freedmen. The authors of the black codes frequently used Northern laws as examples. There was no attempt to re-enslave the black people, but to keep them orderly and out of trouble. Mecklin argues that Northern Radicals misunderstood the intentions of Southern leaders and forced a Reconstruction that ruined race relations and encouraged lawlessness and sectionalism in the South for many decades.

971.   Meredith, William J. F. "The Black Codes." *Negro History Bulletin* 3 (February 1940): 76-77.   Meredith describes black codes in Mississippi, South Carolina, Louisiana, North Carolina, Virginia, and Florida.

972.   Mering, John Vollmer. "Persistent Whiggery in the Confederate South: A Reconsideration." *South Atlantic Quarterly* 69 (Winter 1970): 124-143.   The concept of "persistent whiggery" as set forth by several historians, such as Thomas B. Alexander, David Donald, and C. Vann Woodward, is inconsistent and unusable as an historical tool. It is difficult to prove that Whigs continued to project their political and economic philosophy from the time the Whig Party expired following the 1856 presidential election until well into Reconstruction. Mering criticizes the methods used by historians to identify persistent Whigs. Postwar Whiggery is usually identified based on the political and social background of a political candidate, the policies that they supported, and the individuals who voted for them. Historians have offered identifiers that have been misinterpreted or exaggerated.

973.   Miller, Steven F., Susan E. O'Donovan, John C. Rodrique, and Leslie S. Rowland. "Between Emancipation and Enfranchisement: Law and the Political Mobilization of Black Southerners During Presidential Reconstruction, 1865-1867." *Chicago-Kent Law Review* 70 (1995): 1059-1077.   Four members of the Freedmen and Southern Society Project at the University of Maryland, College Park selected documents written from July, 1865 to July, 1867 by black advocates for civil rights.

The documents are petitions to state and local government officials demanding justice for the freedmen. The documents were written in an environment of postwar government restrictions on black freedom and President Johnson's emphasis on local autonomy. (See also # 8)

974.   M'Neilly, James H. "Reconstruction and the Ku-Klux." *Confederate Veteran* 30 (March 1922): 96-97.   Rev. M'Neilly writes an emotional critique of Northern methods of winning the war and forcing unwanted racial and political changes in the South. He defines the Klan as an instrument used to restore order and uphold the heritage of the South and the Confederacy.

975.   Moneyhon, Carl. "The Failure of Southern Republicanism." In *The Facts of Reconstruction: Essays in Honor of John Hope Franklin.* Baton Rouge: Louisiana State University Press, 1991. Pp. 99-119.   Moneyhon emphasizes the lack of consensus among historians about the failure of Southern Republicanism and suggests that historians direct their attention away from soley political analyses toward social and economic approaches from a regional perspective.   Existing research on the failure of Southern Republicans focuses on racism among white Republicans and the South in general; conservatism among Republicans toward the place of government in society, the lack of a unified program, decreasing black support for moderate Republicans, and financial mismanagement.

976.   Olsen, Otto H. (ed.). *Reconstruction and Redemption in the South.* Baton Rouge: Louisiana State University, 1980. 250p.   Includes 6 essays intended to provide new studies of Republican efforts to rule the South in 6 states. The essays serve as introductions to Reconstruction politics in Florida (see # 1608), Alabama (see # 1411), Mississippi (see # 2096), Virginia (see # 2734), North Carolina (see # 2251), and Louisiana (see # 1927). The essays are particularly concerned with why Southern Republicans failed in their efforts to control state politics.

977.   Owens, Susie Lee. "The Union Leagues of America: Political Activities in Tennessee, the Carolinas, and Virginia, 1865-1870." Ph.D. New York University, 1943.

978.   Pavenstedt, Edmund W. "Mediaeval Carpet-Baggers." *South Atlantic Quarterly* 32 (April 1933): 173-189.   Pavenstedt compares the plunder of the South by carpetbaggers and their scalawag and black followers with the treatment of the lower Languedoc in France by the successful invasion of crusaders sponsored by Pope Innocent III in 1229.

979.   Perman, Michael. "Counter Reconstruction: The Role of Violence in Southern Redemption." In *The Facts of Reconstruction: Essays in Honor of John Hope Franklin.* Baton Rouge: Louisiana State University Press, 1991. Pp. 121-140.   Perman analyses historical writing on the origin and impact of violence as a form of intimidation of blacks and resistance against Reconstruction governments. He reviews Franklin's revisionist interpretation regarding the role of the Ku Klux Klan and later studies that discuss the influence of the Klan on the downfall of

Republican state governments in the South. Perman reviews studies on the internal problems within the Republican community as a key to understanding why Reconstruction governments failed. In fact, these governments were overthrown in a movement consistent with prewar attempts at autonomy.

980.   Perman, Michael. *The Road to Redemption: Southern Politics, 1869-1879*. Chapel Hill: University of North Carolina Press, 1984. 353p. Bibl. Perman approaches the period of Reconstruction within a particular framework - that an examination of Southern politics would benefit from a regional rather than a local perspective; that Reconstruction should be viewed within the continuum of Southern history rather than compartmentalized and separated from the years that followed; and that it would be beneficial to examine how, rather than why, Reconstruction failed. In particular, Perman examines how the dynamics of the political parties in the South contributed to the failure of Reconstruction and how the period created a Democratic Party that juggled the interests of several factions and coalitions. The leaders of the Democratic Party that emerged from Reconstruction provided no agenda or focus to move the New South forward in the years that followed.

981.   Perman, Michael. "Southern Politics and American Reunion, 1865-1868." Ph.D. University of Chicago, 1969.

982.   Pope, Ida Waller. "Violence as a Political Force in the Reconstruction South." Ph.D. University of Southwestern Louisiana, 1982. 285p.

983.   Powell, Lawrence N. "The Politics of Livelihood: Carpetbaggers in the Deep South." In *Region, Race, and Reconstruction: Essays in Honor of C. Vann Woodward*. New York: Oxford University Press, 1982. Pp. 315-347.   Powell writes that most carpetbaggers arrived in the South prior to the Reconstruction Acts of 1867 seeking economic opportunity or a chance to help the freedmen, but economic problems led many of them into Republican politics. Politics became their livelihood and many of them took advantage of government mismanagement by seeking additional income through corruption. Powell points to the infighting among scalawags, carpetbaggers, and blacks for power and over the direction of social reform that contributed to the failure of the Republican Party to prosper in the South.

984.   Rabinowitz, Howard N. "From Reconstruction to Redemption in the Urban South." *Journal of Urban History* 2 (February 1976): 169-194. Tbls. Rabinowitz examines the participation of Radicals, white and black, in urban politics. He traces black officeholders, voting, and the influence of Radical rule in Atlanta, Raleigh, Nashville, Richmond and Montgomery. Once conservatives were in control of state legislatures, they assisted urban conservatives with controlling or eliminating Radical power through gerrymandering and denying public employment to blacks.

985.   Rabinowitz, Howard N. (ed.)   *Southern Black Leaders of the Reconstruction Era*. Urbana: University of Illinois Press, 1982. 422p. Ports.

This book includes 14 essays that illustrate the role of black leaders in Reconstruction and in American history in general. They offer contemporary research into people and topics that form a counterpoint to either the old negative images or the total disregard of black leaders in Reconstruction that emerged from the writings of white historians of the early 20th century (e.g. William Dunning, James Ford Rhodes). The essays focus on the following: Blanche K. Bruce (see # 2091); John R. Lynch (see # 2087); Josiah T. Walls (see # 1588); James T. Rapier (see # 1404); James O'Hara (see # 2212); Holland Thompson (see # 1394); Aaron A. Bradley (see # 1742); William Finch (see # 1711); Benjamin A. Boseman, Jr. (see # 2360); and George T. Ruby (see # 2627). Other essays cover delegates to conventions (see # 958), leaders in New Orleans (see # 1915), Richmond City Councilmen (see # 2715), and legislators in South Carolina (see # 2364). In the last essay, the "Afterword", August Meier reflects on what has been learned from the other essays in the book and reviews the nature of black leadership in Reconstruction. Meier also proposes new areas of research.

986.   Rabinowitz, Howard N. "Three Reconstruction Leaders: Blanche K. Bruce, Robert Brown Elliott, and Holland Thompson." In *Black Leaders of the Nineteenth Century.* Urbana: University of Illinois Press, 1988. Pp. 191-217. Bruce of Mississippi, Elliott of South Carolina, and Thompson of Alabama are studied as examples of black leaders who contradict the orthodox depiction of black leaders as corrupt, lazy, and ignorant. While they represent the typical Southern leaders of their race during Reconstruction who were usually literate and politically moderate, these three men also illustrate diversity in backgrounds, achievements and political motivations and styles. Their stories make clear the need to study black leaders of the time as individuals with their own strengths and weaknesses that reflect the period in which they lived.

987.   Rable, George C. *But There Was No Peace: The Role of Violence in the Politics of Reconstruction.* Athens: University of Georgia Press, 1984. 257p. Bibl. Ills.   Rable examines Southern, white violence as an expression of reactionary counterrevolution against Northern attempts to remake Southern society. He draws from social science research on revolution and counterrevolution, mob behavior, and 20th century race relations to offer incite into what Reconstruction violence revealed about the white South. Rable disagrees with historians who criticize the federal government's plan of Reconstruction because it lacked sufficient radicalism or consistency in policy and enforcement. The truth is that the white reaction against Reconstruction was based on the continuation and intensification of sectional differences. The violence was a continuation of the war, and it proved successful in overthrowing Republican rule and black hopes for racial equality. (See also Rable's "But There Was No Peace: Violence and Reconstruction Politics." 2 Vols. Ph.D. Louisiana State University, 1978. 778p.)

988.   Ranck, James B. *Albert Gallatin Brown: Radical Southern Nationalist.* New York: D. Appleton-Century Co., 1937. 320p. Bibl. Maps. Port.   Brown was a "fire eating" Southern nationalist and proponent of slavery who seemed more conservative than Jefferson Davis and the aristocratic planter class. Following the

war, his writings and public activities reveal a changed man. His Southern nationalism took on a national focus, and he accepted the principles of Republican Reconstruction except for taxation policies and corruption. Brown sought a fusion of conservative Republicans and Democrats by the 1870s. He combined devotion to the South with support for postwar changes in national power, racial harmony, public aid to farmers, and internal improvements.

989.   Randel, William P.   *The Ku Klux Klan: A Century of Infamy.* Philadelphia: Chilton books, 1965.   300p.   Bibl.   Ills.   Randel traces Klan violence and intimidation from its original inception on December 24, 1865 to its continuing existence in the 1960s. The creation of a white supremacist society has been its theme. The chapters on Reconstruction focus on the Klan's power in North Carolina, South Carolina, Florida, and Georgia and its hate against scalawags, Northern teachers, and the Freedmen's Bureau. Randel also discusses the literary battle over the Klan's methods and purpose, and the South's general resistance to change. He views the Klan's successes as evidence of the power of a violent, determined minority in society.

990.   Raum, Green Berry.   *The Existing Conflict Between Republican Government and Southern Oligarchy.*   Washington, D. C.: n.p., 1884.   479p. Raum reviews Southern, Democratic abuses against blacks and their white Republican supporters from the beginning of Reconstruction until early 1884. His argument is completely on the side of the Republican Party in its expressed campaign against the South's denial of free speech and a free ballot for all people. He emphasizes the reactionary violence of the Ku Klux Klan and the political terrorism in support of Democratic power. The Democratic return to power was a revolution that denied the basic rights of republican government.

991.   Rhodes, James Ford.   "Negro Suffrage and Reconstruction." *Massachusetts Historical Society, Proceedings.* Ser. 2, 18 (December 1904): 465-467; 19 (January 1905): 34-37.   Rhodes suggests that it was a mistake to grant suffrage to the freedmen in Reconstruction. He offers Hermann Von Holst as one who retracted his support for black suffrage. At the January, 1905 meeting Rhodes does not retreat from this position, but instead he emphasizes that the Republicans in Congress believed that suffrage was necessary for the self protection of blacks and loyal whites. Rhodes extols the virtues of the Republicans who refused to seek harsh retribution against the South after the rebellion.

992.   Robinson, Armistead. "Beyond the Realm of Social Consensus: New Meanings of Reconstruction for American History." *Journal of American History* 68 (September 1981): 276-297.   The politics of Reconstruction in the South was marked by the impact of conflicts based on social status, class, and race that contradict the social consensus interpretation of American history in the mid to late 19th century. There were social and economic conflicts between upcountry yeomen and Whig planters, blacks of various class divisions, and freedmen and antebellum free blacks about issues of political compromise. These issues weakened the Southern Republican Party and destroyed whatever biracial unity existed.

993.   Rose, Mrs. S. E. F. *The Ku Klux Klan or Invisible Empire*. New Orleans: L. Graham Co., 1914. 84p. Ills.   Rose glorifies the Ku Klux Klan of Reconstruction days and states that it was a necessary and patriotic organization. The book was written for the education of youth.

994.   Russ, Barbara. "The Right to Vote: The Enforcement Acts and Southern Courts." *Prologue* 21 (Fall 1989): 231-237. Ill. Ports.   Rust illustrates the usefulness of documents from the National Archives for investigating the impact of the Enforcement Acts of 1870 and 1871. Both acts were intended in part to safeguard the right of blacks to vote in Southern state elections. Rust describes how the laws were applied in two cases in Louisiana, one from disgruntled Republican office seekers who claimed that they lost elections because blacks were denied a vote in the 1872 election, and the other related to the deadly riot that took place in Colfax in Grant Parish in 1873. In both cases court decisions weakened the acts. By the end of Grant's second term his administration no longer strongly pursued voting rights cases. Congressional acts in 1878 and 1894 killed the provisions that were meant to enforce the 15th Amendment.

995.   Russ, William A. Jr. "The Negro and White Disfranchisement During Radical Reconstruction." *Journal of Negro History* 19 (April 1934): 171-192. Radical Republicans merged the issues of black enfranchisement and white disenfranchisement, because they offered an opportunity for the Republican Party to gain and maintain power in the Southern states. Ironically it was blacks who did not really support white disenfranchisement. Without the influence of carpetbaggers and scalawags, the freedmen would have welcomed former rebels into politics as a sign of equality. Russ points out that without white disenfranchisement, blacks would have lost political influence more quickly under the enhanced power of the Democratic Party.

996.   Russ, William A. Jr. "The Price Paid for Disfranchising Southerners in 1867." *South Atlantic Quarterly* 44 (January 1945): 23-41.   Russ explains that a high price was paid by the South and the nation in general by the elimination of the Southern aristocracy from holding national and local public offices. The South lost the advantage of highly experienced and polished statesmen who had to stand back and watch the expansion of national authority and the lowliest class of blacks and scalawags rule their state. The absence of the traditional leaders sapped their spirit and allowed the quick economic domination of the industrial North. The expansion of big business in the South led to the expansion of government. The loss of good leadership hurt the South for many years.

997.   Russ, William A. Jr. "Registration and Disfranchisement Under Radical Reconstruction." *Mississippi Valley Historical Review* 21 (September 1934): 163-180. Tbl.   When congressional action stipulated the disenfranchisement of former Confederates, the reaction in the South was confusion about who would be automatically denied the rights of U.S. citizenship. Russ discusses this reaction, how registrars implemented the disenfranchisement, and the impact of disenfranchisement on the South and its relationship with the North. He concludes

that the policy was intended as a scheme to temporarily turn the South into a Republican stronghold, but it resulted in generating greater animosity toward blacks, Republicans, and the North. It also played a role in producing modern industrial America by temporarily eliminating a Southern-Western political alliance in Congress that would have opposed legislation partial to the industrial North.

998.   Russ, William A., Jr. "Was There Danger of a Second Civil War During Reconstruction?" *Mississippi Valley Historical Review* 25 (June 1938): 39-58.   In general the South did not want to resist what they considered to be reasonable change forced upon them by the North after the Civil War. This was the case prior to the Reconstruction Acts of 1867 when the Southern states followed President Johnson's Reconstruction plan. With the onset of Congressional Reconstruction, much more resistance materialized, and there was talk of a second civil war when Radicals in Congress sought the removal of the president and the Ku Klux Klan violently resisted Republican rule.

999.   Scroggs, Jack B. "Carpetbagger Constitutional Reform in the South Atlantic States, 1867-1868." *Journal of Southern History* 27 (November 1961): 475-493.   Scroggs examines the activities of carpetbaggers in Virginia, North Carolina, South Carolina, Georgia, and Florida. Carpetbaggers were influential in pushing provisions through state constitutional conventions to extend political participation of blacks and poor whites, to reform apportionment of the electorate, increase the number of elective offices, and establish public education. Even though these Northern transplants successfully worked for political democracy, they generally opposed revolutionary economic reform that would redistribute land to the freedmen. Scroggs seeks to revise the traditional negative view of carpetbaggers.

1000.   Scroggs, Jack B. "Carpetbaggers Influence in the Political Reconstruction of the South Atlantic States, 1865-1876." Ph.D. University of North Carolina, 1951. 318p.

1001.   Scroggs, Jack B. "Southern Reconstruction: A Radical View." *Journal of Southern History* 24 (November 1958): 407-429.   Scroggs examines correspondence from Southern Republicans from Virginia, North Carolina, South Carolina, Georgia, and Florida to congressional Radicals. The letters reveal the lack of cooperation between congressional and local Southern Republicans who held divergent ideologies, and the unsuccessful efforts to form consistent policies to maintain support for the Republican Party. The revolutionary changes attempted by Northerners showed how naïve they were about Southern traditions.

1002.   Sefton, James E. "A Note on the Political Intimidation of Black Men by Other Black Men." *Georgia Historical Quarterly* 52 (December 1968): 443-448. Sefton cites Army and congressional reports in 1871 and 1876 that indicate intimidation by black Republicans against blacks who favored the Democrats. He believes there is only meager evidence.

1003.   Sefton, James E. *The United States Army and Reconstruction, 1865-1877.* Baton Rouge: Louisiana State University Press, 1967. 284p. App. Bibl. Ills. Tbls. Sefton examines the role of the Army in the postwar occupation of the South and the implementation of Reconstruction policies. While there was a tug-of-war between the president and Congress regarding policy, there was no competition related to authority over the Army in the South. Between 1865 and 1877 the Army sought to follow orders or the policies of the government, but they had to adjust to shifting and confusing policies or simply   periods of no policy at all. In this role they performed well, but in the role of protector of the freedmen or enforcer of policies that Congress hoped would transform Southern society, the Army's task was too great. The appendices include "The Structure of Army Commands" in the South in chronological order and a table illustrating "Numbers and Locations of Troops" in each state from 1865 until October, 1876.

1004.   Silverman, Catherine.   "'Of Wealth, Virtue, and Intelligence':   The Redeemers and Their Triumph in Virginia and North Carolina, 1865-1877." Ph.D. City University of New York, 1972. 332p.

1005.   Silvestro, Clement Mario.   "None But Patriots: The Union Leagues in Civil War and Reconstruction." Ph.D. University of Wisconsin, 1959. 449p.

1006.   Singletary, Otis A. *Negro Militia and Reconstruction.* Austin: University of Texas Press, 1957. 181p. Bibl. Ill.   Congress authorized the militia in an effort to reduce violence in the Southern states and help establish and protect Republican state governments. While the militia consisted mostly of black soldiers, there were significant numbers of whites who served in every state, particularly in Tennessee, Louisiana, and North Carolina. Whites considered the black militia an insult to their since of racial propriety. The militias failed because Republican governors refused to deploy them out of fear of a race war. Their weakness hastened the downfall of the Republican Party in the South by lifting white resentment to its height. (See also Singletary's "The Negro Militia Movement During Radical Reconstruction." Ph.D. Louisiana State University, 1954.)

1007.   Singletary, Otis A. "The Negro Militia During Radical Reconstruction." *Military Affairs* 19 (1955): 177-186.   Republican governments in the South organized militias to protect their regimes, white Republicans, and freedmen from whites who responded violently to changes in state government and race relations. The militias, consisting mainly of blacks, were ill treated by national and state officials, as well as Southern whites who responded violently to the presence of uniformed and armed blacks. Singletary explains that historians have exaggerated the negative and positive behavior of black militias, but the most important factor in the rejection of the militias was their racial composition.

1008.   Taylor, Richard. *Destruction and Reconstruction: Personal Experiences of the Late War.* Edited by Richard B. Hartwell. New York; Longmans, Green and Co., 1955. 380p. (Rpt. of New York: Appleton, 1879)   Taylor, son of President Zachary Taylor, was an officer in the Confederate Army. He describes and analyses the experiences of the war and devotes two chapters to Reconstruction. Although he never requested a pardon, his book illustrates how he attempted to influence presidents and congressional politicians regarding the course of Reconstruction.

1009.   Thompson, C. Mildred. Carpetbaggers in the United States Senate." In *Studies in Southern History and Politics*. New York: Columbia University Press, 1914. Pp. 159-176.   The carpetbaggers who served in the U.S. Senate between 1869 and 1873 were dominated by individuals who were either corrupt or lacking in distinction. Thompson reviewed the contribution of these men with an emphasis on their support for Radical legislation, such as the Enforcement Acts, their powers to distribute federal offices in their states, and their disinterest in truly national legislation. The carpetbaggers contributed to and encouraged a low moral tone in the Congress. Thompson discusses William Pitt Kellogg of Louisiana, Hiram Revels of Mississippi, and George Spencer and William Warner of Alabama.

1010.   Thornton, J. Mills, III. "Fiscal Policy and the Failure of Radical Reconstruction in the Lower South." In *Region, Race, and Reconstruction: Essays in Honor of C. Vann Woodward*. New York: Oxford University Press, 1982. Pp. 349-394. Charts, Graphs.   Thornton deemphasizes racism among whites who owned small farms to explain the weak support for the Republican Party in the Southern states. Instead he compares antebellum and postbellum fiscal policies in the South as a method for determining the behavior of white farmers. He concludes that whites rejected the Republican Party because it increased real estate taxes to fund Reconstruction. Higher taxes drove them into the Democratic Party that promptly lowered real estate taxes after they took power.

1011.   Trelease, Allen W. *White Terror: The Ku Klux Klan Conspiracy and Southern Reconstruction*. Baton Rouge: Louisiana State University Press, 1995. Illus. Bibl essay. 557p. (Rpt. of original 1971 edition by LSU Press)   Trelease analyzes the ideological basis and activities of the Klan from 1866 to 1872. He demonstrates the central theme that tied Klan organizations together no matter what state or county they were from - the maintenance of white supremacy. He emphasizes the terrorist nature of the Klan and that such activities were intended to force blacks out of specific regions, threaten them if they exercised the vote, ensure that they would not own or rent land, and generally attempt to force them to accept peonage and second class citizenship. Trelease explores the tradition of white supremacy in the South and the basis for widespread acceptance of violence as a means to achieve social and political ends. He emphasizes the falseness of many traditional historical treatments depicting the Klan as a savior of the South, and he presents a positive image of Southern Republicans.

1012.   Trelease, Allen W. "Who Were the Scalawags." *Journal of Southern History* 29 (November 1963): 445-468. Tbls. Map.   In this statistical study of Southern, white Republican voting patterns in counties throughout the South, Trelease focuses on the presidential election of 1872 and gives additional information on presidential and state elections from 1868 to 1876. He identifies where white Republicans were located and who they were. Trelease identified different groups of white Republicans, including the largest group comprised of hill country farmers. This strongly Unionist group identified with Republican Party values of egalitarianism, political and social reform, and government aid for economic development. Trelease states that his focus on hill country farmers was a departure from previous studies by David Donald (see # 2080) and Thomas Alexander (e.g. see # 915). In an exchange of letters (*Journal of Southern History* 30 (May 1964): 253-257) Donald disagrees that 1872 was a representative election and says that Trelease's methodology misses Republican support in the Black Belt counties.

1013.   Verney, Kevern John. "Contrast and Continuity: 'Black' Reconstruction in South Carolina and Mississippi, 1861-1877." Ph.D. University of Keele [Great Britain] 1987. 402p.

1014.   Walton, Hanes, Jr. *Black Republicanism: The Politics of the Black and Tans.* Metuchen, N.J.: Scarecrow Press, Inc., 1975. App. Bibl.   Walton examines the development of black participation in the Republican Party in the South and at the national level. He discusses the development of factions with the Republican Party, particularly along racial lines, and offers a state-by-state description of Republican Party developments with emphasis on the former Confederate states. Black and tan Republican organization continued in some form in some areas up to the 1960s. In appendices Walton lists the names and states of Southern black delegates to the Republican National Conventions from 1868 to 1944.

1015.   Weeks, Stephen B.   "The History of Negro Suffrage in the South." *Political Science Quarterly* 9 (December 1894): 669-703.   Weeks surveys black suffrage from the early eighteenth century until the mid-1890s. References to Reconstruction are written from the perspective that universal suffrage for the freedmen was wrong because the freedmen were unprepared to exercise the vote in an intelligent, independent manner. The suffrage restrictions enacted by the 1890s emphasized the importance of education in voting, and Southern poll taxes were consistent with similar taxes in the North.

1016.   Wilson, D. L. and J. C. Lester.   "The Ku Klux Klan: Its Origin, Growth, and Disbandment." *Century Magazine* 28, ns6 (May-October 1884): 398-410. The authors state that their history of the Klan is the first historical account based on solid sources of information. They explicitly state that their sources cannot be revealed, but they assure readers that the information is accurate. The authors recognize that violence perpetrated by the Klan was tragic, but believe that the organization was unjustly criticized by its Northern detractors.

1017.   Wilson, Theodore Brantner. *The Black Codes of the South.* University: University of Alabama Press, 1965. 177p. Bibl.   Wilson analyses the content and purpose of the codes and their influence on the election of 1866 and Radical Reconstruction. He argues that the codes were not as severe as Northern Radicals described. The codes were ultimately a minor issue among many others that led to

Northern public support for Radical Reconstruction. The codes were used as propaganda to whip up support, but the Northern public cared little for the welfare of the blacks. Instead they were concerned about the lack of Southern contrition, the election of former rebels, and violent unrest. (See also Wilson's Ph.D. dissertation with the same title from University of Florida, 1963.)

1018.   Wood, Forrest G. "On Revising Reconstruction History: Negro Suffrage, White Disfranchisement, and Common Sense." *Journal of Negro History* 51 (April 1966): 98-113.   The notion that black suffrage and white disenfranchisement led to black domination of Southern politics is totally unsubstantiated. Wood examines voter registration statistics and concludes that blacks never dominated politics in any state, even in South Carolina, Mississippi, and Louisiana, where the black population had an advantage. Wood notes that poor whites opposed black suffrage because it put blacks on par with whites and enhanced the power of the planter class that would influence the direction of black voting.

1019.   Work, Monroe N. "Some Negro Members of Reconstruction Conventions and Legislatures and Congress." *Journal of Negro History* 5 (January 1920): 58-125.   Work provides lists, correspondence, and other descriptions of black participants in politics in the Southern states. Following this information is a document from the papers of James G. Thompson in which he describes his political experiences in South Carolina following the conclusion of the war in 1865.

1020.   Zimmerman, Hilda Jane. "Penal Systems and Penal Reform in the South Since the Civil War." Ph.D. University of North Carolina, 1948.

Aid and Education: Freedmen's Bureau and Voluntary Organizations

1021.   Adams, Paul K. "Speaking Plainly: James P. Wickersham on Education and Reconstruction." *Journal of Lancaster County Historical Society* 90, 2 (1986): 87-101.   Wickersham, a Lancaster County, Pennsylvania, teacher, educational administrator, and 1866 president of the National Teachers Association, spoke out strongly against the idea that a quick transition to reunion would produce good citizens among white and black Southerners. He believed that the South ought to reform its systems of education through a nationally coordinated program of free public schools that would educate citizens equally, irrespective of color or economic status, based on a conservative, democratic, nationalistic approach. This program would be partially funded by Congress and would help draw the nation together into a patriotic union. He sought, unsuccessfully, congressional approval of funds to assist public schools in the South.

1022.   Alexander, Philip Wade. "John Eaton, Jr., Preacher, Soldier and Educator." Ph.D. George Peabody College for Teachers, 1939.

1023.   Anderson, James D. "Ex-Slave and the Rise of Universal Education in the New South, 1860-1880." In *Education and the Rise of the New South.* Edited by Ronald K. Goodenow and Arthur O. White. Boston: G. K. Hall, 1981. Pp. 1-25. The freedmen responded immediately to their emancipation by seeking educational opportunities provided by the Freedmen's Bureau and benevolent societies, they were largely responsible for initiating the organization of schools and an educational program.   The self education movement, based on the communalism of the slave society, extended to sabbath schools and influenced the interest in white Southerners in universal education.

1024.   Anscombe, Francis Charles.   "Contributions of the Quakers to the Reconstruction of the Southern States." Ph.D. University of North Carolina, 1926.

1025.   Armstrong, Warren B.   "Union Chaplains and the Education of the Freedmen." *Journal of Negro History* 52 (April 1967): 104-115.   During the Civil War some freedmen got a taste of positive change in their lives when they experienced the efforts of U.S. Army chaplains to educate them.   Armstrong quotes several chaplains who believed that education was necessary so that the freedmen could become a part of American society.   An extensive effort to look after the needs of freedmen was ordered by Gen. Grant as a way to maintain order among the freedmen who were drawn to his army.   Grant ordered Chaplain William Eaton, who maintained a school for the 12th U.S. Colored Troops, to direct black affairs in the Department of Tennessee from November, 1862 until the spring of 1865.   Eaton considered education to be an important part of his charge.   The program assisted in the transition from slavery to freedom.

1026.   Armstrong, William H.   *A Friend to God's Poor: Edward Parmelee Smith.* Athens: University of Georgia Press, 1993. 518p. Bibl. Illus. Ports.   Armstrong describes Smith's contributions as a leader among Christian evangelicals in the struggle to help the poor and spread the faith.   Regarding the period of Reconstruction, Smith was a minister and field agent associated with the American Missionary Association in Cincinnati. He supervised the teachers preparing to teach freedmen, and he worked with the Freedmen's Bureau to obtain material and financial assistance in the A.M.A.'s relief and educational efforts. Smith helped organize many black schools, including Fisk University, Atlanta University, Hampton Institute, Tougaloo College and Talledega College.   He was appointed president of Howard University for a short time in December, 1975.   Whether working as an educator or missionary, his goal was to uplift the poor and strengthen the faith.

1027.   Bean, Richard J.   "Yankee Teacher in the Reconstruction South." *Educational Forum* 32 (March 1968): 277-285.   Bean briefly describes the efforts and experiences of Northern teachers to improve education and to reform in the South.

1028.   Beard, Augustus Field.   *A Crusade of Brotherhood: A History of the American Missionary Association.* Boston: Pilgrim Press, 1909. 334p. Ills. Ports.

Beard surveys the work of the A.M.A. in building and organizing churches and schools for the freedmen. His focus is on education, particularly the founding of several colleges and teacher education institutions throughout the South. Beard emphasizes the dedication of the A.M.A., not only during the war and Reconstruction, but for decades afterward.

1029.   Bennett, Clifford T. and Margaret L. Dwight. "Literacy and Liberty: The Development of Public School Education for Blacks During Reconstruction." ERIC Doc. #177248. 1979. 14p.   Provides a brief description of efforts to establish public schools for freedmen sponsored by churches, philanthropic organizations, and the Freedmen's Bureau. The emphasis is on the efforts of blacks to seek educational opportunities despite the obstacles of white obstruction and lack of government aid.

1030.   Bentley, George R. *A History of the Freedmen's Bureau.* New York: Octagon Books, 1970 298p. Bibl. (Rpt. of Washington: American Historical Association, 1955)   Bentley provides a straight forward history of the origins, politics, and functions of the bureau with heavy reliance on the 1904 book by Peirce (see # 1108) and bureau documents. He believes that the bureau was a force for good, but he is critical of the way agents often encouraged freedmen to participate in politics. Agents showed political bias and exacerbated race relations in the South. (See also Bentley's *A History of the Freedmen's Bureau*, Ph.D., University of Wisconsin, 1949.)

1031.   Blassingame, John W. "The Union Army as an Educational Institution for Negroes, 1862-1865." *Journal of Negro Education* 34 (Spring 1965): 152-159. The Army engaged in early efforts to educate freedmen. Thousands of black troops received at least a rudimentary education by the end of the war. Some of the people involved were John Eaton (Dept. of Tennessee), Lt. Col. J. B. Kinsman (Dept. of North Carolina and Virginia), and Maj. Gen. Nathaniel Banks (Dept. of the Gulf).

1032.   Bond, Horace Mann. *The Education of the Negro in the American Social Order.* New York: Octagon Books, 1966. 531p. Bibl. Graphs. Tbls. (Rpt. with new material based on 1934 edition by Printice Hall)   In chapters 2-4 Bond focuses on the goal of equality of educational opportunity in integrated schools, but even those whites who accepted black education would not approve of integration. Compromise was not possible, and separate schools led to unequal financing and equipping either from the beginning or after Democrats regained control of the government.

1033.   Boromé, Joseph Alfred (ed.). "Robert Purvis, Wendell Phillips, and the Freedmen's Bureau." *Journal of Negro History* 42 (October 1957): 292-295. Purvis was one of the persons President Johnson invited to replace Gen. O. O. Howard as head of the Freedmen's Bureau. Johnson sought a black man as replacement, because he knew that white employees would quit and thus weaken the bureau that he opposed. Every person invited declined, including Purvis. In a letter dated September 13, 1867, Phillips responded to Purvis' request for counsel by urging him not to accept because Johnson sought to destroy the bureau.

1034.   Boyd, Willis Dolmond.   "Negro Colonization in the Reconstruction." *Georgia Historical Quarterly* 40 (December 1957): 360-382.   The American Colonization Society organized in 1817 and assisted thousands of blacks with emigration to Liberia, during the Civil War.   William McLain and William Coppinger directed the society and sought funding and support among whites and blacks.   By 1870 their efforts failed to generate enthusiasm among freedmen. Whites did not want to finance the speculative program, and also did not want to loose a large mass of menial laborers.

1035.   Bronson, Louis Henry.   "The Freedmen's Bureau: A Public Policy Analysis." D.S.W. University of Southern California, 1970. 355p.

1036.   Brown, Ira V. "Lyman Abbott and Freedmen's Aid 1865-1869." *Journal of Southern History* 15 (February 1949): 22-38.   Abbott, a product of a Puritan, New England tradition, served as executive secretary of the American Freedmen's Union from 1865 until 1869. The organization brought together nondenominational societies to provide relief and education for Southern blacks and whites. Abbott sought to enhance popular intelligence and popular morality. His fund raising efforts were in competition with other organizations, mostly denominational groups that combined aid with proselytizing. The A.F.U. disbanded after Southern states began to implement public education programs of their own.

1037.   Butchart, Ronald E.   *Northern   Schools,   Southern   Blacks,   and Reconstruction.* Westport: Greenwood Press, 1980. 309p. Bibl. Tbls.   Given the choices between either land confiscation and distribution or education, Northern white leaders of secular and sectarian organizations favored education as a way for the freedmen to learn about freedom and responsibility and to uplift them from their lowly state.   Leaders believed that if this could be done, the freedmen would gradually become a part of the wider community and achieve higher economic and social status. Butchart argues that education was merely a panacea for solving the problems of the freedmen in the South. In truth, the ideology underlying education was based on capitalist domination of a class and orienting the freedmen to accommodate to Northern and Southern white society. The promise of education was quickly dispelled. The economic and social welfare of blacks would have been served better by providing them with land as a path to independence and freedom. (See also Butchart's "Educating for Freedom: Northern Whites and the Origins of Black Education in the South, 1862-1875." Ph.D. State University of New York at Binghamton, 1976. 579p.)

1038.   Butchart, Ronald. "Recruits to the 'Army of Civilization': Gender, Race, Class, and the Freedmen's Teachers, 1862-1876." *Journal of Education* 172 (1990): 76-87.   Butchart reveals characteristics of Northern teachers of the freedmen based on recent studies. His database of 5,980 teachers who worked with the freedmen reveals the importance of Northern and Southern black participation and variations in age, class, and gender.

1039. Butchart, Ronald. "'We Best Can Instruct Our Own People': New York African Americans in the Freedmen's Schools, 1861-1875." *Afro-Americans in New York Life and History* 12 (January 1988): 27-49. Tbls. As part of a larger examination of the backgrounds and motives of Northern teachers who taught freedmen in the South during and after the Civil War, Butchart focuses on a group of 51 black teachers from New York. The group was well educated, more strongly abolitionist than their white counterparts, and closely identified with black brethren in the South. Their ability to cope with the hardships associated with teaching in the South indicated their dedication and good will.

1040. Chang, Perry. "'Angels of Peace in a Smitten Land': The Northern Teachers' in the Reconstruction South Reconsidered." *Southern Historian* 16 (Spring 1995): 26-45. Chang examines the contributions of the teachers to the lives of freedmen and the difficulties that they encountered with rejection, their own racial attitudes, and the internal disputes among Northern aid organizations. The teachers failed to transform Southern society and uplift the ex-slaves, but they still had a positive impact on their students and their own lives. They set a precedent for future aid and civil rights workers in the 20th century.

1041. Colby, Ira C. "The Freedmen's Bureau: From Social Welfare to Segregation." *Phylon* 46 (September 1985): 219-230. Tbl. Colby outlines the welfare and educational services offered by the bureau and notes that these services have made the agency appear heroic. Despite all of the positive activities of the bureau, it also encouraged segregation by offering services mainly for blacks, and both Congress and the Freedman's bureau organization never established clear, comprehensive goals for the agency. The bureau established a pattern for future racism and segregation.

1042. Cooke, Michael Anthony. "The Health of Blacks During Reconstruction, 1862-1870." Ph.D. University of Maryland, College Park, 1983. 254p.

1043. Cox, John and LaWanda. "General O. O. Howard and the 'Misrepresented Bureau'." *Journal of Southern History* 19 (November 1953): 427-456. Freedmen's Bureau records show that the bureau has been grossly misrepresented in historical literature. The authors refute major criticism of the organization, with particular emphasis on the integrity, efficiency, and morality of Gen. Howard and military discipline throughout the bureau. The negative descriptions of corruption, instigation of racial conflicts, and lax administration were due to the interposition of an agency run by a military occupation force composed of Northerners who presumably did not understand Southern ways and who administered dramatic changes in political, economic, and social affairs. Many of the past histories of Reconstruction were written with pro-Johnson interpretations that were naturally biased against the bureau.

1044. Curry, J. L. M. *Education of the Negroes Since 1860.* Baltimore: Trustees of the John F. Slater Fund, 1894. 32p. Tbls. (Occasional Paper, No. 3) Curry, secretary of the trustees of the John F. Slater Fund, focuses mainly on the development of black education in the South during the Civil War and Reconstruction. He writes about the contributions of the U.S. Army, Freedmen's Bureau, missionary organizations, the Peabody Education Fund, and the Slater Fund (post-Reconstruction). Included are several statistical tables illustrating school enrollment and finances.

1045.   DeBoer. Clara Merritt. *His Truth Is Marching On: African Americans Who Taught the Freedmen for the American Missionary Association, 1861-1877.* New York: Garland Publishing, 1995. 401p. Bibl. Ill. The American Missionary Association was the key institution in establishing and maintaining schools for freedmen. DeBoer emphasizes the contributions of black teachers and administrators in the A.M.A.'s program during and after the Civil War. The stereotype of the white, New England schoolmarm was real, but it must not overshadow the diversity within the A.M.A. DeBoer provides background on many of the black participants. The letters of black A.M.A. workers that are part of the Amistad Research Collection and the A.M.A. archives are the basis for this study. (See also DeBoer's "The Role of Afro-Americans in the Origin and Work of the American Missionary Association, 1839-1877." Ph.D. Rutgers University, 1973. 844p.)

1046.   Donald, Henderson H. *The Negro Freedman: Life Conditions of the American Negro in the Early Years After Emancipation.* New York: Henry Schuman, 1952. 270p. Bibl. Donald's survey is divided by topics: labor; food, clothing and shelter; family life, education, recreation and social life; crime; race relations; and political participation. In general, Donald presents a negative image of the way that the freedmen struggled to adjust to new conditions.

1047.   Drake, Richard B. "The American Missionary Association and the Southern Negro, 1861-1888." Ph.D. Emory University, 1957. 307p.

1048.   Drake, Richard B. "Freedmen's Aid Societies and Sectional Compromise." *Journal of Southern History* 29 (May 1963): 175-186. Freedmen's aid societies approached the postwar South with the same type of spiritual fervor that motivated the antislavery campaign. Organizations, such as the American Missionary Association, the New England Freedman's Aid Society, and the American Freedmen's Union Commission, allied with former abolitionists and Radical Republicans to work towards educating freedmen. But in the late 1860s most aid societies withdrew and the Northern Methodist and Baptist churches concentrated on reuniting with the Southern branch. By the mid-1870s most Northerners left the freedmen to receive help from state and local governments.

1049.   DuBois, W. E. B. "The Freedmen's Bureau." *Atlantic Monthly* 87 (March 1901): 354-365. The bureau had too short a history to have a lasting, positive impact. Its successes in labor, black proprietorship, free public schools, and black participation in the courts must be weighed against the failures, including black relations with former masters, paternalism that discouraged self reliance, and the distribution of land. The bureau's legacy is what it was not allowed to accomplish because of government restrictions and Southern white hostility.

1050.   "Educating the Negro After the Civil War." *Negro History Bulletin* 3 (November 1939): 22-24. Ills. Ports.   Provides a brief history covering the period from 1865 to after World War I. The major focus is on the institutional framework during Reconstruction for providing education and the contributions and challenges of freedmen aid societies, the Freedmen's Bureau, and teachers.

1051.   Eggleston, G. K. "The Work of Relief Societies During the Civil War." *Journal of Negro History* 14 (July 1929): 272-299.   Private and private relief organizations played a major role to assist freed slaves with material needs and education.   Private organizations included sectarian societies, such as the American Missionary Association, that served several Protestant denominations. Nonsectarian organizations, mostly from New York, Philadelphia, and Boston, were particularly active during the early years of the war. Black societies also contributed to relief efforts.   There were so many organizations participating that there was great confusion, lack of coordination, and wasted resources.

1052.   Everly, Elaine C.   "Freedmen's Bureau Records: An Overview." *Prologue* 29 (Summer 1997): 95-99. Ill.   Everly discusses the value of the large collection of documents produced by the bureau during and after the Civil War until 1872 when the agency ceased to exist.   She also describes related groups of documents produced by U.S. government agencies, such as the Quartermaster Generals Office, that collected documents on freedmen in Washington, D. C. The Freedmen's Bureau collection and other agency documents provide incite into the lives of freedmen and the federal government's attempt to aid their transition to freedom.

1053.   Everly, Elaine C. "Marriage Registers of Freedmen." *Prologue* 5 (Fall 1973): 150-154. Ills.   Everle writes about the marriage certificates and registers of former slaves that exist in the documentary collections at the National Archives. In general, the Freedmen's Bureau was charged with guaranteeing the availability of legal marriages. State laws were usually followed, but in cases where freedmen were denied a marriage ceremony, bureau officers did it themselves or arranged for it. The records offer information about slave families because many of the couples were married prior to emancipation.

1054.   Foster, Gaines, M. "The Limitations of Federal Health Care for Freedmen, 1862-1868." *Journal of Southern History* 48 (August 1982): 349-372. Tbls. During and after the Civil War the federal government was not organized to provide health services to the mass of freedmen who previously relied on their masters for health care. The Union Army and later the Freedmen's Bureau and freedmen's aid societies established facilities and provided health personnel in the South, but their efforts were inadequate. Health programs were effected by racism, opposition to a large scale welfare program run by the federal government, and the government's limited capabilities. In general freedmen had to rely on their employers for health care, thus perpetuating black reliance on whites and leading to an increase in black mortality after emancipation.

1055.   Franklin, John Hope. "Jim Crow Goes to School: The Genesis of Legal Segregation in Southern Schools." *South Atlantic Quarterly* 58 (Spring 1959): 225-235.   Franklin emphasizes that Jim Crow, the deliberate discrimination and segregation of blacks based on their inferiority to the white race, originally developed in the North and was emulated by the South after the Civil War. He focuses on Jim Crow in the development of education after the war. The practice became entrenched in the South during Reconstruction and taught children of all races that race means more than brains in the public schools.

1056.   Franklin, John Hope.   "Public Welfare in the South During the Reconstruction Era, 1865-1880." *Social Services Review* 44 (December 1970): 379-392.   After the Civil War Southern governments gradually changed from their traditional objection to government sponsored welfare to the beginning of programs to assist the poor and persons with mental and physical disabilities.   State governments also took responsibility for financing education and seeking ways to ameliorate and avoid mass epidemics. Franklin emphasizes that white Southerners changed slowly and often reluctantly, and the changes were usually done only with the needs of whites in mind. Yet progress was made and should be recognized as a positive outcome of Reconstruction.

1057.   Fraser, Walter J., Jr. "John Eaton, Jr., Radial Republican: Champion of the Negro and Federal Aid to Southern Education, 1869-1882." *Tennessee Historical Quarterly* 25 (Fall 1966): 239-260.   In March, 1870 Eaton became commissioner of the Bureau of Education in the Department of Interior. He had experience dealing with the education of freedmen in Tennessee, and he was a staunch supporter of President Grant and the Republican Party. Eaton worked to convince Congress that it had a moral responsibility to provide educational assistance to the freedmen and he worked with authorities in the South to improve public education for everyone. He worked from the premise that education offered hope for the future of black Americans and the reduction of racism.

1058.   Gara, Cyrus (ed.). "Teaching Freedom in the Post-War South." *Journal of Negro History* 40 (July 1955): 274-276.   Printed is one letter dated March 26, 1867 regarding the work of Catherine R. Bent, a Yankee schoolmistress, who taught freedmen in Gainesville, Florida. The letter, written by a friend, explains Bent's dedication in a hostile and isolated atmosphere toward Northern teachers.

1059.   Gibson, Lucretia M. "William Henry Gibson." *Negro History Bulletin* 11 (June 1948): 199, 215.   William Gibson taught in schools organized by the American Missionary Association and the Freedmen's Bureau in Kentucky during 1866.   His appointment as a mail agent for the Louisville and Nashville Railroad provoked some white employees into violent racial incidents.

1060.   Gray, Charles. "The Freedmen's Bureau: A Missing Chapter in Social Welfare History." D.S.W. Yeshiva University, 1994. 204p.

1061.   Griffin, Paul R.   "Black Founders of Reconstruction Era Methodist Colleges: David A. Payne, Joseph C. Price, and Isaac Lane, 1863-1890." Ph.D. Emory University, 1983. 276p.

1062.   Groff, Patrick.   "The Freedmen's Bureau in High School History Textbooks." *Journal of Negro Education* 51 (Fall, 1982): 425-433.   Groff examines 36 textbooks published between 1971 and 1980 and finds that only four tell the truth about the bureau while the others perpetuate myths. Groff believes that the bureau helped to extend the servitude of the freedmen through its labor policy and general support of the black codes prior to 1867.

1063.   Harvey, William Bernard. "Educational Imperialism in the South: An Analysis of Schooling Opportunities For Blacks in the Southern United States From 1865 to 1954." Ed.D. Rutgers University, 1981. 239p.

1064.   Hoffert, Sylvia D. "Yankee Schoolmarms and the Domestication of the South." *Southern Studies* 24 (Summer 1995): 188-201.   Yankee schoolmarms sought to change the character and traditions of the freedmen by teaching them the proper way to live in society. They sought to make the South more like the North and to establish a basis for national unity. Their experiment in social engineering failed because they disregarded differences in cultures and because funding for the Freedmen's Bureau ended in early 1870.

1065.   Holliday, Joseph E. "Freedmen's Aid Societies in Cincinnati, 1862-1870." *Bulletin of the Cincinnati Historical Society* 22 (July 1964): 169-185.   Both sectarian and nonsectarian organizations in Cincinnati helped black refugees during the war and assisted them with relief and education during Reconstruction. During the postwar years the Western Freedman's Aid Commission, dominated by evangelical clergy, became associated with the American Missionary Association in efforts to raise funds for its work in the South. Methodists in Cincinnati were particularly active in the aid societies, as were the Society of Friends which took a leading role in the Contraband Relief Association. Organizations such as these encouraged the federal government to establish the Freedman's bureau.

1066.   Holloway, Laura C. *Howard: The Christian Hero*. New York: Funk and Wagnalls, 1885. 235p.   One chapter of this book focuses on O. O. Howard's leadership of the Freedmen's Bureau and on activities that illustrate Howard's humanitarian spirit and strong Christian faith. Holloway examines Howard's entire career up to the mid-1880s in the context of his Christian beliefs.

1067.   Holmes, Anne Middleton.   *The New York Ladies' Southern Relief Association 1866-1867*. New York: Mary Mildred Sullivan chapter, United Daughters of the Confederacy, New York City, 1926. 113p.   The NYLSRA organized to raise and distribute funds to needy persons and organizations in the

South. Most of Holme's book is comprised of letters received by the NYLSRA from persons or organizations needing aid and letters of thanks for aid given. Also included is a list of contributions and the amount of their contributions, a list of persons or organizations receiving aid and the amounts received, and a list of officers of the NYLSRA. In Holmes introduction she describes the plight of Southerners and gives an indication of her opposition to Reconstruction.

1068.   Howard, Oliver Otis. *Autobiography of Oliver Otis Howard, Major General United States Army.* 2 vols. New York: Baker and Taylor, 1907-1908. 610p. Ills. Ports.   Volume 2, part 3 (p. 163-458) covers the period of Reconstruction when Howard was commissioner of the Freedmen's Bureau. He offers his perspective on the bureau and his own actions related to land redistribution, medical care, courts of law, school organization and financing, famine relief, the Ku Klux Klan, higher education including the beginning of Howard University, and the politics surrounding the operation of the bureau. Howard strongly believed in the bureau's work, particularly its support for education, as the major requirement for the future advancement of the freedmen.

1069.   Jones, Lewis W. "The Agent as a Factor in the Education of Negroes in the South." *Journal of Negro Education* 19 (Winter 1950): 28-37.   Jones describes the use of agents hired as educators in rural and urban areas by the Freedmen's Bureau and private organizations. He notes the contributions Barnas Sears, agent for the George Peabody Fund that provided money for black and white education, although Sears assumed that less money was need to run a black school. Likewise agents for the John F. Slater Fund assisted in black education but insisted on segregation and less money for black schools.

1070.   Keesbury, Forrest E.   "Radical Republicans and the Congressional Abandonment of the Mixed School Idea, 1870-1875." Ed.D. Lehigh University, 1971. 166p.

1071.   Kelly, Alfred H.   "The Congressional Controversy Over School Segregation, 1867-1875." *American Historical Review* 64 (April 1959): 537-563. Charles Sumner and a few other Radical Republicans spearheaded an attempt to pass federal legislation requiring the integration of public school throughout the nation or at least in the Southern states. There was never a majority in Congress that would support the idea and the attempt to attach it to the Civil Rights Bill of 1875 failed. Most congressmen objected to either race mixing or interference in the rights of the states to regulate schools.

1072.   Knight, Edgar W. "The Influence of Reconstruction on Education in the South." Ph.D. Columbia University, 1913. 100p.

1073.   Knight, Edgar W. *Public Education in the South.* Boston: Ginn and Co., 1922.   482p.   Knight includes three chapters related to the period of Reconstruction. He states that public education was more advanced prior to 1861 than was originally thought and that Reconstruction was more destructive to education in the South than was the Civil War. The corrupt and inept Radical regimes that began in 1868 contributed to the degradation of education by introducing unprepared black children, denying it adequate funding, and, in some cases, insisting or threatening to integrate the races. Education did not begin to recover until the restoration of conservative regimes in state and local governments. Knight includes a chapter about the Peabody Fund which assisted with the funding of public education institutions beginning in Reconstruction and extending into the 20th century. A bibliography follows each chapter.

1074.   Knight, Edgar W. "Some Fallacies Concerning the History of Public Education in the South." *South Atlantic Quarterly* 13 (October 1914): 371-381. The notion that Radical Reconstruction regimes introduced public education to the Southern states is wrong. Reconstruction contributed mandatory provisions for education in state constitutions, black education, and a uniform system of taxation for school support. But states, such as North Carolina, Virginia, and Alabama, had prewar school systems that were not unlike those in the Northeast. While Reconstruction governments brought important education reforms, changes occurred only gradually and were often met with frustration.

1075.   Lieberman, Robert C. "The Freedmen's Bureau and the Politics of Institutional Structure." *Social Science History* 18 (Fall 1994): 405-437. Tbls. Lieberman assesses the performance of the bureau in relation to its organizational structure. He argues that the bureaucratic structure and function of the experimental had a direct impact on success and failure. Lieberman compares the bureau's structure during 1866 and early 1867 with mid-1867 to 1870. He finds that it was more successful with a limited charge under the control of the U.S. Army compared with independent agency status and its expanded tasks and goals established by Congress in the second Freedmen's Bureau Act passed in July, 1866. At the height of Radical Republican power, the bureau's effectiveness steadily diminished because it could not control the political environment and its goals became ambiguous and difficult to assess.

1076.   Lindsay, Irabel Burns. "Some Contributions of Negroes to Welfare Services, 1865-1900." *Journal of Negro Education* 25 (Winter 1986): 15-24. Little attention has been directed to the participation of blacks in organizing and providing public welfare in their communities. Records indicate that blacks contributed time, expertise, and money to assist the freedmen. They worked with benevolent societies and the Freedmen's Bureau in relief and education. When voluntary groups and the bureau left the South, leadership of public welfare was taken up by black churches.

1077.   Low, W. A. "The Freedmen's Bureau in the Border States." In *Radicalism, Racism, and Party Realignment, the Border States During Reconstruction*. Edited by R. O. Curry. Baltimore: Johns Hopkins Press, 1969. Pp. 245-264.   The Freedmen's Bureau benefited the slaveholding border states of Maryland, Kentucky, Delaware, West Virginia, and Missouri. Each state had a different experience, but the bureau's main contribution was its help with

establishing schools for the freedmen. Success varied from one state to another.
The efforts of the Freedmen's Bureau were symbolic of the attempt by the federal
government to secure justice, civil rights, and equality for the former slaves.

1078.   Martin, Sandy Dwayne. "The American Baptist Home Mission Society
and Black Higher Education in the South, 1865-1920." *Foundations* 24 (1981):
310-327.   The American Baptist Home Mission Society was founded in 1832 and
took a clear antislavery position. Missionaries from the predominately white,
Northern organization established secular schools for the freedmen that also would
also teach Christian morality. With the cooperation of black Baptists, the
missionaries established seven institutions of higher education in the South. Martin
emphasizes that the A.B.H.M.S. had more financial resources than the black
organizations and were able to have a long term impact on black education. But by
the end of the 19th century the A.B.H.M.S. found itself in conflict with black
organizations that sought an independent course in black education.

1079.   May, J. Thomas.   "Continuity and Change in the Labor Program of the
Union Army and the Freedmen's Bureau." *Civil War History* 17 (September 1971):
245-254.   There was continuity in the institutional approach to dealing with race
relations from the war to the early years of Reconstruction. Many Freedmen's
Bureau agents were former Army officers who had been involved in maintaining
labor contracts during the war, and they were called on to do the same afterwards.
The Army program was based on the military necessity to maintain order among the
contraband. The same mentality was transferred to the bureau program.

1080.   Mayo, A. D. "The Work of Certain Northern Churches in the Education of
the Freedmen, 1861-1900." In *Report of the Commission of Education for the Year
1902*. Vol. 1. Washington, D.C.: Government Printing Office, 1903. Pp. 285-314.
Mayo describes the work performed by the American Missionary Association, the
Freedmen's Aid Society of the Methodist Episcopal Church, the Presbyterian
Church, the Protestant Episcopal Church, the Society of Friends, and the Home
Mission Society of the Baptist Church of the Northern States. He discusses the
management and financing of their efforts, and lauds their work to increase the
number of Christian faithful and to eliminate illiteracy.

1081.   McFeely, William S. "The Freedmen's Bureau: A Study in Betrayal."
Ph.D. Yale University, 1966. 412p.

1082.   McFeely, William S. "Unfinished Business: The Freedmen's Bureau and
Federal Action in Race Relations." In *Key Issues in the Afro-American Experience.
Vol. II: Since 1865*. Edited by Nathan J. Huggins et. al. New York: Harcourt Brace
Jovanovich, 1971. Pp. 5-25.   The Freedmen's Bureau missed an opportunity
immediately after the Civil War to make lasting changes in race relations and put the
freedmen on the road to economic wellbeing. This chance was lost because
Northerners were not willing to view the reform opportunity from a national
perspective and to dedicate the federal government to the role of the instigator of
reform. The bureau was stymied by its own organization, its paternalism in relations

with the freedmen, the lack of resources for its operations, and negative attitudes in Congress toward the use of a government agency to make reforms.

1083. McFeely, William S. *Yankee Stepfather: General O. O. Howard and the Freedmen*. New York: Yale University Press, 1968. 351p. Bibl. Port. McFeely examines Howard's leadership of the Freedmen's Bureau and whether the bureau accomplished what it was capable of doing. He concluded that the bureau generated great promise and hope that the weight of the federal government would be behind the transformation of ex-slaves to free and equal citizens of the U.S. Howard has been roundly praised for his dedicated work, but McFeely is mainly critical of him and the agency. By his methods and decision making, Howard showed himself to be opposed to using the bureau to bring about equal justice and civil rights for blacks. By the end of 1868 Howard had clearly failed the freedmen because his purpose was to achieve only what white America wanted him to achieve.

1084. McPheeters, A. A. "Interest of the Methodist Church in the Education of Negroes." *Phylon* 10 (1949): 343-350. The Freedmen's Aid Society, organized by the Methodist Episcopal Church in October, 1865, engaged in a program to aid the freedmen's physical, educational, and spiritual needs. The society established Meharry Medical College in 1876 for black students. McPheeters also discusses curriculum development in society schools after Reconstruction.

1085. McPherson, James M. "The New Puritanism: Values and Goals of Freedman's Education in America." In *The University in Society. Vol. 2: Europe, Scotland, and the United States From the 16th to the 20th Century*. Edited by Lawrence Stone. Princeton: Princeton University Press, 1974. Pp. 611-639. App. Puritan values pervade the goals of the Protestant missionaries who traveled to the South during and after the Civil War to establish schools and to educate the freedmen. The education that they taught was based on mainly New England, evangelical or Unitarian principles of Puritan ethics, piety and repression. Their goal was to remake the South, but guilt also motivated them to atone for the sin of slavery and to create a more perfect national society. The missionaries became influential in the black community, but their work would later be seen as narrow and ethnically insensitive white indoctrination.

1086. McPherson, James M. "White Liberals and Black Power in Negro Education, 1865-1915." *American Historical Review* 75 (June 1970): 1357-1386. Tbl. Most of this article deals with the decades following Reconstruction. McPherson describes the increasing friction between the "white liberals," who founded and managed most of the black colleges and schools in the South, and the black leaders and students who wanted more blacks in teaching roles. Only after 1900 did the pace of black control of the schools quicken.

1087. Melder, Keith E. "Angel of Mercy in Washington: Josephine Griffing and the Freedmen, 1864-1872." *Records of the Columbia Historical Society of Washington, D. C.* (1963-1965): 243-272. Ills. Griffing grew up in Connecticut before moving to Northern Ohio with her husband in a community filled with former

New England reform activists. She became active in the antislavery and women's movements. In 1864, as an agent of the National Freedmen's Relief Association of the District of Columbia, she began 8 years of relief and education of poor freedmen. Griffing supported black suffrage and the equality of men and women.

1088.   Mills, Joseph A.   "Motives and Behaviors of Northern Teachers in the South During Reconstruction." *Negro History Bulletin* 42 (January-March 1979): 7-9, 17.   Northern Teachers were motived primarily by humanitarian and religious impulse to help the freedmen. The missionary spirit was a vital qualification for teachers selected by voluntary organizations, such as the American Missionary Association, because Christianity and education were intertwined. Mills frequently cites articles from teachers in the *American Missionary* and the *Congregationalist*.

1089.   Morris, Robert C.   "Educational Reconstruction." In *The Facts of Reconstruction: Essays in Honor of John Hope Franklin*. Baton Rouge: Louisiana State University Press, 1991.   Pp. 141-166.   Morris traces the arguments of historians regarding the Freedmen's Bureau and the educational, cultural, and social programs that it tried to install in the South. The enduring images of freedmen's education has been too simplified and should be revised in light of the complex and contradictory nature of the bureau's activities. The bureau worked with white and black private organizations, such as the American Missionary Association and the African Civilization Society, to formulate mostly moderate approaches to educating blacks. Educators stressed the social control ideology of the Northern elite - self help, preparation for responsible citizenship, and academic preparation.

1090.   Morris, Robert C.   *Reading, 'Riting', and Reconstruction: The Education of Freedmen in the South, 1861-1870*. Chicago: University of Chicago Press, 1981. 341p. Bibl. Ills.   Morris surveys the efforts of Northern secular and religious organizations and the Freedmen's Bureau to offer formal education to the freedmen. His purpose is to present a balanced history that explains the background and motives of the teachers and administrators, as well as the feelings of white Southerners. Northern educators generally set a tone of moderation, social order, and gradual acceptance of blacks as they achieved higher levels of education. (See also Morris's Ph.D. dissertation with the same title from University of Chicago, 1976.)

1091.   Nieman, Donald G.   "Andrew Johnson, the Freedmen's Bureau, and the Problem of Equal Rights, 1865-1866." *Journal of Southern History* 44 (August 1978): 399-420.   The Southern state governments organized by President Johnson in 1865 maintained discriminatory laws in dealing with the freedmen. Johnson believed that the federal government ought to stay out of the affairs of state governments, even if it meant that blacks would not be treated with equality. Gen. O. O. Howard, commissioner of the Freedmen's Bureau, sought increased authority to protect the rights of the freedmen, but Johnson did all he could to prevent the extension of federal authority. Legislative attempts to enforce civil rights for blacks were either blocked by Johnson or did not work effectively.

1092.   Nieman, Donald G. To *Set the Law in Motion: The Freedmen's Bureau and the Legal Rights of Blacks, 1865-1868.* Millwood, N.Y.: KTO Press, 1979. 250p. Bibl.   The Freedmen's Bureau attempted to ensure the civil rights and safety of the freedmen. While Congress had hopes that the agency would be broadly successful, in fact, the bureau lacked the manpower and clear legal authority to fulfill its mission. Attempts to arrange for fair labor contracts and equal justice in military courts were met with local white resistance, indifference from some agents, and President Johnson's amnesty program and support for state power over federal authority. Even the Republican Congress reflected the typical mid-19th century reticence to expand federal authority over the states.

1093.   "A Note on the History of School Segregation." *Journal of Public Law* 3 (Spring 1954): 167-170.   Includes is a table organized by state showing the white/black population as of 1870 and the dates each state passed the 14th Amendment, began segregation in public school, and abolished segregation as of 1954. Only 7 states abolished segregation before the end of Reconstruction - Connecticut (1868), Massachusetts (1874), Michigan (1867), Minnesota (1864), Nebraska (1869), and Nevada (1872). The table was taken from the briefs written for the Segregation Cases of 1953-54 when the U.S. Supreme Court requested that all sides in the case investigate the intent of Congress regarding segregation when the 14th Amendment passed.

1094.   Oakes, James. "A Failure of Vision: The Collapse of the Freedmen's Bureau Courts." *Civil War History* 25 (March 1979): 66-76.   Leaders and agents of the Freedmen's Bureau sought equal justice for the freedmen by eliminating discriminatory laws, insisting on equal treatment in local courts, and using bureau courts when local courts could not be trusted. Their ideology, based on middle class, liberal notions of society in the North, could not defeat the unrelenting resentment of the majority of Southern whites against blacks and the bureau's efforts to change Southern society.

1095.   O'Donnell, James H. III. "Taylor Thistle: A Student at the Nashville Institute, 1871-1880." *Tennessee Historical Quarterly* 26 (Winter 1967): 387-395. O'Donnell follows the educational career of a former slave from Missouri who entered the Nashville Normal and Theological Institute with the desire to become a minister. He points out that his study begins to fill a void in research on the freedmen as individuals.

1096.   Olds, Victoria Marcus. "The Freedmen's Bureau As A Social Agency." D.S.W. Columbia University, 1966. 281p.

1097.   Parker, Marjorie H. "Some Educational Activities of the Freedmen's Bureau." *Journal of Negro Education* 23 (Winter 1954): 9-21.   Parker describes how the bureau provided logistical support for benevolent associations, as well as funds and facilities for schools. The agency gave special attention to higher education resulting in the establishment of many colleges and teacher training schools. Southern whites' initial acceptance of black education deteriorated as the political agenda of many Northern teachers became clear and they appeared to threaten notions of white racial superiority.

1098.   Parmalee, Julius H. "Freedmen's Aid Societies, 1861-1871." U.S. Dept. of Interior, Bureau of Education, *Bulletin* no. 38 (1916): 243-266, 268-302. (Rpt. in *Negro Education: A Study of the Private and Higher Schools For Colored People in the U.S.*, by Thomas J. Jones, 2 Vols., Washington, 1917.)   Includes a review of postwar black education followed by statistics by state and school name and information on participating freedmen's aid societies.

1099.   Parmet, Robert D. "Schools For Freeman." *Negro History Bulletin* 34 (October 1971): 128-132. Ill.   Parmet surveys the wartime measures to educate freedmen but focuses primarily on the efforts of the Freedmen's Bureau, benevolent and religious organizations, and individual benefactors. Collectively their efforts were successful because they contributed to the development of Southern public schools and the education of the freedmen.

1100.   Peirce, Paul Skeels. *The Freedmen's Bureau: A Chapter in the History of Reconstruction*. Iowa City: the University, 1904. 200p. *Bulletin of the State University of Iowa*, New Series, No. 74, March, 1904. (Rpt. by Scholarly Press, 1970.)   Peirce provides critical and favorable comments about the bureau, but in general, he concludes that its positive contributions to assist the freedmen and help return order to Southern society outweigh problems in its administration. The bureau helped form the political identity of the freedmen and align them with the Republican Party for decades. (See also Peirce's "The Freedmen's Bureau." Ph.D. Yale University, 1900.)

1101.   Qualls, Youra Thelma. "Friend and Freedman: The Work of the Association of Friends of Philadelphia and its Vicinity for the Relief and Education of Freedmen During the Civil War and Reconstruction, 1862-1872." Ph.D. Radcliffe College, 1956.

1102.   Rabinowitz, Howard N. "Half a Loaf: The Shift From White to Black Teachers in the Negro Schools of the Urban South, 1865-1890." *Journal of Southern History* 40 (November 1874): 565-594.   Rabinowitz focuses on schools in Atlanta, Raleigh, Nashville, Montgomery and Richmond. These cities represent the typical urban educational environment for blacks in the South where most of the teachers were white, whether schools were integrated or segregated. The change to all black teachers came after 1875 as most schools became racially segregated and black parents and school leaders demanded more black teachers. The change symbolized the black acceptance of segregation, but the demand for change also reflected issues of pride and teacher-student identification. Black parents struggled with white school authorities to get black representation on school boards and better funding for instructional materials and salaries.

1103.   Rachal, John. "Freedom's Crucible: William T. Richardson and the Schooling of the Freedmen." *Adult Education Quarterly* 37 (Fall 1986): 14-22.

Richardson worked to establish evening adult education classes to improve the literacy of black workers living on the Sea Islands.

1104. Richardson, Joe M. "The American Missionary Association and Blacks on the Gulf Coast During Reconstruction." *Gulf Coast Historical Review* 4, 2 (1989): 152-161. Richardson describes the A.M.A. program of relief and education for freedmen that would prepare them for a life of participation in society. A.M.A. missionaries near the coast of the Gulf of Mexico were met with white hostility and occasional violence. Relations between blacks and the A.M.A. were complicated by the frustration of some missionaries with the lack of progress among adults and the desire of freedmen to manage their own affairs, including the administration of schools and classroom teaching. The A.M.A. supported black civil rights and education throughout Reconstruction, but by 1880 the early enthusiasm had diminished.

1105. Richardson, Joe M. *Christian Reconstruction: The American Missionary Association and Southern Blacks, 1861-1890.* Athens: University of Georgia Press, 1986. 348p. Bibl. Ills. The A.M.A. was the most important organization that worked throughout the Civil War and Reconstruction to help Southern blacks by providing basic relief assistance and organizing and managing schools and colleges throughout the South. They regarded their work as a Christian crusade that combined religion and politics to effect social change. The A.M.A. worked with the black community which frequently took the lead in providing funding, students, and teachers. Less successful was the A.M.A.'s effort to establish Congregational churches in the black community, and its other educational efforts were sometimes marred by racism and excessive paternalism by A.M.A. agents.

1106. Sawyer, R. McLaran. The National Educational Association and Negro Education, 1865-1884." *Journal of Negro Education* 39 (Fall 1970): 331-345. At the end of the war the National Teachers' Association and later the National Educational Association supported the idea of granting full civil rights to the freedmen. Eventually the N.E.A. bowed to popular pressure for segregation and disenfranchisement. By the early 1880s the N.E.A. sought to break down sectionalism between North and South and gave in to the white South's insistence that only they knew the proper way of dealing with Southern blacks.

1107. Seifman, Eli. "Education or Emancipation: Schism Within the African Colonization Movement, 1865-1875." *History of Education Quarterly* 7 (Spring 1967): 36-57. Seifman describes the colonization movement led by the American Colonization Society. The debate regarding whether to place resources into colonization or educating freedmen for life in America became pronounced after the Civil War and continued into the early 20th century with the A.C.S. as the lone advocate of colonization.

1108. Small, Sandra E. "The Yankee Schoolmarm in Freedmen's Schools: An Analysis of Attitudes." *Journal of Southern History* 45 (August 1979): 381-402. Negative stereotypes about troublemaking schoolmarms do not fit many of the teachers. Small studied the writings of 12 white, New England women who came to the South to teach and offer relief to the freedmen. The women studied are Anna Gardner, Martha Schofield, Cornelia Hancock, Sarah E. and Lucy Chase, Laura Matilda Towne, Margaret Newbold Thorpe, Susan Walker, Elizabeth Hyde Botume, Harriet Ware, Mary Ames, and Elizabeth Pearson. They showed their progressive attitudes toward aiding the needy freedmen and they worked with religious fervor. The women illustrated the conflicts and contradictions of Northern Republican ideology.

1109.   Small, Sandra Eileen. "The Yankee Schoolmarm in Southern Freedmen's Schools, 1861-1871: The Career of a Stereotype." Ph.D. Washington State University, 1976. 244p.

1110.   Stowe, Harriet Beecher. "The Education of Freedmen." *North American Review* 128 (1879): 605-615; 129 (1879): 81-94.   In part one Stowe, author of *Uncle Tom's Cabin* (1852), examines the history of Southern objections to public schools generally and to the education of blacks. She briefly describes the efforts made during Reconstruction to provide blacks with education. In part two Stowe examines the educational institutions throughout the South that were organized by Christian organizations with the assistance of the Freedmen's Bureau.

1111.   Swint, Henry Lee. *The Northern Teacher in the South 1862-1870*. New York: Octagon Books, 1967. 221p. App. Bibl. (Rpt. of Nashville: Vanderbilt University Press, 1941)   Swint examines the type of Northern organizations that participated in educating the freedmen, the motives and attitudes of the men and women who organized and taught in schools, and the reaction to the Northern educators from the local white population. The attitudes of the freedmen's aid organizations and the teachers they employed were based mainly on a combination of humanitarianism, abolitionist tradition, and religious and pietistic devotion to Christianity. Local whites distrusted their motives and feared their influence on the black population. Swint includes biographical sketches of selected officers of educational organizations, a list of officers grouped by association, and a list of Northern teachers who served in the South between 1862 and 1870 with their home town and service locations. (See also Swint's Ph.D. dissertation with the same title from Vanderbilt University, 1939.)

1112.   Tyack, David and Robert Lowe. "The Constitutional Movement: Reconstruction and Black Education in the South." *American Journal of Education* 94 (February 1986): 236-256.   The authors illustrate how the political power gained by the freedmen and the help of Northern Republicans led to public school programs that had a positive impact on black education during Reconstruction and the decades that followed. Education and a taste of political power contributed to a more promising future future for blacks, despite the return to power of conservative whites in the South. Even though white supremacists showed how legal and political power could enforce social and economic inequality, many gains from Reconstruction remained.

1113.   Vaughn, William Preston. "Partner in Segregation: Barnas Sears and the Peabody Fund." *Civil War History* 10 (September 1964): 260-274.   Sears was selected the general agent for the Peabody Fund, a source of funding donated by George Peabody in 1867 to promote public education in the South. The fund was built at a time when Reconstruction legislatures were beginning new public education programs mandated by new state constitutions.   Sears tried to avoid politics, but he publicly opposed racial integration of schools.

1114.   Vaughn, William Preston. *Schools For All: The Blacks and Public Education in the South, 1865-1877*. Lexington: University Press of Kentucky, 1974. 181p. Bibl.   Vaughn recognizes the important work of the Freedmen's Bureau and Northern benevolent societies in building a foundation for future black education, despite the negative reaction of a large percentage of Southern whites. He discusses the struggle over school integration at both the secondary and college levels, but integration was mainly an unsuccessful issue except in a limited way in Louisiana and South Carolina. Integration was discouraged by Southern whites, by Congress, and by the Peabody Fund, an important private educational funding organization that gave funds to segregated schools in the South to benefit both races. Despite segregation, the progress made by blacks in education was a positive outcome of Reconstruction. (See also Vaughn's "The Sectional Conflict in Southern Public Education: 1865-1876." Ph.D. Ohio State University, 1961. 315p.)

1115.   Warner, Stafford Allen. *Yardley Warner: The Freedman's Friend. His Life and Times With His Journal and Letters Reproduced in an Appendix*. Didcat: Wessex Press, 1957. 331p. Ills.   Portions of this book describe Warner's work with the Friends (Quaker) Freedmen Aid Association of Philadelphia. He traveled extensively in the South between 1866 and 1872 supervising the building and staffing of schools for freedmen of all ages, and he sought to organize teacher training schools so that blacks could be trained as teachers for black schools. Warner communicated with Quakers in Britain about his work in the South. Warner's journal and letters are the basis for this book. The author is his son.

1116.   Weisenfeld, Judith. "'Who is Sufficient for these Things?: Sara G. Stanley and the American Missionary Association, 1864-1868." *Church History* 60 (December 1991): 493-507.   Stanley, a free black from North Carolina who was educated in Ohio, took part in the A.M.A.'s efforts to teach freed black children in Virginia, Missouri, Kentucky, and Alabama from 1864 to 1868. Her devotion to Presbyterianism influenced her Christian approach toward racial equality and was the basis for her charges of racism against specific white A.M.A. teachers and administrators. Stanley promoted the idea of equality to her students, and she wrote stories of her experiences that were published in the *American Missionary*. Her work is representative of the contributions of black women to education in Reconstruction and the racial tensions that existed within the A.M.A.

1117.   West, Earle H. "The Harris Brothers: Black Northern Teachers in the Reconstruction South." *Journal of Negro Education* 48 (Spring 1979): 126-138. William and Robert Harris of Ohio sought to serve God by teaching the freedmen, but unlike their white colleagues, the two black men did not take the cause of political indoctrination (i.e. Republicanism) into the classroom. They sought to wed religion and education for the future success of the former slaves. Both worked in Virginia, and Robert also worked in North Carolina.

1118.   West, Earle H. "The Peabody Education Fund and Negro Education, 1867-1880." *History of Education Quarterly* 6 (Summer 1966): 3-21.   West describes the contributions of the Peabody Education Fund to funding of black schools in the South under the direction of Barnes Sears. The fund promoted black education, but also contributed to the treatment of blacks as second class citizens. Sears believed that it was the organization's Christian duty to promote education among all, but the issues of integration and civil rights were compromised in favor of achieving long term goals.

1119.   Westwood, Howard C. "Getting Justice For the Freedmen." *Howard Law Journal* 16 (Spring 1971): 492-537.   Westwood examines how the Freedmen's Bureau sought to guarantee equal justice for Southern blacks by organizing special legal counsel to be paid by the government. He focuses on the activities of attorneys James C. Carlisle, A. K. Browne, and E. J. Smithars, although bureau agents were also authorized to act as legal counsel for freedmen. The quality and general impact of the service is not examined.

1120.   Wolfe, Allis. "Women Who Dared: Northern Teachers of the Southern Freedmen, 1862-1872." Ph.D. City University of New York, 1982. 227p.

1121.   Wyatt-Brown, Bertram. "Black Schooling During Reconstruction." In *The Web of Southern Social Relations: Women, Family, and Education.* Edited by Walter J. Fraser, Jr. et. al. Athens: University of Georgia Press, 1985. Pp. 146-165. Wyatt-Brown examines the reasons for the problems encountered in educating young freedmen. The education provided by the American Missionary Association and teachers associated with other organizations was based on white, Northern culture. Black children from a rural, peasant setting were used to group, visual learning and had great difficulty with individual cogitation and study. The children experienced competing pressures from their families that wanted them to contribute to the family livelihood, and from local whites, who opposed the education of blacks.

Religion, Family, and Gender

1122.   Abzug, Robert H. "The Black Family During Reconstruction." In *Key Issues in the Afro-American Experience. Vol. II: Since 1865.* Edited by Nathan I. Huggins et. al. New York: Harcourt Brace Jovanovich, 1971. Pp. 26-41.   Abzug provides an alternative view of the post-emancipation black family compared with the story told by historians who have stressed the lack of morality and emotional attachment in black families. He emphasizes the immediate and serious desire among the freedmen to establish a normal family life in freedom. The strong interest in the well-being of their children and the sanctity of their marriages brought new stability, not disintegration to families. The failure of Reconstruction, with its original promise of true freedom, economic opportunity, and personal security, was a blow to black families. Their new freedom was undermined by white violence and economic subjugation.

1123. Angell, Stephen Warder. *Henry McNeal Turner and Black Religion in the South, 1865-1900.* Ph.D. Vanderbilt University, 1988. 670p.

1124. Bailey, Kenneth K. "The Post-Civil War Racial Separations in Southern Protestantism: Another Look." *Church History* 46 (December 1977): 453-473. Race relations in Southern Protestant churches were drastically different prior to and after the Civil War. Before the war a greater feeling of racial togetherness before God existed among whites. After the war, as blacks quickly established their own churches with the encouragement of whites, racial animosity increased and pejorative references to blacks became more common. Segregated churches became a necessity in an environment of Southern white supremacy.

1125. Berkeley, Kathleen C. "'Colored Ladies Also Contributed': Black Women's Activities From Benevolence to Social Welfare, 1866-1896." In *The Web of Southern Social Relations: Women, Family, and Education.* Edited by Walter J. Fraser, Jr. et. al. Athens: University of Georgia Press, 1985. Pp. 181-203. (Rpt. in *Church and Community Among Black Southerners 1865-1900.* New York: Garland, 1994.) In her examination of black women in benevolent societies in Memphis, Berkeley illustrates the leadership that women provided to merge gender with race and class, mostly within the context of Baptist and African Methodist Episcopal church organizations. The Daughters of Zion of Avery Chapel was one such organization that raised funds within the black community to dispense aid to the needy. Berkeley calls for more gender based research to reveal the hidden contributions of women.

1126. Berlin, Ira, Steven F. Miller, and Leslie S. Rowland. "Afro-American Families in the Transition From Slavery to Freedom." *Radical History Review* 42 (1988): 89-121. Ill. The authors publish documents selected by the Freedmen and Southern Society Project at the National Archives. This selection includes letters illustrating the strong family and community ties that existed among the former slaves and how freedom effected these ties during the postwar years. The letters are dated from 1865 to 1867. (See also # 1127)

1127. Berlin, Ira and Leslie S. Rowland (eds.). *Families and Freedom: A Documentary History of African-American Kinship in the Civil War Era.* New York: New Press, 1997. 259p. Ills. This book includes a selection of correspondence previously published in *Freedom: A Documentary History of Emancipation* (see # 8) and in the *Radical History Review* (see # 1126). All letters were written by slaves or former slaves, black soldiers and their families during wartime, as well as various family members during the early years of freedom. They offer insight into the state and hopes of black families during a critical period.

1128.   Bucke, Emory Stevens et. al. (eds). *The History of American Methodism.* 3 Vols. New York: Abindon Press, 1964. Bibl. Ills.   In volume II, chapters 18-19, the author focuses on the restoration of the Methodist Church in the South and the Southern missionary work of Northern Methodists. Postwar church activities that brought Northerners and Southerners together were rife with political, cultural, and racial problems that kept the Methodist Church split, just as it was prior to the Civil War because of slavery. The Southern church lost many white and virtually all black members. Missionary work with freedmen by Northern Methodists is described with particular emphasis on teaching and organizing educational institutions.

1129.   Clinton, Catherine.   "Bloody Terrain: Freedwomen, Sexuality, and Violence During Reconstruction." *Georgia Historical Quarterly* 76 (Summer 1992): 313-332.   Clinton comments that the amount of literature on the rape of white women far exceeds the few studies on the rape of black women. She believes that this is indicative of pervasive racism in academia. Even though freed women had more civil rights after the war and were no longer owned by white masters, their treatment in the postwar period frequently continued as before emancipation. White men inflicted rapes and beatings without much fear that the Southern criminal justice system would punish them.

1130.   Clinton, Catherine. "Reconstructing Freedwomen." In *Divided Houses: Gender and the Civil War.* Edited by Catherine Clinton and Nina Silber. New York: Oxford University Press, 1992. Pp. 306-319.   Clinton focuses on the difficulties faced by freed black women in a white Southern society that showed little respect for them and denied them civil rights. Freedmen's Bureau records and newspapers provide accounts that illustrate the relationship of white male abuse of black women and the vagaries of Southern state laws regarding marriage and children. The white South attempted to establish separate standards for black sexual morality, sexual abuse, and domestic relationships that carried over traditions from slavery. The result was not only severe punishment and abuse but also the physical torture of black women by white men.

1131.   Currie-McDaniel, Ruth. "Northern Women in the South, 1860-1880." *Georgia Historical Quarterly* 76 (Summer 1992): 284-312.   Northern women arrived in the South as teachers or with their husbands. In general, they left with negative impressions regarding social order, cleanliness, insects, food, the enmity of whites, and frequently their interactions with freedmen. The South was often described as a beautiful place, but the experiences of their husbands and their Northern bias and upbringing led the women to reject Southern life as they saw it. Teachers and missionaries were more likely to have feelings of accomplishment.

1132.   Currie-McDaniel, Ruth. "The Wives of the Carpetbaggers." In *Race, Class, and Politics in Southern History: Essays in Honor of Robert F. Durden.*

Edited by Jeffrey J. Crow et. al. Baton Rouge: Louisiana State University Press, 1989. Pp. 35-78. The mix of race, class, and gender are the central issues in this discussion of four Northern women in the South: Emma Spaulding Bryant, wife of John Emory Bryant of Georgia; Blanche Butler Ames, wife of Adelbert Ames of Mississippi; Emma Kilborn Tourgée, wife of Albion Winegar Tourgée of North Carolina; and Etta Stearns, wife of Charles Stearns of Georgia. These women came to the South with negative stereotypes of Southern culture and never discarded them. The author discusses their perceptions of gender relationships and the lack of influence that Republican ideology had on their husbands' traditional ideas about women.

1133.   Daniel, W. Harrison. "English Presbyterians, Slavery and the American Crisis of the 1860s." *Journal of Presbyterian History* 58 (Spring 1980): 50-62. English Presbyterians closely followed events in the U.S. during the Civil War and Reconstruction. They strongly opposed slavery and greeted its elimination with pleasure. Even though hey hoped for leniency toward the South in Reconstruction, but also supported equal legal and civil rights for the freedmen and ensuring that the freedmen had an opportunity for advancement in American society.

1134.   Daniel, W. Harrison. "The Reaction of British Methodism to the Civil War and Reconstruction in America." *Methodist History* 16 (October 1977): 3-20. British Methodists strongly opposed slavery and considered the devastation of the war to be an expression of God's judgment on the nation. After the war they supported full civil rights for American blacks.

1135.   Davis, J. Treadwell. "Obstacles to Reunion of the Presbyterian Church, 1868-1888." *Virginia Magazine of History and Biography* 63 (January 1955): 28-39. The Presbyterian Church in the U.S. split into Northern and Southern churches in 1861 at the commencement of the Civil War. The issue of slavery tore the Church apart, and even after the war, enmity and distrust continued. Despite attempts by the Northern Church to find a way to reunite the two parts of the Church, only cordial relations returned by the 1880s. Politics continued to keep them apart until reunion finally occurred in 1954.

1136.   Farish, Hunter Dickinson. *The Circuit Rider Dismounts: A Social History of Southern Methodism 1865-1900*. Richmond, Va.: Dietz Press, 1938. 400p. App. Bibl. Ports. Farish sympathizes with the Methodist Episcopal Church, South in its efforts to protect itself from agents of the Northern church who invaded the South to reunify the Church and introduce Northern values and theology. The Southerners successfully worked to rehabilitate their church and become active in temperance and education at all levels. The Southern church expressed sympathy with the blacks and sought to ensure their civil rights and freedoms.

1137.   Fleming, John E. "Slavery, Civil War and Reconstruction: A Study of Black Women in Microcosm." *Negro History Bulletin* 38 (August/September 1975): 430-433. Sojourner Truth, Susie King Taylor and Octavia Rogers worked during Reconstruction to improve educational and social conditions for freedmen. They represent how black women struggled to throw off the tradition of slavery.

1138.   Frankel, Noralee. "From Slave Women to Free Women: The National Archives and Black Women's History in the Civil War Era." *Prologue* 29 (Summer 1997): 100-104. Ills.   Two document collections are the focus of this article - the Civil War soldiers pension files (Record Group 15) and the Freedmen's Bureau files (Record Group 105). Both document groups reveal the role of black women in the context of freedmen families and society in general.   The pension files offer information on private and family life reported by black veterans.   Bureau files also provide a wealth of information on families, including relations between men and women, labor, finance, and social structure.

1139.   Fulmer, Hal W. "The Defiant Legacy: Southern Clergy and a Rhetoric Of Redemption For The Reconstruction South." Ph.D.   Louisiana State University, 1985. 221p.

1140.   Gravely, William B. "James Lynch and the Black Christian Mission During Reconstruction." In *Black Apostles at Home and Abroad: Afro-Americans and the Christian Mission From the Revolution to Reconstruction.* Edited by David W. Wells and Richard Newman. Boston: G. K. Hall, 1982. Pp. 161-188.   Lynch, a black preacher in the Methodist Episcopal Church, worked for the general welfare, education, and religious organization of freedmen during and after the war.   His work in South Carolina, Georgia and Mississippi brought him into public prominence as a political exponent of black civil rights and black churches.   As Mississippi secretary of state, he helped organize the first public school system in the state.

1141.   Gravely, William B. "The Social, Political and Religious Significance of the Formation of the Colored Methodist Episcopal Church (1870)." *Methodist History* 18 (1979): 3-25. (Rpt. in *Church and Community Among Black Southerners 1865-1900.* Edited by Donald Nieman. New York: Garland, 1994. Pp. 201-223) Gravely explains the developments leading to the formation of the C.M.E. Church, its property claims against the white Methodist Episcopal Church, South, and the part taken by the African Methodist Episcopal Church and the A.M.E. Zion Church in an unsuccessful attempt to merge the related black churches prior to 1870. The C.M.E. Church distinguished itself from related black Methodist churches by avoiding politics and bringing together a group comprised entirely of former slaves. Politics and religion separated black Methodists.

1142.   Griffin, Farah Jasmine. "Frances Ellen Watkins Harper in the Reconstruction South." *Sage: A Scholarly Journal on Black Women*, Student Suppl. (1988): 45-47.   Griffin examines Harper's letters, articles, and poems to illustrate her focus on black women. Harper was very optimistic about prospects for middle class blacks in Reconstruction, but her perspective changed to a broader and more realistic focus on the problems and concerns of different classes of blacks, as well as the prominence of black women in black society.

1143.   Harvey, Paul. "Redeemed By Blood: White Baptist Organizing in the South, 1865-1895." In *Redeeming the South: Religious Cultures and Racial Identities Among Southern Baptists, 1865-1925*. Chapel Hill: University of North Carolina Press, 1997. Pp. 17-44.   The Baptist Church split into Northern and Southern branches in 1844 over the issue of slavery.   During Reconstruction the Southern branch formed a solid opposition to reforms legislated by Congress and the political and religious influence of Northern politicians, soldiers, and missionaries. Baptists helped to establish white supremacy and entrench the myth of the horrors of Reconstruction.

1144.   Harvey, Paul. "A Wall of the Lord 'Round Me: Black Baptist Organizing in the South, 1865-1895." In *Redeeming the South: Religious Cultures and Racial Identities Among Southern Baptists, 1865-1925*. Chapel Hill: University of North Carolina Press, 1997. Pp. 45-74.   Freedmen left white Baptist churches to seek independence and to get away from white paternalism and racism.   Whites assisted blacks with building churches, but they would not relate to black brethren as equals. Harvey emphasizes the role of the black churches in the social, cultural, and political life of the community.   Baptist organizations and colleges contributed to the development of institutional roots by the end of the 19th century.

1145.   Hayden, J. Carleton. "After the War: The Mission and Growth of the Episcopal Church Among Blacks in the South, 1865-1872." *Historical Magazine of the Protestant Episcopal Church* 42 (December 1973): 403-427.   The growing population of Southern black Episcopalians prior to the war reversed after the war. Most former slaves fled from white Episcopal churches for black led Methodist and Baptist churches. The blacks who found their own Episcopal churches tended to be urban and better educated than the mass of slaves.   Hayden discusses the development of these black churches, and he also examines the work of the Protestant Episcopal Freedmen's Commission, founded in October, 1865, that offered limited assistance with the relief of freedmen and the establishment of schools in the South.

1146.   Heckman, Oliver S. "Northern Church Penetration of the South, 1860-1880." Ph.D. Duke University, 1939.

1147.   Heckman, Oliver S. "The Presbyterian Church in the United States of America in Southern Reconstruction, 1860-1880." *North Carolina Historical Review* 20 (July 1943): 219-237.   The issue of slavery split the Presbyterian Church before the Civil War, and the attempt by the Northern branch to dominate the Southern churches failed. Heckman describes the contributions to relief and education of freedmen of the Northern New School and Old School Presbyterians, particularly in North Carolina and South Carolina.   They continued to have influence through the end of the 19th century.

1148.   Hewitt, Nancy. "Did Women Have a Reconstruction? Gender in the Rewriting of Southern History." *Proceedings and Papers of the Georgia Association of Historians* 14 (1993): 1-11.   Research during the past 20 years has revealed the importance of gender issues in the postwar South. By studying the intersection of women, race, and freedom in Reconstruction, we recognize that women were able to take small steps toward equality when civil rights and freedom were important issues in American society.

1149.   Hildebrand, Reginald F.   "Methodism and the Meaning of Freedom: Missions to Southern Blacks During the Era of Emancipation and Reconstruction." Ph.D. Princeton University, 1991. 292p.

1150.   Hildebrand, Reginald F. *The Times Were Strange and Stirring: Methodist Preachers and the Crisis of Emancipation.* Durham: Duke University Press, 1995. 189p. Bibl.   Black and white Methodist Episcopal missionaries influenced the process of emancipation and the realization and understanding of freedom among former slaves. Hildebrand is particularly concerned with the different approaches toward freedom communicated by missionaries of the African Methodist Episcopal Church, African Methodist Episcopal Zion Church, Colored Methodist Episcopal Church, Methodist Episcopal Church, North, and Methodist Episcopal Church, South.   He finds that there were three main perspectives - black and white Southerners offering a new paternalism characterized by realism, limits on black freedom, and accommodation with white society; Northern blacks supporting the Gospel of Freedom characterized by Republican, middle class values of freedom, work, and racial regeneration, pride, and nationalism; and integrationists who sought to replace white supremacy with a colorblind society without castes.

1151.   Hodes, Martha. "The Sexualization of Reconstruction Politics: White Women and Black Men in the South After the Civil War." *Journal of the History of Sexuality* 3 (January 1993): 402-417.   Strong white objections to sexual relationships between white women and black men began after emancipation when blacks sought equal civil rights in society. In order to maintain or impose white supremacy over blacks, particularly black males, sexual liaisons with white women were deemed abhorrent to a pure white race and the maintenance of white political order. The Ku Klux Klan often directed violent attacks against couples thought to be engaging in an elicit relationship, and reports indicate punishment against black men of a sexual nature in political disputes.

1152.   Hudson, Winthrop S.   "Reconstituting the Nation: Religion and Reconstruction." *Foundations* 8 (October 1965): 331-337.   The cause of the Civil War was national unity, but the victory of the North was not fulfilled in the Reconstruction period. The federal government lacked leadership and allowed the South to lead a successful resistance against reform that delayed the resolution of sectional problems for a later generation.

1153.   Jervey, Edward D. "Motives and Methods of the Methodist Episcopal Church in the Period of Reconstruction." *Methodist History* 4 (July 1966): 17-25. As the Methodist Episcopal Church, North attempted to replace its Southern counterpart and bring freedmen into the fold, their efforts were partially influenced by political motives and personal gain. In general, they contributed to aiding the freedmen in the transition to freedom, but support for the Radicals was partly due to issues relating to church property.

1154.   John, Beverly M. "Culture And Social Change: The Values and Behaviors of African-American People in the South Carolina Lowcountry and Georgia Coastal Region in the Antebellum and Postbellum Periods." Ph.D. University Of California, Berkeley, 1991. 250p.

1155.   Jones, Jacqueline. "Encounters, Likely and Unlikely, Between Black and Poor White Women in the Rural South, 1865-1940." *Georgia Historical Quarterly* 76 (Summer 1992): 332-353.   Most of this book deals with the period after Reconstruction, but it is helpful for any examination of black/white relations in the South following the Civil War. Jones concludes that even poor white women subordinated black women in order to elevate their own image of themselves.

1156.   Jones, Jacqueline. "Women Who Were More Than Men: Sex and Status in Freedmen's Teaching." *History of Education Quarterly* 19 (Spring 1979): 47-59. Like other teachers in the 1860s and 1870s, Northern teachers of freedmen held a lower status and were offered lower pay than their male counterparts. They were also not given management responsibilities. Jones discusses cases of protest against gender discrimination and male domination as they were expressed in diaries and letters of teachers associated with the American Missionary Association.

1157.   Lebsock, Suzanne D. "Radical Reconstruction and the Property Rights of Southern Women." *Journal of Southern History* 43 (May 1977): 195-216. Lebsock explains that the reform of property rights for women that appeared in the 1867-1869 Southern constitutions written by Radical Republicans made significant progress for women's rights.   The reforms were not so much concessions to women's rights as they shielded wives from economic exploitation by their husbands.   The reforms should be seen as very moderate actions taken by what Kenneth Stampp referred to as "essentially conservative" constitutions. Lebsock surveys the changes incorporated in state constitutions throughout the South and compares them with other laws on divorce.

1158.   Maddex, Jack P. "From Theocracy to Spirituality: The Southern Presbyterian Reversal on Church and State." *Journal of Presbyterian History* 54 (Winter 1976): 438-457.   The Southern Presbyterian Church openly supported slavery and the Confederacy much to the consternation of Northern brethren. After the war the Church changed its focus to become apolitical. It claimed to be following prewar ideas, but Maddex explains that they mainly responded to the Confederate defeat and criticism from Presbyterians in the North. The Southerners rewrote their history to eliminate recognition of the Church's role in antebellum and wartime politics.

1159.   Mann, Susan A. "Slavery, Sharecropping, and Sexual Inequality." *Signs* 14 (Summer 1989): 774-798. (Rpt. in *'We Specialize in the Wholly Impossible': A Reader in Black Women's History*. Edited by Darlene Clark Hine et. al. New York:

Carlson Publishing, 1995. Pp. 281-302.)   Mann explores the relationships between sex, race and class as experienced by black women in the transition from slavery to freedom. She finds continuity and reinforcement of discrimination and abuse of black women by both white and black men. Sexual abuse by white men continued, and a patriarchal environment in black sharecropper families reinforced the lower status and inequality of women as reflected in their labor, domestic violence, health, and education.

1160.   Mohler, Mark. "The Episcopal Church and National Reconstruction, 1865." *Political Science Quarterly* 41 (December 1926): 567-595.   The Episcopal Church served as a positive force in the reconciliation between the North and the South following the Civil War. Up to 1861 it was the only Protestant denomination with a national membership, because the church rejected politics as an issue in church policy and the church was led by Rev. J. H. Hopkins who was sympathetic to the Southern cause. Mohler contrasts the Episcopal Church with the postwar relations between Northern and Southern branches of the Methodists, Presbyterians, and Baptists.

1161.   Montgomery, William E. *Under Their Own Vine and Fig Tree: The African-American Church in the South, 1865-1900*. Baton Rouge: Louisiana State University, 1993. 358p. Ills. Ports.   From the beginning of Reconstruction through the end of the 19th century black churches developed into the stabilizing root to the life of Southern blacks. Whether with the help of Northern missionaries or on their own, blacks left white churches to form their own institutions. The leaders of black churches, particularly the preachers, helped to guide the people in religious, educational, political, and social affairs. There was no monolithic black church because the black religious community was greatly fragmented by social status. The fragmentation was also reflected in approaches to race relations and the improvement of former slaves. (See also "Negro Churches in the South, 1865-1915." Ph.D. University of Texas, 1975. 362p.)

1162.   Moore, David O. "The Withdrawal of Blacks From Southern Baptist Churches Following Emancipation." *Baptist History and Heritage* 16 (1981): 12-18.   Baptist theology and a theology of liberation were the basis for the approach of Southern blacks to their new freedom and to white discrimination. White Baptists wanted to retain blacks in their churches so that white domination could be maintained, but the desire for independence and self dignity, and the oppressive nature of white imposed segregation led black Baptists to split away from white congregations.

1163.   Moorhead, James H. *American Apocalypse: Yankee Protestants and the Civil War, 1860-1869*. New Haven: Yale University Press, 1978. 278p. Bibl. Protestant theology played the key role in designing the moral foundation for the Union's approach to the Civil War and its aftermath. The war was interpreted in moral terms as an apocalyptic event that would bring equilibrium to the nation by eliminating slavery and breaking down sectional divisions that were viewed as expressions of selfishness and disloyalty. The expected kingdom of peace that would embrace the nation was an idea that never died completely, but it faltered in the face of Southern obstruction to Northern Protestant ideology. The partial successes achieved by missionary work among the freedmen also revealed that a transformation of society was not imminent. Northern Protestants grew tired of the struggle to reshape the South, and they gave up social idealism in favor of letting blacks find their way with the help of Southern whites. Their goals were too high and the task unrealistic.

1164.   Morrow, Ralph E. *Northern Methodism and Reconstruction.*   East Lansing: Michigan State University Press, 1956. 269p. Bibl.   The Northern Methodist Church responded to peace in 1865 by sending agents to the South to expand membership and to aid the freedmen. This mission and its enthusiasm for abolition conformed with the Church's traditional ambivalence toward black membership.   Southern Methodists opposed expansion of the Northern church among whites, although expansion met some success mainly where there had been the fewest slaves or where Unionists were strong. Northern Methodists contributed to the education and political awareness of the freedmen, but black recruitment into the church could not compete with African Methodist Episcopal churches. Morrow analyses the problems encountered by Northern Methodist agents, including funding Southern projects, racism, and Republican politics. (See also Morrow's "The Methodist Episcopal Church, The South, and Reconstruction, 1865-1880." Ph.D. Indiana University, 1954. 361p.)

1165.   Morrow, Ralph E.   "Northern Methodism in the South During Reconstruction." *Mississippi Valley Historical Review* 41 (September 1954): 197-218.   Leaders of the Northern Methodist Church saw the South as a vast, rich region to expand the teachings of the Church, and they hoped to reunite the Northern and Southern branches that breached in 1844 over the issue of slavery. Methodist missionaries expected to spread Northern Church ideology among whites and freedmen, but their success was limited. Most Southern whites rejected Radical Republican ideology. Some success occurred in the mountain regions of Tennessee, Alabama, North Carolina, and Georgia. The freedmen were subjected to extensive religious and educational instruction by the Church, but they preferred the African Methodist Episcopal Church.

1166.   Murray, Andrew E.   *Presbyterians and the Negro - A History.* Philadelphia: Presbyterian Historical Society, 1966. 270p. Bibl.   By the end of the Civil War Northern Presbyterians united behind the cause of emancipation even though they did not consider it to be the primary goal of the war. They participated in educating freedmen in the South, but few blacks joined the church. Southern Presbyterians disagreed with their Northern brethren about the idea of equal rights for blacks or even equality within the church. By 1877 the Northern Presbyterians turned away from supporting equal rights and accepted racial segregation and Southern white supremacy. The change in approach to race issues followed the pattern of the U.S. in general.

1167.   Pearne, Thomas H. "The Freedmen." *Methodist Review* 59 [4th Ser., vol. 29] (July 1877): 462-481.   Pearne reviews the contributions of Christian churches to the relief and educational work of the American Missionary Association with the freedmen. He emphasizes the work of the Methodist Episcopal Church that supplied more manpower and money than any other group.   Pearne includes statistical comparisons and a discussion of educational institutions founded by all the churches.

1168.   Peterson, Carla L. "Home/Nation/Institutions: African-American Women and the Work of Reconstruction (1863-1880)." In *"Doers of the World": African-American Women Speakers and Writers in the North (1830-1880)*. New York: Oxford University Press, 1995. Pp. 196-238.   This study of black women in Reconstruction focuses on Harriet and Louisa Jacobs, Charlotte Forten, Frances Watkins Harper, Sojourner Truth, Maria Stewart, and Mary Ann Shudd Cary. Through their actions, such as participation in the Freedmen's Bureau, politics, and the press, or their works of fiction and poetry, these women represented the attempt to establish and foster a sense of home and independence in the black community in a new era of freedom.   Their diverse efforts involved labor, political power, and educational advancement. Peterson explains that they may be understood within the context of growing complexity in gender and race relations following the Civil War.

1169.   Rector, W. Henry. "A Reconstruction Episode: Bishop Lay and Episcopal Church Reunion, 1865." *Arkansas Historical Quarterly* 2 (September 1943): 193-201. Port.   Henry C. Lay, missionary bishop of the southwest in Arkansas, joined with his friend Thomas Atkinson, bishop of North Carolina, to seek reconciliation between the Southern and Northern branches of the Protestant Episcopal Church. Both men attended the General Convention of the Protestant Episcopal Church in October, 1865 in Philadelphia, even though they recognized that their positive attitude toward reunion was not shared by many of their brethren in the South.

1170.   Richardson, Joe M. "The Failure of the American Missionary Association to Expand Congregationalism Among Southern Blacks." *Southern Studies* 18 (Spring 1979): 51-73.   The attempt of the A.M.A. to establish Congregational churches in the black community failed because of their lack of understanding and appreciation for the religious needs and traditions of blacks. They were also stymied by black resistance to joining any white church, and the A.M.A.'s view that only educated whites were competent enough to be pastors. Religious segregation encouraged black independence and distrust of whites.

1171.   Richardson, Joe M. "'Labor is Rest to Me Here in This the Lord's Vineyard': Hardy Mobley, Black Missionary During Reconstruction." *Southern Studies* 22 (Spring 1983): 15-20.   Mobley was a former Georgia slave who bought his freedom and eventually served as a missionary for the American Missionary Association. He worked in Georgia, Missouri, and Louisiana as a Congregational minister.

1172.   Roth, Donald Franklin. "'Grace Not Race': Southern Negro Church Leaders, Black Identity, and Missions to West Africa, 1865-1919." Ph.D. University of Texas, 1975. 419p.

1173.   Ruoff, John Carl. "Southern Womanhood, 1865-1920: An Intellectual and Cultural Study." Ph.D. University of Illinois, 1976. 279p.

1174.   Russ, William A., Jr. "The Failure to Reunite Methodism After the Civil War." *Susquehanna University Studies* 1 (1936): 8-16.   The attempt by the Methodist Episcopal Church North to bring the Southern branch back into a unified Church after the schism in 1844 was not successful because Northern Church leaders in the South were equated with carpetbaggers. Also, the Northern Church's requirement that the Southerners announce their loyalty to the Union was unacceptable. Politics, slavery, and old animosities left from 1844 plagued the MEC for many decades. Russ relies mainly on Christian periodicals, particularly the *Western Christian Advocate* and the *Central Christian Advocate*.

1175.   Sommerville, Diane Miller. "The Rape Myth Reconsidered: The Intersection of Race, Class and Gender in the American South, 1800-1877." Ph.D. Rutgers, 1995. 550p. (See also Sommerville's "The Rape Myth in the Old South Reconsidered," *Journal of Southern History* 61 (August 1995): 481-518.)

1176.   Southall, Eugene Portlette. "The Attitude of the Methodist Episcopal Church, South, Toward the Negro From 1844 to 1870." *Journal of Negro History* 16 (October 1931): 359-370.   The Methodist Episcopal Church split over the issue of slavery, but the Southern branch showed concern and active support for the freedmen after the war. The Southern church helped to organize black schools, support black economic prosperity, and seek religious salvation for blacks.

1177.   Stanley, Amy Dru. "Contract Rights In The Age Of Emancipation: Wage Labor And Marriage After The Civil War." Yale University, 1990. 457p.

1178.   Stewart, Rev. Bowyer. *The Work of the Church in the South During the Period of Reconstruction.* Publ. for the Milwaukee Western Theological Seminary by the Young Churchman, 1913. 79p. App.   The Civil War destroyed Episcopal churches, reduced the number of clergy, and put the congregations under pressure of Northern military rule. When the Episcopal Church, South began to rebuild it also had to cope with the migration of blacks to their own churches. Stewart discusses these issues with sympathy for the South. The appendix includes portions of documents from the *Southern Churchman*.

1179.   Stewart, Charles J. "Lincoln's Assassination and the Protestant Clergy of the North." *Journal of the Illinois State Historical Society* 54 (Autumn 1961): 268-293.   Stewart examines the sermons given by 30 Northern, Protestant ministers. Most of the sermons drew connections between the assassination and Reconstruction. The tendency was to call for a policy of punishment against the South or to interpret Lincoln's death by proclaiming that he died so that less leniency would be shown for the South. A few ministers believed that the North was punished for worshipping idols in the form of Lincoln. Stewart proposes that researchers look closely at the influence of the 19th century church on political affairs, particularly on the direction of Reconstruction.

1180.   Stowell, Daniel W. *Rebuilding Zion: The Religious Reconstruction of the South, 1863-1877.* New York: Oxford University Press, 1998. 278p. Bibl. Stowell explores how various organized religions in the South responded to the occupation of Union troops, the defeat of the Confederacy, and the end of slavery. He focuses on the contributions of six Christians to an understanding of white Northern, white Southern, and African American perspectives: Eliza Rhea Anderson Fain (Tennessee Presbyterian), Lucius H. Holsey (Georgia slave), Thomas Hooke McCallie (Tennessee Presbyterian), John H. Caldwell (Georgia Trinity Methodist), and Joanna Patterson Moore (Pennsylvania Baptist teacher and minister in Louisiana and Arkansas). Together they illustrate racial, sectional, and denominational differences in rebuilding religious life during and after the war. (See also Stowell's Ph.D. dissertation with the same title from University of Florida, 1994.)

1181.   Sweet, William W. "Methodist Church Influence in Southern Politics." *Mississippi Valley Historical Review* 1 (March 1915): 546-560.   Politics influenced Northern church activities due to their strong support for Radical Republican ideology. The political message angered the Southern whites, particularly the Ku Klux Klan, and led to violence against church leaders. The Northern Methodists represented both white and black churches, including the Methodist Episcopal Church, North, the African Methodist Episcopal Church, and the African Methodist Episcopal Zion Church. (See also Sweet's "The Methodist Episcopal Church and Reconstruction." *Journal of the Illinois State Historical Society* 7 (October 1914): 147-165; and "The Methodist Episcopal Church and Reconstruction." *Transactions of the Illinois State Historical Society* 20 (1914): 83-94.)

1182.   Sweet, William W. "Negro Churches in the South: A Phase of Reconstruction." *Methodist Review* 104 (May 1921): 405-418.   Sweet describes how the freedmen formed their own churches that promoted education and participation in politics among members. He criticizes the influence of black churches on politics as insensitive to the white population because blacks pushed too hard for reforms and showed a lack of trust in whites. Northern churches and carpetbaggers encouraged participation in politics.

1183.   Swint, Henry L. (ed.). *Dear Ones at Home: Letters From Contraband Camps.* Nashville: Vanderbilt University Press, 1966. 274p. Bibl.   Lucy and Sarah Chase, sisters in a Quaker family of Worcester, Ma., volunteered to work with the freed slaves in Virginia and later in Georgia and Florida. They worked as teachers and aid givers during much of the time from January, 1863 until 1869. Swint provides selected letters that they wrote or letters received from family, friends, and associates. The letters offer descriptions, experiences, and attitudes regarding their work, the life of the freedmen, politics, race relations, and reactions from those who wrote to them from the North.

1184.   Thompson, Ernest Trice. *Presbyterians in the South.* 3 Vols. Richmond: John Knox Press, 1963-1973. Bibl.   Volume 2 covers the years from 1861 to 1890, but most of the book generally focuses on the Reconstruction period. Thompson examines the split between Northern and Southern Presbyterian Church organizations and the frustrating and unsuccessful attempts to reunite them after the war. He offers a negative perspective on Reconstruction as he weaves the general history of the period into a survey of Southern Presbyterian recovery from the war and its relations with Northern brethren, including missionaries who worked in the South.   Thompson also covers Presbyterian educational institutions, the development of the pastorate, and theology in the South.

1185.   Van Tassel, Emily Field. "'Only the Law Would Rule Between Us': Anti-miscegenation, the Moral Economy of Dependency, and the Debate Over Rights After the Civil War." *Chicago-Kent Law Review* 70 (1995): 873-926. Reconstruction is interpreted as a period when the emancipation of the slaves led to a new system of dependency characterized by the persecution of black men by whites in competition for black and white women.   Van Tassell examines the meaning of freedom in the interrelationship of gender, sex, and race with the civil rights of blacks.   Laws against miscegenation existed throughout the South as a symbol of racial and gender dependency or domination.

1186.   Vander Velde, Lewis G.   *The Presbyterian Churches and the Federal Union 1861-1869.* Cambridge: Harvard University Press, 1932. 575p. Tbls. Bibl. The author examines Presbyterian factions, particularly the Old and New School Assemblies of the North and the Southern Churches. He explores the persistent issue of patriotism, abolitionism, the reunification of the Church, the struggle to maintain communication with Northern and Southern branches. Missionary aid work in the South. (See also Vander Velde's Ph.D. dissertation with the same title from Harvard, 1931.)

1187.   Walker, Clarence E. "The A. M. E. Church and Reconstruction." *Negro History Bulletin* 48 (January-March 1988): 10-12.   Between 1863 and 1870 27 African Methodist Episcopal ministers volunteered to establish schools for freedmen, to convert them to the A.M.E. Church and to accumulate Church property. They sought moral perfectibility and economic opportunity for a new social order that followed Republican ideology. The work of the Church was challenged by black and white Northern M.E. churches, the A.M.E. Zion Church, and the Southern born Colored M.E. Church that was promoted by whites as a nonpolitical alternative.

1188.   Walker, Clarence E.   *A Rock in a Weary Land: The African Methodist Episcopal Church During the Civil War and Reconstruction.*   Baton Rouge: Louisiana State University Press, 1982. 157p. Bibl.   This book is about the work of the Northern A.M.E. Church to aid the freedmen. The focus is on the Church's attempt to follow its calling of uplifting the needy by bringing them closer to God and helping to motivate and improve their lives so that the entire black race, and indeed society in general, would form a more useful citizenry in their country. During Reconstruction some of the A.M.E. missionaries, such as Charles H. Pearce in Florida and Henry Turner in Georgia, participated in politics, thus illustrating the political message to promote black civil equality. The A.M.E. goal of an egalitarian society could not be achieved because of the political and social realities in Southern society and American society in general. The Church mission in the South was also stymied by its poor relationship with other missionary groups. (See also Walker's "A Rock in a Weary Land: A History of the African Methodist Episcopal Church During the Civil War and Reconstruction." Ph.D. University of California, Berkeley, 1976.)

1189.   Wallenstein, Peter. "Race, Marriage, and the Law of Freedom: Alabama and Virginia, 1860-1960s." *Chicago-Kent Law Review* 70,2 (1994): 371-437.   The author traces the history of antimiscegenation laws in two states. He emphasizes the laws that appeared during Reconstruction and continued until 1967.

1190.   Washington, James Melvin. "The Origins and Emergence of Black Baptist Separation, 1863-1897." Ph.D. Yale University, 1979. 295p.

1191.   Wheeler, Edward L.   *Uplifting the Race: The Black Minister in the New South 1865-1902.* Lanham: University Press of America, 1986. 146p. App. Bibl. Wheeler focuses mainly on an elite group of 78 black ministers from throughout the South who served as both models and community leaders for the uplift of the freedmen from slaves to full fledged citizens. Whether through politics, education, or temperance, black ministers emphasized that Christianity was the basis for uplifting American blacks, and that uplift would include accommodation to traditional American values. Their leadership called attention to the influence of black Churches, the only institution that was fully controlled by blacks.   An appendix includes a list of the 78 ministers with back ground information. (See also Wheeler's Ph.D. dissertation with the same title from Emory University, 1982.)

1192.   Williams, Burton J.   "Religion and Reconstruction: A Cleric's Conception." *Methodist History* 9 (April 1971): 45-52.   Williams presents the text of an address by Rev. Cyrus R. Rice that describes Rice's support for change in the South but without a complete transformation of Southern society. Until January, 1865 Rice was a member of the Methodist Episcopal Church, South. He joined the Northern church and urged total reconciliation of Northern and Southern churches united under the banner of the Union.

1193.   Williams, Gilbert Anthony. "The *A.M.E. Christian Recorder*: A Forum for the Social Ideas of Black Americans, 1854-1902." Ph.D. University of Illinois, 1979. 186p.

1194.   Wilson, Charles Reagan.   "Robert Lewis Dabney: Religion and the Southern Holocaust." *Virginia Magazine of History and Biography* 89 (January

1981): 79-89.   Dabney, a Presbyterian theologian, warned of impending doom and extinction of the Southern white race because of the impact of the South's defeat on Southern religion and culture. He gave up the idea of emigrating from Virginia, but continued a to fight for the preservation of a distinct Southern church untainted by the North. Wilson believes that the word "holocaust" describes what Dabney saw happening to Southern culture.

1195.   Woodson, Carter G.   *The History of the Negro Church*.   3rd Ed. Washington, D. C.: Associated Publishers, 1972. 322p. Ills. Ports. (First edition published by Associated Publishers in 1921; 2nd edition in 1945)   Chapters 9 and 10 describes the dramatic impact of the Civil War and Reconstruction on various black Christian denominations in the South. Woodson discusses the separation of blacks from white churches and the establishment of separate institutions supported by blacks and usually whites as well. Black denominations also worked to establish and develop religious educational institutions for freedmen, a task that blacks had to do on their own with their own funds. The development of independent black churches offered opportunities to spread the gospel to the freedmen more successfully than prior to the Civil War.

Agriculture, Labor, and Business

1196.   Abbott, Martin. "Free Land, Free Labor, and the Freedmen's Bureau." *Agricultural History* 30 (October 1956): 150-156.   Abbott provides a positive view of bureau's efforts to settle freedmen on the land and to regulate labor contracts. There were many obstacles to success, including strict constitutional requirements that resulted in the return of land to former owners and widespread crop failures, weather problems, and harsh economic conditions in the immediate postwar years. But it was through the efforts of the bureau that blacks were given an opportunity to show that they could and would work effectively without the compulsion of slavery.

1197.   Allen, James S. "The Struggle For Land During the Reconstruction Period." *Science and Society* 1 (Spring 1937): 378-401.   Allen discusses the missed opportunities in 1865 and 1866 to distribute land to the freedmen as a move toward a more democratic society in the South and provide them greater opportunity for future success. Conservative and reactionary forces blocked this possibility and the revolutionary bourgeoisie was weak.

1198.   Alston, Lee J. "Issues in Postbellum Southern Agriculture."   In *Agriculture and National Development: Views on the Nineteenth Century*. Edited by Lou Ferleger. Ames: Iowa State University Press, 1990. Pp. 207-228. Bibl. Alston is concerned with key issues that influenced the development of Southern agriculture from the end of the Civil War to the early 20th century. These issues included decisions about what crops to grow, adjustments to contract labor and sharecropping, the rise of the country merchant and his role as creditor to black farmers, and the plight of independent black farmers. He finds that a new plantation economy arose after the war that was characterized by an economic and political association of plantation owners and merchants. This rural elite held the power that kept the black population from making much economic progress.

1199.   Anderson, George L.   "The South and Problems of Post-Civil War Finance." *Journal of Southern History* 9 (May 1943): 181-195.   Postwar Southern finances were under great stress due to the shortage of money, weakness of banks, and instability caused by Reconstruction politics.   Northern financiers did not include the South in the reformed national banking system, thus retarding economic growth and causing the hoarding of greenbacks. Only in the summer of 1870 did the national banking system come to the South, but the South still did not receive specie payments that would have speeded its redevelopment. This financial policy was the result of Radical politics.

1200.   Brewer, William M.   "Poor Whites and Negroes in the South Since the Civil War." *Journal of Negro History* 15 (January 1930): 26-37.   The difficult race relations between poor whites and blacks were based on the desire of whites to climb out of their economic and social rut by suppressing the efforts of blacks to gain civil rights and economic independence. The whites were held back before the Civil War because slaves held most of the unskilled and semiskilled jobs.   Poor whites not only worked against black progress but became the backbone of the Ku Klux Klan.

1201.   Brinkley, Garland L. "The Decline in Southern Agricultural Output, 1860-1880." *Journal of Economic History* 57 (March 1997): 116-133. Tbls.   Brinkley uses regression analysis to illustrate that the large decline in agricultural output in the South during and after the war was due to the unhealthy condition of the general population. Evidence suggests that hookworm infection increased during the war and caused the general decline of health among thousands of Southerners for many years.

1202.   Burton, Orville V. and Robert C. McGrath, Jr.   *Toward a New South? Studies on Post-Civil War Southern Communities*. Westport: Greenwood Press, 1982. 319p.   This book focuses on developments in Southern urbanization, towns and cities, race and politics, and transitions in plantation society.   Each essay relevant to Reconstruction has been cited separately. (See # 1281, 1767, 2436, 2573, 2798.)

1203.   Byres, Terence J. "The Postbellum South: From Slavery, Through Unfree Labour to Wage Labour." In *Capitalism From Above and Capitalism From Below: An Essay in Comparative Political Economy*. New York: St. Martin's Press, 1996. Pp. 282-341. Tbls.   Byres examines the transition of postwar plantation ownership and labor within the context of Marxian ideology.   There was a natural transition to capitalism in the rural South that involved both the owners (capitalists) and the freedmen (proletariat). This essay is part of a larger work that examines transitions from unfree to free labor and the development of capitalism in Europe and the U.S.

1204.   Campbell, E. G.   "Indebted Railroads-A Problem of Reconstruction." *Journal of Southern History* 6 (May 1940): 167-188.   The federal government assisted Southern railroad companies after the Civil War by selling them government rail equipment.   This allowed the devastated companies to return to operation, but the government expected the companies to repay the debt totaling $5.6 million.   Campbell describes how many of the Southern rail companies were unable to pay their debts.   Extended negotiations with the government resulted in the government reducing the debt and produced a bright spot in the otherwise tense political environment of Reconstruction.

1205.   Clark, Ira G.   "State Legislation and Railroads of the Gulf Southwest." *Southwestern Social Science Quarterly,* Supplement to 41 (1960): 268-282.   This article focuses on railroad expansion and regulation in Texas, Louisiana, Arkansas, Missouri, and Kansas from the 1830s to 1910.   During Reconstruction the corruption and speculation that existed in the former Confederate states under Republican rule was not necessarily due to Radicals alone, nor was it occurring only in the South.   It was the tremendous growth of state aid that was responsible for expansion of the railroads.

1206.   Clifton, James M.   "Twilight Comes to the Rice Kingdom: Postbellum Rice Culture on the South Atlantic Coast." *Georgia Historical Quarterly* 62 (Summer 1978): 146-154.   Rice production in South Carolina, North Carolina, and Georgia dropped dramatically by the end of the Civil War.   During the postwar period production recovered slowly compared with other staple crops, such as cotton, because large plantations disappeared, prices were low, labor and maintenance costs increased, and the freedmen often refused to work in the rice marshes.   By the 1880s production improved, but the South Atlantic states could not compete with new, more efficient techniques used in Louisiana.

1207.   Cohen, William.   "Black Immobility and Free Labor: The Freedmen's Bureau and the Relocation of Black Labor, 1865-1868." *Civil War History* 30 (September 1984): 221-234.   When the system of slave labor collapsed, there were too many laborers in some locations and not enough in others.   The Freedmen's Bureau acted as an employment agency to bring labor and employer together and help to transport indigent laborers to where they were needed.   The bureau based its actions on the idea that helping the freedmen obtain and get to their jobs would reduce the freedmen's dependency on the government.

1208.   Cohen, William.   "Negro Involuntary Servitude in the South, 1865-1940: A Preliminary Analysis." *Journal of Southern History* 42 (February 1976): 31-60. Tbls.   Cohen describes the legal basis for involuntary servitude as it was handed down to future generations by the black codes of 1865-1867 and the laws passed by the Southern states during the decades after Reconstruction.   The continuing system of servitude was embedded in the labor system by sharecropping, tenantry, and the crop-lien system, as well as the treatment of blacks by criminal justice in the Southern states.

1209.   Daniel, Pete. "The Metamorphosis of Slavery, 1865-1900." *Journal of American History* 66 (June 1979): 88-99.   Daniel explains that after the Civil War many freedmen found that they had exchanged one type of slavery for another. Chattel slavery gave way to peonage among agricultural laborers who were forced to stay at the same job for the same employer.   The planters' search for a labor system that they could control led to their use of laws, contracts, violence, and illiteracy to trap sharecroppers into a system of involuntary servitude that persisted into the 20th century.   Daniel compares the aftermath of emancipation in the U.S. with the emancipation of slaves in other countries.

1210.   Davis, Ronald L. F.   *Good and Faithful Labor: From Slavery to Sharecropping in the Natchez District, 1860-1890*. Westport: Greenwood Press, 1982. 225p. App. Bibl. Ills. Maps.   In this case study of Concordia Parish, Louisiana and Adams County, Mississippi, Davis illustrates why and how sharecropping developed in a region of rich land dense with plantations and slaves in the antebellum years. Davis proposes that the freedmen were the main instigators of the sharecropping system because it allowed them to work as families in an environment of freedom and independence.   The planter-merchant alliance and the decreasing price of cotton led to unremitting poverty and dependence for sharecroppers and wage laborers, but this does not outweigh the importance of freedom and independence that sharecropping provided former slaves. (See also Davis' "Good and Faithful Labor: A Study in the Origins, Development, and Economics of Southern Sharecropping, 1860-1880." Ph.D. University of Missouri, 1974. 221p.; and Davis' "Labor Dependency Among Freedmen, 1865-1880." In *From the Old South to the New: Essays on the Transitional South*. Edited by Walter J. Fraser, Jr. and Winfred B. Moore, Jr. Westport: Greenwood Press, 1981. Pp. 155-166.)

1211.   Davis, Ronald L. F. "The U.S. Army and the Origins of Sharecropping in the Natchez District - A Case Study." *Journal of Negro History* 62 (January 1977): 60-80.   In the Natchez District of Adams County, Mississippi and Concordia Parish, Louisiana, Gen. John Eaton, an Army chaplain, was appointed by Gen. U. S. Grant to put the freedmen to work for set wages on private or Army managed plantations. This contributed to the Union war effort, but also taught the freedmen about responsibility and work ethic. The controversy over the benefits of wage labor vs. independent farming for freedmen arose, and it continued after the formation of the Freedmen's Bureau in 1865. The bureau wanted a wage labor system, but freedmen and postwar planters wanted a way to provide for and encourage black independence and protection for the planter.   Sharecropping developed out of these tensions and represented a conservative program in lieu of land distribution to the freedmen.

1212.   DeCanio, Stephen J. "Accumulation and Discrimination in the Postbellum South." *Exploration in Economic History* 16 (April 1979): 182-206.   Tbls. DeCanio uses statistical methodology to demonstrate that the differences between the postwar economic status of blacks and whites in the South was based on the disparity of wealth distribution. The distribution of land to freedmen would have given them the economic foundation to build future wealth, and this could have been done without revolutionary measures. (A rewritten version appears in *Market Institutions and Economic Progress in the New South 1865-1900*, New York: Academic Press, 1981; For an expanded argument see DeCanio's *Agriculture in the Postbellum South: The Economics of Production and Supply*, Cambridge: MIT Press, 1974.)

1213. DeCanio, Stephen J. "Productivity and Income Distribution in the Post-Bellum South." *Journal of Economic History* 34 (June, 1974): 422-446. Tbls. By using regression analysis of census data from all of the former Confederate states except Virginia, DeCanio explains the wide differences in Southern productivity and income distribution among whites and blacks during Reconstruction and the decades that followed. The major emphasis is on economic and geographic factors rather than racial or institutional tradition. DeCanio recognizes the influence of discriminatory laws and deliberate racism among employers, but he concludes that labor market forces were competitive. The main disadvantage for the freedmen was lack of access to land and other nonhuman factors of production that could have led to much higher income and productivity. Economic inequality in the postwar South was at a normal level for a private enterprise market economy and was not inordinately caused by crop selection (cotton) or social and political factors.

1214. Degler, Carl N "Rethinking Post-Civil War History." *Virginia Quarterly Review* 57 ((Spring 1981): 250-67. Degler refers to recent (1970s) interpretations of the postwar Southern economy and society to make the point that historians periodically rewrite history based on the viewpoints and concerns of their generation. In so doing they apply new theories or perspectives that enrich historical interpretation of the past.

1215. Edwards, Thomas J. "The Tenant System and Some Changes Since Emancipation." *Annals of the American Academy of Political and Social Sciences*, [No. 138] 49 (September 1913): 38-46. After the Civil War the freedmen who worked on plantations commonly followed new labor systems, including sharecropping, wage-earning, and standing wage. Edwards describes how the systems worked and briefly compares them with similar labor systems in existence in the early 1910s.

1216. Evans, Arthur S. "The Relationship Between Industrialization and White Hostility Toward Blacks in Southern Cities." *Urban Affairs Quarterly* 25 (December 1989): 322-341. After the freedmen migrated to urban areas, they generally had to cope with entrenched white racism and an expanding white population. Whites increasingly competed and pushed blacks out of jobs that they were traditionally forced to perform. The new industrializing urban areas of the South did not offer blacks any advantages. Rural areas offered opportunities for a better life from 1865 through the early 20th century.

1217. Fields, Barbara Jeanne. "The Advent of Capitalist Agriculture: The New South in a Bourgeois World." In *Essays on the Postbellum Southern Economy*.

Edited by T. Glymph and J. J. Kushma. College Station: Texas A&M Press, 1985. Pp. 73-94.   Fields discusses the development of a Southern capitalist economy after emancipation and compares it with emancipations in other nations.

1218.   Fierce, Mildred C. "Black Struggle For Land During Reconstruction." *Black Scholar* 5 (February 1974): 13-18.   Even though the Confiscation Act of 1862 and proposals for land distribution held out hope to freedmen that they would be provided with the means to be independent, self sufficient free people, their dreams faded with the federal government's disregard for its laws, opposition to handouts to individuals, and the lack of full understanding of the needs of a large emancipated minority.   Fierce suggests that the black's dependency on the government was one of the bitter legacies of Reconstruction.

1219.   Fish, Carl Russell. *The Restoration of the Southern Railroads.* Madison: University of Wisconsin, 1919. 23p. (*University of Wisconsin Studies in the Social Sciences*, No. 2)   Fish focuses on the treatment of Southern railroads by the U.S. Army during the immediate years after the Civil War.   He attributes the early progress at restoring the war torn rail lines to the Army and credit provided by the War Department.   Their efforts illustrate one element of what could have been a highly successful Reconstruction if only economic issues, rather than politics, had been the main focus of national attention.

1220.   Fleming, Walter L. "Forty Acres and a Mule." *North American Review* 182 (May 1906): 721-737.   The ideal of land redistribution was not simply imagined by the freedmen, but was encouraged by the U.S. government in several ways, particularly by the establishment of communities of independent former slaves on confiscated land in South Carolina, Georgia, Florida, Virginia, and Louisiana. Another factor included publicity about the Freedmen's Bureau's role in distributing land and protecting the rights of freedmen.   President Johnson's liberal pardons allowed whites to reclaim their land, but the concept of land redistribution did not die and many freedmen were subjected to swindle and fraud.

1221.   Fleming, Walter L. *The Freedmen's Savings Bank: A Chapter in the Economic History of the Negro Race.* Chapel Hill: University of North Carolina Press, 1927. 170p. App.   Fleming provides a history of the organization, development, and demise of the bank that was incorporated by an act of Congress on March 3, 1865. The fraud and corruption that led to the failure of the institution by June, 1874 and the loss of savings generated distrust in banks among blacks and contributed to economic hardships. The appendix includes documents and statistics related to the freedmen's banks. (See also Fleming's "The Freedmen's Savings Bank," *Yale Review* 15 (May 1906): 40-67; (August 1906): 134-146.)

1222.   Foner, Eric. *Nothing But Freedom: Emancipation and its Legacy.* Baton Rouge: Louisiana State University Press, 1983. 142p.   In three essays Foner examines postemancipation societies in Haiti, the British Caribbean, and the U.S. to arrive at insights about how these societies functioned and to better understand similarities and the unique features of the American experience. He is particularly concerned with the political economy of postemancipation years, including labor, property rights, and political rights and power.   Compared with the other former slave societies, American freedmen had greater opportunities for long run improvement due to the support of federal and state Republican regimes.

1223.   Foner, Eric. "Reconstruction and the Crisis of Free Labor." In *Politics and Ideology in the Age of the Civil War*. New York: Oxford University Press, 1980. Pp. 97-127.   The introduction of Northern labor ideology in the South was meant to convince the freedmen that work was vital to the fulfillment of their material "wants" and to convince white planters that black labor was part of a new free labor market economy.   Planters were skeptical that freedmen would work voluntarily, and they feared the spread of black landholders. Land and free labor went together in Northern ideology, but it would be tarnished by the reality of labor enslavement in Northern industrial environments.

1224.   Frehill-Rowe, Lisa M.   "Postbellum Race Relations and Rural Land Tenure: Migration of Blacks and Whites to Kansas and Nebraska, 1870-1890." *Social Forces* 72 (September 1993): 77-91.   The author explains the basis for the migration and provides a comparative statistical study based on census figures. Economic conditions had an impact on both blacks and whites. White yeomen were influenced by their lowered status relative to blacks, while blacks were strongly influenced by racism and decreasing access to the political system.

1225.   Fritz, Richard G. and James Xander. "The Role of Financial Collapse in the Post-Bellum South."   *Revue Internationale d'histoire de la Banque* 22-23 (1981): 257-275. Tbls.   The authors examines reasons for the slow economic growth of the South. Their statistical analysis focuses on the negative impact of barter exchange rather than money immediately after the war and the positive economic effect of the country stores that served as intermediaries between farmers and banks, as well as suppliers of needed equipment for production.

1226.   Gates, Paul Wallace. "Federal Land Policy in the South, 1866-1888." *Journal of Southern History* 6 (August 1940): 303-330. Tbls.   The Southern Homestead Act of 1866 was designed to open federal lands to freedmen and, for the first year, any person whose loyalty was unquestioned during the war. Republicans sought to extend homesteading, but they also sought to punish and persecute the South by destroying the Southern aristocracy through land confiscation and redistribution to landless classes. Gates suspects that the purchases made prior to 1876 were done by individuals who sold their holdings to lumber companies. He does not address the impact of the 1866 act on the freedmen and landless whites, but he implies that it did not benefit them.

1227.   Gilbert, Abby. "The Comptroller of the Currency and the Freedmen's Savings Bank." *Journal of Negro History* 57 (April 1972): 125-143.   The Freedmen's Savings and Trust Co. opened for business in New York City on April 4, 1865 to receive deposits from former slaves and their descendants and invest the funds in U.S. securities and stocks. Gilbert writes a brief history of the bank and its slide into failure by June 29, 1874 because of poor investments, fraud, speculation, mismanagement, and the Panic of 1873. An investigation by Comptroller of the Currency John Jay Knox revealed the extent of the problems, and for the next 40 years a succession of comptrollers tried unsuccessfully to persuade Congress to approve reimbursements to at least some of the depositors, most of whom deposited less than $50.

1228.   Glymph, Thavolia. "Freedpeople and Ex-Masters: Shaping a New Order in the Postbellum South, 1865-1868." In *Essays on the Postbellum Southern Economy.* Edited by T. Glymph and J. J. Kushma.   College Station: Texas A&M Press, 1985. Pp 48-72.   Planters, freedmen, and Freedmen's Bureau agents struggled to reform the Southern labor system to the satisfaction of all. Planters resisted a system that enhanced the freedom and independence of black laborers. The ex-slaves sought a work situation that emphasized freedom, and they rejected the cash wage system as virtual slavery. The planters struggled to control laborers, and they were eventually successful in undermining the freedmen's concept of free labor by shackling them in debt and peonage in a racist environment.

1229.   Goldin, Claudia. "'N' Kinds of Freedom: An Introduction to the Issues." *Explorations in Economic History* 16 (January 1979): 8-30. Tbls.   Goldin critiques the theories of Ransom and Sutch in *One Kind of Freedom* (see # 1266). She believes that the two authors put too much emphasis on institutional race discrimination for the lagging economy of the South. A more complex economic and social process existed that indicated greater market competition and greater economic and educational opportunities for blacks. (See also # 1263)

1230.   Goodrich, Carter. "Public Aid to Railroads in the Reconstruction South." *Political Science Quarterly* 71 (September 1956): 407-442. Tbls.   Goodrich argues that aggressive state aid to railroads accompanied by corruption and mismanagement was a national phenomena. All of the Southern states participated in the rebuilding and extending rail lines, frequently with Democratic support. The reaction against state aid came from both Democrats and some Radical governments. Goodrich surveys state aid in all of Southern states.

1231.   Griffen, Richard W. "Problems of the Southern Cotton Planters After the Civil War." *Georgia Historical Quarterly* 39 (June 1955): 103-117.   After the war planters had to face a shortage of capital for investment, falling land prices were, and a demoralized labor force.   The freedmen generally could not contribute to a recovery because they refused to work hard and were distracted by politics. Some planters sought foreign laborers. Despite the Reconstruction Acts of 1867 which made matters worse, by 1875 cotton production was back to prewar levels even with the price fluctuations.

1232.   Hahn, Steven. "Hunting, Fishing, and Foraging: Common Rights and Class Relations in Postbellum South." *Radical History Review* 26 (1982): 37-64. Ills.   Black laborers found that white plantation owners sought to exploit their labor and restrict their rights to public gaming on what had been common lands before the war. The restrictions represented the harsh use of authority and power over the freedmen. White farmers and laborers also felt the brunt of the restrictions and some whites recognized a united interest with blacks that created a feeling of "popular radicalism" (p. 57).

1233.   Hesseltine, William B.   "Economic Factors in the Abandonment of Reconstruction." *Mississippi Valley Historical Review* 22 ((September, 1935): 191-210.   Hesseltine defines Reconstruction as the Northern capitalist's attempt to defeat the planter elite and secure the economic subjugation and exploitation of the South.   Politics interfered with the economic rejuvenation of the South when the expansion and preservation of the Republican Party took precedent over economic recovery.   The white South rejected political values espoused by Northern carpetbaggers, and in the case of the Ku Klux Klan, the reaction to Radical Reconstruction was violent.   After the Republican losses in the 1874 election, the Northern economic invasion and exploitation of the South slowed due to Republican appeals for support and promises of future prosperity.

1234.   Hoffman, Edwin D. "From Slavery to Self-Reliance." *Journal of Negro History* 41 (January 1956): 8-42.   Hoffman describes the organization of the Georgia and South Carolina Sea Islands experiment during the Civil War that allowed freed slaves to work the land from themselves.   The project was under the direction of Brig. Gen. Rufus Sexton who led the Army's effort to test freedmen's ability to be free and self-supporting.   The former slaves proved that they could quickly gain self respect and independence.   After the war the Army had the difficult task of taking the land away from the settlers and giving it back to prewar owners. The government lost an opportunity to build a self reliant black population and forced the freedmen to rely on the goodwill of planters and a system of contract labor.

1235.   Hoffnagle, Warren.   "The Southern Homestead Act: Its Origins and Operation." *Historian* 32 (August 1970): 612-629.   The act of June 21, 1866 had the potential of securing the economic and political equality for the freedmen by offering them a chance to purchase federal lands.   Despite the intentions, the legislation failed due to corruption, mismanagement, black illiteracy and poverty, white racism, inadequate staffing by the Freedmen's Bureau, and unsuitable and inaccessible lands.   Hoffnagle examines operations in Alabama, Mississippi, Louisiana, Arkansas and Florida.

1236.   Horowitz, Robert F.   "Land to the Freedmen: A Vision of Reconstruction." *Ohio History* 86 (Summer 1977): 187-199. Ills. Port.   The fact that Reconstruction did not include significant land redistribution to help the freedmen establish an economic base for the future shows how moderate the plan was. The chances of including land distribution was most likely to have occurred, at least legislatively, before the war ended. Congressman James M. Ashley of Toledo, Ohio proposed a Reconstruction plan in 1862 that included confiscation and redistribution of land. Ashley based his plan on the concept that the rebel states had forfeited their status and became territories after secession.   The Constitution, however, was the force that defeated the confiscation proposal.   (See also Horowitz's "James M. Ashley: A Biography," Ph.D., City University of New York, 1973.)

1237.   Howell, Clark. "The Aftermath of Reconstruction: How the South Found Itself." *Century Illustrated Monthly Magazine* 85 (1912-13): 844-853. Ill. Ports. Reconstruction was disastrous for the South because it eliminated the short term economic recovery of the region and generated pessimism in the future.   Significant economic recovery would not begin in earnest until 1880.   The Reconstruction policies of the Radicals could have been avoided had Lincoln not been assassinated. Howell, editor *Atlanta Constitution*, describes black suffrage as counter productive.

1238.   Jaynes, Gerald David. *Branches Without Roots: Genesis of the Black Working Class in the American South, 1862-1882.* New York: Oxford University Press, 1986. 351p. App. Tbls.   Jaynes, an economist, explores the transition from slave labor to free labor and evolving labor relationships between employers and laborers. The study involves consideration of political, social and economic relationships and the meaning of emancipation and freedom in the Southern labor markets during and after Reconstruction.   Jaynes also examines the important influence of the Freedmen's Bureau in labor affairs. Despite a labor system that discouraged black education and economic advancement, black laborers recognized that they were living and working as free people.   The appendices provide an explanation for Jaynes' statistical methodology.

1239.   Lanza, Michael. *Agrarianism and Reconstruction Politics: The Southern Homestead Act.* Baton Rouge: Louisiana State University Press, 1990. 153p. App. Bibl. Tbls.   The Southern Homestead Act of 1866 was an attempt to provide freedmen with federal land for small farms in Alabama, Arkansas, Florida, Louisiana, and Mississippi. It was a positive attempt to establish an economic base for former slaves, but the act failed to achieve this goal and was repealed in 1876. Failure was due to administrative problems of the General Land Offices, racial prejudice, disregard for industrial development, and little recognition of the realities of Reconstruction in the South.   Most of all, Lanza emphasizes the lack of commitment to the program by Republican who were more concerned with their own political success. (See also Lanza's "The Southern Homestead Act." Ph.D. University of Chicago, 1984.)

1240.   Lowenberg, Bert James. "Efforts of the South to Encourage Immigration, 1865-1900." *South Atlantic Quarterly* 33 (October 1934): 363-385.   Historians have misinterpreted the attitude of the South toward immigration in the post Civil War period. Although white planters did not want to import foreign labor, they desperately needed reliable laborers to pull the region out of its critical situation. The freedmen were not trusted as free laborers. Chinese and other nationalities were brought in to do menial labor. Prior to 1877 Southern state governments gradually encouraged immigration, and private agents established businesses to find foreign labor when the need arose. This activity continued into the 1880s and 1890s.

1241.   Magdol, Edward.   *A Right to the Land: Essays on the Freedmen's Community.* Wesport: Greenwood Press, 1977. 290p. Bibl. Illus. Tbls.   This book includes nine related essays that define and affirm the role of blacks in their own emancipation and the reconstruction of their lives and the societies around them.   From 1861 to 1880 freedmen were a self assertive working class that struggled to control the direction of their lives within a society that stifled access to land, fair wages, and equal civil rights.   Self motivation and determination were apparent early in the war after many slaves emancipated themselves. Their drive for education, the rise of black churches, the growing number of black artisans, and the quest for land all contradict theories of emancipation that emphasize learned docility or that were based on white middle class values.   Magdol's introduction is an historiographic essay on contemporary writing on the topic.

1242.   Mandle, Jay R.   "The Role of Markets and Institutions in Postbellum Southern Development." In *Agriculture and National Development: Views on the nineteenth Century.* Edited by Lou Ferloger. Ames: Iowa State University Press, 1990. Pp. 189-206. Bibl.   Researchers should broaden their view of external factors that determined the future of economic success or failure of emancipated blacks in a competitive market. Institutional structures, including racial bias and discrimination, restricted economic resources, and labor options for blacks played a role in their slow development. The same impediments to progress among blacks probably held back economic progress in the South generally. Mandle believes that studies of market theory often disregard various institutional factions that impeded Southern black progress or use statistical methods that overstate black success in accumulating wealth between 1865 and World War I. (See also Mandle's *The Roots of Black Poverty: The Southern Plantation Economy After the Civil War*, Durham: Duke University Press, 1978.)

1243.   Mandle, Jay R.   "Sharecropping and the Plantation Economy in the United States South." In *Sharecropping and Sharecroppers.* Edited by T. J. Byres. London: Frank Cass, 1983. Pp. 120-129.   The postwar plantation economy that relied on sharecropping inhibited economic development of the freedmen and the South. A program of land distribution to the freedmen would have provided a more realistic opportunity for economic advancement.

1244.   Marable, Manning.   "The Land Question in Historical Perspective: The Economics of Poverty in the Blackbelt South, 1865-1920." In *The Black Rural-Landowner-Endangered Species: Social, Political, and Economic Implications.* Edited by Leo McGee and Robert Boone. Westport: Greenwood Press, 1979. Pp. 3-24.   Marable sketches the history of black landownership in the Black Belt with its early emphasis on cotton growing and sharecropping and the gradual acquisition of land. Agriculture and land tenure were the major themes of black history in the South from 1865 until the effects of World War I. Jim Crow helped to commence a decline in black participation in Southern agriculture.

1245.   McKenzie, Robert H.   Postbellum Economic Development in the South: Consequences of Belief." *Southern Studies* 21 (Spring 1982): 27-60.   McKenzie calls on historians to propose new questions, consider different perspectives, and use new methods to explain the lack of economic growth in the South. Economic research has been lacking in favor of political and social studies. He believes that historians should avoid the regional polarity of traditional studies by viewing the Southern economy in a broader, non-regional context of politics, society, culture, business and entrepreneurial development.

1246.   McPherson, Milton M. "Federal Taxes on Cotton, 1862-1868." Ph.D. University of Alabama, 1970. 185p.

1247.   Moore, A. B. "One Hundred Years of Reconstruction of the South." *Journal of Southern History* 9 (May 1943): 153-180.   Moore prepared this paper for his 1942 presidential address to the Southern Historical Association, but the meeting was canceled. Moore blames the continuing economic, social, and political problems in the South on the results of the Civil War and Reconstruction. The main perpetrator, the North, savagely destroyed the economic base of the South and intentionally held it down by treating it as a virtual backwater colony during and after Reconstruction.

1248.   Moran, Jeffrey. "Chinese Labor For the New South." *Southern Studies* N.S. 3 (Winter 1992): 277-304.   Activities to import Chinese laborers to work on Southern plantations failed, due to the costs involved and the lack of Chinese interest in the South, but the scheme was important because it exposed opposing ideas about the future of the region. Many planters sought a return to an economy based on cotton and sugar, and they thought that Chinese laborers, rather than blacks, could fulfill their dream. But other Southerners looked forward to a new South and believed that importing a new race of laborer to rebuild the antebellum economy would hold back the South from broad economic progress.

1249.   Nelson, Scott Reynolds. "Public Fictions: The Southern Railway and the Construction of the South, 1848-1885." Ph.D. University of North Carolina, 1995.

1250.   Novak, Daniel A. *The Wheel of Servitude: Black Forced Labor After Slavery.* Louisville: University Press of Kentucky, 1978. 126p. Bibl.   Novak studies the legal history of black peonage from 1865 until the 1960s. The first three chapters focus on presidential and congressional Reconstruction, a period when peonage got its start with the black codes and with assistance from the U.S. Army, the Freedmen's Bureau, and the Republican Party. Novak includes sharecropping and other postwar labor systems in the systematic effort to recreate a slave-like environment to control black labor.

1251.   Odom, E. Dale. "The Vickburg, Shreveport and Texas: The Fortunes of a Scalawag Railroad." *Southwestern Social Science Quarterly* 44 (December 1963): 277-285.   The experiences of this railroad in northern Louisiana illustrates the financial, political, and legal problems of Southern railroads during Reconstruction.

1252.   Osthaus, Carl R. *Freedmen, Philanthropy, and Fraud: A History of the Freedmen's Savings Bank.* Urbana: University of Illinois Press, 1976. 257p. App. Bibl. Ills. Tbls.   On March 3, 1865 Congress passed an act to incorporate the Freedmen's Savings and Trust Company with the hope of fostering a plan of savings among black soldiers. The great success of the bank illustrated that blacks would work and save money despite their experience in slavery. Osthaus emphasizes the credit due to black bank officials for encouraging depositors and making the system work. Osthaus blames the banks' failure on organizational problems, inadequate oversight, poor decision making and the economic depression of 1873, rather than on fraud. (See also Osthaus's "The Freedmen's Savings and Trust Company: The Tragedy of a Black Bank in Reconstruction America." Ph.D. University of Chicago, 1972.)

1253.   Otto, John Solomon. *Southern Agriculture During the Civil War Era, 1860-1880.* Westport: Greenwood Press, 1994. 171p. Bibl.   Otto recognizes a void in the literature of American agricultural history for the period of Civil War, Reconstruction, and the early years of Redemption. The destruction of property in the war and the freeing of the slaves led to dramatic changes in labor, transportation, markets, farm acreage, private and public land use, and taxes during the 15 years from 1865 to 1880. During the 1870s and the decades that followed, Northern and foreign capitalists contributed to agricultural development by acquiring and investing in businesses, such as railroads, thus leading to greater changes in the nature of Southern agriculture.

1254.   Oubre, Claude F. *Forty Acres and a Mule: The Freedmen's Bureau and Black Landownership.* Baton Rouge: Louisiana State University Press, 1978. 212p. Bibl. Maps. Tbls.   At the end of Reconstruction a small minority of Southern blacks were land owners, despite the Southern Homestead Act of 1866 and attempts by the Freedmen's Bureau to distribute confiscated land. The bureau provided needed aid and support to freedmen, but it did not have the authority to overrule the president's return of confiscated land to prewar owners. Congress refused to act because of constitutional concerns about the rights of private property. Federal lands in the South that were available for purchase reached only a small number of freedmen because of land office inefficiency and lack of knowledge among blacks.   Oubre provides information on homesteading in Mississippi, Alabama, Arkansas, Louisiana, and Florida where most of the federal lands existed.

1255.   Overy, Daniel H., Jr. *Wisconsin Carpetbaggers in Dixie.* Madison: The State Historical Society of Wisconsin for the Department of History, University of Wisconsin, 1961. 81p. Bibl.   In Wisconsin the postwar South was promoted as a new frontier for settlement and business opportunity, but in most areas Wisconsinites were not welcome. These carpetbaggers, who usually did not fit the derogatory stereotype of the thief and political schemer, met with ostracism and threats of violence. Reports were sent home about adjustment problems and the poor quality of the land. As a region for postwar settlement, the South had to compete with the West and with Wisconsin itself. Wisconsinites realized that their own state was still a frontier that offered exciting opportunities. Overy highlights several notable Wisconsinites in the South, including Lewis J. Higby, John S. Harris, Edward Daniels, and Albert T. Morgan.

1256.   Ownby, Ted. "The Defeated Generation at Work: White Farmers in the Deep South, 1865-1890." *Southern Studies* 23 (Winter 1984): 325-347.   Ownby focuses on changes encountered by white farmers in South Carolina, Georgia, Alabama, Mississippi, and Louisiana. The loss of their property and the economic environment required them to borrow large sums of money, focus on speculative crops like cotton, work harder, and sometimes rely on black workers. The new pressures and uncertainties made white farmers and farm workers feel trapped in a slave-like situation. The anger among whites contributed to the emotional state of Southern populism by the 1880s.

1257.   Painter, Carvel. "The Recovery of Confederate Property and Other Assets Abroad, 1865-73." Ph.D. American University, 1973. 485p.

1258.   Pope, Christie Farnham.   "Southern   Homesteads   for   Negroes." *Agricultural History* 49 (April 1970): 201-212. Tbl.   The Southern Homestead Act of 1866 was a proposal pushed by Congressman George W. Julian of Indiana. The intent of the bill was to sell plots of land to freedmen and other Southern loyalists as a way to create an environment for the future success of the former slaves.   In practice the legislation was a complete failure because the opening of General Land Offices was delayed, and freedmen were generally too poor to invest in land, seed, and implements and still feed their families before the first crop. Also, nonresident timber companies used loopholes in the law to gain control of tracts of land for timbering.

1259.   Powell, Lawrence N. "The American Land Company and Agency: John A. Andrew and the Northernization of the South." *Civil War History* 21 (December 1975): 293-308.   Gov. Andrew of Massachusetts organized the American Land Co. and Agency in the fall of 1865 to northernize the South with Northern business capital and know how, and the introduction of the free labor ideology. The creation of wealth and industry in the South was considered vital for making the region more like the rest of the country. The venture failed due to the animosity of Southern whites toward an invasion of Northern business, the poor cotton crop of 1866, and the highly unsettled political environment.

1260.   Powell, Lawrence N. *New Masters: Northern Planters During the Civil War and Reconstruction.* New Haven: Yale University Press, 1980. 253p. App. Bibl.   This analysis of the backgrounds, motives, and activities of Northern planters in the South focuses primarily on cotton planters in South Carolina, Georgia, Florida, Alabama, Mississippi and Louisiana between 1862 and 1868. Powell finds that Northern planters were widespread and had greater enthusiasm for cotton production compared with most other crops. Most of them left the South by mid 1867 because of business failure and poor relations with black laborers and Southern whites. Powell appears to validate the suspicions of whites who viewed the Northern planters as interested in extracting wealth and upsetting race relations.

The exploits of Northern planters are compared with the Forty-niners who rushed to California to seek their fortune in gold. The appendix includes statistical tables showing characteristics of Northern planters. (See also Powell's Ph.D. dissertation with the same title from Yale University, 1976.)

1261. Rabinowitz, Howard N. "The Conflict Between Blacks and the Police in the Urban South, 1865-1900." *Historian* 39 (November 1976): 62-76. The conflict between blacks and police in the 20th century can be traced by to Reconstruction. With emancipation blacks demanded participation in urban police forces and respect from white police. Harsh treatment of blacks by white police led to racial friction, and the presence of black police sometimes led to white riots.

1262. Rabinowitz, Howard N. "Continuity and Change: Southern Urban Development 1860-1900. " In *The City in Southern History: The Growth of Urban Civilization in the South.* Port Washington: Kennikat Press, 1977. Pp. 92-122. Tbls. One third of this essay deals with population growth, economic redevelopment, and the interrelationship of race and economic issues in Southern cities during the Civil War and Reconstruction. Rabinowitz is particularly concerned with New Orleans and Atlanta, but mentions several other cities as well. From 1860 to 1900 Southern cities experienced slow growth relative to the North, and became centers of increasing black poverty and racial discrimination and segregation.

1263. Ransom, Roger L. and Richard Sutch. "Credit and Merchandising in the Post-Emancipation South: Structure, Conduct, and Performance." *Explorations in Economic History* 16 (January 1979): 64-89. Tbls. The authors respond to their critics earlier in the same issue of E.E.H. (see # 1229, 1268, 1293) and explain their economic model for illustrating why the Southern economy lagged behind the nation. (For a general analysis of the direction of future research, see also Gavin Wright, "Freedom and the Southern Economy," *Explorations in Economic History* 16 (January 1979): 90-108.)

1264. Ransom, Roger L. and Richard Sutch. "Ex-slave in Post-Bellum South: A Study of the Economic Impact of Racism in a Market Environment." *Journal of Economic History* 33 (March 1973): 131-148. Tbls. App. Although economic historians of the postbellum South usually deemphasize race as a factor in the economic development of the freedmen and the growth of farm tenantry, Ransom and Sutch support the opposite conclusion. They believe that racial discrimination on the part of white Southern society and the freedman's perception of his predicament, severely depressed the opportunity for black farmers to invest in the future. There was little economic incentive for self improvement because whites blocked the path of progress by restricting black farmers to land tenant contracts and denying them access to financing. The market forces emphasized by most economic historians were not allowed to produce economic advantages for blacks. (See also a related article by Ransom and Sutch that mainly covers years after Reconstruction - "Debt Peonage in the Cotton South After the Civil War." *Journal of Economic History* 32 (September 1972): 641-669; and Gavin Wright's *Old South, New South:*

Revolutions in the Southern Economy Since the Civil War, New York: Basic Books, 1986.)

1265.   Ransom, Roger L. and Richard Sutch. "The Impact of the Civil War and of Emancipation on Southern Agriculture." *Explorations in Economic History* 12 (January 1975): 1-28. Tbls.   The authors criticize the idea that the devastation of the war was the main factor that held back economic growth in the South. Emancipation was more important. Per capita income and productivity dropped after the war because freedmen naturally worked fewer hours compared with slave days. Southern agriculture recovered after population increases replaced the labor lost when the slaves were freed.

1266.   Ransom, Roger L. and Richard Sutch. *One Kind of Freedom: The Economic Consequences of Emancipation*. Cambridge: Cambridge University Press, 1977. 409p. App. Bibl. Maps. Tbls.   The authors, both economists, provide an economic analysis of how the South reconstructed itself in the context of free black labor. Planters and merchant/creditors controlled the process and crafted a restricted type of freedom for most ex-slaves. Labor contracts, sharecropping, and debt peonage were the hallmarks of the new relationship. Racism played a role in the system, but it was not the major factor in its design. As a result of a flawed economic system in the South, the region and its people lagged well behind the rest of the country. Seven appendixes provide supporting statistical data. (See also # 1229, 1263, 1268, 1293, 1299)

1267.   Reid, Joseph D., Jr.   "Sharecropping as an Understandable Market Response: The Post-Bellum South." *Journal of Economic History* 32 (March 1973): 106-130. App. Graph. Tbl.   The development of sharecropping and land rental in Reconstruction was not due principally to freedmen's "land thirst" and planter's racism. Reid emphasizes the economic benefits of distributing risk between landlord and laborer, as well as making use of the planter's close attention to plots distributed to tenants. Sharecropping should have increased agricultural production. Reid includes the text of sharecropper contracts from 1882.

1268.   Reid, Joseph D., Jr.   "White Land, Black Labor, and Agricultural Stagnation: The Causes and Effects of Sharecropping in the Postbellum South." *Explorations in Economic History* 16 (January 1979): 31-55. Tbls.   Reid presents a more positive view of postbellum economic growth in the South in his critique of Ransom and Sutch's *One Kind of Freedom* (see # 1266). Sharecropping, cotton production, and growth of country stores are viewed as indicators and promoters of economic development as revealed in Reid's statistical analysis of farming. Ransom and Sutch interpreted these issues as negative forces in developing the economy in general, particularly in the case of freedmen.

1269.   Reidy, Joseph P.   "Slavery, Emancipation, and the Capitalist Transformation of Southern Agriculture, 1850-1910." In *Agriculture and National Development: Views on the Nineteenth Century*. Edited by Lou Ferleger. Ames: Iowa State University Press, 1990. Pp. 229-264. Bibl. Tbls.   From a Marxist perspective, Reidy explains that the Northern victory in the Civil War and the emancipation of the slaves provided the impetus for the rapid development of capitalism in plantation agriculture and turned slaves into a proletarian class that lacked access to economic resources for improvement. The economic depression of 1873 and the nationalization of agricultural development and labor led to the transformation of a Southern agricultural proletariat into an industrial proletariat in a maturing capitalist environment.

1270.   Robinson, Armistead L.   "The Difference Freedom Made: The Emancipation of Afro-Americans." In *The State of Afro-American History: Past, Present, and Future*. Edited by Darlene Clark Hine. Baton Rouge: Louisiana State University Press, 1986. Pp. 51-74.   By writing about key themes in black emancipation in America, Robinson hopes to contribute to historians' ability to write a new synthesis of emancipation within the broader context of postwar American industrialization. He focuses on labor, social differentiation, and migration in the Southern black community after the Civil War. Following the essay are comments by Eric Foner and Nell Irvin Painter (p. 80-88) on resources and areas of research in emancipation studies.

1271.   Robinson, Armistead L.   "'Warser dan Jeff Davis': The Coming of Free Labor During the Civil War, 1861-1865." In *Essays on the Postbellum Southern Economy*. Edited by T. Glymph and J. J. Kushma. College Station: Texas A&M Press, 1985. Pp. 11-47.   Robinson examines the progressive wartime transformation of Southern planters and laborers from an environment and mentality of slavery to that of capitalist free labor as expounded by the Republican Party. This development led to the changes attempted following the war and contributes to the assessment of the Civil War and Reconstruction as a revolutionary era.

1272.   Rogers, Benjamin F., Jr.   "The United States Department of Agriculture and the South, 1862-1880." *Florida State University Studies* 10 (1953): 71-80. During the postwar years the Department of Agriculture consistently supported the economic reconstruction of Southern agriculture. The help given to Southern farmers produced goodwill towards the commissioners of the department, particularly Isaac Newton, John Stokes, Frederick Watts, and William G. LeDuc.

1273.   Saloutos, Theodore. *Farmer Movements in the South 1865-1933*. Lincoln: University of Nebraska Press, 1960. 354p. Bibl.   In the first three chapters Saloutos examines agricultural problems in the South during Reconstruction including debt, lack of political influence in Congress, the need for a more inflationary monetary policy, reliance on cotton, and the destructiveness of race relations. Also, the Grange (Patrons of Husbandry) took a foothold among Southern farmers in the 1870s, but it never had strong appeal. The problems of farmers during the first postwar decade persisted throughout the rest of the century despite various farmer alliances.

1274.   Saloutos, Theodore. "The Grange in the South, 1870-1877." *Journal of Southern History* 19 (November 1953): 473-487.   The Grange or Patrons of

Husbandry tried to organize Southern farmers after the Civil War, but the movement never succeeded as it did in the Midwest.   There was little anger against monopolistic corporations in the South, and the mostly white organization was impeded by Southern traditions, poor race relations, and the course of Reconstruction politics. The Grange did succeed in showing farmers the benefits of combined action, lessening sectionalism, and agricultural education and training. The Grange set the example for future Southern farmer organizations.

1275.   Saloutos, Theodore.   "Southern Agriculture and the Problems of Readjustment, 1865-1877." *Agricultural History* 30 (April 1965): 58-76.   Racial and social traditions combined with economic changes to create a region that struggled to generate capital, decrease indebtedness, accept agricultural innovations, and regain political clout in Congress. By 1877 the problems of the cotton economy of the South persisted, and it would take generations to overcome them.

1276.   Schmidt, James D. "'Free Labor Still Lives': African-American Uses of the Labor Law in the Reconstruction South, 1864-1868." *Journal of Legal History* 3 (1994): 37-70. Ports.   Schmidt examines how black Southerners were able to skirt the intent of the black codes and successfully fight for their rights a free laborers. The black owned *New Orleans Tribune* helped formulate a philosophy of free black labor, but blacks organized and filed suit to oppose the imposition of contract wage labor and childhood apprenticeships that appeared to be no better than slavery.

1277.   Schmidt, James D. *Free To Work: Labor law, Emancipation, and Reconstruction, 1815-1880*. Athens: University of Georgia Press, 1998. 331p. Bibl.   Schmidt investigates the influence of law on the development of free labor, both ideologically and in practice. He is particularly interested in the evolution of a capitalist labor force in the North, and how the experience played a central role in the Reconstruction of the South following the Civil War. The emancipation of slaves was a key factor in the attempt to force capitalist, bourgeois labor on a mainly agrarian society by the use of legislation, such at the 13th Amendment and "tramp" laws, and the work of the Freedmen's Bureau. The bureau served as a direct instrument of government authority to instill capitalist labor values in Southern society. Despite the inability to transform the South and maintain permanent reforms for the freedmen, the legality and practice of free labor and some other civil rights remained. Both during and after Reconstruction law transformed labor in society and changed it completely by the end of the century. (See also Schmidt's "'Neither Slavery Nor Involuntary Servitude': Free Labor and American Law, ca. 1815-1880." Ph.D. Rice University, 1992. 480p.)

1278.   Schweninger, Loren. "Black Economic Reconstruction in the South."   In *The Facts of Reconstruction: Essays in Honor of John Hope Franklin*. Baton Rouge: Louisiana State University Press, 1991. Pp. 167-188.   Historians of black economic Reconstruction have focused primarily on the impact of market forces, racial discrimination, and the failure of federal and state governments on the transition from slavery to freedom. Schweninger documents black ownership of real estate and personal property in the years just before and after the Civil War by using census statistics. The figures show that black ownership of property increased dramatically from 1860 to 1870 in many areas of the South, particularly in rural areas of the upper South, such as North Carolina, Kentucky and Virginia. The statistics illustrate that many freedmen made great strides in the early years of emancipation. (See also Schweninger's "Property Owning Free African-American Women in the South, 1800-1870," *Journal of Women's History* 1(1990): 13-44 and rpt. in *'We Specialize in the Wholly Impossible': A Reader in Black Women's History*. Edited by Darlene Clark Hine et. al. New York: Carlson Publishing, 1995. Pp. 253-280.)

1279.   Shlomowitz, Ralph. "'Bound' or 'Free'? Black Labor in Cotton and Sugarcane Farming, 1865-1880." *Journal of Southern History* 50 (November 1984): 569-596.   Shlomowitz challenges Jonathan Wiener's (see # 1451) theory that the sharecropping system which developed in the South during Reconstruction was a coercive method of binding the freedmen to the planters' labor designs and that this system originated in class conflict. Shlomowitz reinforces arguments that depict sharecropping as a free market mechanism that allowed freedmen to change jobs, to demand better working conditions, and to create a greater sense of autonomy compared with slave conditions. This situation was more prevalent in cotton farming than cane farming. He cites evidence of competitive labor conditions and wage bidding to bolster his argument.

1280.   Shlomowitz, Ralph. "The Origins of Sharecropping." *Agricultural History* 53 (July 1979): 557-575. Tbls.   An economic framework for the labor-employer relationship between the freedmen and planters is used to explain how sharecropping developed as a viable method of working the land to the relative satisfaction of all parties. The early postbellum gang contracts that approximated work conditions under slavery could not compete, particularly in cotton farming, with an array of other labor relationships and salary distributions. Deciding factors influencing the configuration of the labor-employer relationship were an evolving, informal cost/benefit analysis and the social implications of a work system in an environment in which freedmen sought to express their freedom rather than dependency. Schlomowitz compares the institutional changes in labor relationships in the American South with experiences in other nations.

1281.   Shlomowitz, Ralph. "The Squad System on Postbellum Cotton Plantations." In *Toward a New South? Studies in Post-Civil War Southern Communities*. Westport: Greenwood Press, 1982. Pp. 265-280.   The squad system of labor was used in some plantations during the early years of Reconstruction. It appears to be an intermediate stage in the labor structure between gang wage labor and sharecropping. Shlomowitz uses original contracts and contemporary published literature to find evidence of squads that comprised a small group of persons who worked on a specific plot of land with much greater independence than in gang or individual contract labor. The squad system was mutually agreed upon by planters and laborers, but planters sought to further reduce the size of their working groups leading to family sharecropping. The squad system and sharecropping increased incentives for former slaves to work diligently while offering them a greater sense of independence.

1282.   Shlomowitz, Ralph.   "The Transition From Slave to Freedom: Labor Arrangements in Southern Agriculture, 1865-1870."   Ph.D.   University of Chicago, 1978.

1283.   Shore, Laurence.   *Southern Capitalists: The Ideological Leadership of an Elite, 1832-1885.*   Chapel Hill: University of North Carolina Press, 1986.   282p. Bibl.   Shore analyzes how Southern white elites viewed their situation during and after the Civil War.   In general, white elites made the transition from an agrarian-capitalist, slave based labor system to postwar capitalism that redefined labor as white and dignified.   The elite sought a future that deemphasized agrarianism in favor of industrial development.   Shore defines the transition as the retention of antebellum capitalism and white supremacy with the acceptance of a free labor ideology.   Key players among the "elastic" elite were Lucius Q. C. Lamar of Mississippi and Joe Brown and Benjamin Hill of Georgia.   (See also Shore's "To Dignify Labor: The Ideological Transformation of Southern Leadership, 1832-1880."   Ph.D.   1984.   912p.)

1284.   Smith, John David.   "More than Slaves, Less than Freedmen: The 'Share Wages' Labor System During Reconstruction."   *Civil War History* 26 (September 1980): 256-266.   Among the types of agricultural labor contracts agreed to by freedmen and planters, the share wages system was not frequently used because it employed a gang work system similar to the slave experience.   Smith offers an example of this type of contract at Exeter Plantation near Berkeley, S.C.   The contract dated February 1, 1867 was between the planter, Dr. J. Rhett Motte, and 28 freedmen whose names are listed.

1285.   Smith, Johnie D.   "And the State Became Their Master: An Analysis of the Southern Reconstruction of Labor Systems and Law, 1865-1867."   Ph.D. Wayne State University, 1994.   240p.

1286.   Stover, John F.   "Northern Financial Interests in Southern Railroads, 1865-1900."   *Georgia Historical Quarterly* 39 (September 1955): 205-220.   Ownership of Southern railroads gradually shifted from Southerners to Northerners by the early 1870s as Northern capital was needed to complete unfinished roads or to provide new financing.   After the Panic of 1873 greater amounts of Northern capital entered the Southern railroad industry to bail out failing lines.   During the late 1870s more than half of the Southern lines were under Northern control.   Stover also points out that during Reconstruction corrupt carpetbaggers attempted to build new rail lines or to take over old ones.   By the end of the century Northern influence was nearly complete.

1287.   Stover, John F.   *The Railroads of the South, 1865-1900:   A Study in Finance and Control.*   Chapel Hill: University of North Carolina Press, 1955.   310p. Bibl. Maps. Tbls.   The story of postwar railroads in the South is mainly a combination of rehabilitation, growth, and gradual domination by Northern business interests which was nearly total by 1900. Stover is very critical of the Radical Republican, carpetbagger regimes that either allowed or participated in corruption that resulted in carpetbagger exploitation, high state debt, and deeper depression in the South beginning with the Panic of 1873. Although existing rail lines had nearly recovered by 1870, the 1870s would be a period when most Southern railroads experienced bankruptcy or other serious financial difficulties. This was partly as a result of carpetbagger policies. Stover focuses on railroad history in the former Confederate states east of the Mississippi River, as well as Louisiana and Kentucky, for lines of at least 100 miles. In particular, he writes about the Illinois Central, Louisville and Nashville, and Richmond and Danville.

1288.   Stover, John F. "Southern Railroad Receivership in the 1870s." *Virginia Magazine of History and Biography* 63 (January 1955): 40-52.   Stover examines the negative impact of the Panic of 1873 on the construction of Southern railroads and the Southern railroad business in general. The economic problems lingering from the Civil War followed by economic depression caused a large number of defaults, receiverships, foreclosures, and reorganizations of railroads. Ownership tended to shift from Southern to Northern hands during the 1870s.

1289.   Summers, Mark W.   *Railroads, Reconstruction, and the Gospel of Prosperity: Aid Under the Radical Republicans, 1865-1877.* Princeton: Princeton University Press, 1984. 361p. Bibl.   Railroads became the central issue in the Gospel of Prosperity or the single-minded goal of local and state leaders to rebuild their communities through constructing new or improved rail lines. Republicans considered this to be a public aid program to railroad corporations driven by the frenzied interest at local and state levels for rail lines and by corporate lobbying. One result was widespread corruption among corporations and interest groups. Summers emphasizes that public aid to railroads failed because of parochial interests among local officials, corruption, economic and political rigidity, and economic depression. Republicans bore the blame for the problems, but Summers credits them with trying to make positive changes that would ultimately influence future promoters of the New South. (See also Summers' "Radical Reconstruction and the Gospel of Prosperity: Railroad Aid Under the Southern Republicans." Ph.D. University of California, Berkeley, 1980. 1031p.)

1290.   Sutch, Richard and Roger Ransom. "Sharecropping: Market Response or Mechanism of Race Control?" In *What Was Freedom's Price?* Edited by David Sansing. Jackson: University Press of Mississippi, 1978. Pp. 51-69.   The two economists explain that historians commonly describe sharecropping as a form of racist social control by white landowners. But by emphasizing the aspect of control, historians tend to gloss over the economic basis for sharecropping. This form of postwar agricultural organization emerged as a response to market forces by plantation owners seeking to maximize profits and by the freedmen who sought a more independent working life than they experienced as slave labor. The system was not inherently one of social control, but the authors grant that racial control was certainly incorporated by employers and local merchants to their advantage. As an economic system, the main problem with sharecropping was that it stifled investment and technological progress, thus slowing Southern agricultural development and economic progress among the freedmen.

1291.   Taylor, Rosser H.   (ed.).   "Post-Bellum Southern Rental Contracts." *Agricultural History* 17 (1943): 121-128.   Seven rental contracts between black tenants and landlords are printed. Only the first contract, dated January 1, 1868, is from the Reconstruction period. The others range from 1896 to 1909.

1292.   Tebeau, C. W.   "Some Aspects of Planter - Freedmen Relations, 1865-1880." *Journal of Negro History* 21 (April 1936): 130-150.   The relationship between planters and freedmen were generally good despite conflict over labor contracts, working conditions, and politics. Planters were disposed to be kind to their black workers because blacks were not blamed for the downfall of slavery. Tebeau generally describes the freedmen as ignorant and childlike.

1293.   Temin, Peter. "Freedmen and Coercion: Notes on the Analysis of Debt Peonage in *One Kind of Freedom*." *Explorations in Economic History* 16 (January 1979): 56-63. Tbls.   Temin explains that in *One Kind of Freedom* (see # 1266) Ransom and Sutch present valid concerns about the coercive nature of Southern economic and social institutions, but their data is flawed, and they overstate their case that the coercion and exploitation of black labor held back Southern economic development. (See also 1229, 1268)

1294.   Thompson, Holland. "The Civil War and Social and Economic Changes." In "The Coming of Industry in the South," *Annals of the American Academy of Political and Social Sciences* 153 (January 1951): 11-20.   Thompson summarizes the early transitions in Southern society that were initiated by the Civil War. He emphasizes the diversity of experiences in the South, but generalizes with regard to postwar cotton farming, the decline of the plantation system and the aristocracy that owned them, tenant labor, and the development of Southern industry.

1295.   Turner, Charles W.   "The Chesapeake and Ohio Railroad in Reconstruction, 1865-1873." *North Carolina Historical Review* 31 (April 19540: 150-172.   This case study of the Virginia Central Railroad Company illustrates how one railroad recovered during the period of Reconstruction to emerge in 1873 as a growing, national line. The company became known as the Chesapeake and Ohio Railroad in 1867. In 1869 a New York financier, C. P. Huntington, provided sorely needed capital to maintain the company's growth and gave it a chance to succeed in the future.

1296.   Verney, Kevern J. "Trespassers in the Land of Their Birth: Blacks and Landownership n South Carolina and Mississippi During the Civil War and Reconstruction, 1861-1877." *Slavery and Abolition* 4 (May 1983): 64-78.   Verney cites various examples of the acquisition of land by freedmen and their success as independent farmers. The fact that black landownership was not more pervasive was due to the paltry wages given to black laborers, the restrictions placed on blacks in white society and the lack of support for land distribution from federal authorities. The sambo image that many whites believed as truly indicative of black personality was merely an act for survival during slavery and was quickly dropped by most freedmen.

1297.   Virts, Nancy Lynn.   "Plantations, Land Tenure and Efficiency in the Postbellum South: The Effects of Emancipation on Southern Agriculture." Ph.D. University of California, Los Angeles, 1985. 117p.

1298.   Waller, J. L.   "The Overland Movement of Cotton, 1866-1886." *Southwestern Historical Quarterly* 35 (October 1931): 137-145. Tbls.   The end of the war brought gradual changes to the method and direction that cotton was transported to market.   As railroads were extended, cotton was increasingly transported by rail instead of by river, and increasingly the direction was north and east instead of to Southern markets in New Orleans or Memphis. St. Louis, Cincinnati and Louisville became important locations for the overland movement of cotton, whether the cotton was headed for export or domestic manufacturers. The overland movement, however, was still not as large as traditional transportation methods directed to Southern destinations.

1299.   Walton, Gary M. *Market Institutions and Economic Progress in the New South 1865-1900: Essays Stimulated by One Kind of Freedom: The Economic Consequences of Emancipation.* New York: Academic Press, 1981. 162p. Bibl. Tbls.   This book of seven essays by academic economists analyzes issues raised by *One Kind of Freedom* written by Roger L. Ransom and Richard Sutch (see # 1266). The essays do not focus on the period of Reconstruction *per se*, but on the last decades of the 19th century.   They offer insight into economic and social transformation of emancipation, particularly with regard to the impact of continued concentration on cotton cultivation and the development of sharecropping, merchant credit, and debt peonage. At the center of the changes were the freedman who were not offered the means to succeed economically in the postwar South. The essays contribute to the growing research that investigates the postwar South using the analytical methodologies of economists.

1300.   Washington, Reginald. "The Freedmen's Savings and Trust Company and African American Genealogical Research." *Prologue* 29 (Summer 1997): 170-181. Facim. Ills. Tbl.   Washington discusses the content of records held at the National Archives that were produced by the Freedmen's Savings and Trust Co. The records (Record Group 101), part of the Records of the Comptroller of the Currency, provide significant information about depositors and their families. The bank, which was chartered in 1865 and closed in 1874, proved to be a disaster for thousands of depositors.

1301.   Watkins, Beverly. "'To Surrender All His Estate': The 1867 Bankruptcy Act." *Prologue* 21 (Fall 1989): 206-213. Ill. Port. Tbl.   Following the Civil War Northern companies claimed that Southerners owed them about $300 million in old debts. Congress passed the Bankruptcy Act of 1867 to assist them in obtaining at least part of the debt, and also because of the emergence in the South of a credit system based on crop liens to local merchants and fears of a nationwide economic panic. Watkins explains how the bankruptcy system worked. He offers as an example a description of the bankruptcy of John R. Denty of Marshall County, Mississippi.

1302.   Wayne, Michael S. *The Reshaping of Plantation Society: The Natchez District, 1860-1880*. Baton Rouge: Louisiana State University Press, 1983. 226p. Bibl. Maps. Tbls.   Wayne examines the postwar transition of plantation society in the agriculturally and economically rich region north and south of Natchez along the Mississippi River. The demands of black workers forced an end to the paternalism of slavery and provided them with a greater sense of freedom, but planters eventually allied themselves with merchants in Natchez, New Orleans and other towns. By the 1870s black tenants and laborers were significantly restricted by growing debt to planters and merchants. The evolving economic and social environment of the plantation in the Natchez region eventually favored the planter over the laborer and tenant, keeping the former slaves and their children in a state of economic dependence despite their new freedom.

1303.   Wiener, Jonathan M. "Class Structure and Economic Development in the American South, 1865-1955." *American Historical Review* 84 (October 1979): 970-992.   This essay is followed by comments from Robert Higgs and Harold D. Woodman and a reply from Weiner. Wiener believes that Reconstruction is a key issue in this forum that highlights disagreements about the social impact of the postwar Southern economy. It was in the context of large landholdings and a repressive labor system that the South was held back from economic development and progress experienced in the North.

1304.   Wesley, Charles H. *Negro Labor in the United States 1850-1925: A Study in American Economic History*. New York: Russell and Russell, 1967. 343p. App. Tbls. (Reissue of 1927 edition by Vanguard Press)   In this survey of black labor history, Wesley discusses the challenges that faced most Southern blacks after the Civil War in the transition from slavery to free labor. His main point is that blacks adjusted to their new condition and quickly began to contribute to the economic reconstruction of the South. While they had to cope with prejudice and acts of violence against them, they made significant progress and participated in the national movement to organize black labor. An important development in the postwar period was the organization of industrial education for blacks. This occurred as a response to discussions within the black community about the best path to increase education and labor skills.

1305.   Wilkin, Mary (ed.). "Some Papers of the American Cotton Planters' Association, 1865-1866." *Tennessee Historical Quarterly* 7 (December 1948): 335-361; 8 (March 1949): 49-62.   The A.C.P.A. organized in New York on September 28, 1865 with the intention of rebuilding the cotton plantation business in the South. The correspondence and documents provide information about the organization and membership of the association and its efforts to raise capital for planters.

Documents reveal the condition of cotton plantations and labor in 1865 and 1866 and show that the organization sought funding in the North and in Europe, particularly France.

1306.   Woodman, Harold D. "The Economic and Social History of Blacks in the Post-Emancipation South." *Trends in History* 3 (Fall 1982): 37-56.   In Woodman's bibliographic essay he discusses recent scholarship about the lives of freedmen after the Civil War, particularly regarding the meaning of freedom, labor, agriculture, education, and community. References are made to studies published from the 1860s to the early 20th century. He is encouraged by the growing number of works on social and economic history of black Americans.

1307.   Woodman, Harold D. "Economic Reconstruction and the Rise of the New South, 1865-1900." In *Interpreting Southern History: Historiographical Essays in Honor of Sanford W. Higgenbotham*. Edited by John B. Boles and Evelyn Thomas Nolen. Baton Rouge: Louisiana State University Press, 1987. Pp. 254-307. Woodman's focus is broader than just Reconstruction because economic developments can only be interpreted over a longer period of time than the chronological bounds of political events. Citing literature since the early 1960s, he notes that the few economic interpretations that appeared have tended to argue that the results of the Civil War reflect either a continuity or a discontinuity in Southern history. Economic historians established race as a secondary factor in economic developments.   More important were labor, market forces, and social relations between classes in the South. Woodman calls for more regional comparisons between the West and the South, and the study of the Southern economy within the broader context of American economic development.

1308.   Woodman, Harold D. *King Cotton and His Retainers: Financing and Marketing the Cotton Crop of the South, 1800-1925*. Lexington: University of Kentucky Press, 1968. 386p. Bibl. Ills. Tbls.   Part 5 of this book focuses on the adjustments made by Southern cotton planters to finance their crop and get it to market. Cotton dominated the Southern economy after the Civil War, but the decline of capital assets among the planters following emancipation and the destruction of the war made financing difficult. Northern financiers refused to help, leading to the prewar practice of cotton factor businesses that financed and bought and sold cotton for the planter. During the 1870s factorage firms lost business to country merchants, who helped finance the crop, and railroads that provided transportation to key inland markets directly from the source. The changes in financing and transporting cotton to market did not change the importance of the crop in the Southern economy for many years.

1309.   Woodman, Harold D. *New South-New Law: The Legal Foundations of Credit and Labor Relations in the Postbellum Agricultural South*. Baton Rouge: Louisiana State University Press, 1995. 124p. Cases cited.   In four lectures Woodward explores the legal relationship between landowners, laborers, and merchants. Statutes, court decisions, rules, regulations, and customs formed the basis for postwar Southern agricultural development with emphasis on the control of credit and labor in order to maintain conservative economic and legal power of white property owners and merchants. He discusses crop lien laws that trapped tenants in unending debt and held back agricultural development. Woodman also discusses the social impact of law on Southern society. (See also Woodman's "Post-Civil War Southern Agriculture and the Law." *Agricultural History* 33 (January 1979): 319-337.)

1310.   Woodman, Harold D. "The Reconstruction of the Cotton Plantation in the New South." In *Essays on the Postbellum Southern Economy.* Edited by T. Glymph and J. J. Kushma. College Station: Texas A&M Press, 1985. Pp. 95-119. Woodman recognizes the great changes that the Union victory and emancipation initiated throughout the South, but he also believes that there is preponderant evidence of continuity in Southern society. The continuity of racism and dogged resistance to political, economic, and social change by white society, particularly the planter class, had a great impact on the ability of black laborers to enjoy freedom. Class and race differences between planters, small farmers, tenants, and sharecroppers clashed and resulted in slower economic development in the South.

1311.   Woodman, Harold D. "Sequel to Slavery: The New History Views the Post-Bellum South." *Journal of Southern History* 43 (November 1977): 523-554. Woodman provides a critical analysis of historical writing on the economic and social history of the postwar period. He focuses on the use of statistical methods to explain the development of the Southern economy and the successes and failures of the economy from the perspective of the freedmen. In particular, Woodman examines the works of Robert Higgs, Stephen J. DeCanio, and Joseph D. Reid, Jr. who present a theory of positive postwar development for freedmen, and Roger L. Ranson and Richard Sutch, who focus on the economic stagnation of the South generally and the black laborer in particular. Woodman examines the ideas of Jonathan M. Wiener and Jay R. Mandle who write from a social perspective with emphasis on the continuity of the Southern economy and society from antebellum to postbellum periods.

1312.   Woolfolk, George Ruble. *The Cotton Regency: The Northern Merchants and Reconstruction, 1865-1880.* New York: Bookman Associates, 1958. 311p. Bibl.   Woolfolk agrees that the fifteen years following the war brought on the economic domination of the South by the Northeast and the Midwest. The South was defenseless to exploitation, partly because of adverse court decisions, lack of capital, poor credit conditions, too much emphasis on cotton agriculture, labor instability, the hard money policy, and the Panic of 1873. Woolfolk believes that the exploitation of the South was part of postwar industrial expansion. (See also Woolfolk's Ph.D. dissertation with the same title from University of Wisconsin, 1947.)

1313.   Zeichner, Oscar. "The Legal Status of the Agricultural Laborer in the South." *Political Science Quarterly* 55 (September 1940): 412-428.   Zeichner discusses the legal status and prevalence of labor, sharecropping, and share-tenancy among black agricultural laborers after the Civil War. The legal status of these working situations was generally not set for years after the war depending on the state, but Zeichner cites state legislation and court cases from the period of Reconstruction and the decades that followed that pertain to agricultural labor. He concludes that despite the elimination of slave labor, the plantation system that existed prior to emancipation continued after 1865. Legally, plantation owners maintained control of the land, the crops, and the labor contracts that favored the landlord and offered little promise to the laborer.

1314.   Zeichner, Oscar. "The Transition From Slave to Free Agricultural Labor in the Southern States." *Agricultural History* 13 (January 1939): 22-32.   Zeichner explains the transition from mainly wage labor for the freedmen to widespread use of tenancy and sharecropping.   Planters often abused the wage labor system, and they agreed with black laborers that it was too unpredictable.   The return to cotton farming after the war also contributed to the need for a stable, more controlled labor force.

Selected Studies on Historical Fiction

1315.   Appleby, Joyce. "Reconciliation and the Northern Novelists, 1865-1880." *Civil War History* 10 (June 1964): 117-129.   The majority of the books written in the 15 years after the Civil War emphasized reconciliation between North and South. Historians who credit Southern novelists after 1880 with the reconciliation theme overlook earlier works of Northerners, such as Mary Jane Holmes's *Dr. Wilmer's Love* (1868), John M'Dowell Leavitt's *The American Cardinal* (1871), and Joseph Converse Heywood's *How Will it End?* (1872). When Southern writers used the same theme, Northern readers of romantic fiction quickly accepted it.

1316.   Armour, Robert A.   "History Written in Jagged Lightening: Realistic South vs. Romantic South in *The Birth of a Nation*." *Southern Quarterly* 19 (Winter 1981): 14-21.   Armour explains that D. W. Griffith's own biases and acceptance of Southern myths taint a film that was presented as objective history on Reconstruction.

1317.   Becker, George J.   "Albion W. Tourgée: Pioneer in Social Criticism." *American Literature* 19 (March 1947): 59-72.   Becker seeks to lift Tourgée out of obscurity so that he can be appreciated for his strong commitment to social criticism in his accounts of the South during Reconstruction.   In several fictional works, particularly *A Fool's Errand* (1879) and *Bricks Without Straw* (1880), Tourgée commented on Southern society as he experienced it in North Carolina during and after Reconstruction.   Becker notes that even though the writing is flawed with the romantic style of bad novels of his day, Tourgée dealt with issues of race and democracy in a serious, analytical way.

1318.   Bowman, Sylvia E.   "Judge Tourgée's Fictional Presentation of the Reconstruction." *Journal of Popular Culture* 3 (Fall 1969): 307-323.   Bowman examines how Tourgée's novels on Reconstruction were intended as social commentary and propaganda on Southern racism and Northern political expediency. Tourgée's criticism of white Southerners and their society, based on his experiences in North Carolina, were just as biased as most of the other fictional representations of Reconstruction, but Tourgée's strong support for humanity to all races held meaning for future generations.

1319.   Caccavari, Peter Jerome. "Reconstruction of Race and Culture in America: Violence and Knowledge in Works by Albion Tourgée, Charles Chesnutt, and Thomas Dixon, Jr." Ph.D. Rutgers University, 1993. 323p. (See also Caccavari's "Reconstructing Reconstruction: Region and Nation in the Work of Albion Tourgée," In *Regionalism Reconsidered: New Approaches to the Field*, New York: Garland, 1994. Pp. 119-138.)

1320.   Campbell, Finely Calvin. "The Bloody Chasm; A Descriptive Analysis of Reconstruction in American Literature: 1865-1885." Ph.D. University of Chicago, 1970.

1321.   Davenport, F. Garvin, Jr.   "Thomas Dixon's Mythology of Southern History." *Journal of Southern History* 36 (August 1970): 350-367.   Dixon constructed a mythology of Southern history built on four themes: union, and Southern mission, uniqueness, and burden. His novels, such as *The Clansmen* (1905) and *The Leopard's Spots: A Romance of the White Man's Burden, 1865-1900* (1902), were a reaction to the pressures on white, Anglo-Saxon America for change. One of these pressures was black equality. By depicting the Civil War and Reconstruction era as the beginning of the black threat to white supremacy, Dixon built a concept that placed the South at the lead of a national movement to preserve innocence and fight industrialization, new theories of politics and morals, and black equality. Beating the black threat might lead to the resolution of the other problems.

1322.   DeSantis, Christopher Charles. "Reconstruction and the American Literary Imagination." Ph.D. University of Kansas, 1997. 165p.

1323.   Emerson, A. J.   "A Carpetbagger's View of the Ku-Klux Klan." *Confederate Veteran* 29 (July 1916): 308-310.   Emerson provides extended quotations from Albion Tourgée's *A Fool's Errand* (1879) to illustrate Tourgée's characterization of the Klan.

1324.   Fredrickson, George M. "The Travail of a Radical Republican: Albion W. Tourgée and Reconstruction." In *The Arrogance of Race: Historical Perspectives on Slavery, Racism, and Social Inequality*. Middletown, Conn.:   Wesleyan University Press, 1988. Pp. 94-106.   Fredrickson focuses on Tourgée's *A Fool's Errand* (1879) and what he attempted to accomplish through his political activism as a resident of North Carolina during Reconstruction. Tourgée criticized white Southerners resisting justice for the freedmen and the federal government for its lack of commitment to civil rights and personal security for the freedmen and its insufficient attempt at economic and social reforms.

1325.   Friedman, George Stephen.   "Reconstruction and Redemption in Selected American Novels 1878-1915." Ph.D. Duke University, 1972. 433p.

1326.   Godbold, E. Stanly, Jr.   "A Battleground Revisited: Reconstruction in Southern Fiction, 1895-1905." *South Atlantic Quarterly* 73 (Winter 1974): 99-116. At the end of the 19th century and the beginning of the 20th century Southern writers proliferated and interest in Reconstruction increased. It was a period of economic, political, and social change when Southern industrialization began in earnest, the South participated in a war with Spain and race relations were increasingly on the minds of people. Many Southern fiction writers showed great interest in Reconstruction, but there was no consensus on what life in the South was like during that time. The writers, including George W. Cable, John S. Wise, and Ellen Glasgow approached Reconstruction from their own individual perspectives, usually as a way to find answers to contemporary problems and issues.

1327.   Gross, Theodore L. *Albion W. Tourgée*. New York: Twayne Publishers, 1963. 176p. Bibl.   This book is a literary biography of Tourgée who wrote works of fiction based on his experiences in North Carolina during Reconstruction. Gross focuses on Tourgée's contributions to postwar Southern fiction and his unique place as the only Northern novelist of Reconstruction who experienced the Reconstruction South as an adult. Tourgée's works illustrate his vigorous style of political and social storytelling and preaching, but they also show his strong biases. Two major themes were the necessity for a national educational effort to improve the black community in the South and the force of Christianity to form the moral basis for eliminating racial inequality. On both counts his efforts failed. (See also Gross's "Albion W. Tourgée: Reporter of the Reconstruction."   Ph.D.   Columbia University, 1960.   277p.; and "Albion W. Tourgée: Reporter of the Reconstruction." *Mississippi Quarterly* 16 (Summer 1963): 111-127 in which he characterizes Tourgée as a propagandist of Radical Reconstruction.; also see Roy F. Dibble, *Albion W. Tourgée*. New York: Lemcke and Bueckner, 1921.)

1328.   Gross, Theodore L.   "The Negro in the Literature of Reconstruction." *Phylon* 22 (Spring 1961): 5-14.   Southern writers have dominated fiction dealing with blacks in Reconstruction.   They produced propaganda based on biased conceptions of the black race. Despite the writing of Ohioan Albion Tourgée, who wrote with sympathy about the plight of the freedmen in a hostile white South, racist stereotypes were not only generally accepted in the South but nationwide.   The writing of Thomas Nelson Page, Thomas Dixon, Joel Chandler Harris, Mary Murfree, and Maurice Thompson, published in the early 20th century, depicted a "tragic era" in which carpetbaggers were villains and manipulators of the freedmen.

1329.   Inscoe, John C. *"The Clansman* on Stage and Screen: North Carolina Reacts." *North Carolina Historical Review* 64 (April 1987): 139-161. Ills. Ports.. The stage production in 1905 and film version (*Birth of a Nation*, 1915) of Thomas Dixon's novel of Reconstruction evoked differing emotions in North Carolina based mainly on existing perceptions of race relations.   While the stage production provoked racial animosity, the film stirred nostalgia in the "Lost Cause" and reaction against Northern protest of the film.

1330.   Jones, Howard James.   "Images of State Legislative Reconstruction Participants in Fiction." *Journal of Negro History* 67 (Winter 1982): 318-327. Fictional writing on Reconstruction divides into two genres, conservative and revisionist, just the same way as historical writing has done. Jones explains that there is very little fictional literature on the topic. He surveys the writings of both groups, including conservatives Thomas Dixon, Thomas Nelson Page, Joel Chandler Harris and George Washington Cable; and revisionists Albion Winegar Tourgée, Frank Yerby and Howard Fast. The negative images of Reconstruction have had a lasting impact on Americans, partly due to the influence of Social Darwinism, imperialism, and racism. Conservative novelists reinforced this image.

1331.   MacLeod, Christine. "Telling the Truth in a Tight Place: *Huckleberry Finn* and the Reconstruction Era." *Southern Quarterly* 34 (Fall 1995): 5-16.   The last chapters of Mark Twain's *Huckleberry Finn* should be interpreted in the context of the failure to provide complete freedom to blacks in post-emancipation America. MacLeod suggests that blacks understood and responded to white society with this in mind. The novel reflects this postwar state of mind, particularly during the period between 1876 and 1883, when Twain composed the manuscript and there was a rapid retreat from Reconstruction reforms. MacLeod hopes that an appreciation of the social context of the book will diminish accusations that *Huckleberry Finn* promotes racism.

1332.   Mancuso, Kenneth Luke.   "'The Strange Sad War Revolving': Reconstituting Walt Whitman's Reconstruction Texts in the Legislative Workshop, 1865-1876." Ph.D. University of Iowa, 1994. 280p.

1333.   Ney, Russell B.   "Judge Tourgée and Reconstruction."   *Ohio State Archaeological and Historical Quarterly* 50 (April-June 1941): 101-114.   Nye reviews Tourgée's published writings about his experiences in the North Carolina to show the Ohioan's views toward Reconstruction. Ney is critical of Tourgée's propagandizing with a bias in favor of Republican ideology, but he compliments Tourgée for his temperance, sensibility and intelligence.

1334.   Nolan, Michael Phillip. "Democratic Character in Nineteenth Century American Reconstruction Novels." Ph.D. University of Iowa 1991. 293p.

1335.   Olenick, Monte M. "Albion W. Tourgée: Radical Republican Spokesman of the Civil War Crusade." *Phylon* 23 (Winter, 1962): 332-345.   Tourgée, a Union officer from Ohio, wrote several books based on his experiences with race relations in Greensboro, N.C. after the war. His Reconstruction novels were *A Fool's Errand* (1879), *The Invisible Empire* (1879) and *Bricks Without Straw* (1880). Olnick describes Tourgée contributions to the struggle for race equality, including the years from after Reconstruction when he continued to speak out against racial discrimination and participated in the trial, Plessy v. Ferguson (1896), in which he sought a ruling against "separate but equal."

1336.   Olsen, Otto H. "Tourgée on Reconstruction: A Revisionist Document of 1892." *Serif* 2 (September 1965): 21-28.   Olsen notes that Albion Tourgée was an early voice opposing racial stereotypes that stigmatized blacks as inferior to whites. Printed is a letter from Tourgée to Jeremiah Whipple Jenks dated May 26, 1892 that responds to Jenks' recent lecture on the black race. The former carpetbagger and author of historical fiction condemning white supremacy in Reconstruction challenged Jenks' ideas of black racial inferiority.

1337.   Palmer, Henrietta R. (ed.). *In Dixie Land: Stories of the Reconstruction Era*. By Southern Writers. Illus. By Illa McAfee. New York: Purdy Press, 1926. 226p.   This book is an anthology of 15 short stories or excerpts from novels set in various Southern states during Reconstruction.   In the introduction Palmer comments that even though the works are not high literary achievements, they depict postwar Southern life and culture from the Anglo-Saxon perspective. The authors are Grace E. King, Katherin S. Bonner, Harry S. Edwards, Joel C. Harris, Martha Young, Opie Read, Ambrose E. Gonzales, I. Jenkins Mikell, John Bennett, Kemp P. Battle, Armstead C. Gordon, John S. Wise, John T. Moore, James L. Allen, and Jane J. Heyward. The stories were written between 1878 and 1926.

1338.   Richardson, Emily Stenhouse. "Three Southern Views of Reconstruction, Economic Recovery and Race in the New South, 1865-1900: As Seen in the Life and Work of Thomas Nelson Page, Joel Chandler Harris and George Washington Cable." Ph.D. American University, 1987. 205p.

1339.   Robison, Lori. "The Re-Construction Of Local Color: Writing Region And Race, 1865-1896." Ph.D. Indiana University, 1995. 237p.

1340.   Rowe, Anne Ervin. "The Changing Northern Attitude Toward the Post-Bellum South as Exemplified in the Writings of John De Forest, Albion Tourgée, Constance Woolson, and Lafcadio Hearn." Ph.D. University of North Carolina, 1973. 195p.

1341.   Silverman, Joan L. *"The Birth of a Nation*: Prohibition Propaganda." *Southern Quarterly* 19 (Winter 1981): 22-30.   Silverman discusses D. W. Griffith's movie that brings together stories from Thomas Dixon's Reconstruction novels, *The Clansmen* (1905) and *The Leapard's Spots* (1902), to depict the danger of allowing blacks to drink alcohol. The movie contributed to the passage of the 18th Amendment.

1342.   Tourgée, Albion W. *A Fool's Errand*. New York: Fords, Howard, & Holbert, 1879. 361p.   Tourgée's novels about Reconstruction, including *The Invisible Empire* (New York: Fords, Howard, & Holbert, 1879) and *Bricks Without Straw* (New York: Fords, Howard, & Holbert, 1880), are based on his experiences while living in North Carolina as a farmer, lawyer, and judge. They reflect his consternation with the hatred and violence of Southern whites toward basic civil rights for blacks and resistance to change in Southern society.

1343.   Weissbuch, Ted N.   "Albion W. Tourgée: Propagandist and Critic of Reconstruction."   *Ohio Historical Quarterly* 70 (January 1961): 27-44. Weissbuch examines *A Fool's Errand* and *Bricks Without Straw*, two of Tourgée's novels about Reconstruction in North Carolina.   He describes both books as technically flawed as literary works for various reasons, particularly because of the Radical propaganda and exaggerations of negative aspects of postwar Southern society.   He also faults Tourgée for believing that the South should and could be reformed through education for both blacks and whites.   Tourgée's solutions to postwar problems were off the mark.   His criticism of Southern society was inconsistent with his own contributions to the scandal and corruption of the Radical regime in North Carolina.

1344.   Weissbuch, Theodore N.   "Literary and Historical Attitudes Toward Reconstruction Following the Civil War." Ph.D. University of Iowa, 1964. 261p.

1345.   Williams, Carol Anne.   "A Southern Writer's Retrospective: Betrayal, Rage, and Survival in the Reconstruction Fiction of Grace King." Ph.D. Texas A&M University, 1986. 181p.

1346.   Wilson, Edmund. "Novelists of the Post-War South - Albion W. Tourgée, George W. Cable, Kate Chopin, Thomas Nelson Page." In *Patriotic Gore: Studies in the Literature of the American Civil War*. New York: Oxford University Press, 1962. Pp. 529-616.   Tourgée, Cable, and Page were particularly concerned with issues of race in the postwar South. Wilson examines their literary careers and the influence of their work.

State and Local Reconstruction in the South

Alabama

General History

1347.   Brown, Lynda W. et. al. *Alabama History: An Annotated Bibliography*. Westport: Greenwood Press, 1998. 438p. Chron.   Chapter VII (p. 169-186) includes 146 briefly annotated references to journal articles, dissertations, masters theses, and books on Reconstruction in Alabama. (Note: Brown's section on Reconstruction and my book list many of the same references about Alabama, but she lists M.A. theses while I cover a broader array of sources with longer annotations.)

1348.   Cobb, Henry E. "Negroes in Alabama During the Reconstruction Period, 1865-1875." Ph.D. Temple University, 1953.

1349.   DuBose, John Witherspoon. *Alabama's Tragic Decade: Ten Years of Alabama 1865-1874*. Edited by James K. Greer. Birmingham: Webb Book Co., 1940. 435p. Chron. Ills. Maps.   DuBose, a native Southerner and a member of the White Camellia, originally published his work on Reconstruction as a series of articles in the Birmingham *Age-Herald* in 1912. The articles were mainly based on his experiences. DuBose hoped that Southerners of the 20th century would remember Reconstruction for the Southern heroes of the war who won the struggle against revolutionaries during the postwar period. He examines politics, economics, railroads, education, and the Ku Klux Klan.

1350.   Enzor, Frankie C. "Walter Lynwood Fleming." *Alabama Historical Quarterly* 20 (Winter 1958): 636-646.   Enzor's laudatory article is reprinted from papers of the Pike County Historical Society (v. 1, April 8, 1958). He discusses

Fleming's career and, in particular, his contributions to Reconstruction historiography. Fleming, a native of Alabama, was born in 1874 and died in 1932.

1351.   Fleming, Walter L. *Civil War and Reconstruction in Alabama.* New York: Columbia University Press, 1905. 815p. App. Ills. Maps. Ports. Tbls. Most of this book (565 pages) deals with Reconstruction. Fleming surveys all aspects of the period in topical chapters relating to social, economic, political, educational, and religious developments. There is detailed treatment of the Ku Klux Klan, labor, farming, the Freedmen's Bureau, and the overthrow of the Radical Republican regime in the state. Extensive use of statistical tables and maps provide supporting evidence.   Fleming states that blacks were the central figures in Reconstruction. Although he recognizes positive and negative outcomes for blacks and the South from Reconstruction after 1866, he believes that blacks was well protected and had a promising future under the state laws passed in 1865 and 1866. Radical Reconstruction was unnecessary, disruptive, and produced avoidable pain for both Southern whites and blacks in Alabama. (See also Fleming's Ph.D. dissertation with the same title from Columbia University, 1904.)

1352.   Reid, Robert. "Changing Interpretations of the Reconstruction Period in Alabama History." *Alabama Review* 27 (October 1974): 263-281.   Reid surveys historical writing on Reconstruction in Alabama from the early twentieth century to the 1970s. Revisionism marks the changing nature of historiography, particularly greater objectivity on carpetbaggers, scalawags, participation by blacks, and general assessments of Reconstruction, but Alabama writers have generally maintained a prerevisionist perspective.   He notes that the best single volume on Alabama Reconstruction is Walter L. Fleming's *Civil War and Reconstruction in Alabama* (see # 1351). Reid believes that a new history is needed.

1353.   Stephenson, Wendell H. "Some Pioneer Alabama Historians II: Walter L. Fleming."   *Alabama Review* 1 (October 1948): 261-278.   Fleming was an important historian of Reconstruction in Alabama and the South in general. Stephenson writes a complimentary biographical article describing Fleming's life and contributions to the understanding of Southern history.   Fleming, a student of William A. Dunning at Columbia University, sought to influence the national perception of the South by writing and encouraging other Southern historians to write about the history of their region.

Politics and Law

1354.   "Alabama Citizens of Achievement." *Negro History Bulletin* 5 (March 1992): 134, 143. Ports.   Brief biographical sketches cover the lives of Benjamin Sterling Turner (merchant, congressman), James T. Rapier (congressman), and William Hooper Councill (state legislator, editor, clergy).

1355.   Amos, Harriet E. "Trials of a Unionist: Gustavus Horton, Military Mayor of Mobile During Reconstruction." *Gulf Coast Historical Review* 4, 2 (1989): 134-151. Ills.   Horton, originally from Massachusetts, was a respected businessman and member of the Mobile community until his opposition to secession brought him into conflict with the majority of citizens. He expected that his Unionist sympathies would be honored with a job by U.S. Army commanders, but this did not happen until he was named Republican mayor after the Reconstruction Acts of 1867. Amos describes Horton's public and personal difficulties as a local Republican leader and his conviction for violating the Civil Rights Act of 1866 in his role as judge in Mayor's Court.

1356.   Alexander, Thomas B. "Persistent Whiggery in Alabama and the Lower South, 1860-1867." *Alabama Review* 12 (January 1959): 35-52.   Alexander focuses on the continuous participation of Whigs in Alabama politics from antebellum years through the election of Ulysses S. Grant as president in 1868. Whigs were usually Unionists who participated in governing the state in the immediate postwar period. Alabama Whigs, such as Provisional Gov. Lewis E. Parsons and Gov. Robert M. Patton, had an opportunity to organize a postwar Whig revival that would maintain moderate Reconstruction policies, but sectional conflict and misunderstanding eliminated this possibility. Radical Reconstruction split Whig strength between Republicans and Democrats, and eventually led to Democratic dominance and virtual one party rule.

1357.   Bailey, Richard.   *Neither Carpetbaggers Nor Scalawags: Black Officeholders During Reconstruction of Alabama, 1867-1878.* Montgomery: R. Baily Publishers, 1991. 498p. App. Bibl. Ports. Tbls.   Baily criticizes Walter L. Fleming's influence on negative public perceptions of blacks and carpetbaggers in Alabama during Reconstruction.   Bailey focuses on the important and positive contributions of blacks.   The failure of Republican rule was due mainly to white racism, Democratic political manipulation, and disunity within the Republican Party. Despite the obstacles, black leaders worked to establish schools and the roots for black self esteem, independence, and religious growth.   The appendixes lists black officeholders who served between 1867 and 1884 and provides some background information on each person.   (See also Bailey's "Black Legislators During the Reconstruction of Alabama, 1867-1878." Ph.D.   Kansas State University, 1984. 316p.)

1358.   Bell, William Dudley. "The Reconstruction Ku Klux Klan: A Survey of the Writings on the Klan With a Profile and Analysis of the Alabama Klan Episode, 1866-1874." Ph.D. Mississippi State University, 1973. 395p.

1359.   Brown, Charles A. "A. H. Curtis: An Alabama Legislator 1870-1876 With Glimpses into Reconstruction." *Negro History Bulletin* 25 (February 1962): 99-101. Port.   Brown focuses on the career of Rep. Alexander H. Curtis, a slave until 1859, who served as a legislator from 1870 until 1872 followed by four years in the state senate. He worked on the development of public and religious education, including the State Normal School and University in Marion (1873) and the Alabama Baptist Normal and Theology School in Selma (1878).

1360.   Brown, Charles A. "John Dozier: A Member of the General Assembly of Alabama, 1872-1873 and 1873-1874." *Negro History Bulletin* 26 (December 1962): 113, 128.   Brown briefly mentions Dozier's career as a legislator during Reconstruction.

1361.   Brown, Charles A. "Lloyd Leftwich, Alabama State Senator." *Negro History Bulletin* 26 (February 1963): 161-162. Port.   Leftwich, a former slave, served in the state senate from 1872 until 1876. His family history is described.

1362.   Brown, Charles A. "Reconstruction Legislators in Alabama." *Negro History Bulletin* 26 (March 1963): 198-200.   Brown writes brief biographies and family histories about John William Jones and Mansfield Tyler. Tyler was a Baptist preacher who helped organize the Alabama Colored Baptist State Convention in 1868. Both men served in the legislature during the first half of the 1870s.

1363.   Brown, Charles A. "William Hooper Councill, Alabama Legislator, Editor and Lawyer." *Negro History Bulletin* 26 (February 1963): 171-173.   Brown writes a brief biography and family history of Councill who was a black civil rights leader, editor of the *Negro Watchman* until 1874, and an African Methodist Episcopal clergyman.

1364.   Cash, William McKinley. "Alabama Republicans During Reconstruction: Personal Characteristics, Motivations, and Political Activity of Party Activists, 1867-1880." Ph.D. University of Alabama, 1973. 435p.

1365.   Copeland, Mrs. Kate Murphree.   "Reconstruction in Pike County: Political and Military." *Alabama Historical Quarterly* 22 (Winter 1960): 284-304. Copeland does not offer a general history of Pike County. Her article is more of a compilation of quotations and opinions designed to present a negative view of Republican policies and black civil rights during Reconstruction.

1366.   Damer, Eyre. *When the Ku Klux Rode.* New York: Neale Publishing Co., 1912. 152p. (Rpt. by Westport: Negro University Press, 1970)   This account of Reconstruction in Alabama focuses on the activities of the Klan. The Klan is depicted as a courageous group of men whose purpose was to restore good government and white supremacy. The Radical Republicans in Congress are blamed for a program that allowed blacks and carpetbaggers to rule the state.

1367.   Daniel, Mike. "The Arrest and Trial of Ryland Randolph April-May, 1868." *Alabama Historical Quarterly* 40 (Fall/Winter 1978): 127-143.   Randolph was a staunch Democratic editor of the Tuscaloosa *Independent Monitor* who was associated with the Ku Klux Klan. His arrest and trial for assault and battery against a black man during racial violence in Tuscaloosa is presented as an example of military oppression. Randolph was found not guilty by a military commission, but this may have been done to avoid a constitutional ruling on the Reconstruction Acts regarding his writ of *habeas corpus* that was denied by military authorities.

1368. Brent, Joseph E. "No Compromise: The End of Presidential Reconstruction in Mobile, Alabama, January-May, 1867." *Gulf Coast Historical Review* 7, 1 (1991): 18-37. Ills. Ports. When the U.S. Army occupied Mobile, white citizens quickly reflected a defiant attitude toward Reconstruction reforms, and they were generally unsympathetic with the plight of the ex-slaves. The Army allowed wartime city officials to continue in office, much to the consternation of Unionists. After President Johnson encouraged conservatism, the changes sought by the Republican Congress steadily pushed whites to more defiance and eventually to violence at the time of the Reconstruction Acts in 1867. At least in the case of Mobile, Brent believes that white Southerners were never prepared to compromise their principles by cooperating with moderate reform for equal civil rights for blacks.

1369. Davis, Hugh C. "Hilary Herbert: Bourbon Apologist." *Alabama Review* 20 (July 1967): 216-225. Herbert, a post-Reconstruction congressman from Alabama (1876-1893), has been called an apologist for local whites who took control of the state away from Republicans. In two books (*The Abolition Crusade and Its Consequences* [1912]; *Why the Solid South* [1890]) Herbert set forth his philosophy for Southern culture and resistance to the reforms of Reconstruction. In his writings he discussed the importance of antebellum values of republican government, sectional reconciliation, and paternalism in race relations.

1370. Davis, Thomas J. "Alabama's Reconstruction Representatives in the U.S. Congress, 1868-1878: A Profile." *Alabama Historical Quarterly* 44 (Spring/Summer 1982): 32-49. Tbl. Davis examines the background of the congressmen from Alabama from the time the state reentered the Union until well after the recognized end of Reconstruction. He investigates whether the representatives from 1868 were as ill equipped for service as stated by local Democrats. Davis concludes that the labels, scalawag and carpetbagger, along with the negative connotations implied, revealed Democratic partisanship and did not truly describe the capabilities and character of the representatives who took office on July 21, 1868.

1371. Farish, Hunter Dickinson. "An Overlooked Personality in Southern Life." *North Carolina Historical Review* 12 (October 1935): 341-353. Farish writes with admiration for New Hampshire native Samuel Augustus Hale, a Unionist during the Civil War and a Republican during Reconstruction. Hale strongly opposed the policies of the Radical Republicans and spoke out against them and the evils of carpetbaggers. Hale resided in Tuscaloosa since 1837 and edited *Flag of the Union*, a Democratic newspaper.

1372. Feldman, Eugene. *Black Power in Old Alabama*. Chicago: Museum of African American History, 1968. 69p. App. Bibl. This is an account of James Rapier's contributions to the black struggle for freedom locally and nationally in

Congress. The appendix includes the text of his address in Congress in support of the Civil Rights Bill of 1875.

1373.   Feldman, Eugene.   "James T. Rapier, Negro Congressman From Alabama." *Phylon* 19 (1958): 417-423.   Feldman emphasizes Rapier's work for civil rights and the unionization of black laborers.   As a congressman elected in 1872, he championed the Civil Rights Bill proposed by Senator Charles Sumner, sought to improve race relations, and gave hope to the black community in Alabama.   (See also Feldman's "James T. Rapier-1839-1884." *Negro History Bulletin* 20 (December 1956): 62-66.)

1374.   Fitzgerald, Michael W.   "Radical Republicanism and the White Yeomanry During Alabama Reconstruction, 1865-1868." *Journal of Southern History* 54 (November 1988): 565-596.   The yeomen owned small farms mainly in poor regions of the state, particularly in northern counties. They resented the power and wealth of the planters and generally opposed secession and the war that they were forced to fight. The yeomen's desire to destroy the planter class led them to join Unionist clubs and demand greater attention to their needs. Some of the farmers accepted political equality for the freedmen as a concession leading to a Unionist or Republican alliance of local whites, freedmen, and carpetbaggers. This possibility faded in 1868 as white farmers refused to accept black equality and voted against the 1868 constitution. As agricultural production improved, they turned toward the Democratic Party.

1375.   Fitzgerald, Michael   W.   "Republican   Factionalism   and   Black Empowerment: The Spencer-Warner Controversy and Alabama Reconstruction, 1868-1880." *Journal of Southern History* 64 (August 1998): 473-494.   A heated political rivalry between carpetbagger U.S. senators from Alabama, William Warner and George E. Spencer, illustrated the ideological differences in the Republican Party. It also showed differences about patronage and political influence. Fitzgerald examines how disputes among Republicans gave blacks opportunities to demand jobs and power, but this backfired when the mass of black voters voted against leaders who seemed more concerned for themselves than their people.

1376.   Fitzgerald, Michael W.   "Wager Swayne, the Freedmen's Bureau, and the Politics of Reconstruction in Alabama." *Alabama Review* 48 (July 1995): 188-232. Historians usually describe Gen. Swayne, assistant commissioner of the bureau in Alabama, as conservative, biased toward planters, and a typical representative of Northern white men of his time. Fitzgerald believes that Swayne and the bureau should be reexamined as forces pushing political reform. Swayne viewed his initial conciliatory attitude toward planters in their effort to control black labor as a mistake, because the white establishment wanted no part of Reconstruction. By 1867 Swayne was busy with educational efforts for blacks, and he fully supported Congressional Reconstruction, including black suffrage.

1377.   Fleming, Walter L.   "The Formation of the Union League in Alabama." *Gulf States Historical Magazine* 2 (September 1903): 73-89.   Fleming surveys the organization, activities, and demise of the Union Leagues.   Immediately after the Civil War leagues organized in northern counties and drew many white members, but they withdrew as black members joined and became the predominant members. Fleming believes leagues organized to support the Republican Party in Alabama and to bring political discipline to the black population.   This led to aggressive actions by black members that produced criminal activity and strained race relations.   It was the Union Leagues that made the Ku Klux Klan a necessary organization in the state.

1378.   Fleming, Walter L.   "The Ku Klux Testimony Relating to Alabama."   *Gulf States Historical Magazine* 2 (November 1903): 155-160. Tbl.   Fleming argues that the Congressional committee to investigate affairs in the South was organized in April, 1871 to justify the three Enforcement Acts of 1870 and 1871 and to provide fodder for the 1872 presidential campaign.   He explains that the Democrats who testified were upstanding citizens while nearly all of the Republicans were lowly characters.   Testimony given by Republicans about Klan violence was based on hearsay, while the testimony from Democrats was much more truthful.   The testimony shows the weakness of the Republican's case against the Klan in Alabama.

1379.   Fleming, Walter L.   "Military Government in Alabama, 1865-1866." *American Historical Magazine and Tennessee Historical Society Quarterly* 8 (April 1903): 163-179.   Fleming describes the functions of the military occupation force, court cases tried by military commission, and the problems of order, morale, and organization among the Federal troops.   He is critical of President Johnson's Reconstruction policies.   The Army was commanded by Generals C. R. Woods and Wager Swayne.

1380.   Fleming, Walter L.   "Military Government in Alabama Under the Reconstruction Acts."   *American Historical Magazine and Tennessee Historical Society Quarterly* 8 (July 1903): 222-252.   Fleming surveys the history of military rule under the command of Generals Pope and Swayne.   Even though the public disliked interference from the Federal military, particularly the aggressive measures taken by Pope, they disliked local Republican rule even more.

1381.   Folmar, John Kent.   "Reaction to Reconstruction: John Forsyth and the Mobile *Advertiser and Register*, 1865-1867." *Alabama Historical Quarterly* 37 (Winter 1976): 245-261. Tbls.   As editor of the *Advertiser and Register*, Forsyth revealed a conservative, Democratic bias regarding Reconstruction.   He frequently criticized Republicans by referring to them as Radicals, hoped for the quick demise of the Freedmen's Bureau, and believed that Northern concerns about Southern race relations during presidential Reconstruction were unfounded.   Folmer describes Forsyth as an elitist who built a notable reputation as a Southern journalist.   Seven tables are included that illustrate the breakdown of articles on Reconstruction issues in Forsyth's newspaper.   The survey of the newspaper covers the period from July 18, 1865 to March 31, 1867.

1382.   Grande, Ray.   "Violence: An Instrument of Policy in Reconstruction Alabama."   *Alabama Historical Quarterly*   30   (Fall/Winter 1968): 181-202. Violence in Reconstruction Alabama was rooted in the antebellum traditions of the frontier state, reliance on violence to maintain individual power, and fear of slave revolts.   After the Civil War these traditions continued and were augmented by political passions.   Violence was perpetrated by all elements of society in Reconstruction, including federal soldiers, individual citizens, and "secret Klan-lie organizations of blacks and whites."   (p. 181)   The political nature of the violence was demonstrated by the sharp decline of incidents after the government returned to the hands of native whites   Southern whites demonstrated that violence could be used successfully to achieve a political goal.

1383.   Hennessey, Melinda M.   "Political Terrorism in the Black Belt: The Eutaw Riot."   *Alabama Review* 33 (January 1980): 35-48.   On October 25, 1870 Eutaw, Alabama was the site of one of the worst riots in the state during Reconstruction. The predominately black population of Greene County and white Republicans had already experienced many acts of violence by Ku Klux Klan night riders.   The November, 1870 gubernatorial election became a focal point for racial and political tension.   Although federal troops were stationed near Eutaw, they did not stop political violence.   Republican and Democratic versions of the riot are described. Violence scared away black voters from the polls, thus contributing to the Democratic victory.

1384.   Hennessey, Melinda M.   "Reconstruction Politics and the Military: The Eufaula Riot of 1874."   *Alabama Historical Quarterly*   38 (Summer 1976): 112-125. There was a U.S. military detachment near Eufaula, Alabama, but it did not have an effect on racial intimidation at election time and did not ensure a Republican victory. Despite a black majority in the area, local politics was controlled by Democrats even though Barbour County was controlled by Republicans.   In the election campaign of 1874 white Democrats were determined to take control of state political power and the resulting racial and political tensions led to a riot in Eufaula.   Hennessey focuses on the activities of Elias M. Keils, an Alabama native, who strongly supported the Republicans and served as judge of the city court.   Keils was frequently attacked for his judicial decisions in favor of freedmen and white Republicans.

1385.   Herbert, Colonel Hilary A.   "How we Redeemed Alabama: A Chapter of Reconstruction History.   *Century Illustrated Monthly Magazine* 85 (1912-13): 854-862. Ill. Ports.   Herbert participated in the Democratic Party campaign to regain power in Alabama.   He writes about early efforts to organize against the Republicans and the political campaign of 1874 when black and carpetbagger rule was overthrown.   The leader of the Democratic election drive was attorney W. L. Brogg. Herbert mentions that some violence took place, but describes this as a minor part of the campaign.   The Ku Klux Klan, the "hated organization" (p. 859), played no part in the 1874 campaign.

1386.   Hollman, Kenneth W. and Joe H. Murray, Jr.   "Alabama's State Debt History, 1865-1921."   *Southern Studies* 24 (Fall 1985): 306-325.   This survey focuses on the period from 1868 to 1873 as a period of exploding debt in Alabama due to the attempt of Reconstruction governments to finance the expansion and repair of the state's railroad system. The authors believe that the immediate postwar government and the post-Reconstruction governments were much more conservative and fiscally responsible.

1387.   Hume, Richard. "The Freedmen's Bureau and the Freedmen's Vote in the Reconstruction of Southern Alabama: An Account by Agent Samuel S. Gardner." *Alabama Historical Quarterly* 37 (Fall 1975): 217-224.   After the Reconstruction Acts of 1867 Alabama became the first former Confederate state to complete voter registration and call a constitutional convention. This accomplishment was due to the vigorous efforts of the Freedmen's Bureau, under the direction of Assistant Commissioner Major Gen. Wager Swayne. Local agents, such as Samuel Gardner, a native of Massachusetts, participated in organizing voter registration efforts and explaining to freedmen their rights as citizens. A copy of one of Gardner's reports dated July 23, 1867 about his visit to Monroe and Clarke counties is reprinted. Gardner explains how local whites attempted to discourage communication with the freedmen.

1388.   Hunnicutt, John L. *Reconstruction in West Alabama: The Memoirs of John L. Hunnicutt.* Edited by William Stanley Hoole. Intro. by Allen J. Going. Tuscaloosa: Confederate Publishing Co., 1959. 145p. Bibl. Ills. Port. Map. Hunnicutt was just fifteen years old when the war ended. His memoir of experiences during Reconstruction indicates that he was an organizer and active member of the Ku Klux Klan. He describes his acts of intimidation against blacks and gives an indication of the racial and political tensions. Hoole's preface takes a conservative, Southern white perspective on Reconstruction.   In the introduction Going provides a brief summary of Reconstruction in Alabama.

1389.   Mahaffey, Joseph H. (ed.). "Carl Schurz Letter From Alabama, August 15-16, 1865." *Alabama Review* 3 (April 1950): 134-145.   President Johnson asked Carl Schurz to visit the postwar South in the summer of 1865 to report on conditions, but the trip was made by Schurz with the intention of writing supporting the view of Republicans who opposed the President. Schurz received monetary support and advice from his Republican friends, and his report was based on interactions with Radical soldiers, politicians, and Freedmen's Bureau agents. Mahaffey edits and prints a letter that has never been published before that he presents as illustrative of Schurz' bias. Most of the letter is a description of his travels rather than political commentary.

1390.   McMillan, Malcolm Cook. *Constitutional Development in Alabama, 1798-1901: A Study in Politics, the Negro, and Sectionalism.* Chapel Hill: University of North Carolina Press, 1955. Pp. 90-189. Bibl. (*James Sprunt Studies in History and Political Science*, 37)   A large portion of this book includes a discussion of constitutional issues brought about by the victory of the North in the Civil War.   Important issues were the enfranchisement of the freedmen, reapportionment of the legislature, public education, finance, and the balance of power between Conservatives and Radicals.

1391.   McNair, Cecil E.   "Reconstruction in Bullock County."   *Alabama Historical Quarterly* 15 (1953): 75-125.   This history of Bullock County begins in December, 1866 when the county was formed.   In this M.A. thesis written at the University of Alabama in 1931, the principle sources of information are two Union Springs newspapers, Fleming's *Civil War and Reconstruction in Alabama* (see # 1351), and interviews with Union Springs residents.   The county had a black majority, but white conservatives regained power in the elections of August and November, 1876.

1392.   Myers, John B.   "The Freedmen and the Law in Post-Bellum Alabama, 1865-1867."   *Alabama Review* 23 (January 1970): 56-69.   Except for the elimination of slavery, white Alabamians generally sought to exclude the blacks from any sort of equal status in society.   The constitutional convention that began on September 12, 1865 refused to define their legal status, and the legislature that convened on November 20 focused on control of the freedmen rather than recognizing or granting them basic rights.   The Black Code of Alabama severely restricted their basic rights, thus leading to a high rate of black imprisonment and racial discrimination.   The actions of the white leadership contributed to the Northern mood that led to the passage of the first Reconstruction Act on March 2, 1867.

1393.   Owens, Harry P.   "The Eufaula Riot of 1874."   *Alabama Review* 16 (July 1963): 224-237.   The riot in Barbar County was the result of racial and political tensions that progressively worsened beginning with the introduction of Radical Reconstruction in 1867.   Conservative whites feared a black Republican victory in local and statewide elections and sought to prevent blacks from voting.   Owens also blames the white city counsel and Judge Elias M. Keils, who made ruling sympathetic to the freedmen.   The riots successfully prevented blacks from voting and contributed to the Democratic victory over Republican congressional incumbent J. T. Rapier.

1394.   Rabinowitz, Howard N.   "Holland Thompson and Black Political Participation in Montgomery, Alabama."   *Southern Black Leaders of the Reconstruction Era.*   Edited by Howard N. Rabinowitz.   Urbana: University of Illinois Press, 1982. Pp. 249-280. Ills.   Thompson, a former slave, was a successful politician at the local and state level. He developed a political following based on his activities to organize blacks for political participation, his work with the black Baptist Church organization and the American Missionary Association, and his dedication to establishing schools for black and white children.   White leaders selected Thompson as a city councilman in Montgomery, and he won election to the state legislature. Rabinowitz explains Thompson's accomplishments, but he faded into obscurity by the time of his death in 1887.   He represents the capabilities of black leadership after the Civil War.

1395. Rhodes, Robert S. "The Registration of Voters and the Election of Delegates to the Reconstruction Convention in Alabama." *Alabama Review* 8 (April 1955): 119-142. Conservative whites generally took little or no part in the registration of voters and the election of delegates to the Alabama Constitutional Convention that began in November, 1867. The election of Northerners, Southern loyalists, and blacks drew a highly negative response from the conservative press. Rhodes emphasizes that the delegates were honest men of principle. Better understanding among conservatives and Republicans might have led to a less difficult period of Reconstruction than actually occurred.

1396. Rogers, William Warren. "Agrarianism in Alabama 1865-1896." Ph.D. University of North Carolina, 1954. 580p.

1397. Rogers, William Warren. "The Boyd Incident: Black Belt Violence During Reconstruction." *Civil War History* 21 (December 1975): 308-329. Alexander Boyd, Republican and Solicitor General for Greene County, Alabama, tried to prosecute the perpetrators of murders of local black men when he was murdered by members of the Ku Klux Klan on March 31, 1870. Despite the Republican majority in the county, the murder of a white Republican official intimidated so many Republican voters that the Democrats were victorious in the local elections of 1871.

1398. Rogers, William Warren, Jr. *Black Belt Scalawag: Charles Hays and the Southern Republicans in the Era of Reconstruction.* Athens: University of Georgia Press, 1993. 179p. Bibl. Ports. Hays was a slave-holding planter who opposed secession, but he remained loyal to the South throughout the war. After the war Hays abhorred the conservative refusal to recognize postwar realities, including the necessity of accepting equal civil rights and justice for Alabama freedmen. He became a Republican for this reason and because he saw opportunities for political advancement. Hays disagreed with Radical approaches in the South, but he spoke out against Klan violence and in favor of legislative reform as a member of the state legislature. Hays' story contributes to the rehabilitation of Southern white Republicans. (See also Rogers' "Scalawag Congressman: Charles Hays and Reconstruction in Alabama." Ph.D. Auburn University, 1983. 289p.; and "'Politics is Mighty Uncertain': Charles Hays Goes to Congress." *Alabama Review* 30 (July 1977): 163-190 which is mainly devoted to a description of Hays' successful campaign for Congress.)

1399. Rogers, William Warren, Jr. "The Eutaw Prisoners: Federal Confrontation With Violence in Reconstruction Alabama." *Alabama Review* 43 (April 1990): 98-121. The arrest and conviction by federal authorities of several perpetrators of political violence in Eutaw on March 14, 1868 was an exceptional response to the growing violence against freedmen and white Republicans. Federal troops generally could not maintain order, and local officials simply refused. The beating of Joseph B. F. Hill, a local, white Republican and Methodist preacher, was widely publicized by the military as a case in which violence against Republicans would not be tolerated. In Greene County and throughout the state, the conservative press complained loudly about the conviction, and violence increased until the Republicans lost power in 1870.

1400.   Russ, William A., Jr.   "Disfranchisement in Alabama Under Radical Reconstruction." *Susquehanna University Studies* 2 (March 1943): 334-346.   In this account of the disenfranchisement of many whites by the Alabama constitution, Russ explains that the policy was vindictive and doomed to fail.   In fact, Republicans needed the disenfranchisement law to obtain power. When the restriction was removed, Republicans quickly lost power.

1401.   Schweninger, Loren.   "Alabama Blacks and the Congressional Reconstruction Acts of 1867." *Alabama Review* 31 (July 1978): 182-198. Schweninger seeks to dispel lingering stereotypes of freedmen that were made popular by past historians, such as Walter L. Fleming.   While Fleming accused blacks of laziness and insisting on land confiscation and redistribution, Schweninger concludes that such accusations are fallacious.   In fact, from March to October, 1867, the freedmen responded to the Reconstruction Acts by holding meetings where they called on blacks and whites to work together and demanded all the rights of citizenship.   Both the Democrats and conservative Republicans ignored the moderate tone of black leaders and ensured the failure of the Republican Party.

1402.   Schweninger, Loren.   "Black Citizenship and the Republican Party in Reconstruction Alabama." *Alabama Review* 29 (April 1979): 83-103.   The state Republican convention that met in June, 1867 revealed that Alabama Republicans were badly split between conservatives who did not believe in racial equality and the more moderate to liberal faction that equal rights for freedmen.   Both sides had a mixture of carpetbaggers and scalawags.   The conservative Republicans were represented by former Union general Willard Warner and former Alabama Whig William H. Smith.   Opposing them were men such as James Rapier, a black, and George E. Spencer, a carpetbagger who became U.S. senator.   The split in the party was the main reason for the party's failure and the failure of Reconstruction in the state.

1403.   Schweninger, Loren.   *James Rapier and Reconstruction.*   Chicago: University of Chicago Press, 1978. 248p. Bibl. Chron. Tbl.   Rapier's life as a free black from Alabama was full of accomplishment and public service.   His career proves that blacks could and did make vital contributions to American society despite the racial barriers and prejudices of 19th century America.   He belies the criticism and depredation from early 20th century historians who barely mentioned black leaders in their accounts of Reconstruction except to illustrate their own racial stereotypes.   (See also Schweninger's Ph.D. dissertation with the same title from University of Chicago, 1972.)

1404.   Schweninger, Loren.   "James T. Rapier of Alabama and the Noble Cause of Reconstruction."   In *Southern Black Leaders of the Reconstruction Era.*   Edited by Howard Rabinowitz.   Urbana: University of Illinois Press, 1982. Pp. 79-99. Port. Tbls.   .   Rapier dedicated himself to helping fellow blacks, supporting equal civil rights, and building a united Republican Party in Alabama that could respond to multiple interests. His support was strong among black voters, who helped to elect him to Congress in 1872. When the cause of equal rights failed Rapier favored black emigration to Kansas. Schweninger criticizes historians who accuse Rapier of self promotion.

1405. Sloan, John Z. "The Ku Klux Klan and the Alabama Election of 1872." *Alabama Review* 18 (April 1965): 113-123. The results of the gubernatorial elections of 1870 and 1872 are depicted as part of a plan by carpetbagger and Republican U.S. Senator George E. Spencer to gain control of state politics. Sloan believes that the KKK did not play a part in the elections, except as a tool by Spencer to use Klan violence to further his campaign. Sloan describes the Klan as a protector of whites and believes that the Enforcement Act (Ku Klux Klan Act) of April 20, 1871 was passed for political reasons rather than the perception of widespread Klan violence.

1406. "State Militia of Alabama During the Administration of Lewis E. Parsons, Provisional Governor June 21st 1865 to December 18, 1865." *Alabama Historical Quarterly* 14 (1952): 301-322. Included are documents and letters related to the authorization and organization of the state militia during the military occupation in 1865. Also there are lists of militia soldiers from various counties, including Barbour, Dekalb, Lebanon, Macon, Sumter, Tallapoosa, and Tuscaloosa. Among the documents are a letter to the people of Alabama from Gov. Lewis Parsons and letters written by officers of the militia about conditions in their area.

1407. Steryx, H. E. "William C. Jordan and Reconstruction in Bullock County, Alabama." *Alabama Review* 15 (January 1962): 61-73. Jordan was a plantation owner and Unionist Whig who resisted the emancipation of his slaves and persistently fought a political battle against Radical Republicans in Bullock County. His effort to gather black support for the Democratic Party failed and black workers boycotted his plantation. Jordan's campaign against Republicans and their black supporters ended with the Democratic victory in the 1876 election.

1408. White, Kenneth B. "Black Lives, Red Tape: The Alabama Freedmen's Bureau." *Alabama Historical Quarterly* 43 (Winter 1981): 241-258. When the Freedmen's Bureau came to Alabama there was optimism among the freedmen that the organization would greatly assist with the implementation of racial justice. The optimism faded quickly because the bureau proved to be a chaotic organization that could not function effectively due to staff shortages, bureaucratic tie ups, the constant change of personnel, the lack of sufficient military support, and mismanagement.

1409. White, Kenneth B. "Wager Swayne: Racist or Realist?" *Alabama Review* 31 (April 1978): 92-109. Freedmen's Bureau records reveal that Swayne's actions as assistant commissioner for the bureau in Alabama from August, 1865 to early 1868 illustrate that he was not a radical or a conservative. He was a person who lacked experience in race relations, did not understand the Southern character, and held racial views consistent with other educated, politically moderate, Northern men of his time. His sincere attempt to have an impact on justice for the freedmen faltered, because he refused to use military power to back up decisions. His "unconscious racism" (p. 109) and naiveté clouded his understanding and decision-making regarding issues such as labor contracts, education, and relief.

1410.   Wiggins, Sarah Woolfolk [Woolfolk, Sarah Van V.] "Alabama Attitudes Toward the Republican Party in 1868 and 1964." *Alabama Review* 20 (January 1967): 27-33.   Woolfolk illustrates the changing attitudes of white Alabamians by contrasting the reactions to political defections in 1868 and 1964. Local newspapers heaped scorn on Alexander H. White for switching from the Democrats to the Republicans in 1868, but State Rep. Alfred Goldthwaite received mostly praise when he became a Republican in 1964 in protest against Democratic support for civil rights. In both 1868 and 1964, most whites opposed racial reforms.

1411.   Wiggins, Sarah   Woolfolk.   "Alabama-Domestic Bulldozing and Republican Folly." In *Reconstruction and Redemption in the South*. Edited by Otto Olsen. Baton Rouge: Louisiana State University, 1980. Pp. 48-77.   Alabama politics during Reconstruction was characterized by a two party system. The Democrats actively participated in politics and even won a gubernatorial election in 1870. Republicans allowed their opponents to build power in the state by spending most of their time quarreling and taking only moderate actions in favor of civil rights for blacks. White Democrats learned that they could successfully organize their resources and intimidate black voters.   Intimidation and fraud led to Democratic victory in 1874. Wiggins believes that both parties could be blamed for instances of economic and political fraud. Wiggins includes a bibliographic essay.

1412.   Wiggins, Sarah Woolfolk [Woolfolk, Sarah Van V.]   "Amnesty and Pardon and Republicanism in Alabama." *Alabama Historical Review* 26 (Summer 1964): 240-248.   Among the many reasons historians have offered for the failure of Reconstruction in the South, Woolfolk focuses on the withdrawal of scalawag support for the Republican Party. Local white support for the party in Alabama was hurt because many potential supporters were politically disabled by the 14th Amendment until the 1872 General Amnesty Act. They believed that they were not given enough political power. Their sentiments are reflected in letters written by David P. Lewis to B. F. Butler and J. J. Giers in 1870. In 1872 Lewis became Republican governor of the state.

1413.   Wiggins, Sarah Woolfolk [Woolfolk, Sarah Van V.] "Carpetbaggers in Alabama: Tradition Versus Truth." *Alabama Review* 15 (April 1962): 133-144. (Rpt. in *From Civil War to Civil Rights-Alabama 1860-1960: An Anthology From The Alabama Review*. Tuscaloosa: University of Alabama Press, 1987. Pp. 67-76.) Not all of the Northerners who came to Alabama after the Civil War conform to the negative stereotype of the carpetbagger that has persisted for many years. There were individuals who fit the mold of dishonesty and selfishness, but other Northerners were accepted by local residents. Carpetbaggers in Alabama were much less influential in state Republican politics than widely perceived at the time with regard to their numbers and compared with the number of local Republicans. Those who sought to integrate themselves into the economic life of the community do not fit the stereotype, but they subtly contributed to changing the social structure.

1414.   Wiggins, Sarah Woolfolk [Woolfolk, Sarah Van V.] "Five Men Called Scalawags." *Alabama Review* 17 (January 1964): 45-55. (Rpt. in *From Civil War to Civil Rights-Alabama 1860-1960: An Anthology From The Alabama Review.* Tuscaloosa: University of Alabama Press, 1987. Pp. 57-66.)   Woolfolk examines the backgrounds of Republicans Samuel F. Rice, Alexander H. White, Lewis E. Parsons, David P. Lewis, and Alexander McKinstry who serve as examples of native Republicans who do not fit the stereotype of the poorly educated, white yeoman Unionist. All five were professionals who joined the Republican Party as an act of realism and with hope of personal gain. Their great influence in the party also belies the notion that carpetbaggers always dominated the party.

1415.   Wiggins, Sarah Woolfolk. *From Civil War to Civil Rights-Alabama 1860-1960: An Anthology From the Alabama Review.* Tuscaloosa: University of Alabama Press, 1987. 535p. (For relevant essays see # 1413, 1414, 1448)

1416.   Wiggins, Sarah Woolfolk [Woolfolk, Sarah Van V.] "George E. Spencer: A Carpetbagger in Alabama." *Alabama Review* 19 (January 1966): 41-52.   While the stereotype of the greedy, corrupt carpetbagger did not apply to all Northerners who came to the South and participated in politics, it certainly applies to Spencer. The native of New York became a Republican U.S. senator in July, 1868 and proceeded to do all that he could to manipulate Alabama politics to enhance his own powers of federal patronage. He participated in voter manipulation, embezzlement, and the betrayal of political colleagues.

1417.   Wiggins, Sarah Woolfolk [Woolfolk, Sarah Van V.] "J. A. Yordy and Alabama Ostracism of Republicans." *Alabama Review* 20 (July 1967): 232-234. Yordy, an Ohio carpetbagger, was vilified by the Eutaw *Whig and Observer* and denied service at a Sumter County hotel after casting votes in the state senate. Wiggins believes that similar ostracism in newspapers and private papers was unusual.

1418.   Wiggins, Sarah Woolfolk. (ed.) *The Journals of Josiah Gorgas 1859-1878.* Tuscaloosa: University of Alabama Press, 1995. 305p. Bibl. Ills. Ports. Gorgas was born in Pennsylvania but married a Southerner and forsook his appointment in the U.S. Army to join the Confederacy. His journals during Reconstruction provide information about his work and family, and his experience in politics and Southern society. Wiggins provides biographical sketches of Gorgas' family and friends.

1419.   Wiggins, Sarah Woolfolk.   "The Life of Ryland Randolph as Seen Through His Letters to John W. DuBose." *Alabama Historical Quarterly* 30 (Fall and Winter 1968): 145-180.   Randolph, a staunchly conservative and highly controversial editor in of the Tuscaloosa *Independent Monitor* from 1867 to 1871, heaped scorn on the Republicans and those Democrats who were not conservative enough. His newspaper was suppressed by military order. Wiggins provides extensive biographical background on Randolph based on letters that he wrote to DuBose between May, 1900 and May, 1903. DuBose was a "war-ruined planter" who became a journalist and local historian. Extensive quotations are made about Randolph's wartime service for the Confederacy, attempts to assassinate him, and his criticism of the University of Alabama during Reconstruction years.

1420.   Wiggins, Sarah Woolfolk. "Ostracism of White Republicans in Alabama During Reconstruction." *Alabama Review* 27 (January 1974): 52-64.   Ostracism of white Republicans was widespread after the formation of the state Republican Party in June, 1867. Republicans were made to feel unwanted, and deliberate attempts were made by the press to dissuade people from socializing with them or patronizing their businesses. Scalawags were subject to harsher treatment compared with carpetbaggers. Republicans were viewed as radicals who sought to increase black equality and control state politics.

1421.   Wiggins, Sarah Woolfolk. "The 'Pig Iron' Kelley Riot in Mobile, May 14, 1867." *Alabama Review* 23 (January 1970): 45-55.   Political and racial tensions ran high in Mobile following the passage of the Reconstruction Acts in March, 1867. When Pennsylvania congressman, Judge William Darrah Kelley, came to town on his speaking tour of the South to promote the Republican Party, a disturbance occurred that Wiggins describes as the most serious riot that occurred in the state during Reconstruction. It led to the reorganization of the city government by the U.S. military command and the recognition by Alabama newspaper editors that such disturbances could only hurt the South by alienating Northern Republicans.

1422.   Wiggins, Sarah Woolfolk [Woolfolk, Sarah Van V.]   "The Political Cartoons of the Tuscaloosa *Independent Monitor* and Tuscaloosa *Blade*, 1867-1873. *Alabama Historical Quarterly* 27 (Spring/Summer 1965): 140-165.   Ryland Randolph edited the *Independent Monitor* from 1868 to 1871 and the *Blade* from 1871 to 1875. Under his direction both newspapers were strongly Democratic and much more strident in tone than most other newspapers. Woolfolk highlights the many political cartoons that were used to attack the Republican Party, carpetbaggers, and blacks. The cartoons, made from woodcuts by unknown artists, were unusual among Alabama newspapers, but they served as an effective media for attacking opponents of conservative Democrats. Twenty-one woodcuts are reproduced in this article.

1423.   Wiggins, Sarah Woolfolk [Woolfolk, Sarah Van V.]   "Press Reaction in Alabama to the Attempted Assassination of Judge Richard Busteed." *Alabama Review* 21 (July 1968): 211-219.   When U.S. District Judge Busteed was shot on December 28, 1867 by U.S. District Attorney Lucien Van Buren Martin, the reaction of the Alabama press seemed in contradiction to the earlier vilification of Busteed who came South in 1865 from New York City. The press disliked Busteed, but they may have been much harder on him if he had been a scalawag.

1424.   Wiggins, Sarah Woolfolk. "A Proposal for Women's Suffrage in Alabama in 1867." *Alabama Historical Quarterly* 32 (Fall-Winter 1970): 181-185.   On March 20, 1867 Massachusetts carpetbagger Pierce Burton, who would later be a delegate to the 1867 constitutional convention, a representative in the state House of Representatives   (1867-1871),   and candidate for lieutenant governor in 1870, published an article in the Demopolis *New Era* proposing that women be offered the right to vote in the state.   The proposal was ignored, but was later published again in the *Livingston Journal* in 1870, which is the source used by Wiggins.   In his proposal Burton suggests that female suffrage, offered on the basis of property ownership or literacy, would restore confidence and intelligence to the political process.

1425.   Wiggins, Sarah Woolfolk. *The Scalawag in Alabama Politics, 1865-1881.* University: University of Alabama Press, 1977. 220p. App. Bibl. Ills. Maps. Tbls. Wiggins uses census reports to establish that most scalawags did not fit the stereotype of the poor, ignorant white male from the northern counties of the state. They were well educated and experienced, and they tended to be men who held realistic views of politics and economic advancement in the immediate postwar period.   Scalawags complained about their lack of government appointments, but Wiggins shows that they clearly dominated federal and state political and judicial positions compared with carpetbaggers.   The appendix lists Republican nominations and appointments in Alabama from 1868 to 1881 with an indication of status - scalawag, carpetbagger or black.   (See also Wiggins' "What is a Scalawag?" *Alabama Review* 25 (January 1972): 56-61; and Wiggins' [ie. Woolfolk's] "The Role of the Scalawag in Alabama Reconstruction."   Ph.D.   Louisiana State University, 1965. 309p.)

1426.   Wiggins, Sarah Woolfolk.   "Unionist Efforts to Control Alabama Reconstruction, 1865-1867." *Alabama Historical Quarterly* 30 (Spring 1968): 51-64.   Unionists, who were mainly farmers and prewar Whigs from north Alabama, sought to take control of state politics from plantation owners of the Black Belt immediately after the Civil War.   Unionists Lewis E. Parsons, appointed provisional governor on June 21, 1865, and Robert M. Patton, elected governor in December, 1865, sought to comply with President Johnson's Reconstruction plan.   The power of the Unionists declined after the Reconstruction Acts of 1867.   Even though the Unionists sought a moderate regime and participation in the fledging Republican Party, most of them were excluded from political participation by the 14th Amendment.   Black suffrage shifted power back to the Black Belt.

1427.   Williamson, Edward C.   "The Alabama Election of 1874." *Alabama Review* 17 (July 1964): 210-218.   The election pitted Democrat and former Unionist George Smith Houston against Republican and former Confederate leader David P. Lewis.   Both men were from northern Alabama.   The election was marred by Democratic intimidation of voters and Republican corruption.   The Democratic victory provided the opportunity to end reforms and focus on industrial development, and it also revealed the Democratic alignment with the business interests in the national Republican Party.

1428.   Wood, George A.   "The Black Code of Alabama."   *South Atlantic Quarterly* 13 (October 1914): 350-360.   Wood examines the black code in Alabama as representative of the black codes established throughout the former Confederate states to regulate the lives of the freedmen.   He objects to the idea that they were thinly disguised slave codes, and believes that the most objectionable laws relating to vagrancy and apprenticeships of young boys were actually patterned after circulars distributed by the Freedmen's Bureau.

Agriculture, Labor, and Business

1429.   Barney, William L.   "The Ambivalence of Change: From Old South to New in the Alabama Black Belt, 1850-1870."   In *From the Old South to the New: Essays on the Transitional South*.   Edited by Walter J. Fraser, Jr.   and Winfred B. Moore, Jr.   Westport: Greenwood Press, 1981.   Pp. 33-41.   Residents of Dallas County's responded in the 1850s to attempts by local Whigs to transform the economy from plantation based to the Northern model of commercial, banking and manufacturing interests was rejected as Yankeeism and a threat to Southern rights and independence.   Similar calls for change following the war evoked the same response based on the fears of planters and white yeomen to surrender their traditional self image.   The New South was based not on change but on the values and mythologies of the Old South.

1430.   Dykema, Frank E.   (ed.).   "An Effort to Attract Dutch Colonists to Alabama, 1869."   *Journal of Southern History* 14 (May 1948): 247-261.   Labor shortages in the South following the Civil War led to efforts to import labor.   In a letter from John W. Lapsley, president of Shelby Iron Co. in Shelby County, to Rev. Albertus C. van Raolte, founder of a Dutch colony at Holland, Michigan, Lapsley responds to an inquiry from van Raolte by describing the economic and living conditions in northcentral Alabama with the idea that Dutch workers could be enticed to come to the state.

1431.   Fitzgerald, Michael W.   "The Ku Klux Klan: Property Crime and the Plantation System in Reconstruction."   *Agricultural History* 71 (Spring 1997): 186-206.   Agricultural disruptions due to emancipation drew the planter class into the Klan in northern and western Alabama in an attempt to control the labor of freedmen.   When agriculture improved and black labor became more settled, planters withdrew much of their active support and offered mainly moral support to farmers and white laborers who stepped up violent activities against blacks suspected of petty thefts.   Property crime became the major motive for Klan punishment.   By 1868 planters did not direct the Klan, but they offered their tacit approval as long as it did not disrupt labor or cause trouble with federal authorities.

1432.   Fitzgerald, Michael W.   "Railroad Subsidies and Black Aspirations: The Politics of Economic Development in Reconstruction Mobile, 1865-1879."   *Civil War History* 39 (September 1993): 240-256.   Local urban issues could play a greater role in postwar economic development than the influence of national politics. Mobile's financial problems after the loss of cotton trade and the carryover of prewar debt does not follow the traditional historical interpretations that blamed blacks and carpetbaggers for corruption and fiscal mismanagement.   Local Republican leaders were themselves split over the level of debt to incur in order to get economic activity going after the war. City debt increased because of railroad expansion and harbor and wharf projects, but debt increases also occurred after the Democrats took control in 1873.

1433.   Fitzgerald, Michael W. "'To Give Our Votes to the Party': Black Political Agitation and Agricultural Change in Alabama, 1865-1870." *Journal of American History* 76 (September 1989): 489-505.   Politics effected the structure of postwar agriculture. The development of tenant farming occurred because the freedmen sought the maximum of independence. They were influenced by the slave-like image of gang labor and their politicization by Freedmen's Bureau agents, Loyal Leagues, and the Republican Party. Tenantry led to the dispersal of the freedmen in the countryside and greater exposure to violence from the Ku Klux Klan.

1434.   French, Melodee J. "The *Rural Alabamian*, A Journal of Progressive Agriculture and Improved Industry, 1872-1873. *Alabama Review* 40 (July 1987): 199-215. Port.   The *Rural Alabamian*, edited by Charles C. Langdon, appeared for only two years from 1872-1873, but it represented an early attempt at a new type of agricultural journalism in the postwar South. The journal generally took a progressive, educational approach to helping Alabama farmers learn farming conditions and techniques, such as crop rotation and diversification, uplift farmer morale, provide information and entertaining reading, and opinions on farming issues. Langdon and other writers commented on existing labor issues, including sharecropping, black labor, and the use of immigrants as laborers.

1435.   Griffen, Richard W. "Cotton Fraud and Confiscations in Alabama, 1863-1866." *Alabama Review* 7 (October 1954): 265-276.   During the early years of Reconstruction the federal government sent treasury agents to the South to confiscate cotton that was believed to be owned by the U.S. or that was formerly owned by the Confederate government. Griffen describes how the agents illegally seized millions of dollars worth of cotton owned by Alabama planters.   The corruption included bribery of U.S. Army officers. It took years for claimants to receive compensation.

1436.   Jay, John C. "General N. B. Forrest as a Railroad Builder in Alabama." *Alabama Historical Quarterly* 24 (Spring 1902): 16-31.   Jay offers a brief account of Nathan Bedford Forrest's interest and activities in The Selma, Marion and Memphis Railroad Co. (formerly known as The Cahala, Marion and Greensboro Railroad Co.), incorporated by the Alabama state legislature on December 21, 1868.

1437.   Jones, Judge Walter. "Alabama's Economic Loss Due to Reconstruction." *Alabama Lawyer* 14 (April 1953): 147-155.   Jones describes the near total ruin of Alabama's economy, society, and education system by the military occupation and the corrupt Republican regime. He refers to the loss of black labor, ruinous taxes, the theft of public lands, and the destruction of the University of Alabama.

1438.   Krebs, Sylvia. "The Chinese Labor Question: A Note on the Attitudes of Two Alabama Republicans." *Alabama Historical Quarterly* 38 (Fall 1976): 214-217.   In 1869 state authorities discussed importing Chinese laborers to Alabama. Both Gov. William H. Smith and Commissioner of Industrial Resources John C. Keffer opposed the idea because they believed that cheap Chinese labor would hurt the wages of both whites and blacks. They also believed that the Chinese would not spend their earnings and that their immorality would lead to their imprisonment. The stereotypes of Chinese were not tested because very few of them came to Alabama.

1439.   Kyriakoudes, Louis M. "The Rise of Merchants and Market Towns in Reconstruction - Era Alabama." *Alabama Review* 49 (April 1996): 83-107. Tbls. After the Civil War cotton financing and marketing in Alabama shifted from Mobile to many merchant centers throughout the state, particularly in the Black Belt and the northern hill country. The path of railroads and the development of sharecropping and tenant farming encouraged this growth. Kyriakoudes uses statistics to illustrate how the change occurred. Opponents of this scenario of merchant growth should take a closer look at what really happened.

1440.   McKenzie, Robert H. "Reconstruction Historiography: The View From Shelby." *Historian* 36 (February 1974): 207-223.   The company papers of the Shelby Iron Works reveal a history of Reconstruction different from the standard literature on the period. Shelby eagerly sought after Northern investors to keep the business going, had little involvement in politics, and experienced no trouble from occupying troops.   The Shelby experience seems to reinforce Reconstruction revisionists, but McKenzie acknowledges the complexity of life during the period. He calls for research on the impact of economic development as a factor in local and rural experiences during Reconstruction.   (See also McKenzie's "A History Of The Shelby Iron Company, 1865-1881," Ph.D. University of Alabama, 1971. 460p.)

1441.   McKenzie, Robert H. "The Shelby Iron Company: A Note on Slave Personality After the Civil War." *Journal of Negro History* 58 (July 1973): 341-348.   McKenzie uses business records to determine whether freedmen acted independently, assertively, or passively during the early days of freedom. He concludes that freedmen at Shelby did not immediately leave the town seeking independence, but were non-assertive in the sense that they waited for help from the plant management to return to their former homes, to continue their work, and to receive adequate food.   McKenzie addresses issues raised by Stanley Elkins in *Slavery* (Chicago, 1959) regarding the psychological effects of slavery on the slave.

1442.   Moore, A. B. "Railroad Building in Alabama During the Reconstruction Period." *Journal of Southern History* 1 (November 1935): 421-441.   During Radical Reconstruction in Alabama rail line construction expanded from a few hundred miles to 1,737 miles. Many lines lay unfinished while others were of inferior quality. Moore states that the "Carpetbag-Scalawag-Negro regime" was responsible for this expansion, much of which was needed, but the regime acted in a "typically costly and shameful" (p. 441) way in its loss of state funds through fraud, pillage, plunder, and manipulation. Moore blames Alabama's Republican governments for the inefficiencies and mismanagement of rail construction.

1443. Myers, John B. "The Alabama Freedmen and the Economic Adjustment During Presidential Reconstruction, 1865-1867." *Alabama Review* 26 (October 1973): 252-266. With the chaotic state of the economy immediately after the Civil War, the freedmen needed assistance to adjust to their new economic situation. Federal institutions, including the Freedmen's Bureau and the Freedmen's Saving Bank, attempted to assist them with work contracts, personal security, and encouragment to save their money. The Homestead Act of 1866 offered an opportunity for land ownership, but in Alabama the act was a failure. Only through consistent help did the freedmen have a chance of success.

1444. Myers, John B. "Black Human Capital: The Freedmen and the Reconstruction of Labor in Alabama, 1860-1880." Ph.D. Florida State University, 1974. 271p.

1445. Myers, John B. "The Freedmen and the Labor Supply: The Economic Adjustment in Post-Bellum Alabama, 1865-1867." *Alabama Historical Quarterly* 32 (Fall/Winter 1970): 157-166. White employers did not expect blacks to work without the compulsion of slavery, but by 1866, black workers showed that they could work successfully when given a fair contract. The Freedmen's Bureau in Alabama struggled to work out fair contracts and ensure that freedmen were working. In some cases Alabama planters attempted to use immigrant labor from China and Europe. Even with a better labor situation by 1867, the freedmen still had little control over their lives and lacked self sufficiency and integration into society. They required more help than they had received.

1446. Schweninger, Loren. "James Rapier and the Negro Labor Movement, 1869-1872." *Alabama Review* 28 (July 1975): 185-201. Rapier, a free black from Florence, Alabama, served in various public offices during Reconstruction, including U.S. congressman beginning in 1873. His concern for the rights of black workers in the state, as well as nationwide, led him to help organize the National Negro Labor Union in 1869 and the first Southern state affiliate in 1871. Rapier also sought federal assistance to help blacks purchase homesteads, and he pushed for reforms in the Alabama public school system. Despite his efforts, all of these initiatives resulted in little support from the national Republican Party and little success. The economic and political plight of the freedmen in Alabama actually worsened by the early 1870s.

1447. Vandiver, Frank E. "Josiah Gorgas and the Brierfield Iron Works." *Alabama Review* 3 (January 1950): 5-21. Gorgas's lack of success in the iron works business from 1866 to 1868 indicated the problems encountered by businessmen during the postwar period. Transportation, labor and maintenance costs were extremely expensive. The iron market was limited and prices were depressed. The most important problem was insufficient financing.

1448.   Wiener, Jonathan M. "Female Planters and Planters' Wives in Civil War and Reconstruction: Alabama, 1850-1870." *Alabama Review* 30 (April 1977): 135-149. Tbls. (Rpt. in *From Civil War to Civil Rights, Alabama 1860-1960: Anthology From the Alabama Review*. Tuscaloosa: University of Alabama Press, 1987, pp. 94-105.)   Wiener uses the manuscript census for the years 1850-1870 covering five Black Belt counties to correct the notion that there was a significant increase in the number of women planters after the Civil War. In fact, the census shows no increase in the female planters in the region studied. Among the plantation class, there was continuity with prewar days. Wiener also compares the status and characteristics of female planters from 1860 and 1870 regarding their births, age, marital status, and size of plantation.

1449.   Wiener, Jonathan M. "Planter-Merchant Conflict in Reconstruction Alabama." *Past and Present* 68 (August 1975): 73-94. Tbl.   Wiener uses the U.S. censuses of 1850-1870 in his study of Marengo County in the Black Belt region. He finds evidence that the planter elite, consisting of the top 10% of large landowners, not only maintained their power after the Civil War, but increased it. Also, the make-up of this planter elite was substantially the same group from prewar days. Planter persistence occurred largely because the federal government did not redistribute land to the freedmen. Furthermore, Wiener examines how planters assumed a dual role as merchants to the black tenants that gave them control over labor with the power of crop liens that strapped tenants to the land making them forever in debt to the planter. Not only did the planter elite persist, they grew stronger.

1450.   Wiener, Jonathan M. "Planter Persistence and Social Change: Alabama, 1859-1870." *Journal of Interdisciplinary History* 7 (Autumn 1976): 235-260. Tbls. Wiener uses the manuscript censuses from 1850-1870 to dispute the theory that the Civil War destroyed the planter elite. He focuses on five counties in the western Black Belt of Alabama, including Greene, Marengo, Sumter, Perry, and Hale Counties. From his statistical analysis, he concludes that even though many planter elite lost much of their wealth and social position for various reasons, a remarkable number of them maintained their land and adjusted their lives to cope with the new postwar environment. Wiener studies social and political factors that may explain how a large number of planter elite persisted, such as the location of the plantation, the presence of sons who took possession of the land, and the age of the planters.

1451.   Wiener, Jonathan M. *Social Origins of the New South: Alabama, 1860-1885*. Baton Rouge: Louisiana State University Press, 1978. 247p. App. Map. Tbls.   Wiener focuses on the social and economic development of westcentral Alabama counties, including Hale, Greene, Sumter, Marengo, and Perry. In this region a new, prosperous middle class did not become strong, because the state remained under the economic control of a persistent Old South planter elite. New South ideologists, with their focus on industrial development, made little headway against the planters who maintained control over labor in the form of a repressive sharecropping system, and who extended their power as planter-merchants. Planter domination resulted in the stagnation of state agriculture and industry until the 20th century.

Society, Education, and Religion

1452.   Amos, Harriet E. "Religious Reconstruction in Microcosm at Faunsdale Plantation." *Alabama Review* 42 (October 1989): 243-269.   Located in Marengo County in the Canebreak, Faunsdale was the site of an Episcopal mission directed specifically toward the slave population. Amos explains that prior to emancipation, slaves were reluctant to attend church because of the lack of emotion in Episcopalian religious services and the constant emphasis on discipline and morality. When Southern blacks broke away from white churches after the war, rector William A. Stickney's influence at Faunsdale held freedmen in the church temporarily through contractual labor arrangements. The experience at Faunsdal is viewed as atypical.

1453.   Bethel, Elizabeth. "The Freedmen's Bureau in Alabama." *Journal of Southern History* 14 (February 1948): 49-92.   The Freedmen's Bureau established an office in Alabama in July, 1865 under the direction of Brig. Gen. Wager Swayne. Bethel describes the limited success of the bureau. It did a good job of distributing relief and organizing education for the freedmen, but it's attempt to regulate labor and justice was hurt by poor economic conditions and racial animosity. The bureau also generated local hostility from the involvement of its agents in politics.

1454.   Bond, Horace Mann. *Negro Education in Alabama: A Study in Cotton and Steel.* Washington, D. C.: Associated Publishers, Inc., 1939. 358p. Bibl. Ills. Maps.   The first 7 chapters (147 pages) touch on the issues of education during Reconstruction. Mann extends his discussion in the rest of the book up to the 1930s. He examines the influence of social, economic, and political forces on the development of a statewide education system. Social and economic problems led to inadequate funding, and whites would not accept the ideology of Northern humanitarian educators who criticized Southern traditions and encouraged blacks to become educated and strive for their rights as citizens. Local whites demanded control over the education of freedmen. (See also Bond's "Social and Economic Influences on the Public Education of Negroes in Alabama 1865-1900." Ph.D. University of Chicago, 1939.)

1455.   Bond, Horace Mann.   "Social and Economic Forces in Alabama Reconstruction." *Journal of Negro History* 23 (July 1938): 290-348.   Bond refers to a combination of humanitarianism for black and white landless classes and the power of capitalist expansion. The Freedmen's Bureau and Northern missionaries represent the humanitarians who were most effective until the late 1860s when the focus changed from providing help to rebuilding railroads and financing state debt.

After 1868 the Republican Party concentrated more on economic issues rather than social and political reform.

1456.   Boney, F. N. (ed.). *A Union Soldier in the Land of the Vanquished: The Diary of Sergeant Matthew Woodruff, June-December, 1965.* University, Al.: University of Alabama Press, 1969. 103p. Bibl.   Woodruff's diary deals mainly with his personal life while attached to his army unity in Alabama. In April, 1866 the Army listed him as a deserter shortly before his unit was mustered out.

1457.   Cook, Majorie Howell. "Restoration and Innovation: Alabamians Adjust to Defeat, 1865-1867." Ph.D. University of Alabama, 1968. 231p.

1458.   Curtin, Mary Ellen.   "Legacies Of Struggle: Black Prisoners In The Making Of Postbellum Alabama, 1865-1895."   Ph.D.   Duke University, 1992. 334p.

1459.   Doss, Harriet E. Amos. "White and Black Female Missionaries to Former Slaves during Reconstruction." In *Stepping Out of the Shadows: Alabama Women, 1819-1990.* Edited by Mary Martha Thomas. Tuscaloosa: University of Alabama Press, 1995. Pp. 43-56. Ills.   The missionaries were usually white women who sought to spread their Victorian American culture among the blacks and experience a personal challenge. Their belief in white superiority was clear, but their goal was to make good citizens and Christians. Black female missionaries also served as teachers, but they were in the minority during Reconstruction. Doss discusses the work of the American Missionary Association and the post-Reconstruction work of the Women's Baptist Home Mission Society and the Women's American Baptist Home Mission Society beginning in the late 1870s.

1460.   Fleming, Walter L. "The Churches of Alabama During the Civil War and Reconstruction." *Gulf States Historical Magazine* 1 (November 1902): 105-127. By 1861 all Christian denominations in the North and the South except Roman Catholic had separated on the issue of slavery. In Alabama the occupation of the South by the Union Army led to Army regulations against prayers for the Confederacy and the influx of Northern church officials charged with bringing about the disintegration of the Southern organizations and the reunion of the brethren. Former black members of white churches were persuaded by Northern missionaries and the Freedmen's Bureau to form their own churches associated with the Northern organizations. Fleming is particularly concerned with the Methodists, Baptists, Presbyterians, and Episcopalians. He emphasizes that the reconstruction of the Southern churches was just another form of political reconstruction. Both failed to break the Solid South.

1461.   Folmar, John Kent (ed.). "Post Civil War Mobile: The Letters of James M. Williams, May-September, 1865." *Alabama Historical Quarterly* 32 (Fall/Winter 1870): 186-198.   Williams, a native of Ohio, moved to the South in 1858, supported Southern succession, and served in the Confederate Army. Included here are postwar letters written to his wife from their hometown of Mobile to her temporary residence in central Alabama. He writes about the difficulties of his life in Mobile during the first few months of peace.

1462.   Gilmour, Richard A. "The Other Emancipation: Studies in the Society and Economy of Alabama During Reconstruction." Ph.D. Johns Hopkins University, 1972. 310p.

1463.   Hassan, Gail S. "Health and Welfare of Freedmen in Reconstruction Alabama." *Alabama Review* 35 (April 1982): 94-110. Hassan examines the free medical care offered by the Freedmen's Bureau in Alabama, particularly in the town of Garland. She describes how a "home colony" was organized to help employ and look after the welfare of needy freedmen and how the colony became a hospital. By the end of December 1868 the bureau discontinued medical services in the state, but it had given vital and urgent medical care to thousands of freedmen who could not provide for themselves.

1464.   Hesseltine, William B. and Larry Gara. "Confederate Leaders in Post-War Alabama." *Alabama Review* 4 (January 1951): 5-21. Despite the hardships and disabilities placed on the state and on former Confederate leaders, they found ways to maintain their influence and have a positive impact on state politics and society. Hesseltine and Gara show sentiment in favor of the old leadership and against Republican Reconstruction. Some of the former Confederates mentioned include W. W. Allen, David Peter Leuris, A. S. Walker, George Goldthwaite, and William Russell Smith.

1465.   Howard, Gene L. *Death at Cross Plains: An Alabama Reconstruction Tragedy.* University: University of Alabama Press, 1984. 151p. Bibl. Ills. Ports. Map. Howard tells the story of Canadian minister and teacher William Luke, who came to Alabama in 1869 to teach black students at Talladega College. The local Ku Klux Klan executed him along with three blacks on July 11, 1870. Luke, a sincere but naive man, erred by not understanding the feelings of the white community in the period of Radical Reconstruction.

1466.   Kolchin, Peter R. *First Freedom: The Response of Alabama's Blacks to Emancipation and Reconstruction.* Westport: Greenwood Press, 1972. 215p. Bibl. Maps. Tbls.   Unlike most earlier studies, Kolchin concentrates on the attitudes and responses of blacks to emancipation, race relations, and politics. He uses Alabama as a case study to show that freedmen were proactive in claiming freedom, and this resulted in migration, new labor relationships, political organization, the strengthening of black families, emphasis on education, and the formation of black churches. Freedom changed the black social structure. The changes that occurred during the first few years of freedom established the pattern for the future. (See also Kolchin's Ph.D. dissertation with the same title from Johns Hopkins University Press, 1970)

1467.   Krebs, Sylvia. "Funeral Meats and Second Marriages: Alabama Churches in the Presidential Reconstruction Period." *Alabama Historical Quarterly* 37 (Fall

1975): 206-216.   The end of the war brought movements to unite Northern and Southern branches of churches, particularly the Methodist Episcopal Church and the Protestant Episcopal Church. The Methodists were stymied by racial issues, the influence of Northern missionaries, and lingering sectional distrust by church leaders. The Protestant Episcopal Church united quickly due to the lack of prewar abolitionist fervor displayed by its leadership in the person of Bishop Richard Wilmer. In general, Alabama churches failed to inspire Protestants and struggled to regain their influence.

1468.   Landers, Mary Gene. "Public Pre-Collegiate Education in Alabama during Reconstruction, 1868-1875." Ph.D. University of Alabama 1975. 179p.

1469.   McKenzie, Robert H. "William Russell Smith: Forgotten President of the University of Alabama." *Alabama Review* 37 (July 1984): 163-182. Port.   Smith served as president of the university from June 29, 1870 until his resignation on June 19, 1871. McKenzie relies on the newspaper articles of a Ku Klux Klan leader and editor of the Tuscaloosa *Independent Monitor*, the theories of other historians, and comments by Smith's family and friends to conclude that tension between Smith and the Radical Republican Board of Regents may have influenced his resignation. Indications are that he was a moderate Republican who switched to the Democrats, but the use of political labels in the complicated environment of Reconstruction can be hazardous.

1470.   Montgomery, Margaret L. "Alabama Freedmen: Some Reconstruction Documents." *Phylon* 13 (1952): 245-251.   Portions of the diary written by Talladega County planter James Mallory are published. Mallory describes labor conditions on his land. Also printed are documents from the Convention of Colored People held in Mobile in November, 1865 that illustrate the dedication of freedmen to accept responsibility to work and educate their families.

1471.   Myers, John B.   "The Education of the Alabama Freedmen During Presidential Reconstruction, 1865-1867." *Journal of Negro Education* 40 (Spring 1971): 163-171.   Alabama freedmen sought educational opportunities with a passion in order to guarantee their freedom and self sufficiency. Benevolent and missionary associations, such as the Pittsburgh Freedmen's Aid Commission and the Freedmen's Bureau, provided leadership and manpower to organize schools. Despite the opposition of whites who wanted to control the schools, efforts to educate freedmen during the early postwar years were very successful.

1472.   Myers, John B. "Reaction and Adjustment: The Struggle of Alabama Freedmen in Post-Bellum Alabama, 1865-1867." *Alabama Historical Quarterly* 32 (Spring/Summer 1970): 5-22.   Alabama freedmen faced a chaotic and dangerous environment during the early years of their emancipation. Like many other people in the state, they had to deal with lawlessness, violence, and the lack of sanitary food and shelter. The freedmen were particularly prone to be victims of violence as whites reacted with disgust to the idea of racial equality and equal rights for all citizens. The Alabama Freedmen's Bureau, directed by Gen. Wager Swayne, attempted to provide some relief and protection to freedmen, but the bureau's powers were limited.

1473.   Oldshue, Jerry C.   "Remembering Education in Hale County During Reconstruction." *Alabama Review* 41 (October 1988): 289-298.   Oldshue reprints selected comments about Greene Springs School in Hale County during the 1870s. The comments were recorded by J. Nicholene Bishop in 1940 and later written down as an unpublished manuscript entitled "Our Settlement." Bishop comments about the education of black students in the county and other general educational issues.

1474.   Patin, Robert.   "Alabama Newspaper Humor During Reconstruction." *Alabama Review* 17 (October 1964): 243-260.   Political and racial humor appeared in five Montgomery newspapers - the *Daily Mail*, *Weekly Mail*, *Daily Advertiser*, *Weekly Advertiser* and *Daily Post*.   The humor made fun of Republicans, particularly blacks.   Racial jokes made reference to kissing, drinking and other social and personal relations.   Patin suggests that the humor was a defense against enemies and a cure for other social problems.

1475.   Richardson, Joe.   "'To Help a Brother On': The First Decade of Talladega College." *Alabama Historical Quarterly* 37 (Spring 1975): 19-37.   Talladega College was founded by the American Missionary Association in early 1867 in cooperation with the Freedmen's Bureau.   The school was part of the efforts made by the A.M.A. and the bureau to establish educational institutions for the freedmen. Richardson describes the early development of the school, how it dealt with white violence, and the difficulties of dealing with A.M.A. administrators in the North.

1476.   Rogers, William Warren.   "Alabama Newspaper Mottoes From 1865 to 1900." *Alabama Historical Quarterly* 20 (Fall 1958): 364-370.   Most of this article covers the years of Reconstruction.   Rogers emphasizes that newspaper mottoes expressed opinions regarding politics, religion, and regions, but each newspaper was very independent.   During Reconstruction newspapers had a powerful impact on public opinion.

1477.   Rogers, William Warren.   "The Establishment of Alabama's Land Grant College." *Alabama Review* 13 (January 1960): 5-20.   In February, 1867 the Alabama legislature passed a law authorizing the state to take part in the benefits of the Morrill Act, a federal law assisting the states with the establishment of colleges emphasizing instruction of agriculture and the mechanical arts.   Due to the problems of Reconstruction, little progress was made until 1871 when the state finally began the process of finding an appropriate location.   Rogers describes how Auburn was selected as the cite of a college and how farmers and leaders in the state accepted the concept of progressive education.

1478.   Scherer, Robert G.   "William Burns Paterson: 'Pioneer as Well as Apostle of Negro Education in Alabama." *Alabama Historical Quarterly* 36 (Summer 1974): 121-150.   Paterson, a native of Scotland who arrived in America in 1867, settled in Alabama in 1870.   In 1871 he became a teacher of freedmen and devoted most of his life to education. He became President of Alabama State College (1878-1915) and opposed Booker T. Washington's philosophy of industrial training for blacks.

1479.   Schweninger, Loren.   "The American Missionary Association and Northern Philanthropy in Reconstruction Alabama." *Alabama Historical Quarterly* 32 (Fall and Winter 1970): 129-156.   Northern philanthropic and aid societies were active in the distribution of aid in Alabama, although the state received less aid than most of the other Southern states. The American Missionary Association was particularly active in providing food and clothing, establishing schools, training teachers, helping churches, and organizing temperance associations. The efforts of missionaries, such as Justus and Henry Brown, were important and at least partially successful.   Schweninger emphasizes that the A.M.A., like other missionary societies, was not the fanatical and evil organization described by historian Walter Lynwood Fleming.

1480.   Smith, James R.   "A Southerner on Reconstruction: Letter of James R. Smith, of Livingston, Alabama July 5, 1867." *Moorfield Antiquarian* 1 (1938): 290-195.   Smith's letter is addressed to Sophar Mills of New York City regarding his perspective on the war, the situation in the South, and the future of his business and family.

1481.   Steeh, Charlotte Andrea Goodman.   "Racial Discrimination in Alabama, 1870-1910." Ph.D. University of Michigan, 1975. 339p.

1482.   Stewart, Edgar A. (ed.).   "The Journal of James Mallory, 1834-1877." *Alabama Review* 14 (July 1961): 219-232.   Mallory was a planter in Talladega County, Alabama.   Among the comments that Stewart chose to publish from Mallory's journal are critical opinions about life and politics in the postwar years.

1483.   White, Kenneth B.   "The Alabama Freedmen's Bureau and Black Education" The Myth of Opportunity." *Alabama Review* 34 (April 1981): 107-124.   The education of the freedmen got a start in Alabama through the efforts of Wager Swayne, assistant commissioner of the Freedmen's Bureau, and Rev. Charles W. Buckley, head of the new educational program. They made important progress between the summer of 1865 and the end of 1867, but after their departure in early 1868 the educational program was plagued by inconsistent leadership.   Just as important as leadership problems were the strong white opposition to black education, the deep seated racism of the period, and the lack of funding to expand the program effectively.

1484.   Wilmer, Richard H. *The Recent Past From a Southern Standpoint: Reminiscences of a Grandfather.* New York: Thomas Whitlaker, 1887. 281p. App. Ports.   Wilmer was Protestant Episcopal Bishop of Alabama during Reconstruction. A portion of his memoirs include his opinions about slavery, his problem with national allegiances in his prayers during the military occupation, military orders to stop conducting religious services, and the split between the

Northern and Southern branches of the church. Wilmer favored succession during the Civil War.

Arkansas

General History

1485.   Ellenburg, Martha A. "Reconstruction in Arkansas." Ph.D. University of Missouri, 1967. 308p.

1486.   Staples, Thomas S. "Reconstruction in Arkansas, 1862-1874." Ph.D. Columbia University, 1923. 451p. (Rpt. in *Columbia University Studies*, vol. 109, no. 245)

1487.   Thomas, David Y. *Arkansas in War and Reconstruction 1861-1874*. Little Rock: Arkansas Division, United Daughters of the Confederacy, 1926. 44p. Ports. Ills.   Only about 10% of this book discusses the major events of Reconstruction in Arkansas, and it relies mainly on Staples' work (see # 1486).

1488.   Thompson, George H. "Arkansas Reconstruction 1864-1874." In *Historical Report of the Secretary of State Arkansas*. Little Rock: Secretary of State, 1978. Pp. 89-125. Maps. Tbls.   This article is part of a history of Arkansas written in 13 essays. Thompson writes a narrative of postwar politics, economics, and society in the state from the organization of a wartime Unionist government by President Lincoln to the end of Republican rule. He emphasizes the importance of local geography, patriotism, and leadership personalities in the course of Reconstruction issues, such as race relations. Several maps and tables compare the three main regions of the state - northwest, delta, and southwest - regarding the classification of the electorate and categories of debt.

1489.   Thompson, George H. *Arkansas and Reconstruction: The Influence of Geography, Economics, and Personality*. Port Washington, NY: Kennikat Press, 1976. 296p. Bibl. Maps. Ports. Tbls.   Thompson's approach to Reconstruction emphasizes the importance of the personalities of key people, particularly Unionists David Walker and Augustus H. Garland. The interaction of influential and changing personalities played a more important role in Reconstruction than party loyalties. Although Arkansas was a substantially Unionist state on the eve of the Civil War and during Reconstruction, the struggle between geographic regions and political factions merged in an environment that continued to encourage the tradition of local political control.

Politics and Law

1490.   Atkinson, James H. "The Adoption of the Constitution of 1874 and the Passing of the Reconstruction Regime." *Arkansas Historical Quarterly* 5 (Autumn 1946): 288-296.   The fall of Republican rule in Arkansas began with the Democratic victory in the June, 1874 election to call a constitutional convention. Democratic delegates held a majority of the convention seats and thus were able to control the proceedings. The electoral victory of the new constitution in October led to the resignation of Republican Gov. Baxter. Atkinson does not describe the new constitution itself or how it differed from the 1868 document.

1491.   Atkinson, James H. "The Arkansas Gubernatorial Campaign and Election of 1872." *Arkansas Historical Quarterly* 1 (December 1942): 307-321.   This description of the election is based mainly on newspaper accounts from the *Van Buren Press* and the Little Rock *Daily Gazette*. The gubernatorial election pitted Joseph Brooks, representing the Reform Republicans or "Brindetails" made up mostly of "disappointed carpetbaggers and their Negro followers" (p. 308); and Elisha Baxter, a local Unionist representing the regular Republicans, also known as "Minstrels", who were dominated by U.S. Senator Powell Clayton and allied with Republican supporters of President Grant. After the Liberal Republican ticket collapsed during the campaign, the Democrats supported Brooks.

1492.   Atkinson, James H. "Brooks-Baxter Contest." *Arkansas Historical Quarterly* 4 (Summer 1945): 124-149.   The contested results of the Arkansas gubernatorial election of November 5, 1872 led to a period of uncertainty and violence that extended until May 20, 1874. The election pitted regular Republican, Elisha Baxter against reform Republican, Joseph Brooks. Baxter ultimately prevailed with the assistance of President Grant and military support.

1493.   Atkinson, James H. "Clayton and Catterson Rob Columbia County." *Arkansas Historical Quarterly* 21 (Summer 1962): 153-157.   Printed in this article is a letter dated January 12, 1869 from three land owners to President Johnson. They complain about martial law in the state that was begun by Gov. Powell Clayton, and refer to acts of violence by blacks and the state militia commanded by Gen. Robert F. Catterson. They ask Johnson and President-elect Grant to send an "unprejudiced officer" to investigate the violence in the county.

1494.   Baker, Russell P. "James H. Howard." *Arkansas Historical Quarterly* 35 (Winter 1976): 360-365.   Howard began the Civil War as a supporter of the Confederacy in Arkansas, but he moderated his views when he ran for political office in 1866. Eventually he espoused strong Radical Republican views during his campaign for the state senate in 1870. The conservative press was particularly critical of Howard due to his changing public views, but he had so much support in the legislature that a new county was named in his honor.

1495. Berry, Conrid Clyde III. "Arkansas and Abraham Lincoln: Wartime Reconstruction and the Presidential Plan for the State." Ph.D. University of Mississippi, 1992. 221p.

1496. Brittain, Joseph Matt. Negro Suffrage and Politics in Arkansas Since 1870. Ph.D. Indiana University, 1958. 245p.

1497. Bullock, Neal T. "Pope County Militia War." *Arkansas Valley Historical Papers* no. 33 (June 1965): 1-7. Bullock tells stories of the violence in Pope County throughout Reconstruction. He describes the fight against the carpetbagger regime as a heroic act.

1498. Burnside, William H. *The Honorable Powell Clayton.* Conway, Arkansa: UCA Press, 1991. 132p. Bibl. Clayton, a Union officer from Pennsylvania and Kansas, settled in Arkansas in 1865 and became a controversial Republican governor (1868-1870) and U.S. senator (1871-1877). Burnside believes that Clayton was ambitious but had only positive motives for entering Arkansas politics. As governor, Clayton was highly successful in resolving problems of the state.

1499. Clayton, Powell. *The Aftermath of the Civil War, In Arkansas.* New York: Neale Publishing Co., 1915. 378p. The author was the Republican governor of Arkansas from 1868 to 1871 followed by a period in the U.S. Senate from 1871 to 1877. In his memoir Clayton attempts to correct misimpressions and false information spread by Democratic opponents at the time of his service and in histories written by them. He defends his administration and criticizes those who led his impeachment. Clayton expresses disappointment with how Democratic administrations not only dismantled the achievements of Republican governments, but also governed corruptly. (See also criticism of Clayton's book in U. M. Rose, "Clayton's *Aftermath of the Civil War in Arkansas*," *Publications of the Arkansas Historical Association* 4 (1917): 57-65.)

1500. Cowen, Ruth Caroline. "Reorganizing of Federal Arkansas, 1862-1865." *Arkansas Historical Quarterly* 18 (Summer 1959): 32-57. President Lincoln attempted to reorganize the government of Arkansas after Union troops captured Little Rock in September, 1863. Many Unionists wanted to promote Lincoln's plan, but it failed because Radical Republicans in Congress believed it was too lenient and the military occupation of the state did not establish the right conditions for a return to statehood.

1501. Cypert, Eugene. "Constitutional Convention of 1868." *Publications of the Arkansas Historical Association* 4 (1917): 7-56. Includes details of the proceedings of the convention that was attended by Cypert's father Jesse Cypert.

1502. Donovan, Timothy and Williard B. Gatewood, Jr. (eds). *The Governors of Arkansas: Essays in Political Biography.* Fayetteville: University of Arkansas Press, 1981. 300p. Bibl. Includes essays on the Reconstruction governors:

Unionist Isaac Murphy (1864-1868), Republicans Powell Clayton (1868-1871) and Elisha Baxter (1873-1874), and Democrat Augustus Hill Garland (1874-1877).

1503.   Driggs, Orval Truman, Jr. "The Issues of the Powell Clayton Regime, 1868-1871." *Arkansas Historical Quarterly* 8 (Spring 1949): 1-75.   Driggs' masters thesis, written at the University of Arkansas, focuses on the divisive environment that existed in Arkansas after the Republican Party took control of state politics in 1868.   Clayton, a Pennsylvania carpetbagger and former Union officer, sought to lead Radical reforms, but violent opposition, Republican Party divisions between local Unionists and carpetbaggers and Clayton's impeachment led to the political chaos surrounding the gubernatorial election in November, 1872.   Despite Republican mismanagement and party disunity, Clayton achieved some lasting reforms in welfare and education, tax equalization and government assistance to business.

1504.   Ewing, Cortez A. M.   "Arkansas Reconstruction Impeachments." *Arkansas Historical Quarterly*   13 (Summer 1954): 137-153.   The politics of Reconstruction led to the impeachment of Gov. Powell Clayton and state Supreme Court Justice John McClure.   Both Republicans had enemies among conservative Republicans and Democrats.   Clayton was the object of an impeachment in 1871 after he refused to give up the governor's office to a political enemy, Lt. Gov. James M. Johnson, even though he was appointed to the U.S. Senate.   He angered many whites with martial law against the Ku Klux Klan and his support for arming a black militia.   McClure was impeached after he ruled against Clayton's enemies. Both men avoided a conviction.

1505.   Fehrenbacher, Don E. "From War to Reconstruction in Arkansas."   In *Lincoln in Text and Context*.   Stanford: Stanford University Press, 1987.   Pp. 143-156.   Lincoln's efforts to form a loyal government in Arkansas was mainly a wartime political move to isolate the Confederacy and bring the war to an end.   The president's efforts in Arkansas represent his flexibility and willingness to change his plans based on the existing political and military situation.   Lincoln's policy in Arkansas was not radical because he never requested civil rights for blacks in the new constitution, and he continued to speak of goodwill as an ingredient in his Reconstruction plan.

1506.   Feistman, Eugene G. "Radical Disfranchisement in Arkansas 1867/1868." *Arkansas Historical Quarterly*   12 (Summer 1953): 126-168. Bibl. Tbls.   The constitutional convention of 1868, controlled by 23 carpetbaggers and 8 blacks, accepted the disenfranchisement of certain classes of rebels.   Feistman briefly compares the Arkansas convention with other Southern state conventions and concludes that the state's disenfranchisement law was relatively vindictive.   Three appendices include a table of voter registration by county and race; a list of delegates to the constitutional convention by county, occupation and vote on the constitution; and a table showing votes for and against the convention and the constitution by county.

1507.   Halliburton,   William   H.   "Reconstruction   in   Arkansas   County," *Publications of the Arkansas Historical Association*   2   (1908):   478-520. Halliburton focuses on the administrative structure of both the local government and the judiciary during the years of Reconstruction.

1508.   Harrell,   John   M.   *The   Brooks   and   Baxter   War: A   History   of   the Reconstruction Period in Arkansas.*   St. Louis: Slawson Printing, 1893.   276p. Ills. Ports.   This book was written by Darley Raynor, a native of Little Rock. Harrell   published   Raynor's   manuscript   that   provides   a   narrative   of   political Reconstruction in Arkansas by one who lived through it.   It includes an appendix that reprints selected documents related to the violent result of the clash between Republican Gov. Elisha Baxter and his opponent in the 1872 election, Joseph Brooks, a favorite of conservative Republicans and Democrats.

1509.   Hepp, Judy. "The Mayors of Reconstruction Little Rock." *Pulaski County Historical Society Review* 20 (March 1972): 1-4.   Hepp provides brief information on Dr. J. J. McAlmont (January, 1866-January, 1867), J. Hopkins (January, 1867-February, 1868), John Wassell (February, 1868-January, 1869), A. K. Hartman (January,   1869-November,   1869),   Jefferson   George   Botsford   (January,   1870-November, 1871), Robert F. Catterson (November, 1871-November, 1873), and Frederick Kramer (April, 1873-March, 1875, 1881-1887).

1510.   Hesseltine, William B. and Larry Gara.   "Arkansas' Confederate Leaders After the War." *Arkansas Historical Quarterly* 9 (Winter 1950): 259-269.   The contributions of local Confederate leaders are described, including their influence on the memory of the Lost Cause in Arkansas.   The authors write with a sentimental tone.

1511.   Hume,   Richard   L.   "The   Arkansas   Constitutional   Convention   of   1868:   A Case Study in the Politics of Reconstruction." *Journal of Southern History* 39 (May 1973): 183-206. Tbls.   Hume examines the backgrounds and voting records of the convention delegates on key issues of fundamental importance to the freedmen.   Of the 75 delegates, 45 were Southern whites, 8 were blacks, and the rest were from outside the region.   Hume focuses mostly on Southern whites because the internal split among them gave the balance of power to the Radical faction.

1512.   Johnson, Benjamin S.   "The Brooks-Baxter War." *Publications of the Arkansas Historical Association* 2 (1908): 122-173.   Johnson served in the Confederate Army and became an attorney in Pine Bluff and Little Rock after the war. This account of the violent dispute after the 1872 election between Republican factions is based on a variety of reprinted documents, including extensive quotations from the *Arkansas Gazette.*   In the dispute between Gov. Elisha Baxter and conservative Joseph Brooks, Johnson concludes that fraud occurred.   Brooks forced Baxter to flee from office and briefly replaced him, but Baxter regained his office after federal intervention.

1513.   Kelley, Michael P. "Partisan or Protector: Powell Clayton and the 1868 Presidential Election." *Ozark Historical Review* 3 (Spring 1974): 44-58. Historians have accused Republican Powell Clayton of rejecting election returns from more than a dozen counties to ensure a Republican victory in the state and national elections of 1868. Due to Ku Klux Klan violence against Republicans and the resignation of voter registrars, Clayton decreed that registrations in 14 counties would be rejected. No elections were held in those counties. Although the counties may have given a majority to the Democrats, Kelley believes that Clayton acted without political bias. The loss of votes was the fault of Democrats who promoted violence and intimidation prior to the election.

1514.   Ledbetter, Cal, Jr. "The Constitution of 1868: Conqueror's Constitution or Constitutional Continuity?" *Arkansas Historical Quarterly* 44 (Spring 1985): 16-41.   Ledbetter investigates how the constitution of 1868 compares with American constitutional theories and the state constitutions prior to and after Radical Reconstruction. He concludes that while the process of writing the document in 1867 was unusual, the content was not inconsistent with other constitutions, including the more conservative state constitution of 1874. The 1868 document established an activist government in state society and reflected the goals of reform-minded Republican framers whose outlook was similar to future populist and progressive politicians.

1515.   Leslie, James W. "Ferd Havis: Jefferson County's Black Republican Leader." *Arkansas Historical Quarterly* 37 (Autumn 1978): 239-251. Port. Ills. Ferdinand Havis, born a slave in Desha County, Arkansas, became a barber in Pine Bluff in 1870 and began a long period of participation in the local Republican Party as elected city alderman (1871, 1873) and state legislator (1872). Havis supported regular Republican Elisha Baxter in the 1872 election. He continued to work with the Republican Party until his death in 1913.

1516.   Littlefield, Daniel F., Jr. and Patricia Washington McGraw. "The *Arkansas Freeman*, 1869-1870 - Birth of the Black Press in Arkansas." *Phylon* 40 (March 1979): 75-85.   The *Arkansas Freeman*, the first black newspaper in Arkansas began publication in Little Rock on August 21, 1869 and ceased sometime during the summer of 1870. Rev. Tabbs Gross, editor and owner, hoped to provide a Republican paper that blacks could trust instead of the *Morning Republican* that served as an organ of the local Republican Party. Gross's moderate approach made him popular with the conservative *Daily Arkansas Gazette* and split local Republicans over issues of policy and power distribution within the party.

1517.   McCaslin, Richard B. "Reconstructing a Frontier Oligarchy: Andrew Johnson's Amnesty Proclamation and Arkansas." *Arkansas Historical Quarterly* 49 (Winter 1990): 313-329.   Johnson's amnesty proclamation of May 29, 1865 was consistent with Lincoln's policy, although Johnson increased the number of exceptions. Despite the exceptions, most Arkansas residents who were counted as exceptions and who applied for amnesty were successful. McCaslin concludes that the liberal amnesty policy allowed conservatives to continue their political initiatives in postwar Arkansas and stall or stunt reforms in education, black political rights, and economic growth. Amnesty contributed to a climate that produced tenant farming and racial segregation.

1518.   Monks, William. *A History of Southern Missouri and Northern Arkansas. Being An Account of the Early Settlements, the Civil War, the Ku Klux, and Times of Peace.* West Plains, Mo.: West Plains Journal Co., 1907. 247p. Ports. Ills. Monks joined the militia that helped to defeat the Ku Klux Klan in Arkansas. A portion of this book is his account of activities to uphold the law in the state.

1519.   Mulhollan, Paige E. "Arkansas General Assembly of 1866 and its Effect on Reconstruction." *Arkansas Historical Quarterly* 20 (Winter 1961): 331-343. In 1866 there seemed to be a possibility that Arkansas would be admitted to the Union as long as the legislature passed the 14th Amendment. The new legislature, elected on August 7, 1866, contained mostly Democrats, including prewar legislators and former Confederate politicians and army officers. This conservative group rejected black civil rights, including suffrage, education reforms, and the 14th Amendment. Mulhollan concludes that the recalcitrance of the Arkansas General Assembly increased the certainty of Congressional Reconstruction in the state. Gov. Isaac Murphy, elected in 1864, attempted to moderate several legislative initiatives by using his veto power, but the vetoes were defeated.

1520.   Neal, Diane and Thomas W. Kremm. "Loyal Government on Trial: The Union and Arkansas." *Southern Studies* 25 (Summer 1986): 148-162.   The authors describe how Arkansas Unionists attempted to organize a loyal government following President Lincoln's Reconstruction plan. But Congress refused to accept the elected senators of the rump state because they were part of the disloyal class even though they were Unionists. This was a clear rebuke of Lincoln's policies.

1521.   Neal, Diane. "Seduction, Accommodation, or Realism? Tabbs Gross and the *Arkansas Freeman*." *Arkansas Historical Quarterly* 48 (Spring 1980): 57-64. Gross, who bought his freedom from slavery in Kentucky, arrived in Arkansas in 1867 and founded the *Arkansas Freeman* two years later. In the first black owned and edited newspaper in the state, Gross criticized the Republican Party because the leadership refused to support blacks for elective office or for patronage positions. He used the praise that he received from Democrats and his persistent calls for black independence to force concessions from the Republicans. Gross's support for Liberal Republicans indicated a realistic approach toward civil rights, but the strength of white supremacy in defeated him.

1522.   Nunn, Walter. "The Constitutional Convention of 1874." *Arkansas Historical Quarterly* 27 (Autumn 1968): 177-204. Ills. Ports.   The political chaos in Arkansas in the early 1870s led to public support for rewriting the state constitution. Republican Gov. Elisha Baxter, was a moderate, bipartisan politician who supported the restoration of voting privileges to ex-Confederates in 1873. His victory in the "Brooks-Baxter War" between Republican factions led to the call for a constitutional convention that Democrats believed they could dominate. Democrats comprised a large majority of convention delegates, and the new constitution was the first evidence of the downfall of Reconstruction in Arkansas.

1523.   Palmer, Paul C. "Miscegenation as an Issue in the Arkansas Constitutional Convention of 1868." *Arkansas Historical Quarterly* 24 (Summer 1965): 99-119. The issue of miscegenation caused excited debate at the 1868 convention, but the debate was not between supporters and opponents. Instead it focused on whether the constitution should or should not include a passage forbidding it. Palmer states that no one defended mixed race marriages, but several delegates did not want restrictions placed in the constitution. The constitution passed without restrictions, but the issue was used by conservatives to attack the Radicals and raise fears among white citizens. Ironically, a state law approved in 1838 already banned such marriages.

1524.   Parker, David L. "Officials of Pulaski County, Arkansas During the Period of Reconstruction: 1864-1974." *Pulaski County Historical Review* 18 (December 1970): 43-50. Bibl.   Parker offers capsule information on 21 officials who served the county. He identifies among them 5 carpetbaggers, 13 white Southerners (not scalawags), and 3 blacks. The blacks and carpetbaggers did not hold powerful positions, and they did not control county affairs. Power was in the hands of the local whites who do not fit Parker's definition of scalawags.

1525.   Reynolds, John Hugh.   "Presidential Reconstruction in Arkansas." *Publications of the Arkansas Historical Association* 1 (1906): 352-361.   Includes a brief description of the efforts of local Unionists (formerly Whigs) during the Civil War to reconstruct the state for reentry into the Union in accordance with Lincoln's 10% plan. In terms of the numbers of votes caste, the election of officials in 1864 was more successful than expected.

1526.   Reynolds, Thomas J. "Pope County Militia War (July 8, 1872 to February 17, 1873)." *Publications of the Arkansas Historical Association* 2 (1908): 174-198. Reynolds tells a detailed story of the lawlessness and violence that existed in Pope County. His account is based on his own observations, what he heard, and some documentation that is not revealed.

1527.   Ross, Margaret. "Retaliation Against Arkansas Newspaper Editors During Reconstruction." *Arkansas Historical Quarterly* 31 (Summer 1972): 150-165. Ross describes 4 incidents of attempted suppression or intimidation of conservative newspapers following the introduction of military and Radical Republican rule in 1867. She refers to incidents involving the *Constitutional Eagle* of Camden, the *Southern Vindicator* of Pine Bluff, the *Southern Standard* of Arkadelphia, the *White County Record* of Searcy, and the *Arkansas Gazette* of Little Rock that got into trouble after publishing highly critical articles against military and Republican officials.

1528.   Russ, William A., Jr.   "The Attempt to Create a Republican Party in Arkansas During Reconstruction." *Arkansas Historical Quarterly* 1 (September

1942): 206-222.   Russ provides a chronological description of how the state, under the supervision of Gen. E. O. C. Ord, fulfilled the requirements of the Reconstruction Acts of 1867.   Congressional Reconstruction was intentionally designed, in part, to disenfranchise disloyal whites and enfranchise the blacks to ensure Republican victories in state and federal elections.   Russ criticizes President Johnson's inept actions and the extreme nature of Reconstruction as designed by Congress.

1529.   Russ, William A., Jr. "Presidential Disfranchisement in Arkansas (1863-1865)." *Susquehanna University Studies* 1 (January 1940): 185-196; (1865-1874) 2 (March 1941): 225-239.   Russ traces the issue of disenfranchising white voters to ensure Republican domination from Lincoln's unsuccessful efforts to bring Arkansas   back   into   the   Union   beginning   in   1862-1863   through   the disenfranchisement based on the Reconstruction Acts, the 14th Amendment, and the state constitution.   Russ takes the perspective that disenfranchisement was unconstitutional and led to the influence of ignorant blacks and corrupt Northern and local Republicans.

1530.   Singletary, Otis A.   "Military Disturbances in Arkansas During Reconstruction." *Arkansas Historical Quarterly* 15 (Summer 1956): 140-150. Violence was part of the political scene in Arkansas during Reconstruction, and it came in waves. Singletary focuses on two violent periods. The first occurred after Gov. Powell Clayton, elected in July, 1868, quickly organized a militia with black troops and declared martial law following a period of disorder prior to the elections in November. Singletary also describes the Brooks-Baxter War of 1874 when the Regular Republicans and Liberal Republicans fought each other over who should be governor. The Republican Party in the state hastened its own demise as a political power.

1531.   Skeeters, Martha.   "The Negro and the Arkansas State Constitutional Convention of 1868: A Change in Political Emphasis." *Trinity Valley Historical Review* 1 (Spring 1969): 47-69.   Skeeters emphasizes the growing participation of blacks at the 1868 convention compared with the 1867 convention in Arkansas. Black members struggled to be treated equally in the sessions and in the new constitution, despite the conservatives' disdain for them and the systematic attempt by white Republicans to dominate them and provide them with only rudimentary rights. Black participants, such as G. H. Grey, a black carpetbagger, represented the increasing confidence of black citizens.

1532.   Smith, John I. *The Courage of a Southern Unionist: A Biography of Isaac Murphy, Governor of Arkansas, 1864-1868.* Little Rock: Rose Publishing, 1979. 152p. Bibl. Ports.   Smith compliments Murphy's moderate Unionist government that was formed as part of President Lincoln's Reconstruction policies in April, 1864.   Smith rejected Radical reform proposals, led an honest government, and sought to advance public education in the state.   His Unionism was rejected by conservatives and his moderate politics was rejected by the Radical Republicans. He stands in contrast to the destructive carpetbaggers who replaced him.

1533.   St. Hilaire, Joseph M.   "The Negro Delegates in the Arkansas
Constitutional Convention of 1868:   A Group Profile." *Arkansas Historical
Quarterly* 33 (Spring 1974): 38-69. Tbl.   There were eight black delegates at the
1868 constitutional convention. St. Hilaire examines their activities and concludes
that despite their lack of political experience, they performed well and showed
varied interests and skills.   An examination of 13 votes shows that with few
exceptions they voted Republican, but this did not mean that they supported only the
most radical positions even regarding black rights. This evidence contradicts the
negative description of black participants in the convention by historians William A.
Dunning and Thomas Staples.

1534.   Swinney, Everette.   "United States v. Powell Clayton."   *Arkansas
Historical Quarterly* 26 (Summer 1967): 143-154. Port.   The prosecution of Gov.
Powell Clayton by U.S. District Attorney William G. Whipple in 1871 is described
as one of the few uses of the Enforcement Acts passed by Congress in 1870 and
1871.   Clayton was accused of fraud by illegally manipulating the Congressional
election.   But Swinney believes that the case was politically motivated due to the
strong rivalry between Republican factions.   Clayton's victory against the
prosecution shows that the Enforcement Acts were not vigorously instituted in
Arkansas, partly because the Ku Klux Klan was no longer a factor after 1870 and
because political use of the law in fraud cases was discredited.

1535.   Thompson, George H. "Leadership in Arkansas Reconstruction." Ph.D.
Columbia University, 1968. 490p.

1536.   Thompson, George H.   "Reconstruction and the Loss of State Credit."
Arkansas Historical Quarterly 28 (Winter 1969): 293-308. Ports.   The expansion
of public debt has been viewed as illustrative of Republican malfeasance and
dishonesty, but Thompson believes that, in general, this was not the case. Gov.
Powell Clayton sought to improve the credit of the state and provide vital
improvements of natural resources and railroads. The fact that the debt program
failed does not necessarily reveal dishonesty, but the state's ability to develop its
resources certainly suffered for decades.

1537.   Westwood, Howard C. "The Federals' Cold Shoulder to Arkansas' Powell
Clayton." *Civil War History* 26 (September 1980): 240-255.   Clayton, a former
Union officer, became Republican governor on July 2, 1868 and set out to establish
order as the basis for economic development. The Ku Klux Klan jeopardized his
administration by terrorizing the state. When Clayton's call for federal military
power to eliminate the Klan was unsuccessful, he proclaimed martial law in every
county in 1869. Martial law embittered white conservative even more and destroyed
any chance for the success of the Republican Party in Arkansas.

1538.   Woodward, Earl F. "The Brooks and Baxter War in Arkansas, 1872-
1874." *Arkansas Historical Quarterly* 30 (Winter 1971): 315-336. Ills. Ports.
Woodward attributes the chaos and violence in the state elections of 1872 to the
wide breach in the state Republican Party that mirrored the regular Republican-

Liberal Republican split at the national level. Joseph Brooks, Liberal Republican candidate for governor, was closely associated with Democrats in the election. But it was Elisah Baxter, a regular Republican, who ultimately won with President Grant's help and led the state out of Reconstruction. His policies led to a new state constitution in 1874 and closer personal relations with Democrats following his support for enfranchising former Confederates and for legislation unfriendly to railroads.

1539.   Worley, Ted R.   (ed.).   "Letters to David Walker Relating to Reconstruction in Arkansas, 1866-1874." *Arkansas Historical Quarterly* 16 (Autumn 1957): 319-326.   Printed are letters from four correspondents to Judge David Walker. The letters are from supporters of the Democratic Party who remark about local and national Reconstruction issues, including *Ex parte* McCardle argued before the U.S. Supreme Court, the state constitution, the Democratic Party, the election of 1874, and the opinions expressed in the *Arkansas Gazette*. The four correspondents were Isaac Murphy, W. E. Woodruff, Jr., George S. Watkins, and T. M. Gunter.

Agriculture, Labor, and Business

1540.   Carmichael, Maude.   "Federal Experiments With Negro Labor in Abandoned Plantations in Arkansas: 1862-1865." *Arkansas Historical Quarterly* 1 (June 1942): 101-116.   Carmichael describes the U.S. Army's program to organize black refugees as laborers and leasees to work on the land. This successful program in Arkansas taught federal authorities that blacks wanted to be free and that they could and would work. He credits the work of Maj. Gen. Lorenzo Thomas and Maj. W. G. Sargent. The program was a precursor to the Freedmen's Bureau that built on what was learned about the freedmen during the war.

1541.   Carmichael, Maude.   "The Plantation System in Arkansas, 1850-1876." Ph.D. Radcliffe College, 1935.

1542.   Lovett, Bobby L.   "Some 1871 Accounts For the Little Rock, Arkansas Freedmen's Savings and Trust Company." *Journal of Negro History* 66 (Winter 1981-82): 326-328.   The bank records of the Little Rock branch of the Freedmen's Savings and Trust Co.   (June, 1870-July, 1874) offer information about the socioeconomic activities of blacks during Reconstruction.   Lovett used account application cards to reveal that blacks owned many businesses or were employed in a variety of occupations owned by blacks and whites.

1543.   Moneyhon, Carl H.   "From Slave to Free Labor: The Federal Plantation Experience in Arkansas." *Arkansas Historical Quarterly* 53 (Summer 1994): 137-160. Map.   The wartime experiment to provide labor for freedmen near Helena, Arkansas involved labor contracts with whites who leased plantations. Federal authorities, whether it was the Army, the Treasury Department, or the Freedmen's

Bureau, wanted to provide a basis for order among the freedmen who left their homes to seek freedom among the Northern Army as well as a foundation on which the former slaves could learn the responsibilities of freedom. Moneyhon describes how the difficulties encountered by the freedmen generated mostly distrust in the contract labor system and little economic independence.

1544.   Moneyhon, Carl H. "The Impact of the Civil War in Arkansas: The Mississippi River Plantation Counties." *Arkansas Historical Quarterly* 51 (Summer 1992): 105-118.   Moneyhon examines the impact of the Civil War on Chicot and Phillips Counties to test theories about planter class persistence from antebellum to postbellum periods. He finds that the higher the class status the greater the chances that people were able to hold on to their economic and social position. Even though rich planters lost wealth in the form of slaves, live stock or other materials, they held on to their land and had a basis to persist in the postwar years. Moneyhon suggests that the elite planter class maintained their position, but he also describes the devastating impact of the war on lower classes.

1545.   Watkins, Beverly. "Efforts to Encourage Immigration to Arkansas, 1865-1874." *Arkansas Historical Quarterly* 38 (Spring 1979): 32-62.   In an effort to rebuild the state economy Unionist leaders wanted to attract more people to the state to fill labor shortages following emancipation. The Arkansas Immigrant Aid Society (1865) and the German Immigrant Aid Society (1867) were formed to promote and assist new immigrants, and in 1868 Gov. Powell Clayton signed a bill creating a state commissioner of immigration. Despite various efforts only a few thousand immigrants arrived. Watkins demonstrates that political chaos in the state during the postwar years hurt efforts to encourage immigration. Even so, the state population increased dramatically between 1860 and 1880 due to migration from other parts of the U.S.

1546.   Worley, Ted. R. (ed.). "Tenant and Labor Contracts, Calhoun County, 1869-1871." *Arkansas Historical Quarterly* 13 (Spring 1954): 102-106.   Worley prints three contracts between tenants, laborers and landowner John C. Barrow.

Society, Education, and Religion

1547.   Boyett, Gene W.   "The Black Experience in the First Decade of Reconstruction in Pope County, Arkansas." *Arkansas Historical Quarterly* 51 (Summer 1992): 119-134.   Boyett surveys Reconstruction in a region of Arkansas outside of urban areas and counties in which large numbers of freedmen lived. Pope County in northwestern, rural Arkansas was the scene of important changes as a result of emancipation and Republican government. He discusses population trends, sharecropping, race relations, and education. The upland experience must be part of an overall view of Reconstruction.

1548.   Finley, Randy. *From Slavery to Uncertain Freedom: The Freedmen's Bureau in Arkansas, 1865-1869.* Fayetteville: University of Arkansas Press, 1996. 229p. Bibl. Maps. Tbls.   Finley concentrates on the role of the bureau in the transition to the new realities of the postwar years. He is concerned with how blacks established a new identity in freedom and sought to express that freedom through economic opportunity, education, self help, the establishment of new churches, protection of oneself and family, and a new relationship with whites. The bureau played a positive role in this process through support, guidance, sympathy, and extending the authority of the federal government. Blacks had much control over their own lives, but the bureau helped make life better. (See also Finley's "The Freedmen's Bureau in Arkansas." Ph.D. University of Arkansas, 1992. 559p.)

1549.   Finley, Randy. "In War's Wake: Health Care and Arkansas Freedmen, 1863-1868." *Arkansas Historical Quarterly* 51 (Summer 1992): 135-163. Ill. Tbls.   Finley defines the health care challenges faced by freedmen in Arkansas from the time of their emancipation until the Freedmen's Bureau began to lose its funding in 1867. With the freedmen having little or no means to care for themselves when sick and with deteriorating health conditions during and after the war, the Army and later the bureau coordinated medical care in clinics and hospitals that barely met the rudiments of health care. Findley discusses the cultural problems involved in understanding disease differences and treatments between whites and blacks, difficulties providing doctors, and the maintenance of healthy conditions so that disease could be avoided. He also notes the assistance given by white planters to the health of the freedmen.

1550.   Gerstacker, Frederick. "Arkansas After the War: From the Journal of Frederick Gerstacker." Trans. and edited by Anita and Evan Burr Burey. *Arkansas Historical Quarterly* 32 (Autumn 1973): 255-273. Port.   Gerstacker was a German writer who visited Arkansas and other places in the U.S. in 1867. He comments on his experiences in the state and the mood of people during the first year of Radical Reconstruction. The comments were later published in his book, *Neue Reisen durch die Vereinigten Staaten, Mexiko, Ecuador, West Indien und Venezuela* (Jena: H. Costenoble, 1868). His comments mainly describe the hardships of the time.

1551.   Graves, John Williams. "Town and Country: Race Relations and Urban Development in Arkansas, 1865-1905." Ph.D. University of Virginia, 1978. 448p.

1552.   Greenstreet, Terri. "Reconstruction in Izard County." *Izard County Historian* 14 (October 1983): 17-26.   Greenstreet describes the frequent violence that occurred in Izard County located in the hill country of northern Arkansas. The Freedmen's Bureau was unable to cope with the lawlessness, much of which was blamed on carpetbaggers and the state militia. Greenstreet also describes the state of education in the county from 1866 to 1868.

1553.   Gwaltney, Francis Irby. "A Survey of Historic Washington, Arkansas - Washington in Reconstruction." *Arkansas Historical Quarterly* 17 (Winter 1958):

386-392.   In this brief account of early Reconstruction in Washington, Arkansas, the main emphasis is placed on the transition of blacks from slavery to freedom and the role of the Freedmen's Bureau in caring for the interests of the freedmen. Gwaltney is also concerned with the activities and comments of John Eaton, who edited the *Washington Telegraph* during and after the war and was a member of the state legislature beginning in 1866 and the constitutional convention of 1874.

1554.   Hobby, Selma P. "The Little Rock Public Schools During Reconstruction, 1865-1874." Ed.D. University of Arkansas, 1967. 166p.

1555.   Kennan, Clara B.   "Dr. Thomas Smith, Forgotten Man of Arkansas Education." *Arkansas Historical Quarterly* 20 (Winter 1961): 303-317.   Kennan describes the achievements of Pennsylvania native Thomas Smith who came to Arkansas in 1864 as a physician.   Smith became a central figure in instituting tax supported public schools as a member of the 1868 constitutional convention and as the first elected state superintendent of education.   He was also a founder of the University of Arkansas.   After his defeat for reelection in 1872 at the hands of a Claytonite Republican and the return of power to conservatives, the constitution was rewritten in 1874 and the educational system deteriorated.

1556.   Kennedy, Thomas C. "The Rise and Decline of a Black Monthly Meeting: Southland, Arkansas, 1864-1925." *Arkansas Historical Quarterly* 50 (Summer 1991): 115-139. Ports. Ill.   When Clavin and Alida Clark were sent to Helena, Arkansas to establish an orphanage for black children in 1864, they brought with them their traditional Quaker convictions and the ideals of the "renewal movement." This movement included a new, active approach to proselytizing that led to the conversion of freedmen in Southland where the Quakers established a school in 1866.   The Clarks and other Quaker leaders sought to reform the behavior of freedmen to conform with Quaker teachings regarding abstinence from drinking alcohol, ways of speech, and appropriate reading materials. (See also # 1557)

1557.   Kennedy, Thomas C. "Southland College: The Society of Friends and Black Education in Arkansas." *Arkansas Historical Quarterly* 42 (Autumn 1983): 207-238. Ills. Tbls.   In April, 1864 Quakers from Indiana arrived in Helena, Arkansas to establish an orphanage for children of slaves. The Friends' Freedmen Committee combined its efforts with the Freedmen's Bureau to run the orphanage until 1866 when land was purchased and a new building constructed that eventually became known as Southland College in 1876. Throughout this period the orphanage and school were under the direction of Calvin and Alida Clark of Wayne County, Indiana. Kennedy tells the history of the school until it closed in 1925. (See also # 1556)

1558.   Lovett, Bobby L.   "African Americans, Civil War, and Aftermath in Arkansas." *Arkansas Historical Quarterly* 54 (Autumn 1995): 304-358.   Lovett emphasizes the participation of freedmen in the victory of the Union Army in Arkansas and other areas of the South as well as their role in the changes that took place after the war ended.   During Reconstruction they took part in Republican politics, reformed their churches, and initiated education with the assistance of the Freedmen's Bureau and Northern missionary societies. Lovett also emphasizes the many problems in race relations and the weakness in economic independence among freedmen that persisted well into the 20th century. He lists units of U.S. black troops that wholly or partly served in Arkansas.

1559.　Nash, Horace D.　"Blacks in Arkansas During Reconstruction: The Ex-Slave Narratives." *Arkansas Historical Quarterly* 48 (Autumn 1989): 243-254. Nash reviews the transition from slavery to freedom in Arkansas based on Works Project Administration interviews with ex-slaves. He is mainly concerned with immigration to Arkansas from other states, the Ku Klux Klan, and education. He concludes that the interviews are a rich source for researching slavery and Reconstruction.

1560.　Newberry, Farrar.　"The Yankee Schoolmarm Who 'Captured' Post-War Arkadelphia." *Arkansas Historical Quarterly* 17 (Autumn, 1958): 265-271. Newberry describes the successful teaching career of Mary Connelly, a native of Newberry, New York, who taught in Camden, Arkansas before the war and later in Arkadelphia until the end of Reconstruction. She was involved with establishing a school, teaching in the Presbyterian Church and organizing Arkadelphia's first library. She left the state in 1876.

1561.　Pearce, Larry Wesley.　"Enoch K. Miller and the Freedmen's Bureau." *Arkansas Historical Quarterly* 31 (Winter 1972): 305-327. Port.　Miller, a former Union soldier and chaplain, came to Arkansas in January, 1867 as a missionary for the American Missionary Association and as an assistant superintendent of education for the Freedmen's Bureau. He organized schools and emphasized training black teachers and administrators to manage their own schools. Pine Bluff was the center of his activities and was the location of a future normal school for teacher training.

1562.　Pearce, Larry Wesley.　"The American Missionary Association and the Freedmen in Arkansas, 1863-1878." *Arkansas Historical Quarterly* 30 (Summer 1971): 123-144; "The American Missionary Association and the Freedmen in Arkansas, 1866-1868." 30 (Autumn 1971): 242-259; The American Missionary Association and the Freedmen in Arkansas, 1868-1878." 31 (Autumn 1972): 246-261.　In a series of articles taken from his honors college thesis, Pearce describes the work of the A.M.A. and the Freedmen's Bureau to provide schools and teachers for the freedmen from the time of the Union Army occupation of the state until after Reconstruction. Pearce tells a story of struggle and adjustment for the teachers who had to cope with racial conflict, and constant financial difficulties with organizing and maintaining schools. He emphasizes the work of William Colby, the bureau's general superintendent of schools in Arkansas, his assistant, A.M.A. missionary Enoch K. Miller, and many A.M.A. teachers. The A.M.A. discontinued activities in the state in 1878.

1563.   Richards, Ira Don. "Little Rock on the Road to Reunion, 1865-1880."
Arkansas Historical Quarterly 25 (Winter 1966): 312-335. Ills.   Richards offers a
narrative of Little Rock history during the postwar years with an emphasis on city
politics, business and economics, railroads, social life, and education. The city did
not experience substantial damage during the war. He characterizes the postwar
years as a time of social and economic readjustment and growth, despite the political
mishandling of city affairs by both local Republican and Democratic
administrations.

1564.   Richter, William L. "'A Dear Little Job' Second Lt. Hiram F. Willis,
Freedmen's Bureau Agent in Southwestern Arkansas, 1866-1868." *Arkansas
Historical Quarterly* 50 (Summer 1991): 158-200.   Richter describes Willis'
activities to help the freedmen in and around Sevier County, particularly with
contract disputes, family issues, and responding to violence and intimidation from
local whites. Willis's work was made difficult by unruly soldiers and the natural
inclination of local whites to resent any outside interference in the county. He was
murdered on October 24, 1868.

1565.   Rothrock, Thomas. "Joseph Carter Corbin and Negro Education in the
University of Arkansas." *Arkansas Historical Quarterly* 30 (Winter 1971): 277-
314.   Rothrock examines Corbin's entire career as a leader in black education in
Arkansas beginning with his arrival in the state in 1872. During the last years of
Reconstruction in the state, the Ohio native edited the *Daily Republican* and won
election in 1872 to the post of superintendent of public instruction as a Claytonite
Republican. As *ex officio* president of the Arkansas Industrial University (i.e.
University of Arkansas) in Fayetteville, he successfully pushed for support of
legislation to fund a normal college for black students in Pine Bluff. Corbin became
the first principal of the college in 1875, and the rest of his career revolved around
his work for the college.

Delaware

1566.   Gauger, John H.   "A Delaware Experiment With Reconstruction
Nullification." *Delaware History* 21 (Spring-Summer 1985): 164-185.   Gauger
describes public opinion and the legislative background to the General Assembly's
nullification of the national Civil Rights Act of 1875. Democrats dominated state
politics, and they rejected racial equality in public places and what they considered
to be a Republican ploy to gain political advantages. The nullification law remained
in the state statutes until a U.S. Supreme Court decision in 1961.

1567.   Hancock, Harold B.   "Reconstruction in Delaware." In *Radicalism,
Racism, and Party Realignment, the Border States During Reconstruction*. Edited
by R. O. Curry. Baltimore: Johns Hopkins Press, 1969. Pp. 188-219. Map.
Hancock examines the economic and political situation in Delaware after the Civil
War with particular focus on the struggle of black citizens to attain equal civil rights.

The racism in the white population and the continuous domination of state politics by the Democrats since the 1850s made for a slow and difficult transition in a state that was more southern than northern in character. The end of the war brought new economic opportunities for blacks and whites in Delaware in both rural and urban settings, and the state was unencumbered by military occupation or political turmoil and violence.

1568.   Hancock, Harold B.   "The Status of the Negro in Delaware During the Civil War, 1865-1875." *Delaware History* 8 (1968-1969): 57-66.   Democrats dominated politics in Delaware during the decade after the Civil War.   Slaveholders and supporters of states' rights prompted the General Assembly to reject the 13th Amendment as well as the 14th and 15th Amendments.   Democrats rejected any notion that blacks could be equal citizens with whites and many Republicans agreed. Despite laws granting blacks citizenship and civil rights, Democrats effectively excluded most blacks from voting, and racial descrimination in employment and the use of public places pervaded the state.

Florida

General History

1569.   Davis, William Watson.   *The Civil War and Reconstruction in Florida.* Ph.D.   Columbia University, 1913.   747p.   (Rpt. Ph.D. dissertation, Columbia University, 1913; Gainesville: University of Florida Press, 1964. Introduction by Fletcher Green)   Davis' dissertation has been a key source for the history of Florida during Reconstruction. Some of his opinions on specific issues are more moderate than other historians at the time and closer to the revisionists of later years, such as his description of good and bad carpetbaggers, but he sympathizes with white Southerners' anxiety about black voter domination and their opposition to forced change. In the facsimile reprint Green discusses Davis' book as it relates to Dunning and revisionist historiography.

1570.   Parks, Albert Stanley.   "The Negro in the Reconstruction of Florida." *Quarterly Journal, Florida Agricultural and Mechanical University, Tallahassee* 6, 4 (1936): 35-61.   In this brief survey of the role of blacks in postwar Florida from 1865 to 1877, Parks reveals his conservative sympathies regarding the capabilities and needs of blacks as citizens and Republican politics in the state, but he also discusses black initiatives in religious organization and in education. He touches on labor relations, as well as the role of the Freedmen's Bureau and the influence of the Ku Klux Klan.

1571.   Richardson, Joe Martin.   *The Negro in the Reconstruction of Florida 1865-1877.* Tallahassee: Florida State University, 1965. 255p. Bibl. (*Florida State University Studies*, 46)   In his examination of the role of blacks in postwar Florida, Richardson reviews their adjustment to freedom and their participation in politics, labor, agriculture, religion and education. He is generally positive about the benefits of Reconstruction based on the progress of black citizens in acquiring property, organizing schools and churches, and through participation in local, state, and national government. The tone of Reconstruction politics in Florida was moderate process, and positive contributions were made by blacks and Republicans in government reform. (See also Richardson's Ph.D. dissertation with the same title from Florida State University, 1964.)

1572.   Shofner, Jerrell H.   *Nor is it Over Yet: Florida in the Era of Reconstruction, 1863-1877.*   Gainesville: University Presses of Florida, 1974. 412p. Bibl.   Shofner seeks to correct the misinterpretations of earlier writers on Reconstruction in Florida, particularly the work of William Watson Davis (see # 1569) whose bias in favor of white supremacy marred a well researched work. Shofner emphasizes political, social, and economic developments.   Important to understanding of Reconstruction in Florida are the political advantages that allowed conservatives to gain influence, such as the factions within the Republican Party. Traditional critics of Republican misrule overlook the significant economic development and conservative financial policies of the government.

Politics and Law

1573.   Beatty, Bess.   "John Willis Menard: A Progressive Black in Post-Civil War Florida." *Florida Historical Quarterly* 59 (October 1980): 123-143.   While residing in Louisiana, Menard became the first black man to be elected to the U.S. House of Representatives, although he was never seated.   When he arrived in Florida in 1871 his leadership skills, education, and political experiences made him an important grassroots figure in the state during Reconstruction and subsequent years. Menard was a moderate Republican who worked for racial harmony, and he criticized carpetbaggers and scalawags for their racism.   Eventually he rejected white racism in the political parties and considered organizing an independent party.

1574.   Bentley, George R.   "The Political Activity of the Freedmen's Bureau in Florida." *Florida Historical Quarterly* 28 (July 1949): 28-37.   Col. Thomas W. Osborn took command of the Florida bureau in September, 1865 and quickly gained the confidence of local conservatives for his ability to work with white authorities and his strict disciplinary actions against freedmen prior to their enfranchisement. But Osburn and other assistant commissioners after him gained influence in the Republican Party and helped secure for the party the support of blacks.

1575.   Brown, Canter, Jr.   *Florida's Black Public Officials, 1867-1924.* Tuscaloosa: University of Alabama Press, 1998. 252p. App. Bibl.   Brown provides a brief narrative describing the participation of Florida blacks in public office followed by a directory with biographical sketches of individuals.   An appendix lists the individuals by offices held, and by county and office.   Brown emphasizes that his work illustrates that blacks sought and participated in political life in Florida to a greater extent than has been understood.

1576.   Brown, Canter, Jr.   *Ossian Bingley Hart: Florida's Loyalist Reconstruction Governor.* Baton Rouge: Louisiana State University Press, 1997. 320p. Bibl. Ports.   Brown tries to pull Hart out of historical obscurity with this laudatory biography of a man who was a prewar member of the Know-Nothing Party and a strong Unionist during the war. In March, 1867 he organized the state Republican Party, and he later became a justice in the state Supreme Court (1868-1873), U.S. senator (1870-1874), and governor in early 1874. Brown emphasizes Hart's role in Reconstruction politics, particularly his support for black civil rights and his high reputation for honesty and sincerity in his public activities. (See also Brown's Ph.D. dissertation with the same title from Florida State University, 1994.)

1577.   Brown, Canter, Jr. "'Where are now the hopes I cherished?' The Life and Times of Robert Meacham." *Florida Historical Quarterly* 69 (July 1990): 1-36. Meacham defeats the traditional white Southern stereotype of the ignorant, corrupt black in Southern politics during Reconstruction. The Gadsden County, Florida native became a minister in the African Methodist Episcopal Church, participated in the constitutional convention of 1868, and won election to the state legislature. He lost political influence after the Democrats' return to power, but continued as a clergy in the A.M.E. Church.

1578.   Carson, Ruby Leach. "William Dunnington Bloxham: The Years to the Governorship." *Florida Historical Quarterly*   27 (January 1949): 205-236. Bloxham, a wealthy planter from Leon County before the war, organized Democrats for elections during postwar years and was, himself, nominated and lost an election for Lt. Governor in 1870. His defeat was attributed to Republican fraud and the election was reversed after an appeal in 1872. He continued to work for other Democratic candidates, and enhanced his reputation as an orator and leader. In 1880 Bloxham won the gubernatorial election.

1579.   Clark, James C.   "John Wallace and the Writing of Reconstruction History." *Florida Historical Quarterly* 67 (April 1989): 409-427.   Wallace was a former slave who served in the Union Army. In 1866 he worked as a teacher on the Florida plantation of William D. Bloxham, and in 1868 he entered politics. Through his experience as a state legislator (1870-1874) and senator (1874-1878), he developed a strong distrust for many Republicans, both white and black. Frequently he voted with the Democrats on key issues. In 1888 he published a book on Reconstruction in Florida (see # 1616) that may have been written to influence the 1888 gubernatorial campaign.

1580.   DeCoursey, Irene A. "Two Leaders in Florida." *Negro History Bulletin* 5 (March 1942): 131. Ports.   DeCoursey sketches the lives of Jonathan C. Gibbs (state senator, state superintendent of public instruction) and Josiah T. Walls (state legislator, U.S. congressman in 1872).

1581.   Ewing, Cortez. Florida Reconstruction Impeachments." *Florida Historical Quarterly* 30, 4 (1958): 299-318.   Ewing examines the impeachment of Gov. Harrison Reed and Judge James T. Magbee. Reed, governor from 1868 to 1872, angered many Republicans by appointing secessionist Democrats to office and vetoing legislation. Four attempts to remove him from office for corruption were unsuccessful. Magbee, a supporter of Reed's Republican faction, was charged with corruption and malpractice by the legislature, but his impeachment was eventually dropped due to delays and Reed's increasing influence among legislators.

1582.   Flory, Claude R. "Marcellus L. Stearns: Florida's Last Reconstruction Governor." *Florida Historical Quarterly* 44 (January 1966): 181-192.   Flory provides a brief biographical sketch of Stearns with particular emphasis on his time in Florida from 1867 to 1878. The Maine native came to Florida as an agent of the Freedmen's Bureau in Quincy and became involved in Republican politics in various elected posts, including governor in 1874. Flory compliments Stearns contributions to educating the freedmen, and disputes John Wallace's charges of corruption against him (see # 1616).

1583.   Fryman, Mildred. "Career of a 'Carpetbagger': Malachi Martin in Florida." *Florida Historical Quarterly* 56 (January 1978): 317-338.   Martin fought with the Union Army and then served with the federal occupation forces in Tallahassee in the summer of 1865. In 1866 he resigned from the military and became involved with farming, Republican politics, and prison management. Allegations that he was a cruel prison manager have not been convincingly documented. While Martin sought personal gain in Florida, he also made positive contributions that received little recognition due to his image as a carpetbagger.

1584.   Gilliam, Farley M. "The 'Black Codes' of Florida." *Apalachee* 6 (1963-1967): 111-120.   The black codes of Florida severely restricted the civil rights of blacks. The basis of the laws were white racism and the belief that blacks would not work and were unprepared for citizenship. The laws were only effective from early 1866 until the spring of 1867, but they influenced state law for many years.

1585.   Hume, Richard L. Membership of the Florida Constitutional Convention of 1868: A Case Study of Republican Factionalism in the Reconstruction South." *Florida Historical Quarterly* 51 (July 1972): 1-22.   The bitter factions and final result of the Florida constitutional convention of 1868 set it apart from other Southern conventions during Reconstruction. Hume offers a detailed examination of the delegates attending the convention held in Tallahassee managed by Radical Republicans Liberty Billings and William Saunders ("mule team") and the splinter convention of moderate and conservative Republicans that first met at Monticello before rejoining and overpowering the Radicals. The factions permanently weakened the Republican Party in Florida. An alphabetical list of delegates is provided with race, votes on key issues, and political classification.

1586.   Jackson, Jesse Jefferson. "Republicans and Florida Elections and Election Cases, 1877-1891." Ph.D. Florida State University, 1974. 355p.

1587.   Klingman, Peter D. *Josiah Walls: Florida Black Congressman of Reconstruction.* Gainesville: University Presses of Florida, 1976. 157p. Bibl. Walls, originally a slave in Virginia, served in the Union Army and became an important political figure during Florida's Reconstruction as a state senator and U.S. congressman who fought for civil and economic rights for blacks as well as public improvements.   Klingman's biographical work offers a good overview of Reconstruction politics in Florida.

1588.   Klingman, Peter D. "Race and Faction in the Public Career of Florida's Josiah T. Walls." In *Southern Black Leaders of the Reconstruction Era.* Edited by Howard Rabinowitz. Urbana: University of Illinois Press, 1982. Pp. 59-78. Port. Kingman describes the political career of Walls, a former black officer in the Union Army, who stayed in Florida after the war and built a political force in Alachua County. Walls served two terms in Congress beginning in 1870, but his career as a black Republican was stymied by the divisions within the party and the party's domination by whites. (See also Klingman's "Josiah T. Walls and the Black Tactics of Race in Post Reconstruction Florida." *Negro History Bulletin* 37 (April/May 1974): 242-247.)

1589.   Klingman, Peter D. "Rascal or Representative? Joe Oats of Tallahassee and the 'Election of 1866'." *Florida Historical Quarterly* 51 (July 1972): 52-57. Oats was sent to Washington to represent Leon County at the National Negro Congress of 1866.   Critics accuse Oats of squandering his travel funds, but Klingman corrects this percpetion, at least in part, by demonstrating that Oats did attend the congress and was among a group that met with President Johnson about renewing the Freedmen's Bureau.

1590.   Manley, Walter W., II (ed.). *The Supreme Court of Florida and its Predecessor Court, 1821-1917.* Gainesville: University Presses of Florida, 1997. 454p. Ports.   Part 3 (pp. 187-258) focuses on the Civil War and Reconstruction. The outstanding features of the court during this period were its stability, the progressively stronger image it gained during Reconstruction, and its ability to concentrate on legal, rather than political issues. Biographies of chief justices are included.

1591.   Meador, John A., Jr. "Florida Political Parties, 1865-1877."   Ph.D. University of Florida, 1964. 280p.

1592.   "Notes on Reconstruction in Tallahassee and Leon County." *Florida Historical Society, Quarterly* 5 (January 1927): 153-158.   This unsigned article provides brief information about the perspective of Conservatives in Leon County. Due to the black voter majority in the region, Conservatives had little influence until their victory in 1876, but they did organize the Constitutional Union Club in 1868 and later a Reform Club in 1876.   Reconstruction was considered to be a dark time for the city and county.

1593.   Osborn, George C. (ed.). "Letters of a Carpetbagger in Florida, 1866-1869." *Florida Historical Quarterly* 36, 3 (1958): 239-285.   Thirty letters are printed that were written by Daniel Richards, a native of Illinois, to his close friend Elihu B. Washburne, who served in the U.S. House of Representative from the same state. Richards went to Florida as a tax collector, but in 1867 he agreed to help the Republican national committee organize the state Republican Party. Washburne chaired a Congressional committee investigating political conditions in Florida, Louisiana and Texas. The letters illustrate Richards' impressions of the political and racial problems besetting the state.

1594.   Peek, Ralph L.   "Aftermath of Military Reconstruction, 1868-1869." *Florida Historical Quarterly* 43 (October 1964): 123-141.   Florida's new constitution and the installation of the Republican state government in 1868 provoked acts of violence by staunch conservatives who opposed equal rights for blacks and the domination of the Republican Party in state and local politics. Assistance from the U.S. Army was requested even as troops were being withdrawn from the state or to strategic areas by the end of the year. The end of military Reconstruction seemed to be a signal to many conservatives that violence and intimidation could be exercised as a tool to return the Democrats to power and eliminate blacks as a political force in the state.

1595.   Peek, Ralph L. "Curbing Voter Intimidation in Florida, 1871." *Florida Historical Quarterly* 43 (April 1965): 333-348.   The Grant administration responded to widespread intimidation of black voters by white Democrats in the South by enacting the Enforcement Acts of 1870-71. Democrats in Florida reacted to the new laws with outrage and accused the federal government of violating states' rights and democratic government. The laws probably helped reelect Republican state governments in 1870 and 1872 by slim margins.

1596.   Peek, Ralph L. "Election of 1870 and the End of Reconstruction in Florida." *Florida Historical Quarterly* 45 (April 1967): 352-268.   Democrat William D. Bloxham won the election for lieutenant governor in 1870 after an appeal to the state supreme court in 1872. The closeness of the election and the ruling in favor of Bloxham represent the resurgence of the Democratic Party in Florida. Republicans were totally dependent on black votes, but blacks were subject to white violence and intimidation in counties with black voter majorities. Even though moderate Republicans won the legislature in 1872, they abandoned the freedmen in favor of accommodation with white conservatives. Both Republicans and Democrats share the blame for misrule during Reconstruction.

1597.   Peek, Ralph L. "Lawlessness and the Restoration of Order in Florida, 1868-1871." Ph.D. University of Florida, 1964. 231p.

1598.   Peek, Ralph L. "Lawlessness in Florida, 1868-1871." *Florida Historical Quarterly* 40 (October 1961): 164-185.   Peek offers an account of the violence against blacks and Republicans in northcentral and northern counties of Florida. He concludes that young, upper class men usually carried out acts of violence with the intention of defeating the Republican governments and stopping black domination and their practice of civil rights. There is no evidence that the Ku Klux Klan existed in Florida, but a similar organization, the Young Men's Democratic Clubs, was active. When white violence finally subsided after the Enforcement Act of 1871, white power throughout most of Florida was nearing victory.

1599.   Peek, Ralph L. "Military Reconstruction and the Growth of Anti-Negro Sentiment in Florida, 1867." *Florida Historical Quarterly* 47 (April 1969): 380-400. Military Reconstruction shifted power to the Republicans and their black supporters and enraged white conservatives. They responded with increasing violence and resistance against the blacks and white Republicans, particularly after the formation of the new government in July, 1868. Even moderate Republicans did not support black equal rights. The moderates controlled state politics without support from most black citizens.

1600.   Poyo, Gerald G.   "Cuban Revolutionaries and Monroe County Reconstruction Politics 1868-1876." *Florida Historical Quarterly* 55 (April 1977): 407-422.   Cuban refugees from the revolution in Cuba opposed slavery and naturally supported the Republicans with a bloc vote that helped the party win elections in Key West and Monroe County. But the Grant administration's refusal to get deeply involved in Cuba led to defections to the Democrats, and the Republicans lost political power in the county. The Cubans sought a new strategy to assist the revolution in Cuba.

1601.   "Quincy Conservative Convention." *Florida Historical Quarterly* 18 (January 1940): 267-269.   The Conference of Conservatives held March 31, 1868 at Quincy, Florida was attended by representatives from western Florida counties for the purpose of opposing the Republican constitution and nominating a slate of Conservatives for state and Congressional offices. Receiving the nomination for governor was Col. George W. Scott, a native of Pennsylvania, who moved to Florida in 1850. The article lists the names of persons nominated as delegates to the National Democratic Convention.

1602.   Richardson, Joe M. "Florida Black Codes." *Florida Historical Quarterly* 47 (April 1969): 365-379.   The black code in Florida was among the most severe of the codes enacted in the South. Richardson attributes this to the attitude of white Floridians who did not experience significant destruction in their state during the war and attempted to return the state to prewar conditions as closely as they could. Prior to the Reconstruction Acts of 1867 the state legislature refused to modify the black code, despite negative Northern opinion and the work of the Freedmen's Bureau to uphold equal civil rights for the freedmen.

1603.   Richardson, Joe M. "Jonathan C. Gibbs: Florida's Only Negro Cabinet Member." *Florida Historical Quarterly* 42 (April 1964): 363-368.   Gibbs was a shining example of the many capable black men who participated in Florida's Reconstruction government.   The well educated Presbyterian minister from Philadelphia received a church appointment in Florida in 1867 and later served as a delegate at the constitutional convention in 1868, secretary of state under Gov. Harrison Reed, and superintendent of public instruction under Gov. Ossian B. Hart.

1604.   Russ, William A., Jr.   "Disfranchisement in Florida During Radical Reconstruction." *Susquehanna University Studies* 4 (March 1950): 162-181. Russ describes the debate over disenfranchisement in Florida's constitutional convention of 1868 as mainly between vindictive Radicals and moderate Republicans. The moderates won by aligning disenfranchisement closely with the restrictions in the 14th Amendment. This was enough to satisfy Congress. Even with disenfranchisement, whites held a majority in Florida, but the gerrymandering of districts led to the election of blacks and other Republicans to the legislature. Significant disenfranchisement was never achieved, partly with the cooperation of the Federal Army.

1605.   Shofner, Jerrell H.   "Andrew Johnson and the Fernandina Unionists." *Prologue* 10 (Winter 1978): 211-223. Ill. Ports.   Shofner focuses on the controversies surrounding the federal confiscation of land in Fernandina based on nonpayment of property taxes. Emotions ran high when President Johnson favored the return of confiscated land to its prewar owners, but much of the land had already been purchased. Individuals and the Florida Railroad Co. succeeded in regaining most of the land. This alienated white Unionists and disregarded the economic needs of the freedmen. Property rights took precedence in Congress, which eventually reimbursed prewar property owners for land not returned.

1606.   Shofner, Jerrell H.   "The Constitution of 1868." *Florida Historical Quarterly* 41 (April 1963): 356-374.   The path to the constitution was confused by the split between moderate and radical Republicans over political rights for certain groups of whites and the distribution of power in the state. Two conventions were held, the moderate one led by Freedmen's Bureau Assistant Commissioner George C. Osburn that resulted in the Monticello Constitution, and the radical one led by carpetbaggers Daniel Richards and Liberty Billings that produced another document. Congress favored the moderate document, and moderates won the subsequent elections with the support of many white Floridians. To say that Florida was ruled by Radical Republicans would be a gross exaggeration.

1607.   Shofner, Jerrell H.   "Custom, Law, and History: The Enduring Influence of Florida's 'Black Code,'" *Florida Historical Quarterly* 55 (January 1977): 277-298.   Reconstruction in Florida was marked by the struggle to make custom and law consistent with regard to race relations. The provisional government after the Civil War enacted black codes to place freedmen in nearly the same economic and social environment that existed prior to the war. Even with the Republican regime the overwhelming predominance of white supremacists made black civil rights difficult to enforce. Shofner describes how the black codes were used as the basis of future laws that bound blacks to an existence of dependence, subjugation, and white violence until the second half of the 20th century.

1608.   Shofner, Jerrell H. "Florida: A Failure of Moderate Republicanism." In *Reconstruction and Redemption in the South.* Edited by Otto Olsen. Baton Rouge: Louisiana State University Press, 1980. Pp. 13-46. Bibl.   White Republican moderates who controlled state government frequently agreed with Conservative-Democrats about policy issues. Moderates, led by Governors Harrison Reed (1868-1872) and Ossian B. Hart (1872-1876), reached an accommodation with Democrats. Republicans failed in Florida because of fundamental disagreements between moderates and Radicals and the federal government's inability to enforce the Reconstruction Acts in the state. Blacks participated in politics and enjoyed new freedoms, but their desire for civil rights was never seriously supported by moderate Republicans.

1609.   Shofner, Jerrell H. "Florida Courts and the Disputed Election of 1876." *Florida Historical Quarterly* 48 (July 1969): 26-46.   The disputed election in Florida included the gubernatorial election as well as the presidential election. Republicans and Democrats opposed each other in state courts over the lawfulness and validity of State Canvassing Board rulings that ultimately resulted in the election of Democrat George F. Drew.

1610.   Shofner, Jerrell H. "Florida in the Balance: The Electoral Count of 1876." *Florida Historical Quarterly* 47 (October 1968): 122-150.   Shofner describes the closeness of the election in the state and the legal battles over possible fraudulent results from various counties. The canvassing board, dominated by Republicans, awarded the governor's office to the Democratic candidate, but then decided, incorrectly according to Shofner, in favor of Republican presidential candidate Rutherford B. Hayes.

1611.   Shofner, Jerrell H. "Florida's Political Reconstruction and the Presidential Election of 1876." Ph.D. Florida State University, 1963. 386p.

1612.   Shofner, Jerrell H. "Fraud and Intimidation in the Florida Election of 1876." *Florida Historical Quarterly* 42 (April 1964): 321-330.   Shofner provides a brief account of the tensions between Republicans and Democrats prior to the election as well as charges of fraud in voting and vote counting. There was no question that the Democratic candidate for governor, George F. Drew, was elected, partly with the support of wealthy Republicans, but the election for President was a different matter. The Republican dominated canvassing board changed the outcome in favor of Rutherford B. Hayes instead of Samuel J. Tilden. It was the canvassing board, rather than fraud and intimidation, which most influenced the outcome.

1613.   Shofner, Jerrell H. "A New Jersey Carpetbagger in Reconstruction Florida." *Florida Historical Quarterly* 52 (January 1974): 286-293.   Captain George B. Carse of New Jersey was an example of a highly respected Northerner in Florida who does not fit the traditional stereotype of the plundering carpetbagger. He came to Florida in 1867 as an agent for the Freedmen's Bureau and was known for his fairness and judgment. His involvement in the Republican administration of Gov. Harrison Reed led to accusations against him from Republican opponents.

When Carse left Florida in 1870 he received many kind words from white conservatives.

1614.   Shofner, Jerrell H. "Political Reconstruction in Florida." *Florida Historical Quarterly* 45 (October 1966): 145-170.   Florida differed from most of the former Confederate states during Reconstruction because it was never controlled by Radical Republicans.   Moderates among the Republicans and Democrats controlled the governor's office.   Governors Harrison Reed and Marcellus Stearns held a middle ground between white conservatives and the freedmen.   Racial issues, political infighting, and strong opposition from the Democratic Party made governing difficult.   Both parties should be blamed for government stalemate, mismanagement, and corruption.

1615.   Shofner, Jerrell H. "Wartime Unionists, Unreconstructed Rebels and Andrew Johnson's Amnesty Program in the Reconstruction Debacle of Jackson County, Florida." *Gulf Coast Historical Review* 4, 2 (1989): 162-171.   Map. Shofner explains that rising tension and dissatisfaction among local Unionists in Jackson County with President Johnson's lack of control over Reconstruction and the granting of suffrage to blacks by Congress led to their abandonment of support for the president and contributed to the environment of violence.   By the late 1860s Unionists and former Confederates united in their resistance to Reconstruction.   The Jackson County War from February, 1869 to the summer of 1871 was the result.

1616.   Wallace, John.   *Carpetbag Rule in Florida: The Inside Workings of the Reconstruction of the Civil Government in Florida After the Close of the Civil War.* Kennesaw, Ga.: Continental Book Co., 1959. 444p. App. (Rpt. of Jacksonville: DaCosta Printing, 1888)   Wallace, an ex-slave who served in both houses of the Florida legislature during Reconstruction, recounts the political history of Florida in the postwar years.   The time of promise for the freedmen was setback by the corruption and unfulfilled promises of the carpetbaggers and the fractious nature of the Republican Party in the state.   Wallace believed that blacks should not be blamed for corruption and that the return of the Democrats in 1877 was best for the state because it led to real promise and progress for blacks.   The appendix includes the state constitution of 1868 and related letters.

1617.   Williamson, Edward C. (ed.). "The Election of 1876 in Florida by Marcellus L. Stearns, Republican Candidate for Governor." *Florida Historical Quarterly* 32 (October 1953): 81-91.   Stearns originally came to Florida in 1866 as an officer in the Freedmen's Bureau. The Union Army veteran from Maine became involved with Republican politics and eventually was elected as Lt. Governor in 1872 with Gov. Ossian B. Hart. When Hart died in 1874 Stearns replaced him. Two documents relate to his unsuccessful bid for reelection in 1876 against Democrat George F. Drew. Stearns charged the Democrats with fraud in the election.

1618.   Williamson, Edward C. (ed.). "Florida's First Reconstruction Legislature: A Letter of William H. Gleason." *Florida Historical Quarterly* 32 (July 1953): 41-

43.   Gleason, a native of Wisconsin, came to Florida in 1866 as a real estate developer and later became a leader of Northern settlers in South Florida. In 1868 he won the election for Lt. Governor in the administration of Republican Harrison Reed. In a letter dated October 30, 1890 to Dr. G. W. Holmes, Gleason describes the process of appointments in the legislature and reflects on racial problems in Florida.

Agriculture, Labor, and Business

1619.   Carper, Noel Gordon. "The Convict-Lease System in Florida, 1866-1923." Ph.D. Florida State University, 1964. 429p.

1620.   Clark, Patricia P. "Florida, 'Our Own Italy': James F. B. Marshall's Post-Civil War Letters to Edward Everett Hale." *Florida Historical Quarterly* 59 (July 1980): 53-71.   Marshall's letters to Hale were written during Marshall's tour of Florida during January-March, 1867. As an agent for the New England Emigrant Aid Company, he assessed the economic, transportation, and climatic environment in the state for the purpose of building a community of Northerners. In particular he comments on the availability of land and railroads. He also compares the immigration of Northerners to the South with what took place in Italy after the invasion of the Goths and Lombards. Five letters are printed. (See also Clark's "A New England Emigrant Aid Company Agent in Postwar Florida: Selected Letters of James F. B. Marshall, 1867." *Florida Historical Quarterly* 55 (April 1977): 457-477; and "J. F. B. Marshall: A New England Emigrant Aid Company Agent in Post-War Florida, 1867." *Florida Historical Quarterly* 54(July 1975): 39-60.)

1621.   Clarke, Robert L. "Northern Plans for the Economic Invasion of Florida, 1862-1865." *Florida Historical Quarterly* 28 (April 1950): 262-270.   Clarke describes a scheme to transfer wealth from Florida to the North by encouraging immigration of Northerners to the state to create a market for Northern goods and services. The project was organized by the New England Emigrant Aid Company that hoped to garner support from freedmen and take advantage of the disenfranchisement of many whites. Their goal was Republican rule and support for business interests in the North. (See also # 1631)

1622.   Eckert, Edward K. "Contract Labor in Florida During Reconstruction." *Florida Historical Quarterly* 47 (July 1968): 34-50.   Contract labor on Florida plantations was common because the Freedmen's Bureau and government officials insisted on creating order and the right conditions for economic development. Eckert explains that freedmen were not much better off under contract labor than during slavery. This was particularly the case with wage contracts, because workers often were forced to remain on the plantations to repay debts to the owner. Cotton planter John Haile compiled a business ledger that reveals much about the contract system.

1623.   Fenlon, Paul E. "The Struggle for Control of the Florida Central Railroad, 1867-1882." *Florida Historical Quarterly* 34 (January 1956): 213-235.   The Florida Central Railroad became the focus of a struggle between Republicans and Democrats that ended in federal court. The principle player throughout the period was attorney Edward M. L'Engle, a native Floridian. The affair illustrates the postwar chaos in Southern business and economics.

1624.   Haulman, C. A. "Changes in the Economic Power Structure in Duval County, Florida, During the Civil War and Reconstruction." *Florida Historical Quarterly* 52 (October 1973): 175-184.   Haulman tests the revisionist theme that Reconstruction was not highly disruptive to the Southern economy and was generally beneficial. He examines census records of Duval County to compare sources of wealth between 1850 and 1870. He finds that less than half of wealthy persons prior to the war were still considered wealthy by 1870.   During Reconstruction newcomers from the North dominated wealth in the county. They contributed positively to economic recovery of the county.

1625.   Paisely, Clifton. "Tallahassee Through the Storebooks: Era of Radical Reconstruction, 1867-1877." *Florida Historical Quarterly* 53 (July 1974): 49-65. The postwar economy of Tallahassee was healthy and continued to prosper throughout the years of Reconstruction despite higher taxes and periods of depression and inflation. An example of a prosperous merchant was hardware store owner William P. Slusser, whose store books are the main source for Paisley's article.

1626.   Richardson, Joe M.   "The Freedmen's Bureau and Negro Labor in Florida." *Florida Historical Quarterly* 39 (October 1960): 167-174.   The bureau in Florida was particularly successful at getting freedmen back to work after the war. Their goal was to force freedmen to follow contracts made with employers, who were usually planters, and to force employers to offer fair contracts that included food. Even though the bureau was the object of great resentment among whites, it frequently tolerated inadequate wages and expected laborers and employers to follow their contracts in order to avoid complete disorder.

1627.   Shofner, Jerrell H. "A Merchant-Planter in the Reconstruction South." *Agricultural History* 46 (April 1972): 291-296.   Shofner emphasizes the economic problems of postwar Florida through the experience of Adam L. Eichelberger, a planter and merchant from Marion County. A lack of fluid capital for investment, the unpredictability of agriculture, and poor business decision-making brought on financial disaster for Eichelberger. The economic problems of the region brought suffering to many black laborers who depended on wages that sometimes did not materialize.

1628.   Shofner, Jerrell H. "Militant Negro Laborers in Reconstruction Florida." *Journal of Southern History* 39 (August 1973): 397-408.   Black laborers in Florida took an active part to improve their lives. They were very active locally and nationally in labor organizations, such as the National Labor Union until about 1870 and the National Union of Negro Labor until the early 1870s. Dockworkers, lumbermen, longshoremen, and millworkers in various Florida locations made demands and threatened strikes to get better pay and working conditions. Several Florida labor laws were passed between 1868 and 1875 as a result of demands from black laborers.

1629.   Shofner, Jerrell H.   "Negro Laborers and the Forest Industries in Reconstruction Florida." *Journal of Forest History* 19 (October 1975): 180-191. Ills.   During the Reconstruction years tremendous growth occurred in the Florida lumber industry at the same time cotton production declined.   Freedmen took advantage of employment opportunities that offered good wages and steady work. Shofner describes how the industry operated in the 1870s, the challenges of the lumber workers, and the contributions of blacks to the industry, including their participation in labor organizations.

1630.   Shofner, Jerrell H.   "The Pensacola Workingman's Association: A Militant Negro Labor Union During Reconstruction." *Labor History* 13 (Fall 1972): 555-559.   Black dock workers of the P.W.A. showed how aggressive action on their part could produce positive results.   In December, 1872 and January, 1873 the stevedores used violent tactics to keep Canadian seasonal workers from competing for a limited number of jobs on the Pensacola docks.   They produced a minor international incident, but in 1874 the Florida legislature passed a residency requirement for a stevedore's license.   The black stevedores, who comprised the majority of dock workers, showed that violence and collective action could force change.

1631.   Smith, George W.   "Carpetbag Imperialism in Florida, 1862-1868." *Florida Historical Quarterly* 27 (October 1948): 99-130; 27 (January 1949): 260-299.   From the time that the Union occupied parts of Florida, Northern business interests tried to take advantage of business opportunities, frequently in cooperation with Florida Unionists.   Smith describes prewar economic interaction between the state and the North, and the various schemes and enterprises for profit sought by carpetbaggers, such as Lyman K. Stickney and Eli Thayer. (See also # 1621)

1632.   Sowell, David.   "Racial Patterns of Labor in Postbellum Florida: Gainesville, 1870-1900." *Florida Historical Quarterly* 63 (April 1985): 434-444. During the 1870s and 1880s black workers gave up farm labor for jobs as unskilled and semiskilled laborers.   Over the course of both decades the black professionals increased by only a small number, but the sight of upwardly mobile blacks led to broad support for Jim Crow laws by the 1890s.   Sowell recognizes racial continuity among workers in the socioeconomic environment of the urban South during the 19th century.

Society, Education, and Religion

1633.   Agresti, Barbara Finlay. "Household and Family in the Postbellum South: Walton County, Florida, 1870-1885." Ph.D. University of Florida, 1976. 261p.

1634.   Floyd, Marilyn J. and Harry A. Kersey, Jr. "Harriet Beecher Stowe and Negro Education in Florida." *Negro Educational Review* 28 (January 1997): 19-27. Stowe's contributions to black education were based on the idea that social and environmental factors were more important in educational development than racial differences. Stowe helped build a school in Madarin, Florida.

1635.   Foster, John T., Jr. and Sarah Whitmer Foster. "The Last Shall Be First: Northern Methodists in Reconstruction Jacksonville." *Florida Historical Quarterly* 70 (January 1992): 256-280. Ill.   Northern Methodist Episcopal missionaries promoted religious practice and education among the freedmen, and some became involved in local Republican politics and encouraged Northern immigration to the South.   Beginning in 1864 John Sanford Swaim of New Jersey worked in Jacksonville to carry out the Church's program of aid, organizing black churches, and establishing schools for freedmen, such as Cookman Institute.   These activities overshadow the stereotype of the selfish carpetbagger.   (See also Foster's "John Sanford Swaim: A Life at the Beginning of Modern Florida." *Methodist History* 26 [July 1988]: 229-239.)

1636.   Foster, John T., Jr., Herbert B. Whitmer, Jr., and Sarah W. Foster. "Tourism Was Not the Only Purpose: Jacksonville Republicans and Newark's *Sentinel of Freedom*." *Florida Historical Quarterly* 63 (January 1985): 318-324. The *Sentinel of Freedom* newspaper published letters from Northern transplants in Florida during Reconstruction. The authors discuss letters believed to be from John Sanford Swaim and his son Jacob W. Swaim, both living in Duval County. Their letters refer to the physical and emotional conditions in postwar northeastern Florida. The men encouraged tourism, but also attempted to draw Northerners to the area to enhance Republican power.

1637.   Glunt, James David. "Plantation and Frontier Records of East and Middle Florida, 1789-1868." Ph.D. University of Michigan, 1931.

1638.   Hall, Robert L. "The Gospel According to Radicalism: African Methodism Comes to Tallahassee After the Civil War." *Apalachee: The Publication of the Tallahassee Historical Society* 8 (1978): 69-81. (Rpt. in *Church and Community Among Black Southerners 1865-1900*. Edited by Donald G. Nieman. New York: Garland, 1994.)   The African Methodist Episcopal Church began in Philadelphia in 1787, and by the beginning of the Civil War it had expanded into several regions of the South. In Tallahassee, Florida the A.M.E. church was established in June, 1865 and spread quickly within a few years under the leadership of Rev. Charles H. Pearce. Hall attributes the popularity of the church to its Radical political message and the political influence of ministers like Pearce who was elected to the state senate in 1868 and later became Superintendent of Public Instruction for Leon County.

1639.   Hall, Robert L. "Tallahassee's Black Churches, 1865-1885." *Florida Historical Quarterly* 58 (October 1979): 185-196.   Hall examines the formation and function of black churches following the Civil War. Some churches, such as the Bethel African Methodist Episcopal Church established in 1866 became a focal point for local and state politics, education, social interaction, and religious and moral instruction. To some extent black churches contributed to white expectations for the establishment of social controls over the black community.

1640.   Hall, Robert L. "'Yonder Come Day':   Religious Dimensions of the Transition From Slavery to Freedom in Florida." *Florida Historical Quarterly* 65 (April 1987): 411-432.   Emancipation led to the rejection of white churches by the freedmen in favor of establishing their own churches led by black ministers. Black churches were focal points for both literacy, education, and Republican politics, and black ministers held great influence in their communities. Black churches symbolized freedom and the beginning of a new social relationship between the races.

1641.   Kharif, Wali Rashash. "The Refinement of Racial Segregation in Florida After the Civil War." Ph.D. Florida State University, 1983. 283p.

1642.   Laurie, Murray D. "The Union Academy: A Freedmen's Bureau School in Gainesville, Florida." *Florida Historical Quarterly* 65 (October 1986): 163-174. During 1867-1868 the Freedmen's Bureau coordinated the acquisition of land and the building of the Union Academy, a school for black children in Gainesville. Local black artisans donated their labor to help build a new school building. The teachers were New England ladies who were paid by private organizations, such as the Freedmen's Union Commission in New York. The academy symbolized the progress in black education.

1643.   Richardson, Joe M. "An Evaluation of the Freedmen's Bureau in Florida." *Florida Historical Quarterly* 41 (January 1963): 223-238.   The bureau in Florida received favorable ratings from many whites and blacks, and even from the government investigators appointed by President Johnson. Richardson describes the bureau's activities - distributing food, coordinating labor, organizing education efforts, and attempting to safeguard fair justice for the freedmen. He notes that the agency's notable failure was its inability to resolve racial tensions, but the bureau performed as well as any other organization could have in the same circumstances.

1644.   Richardson, Joe M. "The Freedmen's Bureau and Negro Education in Florida." *Journal of Negro Education* 31 (Fall 1962): 460-467.   From 1865 to 1870 the bureau built a record of accomplishment organizing and constructing schools for the freedmen. The great expansion of black education led to the establishment of a teacher training school in Jacksonville in April, 1866.

1645.   Richardson, Joe M. "A Northerner Reports on Florida: 1866." *Florida Historical Quarterly* 40 (April 1962): 381-390.   Printed is the report of October 15, 1866 of A. E. Klinne, a teacher in schools operated by the National Freedman's Relief Association, on his investigation of social conditions, race relations, and the work of Freedmen's Bureau agents in East Florida. Klinne emphasizes the importance of looking after the rights of the freedmen and working to eliminate prejudice against them. Richardson includes explanatory footnotes elaborating on the text.

1646.   Richardson, Joe M. "'We Are Truly Doing Missionary Work': Letters From the American Missionary Association Teachers in Florida, 1864-1874." *Florida Historical Quarterly* 54 (October 1975): 178-195.   By 1866 more than 350 teachers associated with the American Missionary Association were working in the South. Florida never had more than 15 A.M.A. teachers in any one year. They took on the responsibility of teaching freedmen in both day, evening, and Sabbath schools. Richardson provides 11 letters written by A.M.A. teachers from 1864 to 1872.

1647.   Roberts, Derrell. "Social Legislation in Reconstruction Florida." *Florida Historical Quarterly* 43 (April 1965): 343-360.   Roberts examines social reforms legislated by Democratic and Republican administrations in Florida during the postwar years. The Florida legislature passed various acts related to providing education for the freedmen and white citizens, reforming and upgrading the penal system, providing facilities for the mentally ill, and general assistance to the aged, Confederate veterans, and the freedmen. Roberts considers these actions be the basis for later public welfare reforms in the 20th century.

1648.   Rosen, F. Bruce.   "The Development of Negro Education in Florida during Reconstruction: 1865-1877." Ph.D. University of Florida 1974. 286p.

1649.   Rosen, F. Bruce. "The Influence of the Peabody Fund on Education in Reconstruction Florida." *Florida Historical Quarterly* 55 (January 1977): 310-320. The Peabody Fund provided money for primary education, particularly in the urban areas, of Florida and other Southern states, but it was administered by Rev. Barnas Sears in a very conservative fashion. Segregation was encouraged, and black schools received proportionately less funding than white schools.

1650.   Vance, Maurice.   "Northerners in Late Nineteenth Century Florida: Carpetbaggers or Settlers?" *Florida Historical Quarterly* 38 (July 1959): 1-14. Tbls.   Northerners who came to Florida after the Civil War were labeled as individuals seeking political power in the Republican regime. Vance explains that a statistical analysis of population and occupational trends among Northerners in several Florida counties show that they made up less than 5% of the population prior to the late 1880s and that the majority of them were artisans and merchants. The majority were settlers, not carpetbaggers.

Georgia

General History

1651.   Avery, Isaac Wheeler. *The History of the State of Georgia From 1850 to 1881, Embracing the Three Important Epochs: The Decade Before the War of 1861-65; The War; The Period of Reconstruction...* New York: Brown & Derby, 1881. 714p. Ports.   In the chapters focusing on Reconstruction, Avery describes the period as a type of crucifixion of Georgia by belligerent Northern Radicals, ignorant blacks, and power hungry local whites.

1652.   Conway, Alan. *The Reconstruction of Georgia.* Minneapolis: University of Minnesota Press, 1966. 248p. Bibl.   Conway, a British historian, provides an survey of the Reconstruction years in Georgia.   The period was marked by increasingly conservative governments, defiance against a weak and brief Republican regime, and the quick return of the Democrats to a majority in the legislature in 1871. In December, 1871 a Democrat won the gubernatorial election. His book is the first on Reconstruction in Georgia since Thompson's work (see # 1655) in 1915. Conway criticizes Thompson's conservative interpretation in favor of a more objective perspective.

1653.   Drago, Edmund L.   "Black Georgia During Reconstruction."   Ph.D. University of California, Berkeley, 1975.

1654.   Terry, Steve M.   "Depiction of the Reconstruction Period in Georgia History Textbooks." *Georgia Social Science Journal* 14 (Spring 1983): 5-10., Until the late 1970s traditional, negative interpretations of Reconstruction prevailed in Georgia history textbooks. Revisionists interpretations were partially incorporated into the textbooks.

1655.   Thompson, C. Mildred. *Reconstruction in Georgia: Economic, Social, Political 1865-1872.* Ph.D. Columbia University Press, 1915. 415p. (Also published by Columbia University Press in *Studies in History, Economics and Public Law*, vol. 64, no. 1 [no. 154]).

1656.   Woolley, Edwin C.   "Reconstruction of Georgia." Ph.D.   Columbia University, 1901. 112p. (*Columbia University Studies in the Social Sciences*, 36; AMS Press, 1970)

1657.   Wynes, Charles E.   "Part Four, 1865-1890." In *A History of Georgia*. Edited by Kenneth Coleman. Athens: University of Georgia, 1977. Pp. 205-254. Ills. Ports.   In three chapters Wynes devotes much of his attention to postwar Reconstruction. The chapter on politics emphasizes the relative unimportance of Republican government in Georgia, because it existed for only four years under Gov. Rufus Bullock and was not nearly as corrupt as critics have described. More important for Georgia politics was the Democratic "bourbon" regime that followed, with its fiscal tightness, business perspective, and conservatism that stymied development for decades. Wynes also addresses labor problems, the slow growth of free public education that was extended to all races, the racial segregation of churches, prison reform, and literary culture in the state.

Politics and Law

1658.   Abbott, Richard H.   "Jason Clarke Swayze, Republican Editor in Reconstruction Georgia, 1867-1873." *Georgia Historical Quarterly* 79 (Summer 1995): 337-366.   Perhaps the most successful Republican newspaper in Georgia was the *American Union*, located in Griffin and Macon. In August, 1867 Swayze purchased the newspaper and set out to take a leadership role in organizing local freedmen and whites into a coalition for the Republican Party, but blacks preferred their own leaders, and he was never able to rally white support. Most of the whites despised him for his constant barrage of criticism against Southern chivalry. Despite constant financial turmoil and threats against him, his newspaper continued to appear until autumn of 1872.

1659.   Abbott, Richard H.   "The Republican Party Press in Reconstruction Georgia, 1867-1874." *Journal of Southern History* 61 (November 1995): 725-760. The fortunes of Republican newspapers and their owners in Georgia depended on the success of the Republican Party. From a total of six daily and weekly papers in 1868, the number of papers dwindled to one by 1876. The editors fought for political influence and patronage, and reflected the bickering that existed among Republicans over the issue of civil rights for freedmen. Racial bias was typical of the Republican editors who wanted to appeal to the interests of whites in order to gain subscribers and advertisers. Abbott reviews many newspapers from throughout Georgia, particularly Jason Clarke Swayze's *American Union* (Griffin, Macon), John Emory Bryant's *Loyal Georgia* (Augusta) and Samuel Bard's *Daily New Era* (Atlanta).

1660.   Bacote, Clarence A.   "William Finch, Negro Councilman and Political Activities in Atlanta During Early Reconstruction." *Journal of Negro History* 40 (October 1955): 341-364.   Born a slave in Washington, Ga., Finch became a successful businessman in Atlanta after the Civil War. After Georgia was readmitted to the Union in July, 1870, he was elected to the city council and proceeded to work for the establishment of public schools and city improvements. Finch's work serves as an example of the positive contributions made by black Republicans in public office.

1661.   Brandon, William P.   "Calling the Georgia Constitutional Convention of 1877." *Georgia Historical Quarterly* 17 (September 1933): 189-203.   The Democrats regained total control of the state government in 1872 with the installation of James M. Smith as govenor, but for several years a debate raged regarding the rewriting of the 1868 constitution. The 1868 document was objectionable to many Democrats simply because it was written by a convention dominated by Republicans. Many Republicans and the urban press, particularly the *Atlanta Constitution*, opposed changing the constitution, possibly because of fears that the government would revert to its antebellum structure.

1662. Bryant, Jonathan M. "'We Have No Chance of Justice Before the Court': The Freedmen's Struggle for Power in Greene County, Georgia, 1865-1874." In *Georgia in Black and White: Explorations in the Race Relations of a Southern State, 1865-1950*. Edited by John C. Inscoe. Athens: University of Georgia Press, 1994. Pp. 13-37. Notes. The freedmen's struggle for civil rights in Georgia is traced through the career of ex-slave Abram Colby, who became an influential local leader and state legislator from Greene County in the eastern piedmont region. Colby, who was the personification of black self assertion, stood up to Ku Klux Klan attempts to destroy him, but this resulted in a severe beating and attempts on his life. The rejection of blacks as political participants by moderate Republicans led Colby and others to decide that the state Republican Party cared little about equal rights and justice. (See also # 1755)

1663. Bullock, Hon. Rufus B. "Reconstruction in Georgia 1868-1870." *Independent* 55 (March 19, 1903): 670-674. Bullock, the Republican governor of Georgia from 1868 until his resignation in late 1871, remembers the Reconstruction days as a time when Georgians approached reform in a conservative manner and made the best of a bad situation. His article is also a defense of his stewardship.

1664. Busbee, Westley F., Jr. "Presidential Reconstruction in Georgia, 1865-1867." Ph.D. University of Alabama, 1973. 444p.

1665. Cashin, Edward J., Jr. *"The Banner of the South*, A Journal of the Reconstruction Era." *Richland County History* 6, 1 (1974): 12-72. *The Banner of the South*, a weekly literary journal edited by Father Abram J. Ryan and published in Augusta, Georgia from 1868 to 1870, took up the cause of the Old South by publishing sentimental poems and articles about The Lost Cause. Ryan opposed black civil rights, and he criticized the North and Republican policies. He also led attacks against sources of anticatholicism. The journal ceased after Ryan was forced to leave the Diocese, apparently for reasons unrelated to his journal.

1666. Cason, Roberta F. "The Loyalty Leagues in Georgia." *Georgia Historical Quarterly* 20 (June 1936): 125-153. During the Civil War loyalty leagues had large numbers of white participants, but when blacks were brought into the organizations after the war, whites began to leave. Cason writes that the leagues encouraged racial animosity and manipulated the freedmen by offering poor advice and encouraging labor unrest and political instability.

1667. Cook, James F. *Governors of Georgia*. Huntsville, Al.: Strode Publishers, 1979. Pp. 154-173. Bibl. Ports. Cook provides brief biographical sketches of Georgia's Reconstruction governors, including James Johnson (1865), Charles Jones Jenkins (1865-1868), Thomas Howard Ruger (1868), Rufus Brown Bullock (1868-1872).

1668.   Coulter, E. Merton. "Aaron Alpeoria Bradley, Georgia Negro Politician During Reconstruction Times, Part I." *Georgia Historical Quarterly* 51 (March 1967): 15-41; "...Part II." 51 (June 1967): 154-174; "...Part III." 51 (September 1967): 264-306.   Coulter describes Bradley, who was elected to the state Senate in 1868, as having a fiery, unpredictable personality, and one who displayed a scheming and sometimes dishonest behavior. Bradley appealed to a strong dedicated group of followers from the black community in Savannah. Coulter relies heavily on newspaper accounts and opinions. He also provides insight into the interaction of politics and journalism during Reconstruction.

1669.   Coulter, E. Merton. "Henry M. Turner: Georgia Negro Preacher-Politician During the Reconstruction Era." *Georgia Historical Quarterly* 48 (December 1964): 371-410.   Turner, a former slave who was freed as a youth, arrived in Georgia as a U.S. military chaplain assigned to the Freedmen's Bureau. Coulter explains that Turner's great oratorical skills as an African Methodist Episcopal minister led to his involvement in politics as an advocate for black rights and political participation, but he also tried to appease conservative whites. Coulter claims that even though Turner was admired by whites for his intellect, he led an immoral and dishonest life and was an inflammatory agent in the black community.

1670.   Coulter, E. Merton. *Negro Legislators in Georgia During the Reconstruction Period.* Athens: Georgia Historical Quarterly, 1968. 209p. Bibl. Ports.   Coulter examines the careers of Henry M. Turner, Aaron Alpeoria Bradley, and Tunis G. Campbell. He refers to them as examples of the best of Georgia's black political representatives even though they committed illegal and immoral acts and were generally unfit for public service. The three men are the focus of Coulter's general condemnation of black suffrage and officeholding.

1671.   Coulter, E. Merton. "Tunis G. Campbell, Negro Reconstructionist in Georgia." *Georgia Historical Quarterly* [Part I] 51 (December 1967): 401-424; [Part II] 52 (March 1968): 16-52.   Coulter reviews Campbell's political career. Campbell became a virtual autocrat of St. Catherine Island and its freed inhabitants, and later had great influence over blacks in McIntosh and Darien Counties. His influence and power resulted in his election to the constitutional convention in 1867 and the state senate in 1868. Whites held Campbell in suspicion because of his cunning and charismatic personality, and behavior that led to several indictments and prison sentences.

1672.   Daniell, Elizabeth Otto. "The Ashburn Murder Case in Georgia Reconstruction." *Georgia Historical Quarterly* 59 (Fall 1975): 296-312.   George W. Ashburn, a native Southerner who resided in Columbus, Ga. prior to the Civil War, was murdered on March 31, 1868. The local white population scorned him because he was a delegate to the 1867-1868 constitutional convention, and he supported the Republican Party. Ashburn's case illustrates the extreme emotions felt by whites against Radical Republican rule and the scalawags who participated and encouraged it.

1673. Dickerson, Donna L. "Patronage and the Press: General John Pope and Newspapers in Reconstruction Georgia." *Atlanta History* 36 (Summer 1992): 27-39. Ports. As the district commander for Georgia, Pope followed the letter of the Reconstruction Acts of 1867 as he interpreted them. This included the participation of blacks in the political process and the submission of the district to military rule over existing civil authority. The defiance of the Democratic press provoked Pope to order public officials not to advertise in disloyal newspapers. This act effectively eliminated their patronage income and was a form of censorship. President Grant opposed Pope's order.

1674. Drago, Edmund L. *Black Politicians and Reconstruction in Georgia: A Splendid Failure*. Baton Rouge: Louisiana State University Press, 1982. 201p. App. Bibl. Black politicians in Georgia lacked the sophistication and experience of the free blacks of Charleston and New Orleans who were political leaders in their communities. They lacked the persistence to achieve a political goal without compromise, and they could not overcome the resistance of whites to their political participation. Reconstruction in Georgia was a failure, but the independence and self reliance of freedmen grew, and they continued to seek the civil rights promised by federal legislation. The appendix lists information on black legislators and delegates to the constitutional convention from 1867 to 1872.

1675. Drago, Edmund L. "Georgia's First Black Voter Registrars During Reconstruction." *Georgia Historical Quarterly* 78 (Winter 1994): 760-793. Ills. Tbl. Drago examines the political environment in Georgia and the process that led to the appointment of 52 black registrars who helped with the registration of 80% of male freedmen during the summer of 1867. Black registrars were chosen by white registrars, a process that whites used to pick nonpolitical, literate, middle class blacks. He describes the factions within the black community and resistance among whites that eventually undermined black voting rights. But Drago emphasizes the positive reforms that produced biracial registration boards and might have been more successful with closer federal supervision of elections. A table lists characteristics of black voters.

1676. Duncan, Russell. *Entrepreneur For Equality: Governor Rufus Bullock, Commerce, and Race in Post-Civil War Georgia*. Athens: University of Georgia Press, 1994. 278p. Bibl. Port. As Republican governor from 1868 to 1872, Bullock did not conform to the demonic depiction of post-Reconstruction by historians. In this biography of Bullock, Duncan emphasizes his attempt to ensure as much civil rights for the freedmen as was politically possible, although he could have done more. Conservative Democrats lambasted Bullock as a crook and a destroyer of traditional white domination. Bullock failed because of his limited approach to building political support among blacks and lower class whites, and he lacked support from the Grant administration during the 1871 gubernatorial election. Compared with the governors that followed, Bullock was the best for black citizens until Jimmy Carter in 1970. (See also Duncan's "Rufus Brown Bullock, Reconstruction, and the 'New South', 1834-1907: An Exploration into Race, Class,

Party, and the Corruption of the American Creed." Ph.D. University of Georgia, 1988. 453p.)

1677. Duncan, Russell. *Freedom's Shore: Tunis Campbell and the Georgia Freedmen.* Athens: University of Georgia Press, 1986. 175p. Bibl. Ills. Map. Ports. Tbls. Campbell participated in the Sea Islands experiment in 1863 and later organized blacks in Macintosh County as a Freedmen's Bureau agent. As a bureau agent and politician, he became a powerful influence on the black community's perception of their power and ability to prosper in a capitalist economy. Campbell built a separatist black society that allowed blacks to withstand four years of Democratic government that took over the state in 1871. The legacy of black power extended for 40 years.

1678. Duncan, Russell. "A Georgia Governor Battles Racism: Rufus Bullock and the Fight for Black Legislators." In *Georgia in Black and White: Explorations in the Race Relations of a Southern State, 1865-1950.* Edited by John C. Inscoe. Athens: University of Georgia Press, 1994. Pp. 38-64. Rufus Brown Bullock, a native of New York, was elected Republican governor of Georgia in 1868. He became a strong advocate of equal civil rights for all races, even though most state Republicans sought to compromise the rights of freedmen in favor of political peace with the Democrats. Democrats and the Ku Klux Klan successfully organized to steal the 1870 legislative election, and eventually chased Bullock out of office and the state in 1872. After his return to Georgia, he continued to speak out in favor of equal rights.

1679. Felton, Rebecca. *My Memoirs of Georgia Politics.* Atlanta: Index Printing Co., 1911. 680p. Felton was the wife of William H. Felton, a physician, plantation owner, and a Democratic congressman after the return of the Democratic Party to power. She provides the perspective of a white Southerner loyal to the cause of white domination in the South. Felton follows the career of her husband and events in Georgia. She includes letters written by Dr. Felton and acquaintances.

1680. Fitzsimons, Theodore B., Jr. "The Camilla Riot." *Georgia Historical Quarterly* 35 (June 1951): 116-125. The riot took place on September 19, 1868. The political atmosphere in Georgia was full of tension between most of the local whites and the Republicans. Fitzsimons blames the riot on black marchers. The racial confrontation and the legislature's removal of black members convinced Congress to withhold recognition of Georgia for three more years.

1681. Formwalt, Lee W. "The Camilla Massacre of 1868: Racial Violence as Political Propaganda." *Georgia Historical Quarterly* 71 (Fall 1987): 399-426. Formwalt describes and analyzes the events of September 19, 1868 when local whites carried out the massacre of blacks who sought to attend a political rally in Camilla, Ga. News of the incident was used by Democrats and Republicans in the election nationwide, and it helped to convince Congress that Georgia should return to military rule.

1682.   Formwalt, Lee W. (Ed.). "Petitioning Congress for Protection: A Black View of Reconstruction at the Local Level." *Georgia Historical Quarterly* 73 (Summer 1989): 305-322.   Representatives of the Civil and Political Rights Association, a black organization in the 2nd Congressional district in southwestern Georgia, sent a petition to Congress describing many acts of violence and intimidation carried out by local whites against the black community. The printed document represents the freedmen's lack of confidence in local white Republicans to protect them and their rights.

1683.   Garrison, Ellen Barries. "Old South or New?   Georgia and the Constitution of 1877." Ph.D. Stanford University, 1981. 321p.

1684.   Goetchius, Henry R. *Litigation in Georgia During the Reconstruction Period.* Atlanta: Franklin Printing, 1910? 42p. Tbl. of Cases Cited.   Goetchius reviews the most prolific litigation issues in the Georgia courts in the context of the Reconstruction period.   He discusses cases related to relief and stay laws, Confederate contracts, the status of the slave, and ownership of property.   The unusual postwar period led to unusual litigation with no precedent in statutory or constitutional law. Many cases were decided solely based on their own merits. The loosening of form and procedure in litigation during Reconstruction may have contributed to their liberalization in future decades.

1685.   Hill, B. H. "Address of Honorable B. H. Hill Before the Georgia Branch of the Southern Historical Society at Atlanta, Georgia, February 18, 1874." *Southern Historical Society Papers* 14 (1886): 484-505.   The Southern Historical Society belatedly published a speech given by Benjamin Hill, a former Confederate General, regarding the treatment of the South in Reconstruction. Hill's words are sentimental and full of resentment towards the plunderers of the South and a Republican Congress that sought change through coercion.

1686.   Johnson, Herschel V. "From the Autobiography of Herschel V. Johnson, 1856-1867." *American Historical Review* 30 (January 1925): 311-336.   Johnson, a former U.S. senator (1848-1849) and governor (1853-1857), was a Unionist and a strong supporter of states' rights and nonintervention on the issue of slavery. A small portion   (pages 334-336) includes comments on his participation in the formation of the Georgia government in 1865, his appointment to the U.S. Senate, and political events leading to his withdrawal from politics and his disenfranchisement by the end of 1867.

1687.   Jones, B. A., H. M. Bacote, B. H. Nelson, and William S. Braithwaite. "Workers of Merit in Georgia." *Negro History Bulletin* 5 (March 1942): 129-130. Ports.   Two of the five brief biographical sketches cover black participants in Reconstruction: Jefferson Franklin Long, a congressman in 1870, and Henry McNeil Turner, a leader in Methodist Episcopal Church South, Republican organizer, and state legislator from 1868 to 1870.

1688.   Mahaffey, Joseph H.   (ed.).   "Carl Schurz's Letters From the South." *Georgia Historical Quarterly* 35 (September 1951): 222-257.   Schurz toured the South at the request of President Johnson.   Printed are five of his correspondences about conditions in Georgia.   His letters were later used to support the Radical Republican approach toward Reconstruction.   He was actually encouraged by friends, such as Sen. Charles Sumner of Massachusetts, to build a case against Johnson's Reconstruction plan.

1689.   Mathis, Robert Neil.   "The Ordeal of Confiscation: The Post-Civil War Trials of Gazaway Bugg Lamar." *Georgia Historical Quarterly* 63 (Fall 1979): 339-352.   Lamar was a wealthy Georgia planter, merchant, banker and steamboat proprietor who lost a fortune to federal confiscation and was placed in prison on suspicion that he participated in the assassination of President Lincoln.   His legal battles resulted in compensation of $570,000 during his life and additional posthumous suits by his family that did not cease until 1919.

1690.   Matthews, John M.   "Jefferson Franklin Long: The Public Career of Georgia's First Black Congressman." *Phylon* 42 (June 1981): 145-156.   Long, born a slave in the Georgia Black Belt, became politically active during Reconstruction as a Republican Party organizer and public speaker.   His faith in the party weakened when white Republicans helped to remove all black legislators from office based on a legal technicality.   In 1870, when the Republicans lost their majority in the legislature, Long was elected to Congress, but only for the third session that lasted a few weeks.

1691.   Matthews, John M.   "Negro Republicans in the Reconstruction of Georgia." *Georgia Historical Quarterly* 60 (Summer 1976): 145-164.   Blacks welcomed the Republican Party as the provider of freedom and civil rights, but they found that moderate Republicans were not interested in them, and the Radicals only spoke about their support without allowing freedmen to participate in the leadership of the party.   The freedmen felt betrayed, and the inability of the Republicans to hold on to their support contributed to the quick demise of the Republican Party by 1871.

1692.   McDaniel, Ruth Currie.   *Carpetbagger of Conscience: A Biography of John Emory Bryant*.   Athens: University of Georgia Press, 1987. 238p. Bibl. Ills. Bryant arrived in Georgia as a Freedmen's Bureau agent in 1865 after serving as an officer in the Union Army.   He became excited by the ideals of Radical Republicanism in his struggle to change Southern society.   Despite his commitment to equal rights for freedmen, free labor and free schools, he typified the Northern white Republican male rejection of gender equality, and he recognized the nagging reality that racial equality was ultimately impossible.   Bryant was not the evil carpetbagger of Southern lore, but a devoted, complicated, and contradictory idealist. (See also McDaniel's "Georgia Carpetbagger: John Emory Bryant and the Ambiguity of Reform During Reconstruction." Ph.D. Duke University, 1973. 277p.)

1693.   Mellichamp, Josephine. *Senators From Georgia.* Huntsville, Al.: Strode Publishers, 1976. Pp. 144-161. Bibl. Ports.   This book includes brief biographical sketches of senators serving during Reconstruction, including Homer V. M. Miller (1971), Joshua Hill (1871-1873), Thomas M. Norwood (1871-1877), and John B. Gordon (1873-1880, 1891-1897).

1694.   Mitchell, Eugene Muse. "H. I. Kimball; His Career and Defense." *Atlanta Historical Journal* 3 (October 1938): 249-283.   Kimball arrived in Atlanta in 1867 and became closely associated with Republican Gov. Rufus Bullock.   He became the subject of accusations of fraud and corruption within the Bullock administration. Mitchell describes the accusations and reprints newspaper articles from 1874 that brought the subject back to life and caused Kimball to defend himself once more.

1695.   Moore, John Hammond. "In Sherman's Wake: Atlanta and the Southern Claims Commission, 1871-1880." *Atlanta Historical Journal* 29 (Summer 1985): 5-18. Tbl.   Moore reviews the purposes of the Claims Commission and the claims of many applicants from Fulton and DeKalb Counties. He illustrates the challenge that faced persons who claimed wartime loyalty to the Union and who lost property to the U.S. Army during the war. A list of 400 claimants from both counties is provided showing names and how the commission disposed of their claims. Only 67 of 400 claimants received any compensation.

1696.   Nathans, Elizabeth Studley. *Losing the Peace: Georgia Republicans and Reconstruction, 1865-1871.* Baton Rouge: Louisiana State University Press, 1968. 268p. App. Bibl. Tbls.   Nathan examines the rise and fall of Republican power in Georgia. In retrospect, the failure of the state Republican regime seemed inevitable, but Nathans argues that a real chance existed for a longer and more successful period of Republican rule. There was a natural alliance of blacks and white yeomen, but their social and political differences helped split the party and eventually led to the migration of whites to the Democrats. Democrats were united by the culture of white supremacy, perceptions of Republican corruption, and fear of black power.

1697.   Osthaus, Carl R. "From the Old South to the New South: The Editorial Career of William Tappan Thompson of the *Savannah Morning News.*" *Southern Quarterly* 14 (April 1876): 237-260.   Thompson, originally from Ohio and Philadelphia, became an ardent Southern spokesman and apologist from the 1830s until his death in 1882. He founded the *Savannah Daily Morning News* in 1850 and used it to promote Southern prosperity and distinctiveness until it closed in 1864. Tappan joined the *Daily Herald* in 1865 and eventually transformed it into a voice against Reconstruction and racial equality that reflected the ideas of conservative white Georgians. He symbolized the continuity of the white South's self image from antebellum to postbellum years.

1698.   Parks, Joseph H. *Joseph E. Brown of Georgia.* Baton Rouge: Louisiana State University Press, 1977. 612p. Bibl. Ills. Ports.   Parks explains how Brown, governor of Georgia during the Confederacy, refused to disappear politically after the defeat of the South. Brown took a pragmatic approach toward Congressional

Reconstruction by supporting the 14th Amendment and black suffrage as the price to return Georgia to the Union and direct the state toward the future. Becoming a Republican enhanced his influence, but he had to deflect criticism from Democrats and the conservative press. When Republicans lost control of the legislature in 1870, Brown emerged as a Democrat who concentrated on building personal wealth and political influence. He was appointed to the U.S. Senate in 1880. Parks describes Brown as the most influential man in Georgia from 1857, when he was first elected governor, until the late 1880s.

1699.   Pearce, Haywood J. *Benjamin H. Hill: Secession and Reconstruction.* Chicago: University of Chicago Press, 1928. 330p. Bibl.   In this political biography, Pearce depicts Hill, a prewar Whig, as a moderate who attempted to make peace between abolitionists and proponents of slavery, between Unionists and separatists, and between Congressional reconstructionists and Southern rejectionists of defeat. Although Hill opposed Reconstruction, in 1870 he preached acceptance of the program as a way for local and national Democrats to regain power. This tactic led to political defeats and his rivalry with former governor Joseph E. Brown, but he won a seat in Congress in 1874. Pearce absolves Hill of accusations of wrong doing and opportunism, and he champions him as an American patriot. (See also Pearce's Ph.D. dissertation with the same title from University of Chicago, 1928.)

1700.   Phillips, Ulrich B.   (ed.).   *The Correspondence of Robert Toombs, Alexander H. Stephens, and Howell Cobb.* In *Annual Report of the American Historical Association for the Year 1911.* Vol. II. Washington: GPO, 1913. 759p. Chron calendar.   The selected correspondence of three prominent Georgians of the antebellum and Civil War years cover the period from 1844 to 1882. Sixty-five letters written by or to Cobb and his wife, Toombs, or Stephens were published. The correspondence from the Reconstruction period involves many different friends and family, and deals mainly with Southern and national politics of Reconstruction, state and national elections, economic issues, and personal affairs. Also included is a calendar of letters previously published with brief citations to the sources, a calendar of letters published in this book, and a chronology of the lives of all three men.

1701.   Reagan, Alice E.   "The Reconstruction and Redemption of the Fundamental Law: Constitutional Revision in Georgia, 1865-1877." *Southern Historian* 6 (Spring 1965): 28-39.   Reagan examines and compares the Georgia constitutions of 1865, 1868, and 1877. The 1865 document made changes demanded by President Johnson's Reconstruction plan. In 1868 the constitution was liberalized by the influence of Congressional Reconstruction and compromises accepted by local moderate Republicans and Democrats. After the Republican regime fell in 1871, it took the conservative Democrats until 1877 to organize a new convention under the control of the social and political elite. This reactionary group sought the elimination of reforms, state aid to the needy, and the reduction of voting power among both blacks and poor whites.

1702. Redkey, Edwin S. (comp and ed.). *Respect Black: The Writings and Speeches of Henry McNeil Turner*. New York: Arno Press and the New York Times, 1971. 199p. Port. Turner was a militant, black nationalist who advocated the emigration of American blacks to Africa after it became obvious that promises of real freedom and equal rights in the U.S. would not materialize after the Civil War. During Reconstruction he was active in the organization of the African Methodist Episcopal churches in Georgia, state Reconstruction politics, and briefly in the Freedmen's Bureau. This book prints selections of Turner's writings, including seven documents on emancipation, politics, and early ideas on colonization during Reconstruction. The other documents cover issues from 1880 to 1906 on American wars overseas, Turner's travels to Africa, and race relations in America. (See also John Dittmer, "The Education of Henry McNeal Tuner," in *Black Leaders of the Nineteenth Century*. Ed. by Leon Litwack and August Meier. Urbana: University of Chicago, 1988. Pp. 252-272.)

1703. Reed, John C. Esq. "Reminiscences of Ben Hill." *South Atlantic Quarterly* 5 (April 1906): 134-149. Reed compliments Hill in all respects except for his public support for the 15th Amendment.

1704. Roberts, Derrell C. *Joseph E. Brown and Politics of Reconstruction*. University: University of Alabama Press, 1973. 159p. App. Bibl. Brown rebounded from his political downfall at the end of the Civil War by making a huge amount of money for himself in real estate, railroads, mining, convict labor, and agriculture. The former Confederate governor combined his economic success with continued participation in state politics by taking the dangerous position of supporting whatever Republican policy prevailed at the time. His journey from Confederate leader, to Republican by 1867, to Liberal Republican in 1872, and back to Democrat in 1876 produced political enemies, but his political skills eventually led to a ten year career in the U.S. Senate from 1880 to 1891. Roberts believes that Brown made his fortune legally. Appendices include a list of Georgia governors (1850-1900), U.S. senators (1865-1900), and congressmen (1865-1895).

1705. Roberts, Derrell C. "Joseph E. Brown and the Florida Election of 1876." *Florida Historical Quarterly* 40 (January 1962): 217-225. Although Brown lost his political power after the Northern victory in war, his support for Ulysses S. Grant in the presidential election of 1868 did not serve him well with white Democrats. But in 1876 he helped the national Democratic Party to investigate the dispute in Florida over the national election results. He publicly stated that the Democrats lawfully won the election. This work boosted his image in Georgia, and he was eventually elected to the U.S. Senate in 1880.

1706. Roberts, Derrell C. "Robert Toombs: An Unreconstructed Rebel on Freedmen." *Negro History Bulletin* 28 (Special Summer Issue 1965): 191-192. The former U.S. senator from Georgia fled the U.S. for Cuba and France after the war until his return in 1867. Toombs staunchly opposed to civil rights reforms for the freedmen, and he blamed Northern politicians and carpetbaggers for the South's problems.

1707.   Roberts, Lucien. "The Political Career of Joshua Hill, Georgia Unionist." *Georgia Historical Quarterly* 21 (March 1937): 50-72.   Hill was a longtime Unionist who helped organize the Constitutional Unionist Party that nominated John Bell for president in 1860. He gave tacit support to the Confederacy, but after the war he tried to influence the process of Reconstruction through the Republican Party. Hill actively opposed the Radicals in Congress and supported incremental change in race relations. Roberts believes that Hill's convictions were torn between love of state and love of country.

1708.   Rogers, William Warren (ed.). "Nelson Tift Applies For Pardon 1865." *Georgia Historical Quarterly* 51 (June 1967): 230-232.   Tift's letter requesting a pardon from President Johnson is printed. Prior to the war Tift was a resident of Albany, Ga., where he edited the *Patriot*.

1709.   Rogers, William Warren, Jr. "'Not Reconstructed by a Long Ways Yet': Southwest Georgia's Disputed Congressional Election of 1870." *Georgia Historical Quarterly* 82 (Summer 1998): 257-282. Ills. Ports.   The election of December, 1870 in the 2nd Congressional district revealed racial and political divisions that led to voter intimidation, violence and fraud on the part of determined white Democrats. Georgia had recently returned to the Union for the second time, but most whites in southwestern Georgia counties did not respect the Reconstruction laws. The congressional election pitted Democrat Nelson Tift against Republican Richard Whitely. Rogers examines the highly partisan election campaign in a district where blacks outnumbered whites.

1710.   Russ, William A., Jr. "Radical Disfranchisement in Georgia, 1867-1871." *Georgia Historical Quarterly* 19 (September 1935): 175-209.   Radical Reconstruction failed in Georgia partly because Congress was unable to disenfranchise many white voters in accordance with the Reconstruction Acts of 1867. White Georgians were so recalcitrant and put up so much resistance to disenfranchisement that the whites held a slim majority over blacks in the number of registered voters. Passive and active resistance wore down Congress and led to the return of Democratic power in Georgia in 1871.

1711.   Russell, James M. and Jerry Thornbery. "William Finch of Atlanta, the Black Politician as Civic Leader." In *Southern Black Leaders of the Reconstruction Era*. Edited by Howard N. Rabinowitz. Urbana: University of Illinois Press, 1982. Ill. Port. Pp. 309-334.   Finch, a former slave and skilled tailor from Athens, Georgia, became a central figure in Atlanta politics as a local leader for political equality, the development of elementary and higher education, and municipal services. As a city councilman in the late 1860s and early 1870s, he was a pragmatic, idealistic politician who worked with white leaders and sought support from Democrats as well as Republicans. His political career also illustrates that political opportunities for blacks existed in Atlanta for several years after the war.

1712.   Shadgett, Olive Hall. "James Johnson, Provisional Governor of Georgia." *Georgia Historical Quarterly* 36 (March 1952): 1-21.   Shadgett describes

Johnson's tenure as provisional governor from January 16, 1865 until December 19, 1865.

1713. Shadgett, Olive Hall. *The Republican Party in Georgia: From Reconstruction Through 1900.* Athens: University of Georgia Press, 1964. 210p. App. Bibl. Shadgett emphasizes the unstable nature of Republican rule in Georgia brought on by corruption in the government of Gov. Rufus Bullock, the Republicans' identification with blacks and Radicals and internal factions. Most of the book deals with the post-Reconstruction period that was noted for the continued existence of the Republican Party through the end of the century. The appendices list Republican members of Congress, presidential electors, delegates to the party national conventions, and state central committee heads. (See also Shadgett's Ph.D. dissertation with the same title from University of Georgia, 1962.)

1714. Shingleton, Royce. "Atlanta Becomes the Capital: The Role of Richard Peters." *Atlanta Historical Journal* 28 (Winter 1984-1985): 39-50. Ills. Map. Peters was a leader in the effort to move the state capitol from Milledgeville to Atlanta in 1868 based on his relationship with district military commanders, his offer of land for buildings, and the ready agreement of local officials. Gen. George G. Meade, a district commander, believed that it would make his command easier as well. Peters, a Whig and reluctant Confederate, became a Republican after the war and then a Democrat by the end of Reconstruction. For this reason credit for the capitol transfer has been obscured.

1715. Smith, W. Calvin. "The Reconstruction 'Triumph' of Rufus B. Bullock." *Georgia Historical Quarterly* 52 (December 1968): 414-425. Bullock was elected governor in 1868, but moderate Republicans and Democrats united to oppose his radical politics, including the 15th Amendment, and removed elected black members from the legislature. Bullock's "triumph" was the restoration of military Reconstruction in Georgia and the restoration of black legislators, but the Republican Party was irreparably split. Bullock's involvement in corruption led to the Republican defeat in the November, 1870 election.

1716. Southland, Daniel E. "Edwin DeLeon and Liberal Republicanism in Georgia: Horace Greeley's Campaign for President in the Southern State." *Historian* 47 (November 1984): 38-57. DeLeon was a Democrat who led the Greeley campaign in Georgia. His views of Greeley depart from the commonly accepted idea that Democrats who supported the candidate did so as a way to bring home rule back to the South, improve the chances of sectional reconciliation, and enhance Democratic power. DeLeon actually liked Greeley, and as campaign manager and editor of the *Savannah Republican*, he promoted his candidate. Georgians were more concerned with gaining home rule through local elections, but DeLeon helped Greeley win the state.

1717. Studley, Elizabeth N. "Shaping a New Era: The Politics of Georgia Reconstruction, 1865-1872." Ph.D. Johns Hopkins University, 1966.

1718.   Tankersley, Allen P. *John B. Gordon: A Study in Gallantry*. Atlanta: Whitehall Press, 1955. 400p. Bibl. Ports. Ills.   Gordon has held a high place of honor in Georgia because of his service as an officer in the Confederate Army, his Southern loyalty and political service in Congress during Reconstruction, and his part as a national Democratic leader and governor of the state in the 1880s. Gordon's revulsion to Georgia's Republican government, black labor troubles, and black political organization led to his participation and possible leadership in the Ku Klux Klan. After his election to the U.S. Senate in 1873, he became an outspoken apologist for the South in his effort to bring Reconstruction to an end.   Gordon became known for decades as one who sought to heal sectional differences and promote American nationalism while maintaining Southern distinctiveness.

1719.   Taylor, Arthur R. "From the Ashes: Atlanta During Reconstruction, 1865-1876." Ph.D. Emory University, 1973. 444p.

1720.   Tebeau, C. W. "Visitors' Views of Georgia Politics and Life, 1865-1880." *Georgia Historical Quarterly* 26 (March 1942): 1-15.   Tebeau briefly describes the impressions of several travelers in Georgia after the Civil War. Among the persons cited are Robert Somers (Glasgow *Morning Journal* until his trip), Sidney Andrews *(Boston Advertiser* and *Chicago Tribune)*, J. T. Trowbridge and Charles Nordhoff *(New York Herald)*. Travelers who left diaries frequently commented on the mood of the people, freedmen and race relations, and the rebuilding of Atlanta and Savannah.

1721.   Ward, Judson C., Jr. "The Republican Party in Bourbon Georgia, 1872-1890." *Journal of Southern History* 9 (May 1943): 196-209.   Republican Party control of Georgia during Congressional Reconstruction was never firm even after the election of Rufus B. Bullock as governor in 1868. Control of the legislature was split with the Democrats and after the 1870 election the Democratic Party controlled both houses. Bullock's resignation in October, 1871 led to the election of Democrat James M. Smith who took office in January, 1872. From that point the Republicans steadily lost control of their legislative and Congressional seats and were crushed by white supremacy.

1722.   Watts, Eugene J. "Black Political Progress in Atlanta: 1868-1895." *Journal of Negro History* 59 (July 1974): 268-286.   Beginning in 1868 blacks played a role in Atlanta politics as voters, officeholders, candidates, and rally participants. Both Republican and Democratic candidates attempted to woe the black vote, but during Reconstruction blacks had an impact only in the election of 1870 and several elections between 1877 and 1891. The role of blacks in Atlanta politics was never great, and their rights were practically eliminated in the 1890s.

1723.   Wight, Willard E. "Negroes in the Georgia Legislature: The Case of F. H. Fyall of Macon County." *Georgia Historical Quarterly* 44 (March 1960): 85-97. After the spring elections of 1868 there were 29 members of the state legislature who were classified as black, including 4 who had features that made them appear more Caucasian than Negroid. Fyall was one of the four and his eligibility was challenged on the basis of his race and his ancestral background. Wight explains the case that resulted in the dismissal of Fyall, along with all other black legislators based on their ineligibility.

1724.   Wight, Willard E. (ed.).   "Reconstruction in Georgia: Three Letters." *Georgia Historical Quarterly* 41 (March 1957): 81-89.   Higbee, a native of Vermont who moved to Georgia before the Civil War, became a Radical politician in the Reconstruction legislature.   In late April, 1868 he wrote to Maj. John R. Lewis, Assistant Inspector General of the Sub-District of Georgia, to describe how U.S. troops were befriended by enemies of Reconstruction even though they were sent to maintain order and protect the freedmen.

1725.   Wotton, Grigsby H. "New City of the South: Atlanta, 1843-1873." Ph.D. Johns Hopkins University, 1973. 450p.

1726.   Wynne, Lewis N. and Milly St. Julien. "The Camilla Race Riot and the Failure of Reconstruction in Georgia." *Journal of Southwest Georgia History* 5 (Fall 1987): 15-37. Ills.   The riot in Camilla in Mitchell County on September 19, 1868 symbolized the failed policies of Republican Reconstruction in Georgia and the increasingly violent rejection by whites of freedmen's demands for equal civil and political rights. The authors illustrate how the riot was a logical development in Reconstruction race relations given the postwar history of the state and an environment of Republican coercive reforms.

1727.   Wynne, Lewis N. *The Continuity of Cotton: Planter Politics in Georgia, 1865-1892*. Macon: Mercer University Press, 1986. 200p. Bibl. Tbls.   Wynne focuses on the planters' struggle in Georgia to rebuild their power and wealth destroyed by the Civil War by trying to control political activities. They met strong resistance from a growing class of merchants, industrialists, independents, and Republicans. By 1870 the Democratic Party regained control of state government, but it took several years and a coalition with industrialists before the planters substantially regained their former power. The state constitution of 1877 became the foundation for a revived planter class that was just as dominant as it was in 1861. (See also Wynne's "Planter Politics in Georgia, 1860-1890." Ph.D. University of Georgia, 1980. 486p.)

Agriculture, Labor, and Business

1728.   Armstrong, Thomas F. "From Task Labor to Free Labor: The Transition Along Georgia's Rice Coast, 1820-1880." *Georgia Historical Quarterly* 64 (Fall 1980): 432-447.   Prior to the Civil War task labor allowed slaves greater work autonomy and free time compared with working on a time schedule. After the war the freedmen insisted on maintaining the same task oriented work environment, but within the confines of a mutually agreed contract. By 1880 the changing nature of labor in the South and increasing competition from rice production in other regions and from other industries, such as timber, eventually depressed the rice industry in coastal Georgia.

1729.   Belser, Thomas A., Jr. "Alabama Plantation to Georgia Farm, John Horry Dent and Reconstruction." *Alabama Historical Quarterly* 25 (Spring/Summer 1963): 136-148.   Dent was apparently an exception to historians' generalizations that Radical Reconstruction ruined the Southern plantation class. Dent, a native of Rhode Island who moved to Barbour County in 1837, had his fortune in slaves diminished by emancipation, but he retained his land.   His plantation journal describes his reaction to the loss of slave labor and his subsequent move to a farm in Cave Springs, Georgia in 1866.   During Reconstruction he continued to build his wealth while remaining outside of politics.

1730.   Brooks, Robert Preston. "The Agrarian Revolution in Georgia 1865-1912." Ph.D. University of Wisconsin, 1914. (See also *Bulletin of the University of Wisconsin*, No. 639, History Series, Vol. 3, no. 3: 393-524; AMS Press, 1914).

1731.   Cimbala, Paul A. "The Freedmen's Bureau, the Freedmen, and Sherman: Grant in Reconstruction Georgia, 1865-1867." *Journal of Southern History* 45 (November 1989): 597-632.   During 1865 and 1866 freedmen benefited from Gen. William T. Sherman's Special Field Order No. 15 that provided land along the Georgia coast.   President Johnson's policy, however, eventually restored the lands to the antebellum owners.   The bureau, led by Gen. Rufus Sexton and Gen. Davis Tillson hoped that the experience of free labor would put the freedmen on the road to economic independence, but the concept failed.   Even so the labor system offered possibilities for independence and the negotiation of wages and working conditions. (See also Cimbala's "The 'Talisman Power': Davis Tillson, the Freedmen's Bureau, and Free Labor in Reconstruction Georgia, 1865-1866." *Civil War History* 28 (June 1982): 153-171 for an elaboration on Tillson's efforts that were stymied by persistent resistance of the planters and local courts.)

1732.   Doster, James F. "The Georgia Railroad and Banking Co. in the Reconstruction Era." *Georgia Historical Quarterly* 48 (March 1964): 1-32.   The company emerged from the Civil War intact and profitable, and was able to take advantage of the expanding need for rail service as the Southeast gradually recovered from the destruction of war.   The company was successful under the leadership of President John P. King.

1733.   Engerrand, Steven W. "'New Scratch or Die': The Genesis of Capitalistic Agricultural Labor in Georgia, 1865-1880." Ph.D. University of Georgia, 1981. 270p.

1734.   Flynn, Charles L., Jr. *White Land, Black Labor: Caste and Class in Late Nineteenth-Century Georgia*. Baton Rouge: Louisiana State University Press, 1983. 196p. Bibl.   Flynn explains how the relationship between white landowners and laborers represents the tensions between class and caste throughout the South.   Virtually all whites believed that all classes of people of their race were equals and that blacks were an underclass, but Flynn shows that individual white landowners sought advantages over whites in economic classes above and below themselves. This class rivalry and the tenacious racial class system based on labor manipulation and political violence combined to stymie economic prosperity for all.

1735.   Formwalt, Lee W. "Antebellum Planter Persistence: Southwest Georgia-A Case Study." *Plantation Society in the Americas* 1 (October 1981): 410-429. Tbls. Formwalt uses Wiener's studies (see # 1449-1451) as a model for his research on the survival of planter elite during and after the Civil War.   He finds that in southwestern Georgia counties the planter elite tended to retain their land but at a lower percentage than in Weiner's study of western Alabama. In both cases the war had little effect when compared with persistence from 1850 to 1860. Factors other than the war seem to influence the rate of planter survival.

1736.   Gottlieb,   Manuel.   "The   Land   Question   in   Georgia   During Reconstruction." *Science and Society* 3 (Summer 1939): 356-388.   Freedmen in Georgia eagerly sought land as a symbol of their freedom.   U.S. government officials began a rumor that land distributions would be made, but Gottlieb argues that Georgia Republicans generally opposed confiscation and redistribution of land. The Radicals who might have supported the proposal were weak, as illustrated at the 1867 constitutional convention.

1737.   Hahn, Steven H. "The Roots of Southern Populism: Yeoman Farmers and the Transportation of Georgia's Upper Piedmont, 1850-1900."   Ph.D.   Yale University, 1979. 490p.

1738.   House, Albert V., Jr.   "A Reconstruction Share-Cropper Contract on a Georgia Rice-Plantation." *Georgia Historical Quarterly* 26 (June 1942): 156-165. House briefly covers the historiography of postwar black labor with emphasis on wage, lien, and share cropper contracts in Georgia. He prints a portion of Charles Manigault's diary and a tenant contract. In order to keep his land under cultivation, Manigault had to rent portions of his plantation to tenants.

1739.   McGuire, Peter S. "The Railroads of Georgia, 1860-1880." *Georgia Historical Quarterly* 16 (September 1932): 179-215.   McGuire focuses on the physical regeneration, expansion, and business of railroads in the state after the Civil War.   He also describes corruption in the public issuance of bonds and political payoffs that contributed to the pressure to expand the railroads.

1740.   McLeod,   Jonathan   W.   *Workers   and   Workplace   Dynamics   in Reconstruction-Era Atlanta: A Case Study.* Los Angeles: University of California at Los Angeles, 1989. 135p. Bibl. Ills.   Atlanta responded to peace in 1865 by developing a dynamic economy based on railroads, iron mills, manufacturing, food processing, construction, and services such as hospitality, retail trade and domestics. Growth led to friction between employers and workers, and workers were themselves stratified by industry and level of skills. Attempts to unionize workers was stymied by these differences, but perhaps the most corrosive element working against successful unionization was racism. (See also McLeod's "Black and White Workers: Atlanta During Reconstruction." Ph.D. University of California, Los Angeles, 1987. 392p.)

1741.   O'Donovan, Susan Eva. "Transforming Work: Slavery, Free Labor, and the Household in Southwest Georgia, 1850-1880." Ph.D. University of California, San Diego, 1997. 536p.

1742.   Reidy, Joseph P. "Aaron A. Bradley: Voice of Black Labor in the Georgia Lowcountry." In *Southern Black Leaders of the Reconstruction Era*. Edited by Howard N. Rabinowitz. Urbana: University of Illinois Press, 1982. Pp. 281-308. Bradley was a major force in the struggle of lowcountry blacks to gain political and social rights as free citizens. In the Savannah region he demanded equal rights and access to land as the basis for future black success. The former slave organized black laborers, but he generated tension with white leaders and some black organizations as well.

1743.   Reidy, Joseph P. *From Slavery to Agrarian Capitalism in the Cotton Plantation South: Central Georgia, 1800-1880*. Chapel Hill: University of North Carolina, 1992. 360p. App. Bibl.   A substantial portion of this book deals with postwar changes to economic relationships between elite, white planters, freedmen, and small landholding whites in the central Georgia counties of Jones, Twiggs, Crawford, Houston, and Monroe. Reidy traces the transformation of Southern agricultural organization during Reconstruction from slave oligarchy to agrarian capitalism and finally to industrial capitalism ruled by the planters. The freedmen were unwillingly pushed by political and statutory forces into being a rural proletariat. The planter capitalists successfully sought control over black labor and, simultaneously, they also pushed small white landowners and laborers into a position of political and economic weakness that would generate agrarian unrest by the 1880s.

1744.   Roberts, Derrell C. "Joseph E. Brown and the Western & Atlantic Railroad." *Atlanta Historical Journal* 39 (Spring 1985): 5-40. Ills.   Former Governor Brown became a Republican during Reconstruction and used his connections and financial skills to contribute to the expansion of the Western & Atlantic Railroad. His methods were questioned, because he directed state business to his own enterprises, and he may have been involved in fraud, but he contributed to the expansion of transportation that had a great impact in Atlanta and throughout Georgia.

1745.   Stephens, Lester D. "William Louis Jones and the Advancement of Scientific Agriculture in the South During the Era of Reconstruction." *Georgia Journal of Science* 49 (1991): 72-80.   As a planter, teacher, agricultural administrator, and editor of the *Southern Cultivator*, Jones promoted agricultural experimentation and scientific methodologies among well-to-do Southern farmers after the Civil War. Stephens traces Jones' career and cites responses to Jones' ideas that were published in his periodical. The former slaveholder accepted emancipation and a wage labor system, but he continued to believe that blacks were not good workers as free people and that only with paternalism and coercion would they be productive.

1746.   Stover, John F. "Georgia Railroads During the Reconstruction Years." *Railroad History* 134 (1976): 56-65.   The terrible condition of Georgia railroads after the Civil War was reversed by the end of Reconstruction with repairs and additions to rail lines, but Stover criticizes the corrupt administration of Gov. Rufus Bullock for giving generous funding to the railroad industry.

1747.   Thompson, William Y. "Robert Toombs and the Georgia Railroads." *Georgia Historical Quarterly* 39 (March 1956): 56-64.   Thompson analyses Toombs' philosophy and approach toward railroad services and its relationship to state regulation from the early 1870s until 1877 when a new state constitution was considered. He actively sought to regulate rail services so that they would serve the people of Georgia and not receive special favors. Toombs deplored the graft and plundering that occurred in state financing of railroads during Republican administrations.

1748.   Werner, Randolph Dennis. "Hegemony and Conflict: The Political Economy of a Southern Region, Augusta, Georgia, 1865-1895." Ph.D.   University of Virginia, 1977. 463p.

1749.   Wynne, Lewis N. "The Role of Freedmen in the Post Bellum Cotton Economy of Georgia." *Phylon* 42 (December 1981): 309-321.   Freedmen resisted any type of labor arrangement that put them in a position similar to slavery. Freedmen's Bureau agents tried to balance fair wages and working conditions by insisting that freedmen agree to terms so that labor would be available. This conflict led to the widespread use of sharecropping in Georgia, but blacks still did not gain much economic improvements because they could not acquire enough land.

Society, Education, and Religion

1750.   Armstrong, Thomas F. "The Building of a Black Church: Community in Post Civil War Liberty County, Georgia." *Georgia Historical Quarterly* 66 (Fall 1982): 346-367.   The interaction of religion and politics in the Midway district of Liberty County split the local black community as it sought to build independent black churches. Congregationalist ministers Floyd Snelson and W. A. Golding feuded for control of the church and its members. White Democrats sought to influence the church for political support and encouraged further divisions among blacks.

1751.   Blassingame, John W. "Before the Ghetto: The Making of the Black Community in Savannah, Georgia, 1865-1880." *Journal of Social History* 6 (Summer 1973): 463-488. Map. Tbls. (Rpt. in *Church and Community Among*

Black Southerners 1865-1900. Edited by Donald Nieman. New York: Garland, 1994.)   Savannah serves as a case study of how different Southern cities compare with Northern cities with regard to the development of black communities. The theory of black ghettoization and poverty does not apply to postwar cities like Savannah that experienced a dynamic black community where integrated neighborhoods prevailed until the 20th century, and blacks successfully built a deep institutional structure as free people. Blassingame focuses on the demographics of the black community.

1752.   Bonner, James C. The Georgia Penitentiary at Milledgeville 1817-1874." *Georgia Historical Quarterly* 55 (Fall 1971): 303-328.   Bonner devotes several pages to the reforms carried out during Reconstruction. The state improved the prison facility in 1867-1868, but the tone of state management was concerned more with saving money than penal reform. The legislature legalized the lease of prisons and prisoners to private business. The convict lease system was used extensively in these years. Large numbers of blacks in the prison created management problems that did not exist under slavery.

1753.   Botume, Elizabeth Hyde. *First Days Amongst the Contrabands.* New York: Arno Press, 1968. 286p. (Rpt. of Boston: Lee and Shepard Publishers, 1893)   This book is Botume's memoir as a teacher hired by the New England Freedmen's Aid Society from October 1864 until 1869. She describes her activities and gives her perspective on the state and development of blacks in the coastal Georgia region.

1754.   Brown, Titus. "Origins of African American Education in Macon, Georgia, 1865-1866." *Journal of Southwest Georgia History* 11 (Fall 1996): 43-59. Ills.   Brown describes how freedmen organized their own schools in the summer of 1865 until the Western Freedmen's Aid Commission and the Freedmen's Bureau arrived with resources and organization for the expansion of the schools. In November the WFAC transferred responsibility for Macon schools to the American Missionary Association under the direction of Rev. Hiram Eddy. Eddy worked with state and area bureau agents to make a successful beginning to freedmen schools, despite a shortage of funding and resistance from the white community.

1755.   Bryant, Jonathan M. *How Curious a Land: Conflict and Change in Greene County, Georgia, 1850-1885.* Chapel Hill: University of North Carolina Press, 1996. 266p. App. Bibl. Maps.   Bryant explains how life in Greene County changed in northcentral Georgia during the war and Reconstruction. In particular, freedmen demanded equal rights and political power through voting and officeholding, but they were under the constant threat of violence from the Ku Klux Klan and their white supporters. (See also # 1662)

1756.   Caldwell, John H. *Reminiscences of the Reconstruction of Church and State in Georgia.* Wilmington, Del.: J. Miller Thomas, 1895. 23p. Port. Caldwell recalls his participation in the attempted reform of the Methodist Episcopal Church, South and in the introduction of Republican government during

Reconstruction. The Southern preacher decided at the end of the war that he would speak out against slavery and in favor of justice for the black people. He looked toward a "New South" in temper, attitude and economic progress.

1757.   Campbell, William A. (ed.). "A Freedmen's Bureau Diary By George Wagner." *Georgia Historical Quarterly* 48 (June 1964): 333-360.   Wagner, a native of Philadelphia, fought with Union forces and served with the Freedmen's Bureau from 1866 to 1868 in Macon and Americus. Printed here is his diary which provides mostly personal information and daily reports on weather conditions.

1758.   Cimbala, Paul A.   "A Black Colony in Dougherty County: The Freedmen's Bureau and the Failure of Reconstruction in Southwestern Georgia." *Journal of Southwest Georgia History* 4 (Fall 1986): 72-89.   The failed attempt to establish a colony of black landowners in Dougherty County illustrates the weakness of the Freedmen's Bureau to protect the rights of freedmen and the inevitable collapse of Reconstruction generally. The Georgia bureau, particularly under the direction of Assistant Commissioner Gen. Davis Tillson from 1865 to 1867 insisted that freedmen not be given undue assistance such as hand outs of land. This approach was typical of 19th century America, but it guaranteed that blacks would not receive the help and protection that they needed.

1759.   Cimbala, Paul A. "Making Good Yankees: The Freedmen's Bureau and Education in Reconstruction Georgia, 1865-1870." *Atlanta Historical Journal* 29 (Fall 1985): 5-18.   The goal of bureau agents in Georgia was to emphasize the Northern free labor ideology of hard work and independence. In this context agents helped establish schools for freedmen, but they expected private funding for the schools, including funding from the freedmen. The effort to maintain and protect schools and teachers was hampered by hostile whites.

1760.   Cimbala, Paul A. "On the Front Line of Freedom: Freedmen's Bureau Officers and Agents in Reconstruction Georgia, 1865-1868." *Georgia Historical Quarterly* 76 (Fall 1992): 577-611. Ports.   The tone of the bureau's work to assist freedmen varied from one assistant commissioner to another in Georgia, but in general there was much consistency of ideology, policy, and results from one commissioner to another. The assistant commissioners were Gen. Rufus Saxton, Gen. Davis Tillson, and Maj. John Randolph Lewis. Reports from their local agents are testimonies to the difficulties in carrying out their work. Most of the agents showed sincerity in their interaction with freedmen, but the institution of the bureau itself and the determination of local whites to resist changes made success impossible.

1761.   Cimbala, Paul A. *Under the Guardianship of the Nation; The Freedmen's Bureau and the Reconstruction of Georgia, 1865-1870.* Athens: University of Georgia Press, 1997. 395p. Bibl. Ills. Maps. Ports.   Cimbala focuses on what the Georgia bureau sought to accomplish and whether its goals were achieved in the context of the resources provided by Congress and the volatile environment of the time. He documents the consistent commitment of the bureau to help the freedmen begin a free life, as well as the key forces responsible for its demise, including lack of human and financial resources and the active hostility of most white Georgians to freedom, equal justice, and civil rights for black citizens. (See also Cimbala's "The Terms of Freedom: The Freedmen's Bureau and Reconstruction in Georgia, 1865-1870." Ph.D. Emory University, 1983. 608p.; also see # 1797)

1762.   Cooper, Renée F.   "Reconstruction and Education: Voices From the South, 1865-1876." *Prologue* 27 (Summer 1995): 127-133.   Ills.   Using Freedmen's Bureau records at the National Archives, Cooper describes the challenges of teachers and the new freedmen schools in Georgia.

1763.   Coulter, E. Merton. "The New South: Benjamin H. Hill's Speech Before the Alumni of the University of Georgia, 1871." *Georgia Historical Quarterly* 57 (Summer 1973): 179-199.   Hill was an antebellum Whig who opposed secession but became a diligent supporter of the Confederacy and an opponent of Reconstruction. His speech surprised many people, because he cited the failings of the antebellum South, including the institution of slavery, and spoke of the need for Southerners to focus on rebuilding a prosperous, self sufficient society in the future. Hill' remarks were greeted with criticism by the Georgia press. (See also Coulter's "A Famous University of Georgia Commencement, 1871." *Georgia Historical Quarterly* 57 (Fall 1973): 347-360.)

1764.   Coulter, E. Merton. "Slavery and Freedom in Athens, Georgia, 1860-1866." *Georgia Historical Quarterly* 49 (September 1965): 269-293. (Rpt. in *Plantation, Town, and County: Essays on One Local History of American Slave Society*. Edited by Elinor Miller and Eugene D. Genovese. Urbana: University of Illinois, 1974, pp. 337-364.)   In his examination of the transition from slavery to freedom in Athens, Coulter characterizes blacks by their failure to earn "true freedom." He notes that the freedmen acted with selfish, child-like interests in their quest for freedom.   They were probably better off under the benevolent sort of slavery that existed in Georgia.

1765.   Formwalt, Lee W. "Moving in 'That Strange Land of Shadows': African-American Mobility and Persistence in Post Civil War Southwest Georgia." *Georgia Historical Quarterly* 82 (Fall 1998): 507-532.   Ills. Tbls.   Formwalt uses information from the census, state tax digests, and other sources to investigate the degree of mobility among freedmen in Dougherty County in southwestern Georgia and whether they stayed close to their preemancipation homes between 1865 and the late 1880s. Persistence and mobility varied over time depending on characteristics such as gender, family status, labor skill and the transition of individual plantations to tenantry and sharecropping. Mobility was an expression of freedom and as a way to escape from difficult economic and violent conditions.

1766.   Garrett, Franklin M. "Atlanta and Environs, 1865." *Atlanta Historical Journal* 15 (Fall 1970): 95-132; "1866," 15 (Winter 1970): 102-141; "1867," 16 (Spring 1971): 68-113; "1868," 16 (Summer 1971): 68-103; "1869," 17(Spring-Summer 1972): 64-94; "1870," 17 (Fall-Winter 1972): 59-95; "1871," 18 (Spring-

Summer 1973): 60-77.   The author surveys Atlanta society, culture, religion, education, economy and politics during Reconstruction.   The series is based on contemporary periodicals, newspapers, directories, and organizational minutes.

1767.   Harris, J. William. "Plantations and Power: Emancipation on the David Barrow Plantation." In *Toward a New South? Studies in Post-Civil War Southern Communities*.   Westport: Greenwood Press, 1982.   Pp. 246-264.   Map. Emancipation led to changes in the power structure between old masters, overseers, and former slaves.   Harris offers the example of David Grenshaw Borrow's plantation in Oglethorpe County, Georgia.   Borrow clearly recognized the greater degree of independence displayed by the freedmen and his lack of power to control them.   Freedmen demanded tenant farming, the establishment of schools and churches on the plantation.

1768.   Hesseltine, William B. and Larry Gara. "Georgia's Confederate Leaders After Appomatox." *Georgia Historical Quarterly* 35 (December 1951): 1-15. After the Civil War the former Confederate leaders of Georgia became the most important resource for the future reconstruction and development of the state.   The authors emphasize the contributions of these leaders to building a new South, and they survey the background of 68 persons who held high military or political offices in the Confederacy.

1769.   Hollingsworth, R. R. "Education and Reconstruction." *Georgia Historical Quarterly* 19 (June 1935):   112-133;   (September 1935): 229-250.   Tbl. Hollingsworth's history of educational reform in Georgia focuses on the organization and funding of free public schools for whites and blacks.   The Republican Reconstruction government made important reforms, but reforms were put in motion by Democrats prior to the war and immediately afterwards. Democratic reforms would have led to the same legislative enactments without Congressional Reconstruction, the misappropriation of education funds, and the influence of carpetbaggers.

1770.   Huffman, Frank J., Jr. "Old South, New South: Continuity and Change in a Georgia County, 1850-1880." Ph.D. Yale University, 1974. 307p.

1771.   Hunter, Tera W. "Household Workers in the Making: Afro-American Women in Atlanta and the New South, 1861-1920." Ph.D. Yale University, 1990. 322p.

1772.   Inscoe, John C. (ed.). *Georgia in Black and White: Explorations in the Race Relations of a Southern State, 1865-1950*. Athens: University of Georgia Press, 1994.   300p.   This book of essays includes four works on the Reconstruction. (See # 1662, 1678, 1796, 1799)

1773.   Johnson, Whittington B.   "A Black Teacher and Her School in Reconstruction Darien: The Correspondence of Hettier Sabattie and J. Murray Hoag, 1868-1869." *Georgia Historical Quarterly* 75 (Spring 1991): 90-105. Ills.

Johnson reprints correspondence between Hoag, an assistant superintendent of education in the Freedmen's Bureau based in Savannah, and Sabattie, a mulatto women who organized and taught at a black-run school in Darien, Georgia located in McIntosh County after the Civil War. The letters relate to the operation of the school and reveal the important work performed by two people who are obscure.

1774.   Jones, Jacqueline. *Soldiers of Light and Love: Northern Teachers and Georgia Blacks, 1865-1873.* Chapel Hill: University of North Carolina, 1980. 273p. App. Bibl. Tbls.   Jones expands on McPherson's work (see # 1085) by focusing on young, elementary school teachers in Georgia during the most active time for Northern teachers and the Freedmen's Bureau in the South.   Jones recognizes this group as an extension of antebellum abolitionism steeped in white middle class values of evangelicalism, self control and hard work. Their crusade to educate freedmen was sincere, but few blacks converted to Congregationalism, relatively few were exposed to education for very long, and the racist notions of the teachers and Southern society stymied educational achievements. The stereotypes of 19th century sexism in early Victorian America were not valid for this group of women. (See also Jones' "The 'Great Opportunity': Northern Teachers and the Georgia Freedmen, 1865-1873." Ph.D. University of Wisconsin, Madison, 1976. 475p.)

1775.   King, Spencer B., Jr. "A Poor Widow Asks For Food: 1865." *Georgia Historical Quarterly* 52 (December 1968): 449-450.   Printed is a letter from a Milledgeville widow to Union General James H. Wilson whose troops were stationed near the town in early May, 1865. By pointing out her destitute state and requesting food, the letter illustrates conditions in an area ravaged by war.

1776.   Kuchler, Eula Turner. "Charitable and Philanthropic Activities in Atlanta During Reconstruction." *Atlanta Historical Bulletin* 10 (September 1965): 12-54; 11 (March 1966): 20-54.   Local government and private religious and nonsectarian organizations contributed to aiding the poor and destitute in Atlanta between 1865 and 1872. Kuchler comments on medical care, orphanages, relief provisions, and education.

1777.   Lee, Anne S. and Everett S. Lee. "The Health of Slaves and the Health of Freedmen: A Savannah Study." *Phylon* 38 (June 1977): 170-180.   A comparison of the health of slaves and freedmen in Savannah from prior to the Civil War until 1869 is based on Dr. W. Duncan's *Tabulated Mortuary Record of the City of Savannah* from January 1, 1854 to December 31, 1869. The authors hypothesize that the health of blacks worsened after the Civil War based on data showing increased mortality from disease and the disruption of settled living conditions that required difficult adjustments.

1778.   Leigh, Frances Butler. *Ten Years on a Georgia Plantation Since the War, 1866-1876.* London: Richard Bentley & Son, 1883. 347p. (Also published as *Principles and Privilege: Two Women's Lives on a Georgia Plantation.* Intro. by Dana D. Nelson. Ann Arbor: University of Michigan Press, 1994. 240p.)   Leigh inherited a plantation after the Civil War. Her book is a chronological narrative of her experience in Georgia during the periods when she visited the plantation from her home in the North. Leigh was an absentee landlord who encountered problems managing her plantation, including maintaining labor. Her narrative and various letters provide impressions of Georgia farming, Southern society, and the black race in its new state of freedom. The 1994 edition includes a diary from the 1830s by Leigh's mother, Fanny Kemble.

1779.   Massey, Kate. "A Picture of Atlanta in the Late Sixties." *Atlanta Historical Journal* 5 (January 1940): 32-36.   Massey describes the dreadful state of life in Atlanta after the war.

1780.   Mitchell, Eugene M. "Atlanta During the Reconstruction Period." *Atlanta Historical Bulletin* 2 (November 1936): 18-24.   This brief narrative describes the political, economic, and social life of the city from 1865 to 1872. Mitchell provides a negative view of Reconstruction.

1781.   Nathans, Sydney. "Fortress Without Walls: A Black Community After Slavery." In *Holding on to the Land and the Lord: Kinship, Ritual, Land Tenure, and Social Policy in the Rural South.* Athens: University of Georgia Press, 1982. Pp. 55-65. (Rpt. in *Church and Community Among Black Southerners 1865-1900.* Edited by Donald Nieman. New York: Garland, 1994. Pp. 173-83)   Nathans explores the postwar experiences of blacks who purchased portions of Paul Cameron's plantation in Hale County. Land ownership and religion combined to form a vital community. Much of his evidence is based on interviews with 20th century descendants.

1782.   Newman, Harvey K. "Piety and Segregation-White Protestant Attitudes Toward Blacks in Atlanta, 1865-1905." *Georgia Historical Quarterly* 63 (Summer 1979): 238-251.   Race relations in Atlanta worsened after the Civil War, partly because of widespread segregation of previously integrated churches and the refusal of whites to help blacks in their struggle for civil rights. White Methodist, Methodist Episcopal, and Baptist church leaders believed in the superiority of the white race and reinforced the caste system.

1783.   Newman, Harvey K. "The Vision of Order: White Protestant Christianity in Atlanta, 1865-1906." Ph.D. Emory University, 1977. 208p.

1784.   Owens, James L. "Blacks in Reconstruction Georgia." *Integrated Education* 14 (1976): 35-37.   Owens briefly reviews how blacks responded to their new freedoms in politics, education, and religion.

1785.   Owens, James L. "The Negro in Georgia During Reconstruction 1864-1872: A Social History." Ph.D. University of Georgia, 1975. 272p.

1786.   Perdue, Robert E. *The Negro in Savannah 1865-1900.* New York: Exposition Press, 1973. 156p. Bibl.   Perdue examines the social, political, and economic conditions of blacks in Savannah after the Civil War. He considers a mixed pattern of race relations, segregation, political participation, education, and urban economy, and also describes the vitality of the Savannah community. Perdue was motivated by the lack of post Civil War studies on urban blacks.

1787.   "Postwar Lawlessness in the Atlanta Area." *Atlanta Historical Bulletin* 11 (June 1966): 32-34.   Reprinted is an article from *The Weekly Atlanta Intelligencer* from May 9, 1866 describing an act of theft and murder near Atlanta. (For a related article see "Brivet Brig. General Frederick W. Benteen," *Atlanta Historical Bulletin* 11 (June 1966): 19-31.)

1788.   Rapport, Sara. "The Freedmen's Bureau as a Legal Agent for Black Men and Women in Georgia: 1865-1868." *Georgia Historical Quarterly* 73 (Spring 1989): 26-53.   Bureau agents in Georgia tried to be fair to both white and black communities, and blacks learned quickly that agents could offer them legal assistance with employer contracts, domestic disputes, and white violence. Agents could act harshly and their ability to protect freedmen was limited, but they were vital to the progress of freedmen during the first few years after the Civil War.

1789.   Rawlings, Kenneth W. "Statistics and Cross-Sections of the Georgia Press to 1870." *Georgia Historical Quarterly* 23 (June 1939): 177-187.   Rawlings provides information on Georgia newspapers during the 1870s with comparative information from the 1850s and 1860s. The newspapers are listed by county and include the name, character (i.e. politics, religion, etc.), frequency, and circulation. The statistics are derived from the U.S. Census and other sources.

1790.   Reidy, Joseph. "Masters and Slaves, Planters and Freedmen: The Transition From Slavery to Freedom in Central Georgia, 1820-1880."   Ph.D. Northern Illinois University, 1982. 521p. (See also # 1743)

1791.   Rogers, George A. and R. Frank Saunders, Jr. "The American Missionary Association in Liberty County, Georgia: An Invasion of Light and Love." *Georgia Historical Quarterly* 62 (Winter 1978): 304-315.   A.M.A. teachers and ministers helped establish Dorchester Academy and the New Midway Congregational Church in Liberty County. The organization worked in the county well into the 20th century.

1792.   Savitt, Todd L. "Politics in Medicine: The Georgia Freedmen's Bureau and the Organization of Health Care, 1865-1866." *Civil War History* 28 (March 1982): 45-64.   The medical department of the Freedmen's Bureau provided health care to indigent freedmen until local health authorities could take full responsibilities. But the temporary nature of the service led to political problems with local white health authorities in Georgia. The medical service, under the leadership of Surgeon John W. Lawton, also encountered insufficient qualified personnel, financing, and supplies, and also communicable diseases, such as small pox. These problems led to the deaths of many people and did not establish a foundation for adequate health care for the freedmen.

1793. Shryock, Richard H. *Letters of Richard D. Arnold, M. D. 1808-1876. Mayor of Savannah, Georgia, First Secretary of the American Medical Association.* Durham, N. C.: Seeman Press, 1929. 178p. App. (*Papers of the Trinity College Historical Society,* Duke University, 18-19). Arnold's letters include many on the subject of Reconstruction in the Savannah area. He wrote to friends and associates about the Confederate defeat, the emancipation of slaves, state politics, and the health and education of the local population.

1794. Smith, Albert C. "Down Freedom's Road: The Contours of Race, Class, and Property Crime in Black Belt Georgia, 1866-1910." Ph.D. University of Georgia, 1982. 313p.

1795. Smith, Albert C. "'Southern Violence' Reconsidered: Arson as Protest in Black-Belt Georgia, 1865-1910." *Journal of Southern History* 51 (November 1985): 527-564. Map. Tbls. Smith examines Terrell and Baldwin counties in his study of violent crime in the South. Historians have long recognized the prevalence of violence, particularly homicide and assault, in Southern culture, and have attributed this behavior to cultural traits found among white Southerners. Smith refers to the South's "acute sense of grievance" prompted by "a history of defeat, occupation, and national ostracism" (p. 528). Arson, however, calls into question the assumptions made about violent crime. In the Georgia black belt arson was usually perpetrated by blacks against whites, was an assault on personal property based on interracial grievances and protest against economic depravation. Historians should consider more complex motivations and racial differences in violent crime in the South.

1796. Smith, Jennifer Lund. "The Ties That Bind: Educated African-American Women in Post-Emancipation Atlanta." In *Georgia in Black and White: Explorations in the Race Relations of a Southern State, 1865-1950.* Edited by John C. Inscoe. Athens: University of Georgia Press, 1994. Pp. 91-105. Notes. Smith focuses on the early years of Atlanta University, organized in 1869 by the American Missionary Association. She surveys the university's benefits to the women and men who attended, and its. influence on educational development of blacks in Atlanta. The study extends to the early 20th century.

1797. Smith, John David. "'The Work It Did Not Do Because it Could Not': Georgia and the 'New' Freedmen's Bureau Historiography." *Georgia Historical Quarterly* 82 (Summer 1998): 331-349. Ports. This review essay on Paul Cimbala's *Under the Guardianship of the Nation: The Freedmen's Bureau and the Reconstruction of Georgia, 1865-1870* (see # 1761) is mainly a discussion on the historiography of the bureau. Smith describes the purposes of the bureau and covers highlights of historical writings since the early 20th century.

1798. Smits, A. C. G. (Edited by L. Moody Simms, Jr.). "A Comment on Savannah in 1866." *Georgia Historical Quarterly* 50 (December 1966): 459-460. Simms provides a letter by Smits of Virginia to Daniel Scanland of Middleburg.

Smits comments on life in Reconstruction Georgia, particularly the local economy and Southern acceptance of defeat and black labor.

1799.   Stowell, Daniel W. "'The Negroes Cannot Navigate Alone': Religious Scalawags and the Biracial Methodist Episcopal Church in Georgia, 1866-1876." In *Georgia in Black and White: Explorations in the Race Relations of a Southern State, 1865-1950.* Edited by John C. Inscoe. Athens: University of Georgia Press, 1994. Pp. 68-90. Port.   Religious scalawags were local white leaders in the Church who sought to rebuild the Georgia Confederation by reuniting with the Methodist Episcopal Church, North and bringing black and white members together. Church leaders organized black congregations and initiated schools for the freedmen.   By 1876 the effort to combine white and black Methodist Episcopal congregations in the state Conference had failed, because white members wanted segregation, and blacks resented white paternalism.   (See also Glenn T. Eskew, "Black Elitism and the Failure of Paternalism in Postbellum Georgia: The Case of Bishop Lucius Henry Holsey," in *Georgia in Black and White,* pp. 106-140.

1800.   Taylor, A. Elizabeth.   "The Origins of the Convict Lease System in Georgia."   *Georgia Historical Quarterly* 26 (June 1942): 113-128.   The convict lease system allowed the state to lease prisoners to commercial firms in return for money.   The state legislature legalized the system in December, 1866 although no leases occurred until 1868.   The system was abolished in 1908.   (See also Taylor's "The Abolition of the Convict Lease System in Georgia," *Georgia Historical Quarterly* 26 (September-December 1942): 273-287.)

1801.   Thompson, C. Mildred.   "The Freedmen's Bureau in Georgia, 1865-6:   An Instrument of Reconstruction." *Georgia Historical Quarterly* 5 (March 1921): 40-49.   Thompson provides a sympathetic view of the Freedmen's Bureau in Georgia led by Assistant Commissioner Gen. Davis Tillson.   She notes that after the experience of postwar reconstruction following World War I, it is easier to appreciate the work of the bureau.

1802.   Thornbery, Jerry.   "The Development of Black Atlanta, 1865-1885." Ph.D. University of Maryland, 1977. 352p.

1803.   Thornbery, Jerry.   "Northerners and the Atlanta Freedmen, 1865-1869." *Prologue* 6 (Winter 1974): 236-251. Ill.   Thornbery examines the impact of Union soldiers, the Freedmen's Bureau, and missionary society workers on the life of the freedmen in Atlanta.   Union soldiers lacked the commitment and interest in providing security for blacks, while the Freedmen's Bureau could not overcome racial prejudice and objections to government welfare programs.   The American Missionary Association helped to organize schools and colleges, and, along with Northern representatives of the Methodist Episcopal Church, tried to encourage religious faith and organization among the freedmen.   In general, their efforts represent the failed attempt to reform the South and to help the freedmen begin a new, promising future.

1804.   Wallenstein, Peter.   *From Slave South to New South: Public Policy in Nineteenth-Century Georgia.*   Chapel Hill: University of North Carolina, 1987. 284p.   Bibl.   Wallenstein shows the relationship between policies on taxation and debt, education, and railroads to illustrate that government policies are interrelated. Postwar Republican government in Georgia was brief and its financial policies were substantially set by wartime tax and debt decisions.   Also, Georgia Republicans had little impact on social policy for blacks and elementary and higher education in general because of racial prejudice, the lack of revenue, and the weak tax structure supporting these issues.   (See also Wallenstein's "From Slave South to New South: Taxes and Spending in Georgia From 1850 Through Reconstruction." Ph.D.   Johns Hopkins University, 1973.   433p.)

1805.   Waring, Martha Gallaudet.   "Notes and Documents: The Striving 'Seventies in Savannah'."   *Georgia Historical Quarterly* 20 (June 1936): 154-171. Waring uses letters written during Reconstruction to help describe social and political conditions in Savannah during the first half of the 1870s. (See also Thomas P. Waring, "Savanah of the 1870s," *Georgia Historical Quarterly* 20 (March 1936): 52-64.)

1806.   Williams, John.   "Hayne's 'The Prostrate South To the Radical North'." *Georgia Historical Quarterly* 49 (March 1965): 98-101.   *Banner of the South* was a periodical published in Augusta, Ga. from March 31, 1868 until October 15, 1870 by Rev. Abram Ryan.   He proposed to keep alive the "tradition and memories and glories of the struggle" of the South.   To this end he published a poem on January 16, 1869   (v. 1, no. 44) by Paul Hamilton Hayne on the trials of "The Prostrate State."   The poem is reprinted.

1807.   Wright, C. T.   "The Development of Education For Blacks in Georgia, 1865-1900." Ph.D.   Boston University, 1977.   283p.

Indian Territories

1808.   Abel, Annie Heloise.   *The American Indian and the End of the Confederacy, 1863-1866.*   Lincoln: University of Nebraska Press, 1993.   419p. Bibl.   (Rpt. of the 1925 edition by Arthur Clark Co. entitled *The American Indian Under Reconstruction*)   Abel focuses on the fortunes of the Cherokee, Choctaw, Chickasaw, Creeks and Seminoles, many of whom owned black slaves and gave varying degrees of support to the Confederacy and the Union. Many Indians fled to Missouri and Kansas during the war.   In general, Reconstruction for the Indians brought permanent dislocation, loss of property including black slaves, and loss of federal protection and rights supposedly guaranteed by prewar treaties.   The so called Treaties of 1866 were the foundation of a bitter Reconstruction for Southern Indians.

1809.   Andrews, Thomas F. "Freedmen in Indian Territory: Post-Civil War Dilemma." *Journal of the West* 4 (July 1965): 367-376.   The freedmen who were slaves of the Choctaw and Chickasaws found themselves in the middle of disputes between the Indian tribes and the federal government over where the freedmen should reside and the disposition of land in Indian territory located in the Oklahoma and Arkansas region. The treaty of July 10, 1866 was intended to form the basis for resolving issues, but the treaty was not followed, particularly with regard to the possible relocation of the freedmen. Freedmen sought to remain in Indian territory and use land in the region. The struggle over this issue contributed to greater congressional attention towards the Oklahoma territory.

1810.   Bolman, Gail. "The Creek Treaty of 1866." *Chronicles of Oklahoma* 43 (Summer 1970): 184-196. Map.   Federal peace commissioners from the Department of Interior met with Creeks and other Indian tribal leaders in September, 1865 to workout formal treaties of peace and Reconstruction. The government's approach varied depending on whether the tribes had been loyal to the Union or the Confederacy, but even loyal Creeks were held in suspicion in the context of the treaty negotiations. Bolman describes the proceedings at Levenworth, Kansas and later meetings in January, 1866 that concluded the treaty process. The Creek treaty abolished slavery and granted exslaves rights of citizenship. Bolman suggests that the treaty was a precursor to Republican Reconstruction plans in general, but the Creek treaty also included the government's plan to claim more Indian lands for white settlers and the expansion of railroads.

1811.   Grinde, Donald A., Jr. and Quintard Taylor. "Red vs. Black: Conflict and Accommodation in the Post Civil War Indian Territory, 1865-1907." *American Indian Quarterly* 8 (Summer 1984): 211-229. Tbls.   After the Civil War the federal government discontinued treaties with the Five Civilized Tribes (Seminoles, Creeks, Cherokees, Chickasaws and Choctaws) and eliminated slavery among the Indians. The tribes were forced to free their black slaves and decide what type of relationship they would have within Indian societies. The blacks who spoke Indian languages and lived in Indian culture were often discriminated against with black codes, particularly among the Chickasaw and Choctaw. Assimilation, acceptance, and civil rights of the freed blacks varied from one tribe to another, and the situation was complicated by the influx of blacks from outside of Indian territory. Indians were persistently wary of being overwhelmed by the increasing black population, and they sought to ensure their own survival.

1812.   James, Parthena Louise. "Reconstruction in the Chickasaw Nation: The Freedmen Problem." *Chronicles of Oklahoma* 45 (Spring 1967): 44-57.   The Treaty of 1866 between the U.S. government and the Chickasaw Nation was supposed to solve the problem of the freedmen among the Chickasaw. Free blacks were not desired among the Indians who feared for their culture and political power on their lands. The treaty failed because the federal government never acted to help move the freedmen or to assist them in Chickasaw territory. The confusion prolonged racial tensions, the lack of civil rights for blacks, and the Chickasaw attempts to cope with the influx of white and black migrants to their land.

1813.   Kensell, Lewis Anthony.   "Phases of Reconstruction in the Choctaw Nation, 1865-1870." *Chronicles of Oklahoma* 47 (Summer 1969): 138-153. Ports. Kensell writes about the changes that took place in Choctaw society following the Civil War. The emancipation of black slaves among the Choctaw caused labor shortages and the migration of freedmen and whites to the Arkansas, Louisiana, and Texas region accelerated the assimilation of Choctaw culture into Anglo-Saxon culture.

1814.   Lambert, Paul F.   "The Cherokee Reconstruction Treaty of 1866." *Journal of the West* 12 (July 1973): 471-489.   The treaty was influenced by a split among the North and South Cherokee that existed since a tribal treaty in 1835 and the division of loyalties between the U.S. and the Confederacy. The long negotiations that began in September, 1866 in Ft. Smith, Arkansas did not conclude until July, 1867 with the Cherokee conceding emancipation and some civil rights for their slaves, railroad rights-of-way, and land for other Indian tribes. Although the treaty produced long term problems for Cherokee factions, the tribe was able to maintain a since of unity and political autonomy for another 40 years. The most influential leaders in the negotiations were Cherokee leader John Ross and U.S. Commissioner for Indian Affairs Dennis N. Cooley.

1815.   Littlefield, Daniel F., Jr. *The Cherokee Freedmen: From Emancipation to American Citizenship.* Westport: Greenwood Press, 1978. 281p. Bibl. Ills.   After the Civil War the black slaves owned by Indians of the Cherokee Nation in Oklahoma were freed and entitled to Cherokee citizenship and the right to own land if they met the stipulations of the Treaty of 1866. Blacks sought equal rights with the Indians and full citizenship, but the Cherokee were reluctant to bring many blacks into the Nation because of racial prejudice and concern for the preservation of their local authority. The problems between the Cherokee and freedmen on one hand and the Cherokee and the U.S. federal government on the other proved so complicated that legal proceedings establishing citizenship and land rights extended into the 20th century.

1816.   McCullars, Marion Ray. "The Choctaw-Chickasaw Reconstruction Treaty of 1866." *Journal of the West* 12 (July 1973): 463-470.   The Reconstruction treaty between the Choctaw and Chickasaw Indian tribes and the U.S., signed on April 28, 1866 in Washington, DC, was the most favorable treaty arranged by any of the Five Civilized Nations even though the two tribes supported the Confederacy. McCullar credits the leadership of Indian negotiators with courage and stubbornness in their insistence on protecting their lands and people. The treaty freed several thousand black slaves and provided for their rights and economic well-being. It also offered a right-of-way through tribal lands to the railroads.

1817.   Micco, Lelinda Beth. "Freedmen and Seminoles: Forging a Seminole Nation." Ph.D. University of California, Berkeley, 1995. 198p.

1818.   Tracey, Patricia Cleland. "Cherokee Reconstruction in Indian Territory." *Journal of the West* 35 (July 1996): 81-85. Ills. Map.   Tracey briefly traces

Cherokee history from their removal to the Indian Territory in Oklahoma region in the 1830s through the 20th century. Post Civil War Reconstruction among the Cherokee has been marked by a long term struggle to maintain the unity of the Cherokee nation and many tribal traditions.

1819.   Trees, May. "Socioeconomic Reconstruction in the Seminole Nation, 1865-1870." *Journal of the West* 12 (July 1973): 490-498.   The Civil War destroyed relations among Indian tribes living in the Indian Territory of the West. The Seminoles, who had been removed from Florida to the West, were forced to sign a treaty in September, 1866 with the U.S. government that cheated them out of land, emancipated their black slaves, required them to accept blacks as equal members of society, and led to their dependency on white America for material assistance. By 1870 the Seminoles had made some economic progress and schools, churches, and missionaries had returned, but in the long run the tribe lost its independence and succumbed to white domination.

1820.   Warren, Hanna R. "Reconstruction in the Cherokee Nation." *Chronicles of Oklahoma* 45 (Summer 1967): 180-189.   Reconstruction in Cherokee territory in northeastern Oklahoma was a time of rebuilding a society that experienced material destruction, population dispersion, internal feuds, and the end of black slavery. Warren describes the difficulties that the Cherokee Nation had coming to term with these issues and agreeing to the federal government's Treaty of 1866 that was signed by the Five Civilized Tribes.

Kentucky

General History

1821.   Coulter, E. Merton. *The Civil War and Readjustment in Kentucky.* Gloucester, Ma.: Peter Smith, 1966. 468p. Bibl. Maps. (Rpt. of Chapel Hill: University of North Carolina Press, 1926)   Coulter emphasizes the independent nature of Kentucky in the war and Reconstruction. Kentuckians sought neutrality but were forced to side openly with the Union. When the war ended conservatives held firm control over the state, and attempts to enact reforms were met with stubborn defiance and violence. Coulter focuses on political developments that shaped Kentucky's unique position in the war and postwar period. Financial, social and educational affairs are also included. (See also # 1824, 1826, 1838)

1822.   Harrison, Lowell H. and James C. Klotter. *A New History of Kentucky.* Lexington: University of Kentucky Press, 1997. 533p. Apps. Bibl. Ills. Maps. Tbls.
        The chapter focusing on Reconstruction emphasizes the slow, difficult adjustment of the state to changes in race relations and the political and demographic differences among Kentuckians on postwar issues. The authors explain that postwar years illustrated that there was still much continuity in the attitudes and outlook of whites from antebellum days that remained as the state

entered the 20th century.   There are chapters with brief references to the Reconstruction period regarding rural and urban life, economics and agriculture, education and equality, and the culture and laws of the state. Appendix B includes a chronological list of biographical sketches of Kentucky governors.

1823.   Lucas, Marion B. *A History of Blacks in Kentucky. Vol. 1: From Slavery to Segregation, 1760-1891.* Frankfort: Kentucky Historical Society, 1992. 430p. Bibl. Graphs. Tbls.   Lucas gives broad coverage to the social, political, and economic challenges that faced the freedmen after the Civil War. Although Kentucky was not part of the Confederacy, in general the state government and the white population sought to create a second class community that could be denied any help whatsoever with starting a new life, gaining an education, and finding work. Lucas emphasizes the struggle that the ex-slaves experienced, but also the progress they achieved in establishing their freedom and independence with some assistance from the Freedmen's Bureau and private missionary organizations. This included building strong families, initiating churches and schools, and struggling to gain civil rights and improved working and living conditions.

1824.   Smith, John David. "E. Merton Coulter, the 'Dunning School,' and *The Civil War and Readjustment in Kentucky.*" *Register of the Kentucky Historical Society* 86 (Winter, 1988): 52-69. Ills.   Smith surveys the responses of contemporaries and later historians to Coulter's *The Civil War and Readjustment in Kentucky* (see # 1821). Revisionist historians after World War II criticized Coulter for his unbalanced and racist treatment of Reconstruction that conformed with the tradition of William Dunning and his students. Even though much of Coulter's book is outdated, it remains the single most important work on the subject because of Coulter's insights and interdisciplinary themes, such as economics, geography, and race, and because no other historian has attempted a revisionist work of the same magnitude.

1825.   Webb, Ross A. *Kentucky in the Reconstruction Era.* Lexington: University Press of Kentucky, 1979. 101p. Bibl.   Reconstruction in Kentucky differed from other Southern states because the state remained loyal to the Union during the Civil War. The tradition of independence and local authority made the postwar government in Kentucky and the white population very reluctant to accept reforms, including the emancipation of slaves, civil rights for the freedmen, and any other imposition, such as the Freedmen's Bureau. Ku Klux Klan violence and intimidation against blacks and white Republicans were widespread, and reforms were made grudgingly. Webb concludes, however, that the painful acceptance of change in Kentucky, or what local journalist Henry Watterson referred to as the "New Departure", laid the foundation for progressive, successful programs in education, economics, and eventually in the broadening of legal rights for blacks.

Politics and Law

1826.   Connelly, Thomas L.   "Neo-Confederation or Power Vaccum: Post-War Kentucky Politics Reappraised." *Register of the Kentucky Historical Society* 64 (October 1966): 257-269.   E. Merton Coulter described post-Civil War Kentucky as a place of Confederate resurgence by a dominant Democratic Party, even though the state did not secede (see # 1821).   Connelly contests this interpretation in his reexamination of state politics in the 1860s and 1870s. Among white Kentuckians, conservatism predominated, but politically there was a power vacuum based on competing interest groups, such as railroads and mining companies, and the general displacement of people and the economy after the war.

1827.   Hartz, Louis. "John M. Harlan in Kentucky, 1855-1877: The Story of his Pre-Court Political Career." *Filson Club History Quarterly* 14 (January 1940): 17-40.   Hartz follows Harlan's political career in Kentucky from Whig, to xenophobic Know Nothing, to staunch conservative opponent of emancipation, to his final acceptance of Republican Reconstruction in 1866. His Republican support ruined his chances in state elections, but it helped him in his confirmation hearings for the U.S. Supreme Court in 1877. He served on the court until 1911.

1828.   Howard, Victor B.   "The Black Testimony Controversy in Kentucky, 1866-1872." *Journal of Negro History* 58 (April 1973): 140-165.   Howard clarifies the extensive efforts of the freedmen and federal authorities in Kentucky to secure the right of black testimony against whites in state and local courts. The state legislature refused to grant this right despite the Civil Rights Act of 1866, a law that state authorities considered to be unconstitutional. The continuous pressure on the state to modify its law of evidence in courts, including the influence of rulings in federal courts (e.g. Blyew-Kennard [i.e. Blyew v. U.S.] case in 1872) and federal legislation, forced the Kentucky legislature to allow black testimony.

1829.   Howard, Victor B. "The Breckinridge Family and the Negro Testimony Controversy in Kentucky, 1866-1872." *Filson Club History Quarterly* 49 (January 1975): 37-56.   The Breckinridge family, which included John C. Breckinridge, former vice-president of the U.S. and presidential candidate in 1860, split over the issue of secession in 1861. Howard focuses on the former vice-president's Unionist uncle, Dr. Robert J. Breckinridge and his sons, Robert and William, who were Confederate officers. All three worked in favor of black testimony. William campaigned for the issue in the newspaper that he edited, the *Lexington Observer and Reporter.*

1830.   Howard, Victor B.   "The Kentucky Press and the Black Suffrage Controversy, 1865-1872." *Filson Club History Quarterly* 47 (July 1973): 215-237. The Democratic press usually opposed black suffrage on the grounds that blacks were either inferior or ignorant and lacking preparation for the responsibility. After the ratification of the 15th Amendment in March, 1870, there were differences of opinion, but the reactionary Democratic newspaper supported violence or other means to deter blacks from voting, until it became clear that their votes would not lead to the feared black domination in local politics. The Republican press approved of black suffrage, but the Republican Party gradually lost many black followers because of the party's refusal to place blacks in leadership positions or in desired offices.

1831.   Howard, Victor B.   "The Kentucky Press and the Negro Testimony Controversy, 1866-1872." *Register of the Kentucky Historical Society* 71 (January 1973): 29-50.   Virtually the entire Democratic press, except for the Louisville *Courier-Journal*, opposed allowing the testimony of blacks in state courts. Many Republican newspapers, including the Louisville *Daily Union Press* and the *Frankfurt Commonwealth*, urged the legislature to give this basic right to black citizens, but they were in the minority. Howard surveys press opinion and notes that by 1871 the position of urban newspapers changed due to the impact of black suffrage and as pressure built within the legal profession and the black community.

1832.   Howard, Victor B.   "Negro Politics and the Suffrage Question in Kentucky, 1866-1872." *Register of the Kentucky Historical Society* 72 (April 1974): 111-133.   The drive to secure suffrage was the central issue for blacks from 1866 until the ratification of the 15th Amendment. In a state dominated by Democrats, blacks began to abandon the Republicans by 1870 and particularly in the 1872 election, but a complete change of support did not happen. The black community split over how to respond to white concessions to their civil rights that occurred only under pressure and not out of sincere support.

1833.   Logan, Lena Crain.   "Henry Watterson, Border Nationalist, 1840-1877." Ph.D. Indiana University, 1942.

1834.   Norris, Majorie M.   "An Early Instance of Nonviolence: The Louisville Demonstrations of 1870-1871." *Journal of Southern History* 32 (November 1966): 487-504.   On October 30, 1870 local black residents protested against segregation on Louisville streetcars. The nonviolent protest resulted in a court ruling against the protesters, but by May, 1871, as protests continued, the Louiville City Railway decided to open the streetcars to all persons. This was a significant victory for Louiville blacks, even with the continuation of all other forms of segregation and discrimination in the city.

1835.   Russ, William A., Jr.   "The Role of Kentucky in 1867." *Susquehanna University Studies* 1 (January 1938): 106-114.   In 1867 politics in Kentucky represented what Republicans wanted to avoid in the other Southern states. White conservative Kentuckians were not under the pressure of Reconstruction and pursued a policy of defiance against radical reforms. Former rebels were elected to Congress and other public offices, partly because Republicans and freedmen could not vote.

1836.   Springer, Helen L.   "James Speed, the Attorney General, 1864-1866." *Filson Club History Quarterly* 11 (July 1937): 169-188.   Speed, a Kentucky Unionist who opposed slavery, served as U.S. Attorney General in the administrations of both Lincoln and Johnson. His moderate Republican ideas became radicalized, and he strongly and openly opposed the Reconstruction policies of President Johnson, including Johnson's objection to black suffrage. Speed helped to organize the Republican Party in Kentucky, but his Republican stance damaged his political career in his home state.

1837.   Wall, Joseph F. *Henry Watterson: Reconstructed Rebel.* New York: Oxford University Press, 1956. 362p. Bibl. Port.   After the Civil War Watterson, editor of the Louisville *Courier Journal*, accepted Republican reform and condemned harsh black codes and the defiant attitude of white Southerners. As a conservative Republican, Watterson worked for black civil rights and recognized the importance of educating the freedmen, but he supported Andrew Greeley and the Liberal Republicans in the national election of 1872 and Samuel Tilden in 1876. Sectional reconciliation was one of Watterson's continuing goals. (See also Wall's Ph.D. dissertation with the same title from Columbia University, 1951.)

1838.   Webb, Ross A. "Kentucky: 'Pariah Among the Elect'." In *Radicalism, Racism, and Party Realignment, the Border States During Reconstruction.* Edited by R. O. Curry. Baltimore: Johns Hopkins Press, 1969. Pp. 105-145. Map.   The idea that Kentucky was partial to the Confederacy during and after the Civil War was based on incorrect interpretations by historians, such as E. Merton Coulter (See # 1821) The economic and social ties to both North and South created split loyalties in the state, but most Kentuckians were strong Unionists who resented any interference of Congress in local affairs, including the abolition of slavery, the imposition of the Freedmen's Bureau, and providing for equal civil rights and education for blacks.

1839.   Webb, Ross A. *Benjamin Helm Bristow: Border State Politician.* Lexington: University Press of Kentucky, 1969. 370p. Bibl. Port.   Bristow was a moderate Republican from Kentucky who supported equal civil rights for blacks. As the U.S. Attorney for the District of Kentucky from 1866 to 1870, he vigorously pursued violators of the Civil Rights Act of 1866 and made Kentucky a test case for the law. Bristow's success in Kentucky led to his appointment as the first Solicitor General of the U.S., and he argued many of the cases related to Reconstruction between 1870 and 1872. He supported both individual responsibility and the government guarantee of individual liberty of all races. He was more effective in the role of prosecutor and private lawyer than as a national politician.

1840.   Wharton, George Christopher. "Henry Watterson - A Study of Selected Speeches on Reconciliation in the Post-Bellum Period." Ph.D. Louisiana State University, 1974. 272p.

Agriculture, Labor, and Business

1841.   Boyd, Carl B., Jr.   "Local Aid to Railroads in Central Kentucky, 1850-1891, Part I." *Register of the Kentucky Historical Society* 62 (January 1964): 4-23; "Part II." 62 (April 1964): 112-133.   Includes information on railroad construction during the years of Reconstruction.   Boyd believes that local aid was important for the growth of rail transporation because there was not enough private funding.

1842.   Coulter, E. Merton.   "Commercial Relations of Kentucky, 1860-1870." Ph.D. University of Wisconsin, 1917.

1843.   Roberts, Derrell C.   "Kentucky Baptist Aid to Reconstruction Georgia." *Register of the Kentucky Historical Society* 79 (Summer 1981): 219-226.   Ports. The Kentucky Baptist Association for the Relief of the South originated on October 8, 1866 to collect and distribute food for destitute fellow Southerners in Georgia after crop failures led to deprivation.   Georgians responded to their predicament by accepting the aid, but they also sought to help themselves through crop diversification, particularly the replacement of cotton acreage with wheat and corn.

Society, Education, and Religion

1844.   Crawford, Robert Gunn.   "History of the Kentucky Penitentiary System, 1865-1923." Ph.D. University of Kentucky, 1955. 383p.

1845.   Howard, Victor B.   "The Struggle For Equal Education for Blacks in Kentucky, 1866-1884." *Journal of Negro Education* 46 (Summer 1977): 305-328. The American Missionary Association and the Freedmen's Bureau established a structure for black education, but their efforts were met by either a lack of concern or blatant hostility from many whites.   The legislature passed funding laws for black education, but the laws were not enforced or placed an unfair tax burden on the black community.   Conditions for black education in Kentucky improved by the early 1880s.

1846.   Howard, Victor B.   *Black Liberation in Kentucky: Emancipation and Freedom, 1862-1884.* Lexington: University Press in Kentucky, 1983. 222p. Bibl. Black Kentuckians struggled to gain their freedom and civil rights in a Southern state that refused to join the Confederacy but tenaciously held on to antebellum race relations for as long as it could.   Thousands of slaves freed themselves and their families through military service in the Union Army.   They sought to maintain strong families, organize their own schools, and maintain pressure for the right to vote and to give testimony in court.   They had to cope with violence from the Ku Klux Klan, Democratic domination, and resistance of most whites to treating them as equals.   By the 1870s the influence of the "New Departure" Democrats brought reforms and the federal government backed away from interference in the state.

1847.   Kellog, John. "The Formation of Black Residential Areas in Lexington, Kentucky, 1865-1887." *Journal of Southern History* 48 (February 1982): 21-52. Maps. Tbls.   Kellog studies urban residential patterns in Lexington by using demographic research methodology to demonstrate how and why racial segregation occurred in housing in a Southern city prior to the availability of efficient mass transportation.   Residential segregation developed as blacks migrated to Lexington after the Civil War.   Segregation developed due to increasing white animosity against and fear of blacks, the need to form a protective community for blacks, and economic realities that required black segregation in low cost housing districts.

1848.   Kimball, Philip Clyde. "Freedom's Harvest: Freedmen's Schools in Kentucky After the Civil War." *Filson Club History Quarterly* 54 (July 1980): 272-288.   The freedmen were required to pay for their own schools in Kentucky immediately following the Civil War until the Freedmen's Bureau arrived in the state in 1866.   Black educators encountered white hostility, poverty, and some black dissension, but the establishment and administration of hundreds of schools in by blacks themselves helped them when the Freedmen's Bureau left the state.   Even after funding came from the legislature in 1874, blacks continued to run their schools apart from white school administration.   The schools for blacks developed into one of the strongest systems in the South.

1849.   Lucas, Marion B. "Kentucky Blacks: The Transition From Slavery to Freedom." *Register of the Kentucky Historical Society* 91 (Autumn 1993): 403-419. Ills.   During the years 1865 to 1870 blacks in Kentucky experienced a difficult and disheartening transition to freedom because of the lack of federal and local assistance and white defiance against changes in race relations.   Lucas describes the efforts of white Kentuckian John G. Fee, an abolitionist who organized assistance for freedmen and worked to find them employment, land, and educational programs. Blacks aggressively sought to improve their own lives by pushing for change, organizing churches, maintaining families and community life, and seeking equal rights as citizens.

1850.   Raphael, Alan. "Health and Welfare of Kentucky Black People, 1865-1870." *Societas* 2 (Spring 1972): 143-157.   Health services to Kentucky freedmen began in the fall of 1865, but services provided by the Freedmen's Bureau were totally inadequate to treat an impoverished population.   After bureau services ceased in 1868-69, health care among blacks worsened, because local doctors and public officials were unsympathetic to their needs.

1851.   Sears, Richard. "John G. Fee, Camp Nelson, and Kentucky Blacks, 1864-1865." *Register of the Kentucky Historical Society* 85 (Winter 1987): 28-45. Ills. Reverend Fee, an abolitionist who was deported from Kentucky prior to the war for establishing an integrated church in Berea, volunteered to serve the spiritual, educational, and relief needs of blacks at Camp Nelson, a primary camp for the enlistment of blacks into the Union Army.   His experiences at the camp confirmed his previous dedication to racial equality, and he attempted to put his ideas into practice at his church in Berea from 1864 to 1904. (For earlier activities of Fee and his colleague see also Sears' *The Kentucky Abolitionists in the Midst of Slavery, 1854-1864: Exiles from Freedom.* Lewiston: Edwin Mellen Press, 1993. 430p.)

1852.   Sears, Richard. *A Utopian Experiment in Kentucky: Integration and Social Equality at Berea, 1866-1904.* Westport: Greenwood Press, 1996. 228p. Apps. Bibl.   Sears emphasizes the leadership of Rev. John G. Fee with helping freedmen at the military training camp at Ft. Nelson in 1864-1865 and fostering racial equality and integration at Berea College beginning in 1866. Fee showed that an integrated community could be successful despite financial problems and opposition from many whites. Sears illustrates how the Berea community developed and changed during the last decades of the 19th century, but Fee's contributions to racial and gender equality within a strong Christian context remained.

1853.   Thomas, Herbert A., Jr.   "Victims of Circumstances: Negroes in a Southern Town, 1865-1880." *Register of the Kentucky Historical Society* 71 (1973): 253-271.   Lexington, like many other Southern cities, experienced a large influx of former slaves from rural areas after emancipation. The influx upset race relations in the city where integrated neighborhoods were widespread.   Immigration led to segregated neighborhoods and a large urban population of poor blacks. The city had few low skilled jobs, and slavery did not prepare the freedmen for jobs that could lead to economic success. The most prosperous blacks were usually persons who were free before the war.

1854.   Webb, Ross A. "'The Past is Never Dead, It's Not Even Past': Benjamin P. Runkle and the Freedmen's Bureau in Kentucky, 1866-1870." *Register of the Kentucky Historical Society* 84 (Autumn 1986): 343-360.   Runkle was a bureau agent and later assistant commissioner of the bureau in Kentucky.   He faced professional and personal challenges during his tenure, including the general disapproval of white Kentuckians.

1855.   Williams, Gary L. "James and Joshua Speed: Lincoln's Kentucky Friends." Ph.D. Duke University, 1971. 256p.

1856.   Wright, George C. *Racial Violence in Kentucky 1865-1940: Lynchings, Mob Rule, and "Legal Lynchings."* Baton Rouge: Louisiana State University Press, 1990. 350p. App. Bibl. Ills. Tbls.   The opening chapter focuses on the widespread violence against blacks during Reconstruction. The precedence was set for future decades of lynchings, mob rule, and the absence of justice for blacks in Kentucky. But blacks established a precedence of resistance. In the appendix Wright lists the victims of lynchings by race, location, date, and reason from 1866 to 1934. Legal executions are also listed from 1872 to 1939.

Louisiana

General History

1857.   Ficklen, John Rose. *History of Reconstruction in Louisiana (Through 1868).* Gloucester, Ma.: Peter Smith, 1966. 234p. (Rpt. of Baltimore: Johns Hopkins Press, 1910)   Ficklen died before the final editing of his book. His account covers mainly politics from 1862 through the presidential and gubernatorial elections of 1868. Ficklen's work, based on published sources, is highly critical of Reconstruction and consistent with the conservative interpretations of William Dunning.

1858.   Highsmith, William E.   "Louisiana During Reconstruction."   Ph.D. Louisiana State University, 1953.

1859.   Lonn, Ella. *Reconstruction in Louisiana After 1868.* New York: G. P. Putnam's Sons, 1918. 538p. Bibl. Maps.   Lonn, a Northern historian, provides a scholarly history of Reconstruction in Louisiana beginning with Republican rule in 1869. She writes very critically of the state government dominated by carpetbaggers and blacks, and she views the restoration of white, Democratic rule in 1877 as the end of a long nightmare for Louisiana that began in 1862 when Union troops occupied New Orleans.   Lonn focuses on the politics of Republican state government, local politics and disturbances in New Orleans, and state and federal elections. (See also Lonn's Ph.D. dissertation with the same title from University of Pennsylvania, 1911.)

1860.   Taylor, Joe Gray. *Louisiana Reconstructed 1863-1877.* Baton Rouge: Louisiana State University, 1974. 552p. Bibl. Charts. Ports. Tbl.   Taylor's survey covers politics, labor, economics, culture and society. He believes that the failure of Reconstruction was inevitable in Louisiana because of intense white racism and aggressive rejection of Reconstruction reforms, divisions among local Republicans, and waning support from the federal government for maintaining Reconstruction. Taylor compliments the 1868 constitution as bringing greater democracy to the state, but succeeding constitutions scuttled the progress even in public education. He criticizes Henry Clay Warmoth for leading a corrupt administration, but William P. Kellogg receives a good evaluation for honesty. Louisiana suffered economically and freedmen were depressed by racism, peonage, and violence. When the Democrats regained control of the state in 1877, in many respects society closely matched that of the prewar years.

Politics and Law

1861.   Abbott, Martin (ed.).   "Reconstruction in Louisiana: Three Letters." *Louisiana History* 1 (Spring 1960: 153-157.   Abbott provides three short letters from Thomas Conway, head of the Freedmen's Bureau in Louisiana for six months in 1865, and Charles H. Fox, a former Union soldier who became involved in Republican politics. Their letters, written in early 1868, provide a bit of background to events in the state.

1862.   Binning, F. Wayne.   "Carpetbaggers' Triumph: The Louisiana State Election of 1868." *Louisiana History* 14 (Winter 1973): 21-39.   The triumph of the carpetbaggers was a victory of white Republicans over the prewar free colored class in New Orleans that sought significant participation in the political process. The split in the Republican Party led to two Republican candidates for governor in 1868, Henry Clay Warmoth of the regular Republicans and James G. Taliaferro of the "pure Radicals."   Warmoth rejected the call of the free colored class for increasing social and political equality of the races.

1863.   Binning, Francis W.   "Henry Clay Warmoth and Louisiana Reconstruction." Ph.D. University of North Carolina, 1969. 393p.

1864.   Bone, Fanny Z. Lovell.   "Louisiana in the Disputed Election of 1876." *Louisiana Historical Quarterly* 14 (July 1931): 408-440; 14 (October 1931): 549-566; 15 (January 1932): 93-116; 15 (April 1932): 234-267.   Bone's M.A. thesis (Louisiana State University, 1928) was published in series format. She describes events related to the election, and provides a detailed chronology of Louisiana history and copies of documents, letters, and newspaper articles on politics during 1874-1877. State and local election returns are also given.

1865.   Burns, Francis P.   "White Supremacy in the South: The Battle of Constitutional Government in New Orleans, July 30, 1866." *Louisiana Historical Quarterly* 18 (July 1935): 581-616.   The riot of July 30 took place because freedmen in New Orleans sought civil rights at the expense of white citizens. Freedmen were encouraged by white radicals to act irresponsibly so that white leaders, such as Dr. Anthony Paul Dostie, could gain power.

1866.   Campbell, Clara L.   "The Political Life of Louisiana Negroes, 1865-1900." Ph.D. Tulane University, 1971. 257p.

1867.   Capers, Gerald M. *Occupied City: New Orleans Under the Federals 1862-1865*. Lexington: University of Kentucky Press, 1965. 248p. Bibl. Maps. In chapter six (p. 120-144) Capers discusses the attempt to build a Reconstruction government in New Orleans in accordance with Lincoln's 10% plan. He emphasizes the political dissension among Unionists and the lack of support for black suffrage. He also examines the interaction of Gen. Nathaniel P. Banks occupation government and the local political leaders, particularly Michael Hahn and J. Madison Wells.

1868.   Caskey, Willie Malvin.   *Secession and Restoration of Louisiana*. University, La.:   Louisiana State University Press, 1938.   318p.   Bibl. Maps. (*Louisiana Studies*, 36; Rpt. in New York: Da Capo, 1970.)   Caskey writes about state politics from the Federal Army occupation in May, 1862 through the New

Orleans riot of July 30, 1866 when Louisiana experienced a gradual process of restoration to locally controlled government. By the time of the riot, restoration was complete in accordance with President Johnson's Reconstruction plan, but the riot in New Orleans contributed to empowering the Radicals in Congress and defeating Johnson's policies. Caskey depicts the government in Louisiana as quite moderate, and he refers to the black codes as moderate and necessary for order. His references to the behavior of freedmen indicate negative stereotypes. (See also Caskey's Ph.D. dissertation with the same title from Vanderbilt University, 1936.)

1869.   Christian, Marcus A. "Men of Worth in Louisiana." *Negro History Bulletin* 5 (March 1942): 137-139.   Ports.   Brief biographical sketches describe Oscar James Dunn (lieutenant governor, 1869-1871); Charles Edmund Nash (U.S. congressman, 1874-1876); Pinckney Benton Stewart Pinchback (state senator, 1868-1871; lieutenant governor, 1871-1872; governor, December, 1871-January, 1872; publisher of New Orleans *Louisianian*); and James Lewis (Freedmen's Bureau agent, U.S. customs inspector, 1867-1868, policeman).

1870.   Christian, Marcus A. "The Theory of the Poisoning of Oscar J. Dunn." *Phylon* 6 (1945): 254-266.   Dunn, a black lieutenant governor in the Henry Clay Warmoth administration, died on November 22, 1871.   Christian explores the possibility that he was poisoned by Republican opponents, but admits that the truth will never be known.

1871.   Clark, Robert T., Jr.   "Reconstruction and the New Orleans German Colony." *Louisiana Historical Quarterly* 23 (April 1940): 501-524.   Clark relies on German and English language newspapers, particularly *Deutche Zeitung*, which shifted from solidly Democratic to Republican sympathies, the *Echo von New Orleans*, an anti-Radical paper, and the *New Orleanser Deutche Presse*, a supporter of the Democrats.   The German community took a moderate position in Reconstruction politics, but it clearly opposed carpetbagger governments. German-Americans were more interested in events in Europe during the 1860s and 1870s that led to German unification.

1872.   Copeland, Fayette. "The New Orleans Press and the Reconstruction." *Louisiana Historical Quarterly* 30 (January 1947): 149-337.   App. Bibl.   In Copeland's M.A. thesis (Louisiana State University, 1937) he surveys the attitudes expressed by editors of New Orleans newspapers. He lists the newspapers with their history during Reconstruction.   Copeland focuses mostly on *The Picayune* (Democrat), the *Crescent* (Democrat), the *Times* (Democrat), the *Commercial Bulletin* (conservative economics), the *Daily Delta* (Democrat), and the *Democrat*. The appendix includes a list of newspapers and other publications in New Orleans that existed between 1866 and 1876. The Republican press is not considered.

1873.   Dart, Henry P.   "The Revolution of 1876 in Louisiana." *Louisiana Historical Quarterly* 14 (April 1931): 212-214.   Dart introduces a series of articles on the election of 1876 in Louisiana. He emphasizes the chaotic domination of Radical Republican rule at the state level on the eve of the election and characterizes it as dominated by blacks who sought dramatic reforms. The fraud of the Republican Returning Board that controlled votes was overcome and the white conservatives returned the state to normalcy.

1874.   Dauphine, James G. "The Knights of the White Camellia and the Election of 1868: Louisiana's White Terrorists; a Benighting Legacy." *Louisiana History* 30 (Spring 1989): 173-190.   The Knights of the White Camellia opposed Republican rule and civil rights for freedmen, and it proved very effective in intimidating blacks and white Republicans in the 1868 election campaign. Democrat Horatio Seymour defeated Ulysses S. Grant in most of the state except in the river parishes where there were large concentrations of Union soldiers.

1875.   Davis, Donald W. 'Ratification of the Constitution of 1868-Record of Votes." *Louisiana History* 6 (Summer 1965): 301-305. Facim.   Davis prints a document that lists a tally of all votes by race and parish that were for and against the ratification of the constitution. The votes appears to have occurred on April 17 and 18, 1868.

1876.   Dawson, Joseph G. III. "General Lovell H. Rousseau and Louisiana Reconstruction." *Louisiana History* 20 (Fall 1979): 373-391.   In the summer of 1868 President Johnson appointed Rousseau commander of the Department of Louisiana to replace commanders who strongly followed Republican Reconstruction policies. When racial clashes became violent during the fall election campaign, he was slow to protect blacks from violence and maintain the peace. Democrats mourned him when he died suddenly on January 7, 1869.

1877.   Dawson, Joseph G. III.   "General Phil Sheridan and Military Reconstruction in Louisiana." *Civil War History* 24 (June 1978): 133-151.   As commander of Louisiana and Texas during 1867, Sheridan sought to carry out the orders of Congress. He was not an advocate of racial equality, but he sympathized with equal justice and civil rights. His interpretation of the Reconstruction Acts was the basis for his removal, but he brought blacks into the political process as voters and jurors, eliminated segregation on New Orleans streetcars, and removed disloyal officials from office.

1878.   Dawson, Joseph G. III. *Army Generals and Reconstruction: Louisiana, 1862-1877.*   Baton Rouge: Louisiana State University Press, 1982. 294p. App. Bibl. Map. Ports.   Sixteen U.S. Army commanders between 1862 and 1877 made decisions that effected politics and society in Louisiana. Dawson explains that many of the decisions were based on prejudice, ideology and local pressures, but he judges their performance very positively. (See also Dawson's "The Long Ordeal: Army Generals and Reconstruction in Louisiana, 1862-1877." 2 Vols. Ph.D. Louisiana State University, 1978. 568p.)

1879.   Dawson, Joseph G. III. (ed.). *The Louisiana Governors: From Iberville to Edwards.* Baton Rouge: Louisiana State University Press, 1990. 297p. Ports. This book of biographical essays includes the Reconstruction governors: George F.

Shepley (1861-1864), Michael Hahn (1864-1865), James Madison Wells (1865-1867), Benjamin Franklin Flanders (1867-1868), Joshua Baker (1868), Henry Clay Warmoth (1868-1872), P. B. S. Pinchback (1872-1873), and William Pitt Kellogg (1873-1876). Each essay provides an interpretation of the governor's career and includes a bibliography. (See also Miriam G. Reeves, *The Governors of Louisiana*, Gretna: Pelican, 1998.)

1880.   DeLatte, Carolyn E.   "The St. Landry Riot: A Forgotten Incident of Reconstruction Violence." *Louisiana History* 17 (Winter 1976): 41-49.   Two weeks of violence in St. Landry Parish erupted on September 28, 1868 and resulted in the massacre of blacks by local whites. DeLatte explains that the tense political atmosphere prior to the 1868 election merely added to fears among whites when rumors emerged of an uprising among black citizens.

1881.   DuFour, Charles L. "The Age of Warmoth." *Louisiana History* 6 (Fall 1965): 335-364.   Dufour surveys Warmoth's political career as one of three strongmen in Louisiana politics from 1835 to 1935. The other two were John Slidell and Huey Long. He emphasizes Warmoth's skill with power and influence as governor from 1868 to 1873 and compares him with Long.

1882.   Edwards, John Carver. "Radical Reconstruction and the New Orleans Riot of 1866." *International Review of History and Political Science* 1 (August 1973): 48-64.   Edwards provides a narrative of the riot of July 30 and concludes that all sides were to blame for the incident, although he emphasizes the responsibility of President Johnson, Mayor John T. Monroe, the New Orleans police force that was full of exConfederates, and Gen. Absalom Baird of the U.S. Army.

1883.   Everett, Donald E.   "Demands of the New Orleans Free Colored Population for Political Equality, 1862-1865." *Louisiana Historical Quarterly* 38 (April 1955): 43-64.   During the Union occupation of New Orleans, the free black community sought a measure of political equality through voting, but they failed to secure the franchise before the war ended. Everett questions whether free blacks truly cared for the rights of the slaves, because they sought to separate themselves from their less fortunate brothers and to find a way to dominate the white population in the postwar period.

1884.   Fleming, Walter L. (ed.). "A Ku Klux Document." *Mississippi Valley Historical Review* 1 (March 1915): 575-578.   Fleming provides a document that he refers to as the "Ritual" of a local secret organization known as "No. 298." The order existed in the Florida parishes of Louisiana between 1872 and 1877.

1885.   Fortier, James T. A. (ed.). *Carpet-Bag Misrule in Louisiana: The Tragedy of the Reconstruction Era Following the War Between the States*. New Orleans: Louisiana State Museum, 1938. 103p. Bibl. Ills. Ports.   This pamphlet was written by the Louisiana State Museum and dedicated to Louisianians who vigorously fought "to maintain White Supremacy as a cardinal principle of wise, stable, and practical government." (p. 1) Reconstruction is strongly denounced in this brief account. Particular attention is placed on the violence that took place in the state to win back lawful rights of the conservative white majority.

1886.   Gonzales, John Edmund. "William Pitt Kellogg, Reconstruction Governor of Louisiana, 1873-1877." *Louisiana Historical Quarterly* 29 (April 1946): 394-495. Bibl.   This article is Gonzales' M.A. thesis (Louisiana State University, 1945). He describes the political career of Kellogg, a Vermont native who came to Louisiana in April, 1865 and rose quickly in power and influence within the Republican Party. Kellogg won the 1872 gubernatorial election, despite Republican disunity, and held office until the Democrats regained control in 1877. Democrats hated him because he was a tool of the Grant administration. Gonzales also discusses Kellogg's activities with regard to New Orleans politics, internal improvements, education, executive powers, election law, and the black citizens.

1887.   Grosz, Agnes Smith. "The Political Career of Pinkney Benton Stewart Pinchback." *Louisiana Historical Quarterly* 27 (April 1944): 526-612. Bibl.   In this M.A. thesis (Louisiana State University, 1943) Grosz depicts Pinchback as a man of great ability, courage, and charisma, but notes that his career was marred by the corruption and political chaos of the period. Pinchback was lieutenant governor in 1871, acting governor from December, 1872 until January, 1873, and elected U.S. senator in 1873 but never took his seat. Although he always championed the cause of black civil rights, but was not a Radical on all issues.

1888.   Harris, Francis Byers. "Henry Clay Warmoth, Reconstruction Governor of Louisiana." *Louisiana Historical Quarterly* 30 (April 1947): 523-653. Bibl.   In his M.A. thesis (Louisiana State University, 1943), Harris depicts Warmoth as a scheming carpetbagger who was appointed in June, 1868 and maintained power based on the votes of the freedmen until 1873. Warmoth had political control of the legislature, but he could not control the corruption in government during his administration. As he moved to the side of the conservative Republican faction and sought Democratic support, he lost his traditional black support.

1889.   Haskins, James. *Pinckney Benton Stewart Pinchback.* New York: Macmillan Publishing Co., 1973. 292p. Bibl. Port.   Pinchback was born a slave of mixed blood on a Virginia plantation in 1836 and rose during Reconstruction to be the governor of Louisiana. Haskins provides a sympathetic biography of a man who was vilified by whites as an example of the corrupt, black, Republican politician. Haskins does not deny that Pinchback participated in corruption, but emphasizes his positive contributions.

1890.   Hennessey, Melinda Meek. "Race and Violence in Reconstruction New Orleans: The 1868 Riot." *Louisiana History* 20 (Winter 1970): 77-91.   Political and racial tensions between black Republicans and white Democrats led to violence in New Orleans and surrounding parishes. Black demands for civil rights progress encouraged the fears of whites, and both sides organized clubs that clashed in late October, shortly before the November elections. The riots intimidated black voters and many stayed away from election polls and helped the Democrats win Louisiana for presidential contender, Horatio Seymour.

1890b.   Hogue, James K.   "Bayonet Rule: Five Street Battles in New Orleans and the Rise and Fall of Radical Reconstruction." Ph.D. Princeton University, 1998. 336p.

1891.   Howard, Perry H.   "Another Look at Reconstruction."   In *Political Tendencies in Louisiana.* Revised and expanded edition. Baton Rouge: Louisiana State University Press, 1971, 1957. Pp. 104-152. Maps. Tbl.   Howard's study is based on the premise that political ecology is defined by geography and its impact on the formation of social classes that tend to follow certain political characteristics. He compares electoral returns with regional political tendencies that were identified from the antebellum period. Political tendencies, as illustrated in maps and tables, may provide greater understanding of regional voting patterns and the influence of regional economics and social stratification in the state.   Appendixes provide supporting statistical information on election returns by election and parish.

1892.   Johnson, Manie White.   "The Colfax Riot of April, 1873." *Louisiana Historical Quarterly* 13 (July 1930): 391-427. Bibl.   In his M.A. thesis (Southern Methodist University, 1929) Johnson describes a racial disturbance in Colfax, a village in Grant Parish in northwestern Louisiana. His story is from the perspective of the white conservatives who opposed Gov. William Kellogg's government and attempts to enforce civil rights for blacks.

1893.   Jones, Howard J.   "Biographical Sketches of Members of the 1868 Louisiana State Senate." *Louisiana History* 19 (Winter 1978): 65-110.   The 1868 senate was atypical compared with earlier senates, but does not conform to the negative descriptions of contemporary journalists, novelists, and later historians. Jones sketches the lives of the following: (blacks) Pinckney Pinchback, Ceasar Antoine, John Randall, Alexander Francois, George Y. Kelso, Julien J. Monette, Curtis Pollard, and Robert Poindexter; (carpetbaggers) John Harris, Chester B. Darrall, Lorenzo B. Jenks, Patricia O'Hara, Joseph Wittgenstein, Christophe Packard, Theodore Coupland, Carlos Wilcox, John Lynch, and Hugh Campbell; (native whites) Edwin Jewell, Frederick Jewell, Reuben White, Thomas C. Anderson, William Offutt, A. B. Bacon, Marcellus A. Foute, Robert N. Ogden, George H. Braughn, John R. Williams, Robert W. Futch, William L. Thompson, Samuel Todd, Dr. Richard Day, Dr. James Egan, Wilbur Blackman, and John Ray.

1894.   Jones, Howard J. "Members of the Louisiana Legislature of 1868: Images of 'Radical Reconstruction' Leadership in the Deep South." Ph.D. Washington State University, 1975. 270p.

1895.   Landry, Stuart Omer. *The Battle of Liberty Place: The Overthrow of Carpet-Bag Rule in New Orleans - September 14, 1874.* New Orleans: Pelican Publishing Co., 1955. 244p. Bibl. Ills. Ports.   Landry believes that the violent confrontation between the White League and the Metropolitan Police was caused by the corrupt Radical Republican regime of Gov. William P. Kellogg and the abuses of the black police against white citizens. The White Leaguers, whose names are listed in the book and whose deeds were memorialized in a monument, are viewed as heroes. Although Kellogg and the Republicans were not permanently overthrown, the events of September 14, 1874 led directly to the total collapse of Reconstruction in the South. Landry frequently quotes from New Orleans newspapers and reports of the incident.

1896.   Lathrop, Barnes F.   (ed.).   "An Autobiography of Francis T. Nicholls, 1834-1881." *Louisiana Historical Quarterly* 17 (April 1934): 246-267.   Nicholls, Louisiana's governor from 1877 to 1880 and 1888 to 1892, wrote a letter to his brother-in-law William W. Pugh, a prominent sugar planter in Assumption Parish, explaining his perspective on the election of 1876. He claims that he had no part in any deals that validated his election in exchange for allowing Rutherford Hayes to win disputed electoral votes from Louisiana.

1897.   Lestage, H. Oscar, Jr.   "The White League in Louisiana and its Participation in Reconstruction Riots." *Louisiana Historical Quarterly* 18 (July 1935): 617-695. Bibl.   In this M.A. thesis (Louisiana State University, 1930) Lestage describes the organization and activities of the White Leagues with particular emphasis on Natchitoches and Red River Parishes during the election campaign of 1874. Violence and intimidation against blacks and white Republicans led to the conservative victory in the state House of Representatives. Support for the League was based on Radical misrule and the demands of blacks for social and political equality.

1898.   Lowery, Walter McGehee.   "The Political Career of James Madison Wells." *Louisiana Historical Quarterly* 31 (October 1948): 995-123. Bibl.   In his M.A. thesis (Louisiana State University, 1947) Lowery describes the former governor of the state from early 1865 until 1867 when Gen. Sheridan removed him from office. Wells attempted to follow opinion instead of leading it. He shifted his policies from support for Republican reforms to favoring the return of power to conservative whites. His failure led him to declare support for Republicans again and for black suffrage. Wells was a conciliator who eased the state into Reconstruction but failed to moderate the strident conservatives who were determined to avoid change.

1899.   McCrary, James Peyton.   "Moderation in a Revolutionary World: Lincoln and the Failure of Reconstruction in Louisiana." Ph.D. Princeton University, 1972. 472p.

1900.   McDaniel, Hilda Mulvey.   "Francis Tillou Nicholls and the End of Reconstruction." *Louisiana Historical Quarterly* 32 (April 1949): 357-513. Bibl. In McDaniel's M.A. thesis (Louisiana State University, 1946) she covers the election campaign and controversy of 1876-1877. Nicholls, a Democrat, became governor in 1877, thus ending Reconstruction and Republican rule in the state. His major challenges as governor (1877-1880, 1888-1892) are also described.

1901.   McGinty, Garnie W. *Louisiana Redeemed: The Overthrow of Carpet-bag Rule, 1976-1880.* New Orleans: Pelican Publishing, 1941. 271p. Bibl. Maps. Approximately half of McGinty's book covers the years of Reconstruction with the greatest emphasis on the 1876 election in Louisiana. Despite the disputed election results, Francis T. Nicholls rightfully won the election, partly as a result of gaining support from some black voters. McGinty laments the lack of change from Republican to Democratic rule. The new regime, like the old, was more concerned with individual desires than the public good.

1902.   Moore, Dosia Williams. *War, Reconstruction, and Redemption on Red River: The Memoirs of Dosia Williams Moore.* Edited by Carol Wells. Ruston, La.: Dept. of History, Louisiana Tech. University, 1990. 135p. Map.   Moore was a white woman who lived in Rapides Parish and northern Natchitoches Parish in central Louisiana. Her memoirs bring together stories of her experiences during the Civil War and Reconstruction and the years afterward. Her words express a clear dislike for Radical government and a paternalistic attitude toward blacks.

1903.   Moore, Frederick W. "The Course of Louisiana Politics from 1862 to 1866." *South Atlantic Quarterly* 1 (April 1902): 128-144.   Moore emphasizes the influence of the Union Army in the development of a loyal government.

1904.   Moore, Frederick W. "Reconstruction in Socialism: A Contribution to the Political History of Louisiana From May 1, 1862, to March 29, 1867, and to the History of Reconstruction in the Southern States Collected From Contemporaneous Sources." Ph.D. Yale University, 1890.

1905.   Moran, Robert E. "Local Black Elected Officials in Ascension Parish (1868-1878)." *Louisiana Studies* 27 (Summer 1986): 273-280.   Ascension Parish maintained a Republican local government throughout the period of Radical Reconstruction because it had a large black majority and did not encounter significant violence against black voters until after the return of Democrats to power. Events in Ascension Parish shows that the stereotype of black domination was overblown. Blacks formed a majority in few decision-making bodies and relied on the help of whites.

1906.   Otten, James T. "The Wheeler Adjustment in Louisiana: National Republicans Begin to Reappraise Their Reconstruction Policy." *Louisiana History* 13 (Fall 1972): 349-367.   The Wheeler Adjustment, devised by Rep. William A. Wheeler, a New York Republican, attempted to resolve the tense political atmosphere in Louisiana following the elections of 1874.   A Congressional committee plan allowed Democrats to have the congressional seats the state Republican returning boards disallowed due to voter intimidation, allowed conflicting claims to be submitted to Congress, and asked the state legislature not to impeach Gov. William P. Kellogg. The plan has been criticized by historians as a Republican compromise, but Otten disputes this claim. The agreement illustrates growing impatience in Congress for resolving political chaos in states still under Reconstruction.

1907.   Penn, James. "The Geographical Variation of Unionism in Louisiana: A Study of the Southern Claims Commission." *Louisiana History* 30 (Fall 1989): 399-418. Maps.   Penn examines the distribution of claims against the federal government to measure the distribution of unionism. Successful claimants had to prove that they remained loyal to the Union throughout the war and did not provide support to the Confederacy. He finds that unionism existed in various areas of the state and included members of different classes. The claims data points to the continued strength of the former Whig party and its emphasis on business and unionism.

1908.   Perkins, A. E. "James Henri Burch and Oscar James Dunn in Louisiana." *Journal of Negro History* 22 (July 1937): 321-334.   Perkins discusses the close relationship between Lt. Gov. Dunn (1868-1871) and Burch, who won several state house and senate elections from East Baton Rouge Parish beginning in 1868. Both black men disliked Gov. Henry Clay Warmoth, because they believed the governor was corrupt and a friend of white conservatives. Perkins also discusses Dunn's mysterious death.

1909.   Perkins, A. E. "Oscar James Dunn." *Phylon* 4 (1943): 105-121.   Dunn rose from slavery to be lieutenant governor of Louisiana from 1868 to 1871. His political career is the focus of this article, particularly his disagreements with Gov. Henry Clay Warmoth that effectively split the state Republican Party. Dunn disproves the Southern stereotype that all black politicians in Reconstruction were dishonest and ignorant.

1910.   Perkins, A. E. "Some Negro Officers and Legislators in Louisiana." *Journal of Negro History* 14 (October 1929): 523-528.   The names of black state and federal elected officeholders in Louisiana are listed along with their terms of office. The list includes Congressman Charles E. Nash, 6 state officers, 32 state senators, 94 state representatives, and 40 delegates of the 1867 state constitutional convention. The list covers the years 1864 to 1896.

1911.   Phelps, Albert. "New Orleans and Reconstruction." *Atlantic Monthly* 88 (July 1901): 121-131.   Phelps's description of Reconstruction in the city reveals his convictions against Republican rule.

1912.   Pitre, Althea D. "The Collapse of the Warmoth Regime, 1870-1872." *Louisiana History* 6 (Spring 1965): 161-187.   Warmoth faced opposition from within the Republican Party and from Democrats. Even among the Radicals, particularly blacks, opponents chaffed at his veto of civil rights reforms and opposition to a public education law. Accusations of misuse of power and financial illegalities led to his impeachment in December, 1872 and January, 1873, but Pitre believes that the allegations were politically motivated.

1913.   Prichard, Walter (ed.). "The Origin and Activities of the White League in New Orleans (Reminiscences of a participant in the Movement)." *Louisiana Historical Quarterly* 23 (April 1940): 525-543.   A letter written by Darrah Albert

Shelby Vaught, a white leaguer, to Prof. John Rose Ficklen is published. The letter, dated May 8, 1894, includes Vaught's descrption of his participation in the league that began in 1873 amidst growing political agitation against Radical rule.

1914.   Rable, George. "Republican Albatross: The Louisiana Question, National Politics, and the Failure of Reconstruction." *Louisiana History* 23 (Spring 1982): 109-130.   Reconstruction failed for various reasons, but one in particular was President Grant's choice to test his Reconstruction policies in Louisiana. Grant put so much effort into maintaining Republican policies in Louisiana that he undercut his entire program for the South. The peculiar nature of politics, culture, and violence in the state made for a very difficult challenge for the president and Congress. The unsuitability of Louisiana as a testing ground for Radical policies provides a different perspective on the failure of Reconstruction compared with the interpretations of the neo-revisionist historians who blame the conservatism of the Republican Party.

1915.   Rankin, David C. "The Origins of Negro Leadership in New Orleans During Reconstruction." In *Southern Black Leaders of the Reconstruction Era.* Edited by Howard N. Rabinowitz. Urbana: University of Illinois Press, 1982. Pp. 155-189. Tbls.   The black leaders in postwar New Orleans consisted mainly of individuals who had been free prior to the war and who came from well-to-do, established families that enjoyed most of the rights of white citizens and viewed themselves as an elite class. Beginning with the capture of New Orleans in April, 1862 they sought to lead the freedmen and push for the emancipation of all slaves, but they generally opposed suffrage except for themselves and a select group of worthy freedmen. The differences between the mulatto elite and the freedmen in the city led to the weakening of their potential political power. Rankin describes the characteristics of the black aristocracy in a table that includes 240 names. (Updates Rankin's earlier study: "The Origins of Black Leadership in New Orleans During Reconstruction," *Journal of Southern History* 40 (August 1974): 417-440.)

1916.   Reynolds, Donald E. "The New Orleans Riot of 1866, Reconsidered." *Louisiana History* 5 (Winter 1964): 5-27.   Reynolds counters the Southern Democratic perspective on the riot of July, 1866. He concludes that responsibility for the massacre of blacks and the mass arrest of Radicals lays with the uncontrolled emotions of lower class whites who opposed the reforms sought by black and white Republicans at the reconvening of the state constitutional convention of 1864. The white riot was a protest against the idea of black suffrage and Radical rule.

1917.   Richardson, Frank L., Col. "My Recollections of the Battle of the Fourteenth of September, 1874, in New Orleans, La." *Louisiana Historical Quarterly*   3 (October 1920): 498-501. Richardson describes the violent confrontation between two groups of former Confederate soldiers (Louisiana's Own and the White League) against the Metropolitan Brigade of the Radicals. Following the article is a letter written by a visitor from New York, Jno. J. Colvin, Jr., who observed some of the revolt. (See also "A New York Yankee in New Orleans Sept. 14, 1874." *Louisiana Historical Quarterly* 3 (October 1920): 502.)

1918. Richter, William L. "James Longstreet: From Rebel to Scalawag." *Louisiana History* 11 (Summer 1970): 215-230. Most Southern whites vilified former Confederate Corps Commander, Lt. Gen. Longstreet, after he expressed moderate views about Reconstruction in 1867. He accepted the Reconstruction Acts as a way to moderate the Radicals and promote civil order. White Republican appreciated Longstreet's comments, but the black press believed that he undermined their efforts to reform the South. The debate, mostly carried on in newspapers, led to the tagging of Longstreet as a traitor and scalawag, but Longstreet did not fit the scalawag image.

1919. Russ, William Jr. "Disfranchisement in Louisiana (1862-1870)." *Louisiana Historical Quarterly* 18 (July 1935): 557-580. Russ discusses the political development of disenfranchisement of persons who would not or could not take the loyalty oaths during wartime and in the postwar period. Republican Governor Henry Clay Warmoth proposed a substantial end to disenfranchisement in 1870 because it simply was not worth maintaining.

1920. Sanson, Jerry Purvis. "White Man's Failure: The Rapides Parish 1874 Election." *Louisiana History* 31 (Winter 1990): 30-58. The White Man's Party was political arm of the White League of Rapides Parish created in March, 1877 to remove Republicans from public office and to emphasize the importance of white domination in society. Their efforts to defeat Republican candidates failed after the Republican Returning Board reversed an apparent conservative victory. Sanson suggests that accusations of violence, intimidation and vote stealing against the W.M.P. were not widespread and that the Returning Board manipulated the election. Parish election results are included. (See also Sanson's "Rapides Parish, Louisiana, During the End of Reconstruction." *Louisiana History* 27 (Spring 1986): 167-182.)

1921. Schoonover, Thomas (translator). "The German Minister Interprets Reconstruction Louisiana." *Louisiana History* 18 (Summer 1977): 335-337. The Prussian Minister to the U.S., Baron Kurd von Schloezer, wrote to his government on January 14, 1975 regarding the Republican Reconstruction policy and Louisiana politics. He comments on the violence in New Orleans and the ineptness of the response of the Grant administration. He views Reconstruction as destructive to the South.

1922. "Semi-Centennial of the 14th September, 1874." *Louisiana Historical Quarterly* 7 (October 1924): 570-657. *L.H.Q.* prints several papers and documents that recall the events of the conservative revolt against the Radicals in New Orleans. There is "History of the Events Leading Up to the Battle" by W. O. Hart (571-595); "The Call to Arms," a petition to white citizens; "General Ogden's Official Report" dated September 14 to Col. E. J. Ellis with a list of White League members (597-601); "The Metropolitan Police Story of the Battle" taken from *the Times Picayune* on September 14 with a list of persons killed and wounded (602-604); "The Republican Party After the Battle of September 14, 1874" by Henry W. Robinson offering the Republican view (604-618); "The 14th of September, 1874, as Viewed By the Supreme Court of Louisiana" by Jas. A. Renshaw (Henry Street et. al. vs. The City of New Orleans, 32 La Ann. 577, Opinion of Mr. Asso. Justice F. P. Poche) (618-620); "The Citizen Soldiery" listing the persons who fought by company or White League and indicating killed and wounded (621-633); and "The Monument at the Head of Canal Street - Ceremonies at the Laying of the Corner Stone" taken from the *Times Democrat* on September 15, 1891 with speeches commemorating the battle (633-657).

1923.   Shoalmire, Jimmie G. "Carpetbagger Extraordinary: Marshall Harvey Twitchell, 1840-1905." Ph.D. Mississippi State University, 1969. 253p.

1924.   Simpson, Amos E. and Vaughn Baker. "Michael Hahn: Steady Patriot." *Louisiana History* 13 (Summer 1972): 229-253.   Hahn, a Unionist, was elected governor of Louisiana in accordance with President Lincoln's Reconstruction plan during the war. He served from February, 1864 until March, 1865. Hahn did not support black suffrage, although he later supported suffrage as a way to gain more support for the Republicans. His reform efforts were opposed by the legislature and the Union Army.   The authors praise Hahn for his honesty, principles, and leadership.

1925.   Snyder, Perry A.   "Shreveport, Louisiana During the Civil War and Reconstruction." Ph.D. Florida State University, 1979. 265p.

1926.   Summers, Mark. "The Moderates' Lost Chance: The Louisiana Election of 1865." *Louisiana History* 24 (Winter 1983): 49-69.   Summers uses Louisiana as a test case to determine whether there was any chance that a moderate political party could succeed in the late war or immediate postwar periods. The former Whigs and National Unionists seemed to offer a middle ground between the Radical Republicans and the Conservative Democrats.   The problems encountered by governors Michael Hahn (1864-1865) and David Wells (1865-1867) illustrate that a truly moderate way was not possible due to the extreme pressure of uncompromising former Confederates and Radicals.

1927.   Taylor, Joe Gray. "Louisiana - An Impossible Task." In *Reconstruction and Redemption in the South*. Edited by Otto H. Olsen. Baton Rouge: Louisiana State University Press, 1980. Pp. 202-235.   Reconstruction was a complete failure in Louisiana despite its early start during the Civil War, the abundance of educated and sophisticated leaders in the black community, and the federal legislation and constitutional amendments intended to provide and protect civil rights.   The Republican Party could not build a strong base of support in the white community, and the Knights of the White Camellia used intimidation, violence, fraud and corruption to defeat them. The failure of Reconstruction also rests on the lack of commitment and will by the North to provide the freedmen with adequate assistance to achieve civil rights and economic independence.

1928.   Taylor, Joe Gray. "New Orleans and Reconstruction." *Louisiana History* 9 (Summer 1968): 189-208.   The cosmopolitan nature of New Orleans might have led to more tolerance in Reconstruction reforms, but in practice most white residents responded with the same negativity as rural whites. They actively opposed equal civil rights for blacks based on black inferiority. Whites put up with Gov. Henry Clay Warmoth's corrupt administration because of his charisma and his moderate race policies, but they despised William P. Kellogg's administration because it was Republican and viewed as illegitimate.

1929.   Tregle, Joseph G., Jr. "Thomas J. Durant, Utopian Socialism, and the Failure of Presidential Reconstruction in Louisiana." *Journal of Southern History* 45 (November 1979): 485-512.   Durant, a New Orleans transplant from Pennsylvania in the early 1830s, followed some of the utopian socialist teachings of Francois Marie Charles Fourier and tried to influence others in the Democratic Party. But Durant opposed slavery and secession, and when the city was occupied by the Union Army, he became involved in formulating the Reconstruction of state government for a swift return to the Union. He favored racial equality and called for revolutionary changes in society and the economy. His plans were undermined by Gen. Banks and Gov. Michael Hahn, a conservative Unionist who eventually turned into a rebel sympathizer.

1930.   Tucker, Robert Cinnamond. "The Life and Public Service of E. John Ellis." *Louisiana Historical Quarterly* 29 (July 1946): 679-770. App. Bibl.   Ellis, a Confederate veteran and lawyer, became deeply involved in the election of 1872 on the side of the Democrats and won election to Congress in 1874. Tucker describes Ellis' activities in New Orleans and state-wide politics during the latter stages of Reconstruction. This article is Tucker's M.A. thesis (Louisiana State University, 1941).

1931.   Tunnell, T. B., Jr. "The Negro, the Republican Party, and the Election of 1876 in Louisiana." *Louisiana History* 7 (Spring 1966): 101-116.   Tunnell explores the U.S. House of Representative's investigation of the disputed election in Louisiana and concludes that black disillusionment with the Republican Party and the attempts of the Democrats to gain black voters proved more important than intimidation. He points out that the U.S. Senate's investigation emphasized voter intimidation as the most important factor, but Tunnell discounts this report because the Senate investigation was very limited.

1932.   Tunnell, Ted (ed.). *Carpetbagger From Vermont: The Autobiography of Marshall Harvey Twitchell.* Baton Rouge: Louisiana State University Press, 1989. 216p. Ports.   Twitchell arrived in Bienville Parish in the fall of 1865 as an agent for the Freedmen's Bureau, and he quickly became a leader in Republican politics and a successful plantation owner. His prominence and his outspoken Northern arrogance made him and his family a target of the White League in newly created Red River Parish. Several family members were murdered in the Coushatta Massacre in 1873, and he nearly lost his own life in 1876. (See also Tunnell's "Marshall Harvey Twitchell and the Freedmen's Bureau in Bienville Parish." *Louisiana History* 33 (Summer 1992): 241-263. He emphasizes that Twitchell was not liked by either the freedmen or the whites because he attempted to take a middle ground on the issue of civil rights.)

1933.   Tunnell, Ted. *Crucible of Reconstruction: War, Radicalism and Race in Louisiana 1862-1877.* Baton Rouge: Louisiana State University Press, 1984. 257p. App. Bibl. Maps.   Tunnell provides thematic essays on Unionism, the role of the black elite, racial politics of carpetbaggers and scalawags in the administrations of Governors Henry C. Warmoth and William P. Kellogg, white opposition to Reconstruction, and Republican corruption and disunity. The appendix includes a list of Louisiana Unionists during the war, members of the constitutional convention of 1867/68, and major officeholders in the federal bureaucracy in Louisiana from 1867 to 1875. (See also Tunnell's "Anvil of Revolution: The Making of Radical Louisiana, 1862-1877." Ph.D. University of California, Berkeley, 1978. 243p.)

1934.   Tunnell, Ted. "Free Negroes and the Freedmen: Black Politics in New Orleans During the Civil War." *Southern Studies* 19 (Spring 1980): 5-28.   The traditions and independence of the large free black population in New Orleans led to demands for equal civil rights after the Union Army occupied the city. Black leaders sought land and labor reforms, but they became dissatisfied with the efforts of the Army, the local white leadership, and President Lincoln's support for Confederate property rights. Free blacks and former slaves recognized that their future freedoms were bound together, but their relationship was paternalistic and emphasized education and religious elevation.

1935.   Uzee, Philip D. "The Beginnings of the Louisiana Republican Party." *Louisiana History* 12 (Summer 1971): 197-211.   The Republican Party in Louisiana drew leadership and support from some of the Unionist "free staters" who organized in 1863 under the direction of Thomas J. Durant. The Republican Party began in the state in 1864 and relied on former Unionists, carpetbaggers, and blacks for support. Most of all they relied on the Grant administration and federal troops to maintain power until their defeat in the 1876 elections.

1936.   Vandal, Gilles. "Albert H. Leonard's Road From White League to the Republican Party: A Political Enigma." *Louisiana History* 36 (Winter 1995): 55-76.   Leonard became prominent in Louisiana politics as editor and part owner of the *Shreveport Times* beginning in December, 1871. His political message was so strongly anti-Radical that he urged support for Henry C. Warmoth's Liberal Republicans as well as the Fusion ticket in 1872. In 1874 he openly called for violence against white Radicals and blacks, but by early 1875 he supported the Wheeler Compromise that allowed Gov. William P. Kellogg to remain governor. His transformation to a Republican by 1878. Leonard's behavior represents the fluid nature of Louisiana politics in the 1870s.

1937.   Vandal, Gilles. "'Bloody Caddo': White Violence Against Blacks in a Louisiana Parish, 1865-1876." *Journal of Social History* 25 (Winter 1991): 373-388. Tbls.   Vandal emphasizes the importance of local or regional variations in the level of deadly violence that existed during Reconstruction. Caddo Parish did not experience war destructiveness, and this led to a high degree of white defiance against Union occupation, emancipation of blacks, and changes in race relations. Vandal suggests that most of the higher than normal level of violence was related to politics prior to the elections of 1868 and 1874. Perpetrators of deadly violence were prominent persons, such as planters, farmers, and public officials. (See also Vandal's "The Policy of Violence in Caddo Parish, 1865-1884." *Louisiana History* 32 (Spring 1991): 159-182. Tbls.)

1938.   Vandal, Gilles. *The New Orleans Riot of 1866: Anatomy of a Tragedy.* Lafayette: Center for Louisiana Studies, University of Southwestern Louisiana, 1983. 238p. App. Bibl. Tbls.   The Republican meeting of July 30, 1866 to revise the state constitution written during 1864 inflamed the white population and led to a violent clash.   Vandal explains that the riot occurred because of the build up of social and racial anxiety and enmity within the white community about attempts to enhance the power of blacks and the Republican Party in general.   The riot could have been prevented if federal military authorities had acted promptly.   (See also Vandal's Ph.D. dissertation with the same title from College of William and Mary, 1978; and "The Origins of the New Orleans Riot of 1866, Revisited." *Louisiana History* 22 (Spring 1981): 135-165 in which he concludes that city leaders tried to calm the city, not instigate a riot, and that the press merely printed accurate descriptions of social tensions, not rumors.)

1939.   Vincent, Charles. "Aspects of the Family and Public Life of Antonie Dubuclet: Louisiana's Black State Treasurer, 1868-1878." *Journal of Negro History* 66 (Spring 1981): 26-36.   The career of Dubuclet as state treasurer between 1868 and 1878 contradicts the highly negative image of black officeholders depicted by many historians.   Dubuclet, born free in Iberville Parish, served as treasurer in Republican and Democratic administrations.   He was admired for his honest and efficient work, but his impact on the state was limited by politics and government corruption.

1940.   Vincent, Charles. *Black Legislators in Louisiana During Reconstruction.* Baton Rouge: Louisiana State University Press, 1976. 262p. App. Bibl. Maps. Ports.   Traditional ideas about the role of blacks in Reconstruction politics have been largely incorrect and based mainly on racial antipathy.   In Louisiana black politicians never held a majority of public offices and did not conform to the stereotype of the ignorant, corrupt, and selfish black politician.   Vincent gives an account of black participation in state government and the impact of Republican factional strife under governors Henry Clay Warmoth and William P. Kellogg. Some of the key black state legislators mentioned are James H. Ingrahm, C. C. Antoine, Robert H. Isbelle, Henry Demas, Oscar Dunn, and P. B. S. Pinchback. Appendices provide lists of black members of the state constitutional convention and the legislature from 1868 to 1876. (See also Vincent's "Negro Legislators in Louisiana During Reconstruction." Ph.D. Louisiana State University, 1973.   304p.)

1941.   Vincent, Charles. "Louisiana's Black Governor: Aspects of His National Significance." *Negro History Bulletin* 42 (April-June 1979): 34-36.   Port. Vincent describes the life of P. B. S. Pinchback, who participated in Louisiana politics from 1867 until about 1892.   Pinchback was a leader in the local and national Republican Party and served in several public offices, including lieutenant governor (1871-1873), acting governor (Dec. 9, 1972-Jan. 13, 1873) and U.S. senator (1873-1876) but was never allowed to take his seat in the Senate. He also worked in newspaper publishing, business, and in the founding of Southern University in New Orleans in 1879.

1942.   Vincent, Charles. "Louisiana's Legislators and Their Efforts to Pass a Blue Law During Reconstruction." *Journal of Black History* 7 (September 1976): 47-56.   Black lawmakers in Louisiana attempted to make business unlawful on the sabbath beginning with the Constitutional Convention of 1867/1868 until 1875. In all cases the proposals were blocked or voted down, mainly by white legislators. Vincent suggests that attempts to pass blue laws were examples of the beneficial programs initiated by black legislators in Reconstruction.

1943.   Vincent, Charles. "Negro Leadership and Programs in the Louisiana Constitutional Convention of 1868." *Louisiana History* 10 (Fall 1969): 339-351. The convention consisted of 49 whites and 49 blacks. The black delegates did not seek social and economic revolution. They were highly responsible men who sought a basis for equal civil rights and reasonable reforms of government, education, marriage, labor, and homestead laws for all citizens.

1944.   Wade, Michael G. "'I Would Rather Be Among the Comanches': The Military Occupation of Southwest Louisiana, 1865." *Louisiana History* 39 (Winter 1998): 45-64.   Wade explains that the military occupation of southwestern Louisiana near New Iberia calmed the chaotic situation after the war. He focuses on the occupation by the 98th Colored Infantry, led by Col. Charles Ledyard Norton, beginning June 1, 1865 and ending after the November elections. Once white residents realized that the occupation would end soon and that President Johnson opposed Radical demands to reform the South, violence increased markedly, particularly violence against blacks. A continued military occupation would have had a positive impact on maintaining order and security in the region.

1945.   Warmoth, Henry Clay. *War, Politics and Reconstruction: Stormy Days in Louisiana.* New York: Macmillan Co., 1930. 285p. App.   Originally from Illinois, Warmoth came South with the Federal Army and got involved in Louisiana politics after the war. He served as the first Republican governor of Louisiana from 1868 until 1872. His enemies sought his impeachment and have accussed him of corruption and dishonesty. This book is Warmoth's memoir of his family background, military career during the Civil War, and experiences as a politician in the state. Warmoth defends his record and reflects on state politics during the postwar years.

1946.   Webb, Allie Bayne Windham. "Organization and Activities of the Knights of the White Camellia in Louisiana, 1867-1869." *Proceedings of the Louisiana Academy of Science* 17 (March 19-20 1954): 110-118.   The Knights of the White Camellia, founded on May 22, 1867 in Franklin, La., was a defender of white morality in Reconstruction.

1947.   Weisberger, Bernard A.   "The Carpetbagger: A Tale of Reconstruction."
American Heritage 25 (December 1973): 70-77.   Ills. Ports.   The "carpetbagger"
in this article is Pinckney B. S. Pinchback, a mulatto born in Macon, Georgia and
educated in Ohio.   Weisberger provides a biography of the man who served as
acting governor from December, 1872 to January, 1873 following Henry Clay
Warmoth's resignation.   He is depicted as ambitious, intelligent, and probably
corrupt, although Weisberger provides no evidence to support this.   Pinchback later
served on the state board of education   (1877), the state constitutional convention
(1879), and as a founder and trustee of Southern University (1883).

1948.   Wetta, Frank J.   "Bloody Monday: The Louisiana Scalawags and the New
Orleans Riot of 1866."   *Southern Studies*, New Series, 2 (Spring 1991): 5-15.
Scalawags, such as Michael Hahn, A. P. Dostie, and Thomas Jefferson Durant, were
influential from 1862 until the riot of July 30 led to the end of their influence.   Wetta
examines the role of the scalawags in the riot and concludes that while their
speeches inflamed hatred against blacks and all local Republicans, the riot was
planned and initiated by former confederates as a way to eliminate Republicans and
secure power for Democrats.   In his footnotes, Wetta lists the names of Louisiana
scalawags.

1949.   Wetta, Frank J.   "'Bulldozing the Scalawags': Some Examples of the
Persecution of Southern White Republicans in Louisiana During Reconstruction."
Louisiana History 21 (Winter 1980): 43-58.   Republicans were roundly ostracized
and intimidated, but scalawags were considered traitors and a low form of beast.
Wetta provides a lengthy list of Louisiana scalawags who held public office after
1868, well after the beginning of the gradual decline of their influence following the
New Orleans riot of 1866.   The Ku Klux Klan, the Knights of the White Camellia,
and the White League contributed to this decline and the destruction of the
Republican Party in the state.

1950.   Wetta, Frank J.   "The Louisiana Scalawags."   Ph.D. Louisiana State
University, 1977. 402p.

1951.   Williams, E. Russ, Jr.   "John Roy: Forgotten Scalawag."   *Louisiana
Studies* 8 (Fall 1974): 240-262.   Roy was a former Whig and Unionist who
supported President Johnson's Reconstruction policies.   After his election to the
state senate in 1868, Roy became a supporter of Gov. Henry Clay Warmoth and later
supported the radical Custom House Republicans in the 1872 election against
Warmoth Republicans.   Roy is characterized as interested mainly in power and
wealth through public office.

1952.   Williams, T. Harry.   "The Louisiana Unification Movement of 1893."
Journal of Southern History 11 (August 1945): 349-369.   (Rpt. in *The Selected
Essays of T. Harry Williams*.   Baton Rouge: Louisiana State University Press,
1983.) In 1872 the New Orleans business community decided that political strife
was depressing commercial activity and economic development.   To reduce
statewide racial and political problems, white citizens formed the Reform Party, led

by Isaac N. Marks and William M. Randolf, to work out a compromise. In 1873 the party became the Unification Party. The movement failed because it never garnered the trust of the black community, Republican and Democratic politicians, and rural whites who generally refused to compromise white supremacy.

1953.   Williams, T. Harry.   *P. G. T. Beauregard: Napoleon in Gray.*   Baton Rouge: Louisiana State University Press, 1955. 345p. Bibl. Ports. Ills.   In this biography of the creole Confederate general from south Louisiana, Williams discusses Beauregard's decision to accept the South's defeat, the end of slavery, and also civil rights for blacks. His only participation in Reconstruction politics was his public support for the New Orleans based Louisiana Unification Movement. Beauregard spent most of his time during and after Reconstruction with a New Orleans transportation business and other commercial enterprises, including the Louisiana Lottery.

1954.   Williams, T. Harry. "The Politics of Reconstruction." In *Romance and Realism in Southern Politics.* Baton Rouge: Louisiana State University Press, 1966. Pp. 17-43. (Originally published by University of Georgia Press, 1961.) In general, Southerners responded to the defeat of the Confederacy by not only rejecting change, but also prewar tolerance for criticism of traditional Southern values and racial ideology. Among the groups that favored pragmatic and realistic changes was the New Orleans based Unification Movement, but it failed to gain broad support among rural whites. The Louisiana planter-business class opposed black suffrage, as did conservative New Orleans newspapers, as mob rule. Williams believes that Reconstruction raised issues that could have been handled more realistically instead of putting off the problems for later generations.

1955.   Wilson, James D. "The Donaldsonville Incident of 1870: A Study of Local Party Dissension and Republican Infighting in Reconstruction Louisiana." *Louisiana History* 38 (Summer 1997): 329-345.   Republican Party dissension in Donaldsonville located in Ascension Parish was based on the factions within the party at the time of the 1870 election. Pierre Landry, a former slave, was elected mayor in 1868 and helped organize a conservative Republican group that worked with Democrats against white violence and power hungry carpetbaggers.   The distrust of Landry's group and the Republicans led by Gov. Henry Clay Warmoth led to a violent confrontation at the time of the election in November. The divisions within the Republican Party contributed to its downfall.

Agriculture, Labor, and Business

1956.   Barnhardt, John D. (ed.). "Reconstruction in the Lower Mississippi." *Mississippi Valley Historical Review* 21 (December 1934): 387-396.   Printed are excerpts of letters written by James A. Payne from Baton Rouge to his step-daughter, Mrs. Kate F. Sterrett, at Point Pleasant, West Virginia. Payne, a native of West Virginia, went to Louisiana for business purposes prior to the Civil War and stayed there throughout Reconstruction. Most of the letters were written during Reconstruction and illustrate Payne's negative perspective on black participation in government and the impact of Reconstruction on his businesses in cotton speculation, smuggling, loaning money, warehousing, and supplying farms with equipment.

1957.   Cohen, Lucy M. *Chinese in the Post-Civil War South: A People Without a History*. Baton Rouge: Louisiana State University Press, 1984. 211p. App. Bibl. Ills. Ports. Map.   Many Southern planters hired Chinese laborers after the war to take the place of black labor that was considered unreliable. Cohen emphasizes the use of Chinese labor in Louisiana between 1865 and 1880. Planters were dissatisfied with them because of cultural differences and their substantial wage demands. The Chinese moved on to sharecropping or retailing and eventually lost their cultural identity through intermarriage and migration to other U.S. regions.

1958.   Cohen, Lucy M.   "Entry of Chinese to the Lower South From 1865 to 1870: Policy Dilemmas." *Southern Studies*, New Series, 2 (Fall/Winter 1991): 281-313.   Chinese workers came to Louisiana and adjacent states from Cuba and China during postwar years until 1870 when the British effectively closed Hong Kong as a port for the recruitment of Chinese labor outside of the British colonies. Cohen focuses on the national and local public policies and international negotiations that had an impact on the recruitment and movement of people.

1959.   Ellis, L. Tuffly.   "The New Orleans Cotton Exchange: The Formative Years, 1871-1880." *Journal of Southern History* 39 (November 1973): 545-564. The deteriorating cotton market in New Orleans after the Civil War was reversed by the organization of the New Orleans Cotton Exchange, founded on January 17, 1871. The founders sought to rebuild the city's position as the principal spot market of the world and a leading futures market for cotton. Despite heavy competition from other markets, the New Orleans exchange was highly successful. It usually stayed out of politics, except for a few situations in which it established a decidedly conservative, anti-Republican position.

1960.   Gray, Andrew (ed.). "The Carpetbagger's Letters." *Louisiana History* 20 (Fall 1979): 431-451.   Several letters written by Abram Piatt Andrew of Indiana are printed. After serving in the Army of the Cumberland, he teamed up with his brother-in-law in 1866 to try farming at Airlie Plantation near Goddrich Landing, La.   The letters to his parents provide details about his financial and farming activities and his life in a new environment. Andrew did not fit the stereotype of the carpetbagger.

1961.   Highsmith, William E.   "Louisiana Landholding During War and Reconstruction." *Louisiana Historical Quarterly* 38 (January 1955): 39-54.   Prior to the war and during the first 15 years afterwards land ownership and wealth were concentrated in a minority.   White yeomen continued to till their small and frequently infertile farms, and blacks commonly stayed on the plantations as sharecroppers living an existence not much different than slavery. Large plantations stayed together with financing from New Orleans banks and the desire of planters to hold their land.

1962.   Highsmith, William E. "Some Aspects of Reconstruction in the Heart of Louisiana." *Journal of Southern History* 13 (November 1947): 460-491. Tbls. Highsmith provides a broad view of the economic, social and political environment in Rapides Parish. He offers a statistical analysis of agricultural and land use in the parish, labor issues on large plantations, political reorganization, and the worsening of race relations during the 1870s. There may be a relationship between economic problems and race problems, but this is unclear for the study.

1963.   Kearns, David Taylor. "The Social Mobility of New Orleans Laborers, 1870-1900." Ph.D. Tulane University, 1977. 190p.

1964.   Lanza, Michael L. "Getting Down to Business: The Public Land Offices in Louisiana During Reconstruction." *Louisiana History* 29 (Spring 1988): 177-182. The problem with the implementation of the Southern Homestead Act of 1866 in Louisiana was the disarray of General Land Offices. Land records were missing or disorganized, and the offices were frequently closed due to the lack of employees. Land offices in Louisiana had the worst record of any Southern state with regard to the number of homestead applications and successful land transactions processed.

1965.   Marquette, C. L. (ed.). "Letters of a Yankee Sugar Planter." *Journal of Southern History* 6 (November 1940): 521-546. Tbls.   Maine entrepreneur Daniel Thompson invested in a sugar plantation in St. Mary's Parish, Louisiana. At Calumet Plantation he conducted a profitable sugar business and used advanced scientific information in the planting and manufacturing of sugar. The letters printed are from Thompson to Cyrus Woodman, a land agent in Wisconsin. A few of the letters written between 1866 and 1876 remark on the sugar industry, black labor, and politics. Most of the letters were written between 1877 and 1889.

1966.   McGinty, Garnie W. "Changes in Louisiana Agriculture, 1860-1880." *Louisiana Historical Quarterly* 18 (April 1935): 407-429.   McGinty compares Louisiana's progress in the postbellum period with the northcentral states and the U.S. in general.   Reconstruction hampered agricultural recovery, and the value of farms decreased. Tenancy among the freedmen became widespread and continued at the end of the century. Louisiana fell far behind the agricultural progress in other parts of country.

1967.   McGuire, Mary Jennie. "Getting Their Hands on the Land: The Revolution in St. Helena Parish, 1861-1900." Ph.D. University of South Carolina, 1984. 263p.

1968.   Messner, William F. *Freedmen and the Ideology of Free Labor: Louisiana 1862-1865.* Lafayette: Center for Louisiana Studies, University of Southwestern Louisiana, 1981. 206p. Bibl. Ills. Ports.   The Republican ideology of free labor stressed individual initiative, hard work and economic orthodoxy. This was the U.S. Army's approach toward freedmen in the Gulf Department parishes of South Louisiana prior to the end of war and became the foundation for programs to help freedmen during Reconstruction. Messner argues that the free labor ideology was inappropriate for a black peasantry that did not have the political and economic power to succeed in a hostile white society. Barriers to the success of blacks reinforced notions of their inferiority.

1969. Millet, Donald J. "The Economic Development of Southwest Louisiana, 1865-1900." Ph.D. Louisiana State University, 1964. 467p.

1970. Oubre, Claude F. "'Forty Acres and a Mule': Louisiana and the Southern Homestead Act." *Louisiana History* 17 (Spring 1976): 125-157. The Southern Homestead Act of 1866 offered freedmen and loyal whites the opportunity to purchase public lands, but many obstacles prevented freedmen from taking advantage of the law in Louisiana, including economic hardship, flooding due to levee disrepair, the chaotic management of the state's single land office, opposition of whites, and competition from business. Oubre questions whether the homestead act really helped poor farmers anywhere in the South.

1971. Prichard, Walter. "The Effects of the Civil War on the Louisiana Sugar Industry." *Journal of Southern History* 5 (August 1939): 315-332. The war devastated the state's sugar industry worth about $200 million by causing crop reductions, loss of seed cane, and damage to the river levees near the cane fields. The industry gradually recovered during Reconstruction, although river flooding and the lack of labor and capital hampered the process. Prichard notes how the industry showed resiliency and innovation in its acceptance of labor saving methods and machinery, but it was hampered by carpetbagger governments and labor shortages.

1972. Rodrigue, John C. "Raising Cane: From Slavery To Free Labor In Louisiana's Sugar Parishes, 1862-1880." Ph.D. Emory University, 1993. 698p.

1973. Schweninger, Loren. "Antebellum Free Persons of Color in Postbellum Louisiana." *Louisiana History* 30 (Fall 1989): 345-364. Maps. Tbls. During Reconstruction most persons of color who were free prior to the war were unable to return to the same economically prosperous life they once had, a life that included the ownership of black slaves and allegiance to the state. This group of Louisiana blacks longed for prewar days when they led more secure lives. Included are tables illustrating black real estate ownership and property values during the antebellum and postbellum decades.

1974. Shugg, Roger W. *Origins of Class Struggle in Louisiana: Social History of White Farmers and Laborers During Slavery and After, 1840-1876.* Baton Rouge: Louisiana State University Press, 1939. 372p. App. Bibl. Shugg examines antebellum and postwar Louisiana from the perspective of social and economic classes, including the small number of wealthy plantation owners and the masses of poor whites. Blacks are not considered in this discussion, except for their struggle for power with poor whites during Reconstruction. The end of

Reconstruction brought defeat to both groups at the hands of the traditional power aristocracy of antebellum days. Conditions for lower class whites worsened in Louisiana and throughout the South during the rest of the 19th century, but by the 1890s this group brought strength to the Populist movement against the established economic power structure. The appendix includes statistical tables on land holdings and wealth by parish prior to and after the war.

1975.   Shugg, Roger W. "Survival of the Plantation System in Louisiana." *Journal of Southern History* 3 (August 1937): 311-325. Tbl.   The popular idea that Southern plantations broke up into many small landholdings was based on incorrect census data from the censuses for 1870-1900. Shugg uses state assessment rolls to study landholdings in Concordia, Iberville, Catahoula, Lafouche, and Natchitoches parishes to show that many plantations not only survived but increased in number after the Civil War. Plantations were often split into small tenant plots, but the plots continued to be owned by one person or corporation. Many plantations survived because large scale agriculture was needed, credit was plentiful in New Orleans, Reconstruction collapsed, and black workers were allowed to support themselves, even if they were forced into peonage.

1976.   Sitterson, J. Carlyle. *Sugar Country: The Cane Sugar Industry in the South, 1753-1950.* Lexington: University of Kentucky Press, 1953. 414p. Bibl. Ills. Maps.   Sitterson discusses postwar adjustments to plantation management, sugar manufacturing, labor, financing, and technological innovations that led to the development of a modern sugar cane industry. Most of his book is an examination of the cane sugar industry in Louisiana, but he also mentions other states, particularly Florida and Texas.

1977.   Sitterson, J. Carlyle. "The Transition From Slave to Free Economy on the William J. Minor Plantation." *Agricultural History* 17 (October 1943): 216-224. The Minor Plantation was a group of mainly sugar plantations owned by William and Henry Minor in Ascension and Terrebonne Parishes. Using the personal correspondence and plantation records of William Minor, Sitterson describes how the transition to freedom for the plantation slaves took place during the Civil War. By the spring of 1865 a new, but still highly restrictive, labor relationship had been established, but poor crops and poor wages contributed to the workers' departure. Labor shortages resulted throughout the sugar growing region by 1867 and brought hardship to the industry and the Minor family.

1978.   Vandal, Gilles. "Black Utopia in Early Reconstruction New Orleans: The People's Bakery as a Case-Study." *Louisiana History* 38 (Fall 1997): 437-452. The People's Bakery was a producer-run cooperative of free blacks who sought to advance the black community economically based on modified Fourierist principles. Black property owners and their workers within the cooperative would share equally in the profits. The utopian concept seemed to offer promise for black progress, but it was unsuccessful from the start due to internal disagreements. The attempt represented one way that blacks tried to take control of their destiny.

1979.   Williams, E. Russ, Jr.   "Louisiana Public and Private Immigration Endeavors: 1866-1893." *Louisiana History* 15 (Spring 1974): 153-173.   Part of this article focuses on the ineffective efforts of the state government to encourage immigration into Louisiana after the Civil War.   The need for labor led to the organization of the Bureau of Immigration on March 17, 1866 and efforts continued throughout the 19th century.

Society, Education, and Religion

1980.   Adamoli, Giulio.   "New Orleans in 1867 - 'Letters from America, 1867.'" *Louisiana Historical Quarterly* 6 (April 1923): 271-279. (Rpt. from *The Living Age* 313 (April 1, 1922).   In three letters Adamoli describes the sites and his activities in New Orleans, including information told to him regarding the condition of blacks and the activities of the Freedmen's Bureau.   His letters mention economic activity and Mardi Gras.

1981.   Beasley, Leon O.   "A History of Education in Louisiana During the Reconstruction Period, 1862-1877."   Ph.D. Louisiana State University, 1957. 328p.

1982.   Blassingame, John W.   *Black New Orleans, 1860-1880*.   Chicago: University of Chicago Press, 1973. 301p.   App. Bibl. Ills. Tbls.   Blassingame focuses on the social and economic culture of blacks in New Orleans during Reconstruction.   This includes labor and landowning patterns, family life, education and intellectual life, and relations with the white community.   He emphasizes the uniqueness of the New Orleans culture and its black community that included a large number of free blacks, and the part this played in the responses of blacks to emancipation and new opportunities.   They gained little politically, but their confidence increased through social organizations, limited success with integration, and greater economic participation.   (See also Blassingame's "A Social and Economic Study of the Negro in New Orleans, 1860-1880." Ph.D. Yale University, 1971. 388p.)

1983.   Brady, Patricia.   "Trials and Tribulations: American Missionary Association Teachers and Black Education in Occupied New Orleans, 1863-1864." *Louisiana History* 31 (Winter 1990): 5-20.   The efforts of the A.M.A. to organize education for freedmen in New Orleans began in December, 1863 with the arrival of two agents, Dr. Isaac G. Hubbs and Rev. Charles Strong.   Internal struggles and misunderstandings within the A.M.A. and differences with the Union troops made the job difficult.   A.M.A. schools remained open only until the fall of 1864.   The Freedmen's Bureau did not have the resources to maintain schools, and it was not until 1869 that the A.M.A. returned to coordinate freedmen education.

1984.   Caldwell, Joe L.   "A Social, Economic, and Political Study of Blacks in the Louisiana Delta, 1865-1880."   Ph.D. Tulane University, 1989. 354p.

1985.   Carleton, Mark T. "The Politics of the Convict Lease System in Louisiana: 1868-1901." *Louisiana History* 8 (Winter 1967): 5-25.   The Republican governments of Henry Clay Warmoth and William P. Kellogg began an infamous system of leasing prison facilities and prisoners to commercial operations. The penal system lacked rehabilitative services and ruined the health of many prisoners.

1986.   Conner, William P. "Reconstruction Rebels: The *New Orleans Tribune* in Post-War Louisiana." *Louisiana History* 21 (Spring 1980): 159-181.   Dr. Louis Charles Roudanez, a free black, founded the *Tribune* in the summer of 1864 after the demise of the French language *L'Union*. Roudanez hired Paul Trévigne and Jean-Charles Houzeau de la Haie to form a team that provided the black community in New Orleans with a major voice for political, social, and economic reform in the South. The *Tribune* was known as a promoter of civil rights, black education, and enhanced power for laborers. Political factions among the writers and funding problems brought an end to the newspaper in 1870.

1987.   Crouch, Barry A. "Black Education in Civil War and Reconstruction Louisiana: George T. Ruby, the Army, and the Freedmen's Bureau." *Louisiana History* 38 (Summer 1997): 287-308.   Ruby is known for his participation in Texas politics, but Crouch examines his work in Louisiana that prepared him for future challenges. Ruby, a free black from New York and Maine, worked as a school teacher and principle in New Orleans and St. Bernard Parish beginning in 1864 and eventually became an agent for the Freedmen's Bureau in charge of establishing schools and investigating the state of black education. Crouch describes Ruby as a typical black carpetbagger who made positive contributions to education and gained valuable experience for a career in public life.

1988.   Engelsman, John Cornelius. "The Freedmen's Bureau in Louisiana." *Louisiana Historical Quarterly* 32 (January 1949): 145-224. Bibl.   In the author's M.A. thesis (Louisiana State University, 1937) he describes the function of the Freedmen's Bureau in Louisiana and the animosity it engendered among the vocal white population. The bureau's positive activities were obstructed by the whites and it brought on other problems by encouraging blacks to strive for social equality when they only wanted personal freedom.

1989.   Fischer, Roger A. "A Pioneer Protest: The New Orleans Street-Car Controversy of 1867." *Journal of Negro History* 53 (July 1968): 219-233.   Racial tension and violence occurred on May 4-5, 1867 in New Orleans when blacks protested segregation of street cars. This had been controversial for decades but only after emancipation and the Reconstruction Acts did disaffection with the practice reach a head.   As a result of the unrest, the street cars were officially desegregated and remained so until 1902 when state law forbid it. The local white press correctly interpreted the reform as a precursor to future change in the blacks' struggle against second class citizenship.

1990.   Fischer, Roger A. *The Segregation Struggle in Louisiana, 1862-1877.* Urbana: University of Illinois Press, 1974. 168p. Bibl.   In postwar Louisiana, particularly New Orleans, blacks who had been free since antebellum days spearheaded an attempt to eliminate as much of the discriminatory practices against blacks as they could. They led a determined campaign to abolish segregation in politics, public transportation, public accommodations, and public schools. Their drive for equality with whites was partially successful and may have contributed to a white backlash in the form of Jim Crow laws in the 1890s. (See also Fischer's "The Segregation Struggle in Louisiana, 1850-1890," Ph.D. Tulane University, 1967.)

1991.   Harlan, Louis R. "Desegregation in New Orleans Public Schools During Reconstruction." *American Historical Review* 67 (April 1962): 663-675.   Harlan explains that the cultural, political, and racial composition of the city led to desegregation and to cooperation between black and white citizens that was unique among cities in the South. Cooperation also took the form of the Unification Movement of 1873 that sought to return home rule to the state, but the attempt failed and interracial cooperation collapsed completely after local Democrats regained power and segregated the schools once again.

1992.   Haywood, Jacquelyn S.   "The American Missionary Association in Louisiana in Reconstruction." Ph.D. University of California at Los Angeles, 1975. 262p.

1993.   Loveland, Anne C.   "The 'Southern Work' of the Reverend Joseph C. Hartzell, Pastor of Ames Church in New Orleans, 1870-1873." *Louisiana History* 16 (Fall 1975): 391-407.   Hartzell's "southern work" with the Methodist Episcopal Church was to promote an atmosphere of reform among the members of the Church, many of whom were carpetbaggers and local Republicans. Local whites rejected his liberalism and efforts to work with black Methodists, and they undermined Hartzell's work for civil rights.

1994.   May, J. Thomas. "The Freedmen's Bureau at the Local Level: A Study of a Louisiana Agent." *Louisiana History* 9 (Winter 1968): 5-19.   The reports of agent W. H. Cornelius indicated that he did not fit the stereotype of Radical Republicans involved in social and political reform. In St. Martins Parish Cornelius relied on the good will and assistance of local whites and intentionally worked within the local political and judicial framework controlled by conservatives. In his relations with whites and freedmen, he focused his attention mainly on rebuilding the agricultural base.

1995.   May, J. Thomas. "The Medical Care of Blacks in Louisiana During the Occupation and Reconstruction, 1862-1868: Its Social and Political Background." Ph.D. Tulane University, 1971. 191p.

1996.   May, J. Thomas. "A 19th Century Medical Care Program For Blacks: the Case of the Freedmen's Bureau." *Anthropological Quarterly* 46 (July 1973): 160-171.   May examines the administration of a bureau hospital in Shreveport, Louisiana to illustrate how conflict over authority and control between bureau officials and U.S. Army officials made administering medical care to the freedmen a difficult task. Native whites resented the federal medical facility and worked to reach a consensus with the Army and the bureau. These issues are compared with problems in offering contemporary government services.

1997.   McTigue, Geraldine M. "Forms of Racial Interaction in Louisiana, 1860-1880." Ph.D. Yale University, 1975. 400p.

1998.   Messner, William F. "Black Education in Louisiana, 1863-1865." *Civil War History* 21 (March 1976): 41-59.   Gen. Nathaniel Banks took command of the Gulf Department in late 1862 and within a few months began to plan for the education of black children based on the idea that it would have a positive influence on social stability, economic development, and the quality of black labor. The Army paid for part of the expenses related to elementary education for blacks in New Orleans and it established schools in rural parishes.   Banks encouraged the state constitutional convention of 1864 to support black education.

1999.   Padgett, James A. (ed.). "Some Letters of George Stanton Dension, 1854-1866: Observations of a Yankee of Conditions in Louisiana and Texas." *Louisiana Historical Quarterly* 23 (October 1940): 1132-1240.   Denison, a native of Vermont, arrived in New Orleans in the spring of 1862 as a customs official, a position he held until June 24, 1865. In his letters he describes his experiences during the Union Army occupation of the city and his travels in Louisiana and Texas during 1865 and 1866. Most of the letters were written to friends and family, including his uncle, Salmon P. Chase.

2000.   Patty, James S. "A Woman Journalist in Reconstruction Louisiana: Mrs. Mary E. Bryan." *Louisiana Studies* 3 (Spring 1964): 77-104. Port.   Bryan wrote editorials for the *Semi-Weekly Natchitoches Times* from 1867 to 1874. She was an ardent defender of the South and opposed Radical Reconstruction. Her comments often reveal racist attitudes. Bryan also wrote about the literary output of Southern women.

2001.   Porter, Betty. "The History of Negro Education in Louisiana." *Louisiana Historical Quarterly*   25 (July 1942): 728-821. Bibl.   In this M.A. thesis (Louisiana State University, 1938) Porter covers prewar and postwar periods with particular emphasis on the efforts made by the Freedmen's Bureau and private organizations. The establishment of institutions of higher education are highlighted, including the founding of Straight University   (1869), New Orleans University (1869), and Leland College (1870). The last section surveys philanthropy for black education, but this was mainly a phenomena of the post-Reconstruction period.

2002.   Rankin, David C. "The Forgotten People: Free People of Color in New Orleans, 1850-1870." Ph.D. Johns Hopkins University, 1976. 342p.

2003.   Rankin, David C. "The Impact of the Civil War on the Free Colored Community of New Orleans." *Perspectives in American History* 11 (1977-1978): 377-416.   Rankin describes how the free black community was destroyed by the war and Reconstruction. Beginning with the Union occupation of the city in May, 1962, free blacks who were affluent and educated lost their special status and struggled to distinguish themselves from freed blacks who they disdained. Union occupiers treated them poorly.

2004. Reed, Germaine A. "David Boyd, L.S.U., and Louisiana Reconstruction." *Louisiana Studies* 14 (Fall 1975): 259-276. After the war Boyd directed the Louisiana State Seminary of Learning and Military Academy (renamed Louisiana State University in 1870). He struggled to maintain and build the school admidst state politics, race issues, and financial upheavals. Boyd developed a good relationship with Gov. Henry Clay Warmoth and received adequate funding, but finances deteriorated under Gov. William Pitt Kellogg to the point of disaster. As a moderate on race issues, but he struggled against integrating the school. Reed's study in based on Boyd's correspondence.

2005. Reed, Germaine A. "David Boyd: Southern Educator." 2 Vols. Ph.D. Louisiana State University, 1970. 712p.

2006. Reed, Germaine A. "Race Legislation in Louisiana, 1864-1920." *Louisiana History* 6 (Fall 1965): 379-392. Reed provides a brief survey of race related legislation passed by the legislature. During Reconstruction this included black laws, public education, civil rights, jury selection, marriage and children, and discrimination in schools for the blind and at Shreveport's Charity Hospital.

2007. Ripley, C. Peter. *Slaves and Freedmen in Civil War Louisiana.* Baton Rouge: Louisiana State University Press, 1976. 237p. Bibl. Reconstruction in wartime Louisiana proved to be the model for the treatment of blacks in other states. The emancipation of slaves in the state as Union troops occupied increasing portions of territory eventually led to military policies related to black labor, education, civil rights, housing, justice, and family security. Blacks were denied most of what they expected from freedom. The Union Army in the Gulf Region, led by Major Gen. Nathaniel P. Banks, sought to assuage white plantation owners or to offer resources to Union soldiers rather than to help the freedmen begin a new economic and social life. In Louisiana and throughout the South the general pattern of Army occupation emphasized the maintenance of order and reunion rather than civil rights for blacks.

2008. Rousey, Dennis C. "Black Police in New Orleans During Reconstruction." *Historian* 49 (February 1987): 223-243. On May 30, 1867 New Orleans became the first Southern city to integrate its police force. The transition was eased by the precedent set earlier in the 19th century, the large number of free blacks who participated in various ways in city life prior to the Civil War, and the high percentage (26% in 1870) of blacks in the population. Rousey examines the role of blacks in the police force and emphasizes their positive contributions.

2009. Schuler, Kathryn Reinhart. "Women in Public Affairs in Louisiana During Reconstruciton." *Louisiana Historical Quarterly* 19 (July 1936): 668-750. In his M.A. thesis (Louisiana State University, 1936) Schuler compares the advances made by women in the North and South, particularly in Louisiana. The South took a more conservative view of women's roles in society. In postwar Louisiana women had to take on greater responsibilities in public welfare, caring for war casualties, journalism, and domestic work. In general, very little progress occurred outside of traditional Southern roles, because white males would not tolerate change.

2010.   Shaik, Mohamed J. "The Development of Public Education for Negroes in Louisiana." Ph.D. University of Ottawa, 1964.

2011.   Somers, Dale A. "Black and White in New Orleans: A Study in Urban Race Relations, 1865-1900." *Journal of Southern History* 40 (February 1974): 19-42.   The cosmopolitan and urban environment of New Orleans helped to make the city a very different place for blacks compared with the rural areas during Reconstruction. The independence of the many free blacks and an environment which bred black leaders and attracted a large black community stymied attempts by whites to establish a segregated and intimidating environment with blacks. The Reconstruction Acts of 1867 and the new Louisiana constitution of 1868 gave additional force to black demands for racial equality in all aspects of urban life. Despite racial tensions, pressure for equal rights and integration were highly successful, but progress deteriorated after Reconstruction.

2012.   Sutherland, Daniel E. "Looking for a Home: Louisiana Emigrants During the Civil War and Reconstruction." *Louisiana History* 21 (Fall 1980): 341-359. Most Louisianians who left their homes after the Civil War either left the country for South America or Mexico, or they fled to Northern and Western states. Sutherland discusses the motivations of these people, including the influence of promotional campaigns directed from other countries.

2013.   Turner, Howard. "Robert Mills Lusher, Louisiana Educator." Ph.D. Louisiana State University, 1944. 300p.

2014.   Vandal, Gilles. "Property Offenses, Social Tension and Racial Antagonism in Post-Civil War Rural Louisiana." *Journal of Social History* 31 (Fall, 1997): 127-153. Map. Tbls.   There was a close relationship between various types of property crimes and the postwar political and social environment in Louisiana. Newspaper reports indicate that property crimes increased dramatically among blacks and whites, and the crimes were often related to the difficult economic situation in Reconstruction. Vandal also examines the phenomenon of gangs that contributed to lawlessness in the countryside and the unstable, conflict ridden nature of the postwar South.

2015.   White, Howard A. *The Freedmen's Bureau in Louisiana.* Baton Rouge: Louisiana State University Press, 1970. 227p. Bibl.   White's case study is organized by topics, including relations with local whites, land distribution, medical care, labor, civil rights, and education. In general, White is highly complimentary of the bureau, despite its limited ability to bring about long term change in the lives of the freedmen. (See also White's Ph.D. dissertation with the same title from Tulane University, 1956.)

Maryland

General History

2016.   Fields, Barbara Jeanne. *Slavery and Freedom on the Middle Ground: Maryland During the Nineteenth Century.* New Haven: Yale University Press, 1985. 268p. Map. Tbls.   In the last two chapters Fields focuses on Reconstruction and emphasizes the difficult transition to freedom for the ex-slaves and the brutality perpetrated against them. She describes the bleakness of their lives and the general dissatisfaction with the results of the postwar period. (See also Fields' "The Maryland Way From Slavery to Freedom." Ph.D. Yale University, 1978. 317p.)

Politics and Law

2017.   Baker, Jean H. *The Politics of Continuity: Maryland Political Parties From 1858 to 1870.* Baltimore: Johns Hopkins University Press, 1973. 239p. App. Bibl. Maps. Tbls.   In the last two chapters and the epilogue Baker explains that the attempt to form a postwar fusion party of conservative Unionists and Democrats failed to materialize despite the efforts of Montgomery Blair. The Democrats remained united as they made constitutional and statutory adjustments to capture elections. Race was always an issue in this white supremacist state, and it was used to ensure adequate fear of black power and strong support for the Democratic Party. Even the enactment of the 15th Amendment did not alter the political continuity from prewar days.

2018.   Blauch, L. E. "Education and the Maryland Constitutional Convention, 1864." *Maryland Historical Magazine* 25 (September 1930): 225-251.   Bringing modern reforms to state education was a major focus of the constitutional convention of 1864. The Unionist majority sought a modern school system supported by taxation. The convention achieved a statewide public school system that did not specifically include or exclude blacks. The convention also disenfranchised many citizens who could not meet a test oath, thus eliminating potential votes against the constitution. The new constitution barely passed with the overwhelming support of soldiers in the field.

2019.   Fuke, Richard Paul.   "Hugh Lennox Bond and Radical Republican Ideology." *Journal of Southern History* 45 (November 1979): 568-586.   Fuke criticizes historians who focus on racism among Radical Republicans and their limited commitment to make difficult changes to help the freedmen. Such failures should not detract from the "progressive nature of Radical ideology." (p. 570)

Bond is an example of a Marylander who was devoted to uplifting the ex-slaves and treating them with dignity and respect. As a judge during Reconstruction, he supported equal political rights, unrestricted educational and economic opportunities for all, and a future of progress in the state.

2020.   Henig, Gerald S. *Henry Winter Davis: Antebellum and Civil War Congressman From Maryland.* New York: Twayne Publishers, 1973. 332p. Bibl. Henig reinforces the positive aspects of Davis's service to Maryland and the U.S. Davis has been criticized for his rash personality and political errors, but recently discovered letters help to show that, despite his imperfections, Davis should be remembered mainly for his ability to keep Maryland in the Union, and lead both the emancipation effort in the state and Republican efforts to formulate an effective Reconstruction. Davis, a former Whig, was partly motivated by his hatred for the Democratic Party.

2021.   Myers, William Starr. *The Self-Reconstruction of Maryland, 1864-1867.* Baltimore: Johns Hopkins Press, 1909. 131p. (*Johns Hopkins University Studies in Historical and Political Science*, Ser. 27, no. 1-2)   "Self-Reconstruction" in Maryland refers to the reform of state laws by Democratic-Conservatives who rejected the Unionist constitution of 1864 because of its radical provisions. Democrats were in the majority, but they had to gain strength between 1864 and 1867 by restoring the vote to former Confederates and uniting against black suffrage. Myers indicates his approval of the conservative government because the public simply wanted to put the war in the past instead of implementing radical reforms.

2022.   Russ, William A., Jr.   "Disfranchisement in Maryland (1861-1867)." *Maryland Historical Magazine* 28 (December 1933): 309-328.   After Maryland was forced to remain in the Union, loyalty oaths were used to restrict potential voters, partly to guarantee Unionist majorities in the legislature. A split among Unionists over disenfranchisement of whites led to a Democratic victory in the state election of 1866. Democrats repealed voting restrictions on whites, placed restrictions on black voters, and demanded compensation for the emancipation of slaves. Russ believes that the state would likely have seceded given a chance and that its defiant response to the Northern military victory contributed to the Radical's push for a severe Reconstruction in the South.

2023.   Wagandt, Charles L. *The Mighty Revolution: Negro Emancipation in Maryland, 1862-64.* Baltimore: Johns Hopkins Press, 1964. 299p. Bibl. Tbls. Wagandt explains that Maryland remained loyal to the Union but resisted the emancipation of slaves as destructive to a way of life and individual property rights. He examines the political struggle among Unionists, Radicals, and Democrats during the war, which itself played a role in the direction of reform in the state. The Radical goal of emancipation was bound up with various personal goals, including elimination of aristocracy, shifting power away from the agricultural counties, and encouraging economic growth and the enlistment of blacks into the Union Army. Radical goals split Maryland Unionists into both conservative and more liberal factions, but the new constitution of 1864 enacted reforms. Much of the reform was reversed by Democrats in 1867.

2024.   Wagandt, Charles L. "Redemption or Reaction? Maryland in the Post-Civil War Years." In *Radicalism, Racism, and Party Realignment, the Border States During Reconstruction*. Edited by R. O. Curry. Baltimore: Johns Hopkins Press, 1969. Pp. 146-189. Map.   In November, 1864, Maryland became the first border state to eliminate slavery, but Radicals were only partially successful at enacting civil rights reforms and the disenfranchisement of rebels in a state dominated by Democrats of the old prewar order. Maryland politics in the postwar years clarify the strong reluctance of the white population to approve further racial reforms that were eventually forced on the state by federal constitutional and legislative action.

2025.   White, Frank F., Jr. *The Governors of Maryland 1777-1970*. Annapolis: Hall of Records Commission, State of Maryland, 1970. 351p. Ports. Biographical sketches for governors during the Reconstruction years include Augustus W. Bradford (January 8, 1862-January 10, 1866), Thomas Swann (January 10, 1866-January 13, 1869), Oden Bowie (January 13, 1869-January 10, 1972), William Pinkney Whyte (January 10, 1872-March 4, 1974), and James Black Groome (March 4, 1874-January 12, 1876).

Agriculture, Labor, and Business

2026.   Fuke, Richard Paul. "Blacks, Whites, and Guns: Interracial Violence in Post-Emancipation Maryland." *Maryland Historical Magazine* 92 (Fall 1997): 327-348. Facim. Ills. Port.   Violence occurred in postwar Baltimore and other parts of the state because ex-soldiers of both races owned guns, and whites in the city refused to have patience with the influx of unskilled, impoverished black laborers from rural areas who competed for jobs or pursued antisocial activities. Black citizens of Baltimore who were free prior to the war were lumped together with migrants in an environment of racial, economic, and social confrontation that led to violent clashes.

2027.   Fuke, Richard Paul. "Peasant Priorities? Tidewater Blacks and the Land in Post-Emancipation Maryland." *Locus* (Denton, Tx.) 3 (1990): 21-45.   Fuke emphasizes the positive nature of the small, but increasing numbers of former slaves who were able to purchase small plots of land in the tidewater counties between 1860 and 1870. Most black landowners were free prior to the war, but the growth of landownership among freedmen represented greater independence, hope, and progress, even if they lived at the subsistence level.

2028.   Fuke, Richard Paul. "Planters, Apprenticeship, and Forced Labor: The Black Family Under Pressure in Post-Emancipation Maryland." *Agricultural History* 62 (Fall 1988): 57-74.   Beginning with emancipation in 1864 black families and planters in Maryland struggled over the freedom of ex-slaves. Planters sought white domination and control over black labor, such as coerced apprenticeships of children, but the freedmen wanted to control the life and labor of their families. By 1868 blacks used the U.S. Army, the Freedmen's Bureau, and the backing of Radical Republicans to force the release of children and the elimination of forced apprenticeships. This victory did not ensure the future economic well being of the freedmen.

Society, Education, and Religion

2029.   Blauch, L. E. "The First Uniform School System of Maryland, 1865-1868." *Maryland Historical Magazine* 26 (September 1931): 205-227.   Blauch describes the organization and implementation of the first public school system in Maryland. Although state law did not specifically exclude black children, the legislature would not agree with the state superintendent's attempt to establish schools for blacks with tax funds collected from blacks. Integrated schools were never considered.

2030.   Browne, Joseph L. "'The Expenses Are Borne by Parents': Freedmen's Schools in Southern Maryland." *Maryland Historical Magazine* 86 (Winter 1991): 407-422.   Browne describes the struggle of blacks in Anne Arundel and Calvert Counties where the financial support for black education came from local and Northern private organizations and black citizens. Funding was secured temporarily from benevolent societies, the Freedmen's Bureau, and the Baltimore Association for the Moral and Educational Improvement of the Colored People. State funds began in 1873 when the black school system was diminished by lack of funding.

2031.   Fuke, Richard Paul. "The Baltimore Association For the Moral and Educational Improvement of the Colored People, 1864-1870." *Maryland Historical Magazine* 66 (Winter 1971): 369-404.   The white population generally opposed black education, but it became a reality through the efforts of the Baltimore Association for the Moral and Educational Improvement of the Colored People. The association agitated for public funding, established schools, and requested assistance from the Freedmen's Bureau, the American Missionary Association, and freedmen's aid societies. In 1867, when the city council agreed to bring black students into the citywide school system, the association began to disband, but it proved that blacks could be educated.

2032.   Fuke, Richard Paul. "Black Marylanders, 1864-1868." Ph.D. University of Chicago, 1973. 415p.

2033.   Fuke, Richard Paul. "A Reform Mentality: Federal Policy Toward Black Marylanders, 1864-1868." *Civil War History* 22 (September 1976): 214-235. Tbl. Many Northerners accepted racism and cared little about the civil rights of the freedmen, but in the 1860s there was a reform mentality among federal officials who helped blacks in various ways. There were federal officials and Unionist

Republicans in Maryland who supported the freedmen's need for land, civil rights, and education, and who worked to eliminate abusive apprenticeships among young blacks. They did not believe in racial equality but in justice and opportunity.

2034.   Fuke, Richard Paul.   "A School For Freed Labor: The Maryland 'Government Farms,' 1864-1866." *Maryland Historian* 26 (Spring-Summer 1985): 11-23.   The "government farms" organized in St. Mary's County by the U.S. Army for black refugees were directed by Lt. Edward F. O'Brien and later Capt. E. B. Gates.   These men performed well in the task of maintaining a safe facility where former slaves could begin to make a transition to freedom and learn the virtues of hard work and self reliance.   After the war the farms were returned to their prewar owners and the Army assisted freedmen with the difficult task of finding them a place to work that would be safe and provide a fair wage.

2035.   Low, W. A.   "The Freedmen's Bureau and Civil Rights in Maryland." *Journal of Negro History* 37 (July 1952): 221-247.   Low believes that the major issues faced by the bureau in Maryland were justice and education for the freedmen. He discusses how the bureau dealt with the widespread use of apprenticeships for young freedmen that bound them into a type of virtual slavery as a way to insure labor and social control.   In 1866 the bureau actively sought to end this practice, but only in 1868, after the implementation of the Reconstruction Acts of 1867, did apprenticeships disappear.

2036.   Low, W. A.   "The Freedmen's Bureau and Education in Maryland." *Maryland Historical Magazine* 47 (March 1952): 29-39.   Low describes the major, positive role played by the bureau in organizing and providing resources for public education facilities for freedmen.   During 1865 and 1866 the bureau and freedmen schools had to endure widespread resentment and violence by local whites, but eventually this behavior dissipated and the state became more interested in public education.

2037.   Low, W. A.   "Methodism and the Beginning of Higher Education of Negroes in Maryland." *Quarterly Review of Higher Education Among Negroes* 18 (October 1950): 137-149. Tbls.   Fund raising by the Methodist Episcopal Church and the work of its Freedmen's Aid Society in 1866 contributed to the founding of schools of higher education throughout much of the South.   Low discusses the society's work in Maryland from Reconstruction until the early 20th century.   The Church organized Centenary Biblical Institute in 1866 which led to the founding of Morgan State College and Maryland State College.

2038.   Thomas, Bettye C.   "Public Education and Black Protest in Baltimore 1865-1900." *Maryland Historical Magazine* 71 (Fall 1976): 381-391.   Thomas reviews the history of public education in Baltimore and the influence of the American Missionary Association and the Baltimore Association for the Moral and Educational Improvement of the Colored People.   Not until 1867 did the city counsel support public education for blacks, but from that time until the end of the century blacks protested poor facilities and the predominance of white teachers.

Mississippi

General History

2039.   Abney, M. G. "Reconstruction in Pontotoc County." *Publications of the Mississippi Historical Society* 11 (1910): 229-269. App.   Abney examines mainly political and racial issues, and also includes information on public schools, black religious organizations, economic conditions, and the activities of the Ku Klux Klan. The appendix includes names of officials and various statistics about the Pontotoc County.

2040.   Bowman, Robert. "Reconstruction in Yazoo County." *Publications of the Mississippi Historical Society* 7 (1903): 115-130.   Bowman, a former Confederate soldier, lawyer, and politician, emphasizes the harshness of Reconstruction in Yazoo County beginning in 1870 when the first Radical Reconstruction government took office.   As in other counties, Yazoo was the scene of violence during the 1875 election.

2041.   Braden, W. H. "Reconstruction in Lee County." *Publications of the Mississippi Historical Society* 10 (1909): 135-146.   Braden emphasizes that few Republicans lived in Lee County and none held any public office. Most blacks were cooperative despite the attempt of the Freedmen's Bureau to generate Republican support.   The Ku Klux Klan successfully reduced trouble from the freedmen. Names of many Democratic officeholders are given. The main political suspense was between Democrats and former Whigs.

2042.   Brown, Julia C. "Reconstruction in Yalobusha and Grenada Counties." *Publications of the Mississippi Historical Society* 12 (1912): 214-282.   This survey of Reconstruction in 2 counties is from the perspective of local whites. Brown touches on various topics including the Ku Klux Klan, Freedmen's Bureau, education, economy, and religion. Race relations or the maintenance and control of blacks was the central issue. Also included is a list of county officials and statistical data from the U.S. census.

2043.   Browne, Fred Zollicoffer. "Reconstruction in Okitibbeha County." *Publications of the Mississippi Historical Society* 13 (1913): 273-298. App.   The focus is on politics, race relations, and the Ku Klux Klan. An appendix includes the names of selected officials and statistics on slave ownership, population, farms, manufacturing, and finances in the county.

2044.   Coleman, Edward Clarke, Jr. "Reconstruction in Attala County." *Publications of the Mississippi Historical Society* 10 (1909): 147-161.   Coleman emphasizes that Attala County did not experience widespread devastation from the war. During Reconstruction it had the distinction of being prosperous and without corruption. The Ku Klux Klan was active and helped keep blacks under control. He discusses local politics from the perspective of white conservatives.

2045.   Conerly, Luke Ward.   *Pike County Mississippi 1798-1876:   Pioneer Families and Confederate Soldiers, Reconstruction and Redemption.* Nashville: Brandon Printing Co., 1909.   356p.   Ills.   Ports.   (Rpt. by University Microfilms International, 1979)   Conerly devotes significant attention   (p. 226-356) to life during Reconstruction in Pike County and his general perspective on the period in Mississippi.   He writes sympathetically about conservative, Southern whites who were forced to cope with black, Radical rule.   He describes crime, politics, military occupation, social life, and the activities of the Ku Klux Klan.   Conerly devotes much of the book to a list of Confederate soldiers from Pike county and recounting the early history and wartime events of the area.

2046.   Connolly, Michael Brian.   "Reconstruction   in   Kemper   County, Mississippi."   Ph.D.   Old Dominion University, 1989.   173p.

2047.   Cooper, Forrest.   "Reconstruction in Scott County."   *Publications of the Mississippi Historical Society* 13 (1913):   99-221.   App.   Cooper surveys political, social, economic, and educational activities from the perspective of white, Democratic partisans.   He also discusses the Freedmen's Bureau, Loyalty Leagues, and the Ku Klux Klan.   Statistics and copies of letters are printed in the appendix.

2048.   Edwards, Thomas S.   "'Reconstructing' Reconstruction: Changing Historical Paradigms in Mississippi History."   *Journal of Mississippi History* 51 (August 1989):   165-180.   Historians' interpretations of Reconstruction in Mississippi have changed during the 20th century.   Edwards refers to a call by historian Gene Wise for historians to examine historical conventions and paradigms for a better understanding of their profession that will ultimately reduce prejudices and biases that emerge in their research.   Edwards examines the work of James W. Garner, Vernon L. Wharton, and William C. Harris.

2049.   Garner, James Wilford.   *Reconstruction in Mississippi.*   New York: Macmillan, 1901.   422p.   Garmer provides a broad history of political, economic, and social life.   His work is important for its emphasis on Reconstruction at the state level and his moderate tone toward Reconstruction compared with other works at the time.   Garner does not view all carpetbaggers as evil, and he is complimentary of educational reforms.   But he is critical of the government of Republican carpetbaggers, scalawags, and blacks following the passage of the 1869 constitution. He views white violence as a natural response to Republican rule, and credits the victory of the Democrats in 1875 to disunity among the Republicans and dissatisfaction with their regime.   In the introduction to the 1968 edition, Richard Current compliments Garner's accuracy and ability to shed biases.   This introduction was reprinted in *Arguing with Historians: Essays in the Historical and the Unhistorical* (Middletown: Wessleyan University Press, 1987), 97-114.   (See also Garner's Ph.D. dissertation with the same title from Columbia University, 1902.)

2050.   Harris, William C.   *The Day of the Carpetbagger: Republican Reconstruction in Mississippi.*   Baton Rouge: Louisiana State University Press, 1979.   760p.   Bibl. Ill. Map. Ports.   Harris provides a comprehensive survey of

Mississippi politics, economy, agriculture, daily life and education from 1867 through 1876. He believes that Reconstruction offered the state opportunities for political and social reforms. The myths and unsolved problems of Reconstruction persisted after 1876 because white citizens rejected Republican rule, black civil rights, and the opportunity to remake their society.

2051.   Harris, William C.   "The Reconstruction of the Commonwealth, 1865-1870." In *A History of Mississippi.* Vol. I. Edited by Richard Aubrey McLemore. Hattiesburg: University College Press of Mississippi, 1973. Pp. 542-570. Harris examines the period of adjustment to peace, initial rebuilding of infrastructure, presidential Reconstruction and military occupation following the Reconstruction Acts of 1867. He uses primary sources and explains the current interpretations of the period.

2052.   Kendal, Julia. "Reconstruction in Lafayette County." *Publications of the Mississippi Historical Society* 13 (1913): 223-271.   Kendal focuses mainly on political activities, race relations, the Ku Klux Klan, education, and religion. An appendix includes the names of selected officials and statistics on slave ownership, population, farms, manufacturing, and finances in the county.

2053.   Kyle, John W. "Reconstruction in Panola County." *Publications of the Mississippi Historical Society* 13 (1913): 9-98. App.   Kyle emphasizes the corruptness and base nature of Republican rule in Panola County. He provides extensive descriptions of Republican leaders and organizations, including the Loyalty League and Freedmen's Bureau, and the social, political and economic conditions.

2054.   Lacey, Nannie. "Reconstruction in Leake County." *Publications of the Mississippi Historical Society* 11 (1910): 271-294. App.   Lacey describes social, economic, and political affairs in the county. He emphasizes race relations and politics, but emphasizes that Leake County was quiet during Reconstruction because carpetbaggers were not prominent and the Democrats regained control in 1872. The appendix provides a variety of statistics and names of officials.

2055.   Lynch, John R. *The Facts of Reconstruction.* New York: Arno Press and the New York Times, 1968. 325p. Ports. (Rpt. from Neale Publishing Co., 1913) Lynch, a former slave who won a seat in the Mississippi legislature in 1869 and the U.S. Congress in 1872, wrote this early revisionist history of Reconstruction politics based on his experiences, knowledge, and contacts in his state. He attempts to correct the wholly negative picture of Reconstruction and the part played by the freedmen that appears in the work of James Ford Rhodes (see # 141) and William Dunning (see # 79, 80). The book is semi-autobiographical covering Lynch's postbellum years through the first decade of the 20th century. (See also Lynch's *Reminiscences of an Active Life: The Autobiography of John Roy Lynch*, edited with an introduction by John Hope Franklin, Chicago: University of Chicago Press, 1970, in which he provides first hand information about Reconstruction in Mississippi and his work for the Republican Party.)

2056.   McNeilly, J. S.   "War and Reconstruction in Mississippi: 1863-1890."
Publications of the Mississippi Historical Society 2 (1918): 116-535.   In this book-
length publication, McNeilly, a former Confederate soldier, surveys the last years of
war in Mississippi and the history of Reconstruction. He discusses state politics
from the perspective of a Southern patriot. His survey extends to the 1890 state
constitutional convention, an event considered to be the time when the state emerged
from the "Old South" into a new era and generation.

2057.   Mechelke,   Eugene   R.   "Some   Observations   on   Mississippi's
Reconstruction Historiography."   *Journal of Mississippi History* 33 (February
1971): 21-38.   Mechelke examines historical literature through 1965 to evaluate
the validity of the traditional versus the revisionist interpretations of Reconstruction
as they apply to Mississippi. He concludes that revisionists generally are correct in
their more positive interpretations and that the term "radical" should not be used
when referring to Republican rule or the actions that took while they were in power.
Republican reforms made no fundamental changes in politics or the status of blacks.

2058.   Meltzer,   Milton.   *Freedom   Comes   to   Mississippi: The   Story   of
Reconstruction*.   Chicago: Follett Publishing Co., 1970.   192p.   Bibl. Ill. Map.
Ports.   Written for young readers, this book is based on scholarship of the 1960s
which substantially revised the way historians understand Reconstruction.

2059.   Wallace, Jesse Thomas. "A History of Negroes of Mississippi From 1865
to 1890." Ph.D. Columbia University, 1928. 188p.

2060.   Watkins, Ruth. "Reconstruction in Marshall County." *Publications of the
Mississippi Historical Society* 12 (1912): 155-213.   A broad view of persons and
conditions in Marshall County are described. Emphasis is place on race relations,
the Ku Klux Klan, Loyal Leagues, Freedmen's Bureau, education, religion,
economics, and local government. The appendix includes various statistics about
the county.

2061.   Watkins, Ruth. "Reconstruction in Newton County." *Publications of the
Mississippi Historical Society* 11 (1910): 205-228. App.   Watkins describes the
political, racial, economic, and social conditions in Newton County. She discusses
prominent leaders, election fraud, violence, the Ku Klux Klan, education, and black
churches. The appendix includes various statistics about the county.

2062.   Wharton, Vernon. L. *The Negro in Mississippi 1865-1890*. Chapel Hill:
University of North Carolina Press, 1947. 298p. Bibl. (*James Sprunt Studies in
History and Political Science*, 28)   In his topical approach toward the changing life
of blacks in Mississippi, Wharton emphasizes the broad outlines of attitudes and
events. In particular, he emphasizes white attitudes toward blacks. He offers
sympathy for the plight of blacks but views Reconstruction negatively, partly
because of errors made by the freedmen. Wharton notes the progress of blacks
towards self improvement as achieved by 1890 despite white supremacy. He
includes chapters on agriculture, the Freedmen's Bureau, black codes, politics, race

relations, crime, education, religion, and social life. (See also Wharton's "The Negro in Mississippi, 1865-1900." Ph.D. University of North Carolina, 1939. 526p.)

2063.   Woods, William Leon. "The Travail of Freedom: Mississippi Blacks, 1862-1870." Ph.D. Princeton University, 1979. 318p.

Politics and Law

2064.   Alexander, Thomas B. "Persistent Whiggery in Mississippi: The *Hinds County Gazette*." *Journal of Mississippi History* 23 (April 1961): 71-93.   As an example of how Whig principles continued well after the Civil War, Alexander reprints articles from the *Hinds County Gazette* that were written by the editor, George W. Harper. The articles were written between October 7, 1865 and November 6, 1878.

2065.   Ames, Blanche Butler (comp.). *Chronicles From the Nineteenth Century: Family Letters of Blanche Butler and Adelbert Ames, Married July 21st, 1870.* 2 Vols. (Vol. 1: 1861-1874; Vol. 2: 1874-1899) Clinton, Ma.: Colonial Press, 1957. 625p.   Many of the letters exchanged by Ames and Butler provide extensive firsthand information about politics and life in Mississippi during Reconstruction. Ames, a native of Maine, was appointed military governor of the state in July, 1868 and commander of the Fourth Military District in March, 1869.   He served Mississippi as a Republican U.S. senator and later as governor from 1874 until he was forced to resign under threat of impeachment in March 1876.   Butler was the daughter of Benjamin Butler.

2066.   Ames, Blanche Butler. *Adelbert Ames, 1835-1893: General, Senator, Governor.* New York: Argosy-Antiquarian Ltd., 1964. (First edition North Easton, Ma.: n.p., 1964; also London: Macdonald, 1964) 625p. App. Bibl. Ill. Maps. Ports. This biography of Ames, a New Englander, was written by his daughter for the expressed purpose of telling the true story of her father's life, particularly his years as governor of Mississippi during Reconstruction.   She wishes to correct the distorted views of Ames' career written mostly by historians who showed bias towards the South in Reconstruction and criticized carpetbagger politicians for their corruption and profligate fiscal policies.   Sources include Ames' official papers and correspondence.

2067.   Beckett, R. C.   "Some Effects of Military Reconstruction in Monroe County, Mississippi." *Mississippi Historical Society Publications* 8 (1904): 177-186.   The effects that Beckett refers to are the organization of the Ku Klux Klan and white resistance to "obnoxious" blacks and radical whites.   He defends the violent actions of the Klan as necessary for the preservation of white security and to put blacks in their place.

2068.   Benson, Harry King. *The Public Career of Adelbert Ames, 1861-1876.* Ph.D. University of Virginia, 1975. 342p.

2069.   Bigelow, Martha Mitchell. "Public Opinion and the Passage of the Mississippi Black Codes." *Negro History Bulletin* 33 (January 1970); 11-16. Bigelow believes that the public was so concerned about whether blacks would be allowed to testify in court that little consideration was given to how the North would react to laws restricting other facets of the freedmen's lives. The black codes inflamed Republicans in Congress, but Bigelow believes that Republicans would have found another issue to upset them if the black codes had not existed.

2070.   Blain, William T. "'Banner' Unionism in Mississippi: Choctaw County 1861-1869." *Mississippi Quarterly* 29 (Spring 1876): 207-220.   Unionism and desertions plagued Choctaw County during the war, and afterwards the forces of Unionism attempted to take control of the county. Threats and violence against conservative officeholders did not eliminate local Democrats in the 1869 election even though Republicans won at the state level. The violent methods used by conservative forces to retain power was a forewarning of the broader tactic known as the Mississippi Plan.

2071.   Blain, William T. "Challenge to the Lawless: The Mississippi Secret Service, 1870-1871." *Journal of Mississippi History* 40 (May 1878): 119-131. The Mississippi legislature authorized the secret service authorized in 1870 by at the behest of Gov. James L. Alcorn.   Alcorn wanted the force to use against the increasing number of violent acts in the state, particularly acts perpetrated against blacks and Republican by the Ku Klux Klan. Agents investigated crimes, made arrests, and infiltrated the Klan to gather information. Criminals were identified, but the violence and the widespread support for vigilante groups persisted.

2072.   Bowie, Ben. "The Southern Claims Commission, 1871-1880." *Journal of Mississippi History* 12 (April 1950): 105-115.   Bowie briefly discusses the work of the claims commission with particular reference to claimants in Mississippi. He notes the prevalence of corruption among "special commissioners" and "special agents" who were assigned to investigate and verify claims and the loyalty of the claimants.

2073.   Brock, Euline W. "Thomas W. Cardozo: Fallible Black Reconstruction Leader." *Journal of Southern History* 47 (May 1981): 183-206.   Revisionist historians have tended to depict black leaders as heroes of Reconstruction, but this is an exaggeration in response to the traditional view of blacks as uniformly corrupt as government officials. Cardozo, a free black from Charleston, was well educated, articulate, and experienced as a teacher in the North, South Carolina, and North Carolina.   His interest in politics led him to Vicksburg, Mississippi where he actively sought political opportunities, but the misappropriation of public funds led to his indictment. He played a role in the downfall of the Mississippi Republican Party.

2074. Brough, Charles Hillman. "History of Taxation in Mississippi." *Publications of the Mississippi Historical Society* 2 (1899): 113-124. With regard to Reconstruction, Brough indicates that conservative leaders of the state between 1865 and 1867 performed an admirable job of scaling down indebtedness in a difficult fiscal environment following the war. The onset of Radical Reconstruction bought "retrogression" and "ignorance" to government policy. Taxes and government spending rose steeply, funds were misappropriated, and the freedom of the press was attacked.

2075. Brough, Charles Hillman. "The Clinton Riot." *Publications of the Mississippi Historical Society* 6 (1902): 53-63. Clinton, Mississippi was the scene of a violent confrontation between blacks and whites at a barbecue held on September 4, 1875 as part of the fall election campaign. Brough points out that this was one of several campaign "riots" caused by white frustration with high taxes and the general domination of Republicans and blacks. The violence led to the downfall of Republican rule in the state and confirmed Anglo-Saxon supremacy.

2076. Coker, William L. "The United States Senate Investigation of the Mississippi Election of 1875." *Journal of Mississippi History* 37 (May 1975): 143-163. After the Democrats in Mississippi nearly swept the state elections of 1875, despite the black majority among registered voters, Reconstruction in state came to an end. Radical Republican Senator Oliver P. Morton of Indiana led the call for an investigation into fraud and violence that was assumed to be the method used by Democrats to win the election. Both the debate and the findings of the investigating committee were split along party lines. Morton sought to help black residents of Mississippi, but the entire affair centered around the struggle for political advantage.

2077. Cresswell, Stephen. "Enforcing the Enforcement Acts: the Department of Justice in Northern Mississippi, 1870-1890." *Journal of Southern History* 53 (August 1987): 421-440. Tbl. Congress enacted the Enforcement Acts of 1870 and 1871 in an attempt to quell violence, intimidation, and election fraud perpetuated by the Ku Klux Klan and other local white groups. Cresswell focuses on the response of local whites to federal authorities who sought to enforce the law. Between 1871 and 1884 northern Mississippi accounted for 1/3 of all convictions in the South and showed a 55% conviction rate, but federal authorities had to withstand constant expressions of hate and continued resistance.

2078. Currie, James T. "The Beginnings of Congressional Reconstruction in Mississippi." *Journal of Mississippi History* 35 (August 1973): 267-286. Currie analyses the course of Reconstruction in Mississippi from the appointment of military rule under Maj. Gen. E. O. C. Ord in the spring of 1867 through the end of the state constitutional convention in 1868. Ord dedicated himself to following instructions from Congress, although Currie believes that he probably overstepped his authority by his methods of enforcement (e.g. *Ex parte* McCardle). Currie analyses the delegates at the convention based on statistical research of voting patterns and attendance records. Included is a table of voter registration in 1867 by county, race, and the number of convention delegates.

2079. Currie, James T. "From Slavery to Freedom in Mississippi's Legal System." *Journal of Negro History* 65 (Spring 1980): 112-125. Tbls. Currie examines the legal standing of slaves according to the 1857 slave code in Mississippi and contrasts it with the changes brought about by emancipation. Despite the legal setbacks, including black codes and the reversal of civil rights by post-Reconstruction governments, the legal advances established a foundation for future reforms in the mid-20th century.

2080. Donald, David H. "The Scalawag in Mississippi Reconstruction." *Journal of Southern History* 10 (November 1944): 447-460. Donald alters the traditional, highly negative image of the scalawag. The scalawags of Mississippi were typically wealthy, landholding Whigs prior the the war, and they continued to retain their Whig political perspective in Reconstruction. As political moderates, they distrusted Democrats and sought influence among Republicans. Former Whigs comprised a large portion of Republican officeholders and when carpetbaggers and blacks turned against Gov. James Alcorn and the moderates, the Whigs lost power and reluctantly migrated to the Democrats. It was the Whig abandonment of the Republican Party that brought down Republican rule in Mississippi.

2081. Drake, Winbourne Magruder. "A Mississippian's Appraisal of Andrew Johnson: Letters of James T. Harrison, December, 1865." *Journal of Mississippi History* 17 (January 1955): 43-48. In two letters written by newly elected Congressman James T. Harrison in early December, 1865, he describes his confidence in President Johnson and his concern with the rejection of the Mississippi delegation by the Republican Congress. Drake describes Harrison's background and explains that Mississippians eventually became dissatisfied with Johnson because of his inability to return political and civil affairs to a normal state.

2082. Drake, Winbourne Magruder. "The Mississippi Reconstruction Convention of 1865." *Journal of Mississippi History* 21 (October 1959): 225-256. Drake describes the delegates and the work of the first constitutional convention among the former Confederate states. Under the conditions that prevailed in 1865, the Mississippi convention did the best job it could do, and it intentionally left many decisions to the legislature. Prominent delegates included William Yerger and James T. Harrison. The convention performed much better than the legislature that followed.

2083. Drake, Winbourne Magruder. "A 'Repentant Rebel': Letter From John J. McRae to William L. Sharkey." *Journal of Mississippi History* 8 (October 1956): 302-206. In his letter to Provisional Gov. Sharkey dated July 13, 1865 McRae requested a pardon under President Johnson's amnesty proclamation. McRae, a former governor., U.S. senator and congressman, and an ardent secessionist, filled his letter with humor that alludes to his friendship with Secretary of State William H. Seward.

2084. Ellem, Warren A. "Doing God's Service: Adelbert Ames and Reconstruction in Mississippi." In *Varieties of Southern History: New Essays on a*

Region and its People. Edited by Bruce Clayton and John Salmond. Westport: Greenwood Press, 1996. Pp. 119-136.   Ellam explains how Ames' postwar experiences in the South and in Europe helped to shape his ideas about blacks and Southern white elites.   Ames' horror at white violence against blacks and his growing dissatisfaction with President Johnson's lenient Reconstruction policies led to his full support for Congressional Reconstruction. As a U.S. senator and governor, he believed that he was on a mission to reform Southern state government with pure republican ideology and ensure equal rights for blacks and whites.

2085.   Ellem, Warren A.   "The Overthrow of Reconstruction in Mississippi." *Journal of Mississippi History* 54 (May 1992): 175-201.   Ellem reviews the political developments in Mississippi that led to the white-line "Revolution of 1875" and brought the Democratic Party back to power in the state. The "revolution," known as the Mississippi Plan, focused on white supremacy and the use of violence and intimidation to ensure political victory. The tactics led to Democratic success because disunity plagued the Republican Party and the federal government's support for upholding the law in Mississippi had diminished.

2086.   Ellem, Warren A.   "Who Were the Mississippi Scalawags." *Journal of Southern History* 38 (May 1972): 217-240. Graphs. Map. Tbls.   This quantitative study seeks to expand on Allen W. Trelease's study (see # 1012) and to clarify the disagreement between Trelease and David Donald (see # 2080) regarding the number and political background of scalawags in Mississippi. Ellem examines voter returns from all counties for elections from 1871 to 1873.   While he follows Trelease's basic research methodology, he changes the formula for identifying scalawags and arrives at a different conclusion. He finds that scalawags comprised a small percentage of the white electorate (15%) and that their influence in the Republican Party was a key to the strength of the party in Mississippi.

2087.   Franklin, John Hope.   "John Roy Lynch: Republican Stalwart from Mississippi." In *Southern Black Leaders of the Reconstruction Era.* Edited by Howard N. Rabinowitz. Urbana: University of Illinois Press, 1982. Pp. 39-58. Port.   In this biographical essay Franklin focuses on Lynch's political contributions. He strongly supported the Republican Party in Mississippi, but acted with independence in his support of people and issues. In his service in the state legislature and U.S. House of Representatives, he garnered a reputation as a vigorous and astute politician. In 1901 he published *The Facts of Reconstruction* (see # 2055), a work that was little noticed at the time.

2088.   Gardner, Bettye J.   "William Foote and Yazoo Politics, 1866-1883." *Southern Studies* 21 (Winter 1982): 398-407.   Foote, born a free black in Vicksburg and educated in the North, fought for the Confederacy during the Civil War. Gardner describes his participation in Republican politics in Yazoo City, his support for civil rights, and his struggle to avert racial violence in state elections. He was murdered by a white mob in 1883 after being accused of conspiracy to commit murder.

2089.   Hall, L. Marshall. "William L. Sharkey and Reconstruction, 1866-1873." *Journal of Mississippi History* 27 (February 1965): 1-17.   Hall describes Sharkey's public career following his time as provisional governor of Mississippi from June 13 to October 16, 1865.   Sharkey, a committed conservative Whig and Unionist, fought vigorously against Radical Reconstruction and attempted to organize a political union of Whigs and Democrats in 1868 that could effectively oppose the Republicans.   Sharkey's principles of moderate, conservative politics led him to reject extremists in both the North and the South.

2090.   Hardy, W. H.   "Recollections of Reconstruction in East and Southeast Mississippi." *Publications of the Mississippi Historical Society* 4 (1901): 105-132; 7 (1903): 199-215; 8 (1904): 137-151.   Hardy seeks to demonstrate the ills of government under Republican and black rule.   He is highly critical of the constitutional convention of 1868 for its profligate ways and its disenfranchisement of many whites.   He describes the splits within the Republican Party and the white frustrations with Republican taxation policies and black voting power.   The conservative backlash contributed to the Democratic victory in 1875.   For Hardy, Reconstruction proves that blacks are not fit for governing, voting, or jury duty because they cannot think critically or independently.

2091.   Harris, William C.   "Blanche K. Bruce of Mississippi: Conservative Assimilationist."   In *Southern Black Leaders of the Reconstruction Era*.   Edited by Howard N. Rabinowitz.   Urbana: University of Illinois Press, 1982.   Pp. 3-38.   Port. Bruce's political career in the state began with his arrival in 1867.   His impressive qualities of leadership and judgment led to his accendancy within the state Republican Party.   His friendship with Gov. Adelbert Ames helped him to win an election to the U.S. senate.   Bruce gained the confidence of planters and white Republicans, but in later decades his close association with whites, and his conservative ideas toward black improvement and civil rights, led to his isolation from the black community.

2092.   Harris, William C.   "The Creed of the Carpetbaggers: The Case of Mississippi." *Journal of Southern History* 40 (May 1974): 199-224.   Harris tests the revisionist view that most carpetbaggers were not the scoundrels depicted by early 20th century historians.   Carpetbaggers were a small percentage of the Northern immigrants to the South who were usually economically well off and politically active in the Republican Party.   They sought to reform the South through their leadership in education, the promotion of moderation in race relations, and the removal of disloyal men from power.   From 1870 to 1876, they tried to implement a progressive programs in Mississippi to create their ideal world.

2093.   Harris, William C.   "Formulation of the First Mississippi Plan: The Black Code of 1865." *Journal of Mississippi History* 29 (August 1967): 181-201. Radical Republicans used the Mississippi black code to propagandize against President Johnson's moderate Reconstruction program and convince the Northern public that Southerners refused to accept the results of the Civil War.   Harris believes that Radical Reconstruction was not inevitable, and that the actions of

Southern conservatives provided Radicals with a path to power. He describes the debates in Mississippi regarding civil and political rights for the freedmen.

2094. Harris, William C. "Hiram Cassedy: A Former Southern Nationalist in Defense of the Negro in Mississippi Reconstruction." *Louisiana Studies* 7 (Fall 1968): 252-258.   Cassedy supported civil rights so that freedmen would be protected from unlawful assaults and maltreatment by employers. In a letter written on December 16, 1866, Cassedy expressed confidence that discrimination was fading and resides only among the ignorant.

2095. Harris, William C. "James Lynch: Black Leader in Southern Reconstruction." *Historian* 34 (November 1971): 40-61.   Lynch arrived in Mississippi in early 1867 to promote the Northern Methodist Church among the freedmen. Gradually he combined church activities with participation in the Republican Party and black voter registration. Lynch became widely known as an impressive public speaker, editor of the Jackson *Colored Citizen*, and promoter of black education, landownership, and economic and political equality.

2096. Harris, William C. "Mississippi - Republican Factionalism and Management." In *Reconstruction and Redemption in the South*. Edited by Otto Olsen. Baton Rouge: Louisiana State University, 1980. Pp. 78-112. Bibl. Republicans in Mississippi faltered because they fought among themselves, lacked competent leadership, and mismanged state government. Radical governors, Ridgley C. Powers (1871-1874) and Adelbert Ames (1874-1875), tried to broaden their support among local whites, but their efforts failed because of increasing Radical demands for economic and civil rights reforms, a depression in 1871, and racial and political violence.

2097. Harris, William C. "A Mississippi Whig and the Ascension of Rutherford B. Hayes to the Presidency." *Journal of Mississippi History* 30 (August 1968): 202-205.   Most white Southerners were very unhappy that Hayes won the 1876 presidential election because it seemed to indicate four more years of Radical Republican rule. But Oscar J. E. Stuart, a former Whig, expressed delight in an undated letter that he wrote to the new president shortly after his inauguration.

2098. Harris, William C. *Presidential Reconstruction in Mississippi*. Baton Rouge: Louisiana State University Press, 1967. 279p. Bibl. Maps. Ports. President Johnson's Reconstruction program gave the white population of the state substantial freedom to rebuild the government and bring the state back into the Union. Under the leadership of the appointed governor, William L. Sharkey, successful government reorganization was achieved, but his efforts ultimately failed because of insurmountable problems with restoring and diversifying the economy, and securing funds to rebuild river levees. White leaders incorrectly believed that they could regulate the freedmen as they pleased and reject Reconstruction reforms demanded by Congress. (See also Harris' Ph.D. dissertation with the same title from University of Alabama, 1965.)

2099.   Harris, William C.   "A Reconsideration of the Mississippi Scalawag."
Journal of Mississippi History 32 (February 1970): 3-42.   Harris surveys historical
interpretations about the identities and origins of scalawags.   He finds many were
former Unionist Whigs, and others were simply tired of Democratic misrule and
wanted reforms.   In general, they looked forward to the future and sought a complete
return to the Union under the rule of a vigorous Republican Party.   With varying
enthusiasm, scalawags supported suffrage and civil rights for blacks, but they
maintained a conservative view towards politics and social transformation.   The lack
of support from the national party leaders doomed local Republicans to failure.

2100.   Hartley, William G.   "Reconstruction Data From the 1870 Census: Hinds
County, Mississippi."   *Journal of Mississippi History* 35 (February 1973): 55-64.
Hartley investigates the wealth and public offices held by 52 officials in Hinds
County.   He finds that Northern newcomers to the state held most of the major
public offices and that they held the largest share of the wealth compared with
Southern whites and blacks.   Blacks secured more major offices than Southern
whites, but they were a distant third in minor offices and accumulated wealth.   In an
appendix Hartley lists all 52 names of public officials by age, race, office, state of
birth, real estate holdings, and other wealth indicators.

2101.   Johnston, Frank.   "The Public Services of Senator James X. George."
Publications of the Mississippi Historical Society 7 (1904): 201-226.   Part of this
article deals with George's conference with Gov. Adelbert Ames in October, 1875
that averted a clash between the black militia and white groups.   George is credited
with delivering the state to the Democrats from "negro and alien rulers."   Johnston
also discusses George's activities in state politics from 1876 to 1890, including his
defense of the 1890 constitution in the U.S. Senate.   George is revered as a
Democrat who helped to reestablish white supremacy in Mississippi.   (See also
Johnson's "The Conference of October 15, 1875, Between General George and
Governor Ames," *Publications of the Mississippi Historical Society* 6 (1902): 65-
77.)

2102.   Johnston, Frank.   "Suffrage and Reconstruction in Mississippi."
Publications of the Mississippi Historical Society 6 (1902): 141-244.   Bibl.
Johnston explains the role of suffrage in the process of Reconstruction and how the
issue was resolved by the white leaders of Mississippi when they rewrote the
constitution in 1890.   The legislature's enactment of black codes and rejection of the
14th Amendment were mistakes, but the history of Reconstruction proves that the
states ought to control their own affairs, black suffrage is impractical, and the white
race must be assured of power and good government.

2103.   Jones, J. H.   "Reconstruction in Wilkinson County."   *Mississippi
Historical Society Publications* 8 (1904): 153-175.   The end of the Civil War in
Wilkinson County brought few changes in race relations until the appearance of
carpetbaggers, who sought to influence the freedmen to demand the rights of free
men and vote Republican.   Blacks took part in county politics, including Republican

corruption, but violence was kept to minimum because the races stayed apart and freedmen avoided provoking the whites.

2104.   Leftwich, George J.   "Reconstruction in Monroe County." *Publications of the Mississippi Historical Society* 9 (1906): 53-84.   Leftwich focuses on county politics and the struggle by white conservatives to regain power.   The Ku Klux Klan was active as a tool to punish or intimidate black and white Republicans.

2105.   Lord, Stuart B.   "Adelbert Ames Soldier & Politician: A Reevaluation." *Maine Historical Society Quarterly* 13, 2 (1973): 81-97.   Port.   Lord emphasizes Ames' career as a highly decorated Union Army office in the Civil War, military commander in the South beginning in 1868, and Republican U.S. senator (1869-1873) and governor (1873-1876) from Mississippi.   Lord defends Ames against his critics.

2106.   Magee, Hattie.   "Reconstruction in Lawrence and Jefferson Davis Counties." *Publications of the Mississippi Historical Society* 11 (1910): 163-204. App.   Magee focuses on political conditions, including descriptions of prominent Democrats and Republicans, the Freedmen's Bureau, Loyal Leagues, and the Ku Klux Klan.   The county avoided extreme misrule and violence due to the efforts of local Unionists.   The appendix includes names of officials and various statistics.

2107.   Mann, Kenneth Eugene.   "John Roy Lynch: U.S. Congressman From Mississippi."   *Negro History Bulletin* 37 (April/May 1974): 238-241.   Ports. Lynch won election to Congress three times (1873-1877, 1882) as a Republican. Mann notes that Lynch was a defender of civil rights and security for all Americans, and that his most noteworthy achievement was his defense of the Civil Rights Bill of 1875.

2108.   McNeilly, J. S.   "Climax and Collapse of Reconstruction in Mississippi." *Publications of the Mississippi Historical Society* 12 (1912): 283-474.   McNeilly depicts Gov. Adelbert Ames as a weak and misguided carpetbagger whose failure to stem political and financial anarchy in the state led to his political demise.   The defining event of the late Reconstruction period was the Vicksburg riot that took place amidst the election campaign in July, 1874.   McNeilly comments extensively on excessive taxation, federal-state relations, and political corruption. He quotes liberally from letters, documents, and newspapers.

2109.   McNeilly, J. S.   "The Enforcement Act of 1871 and the Ku Klux Klan in Mississippi." *Publications of the Mississippi Historical Society* 9 (1906): 109-171. The Enforcement Act (Ku Klux Klan Act) of April 20, 1871 was an attempt by Radical Republicans to reinforce Radical rule in the South rather than to protect the civil rights, property, and safety of the freedmen from unwarranted violence from the KKK.   Local Republicans exaggerated Klan influence and violence to force Congress to crack down on white Southerners.   McNeilly expresses sympathy for the response of whites against Radical rule of blacks and carpetbaggers.

2110.   McNeilly, J. S.   "From Organization to Overthrow of Mississippi's Provisional Government: 1865-1868." *Publications of the Mississippi Historical Society.* Centenary Series, 1 (1916): 9-404.   McNeilly focuses on the period prior to the passage of the 1868 state constitution.   He covers the broad scope of national and state politics to illustrate how a moderate state government was overthrown by radicals in Congress leading to misery, violence and white degradation.   He discusses race relations, suffrage, labor, militia, the Freedmen's Bureau, and the national debate on Reconstruction.

2111.   "Men of Worth From Mississippi." *Negro History Bulletin* 5 (March 1942): 135-136. Ports.   Brief biographical sketches cover the lives of Hiram Revels (U.S. senator, minister), Blanche K. Bruce (U.S. senator), John Ray Lynch (state legislator, congressman), and Isaiah T. Montgomery (postwar plantation manager).

2112.   Murphy, James B. *L. Q. C. Lamar: Pragmatic Patriot.* Baton Rouge: Louisiana State University Press, 1973. 294p. Bibl. Port.   Lamar symbolizes the good stateman in postwar Southern history. After his election to Congress in 1872, he worked for a return to home rule.   Lamar's strategy to assume the role of the Southern patriot, to explain the case for the white South, and to gain the trust and sympathy of the North was contrived and inconsistent, but it proved effective. As a national figure and eventually Justice of the U.S. Supreme Court (1888-1893), Lamar maintained an image of moderation and statesmanship, but he never gave up principles of states' rights and Southern distinctiveness.

2113.   Nichols, Irby C. "Reconstruction in DeSoto County." *Publications of the Mississippi Historical Society* 11 (1910): 295-316. App.   Nichols concentrates on describing prominent carpetbaggers and scalawags, and also election campaigns. He clarifies the divisions among Republicans that led to their defeat. The appendix lists names of officials and various statistics about the county.

2114.   Nieman, Donald G. "The Freedmen's Bureau and the Mississippi Black Code." *Journal of Mississippi History* 40 (May 1978): 91-118.   The Mississippi Freedmen's Bureau, locally directed by Col. Samuel Thomas, protested the black code designed to control the freedmen and deny them equal civil rights with whites. The bureau complained about the treatment of the freedmen, but President Johnson refused to involve the federal government in local affairs. bureau agents helped free children of freedmen from "apprenticeships," but it was only after the passage of the Civil Rights Act of 1866 that bureau officials believed that the agency had the authority to protect freedmen from black codes.

2115.   Pereyra, Lillian A. *James Lusk Alcorn: Persistent Whig.* Baton Rouge: Louisiana State University, 1966. 237p. Port.   Alcorn, a Southern Unionist, became Mississippi's first Republican governor in Reconstruction (1869-1871). He sought honest government and cooperated with racial reforms despite growing violence against blacks and criticism from Radical Republicans, particularly Adelbert Ames.   Pereyra characterizes Alcorn's failure as due to his inability to organize a neo-Whig alignment, and his attempt to solve problems with outmoded ideas. As governor and U.S. senator (1871-73) Alcorn tried to bring peace and prosperity to his state. (See also Pereyra's "James Lusk Alcorn: A Biography." Ph.D. University of California, Los Angeles, 1962.)

2116.   Powell, Lawrence N. "Correcting for Fraud: A Quantitative Reassessment of the Mississippi Ratification Election of 1868." *Journal of Southern History* 55 (November 1989): 633-658. Graphs. Map. Tbls.   The Mississippi Constitution of 1868 went down to defeat in the June election despite the majority of black registered voters in the state.   Powell tests ecological regression analysis as a methodology for measuring whether the presence of fraud, violence, and intimidation had an impact on the outcome of the vote. He finds that whites did whatever was necessary in 15 counties to ensure that the constitution failed, including fraud and voter intimidation.

2117.   Power, J. L. "The Black and Tan Convention." *Publications of the Mississippi Historical Society* 3 (1900): 73-83.   Power outlines the post Civil War events leading up to the constitutional convention of 1868 that was derisively labeled Black and Tan. He criticizes the composition, behavior, and product of the convention, mainly because it took power away from many whites and equalized civil rights for whites and blacks.

2118.   Puckett, E. F. "Reconstruction in Monroe County." *Publications of the Mississippi Historical Society* 11 (1910): 103-161. App.   The focus is mainly on political affairs, particularly elections and race relations. Puckett describes the work of the Ku Klux Klan, white election fraud, and intimidation of blacks. Puckett is sympathetic to the cause of conservative whites. The appendix includes the names of officials and various statistics.

2119.   Rainwater, P. L. (ed.). "The Autobiography of Benjamin Grubb Humphreys August 216, 1808-December 20, 1882." *Mississippi Valley Historical Review* 21 (September 1934): 231-255.   Humphreys, a Mississippi Whig who opposed secession, served the Confederacy as a Brigadier-General in the Army. In October, 1865 he won the gubernatorial election and held the office until July, 1868 when the Union Army removed him.   Printed is an autobiography devoted substantially to his experience as governor. Humphreys discusses the necessity of the black codes and his relationship with Army commanders in Mississippi during the transition to Congressional Reconstruction.

2120.   Rainwater, P. L. (ed.). "Letters to and From Jacob Thompson." *Journal of Southern History* 6 (February 1940): 95-111.   Thompson was a congressman and planter from Mississippi prior to the Civil War. When peace came he escaped the U.S. for Ireland and later Nova Scotia where he remained until his return home in the spring of 1869. Five of the ten letters printed were written by Thompson while he was in exile.   He remarks about the course of Reconstruction in Mississippi.

2121.   Riley, Franklin L. "Outline for a County History of Reconstruction." *Publications of the Mississippi Historical Society* 12 (1912): 12-15.   The editor of the *Publications of the Mississippi Historical Society* provides a detailed outline that was used by writers for the periodical's series on Mississippi counties during Reconstruction.

2122.   Ringold, May Spencer. "James Lusk Alcorn." *Journal of Mississippi History* 25 (January 1963): 1-14.   Ringold reviews Alcorn's political career as Republican governor in 1870 and U.S. senator in 1871. She characterizes him as a keen, opportunistic politician who sought power and compromised his ethics to acquire it.

2123.   Robinson, Mary Fisher. "A Sketch of James Lusk Alcorn." *Journal of Mississippi History* 12 (January 1950): 28-45.   Robinson chronicles Alcorn's public life before and after the Civil War. She compliments his performance as governor and U.S. senator during Reconstruction and offers criticism of the Radicals Republicans in the state.

2124.   Rowland, Dunbar, Esq. "The Rise and Fall of Negro Rule in Mississippi." *Publications of the Mississippi Historical Society* 2 (1899): 189-199.   In emotional language Rowland describes Reconstruction as a period of black rule struck down by Mississippians acting in the spirit of Southern patriotism to protect their state, their families, and their property.

2125.   Russ, William A., Jr. "Radical Disfranchisement in Mississippi (1867-1870)." *Mississippi Law Journal* 7 (January 1935): 365-377.   Russ is very critical of the disenfranchisement of former rebels as stipulated in the 14th Amendment, the Reconstruction Acts, and the Mississippi state constitution passed in 1868. By following the example of intransigence to disenfranchisement in Virginia, white Mississippians lengthened military rule and weakened the impact of disenfranchisement laws in the state.

2126.   Sallis, William C. "The Color Line in Mississippi Politics, 1865-1915." Ph.D. University of Kentucky, 1967. 470p.

2127.   Sansing, David G. "Congressional Reconstruction." In *A History of Mississippi.* Vol. I. Edited by Richard Aubrey McLemore. Hattiesburg: University College Press of Mississippi, 1973. Pp. 571-589.   Sansing discusses the period of Republican rule from the election of James L. Alcorn as governor in 1869 to the Democratic election victory and the forced resignation of Gov. Adlebert Ames in 1875. He relies mainly on primary resources and explains current interpretations of the period.

2128.   Sansing, David G. "The Failure of Johnsonian Reconstruction in Mississippi, 1865-1866." *Journal of Mississippi History* 34 (November 1972): 373-390.   In April, 1865 Mississippians were ready to accept the end of slavery and whatever was required, including basic civil rights for blacks, to return their lives to normal. When President Johnson encouraged them to defy radical demands coming from the Republican Party, Johnson's Reconstruction program collapsed. The Mississippi legislature rejected reform and passed a black code. The mood in the state became defiant in favor of returning the state as close to antebellum life as possible.

2129.   Sansing, David G.   "The Role of the Scalawag in Mississippi Reconstruction." Ph.D. University of Southern Mississippi, 1969. 248p.

2130.   Satcher, Buford. *Blacks in Mississippi Politics 1865-1900.* [Washington, DC]: University Press of America, 1978. 213p. App. Bibl. Ill. Tbls.   In his examination of the contributions of blacks to rebuilding Mississippi, Satcher emphasizes that accusations of fraud and corruption against them have been exaggerated. Black politicians were successful at the local level where they took advantage of their majority in many counties. The end of Republican rule in 1875 and the official end of Reconstruction in 1877 did not bring an end to black participation in the state. Until the 1890s blacks continued to vote, hold offices, and create political alliances despite opposition from whites. The appendix lists the names of black politicians, provides information about state and national offices held, and includes voter statistics. (See also Satcher's Ph.D. disseration with the same title from Oklahoma State University, 1976.)

2131.   Simms, L. Moody, Jr.   "'...in the gloomy macrocosm of Lucifer': A Mississippian Comments on the Beginnings of Reconstruction." *Journal of Mississippi History* 30 (August 1968): 193-195.   George Daniel Farrar, a resident of Adams County and a Confederate veteran, wrote his father from Cambridge, Ma., on July 26, 1865 to express his opposition to any change in the prewar constitution of Mississippi. Farrar opposed even President Johnson's Reconstruction plan. The letter is printed.

2132.   Smiley, David L. "Cassius M. Clay and the Mississippi Election of 1875." *Journal of Mississippi History* 19 (October 1957): 252-262.   Clay, a Kentuckian who opposed the Southern concept of states' rights and favored emancipation, took the side of the Union and the Republican Party in 1860. As minister to Russia during the Grant administration, he became so dissatisfied with Grant that he joined the Liberal Republicans and eventually the Democrats. In the state election campaign of 1875 he made many public speeches against Grant and the Republicans. Mississippi Democrats welcomed him to their state, specifically to persuade blacks to vote Democratic.

2133.   Stone, Alfred Holt. "A Mississippian's View of Civil Rights, States Rights, and the Reconstruction Background." *Journal of Mississippi History* 10 (1948): 181-239.   Stone reviews Reconstruction by reprinting contemporary accounts, letters, presidential documents, and legislative texts.

2134.   Stone, Alfred Holt. "Mississippi's Constitution and Statutes in Reference to Freedmen, and Their Alleged Relation to the Reconstruction Acts and War

Amendments." *Publications of the Mississippi Historical Society* 4 (1901): 143-226.   Stone, a lawyer and planter in late nineteenth century Mississippi, distinguishes between the state's laws prior to the Reconstruction Acts in 1867 and the requirements made by the federal government to reenter the political life of the nation.   He characterizes the state's response prior to March, 1867 as knowledgeable, realistic, and sincere.   The Radicals are depicted as hypocritical, particularly regarding the racial laws in Northern states.

2135.   Stone, James H.   (ed.).   "L. Q. C. Lamar Letters to Edward Donaldson Clark, 1868-1885. Part I: 1868-1873." *Journal of Mississippi History* 35 (February 1973): 65-73; "Part II: 1874-1878."   37 (May 1975): 189-201.   Stone presents selected letters written by Lamar to his law partner in Vicksburg.   Lamar wrote strong letters criticizing the federal government and the Republican regime in the state.   He is particularly critical of the Grant administration and Republican Governors James Alcorn and Adelbert Ames.   Lamar also wrote about his meeting with Blanche K. Bruce after he won a seat in the U.S. senate in the 1876 election. (See also "Part III: 1879-1885," *Journal of Mississippi History* 43 (May 1981): 135-164.)

2136.   Sumner, Cecil L.   *The Govenors of Mississippi*.   Gretna: Pelican Publishing Co., 1980. 164p. Bibl. Ports.   Sumner includes biographical sketches of governors William Lewis Sharkey (June 13-October 16, 1865), Benjamin Grubb Humphreys (October 16-June 15, 1868), Adelbert Ames (June 15, 1868-March 10, 1870, January 4, 1874-March 29, 1876), James Lusk Alcorn (March 10, 1870-November 30, 1871), and Ridgley Ceylon Powers (November 30, 1871-January 4, 1874).

2137.   Waldrep, Christopher. "Black Access to Law in Reconstruction: The Case of Warren County, Mississippi." *Chicago-Kent Law Review* 70, 2 (1994): 583-624. Tbls.   Waldrep measures the access that blacks had to legal services in Warren County by reviewing the number that participated on grand juries and how that correlates with the number that brought cases to court when they were victims of crime.   Participation in grand juries and access to courts improved under carpetbagger rule between 1869 and 1874, but the numbers were not high and, in general, access to legal protection was very limited.   The main impediment to black participation was the common law tradition of selecting literate, propertied men.

2138.   Warren, Henry Waterman.   *Reminiscences of a Mississippi Carpet-Bagger*. Holden, Ma., 1914. 110p. Ills. Ports.   Warren, a native of Massachusetts, purchased a cotton plantation in Leake County in 1866.   This book provides Warren's perspective on state politics during the ten years that he lived in the state. He supported Gov. Adelbert Ames and reforms in education and civil rights.   In 1869 he became speaker of the house in the state legislature.

2139.   Wells, W. Calvin. "Reconstruction and its Destruction in Hinds County." *Publications of the Mississippi Historical Society* 9 (1906): 85-108.   Wells emphasizes political and electoral events and racial tensions in the county.   He is particularly concerned with the period before Radical Reconstruction started in 1867 and 1874-1875 when Democrats regained power in the state.

2140.   Wharton, Vernon. L. "The Race Issue in the Overthrow of Reconstruction in Mississippi." *Phylon* 2 (4th Quarter 1941): 362-370.   The accusation that the state and local governments were dominated by ignorant blacks who exhibited inefficiency, extravagance and corruption does not hold up when closely examined. Freedmen predominated in the electorate, but they never came close to gaining control of positions of power. Republicans generally had a record of remarkable honesty, but they were doomed to fail because the white majority objected to Republican rule and would not accept blacks on equal terms. By 1873 the moderate government of Gov. James L. Alcorn could not cope with black demands for greater power and the increasing intimidation and violence against blacks by the white community.

2141.   Williams, James Levon, Jr. "Civil War and Reconstruction in the Yazoo Mississippi Delta, 1863-1875." Ph.D. University of Arizona, 1992. 248p.

2142.   Wilson, Walter. "The Meridian Massacre of 1871." *Crisis* 81, 2 (1974): 49-52.   Wilson describes the reign of terror inflicted on the South by the Ku Klux Klan as illustrated by the Klan killings during a trial in Meridian on March 6, 1871.

2143.   Witty, Fred M. "Reconstruction in Carroll and Montgomery Counties." *Publications of the Mississippi Historical Society* 10 (1909): 115-134.   Witty chronicles political events in two counties from the perspective of local white conservatives. He includes sections on the activities of the Ku Klux Klan, racial tension, a riot in Winona, and the Freedmen's Bureau.

Agriculture, Labor, and Business

2144.   Currie, James T. "Benjamin Montgomery and the Davis Bend Colony." *Prologue* 25th Anniversary Issue (1989): 73-85. Ills. Ports.   Montgomery was a slave of Joseph Davis, brother of Jefferson Davis, near Natchez, Mississippi. Davis left Montgomery in charge of his plantation as he fled from Union troops in 1863, and his land and a neighboring plantation were set aside as a colony for freedmen farmers to show that black farmers could earn an independent living. In 1867 Davis sold his land to Montgomery who led the colony of black farmers through difficult times until Jefferson Davis acquired it. The Davis Bend colony showed the potential benefits of land distribution.

2145.   Currie, James T. *Enclave: Vicksburg and Her Plantations, 1863-1870.* Jackson: University Press of Mississippi, 1980. 257p. Bibl. Ills. Maps. Ports. Vicksburg differed from most of the South because it was the home of the Fourth Military District and the state office of the Freedmen's Bureau, making it a place with a large concentration of federal troops and officials who could ensure that changes were carried out according to federal law. Currie discusses the impact of war and Reconstruction on the city and the educational, political and labor opportunities for freedmen in Warren County. Nearby Davis Bend was noted as a place where former slaves proved that they could successfully engage in agriculture without the force of slavery.

2146.   Currie, James T. "Vicksburg, 1863-1870: The Promise and the Reality of Reconstruction on the Mississippi." Ph.D. University of Virginia, 1975. 289p.

2147.   Dykes, Mary Frances W.   "Public Policy and Mississippi Industrial Growth, 1865-1880." *Mississippi Quarterly* 8 (April 1955): 1-12; (Summer 1955): 22-40.   Dykes does not distinguish between the efforts of the conservative regime immediately after the Civil War and the Republicans who took control in 1867, except that the 1869 constitution allowed for taxation of business at the same rate as other private property.   State officials throughout the period promoted industrialization, but the process was slow and could not compete with the rest of the U.S.

2148.   Futrell, Robert F. "Efforts of Mississippians to Encourage Immigration, 1865-1880." *Journal of Mississippi History* 20 (April 1958): 59-76.   A campaign to import white immigrants to Mississippi failed to bring significant numbers. Some of the newcomers were Northerners seeking profits in cheap cotton plantations, but more organized efforts were made to bring Chinese and Europeans to rural areas to replace black laborers who were considered unreliable.   But poor working conditions, economic problems, and competition with black labor persuaded prospective immigrants to stay away.

2149.   Greenberg, Kenneth S.   "The Civil War and Redistribution of Land: Adams County, Mississippi 1860-1870." *Agricultural History* 52 (April 1978): 292-307. Tbls.   Greenberg compares the holdings of land by values as revealed in the U.S. censuses of 1860 and 1870. He finds that in Adams County, a section of Mississippi that avoided war related destruction and that was mostly Unionist, land redistribution from large plantation owners to smaller land owners was not widespread. In the short term, planter stability based on land values persisted throughout the decade, although this conclusion must be tempered by the reality of lost capital in the form of slaves and the resulting loss of prestige. Greenberg also discusses problems with interpreting the census statistics.   Six tables illustrate statistical data on the changes in land distribution.

2150.   Haws, Robert J. and Michael V. Namorato. "Race, Property Rights, and the Economic Consequences of Reconstruction: A Case Study." *Vanderbilt Law Review* 32 (January 1979): 305-326. Tbls.   In this study of Lafayette County, Mississippi, from 1865 to 1870, the authors argue that racial discrimination, black codes, the use of criminal and vagrancy laws, and the failure to resolve private debt problems resulted in economic stagnation during the early postwar period. These conditions were reinforced by local courts that followed state legislation and acted in

416   *Reconstruction in the United States*

the interests of persons who did not want to reform Southern society. In a follow up "comment," Robert B. Jones criticizes the article for its lack of evidence.

2151.   Hermann, Janet Sharp. *The Pursuit of a Dream.* New York: Oxford University Press, 1981. 290p. Bibl. Ills. Maps Ports.   Joseph Davis, brother of Jefferson Davis, attempted to build a utopian community on the Mississippi plantations at Davis Bend in prewar days. The wealthy farmer and lawyer from Natchez sought an ideal community of prosperity, and he encouraged initiative among his slaves, particularly Benjamin T. Montgomery, who purchased the plantation from Davis in 1866. Montgomery's experience prepared him for a new experiment in collective living and working after the war. After the community declined, Isaiah Montgomery, Benjamin's son, revived the dream by creating a colony at Mound Bayou in 1887. (See also Hermann's "The Black Community at Davis Bend: The Pursuit of a Dream." Ph.D. University of California, Berkeley, 1979. 360p.)

2152.   Hermann, Janet Sharp. "Reconstruction in a Microcosm: Three Men and a Gin." *Journal of Negro History* 65 (Fall 1980); 312-335.   The Davis Bend experiment in black farming was a success, except for disagreements between former slave Benjamin Montgomery and Freedmen's Bureau agent Samuel Thomas. Montgomery was aided by his former owner, Joseph Davis. This peculiar alliance of plantation owner and former slave against the Freedmen's Bureau led to an extended struggle that resulted in Thomas' removal by the Army.

2153.   Humphrey, George D. "The Failure of the Mississippi Freedman's Bureau in Black Labor Relations, 1865-1867." *Journal of Mississippi History* 45 (February 1983): 23-37.   Humphrey argues that the bureau acted as a conservative institution in Mississippi. It was not successful providing aid to blacks, because the overwhelming racism in the state put obstacles in the way of aid and enforcement of civil rights, and many bureau agents held conservative and racist views.

2154.   Rogers, William Warren. "Thomas Gale's New South Letters." *Journal of Mississippi History* 28 (August 1966): 228-236.   Twelve letters written by physician and planter Thomas Gale to his daughter describe life in postwar Mississippi. The letters cover the period from December, 1865 to June, 1883 and all were written from his home in Abydon near the Yazoo River. Gale refers mostly to agricultural and labor issues on his plantation.

2155.   Ross, Steven Joseph. "Freed Soil, Freed Labor, Freed Men: John Eaton and the Davis Bend Experiment." *Journal of Southern History* 44 (May 1978): 213-232.   Davis Bend, 25 miles down the Mississippi River from Vicksburg, Mississippi, was the site of an experiment in independent farming by former slaves. With Eaton's careful planning beginning in 1862, Davis Bend became an example of a successful program organizing freedmen for a new life based on the Republican ideology of free labor. The experiment depended on the confiscation of abandoned plantations, but President Johnson's amnesty to plantation owners precluded land confiscation, and Congressional Republicans believed that confiscation was a violation of the sanctity of property rights.

2156.   Smith, Claude P.   "Official Efforts By the State of Mississippi to Encourage Immigration, 1868-1886." *Journal of Mississippi History* 32 (November 1970): 327-340.   Although Mississippi's constitution of 1868 included provisions for a commission of immigration and agriculture, the office was rarely filled. The Republican legislature feared an influx of whites could shift the balance of political power. In 1873 the office was finally filled with the hope that European immigrants could provide labor and resources to improve the state economy. The effort to attract Europeans failed, because the standard of living in the state was too low and the state had a negative image compared with other parts of the U.S.

2157.   Wayne, Michael Stuart. "Antebellum Planters in the Post-Bellum South: The Natchez District, 1860-1880." Ph.D. Yale University, 1979. 335p.

Society, Education, and Religion

2158.   Anderson, E. H. "A Memoir on Reconstruction in Yazoo City." *Journal of Mississippi History* 4 (October 1942): 187-194.   Anderson tells a story of violence and racism in Yazoo City.

2159.   Bercaw, Nancy Dunlap.   "The Politics of Household: Domestic Battlegrounds in the Transition From Slavery to Freedom in the Yazoo-Mississippi Delta, 1861-1876." Ph.D. University of Pennsylvania, 1996. 437p.

2160.   Ganus, Clifton L, Jr. "The Freedmen's Bureau in Mississippi."   Ph.D. Tulane University, 1953.

2161.   Gibson, J. M. *Memoirs of J. M. Gibson: Terrors of the Civil War and Reconstruction Days*.   Edited by James Gibson Alverson and James Gibson Alverson, Jr. (np), 1966. App.   Writing in 1929 Gibson describes how his family in Vicksburg coped with the war and the social and political difficulties that occurred during Reconstruction. In depictions of constant racial confrontation, he blames the sudden emancipation of the slaves for black lawlessness. He also attributes violence and political corruption to carpetbaggers and black rule.

2162.   Gravely, William B.   "A Black Methodist on Reconstruction in Mississippi: Three Letters by James Lynch in 1868-1869." *Methodist History* 11 (April 1973): 3-18. (Rev. and repub. in *Black Apostles at Home and Abroad*, edited by D. W. Wills and R. Nieman, Boston: G. K. Hall, 1982. Pp. 161-188.)   Lynch, a free black from Baltimore, combined his religious training with political savvy in the struggle for black civil rights and the development of the African Methodist Episcopal Church in Mississippi. He became presiding elder of the Natchez District of the A.M.E. Church after serving the needs of freedmen during the war. The three letters reveal his perspective on the place of blacks in the postwar South and the role of the Church. Politics was a major component of his life, and he was highly respected in the Republican community.

2163.   Hesseltine, William B. and Larry Gara.   "Mississippi's Confederate Leaders After the War." *Journal of Mississippi History* 13 (April 1951): 88-100. The authors describe the postwar careers of prominent citizens of Mississippi, including Jefferson Davis and Lucius Q. C. Lamar, who refused to emigrate in favor of staying in their state to contribute to the rebuilding process.

2164.   Jenkins, Robert L.   "The Development of Black Higher Education in Mississippi (1865-1920)." *Journal of Mississippi History* 45 (November 1983): 272-286.   The origins of black higher education in Mississippi can be found in the period of Reconstruction.   During Reconstruction the Freedmen's Bureau and religious and benevolent societies greatly assisted the beginning of black education. The schools founded during Reconstruction were Tougaloo College (1869), Rust College (1870), and Alcorn State University (1971).

2165.   Legan, Marshall Scott.   "Disease and the Freedmen in Mississippi Reconstruction." *Journal of the History of Medicine and Allied Sciences* 28 (July 1973): 257-267.   Disease is considered an important factor explaining the decreasing numbers of blacks in Mississippi from the beginning of the Civil War through 1866. Freedmen across the state were subjected to the ravages of many diseases, particularly cholera and yellow fever. During Reconstruction racism was a factor in the lack of attention paid to the health of ex-slaves.   The Freedmen's Bureau, along with local authorities, provided health care, but adequate services were not provided

2166.   Moore, Ross H. "Social and Economic Conditions in Mississippi During Reconstruction." Ph.D. Duke University, 1938.

2167.   Morgan, A. T. *Yazoo; or, on the Picket Line of Freedom in the South. A Personal Narrative.* Washington, D.C.: Published by the Author, 1884. 512p. Morgan describes his experiences in Yazoo County, Mississippi during Reconstruction. He grew up in Wisconsin, served in the Union Army, and settled in the South with the hope of making lucrative investments in cotton cultivation. Morgan was a Republican officeholder and married a black woman. He focuses on politics, race relations, and social life in Yazoo.

2168.   Osborne, George C. "The Life of a Southern Plantation Owner During Reconstruction as Revealed in the Clay Sharkey Papers." *Journal of Mississippi History* 6 (April 1944): 103-112.   Osborne describes public and private activities in the postwar life of planter Clay Sharkey of Hinds County.

2169.   Porch, James Milton. "Race Relations Between Black and White Baptists in Mississippi, 1862-1890." Th.D. New Orleans Baptist Theological Seminary, 1974.

2170. Robuck, J. E. *My Own Personal Experience and Observations as a Soldier in the Confederate Army During the Civil War, 1861-1865, Also During the Period of Reconstruction.* Birmingham, Ala., 1947. 136p. Regarding the postwar period in Mississippi from 1865 to the early 1870s, Robuck tells detailed stories about deceitful, corrupt carpetbaggers who, along with Northern teachers, turned docile, friendly blacks into criminals and ranters for political power. He defends the swift justice of whites against black transgressors and describes the Ku Klux Klan as a secret military force designed to enforce peace and proper black behavior.

2171. Smith, Dorothy Vick. "Black Reconstruction in Mississippi, 1862-1870." Ph.D. University of Kansas, 1985. 308p.

2172. Smith, Thomas H. "Ohio Quakers and the Mississippi Freedmen -'A Field to Labor.'" *Ohio History* 78 (Summer 1969): 159-171. Members of the Ohio Yearly Meeting of the Society of Friends (Orthodox) refused to fight in the Civil War, but they helped their country by offering assistance to the freedmen, first with their physical needs and later with education. Elder John Butler worked with Indiana Quakers to raise funds for schools, such as one founded in 1866 in Jackson, Mississippi to teach both industrial and literary skills. Despite the pressures against them, the Quakers maintained their schools until 1875. They were genuinely interested in providing the freedmen with skills for independent living.

2173. Sparks, Randy J. "'The White People's Arms Are Longer Than Ours': Blacks, Education, and the American Missionary Association in Reconstruction Mississippi." *Journal of Mississippi History* 54 (February 1992): 1-27. Freedmen in Mississippi established schools before the arrival of Northern teachers and missionaries. Officials and teachers of the A.M.A. assisted blacks with organizing and building schools, despite the increasing hostility from local whites, such as the Ku Klux Klan. Sparks emphasizes the initiative and proactive efforts of blacks to organize themselves for educational improvement. This effort made it easier for the A.M.A. to provide effective assistance, but historians have disagreed about the nature of the A.M.A.'s role in black education.

2174. Timberlake, Elise. "Did the Reconstruction Regime Give Mississippi Her Public Schools?" *Publications of the Mississippi Historical Society* 12 (1912): 72-93. The idea that public schools began in Mississippi during Reconstruction is a misconception. State law allowed for local taxation for schools since March 4, 1846, and the number of counties taking advantage of this increased over the years. During Reconstruction the system was expanded. Timberlake criticizes the Republican regime for wasting funds, and emphasizes that local whites resented the education offered by Northern teachers.

2175. Waterbury, M. *Seven Years Among the Freedmen.* 2nd Ed. Rev. and enlarged. Chicago: T. B. Arnold, 1891. 198p. Ills. Ports. The author traveled from near Chicago to a remote plantation in Mississippi to serve as a teacher and Christian missionary among the freedmen. She describes her interaction with black children and adults, as well as experiences with the Ku Klux Klan and local politics.

2176.   Williams, Martha Huddleston.   "Education For Freedom: The Noble Experiment of Sarah A. Dickey and the Mount Herman [Mississippi] Seminary." Ph.D. University of Mississippi, 1985. 162p.

2177.   Willis, John Charles.   "On The New South Frontier: Life In The Yazoo-Mississippi Delta, 1865-1920." Ph.D. University of Virginia, 1991. 387p.

Missouri

General History

2178.   DeArmond, Fred.   "Reconstruction in Missouri." *Missouri Historical Review* 61 (April 1967): 364-377. Ills. Port.   In this brief survey DeArmond describes the postwar period as the continuation of vicious guerrilla warfare in Missouri that pitted former Confederates against Unionists.   In this environment Republican reformers, led by Charles D. Drake, revised the state constitution and worked to avoid a return to antebellum politics.   The reforms provided greater freedoms for black citizens and progress in establishing a system of public education.

2179.   Parrish, William E.   *History of Missouri.   Volume III: 1860-1875.* Columbia: University of Missouri Press, 1973. 332p. Bibl.   Parrish covers political, cultural, economic, and urban issues during a time of political turmoil. During Reconstruction in Missouri there was progress in civil rights and education, and optimism about economic development.   Parrish highlights the key political developments during the time of Republican resurgence, the emancipation of slaves, political fragmentation of the Radicals, and the ultimate success of conservatism in 1875.   Key political players in Missouri during the period were Frank P. Blair, B. Gratz Brown, Charles D. Drake, Thomas Fletcher, Joseph W. McClurg, and Hamilton R. Gamble.

Politics and Law

2180.   Barclay, Thomas S. *The Liberal Republican Movement in Missouri 1865-1871.* Columbia: State Historical Society of Missouri, 1926. 288p. Ports. Tbls. Bibl. (Also in *Missouri Historical Review* 20 (October 1925-July 1926):3-78, 262-332, 406-437, 515-564; 21 (October 1926): 59-108.   Missouri Radicals defeated conservative Unionists for political control of the state by the end of the Civil War. They held power until 1872 when the Democrats took advantage of a state Liberal Republican movement led by Carl Schurz that split the Republican Party.   Liberals provided the Democrats with an opportunity to regain power for the next 30 years.

2181.   Barclay, Thomas S. "The Test Oath for the Clergy in Missouri." *Missouri Historical Review* 18 (April 1924): 345-381.   Missouri's test oath enacted in June, 1865, required all clergy to take an oath of loyalty so that they could solemnize marriages. In *Ex parte* Garland the U.S. Supreme Court decided that the law was unconstitutional. The oath was never meant to destroy religious freedom, but it did embarrass the Radicals who themselves were split over the law.

2182.   Dwight, Margaret Leola. "Black Suffrage in Missouri, 1865-1877." Ph.D. University of Missouri, 1978. 314p.

2183.   Kohl, Martha. "Enforcing a Vision of Community: The Role of the Test Oath in Missouri's Reconstruction." *Civil War History* 40 (December 1994): 292-307.   Republicans used the test oath as a punitive measure to disenfranchise supporters of the Confederacy, but the oath also represented an attempt by Republicans to build a new political environment, based on an industrious, free soil community.   But Republicans were able to hold on to power only until disenfranchisement ended in 1870. The return of Democratic dominance revealed the continuity of conservative Missouri politics even with blacks and the influx of new residents from the Northeast.

2184.   Kremer, Gary R. "Background to Apostasy: James Milton Turner and the Republican Party." *Missouri Historical Review* 71 (October 1976): 59-75. Ills. Ports.   Kremer describes Turner's work for black civil rights and the Republican Party that led to his appointment as Minister to Liberia in March, 1871. His high regard for the party diminished by 1878 when he lost faith in the Republican Party's dedication to equal civil rights. By the 1880s he switched his support to the Democrats.

2185.   Kremer, Gary R. *James Milton Turner and the Promise of America: The Public Life of a Post-Civil War Black Leader.* Columbia: University of Missouri, 1991. 245p. App. Bibl.   Turner was a leader for black political rights and education in Missouri during the postwar decades. He worked for the Freedmen's Bureau establishing schools, participated in Republican politics, and in 1871 was appointed by President Grant to be the American Ambassador to Liberia. Turner drew criticism from other blacks for his assimilation into white society and his unbridled patriotism and faith in American institutions. He believed that white racism could be overcome through educational and social advancement. (See also Kremer's "A Biography of James Milton Turner." Ph.D. American University, 1978. 391p.; and a brief sketch in Noah Webster Moore's "James Milton Turner: Diplomat, Educator, and Defender of Rights, 1840-1915," *Bulletin of the Missouri Historical Society* 27 (April 1971): 194-201.)

2186.   Lehmann, Frederick W. "Edward Bates and the Test Oath." *Missouri Historical Society Collections* 4 (1923): 389-401. Port.   Bates was a leader of the Conservatives along with Gen. Francis P. Blair. In Missouri Conservatives believed that the test oaths approved by the Republican constitution were illegal, but Bates recommended that anyone who felt that they were not loyal to the government should take the oath in order to vote. The oath was considered to be humiliating, but Bates focused on the advantages to Conservatives of accepting the oath.

2187.   March, David D. "Charles D. Drake and the Constitutional Convention of 1865." *Missouri Historical Review* 47 (October 1952 - July 1953): 110-123. Drake's proslavery position gradually changed during the war until he was identified with the Radical elements in Missouri.   When the Radicals won control of state government in November, 1864 Drake played a key role in steering the constitutional convention to incorporate emancipation and the "iron-clad" oath that would disenfranchise supporters of secession. Drake insisted on legal equality of the freedmen, but he opposed extending suffrage.

2188.   March, David D. "The Life and Times of Charles Daniel Drake." Ph.D. University of Missouri, Columbia, 1949. 466p.

2189.   McDougal, H. C. "A Decade of Missouri Politics-1860 to 1870. From A Republican Viewpoint." *Missouri Historical Review* 3 (January 1909): 126-153. McDougal surveys the struggle for Missouri to stay in the Union, the rise of the Republican Party, and the enactment of a test oath to quality for voting and holding public office. Republican governments were in office from 1864 to 1870.   The author defends the controversial test oath as well meaning.

2190.   Morrow, Lynn. "Joseph Washington McClurg: Entrepreneur, Politician, Citizen." *Missouri Historical Review* 78 (January 1984): 168-201.   McClurg freed his slaves in 1863 and became a supporter of the Radical Republicans in his Ozark region of Missouri. He won a third term in Congress in 1866 and the governorship in 1868. Splits within the Republican Party and a resurgent Liberal Republican movement led to his defeat in 1870. Morrow emphasizes McClurg's honesty, fiscal conservatism, strong unionism, and support for business and industry in Missouri. (See also James S. Botsford, "Gov. Joseph W. McClurg and his Administration," *Missouri Historical Review* 6 (July 1912): 182-191.)

2191.   Parrish, William E. *Missouri Under Radical Rule, 1865-1870*. Columbia: University of Missouri Press, 1965. 385p. Bibl.   The positive developments of postwar Radical rule in Missouri became the foundation for future growth of the state during the decades following Reconstruction. Progress occurred in civil rights, education, transportation, migration to the state, and in economic development under Radical leadership. The Republican losses in the 1872 state elections were due to widening party divisions between radical Unionists, led by Charles D. Drake, and Liberal Republicans, led by Carl Schurz.   Thirty-five years of continuous Democratic rule followed, but the liberal reforms remained, leading to further social and economic progress.

2192.   Parrish, William E. "Reconstruction Politics in Missouri, 1865-1870." In *Radicalism, Racism, and Party Realignment, the Border States During Reconstruction*. Edited by R. O. Curry. Baltimore: Johns Hopkins Press, 1969. Pp. 1-36.   The victory of the Radical Unionist Party in Missouri in 1864 represented the strength of the nonslaveholding population that had kept the state solidly on the side of the Union in 1861. The attempts of the Radicals to put the state at the forefront of reform produced great turmoil and dissension among Republicans, and resulted in the strengthening of conservative forces. Parrish discusses the legislative and party struggles on suffrage, loyalty oaths, disenfranchisement of rebel sympathizers, education, immigration, and railroads. Radical leaders included Governor Thomas C. Fletcher and Judge Charles D. Drake.

2193.   Peterson, Norma L. *Freedom and Franchise: The Political Career of B. Gratz Brown.* Columbia: University of Missouri Press, 1965. 252p. Bibl. Port. During his public career in the state, from 1852 to 1872, Brown helped organize the state Republican Party and took a strong stand for emancipation and black suffrage, but he opposed a ironclad test oath that he believed would discriminate against freedom of thought. He served as a U.S. senator from 1863 to 1867, Liberal Republican governor in 1871, and vice presidential candidate in 1872. To his colleagues Brown was either too radical or not radical enough. His apparent inconsistency illustrated the complexity of politics in a border state.

2194.   Primm, James N. "The G. A. R. in Missouri, 1868-1870." *Journal of Southern History* 20 (August 1954): 356-375.   The Grand Army of the Republic (G.A.R.) was an organization of Union veterans that became active in Missouri by the summer of 1866. The G.A.R. became strongly identified in Missouri and Northeastern newspapers as a Radical political organization that worked against President Johnson, Democrats, and moderate and conservative Republicans. With the victory of Ulysses S. Grant in the presidential election of 1868, the Missouri branch became nonpolitical and eventually folded by 1871.

2195.   Skinker, Thomas K. "The Removal of Judges of the Supreme Court of Missouri." *Missouri Historical Society Collections* 4 (1914): 243-274.   The contest between Radicals and Conservatives in Missouri is illustrated by the act of Republican removal of Conservative judges and other officials deemed disloyal. Skinker quotes from various partisan publications to describe the controversy.

2196.   Switzler, W. F. "Constitutional Conventions of Missouri, 1865-1875." *Missouri Historical Review* 1 (January 1907): 109-120.   Switzler, a participant at the conventions of 1865 and 1875, briefly describes the early conference as "abnormal" and "revolutionary" and the latter as a significant revision. (See also Isidor Loeb, "Constitutions and Constitutional Conventions in Missouri." *Missouri Historical Review* 16 (January 1922): 189-238.)

Agriculture, Labor, and Business

2197.   Naglich, Dennis. "Rural Prairieville During Reconstruction." *Missouri Historical Review* 87 (July 1993): 387-402. Ills. Ports.   Economic and agricultural adjustments are the focus of Naglich's work on Pike and Lincoln Counties in eastcentral Missouri near the Mississippi River. He discusses the relationship of freedmen with various plantation owners and the activities of freedmen to purchase land and exercise their new right to vote.

2198.   Roediger, David. "Racism, Reconstruction, and the Labor Press: The Rise and Fall of the St. Louis *Daily Press*, 1864-1866." *Science and Society* 42 (Summer 1978): 156-177.   The downfall of the *Daily Press* in 1866 is attributed, in part, to the racism and anti-Republicanism that divided the labor movement in St. Louis.

Society, Education and Religion

2199.   Christensen, Lawrence O. "Black St. Louis: A Study of Race Relations, 1865-1916." Ph.D. University of Missouri, Columbia, 1972. 373p.

2200.   Christensen, Lawrence O. "Schools For Blacks: J. Milton Turner in Reconstruction Missouri." *Missouri Historical Review* 76 (January 1982): 121-135. Ills. Port.   Col. F. A. Seely of the Freedmen's Bureau and Thomas A. Parker, State Superintendent of Schools, hired Turner to travel the state to establish schools for black children. Turner's letters to Seely are used to illustrate the work that was done and the problems that he encountered with local school officials. (For a review of Turner's post-Reconstruction career see also Christensen's "J. Milton Turner: An Appraisal," *Missouri Historical Review* 70 (October 1975): 1-19; and Irving Dillard's "James Milton Turner: A Little Known Benefactor of his People." *Journal of Negro History* 19 (October 1934): 372-411.)

2201.   Holland, Antonio F. and Gary R. Kremer (eds.). "Some Aspects of Black Education in Reconstruction Missouri: An Address by Richard B. Foster." *Missouri Historical Review* 70 (January 1976): 184-198. Ills. Ports.   Foster served with the 62nd U.S. Colored Infantry in the Civil War. After the war he helped organize schools for black children with funds raised by black soldiers. In his address to the State Teachers' Association at St. Louis on May 17, 1869, Foster spoke of the difficulties encountered by schools for black children and how it was necessary to reach more children than only the small fraction then attending.

2202.   Hughes, John Starrett. "Lafayette County and the Aftermath of Slavery." *Missouri Historical Review* 75 (October 1980): 51-63. Ills.   Hughes emphasizes the deteriorating race relations in west central Missouri and the county seat of Lexington. The white community was nervous about the presence of freed slaves, and the Ku Klux Klan sought to maintain control by intimidating both blacks and white Republicans. The Lexington *Weekly Caucasian* espoused white supremacy, including the removal of blacks from the U.S.

2203.   Hunter, Lloyd A. "Missouri Confederate Leaders After the War." *Missouri Historical Review* 67 (April 1973): 371-396. Ills. Ports.   William B. Hesseltine's studies of the careers of Confederate military and civil leaders after the war (see # 1464, 1510, 1768, 2163) form the basis of Hunter's work. Hunter believes that Missourians generally favored Robert E. Lee's flexible approach to postwar conditions in the South even though they frequently spoke with the defiance of Jefferson Davis. Particular mention is made of M. Jeff Thompson, Sterling Price, Warwick Hough, John B. Clark, Sr. (and Jr.), Thomas Caute Reynolds, John Sappington Marmaduke, William Henry Hatch, Francis Marion Cockrell, and George G. Vest.

2204.   Richardson, Joe M. "The American Missionary Association and Black Education in Civil War Missouri." *Missouri Historical Review* 69 (1974-1975): 433-448. Ills.   The leadership of the American Missionary Association in the education of freedmen in Missouri began in earnest in March, 1863 with the arrival of J. L. Richardson in St. Louis. Richardson emphasizes the dedication of the A.M.A. teachers, despite the opposition from the local white community. Most of the support for A.M.A. activities came from the black community.

2205.   Wamble, Gaston Hugh.   "Negroes and Missouri Protestant Churches Before and After the Civil War." *Missouri Historical Review* 61 (April 1967): 321-347.   Wamble examines the records of 35 Protestant, mainly Baptist, churches in Missouri for relations between white and black congregants both prior to and after the Civil War. Integrated churches were common before the war, and they included black slaves. After emancipation when the exercise of freedom led black Protestants to establish their own churches.   Racial segregation among churches usually occurred amicably.

2206.   Williams, Henry Sullivan. "The Development of the Negro Public School System in Missouri." *Journal of Negro History* 5 (April 1920); 137-165.   The Republican dominated state government rewrote the constitution in 1865 to include public education for all children irrespective of color. Implementation of schools for blacks was uneven throughout the state because of Confederate sympathies, but progress was made through the rest of the century. By 1915 Missouri was ahead of every former slave state in providing equal funding of education for black and white students.

North Carolina

General History

2207.   Carson, William W.   "Social and Economic Reconstruction in North Carolina." Ph.D. University of Wisconsin, 1914.

2208.   Davis, J. R. "Reconstruction in Cleveland County." *Historical Papers* of the *Trinity College Historical Society,* Duke University 10 (1914): 5-31.   Davis offers a brief account of Cleveland County after the Civil War, including a description of social and economic conditions, education and churches, local government, Ku Klux Klan activities, and the Democratic and Republican Parties.

2209.   Hamilton, J. G. de Roulhac. "Reconstruction in North Carolina." Ph.D. Columbia University, 1906. 683p. (Rpt. in Raleigh: Edward, 1906; *Columbia University Studies*, v. 141, no. 58 (1914); Gloucester: P. Smith, 1964)

2210.   Ruark, Bryant Whitlock. "Some Phases of Reconstruction in Wilmington and the County of New Hanover." *Historical Papers of the Trinity College Historical Society,* Duke University 11 (1915): 79-112.   Ruark discusses developments in education, the judicial system, health conditions, society, agriculture, business, and politics in New Hanover County. He also refers to political conditions specifically in Wilmington from 1865 through the election of July, 1868.

2211.   Zuber, Richard. *North Carolina During Reconstruction.* Raleigh: North Carolina Division of Archives and History, 1996. 67p. Bibl. (Rpt. of 1966 edition).   Zuber offers a brief summation of politics, industrial development, religion, and education after the war. He seeks to dispel traditional stereotypes and misconceptions, and he mentions the progress made during Reconstruction in education, industry, and the Republican constitution.

Politics and Law

2212.   Anderson, Eric. "James O'Hara of North Carolina: Black Leadership and Local Government." In *Southern Black Leaders of the Reconstruction Era.* Edited by Howard N. Rabinowitz. Urbana: University of Illinois Press, 1982. Pp. 101-125. Port. Tbl. Notes.   O'Hara, raised from infancy in the West Indies, arrived in North Carolina in 1862 and lived there for the the rest of his life. O'Hara's career in local politics from the mid to late 1870s and his service in Congress (1883-1887) illustrate that black participation in politics was anchored in the Republican Party at the county and local levels.

2213.   Balanoff, Elizabeth. "Negro Legislators in the North Carolina General Assembly, July, 1868-February, 1872." *North Carolina Historical Review* 49 (January 1972): 22-55. Ills. Ports. Tbl.   Thirty-four black legislators served as either representatives or senators in the General Assembly between 1868 and 1872. Balanoff surveys the backgrounds and contributions of many in this group and finds that, in general, they were not oriented toward strictly radical proposals. They demanded action to protect personal safety and basic civil rights for blacks, but they took moderate stands on school integration and enfranchising all whites.

2214.   Bond, James E. "Ratification of the Fourteenth Amendment in North Carolina." *Wake Forest Law Review* 20 (Spring 1984): 89-119.   Bond examines local interpretations of the amendment as revealed in the ratification debate in newspapers. He finds that the voluminous public debate and reports on political speeches lead to the conclusion that North Carolinians did not suspect or consider that Section 1 of the 14th Amendment incorporated the Bill of Rights. There was agreement that it protected civil rights, but conservatives were quick to exclude any guarantee of the right to vote.

2215. Boyd, W. K. "William W. Holden." *Historical Papers of the Historical Society of Trinity College*, Series 3 (1899): 39-78, 90-130.   Boyd seeks an unbiased account of Holden's public career as a journalist and governor of North Carolina prior to and during Reconstruction. He believes that Holden's dedication to upholding the law was admirable and that the governor did not deserve to be impeached after Democrats regained control of the legislature.

2216. Brown, Norman D. "A Union Election in Civil War North Carolina." *North Carolina Historical Review* 43 (Autumn 1966): 381-400. Ports.   Unionists attempted to hold an election in January, 1863 to elect a representative to Congress and to bring the state back into the Union. Congress rejected the election due to a small turnout.   The election revealed a class split between slaveholders and nonslaveholders.

2217. Browning, James B. "The North Carolina Black Code." *Journal of Negro History* 15 (October 1930): 461-473.   The black code in North Carolina was one of the most liberal among the Southern states, but it still sought to preserve white domination and to show the freedmen their "place" in society. The code was an expression of social order which, Browning points out, continues in his own day.

2218. Burnstein, Leonard. "The Participation of Negro Delegates in the Constitutional Convention of 1868 in North Carolina." *Journal of Negro History* 34 (July 1949): 391-409.   Of the 120 delegates at the convention of 1868, 13 were blacks. Burnstein uses the *Journal of the Constitutional Convention of North Carolina* (Raleigh, 1868), and a Raleigh newspaper, the *Sentinel*, to provide details of black delegate participation on various issues.

2219. Cotton, William D. "Appalachian North Carolina: A Political Study, 1860-1889." Ph.D. University of North Carolina, 1955. 593p.

2220. Crow, Jeffrey J. "Thomas Settle Jr., Reconstruction, and the Memory of the Civil War." *Journal of Southern History* 62 (November 1996): 689-726. Settle, a former North Carolina Democrat, rejected secession and emerged from the Civil War as an ardent Unionist bent on reforming his state. He participated in Reconstruction as a key person in the Republican Party, a judge, and one who supported party reforms. His campaign for governor against Zebulon Vance in 1876 revealed his ideas about the meaning of the war and the attempts to reform Southern society. Settle cannot be classified as a stereotypical radical scalawag, and he represents the best the Republicans could offer in a highly reactionary state.

2221.   Daily, Douglass L. "The Elections of 1872 in North Carolina." *North Carolina Historical Review* 40 (Summer 1963): 338-360.   Daily describes the state and national election campaigns of 1872 when conservatives sought to recapture the governor's office and maintain control of the legislature, North Carolina Republicans gave tacit support to Liberal Republican Andrew Greeley at the national level, and won the gubernatorial race by a close margin.   But the conservatives actually had more to be happy about, because they held on to the legislature through their alliance with local Liberal Republicans.

2222.   Devin, William A. "Footprints of a Carpetbagger." *The Torch* 17 (April 1944): 16-19, 21.   Devin provides a sketch of Albion W. Tourgée's career in North Carolina that won for him the respect of friend and foe alike.

2223.   Dorris, Jonathan Truman. "Pardoning North Carolinians." *North Carolina Historical Review* 23 (July 1946): 360-401.   As provisional governor, William H. Holden administered the pardon program in North Carolina in accordance with President Johnson's general amnesty of May 29, 1865. With very few exceptions, all individuals who requested pardons received them until Jonathan Worth became governor in November, 1865.   Dorris highlights cases of individuals who were rejected in accordance with the provisions of the 14th Amendment.   Rejections included ex-governors William A. Graham, Henry T. Clark, and Zebulon Baird Vance. He shows how pardons were used for political purposes.

2224.   Drumm, Austin M. "Union League in the Carolinas." Ph.D. University of North Carolina, 1955.

2225.   Escott, Paul D. "White Republicanism and Ku Klux Klan Terror: The North Carolina Piedmont During Reconstruction." In *Race, Class, and Politics in Southern History: Essays in Honor of Robert F. Durden.* Edited by Jeffrey J. Crow et. al. Baton Rouge: Louisiana State University Press, 1989. Pp. 3-34. Maps. Support for the Republican Party in the piedmont region of North Carolina was more complex than many historians have described. Blacks and a large minority of lower class whites supported the Republicans.   White supporters wanted a more democratic social and political environment that would be conducive to their needs. The Klan fought this coalition with violence and brought the Democrats back to power, but the Republican coalition remained viable for decades.

2226.   Evans, William McKee. *Ballots and Fence Rails: Reconstruction on the Lower Cape Fear.* Chapel Hill: University of North Carolina Press, 1967. 314p. Apps. Bibl. Tbls.   Evans examines the political and economic adjustments in the counties of Lower Cape Fear in southeastern North Carolina. The major themes include the struggle for power between Republicans and white conservatives, the new found political rights of the freedmen, and the gradually changing economy in which the two largest industries, rice and naval stores, experienced significant reductions. Republican rule brought stability to the region, despite corruption and the Ku Klux Klan. (See also Evans' Ph.D. dissertation with the same title from University of North Carolina, 1965.)

2227.   Evans, William McKee. *To Die Game: The Story of the Lowry Band, Indian Guerrillas of Reconstruction.* Baton Rouge: Louisiana State University Press, 1971. 282p. Bibl. Map. Ports.   Evans writes about the violence between a band of Lumbee Indians and the Ku Klux Klan in the lowland region of North Carolina near the Lumber River.   The band, led by Henry Berry Lowry and Stephen Lowry, exacted retribution for the killing of Indians, blacks, and white Republicans as well as grievances from prewar days when Indians were denied civil rights and much of their land by white Southerners. Evans concludes that the Republican's call for law and order in the state was never backed up with action, thus leading to Lowry band to apply their own brand of justice.

2228.   Ewing, Cortez A. M.   "Two Reconstruction Impeachments." *North Carolina Historical Review* 15 (July 1938): 204-230. Tbls.   The impeachments described are those of Governor William W. Holden in 1870 and Superior Court Judge Edmund W. Jones in 1871.   The Democratic legislature impeached Holden for declaring martial law in Alamance County and sending a strong military force to put down Ku Klux Klan violence against blacks.   Ewing agrees with the impeachment on these grounds because Holden used martial law for political purposes. Jones, a Republican, drew the ire of Democrats due to drunkenness and other misbehavior.

2229.   Folk, Edgar E. and Bynum Shaw. *W. W. Holden: A Political Biography.* Winston-Salem, N.C.: John F. Blair, 1982. 285p. Bibl. Chron.   Prior to the war Holden was the political editor of the *Raleigh Standard*, the "most powerful newspaper in North Carolina in the 19th century" (p. ix). Originally a secessionist, he turned against the war.   President Johnson appointed him governor in 1865, and in 1868 he won election as a Republican.   The authors argue against accusations of corruption against Holden by emphasizing that he sought to uphold the law and maintain security.   The Ku Klux Klan politically destroyed him with violence, and after he invoked marital law against them in Alamance and Caswell Counties in 1870, the Democratic state legislature impeached and convicted him for abuse of power.

2230.   Graham, William A. *The Papers of William Alexander Graham.* 8 Vols. Edited by Max R. Williams.   Raleigh: North Carolina Department of Cultural Resources, Division of Archives and History, 1957-1992. Ports.   Volumes 6, 7 and 8 include letters and other documents written by or to Graham about the Southern defeat and Reconstruction.   Graham was a former governor (1845-1848) who opposed secession, but remained loyal to his state and the South.   In Reconstruction he supported white supremacy and believed Northern influence in his state was a disaster for Southern civilization.

2231.   Hamilton, J. G. de Roulhac   (ed.).   *The Correspondence of Jonathan Worth.* 2 Vols. Raleigh: Edwards and Broughton, 1909. 1313p. Port.   Worth opposed secession in 1861 but accepted it as reality.   He served in the North Carolina senate and encouraged citizens to fight against the enemies of the Confederacy.   In November, 1865 he defeated Provisional Governor William W. Holden in the gubernatorial election.   Worth was a popular and accomplished governor until the Reconstruction Acts led him to forgo reelection in 1868. Nearly all of the letters printed in both volumes come from Worth's "private tissue letter-books" (p. iii) and represent only a small part of his correspondence. The letters range from February, 1841 to September, 1869. The majority were written by Worth during his years as governor.

2232.   Hamilton, J. G. de Roulhac. "The Elections of 1872 in North Carolina." *South Atlantic Quarterly* 11 (April 1912): 143-152.   Republican Governor Tod R. Caldwell   (1870-1874) ran for reelection against the Conservative candidate, Augustus S. Merrimon, who received support from both the Democratic Party and the Liberal Republicans.   Republican fraud led to Caldwell's victory, but the Conservative/Democratic coalition retained control of the legislature.   Republican power continued into the November national election when President Grant carried the state.

2233.   Hamilton, J. G. de Roulhac. "The North Carolina Convention of 1865-1866." *Proceedings and Addresses of the 14th Annual Session of the State Literary and Historical Association of North Carolina, Raleigh, November 20-21, 1913.* Raleigh: Edwards & Broughton, 1913.   Hamilton reviews the work of the North Carolina constitutional convention and generally praises it for complying with President Johnson's Reconstruction policies.   He refers to the convention as a progressive body that sought to enhance democracy in the state, but the people rejected the proposed constitution in August, 1866.

2234.   Harris, William C.   "Lincoln and Wartime Reconstruction in North Carolina, 1861-1863." *North Carolina Historical Review* 63 (April 1986): 149-168. Ills. Ports.   North Carolina is a case study in the failure of Lincoln's policy of voluntary reconstruction and reunion.   Lincoln shifted to a more proactive policy when he issued the Emancipation Proclamation in December, 1862 and the Proclamation of Amnesty and Reconstruction in December, 1863.

2235.   Harris, William C. *William Woods Holden: Firebrand of North Carolina Politics.* Baton Rouge: Louisiana State University Press, 1987. 332p. Bibl. Ill. Ports.   As governor from 1868 to 1871, Holden's efforts at racial and political reform generated local hatred of him, and he faced impeachment after the new conservative legislature elected in 1870 accused him of fraud, mismanagement, and unlawful use of power to put down the Ku Klux Klan. Harris seeks a thorough, balanced account of Holden's life and the context in which he lived. He discusses the changing opinions of historians about Holden from the conservative, post-Reconstruction perspective that was influenced by strong hatred of Holden, to the revisionists who depicted him as class conscious and ambitious but sincere in his efforts to maintain order during a violent time.

2236.   Harris, William C. "William Woods Holden: In Search of Vindication." *North Carolina Historical Review* 59 (Autumn, 1982): 354-372. Ills. Ports.   After Reconstruction Holden sought to vindicate himself of charges of corruption and violations associated with quelling white violence.   A core of friends assisted

Holden, but it was only after his death in 1892 that kind words about his political and journalistic career appeared in the press and from the political establishment. Harris survey's Holden's political career and indicates that various factors inflamed contemporary opinion against him, including his reputation as editor of the *Raleigh Standard* and his support for black political equality. Until the 1950s most historians vilified Holden.

2237.   Holden, William Woods. *Memoirs of W. W. Holden.* Durham, N. C.: Seeman Printery, 1911. 199p. App. *(John Lawson Monographs of the Trinity College Historical Society,* Duke University, 2)   Holden, provisional governor of North Carolina after the Civil War and later elected Republican governor from 1868 to 1871, dictated his memoirs to his daughter in 1889/1890 when he was 71 years old. According to William K. Boyd, who introduces the work, Holden was infirm and his memory was sometimes inaccurate or incomplete. The book includes the text of various documents from the period of Reconstruction and testimony about the Holden-Kirk War in 1870. The war was Gov. Holden's attempt at a military solution to Ku Klux Klan violence in the state. It contributed to his impeachment in 1871.

2238.   Houghton, Jonathan Thomas Young. "The North Carolina Republican Party: From Reconstruction to the Radical Right." Ph.D. University of North Carolina at Chapel Hill, 1993. 399p.

2239.   Lancaster, James L. "The Scalawags of North Carolina, 1850-1868." Ph.D. Princeton University, 1974. 609p.

2240.   Massengill, Stephen E. "The Detectives of William W. Holden, 1869-1870." *North Carolina Historical Review* 62 (October 1985): 448-487. Facim. Ills. Ports. Tbls.   Gov. Holden hired private detectives to investigate Ku Klux Klan violence in North Carolina, particularly in the north-central counties. The detectives were ineffective and replaced by militia in 1870. The Kirk-Holden war resulted in the lessening of Klan violence but led to Holden's impeachment after conservatives gained control of the legislature in the fall of 1870. Massengill includes the names and backgrounds of detectives.

2241.   McDuffie, Jerome Anthony. "Politics in Wilmington and New Hanover County, North Carolina, 1865-1900: The Genesis of a Race Riot." Ph.D. Kent State University, 1979. 851p.

2242.   McGee, Edward H. "North Carolina Conservatives and Reconstruction." Ph.D. University of North Carolina, 1972. 399p.

2243.   McIver, Stuart. "The Murder of a Scalawag." *American History Illustrated* 8 (April 1973): 12-18. Ills. Ports.   McIver describes the murder of State Senator John W. Stephens by the Ku Klux Klan during the state election campaign in Caswell County on May 21, 1870. The murder, one of many committed by the

Klan prior to the election, could not be traced to any individuals until Klansman John W. Lea spoke about the incident for the first time in 1919.

2244.   McKinney, Gordon.   "The Klan in the Southern Mountains: The Lusk-Shotwell Controversy." *Appalachian Journal* 8 (Winter 1981): 89-104.   Virgil Lusk, a former Confederate officer, joined the Republican Party in North Carolina after the war and became Solicitor of the 12th Judicial Circuit.   He wrote a description of his confrontation with Randolph Shotwell, a leader of the Ku Klux Klan and editor of the Asheville *Citizen*.   McKinney provides a copy of Lusk's document that describes Klan activities in the North Carolina mountains.

2245.   McPherson, Elizabeth Gregory.   "Letters From North Carolina to Andrew Johnson." *North Carolina Historical Review* 27 (July 1950): 336-363; 27 (October 1950): 462-490; 28 (January 1951): 63-87; 28 (April 1951): 219-237; 28 (July 1951): 362-375; 28 (October 1951): 486-516; 29 (January 1952): 104-119; 29 (April 1952): 259-277; 29 (July 1952): 400-431; 29 (October 1952): 569-578.   The letters were taken from the papers of Andrew Johnson at the Library of Congress. Nearly all were written during his presidency, and a few were written as early as 1859 and as late as 1875.   The letters cover a wide range of issues, but they are particularly concerned with pardons, requests for office, thoughts on the condition of the South, and politics in North Carolina.

2246.   Miller, Robert D.   "Samuel Field Phillips: The Odyssey of a Southern Dissenter." *North Carolina Historical Review* 57 (Summer 1981): 263-280.   Ills. Ports.   Miller examines Phillips' career as a Unionist and Whig who supported the Confederacy but lost faith with the Democratic Party by 1865.   He supported black civil rights, including suffrage, in a white ruled government with the hope of avoiding Radical rule.   As Solicitor General of the U.S. from 1872 until 1885, he worked to ensure civil rights for blacks, and he earned the status of Southern dissenter and supporter of racial equality.

2247.   Morrill, James Ray III.   "North Carolina and the Administration of Brevet Major General Sickles." *North Carolina Historical Review* 42 (Summer 1965): 291-305.   Daniel E. Sickles was commander of the Second Military District from the spring of 1867 until August 26, 1867.   Morrill describes how Sickles followed the laws established in the Reconstruction Acts and did not insert himself into partisan politics. Many North Carolinians saw him as a Radical by the time of his departure, but Morrill believes that he acted impartially and lawfully, and he worked to improve justice and civil rights for the freedmen.

2248.   O'Brien, Gail W.   "Power and Influence in Mecklenburg County, 1850-1880. *North Carolina Historical Review* 54 (April 1977): 120-144.   Ills. Ports. Tbls.   O'Brien analyzes the transition from prewar to postwar power structures in the South by testing theories proposed by Eugene Genovese   (i.e. prewar, slaveholding planter domination in a preindustrial society) and C. Vann Woodward (i.e. postwar, Whig influence on industrialization that dominated the planter class). Using census data for Mecklenburg County, a region that included the urban center of Charlotte, O'Brien examines occupations, property values, and social and political participation. He concludes that the power structure in the county changed little during the period studied. The power elites before the Civil War were nonfarm, slaveholding professionals, and the postwar elites came from the same group.

2249.   Olsen, Otto H.   *Carpetbagger's Crusade: The Life of Albion Winegar Tourgée.* Baltimore: Johns Hopkins Press, 1965. 395p. Bibl. Ills. Ports.   Olsen provides a detailed examination of Tourgée's life with particular emphasis on North Carolina during Reconstruction, his literary contributions, and his struggle against the erosion of democracy. Tourgée, a native of Maine and resident of Ohio, fought vigorously against the racist, caste system of the postwar South while living in North Carolina, and after leaving the state, his efforts extended to Northern society as well. Olsen reviews Tourgée's writing career with emphasis on *A Fool's Errand* (see # 1342) and *Bricks Without Straw* (see # 1342). He describes these works as sophisticated and still relevant for understanding 19th century racism. Tourgée's dedicated commitment to equal rights for all citizens placed him ahead of his time. (See also Olsen's "A Carpetbagger: Albion W. Tourgée and Reconstruction in North Carolina." Ph.D. Johns Hopkins University, 1959. 507p.; and "Albion W. Tourgée: Carpetbagger," *North Carolina Historical Review* 40 (Autumn 1963): 434-454 for a character sketch.)

2250.   Olsen, Otto H.   "The Ku Klux Klan: A Study in Reconstruction Politics and Propaganda." *North Carolina Historical Review* 39 (Summer 1962): 340-362. Olsen focuses on the Piedmont region of North Carolina where the Klan was very active, particularly in Alamance, Caswell, and Orange Counties. The Klan was a terrorist organization that succeeded because it had the backing of the conservative press, and it conspired to obstruct legal attempts to convict perpetrators of violence. Olsen stresses the fallacy of KKK propaganda by examining the reasons whites gave for their support of the Klan, including black crime, Union Leagues, and Republican judges. He also emphasizes the controversial rulings of Judge Albion W. Tourgée.

2251.   Olsen, Otto H.   "North Carolina - An Incongruous Presence." In *Reconstruction and Redemption in the South.* Edited by Otto Olsen. Baton Rouge: Louisiana State University Press, 1980. Pp. 156-201.   North Carolina Republicans enjoyed some electoral success with the election of William W. Holden as governor in 1868, but the support of black voters and many whites was not enough to overcome the domination of conservatives in every other facet of society. White conservatives resented alien ideas from the North and used deceit, intimidation and violence to weaken Republican attempts to provide economic and political reforms. The Republican Party was probably doomed to failure anyway, because the party could not build a strong voting base and had no clear ideological approach that was acceptable to most whites citizens.

2252.   Olsen, Otto H. and Ellen Z. McGrew (eds). "Prelude to Reconstruction: the Correspondence of State Senator Leander Sams Gash, 1866-1867." Part I. *North Carolina Historical Review* 60 (January 1983): 37-88; Part II: Nov.-Dec.,

1866, 60 (April 1983): 206-238; Part III: Jan.-March, 1867, 60 (July 1983): 333-366. Ills. Ports.   Gash was a moderate, Unionist Whig who strongly disagreed with secession, but grudgingly recognized its reality. He came from the western mountain region of North Carolina where he prospered as a merchant and slaveholding farmer before emancipation. When the war ended he received a pardon and quickly won a seat in the state senate in 1865 and 1866. Olsen and McGrew provide 28 letters written by Gash and a few written to him by his wife and business associate. Gash's letters illustrate that he did not support radical reforms in civil rights for blacks, and he was generally disappointed with Congressional Reconstruction. Extensive footnotes are included.

2253.   Olsen, Otto H.   "Reconsidering Scalawags."   *Civil War History* 12 (December 1966): 304-320.   Olsen emphasizes the continuity of political differences in North Carolina from prewar to postwar political rivalries and issues revolving around reform, unionism, class, and sectional divisions. The Republican Party, led by William Holden, relied on biracial unity to achieve success, but it failed because Republicans were weakened by internal factions, excessive political idealism, and the inability to protect supporters from violence.

2254.   Padgett, James A. (ed.).   "Reconstruction Letters From North Carolina. Part I, Letters to Thaddeus Stevens." *North Carolina Historical Review* 18 (April 1941): 171-195.   Includes 15 letters printed from the manuscripts of Edward McPherson at the Library of Congress. The letters date from December, 1865 to February, 1868. The writers are various individuals who wrote on a wide range of Reconstruction issues.

2255.   Padgett, James A. (ed.).   "Reconstruction Letters From North Carolina. Part II, Letters to John Sherman." *North Carolina Historical Review* 18 (July 1941): 278-300; (October 1941): 373-388.   The 27 letters printed are from the Sherman manuscripts at the Library of Congress. Sherman was a U.S. senator from Ohio. The letters date from January, 1865 to November, 1877.

2256.   Padgett, James A. (ed.).   "Reconstruction Letters From North Carolina. Part III, Letters to William Tecumseh Sherman." *North Carolina Historical Review* 18 (October 1941): 389-392.   Includes 4 letters from General Sherman's collection at the Library of Congress dating from January, 1865 to September, 1874.

2257.   Padgett, James A. (ed.).   "Reconstruction Letters From North Carolina. Part IV, Letters to Elihu Benjamin Washburne." *North Carolina Historical Review* 18 (October 1941): 393-397.   Includes 3 letters from the Washburne collection at the Library of Congress dating from October 1867 to April, 1871. Washburne was President Grant's Secretary of State in 1869.

2258.   Padgett, James A. (ed.).   "Reconstruction Letters From North Carolina. Part VI, Letters to William E. Chandler." *North Carolina Historical Review* 19 (January 1942): 59-94.   Includes 56 letters or telegrams written from various persons from January, 1868 to January, 1878. Chandler was a New Hampshire

Radical Republican and Assistant Secretary of the Navy from 1865 to 1867. The letters express complaints from Republicans about Democratic state legislation and federal appointments. Padgett includes extensive footnotes.

2259.   Padgett, James A. (ed.). "Reconstruction Letters From North Carolina. Part VII, Letters to Edward McPherson." *North Carolina Historical Review* 19 (April 1942): 187-208.   Includes 29 letters from McPherson's collection at the Library of Congress dating from March, 1865 to February, 1875. McPherson was Clerk of the House of Representatives (1863-1875). The letters deal with newspaper or printer publishing contracts for government documents.

2260.   Padgett, James A. (ed.). "Reconstruction Letters From North Carolina. Part VIII, Letters to Carl Schurz." *North Carolina Historical Review* 19 (July 1942): 280-302.   Includes 23 letters from the Schurz collection at the Library of Congress dating from April, 1865 to October, 1878. Most of the letters deal with Schurz's leadership in the Liberal Republican Party and his participation in President Hayes' cabinet as Secretary of Interior.   A few letters are about the Republicans in North Carolina and national politics.

2261.   Padgett, James A. (ed.). "Reconstruction Letters From North Carolina. Part IX, Letters to Benjamin Franklin Butler." *North Carolina Historical Review* 19 (October 1942): 381-404; 20 (January 1943): 54-82; (April 1943): 157-180; (July 1943): 259-282; (October 1943): 341-370; 21 (January 1944): 46-71.   Includes 163 letters from the Butler papers at the Library of Congress dating from January, 1865 to November, 1877.   There is a mixture of general and commercial correspondence.

2262.   Padgett, James A. (ed.). "Reconstruction Letters From North Carolina. Part X, Letters to James Abram Garfield." *North Carolina Historical Review* 21 (April 1944): 139-157.   Includes 16 letters from the Garfield collection at the Library of Congress dating from April, 1868 to October, 1877. The letters deal with patronage and Republican politics.

2263.   Padgett, James A. (ed.). "Reconstruction Letters From North Carolina. Part XI, Letters to Salmon Portland Chase." *North Carolina Historical Review* 21 (July 1944): 232-238.   Includes several letters from Chase's papers at the Library of Congress dating from September, 1865 to February, 1868 dealing with Republican politics. Chase was an Ohio Republican who served as Secretary of the Treasury from 1861 to 1864 and Chief Justice of the Supreme Court from 1864 to 1873.

2264.   Padgett, James A. (ed.). "Reconstruction Letters From North Carolina. Part XII, Other Letters." *North Carolina Historical Review* 21 (July 1944): 239-247.   Includes letters to Lyman Trumbull (3) in January-April, 1872; Thaddeus Stevens (1) in March, 1867; Edward McPherson (3) in December, 1870; and Benjamin Franklin Wade (1) in February, 1868 (from Albion Tourgée).

2265.   Raper, Horace W. *William W. Holden: North Carolina's Political Enigma.*
Chapel Hill: University of North Carolina Press, 1985.   376p. Bibl. Ills. Ports.
(*James Sprunt Studies in History and Political Science*, v. 59)   President Johnson
appointed Holden, a Democrat, provisional governor in 1865, and in 1868 he was
elected governor as a Republican.   Raper describes Holden as a visionary and
pragmatic leader whose ideas were more attuned with the 20th century South than
Reconstruction.   His progressive approach to reform and his championing of the
rights of blacks set him apart from both Democrats and carpetbag Republicans.
Holden was the most influential public person of his era in North Carolina.   (See
also Raper's "William Woods Holden: A Political Biography." Ph.D. University
of North Carolina, 1951. 432p.)

2266.   Ratchford, B. U. "The North Carolina Public Debt 1870-1878." *North
Carolina Historical Review* 10 (January 1933): 1-20.   Some discussion is included
on the role of Reconstruction governments in the accumulation of debt, principally
from state bonds to aid railroad companies in North Carolina. Ratchford blames the
abuses of the Constitutional Convention of 1868 and the General Assembly (1868-
1870) for significantly increasing state indebtedness. He describes how the state
dealt with the debt after conservatives came back into power.

2267.   Reid, George W. "Four in Black: North Carolina's Black Congressmen,
1874-1901." *Journal of Negro History* 64 (Summer 1979): 229-243.   Of the four
black congressmen prior to 1901, one was elected during Reconstruction. John A.
Hyman, an ex-slave, participated in the state Republican Party and served as a
delegate at the state constitutional convention in 1868. He won election to the state
senate in 1868 and the U.S. Congress in 1874. James E. O'Hara, born in the West
Indies, was a lawyer who worked in Reconstruction politics, but did not win election
to Congress until 1882 and 1884. The later congressmen were Henry Phimmer
Cheatham (elected 1888, 1890) and John Mercer Langston (elected 1890). Reid
notes that all were elected from the predominately black 2nd Congressional District.

2268.   Russ, William A., Jr. "Radical Disfranchisement in North Carolina."
North Carolina Historical Review 11 (October 1934): 271-283.   The
distinguishing feature of the disenfranchisement of former rebels in North Carolina
was its extremely conservative nature. There were many disqualifications under the
Reconstruction Acts, but the state constitution did not disenfranchise anyone. But
this did not stop the election of Republicans to Congress because of the election
manipulation by Gen. E. R. S. Canby, Commander of the Second Military District.

2269.   Weiler, Dagmar. "An Examination Of Political Hegemony: Race, Class,
And Politics In Edgecombe County And Rocky Mount, North Carolina, 1865-
1900." Washington State University, 1991. 229p.

2270.   St. Clair, Kenneth E. "The Administration of Justice in North Carolina
During Reconstruction, 1865-1876." Ph.D. Ohio State University, 1939.

2271.   St. Clair, Kenneth E.   "Debter Relief in North Carolina During Reconstruction." *North Carolina Historical Review*   18 (July 1941): 215-235. Postwar humanitarian issues and preservation of the middle class effected approaches toward debtors.   Many debtors were protected from court actions and property confiscation, and imprisonment for debt was abolished.   The U.S. Supreme Court overruled these actions in favor of middle class creditors and credit contracts.

2272.   St. Clair, Kenneth E.   "Military Justice in North Carolina, 1865:   A Microcosm of Reconstruction."   *Civil War History* 11 (December 1965): 341-350. Martial law in North Carolina reflected the attitudes of the commanding officers, Maj. Gen. John M. Schofield and then Gen. Thomas H. Ruger.   They attempted to establish order, to reestablish a degree of civilian authority, and to uphold the right of testimony by the freedmen.

2273.   Starnes, Richard D.   "'Rule of Reb': Confederate Historical Memory and White Supremacy in North Carolina, 1865-1870." *Southern Historian* 17 (Spring 1996): 45-66.   The Reconstruction period in North Carolina exemplifies how collective and individual memories of the Old South and the Confederate defeat in the Civil War influenced the responses of the white population to Republican politics and black freedom.   By sentimentalizing the military defeat as the "Lost Cause" in the public media, particularly newspapers, and in the aggressive and violent activities of the Ku Klux Klan, memory became the motivation for white resistance to change, the demonization of Northern intruders, and the absolute insistence on white supremacy.   The memory of the Lost Cause remained part of the postwar psyche for decades.

2274.   Trelease, Allen W.   "Republican Reconstruction in North Carolina: A Roll-Call Analysis of the State House of Representatives, 1868-1870." *Journal of Southern History* 42 (August 1976): 319-344. Tbls.   Trelease studies the voting patterns of various groups of legislators during the only sessions when the Republicans outnumbered the Democrats from 1868 to 1870.   He analyses the votes of the Democrats and Republicans and provides detailed voting statistics of scalawags, carpetbaggers and blacks on 190 roll call votes covering a wide range of important issues.   Trelease notes that the scalawags, who comprised 52 of the 87 Republicans (there were 39 Democrats), saw their role as pushing through reforms that would increase democracy in the state.

2275.   Zuber, Richard.   *Jonathan Worth: A Biography of a Southern Unionist.* Chapel Hill: University of North Carolina, 1965. 351p. Bibl. Port.   Worth maintained support for the Union and the principle of state authority.   When he became governor in December, 1865 he worked to uphold state power in the face of federal, military encroachments, Radical Republican proposals, and attempts by conservative whites to persecute the freedmen.   His political views were consistent with President Johnson's Reconstruction program, and he tried to work with both Gen. Daniel E. Sickles and Edwin R. S. Canby to save the state from military rule. (See also Zuber's Ph.D. dissertation with the same title from Duke University, 1961.)

Agriculture, Labor, and Business

2276. Daniels, Jonathan. *Prince of Carpetbaggers*. Philadelphia: J. B. Lippincott Co., 1958. 319p. Port.   The carpetbagger that Daniels refers to is Milton S. Littlefield, a native of New York state, who ended the Civil War as an Union Army general and proceeded to North Carolina. Littlefield purchased the Republican newspaper, *The Standard* (Raleigh), from Governor William Holden and also became involved in the construction and financing of railroads in North Carolina and Florida. In this impressionistic work, Daniels uses Littlefield as the symbol of all that was disgraceful and dishonest with carpetbaggers.

2277. Hinton, Robert. "Cotton Culture on the Tar River: The Politics of Agricultural Labor in the Coastal Plain of North Carolina, 1862-1902." Ph.D. Yale University, 1993. 246p.

2278. Holt, Sharon Ann. "Making Freedom Pay: Freedpeople Working for Themselves, North Carolina, 1865-1900." *Journal of Southern History* 60 (May 1964): 229-262. Tbls.   The focus on the subjugation of freedmen by white landowners disregards the household economy generated by freedmen who independently engaged in work to generate money for family needs and to help schools. Holt focuses on Granville County with an emphasis on the proliferation of family businesses that supplemented contract wages and gave the freedmen the opportunity to feel that they had some power and control over their lives and their communities. These businesses included tobacco and food farming, and various services. (See also Holt's "A Time to Plant: The Economic Lives of Freedpeople in Granville County, North Carolina, 1865-1900." Ph.D. University of Pennsylvania, 1991. 343p.)

2279. Kenzer, Robert C. "The Black Businessman in the Postwar South: North Carolina, 1865-1880." *Business History Review* 63(Spring 1989): 61-87. Ills. Tbls. Kenser explores the data on black businessmen and their establishments from credit evaluations compiled by R. G. Dun and Co. in *The Merchant Agency Reference Book* in addition to other sources such as the U.S. census. R. G. Dun's publication offers detailed information on businesses nationwide from 1841 to 1880. Kenser reviews the data on 126 black establishments to determine the relationship between success of these businesses and whether the owner was free prior to the Civil War or freed after/during the war. He also studies the relationship between black economic opportunity and political power. He concludes that advantages of antebellum freedom, racial mixture, and market conditions were particularly influential to the success of black entrepreneurs. (See also Kenzer's *Enterprising Southerners : Black Economic Success in North Carolina, 1865-1915*. Charlottesville: University Press of Virginia, 1997. 178p.; and "Portrait Of A Southern Community, 1849-1881: Family, Kinship, And Neighborhood In Orange County, North Carolina," Ph.D. Harvard University, 1982. 260p.)

2280. Price, Charles L. "Railroads and Reconstruction in North Carolina, 1865-1871." Ph.D. University of North Carolina, 1959. 628p.

2281.   Trelease, Allen W. "The Passive Voice: The State and the North Carolina Railroad, 1849-1871." *North Carolina Historical Review* 61 (April 1984): 174-204. Ills. Maps. Ports.   There were concerns about government majority ownership of the North Carolina Railroad during the postwar years. Governors Jonathan Worth and William H. Holden both used patronage to control the company. The government was particularly involved after 1868, but evidence indicates that the operation of the railroad was not hampered. Opponents of government influence did not site evidence of mismanagement.

Society, Education and Religion

2282.   Alexander, Roberta Sue. "Hostility and Hope: Black Education in North Carolina During Presidential Reconstruction, 1865-1867."   *North Carolina Historical Review* 53 (April 1976): 113-132. Ills. Ports. Tbls.   Prior to the Reconstruction Acts in 1867 freedmen and Northern benevolent organizations worked hard to provide organized educational opportunities for black children and adults across the state. Blacks took the initiative to raise funds among themselves for education, particularly when donations from the North decreased and assistance from the Freedmen's Bureau was limited. Most whites were not opposed to black education as long as they could control the curriculum and teaching, but they were angered by Northern teachers who encouraged freedom and independence among the former slaves.

2283.   Alexander, Roberta Sue. "North Carolina Churches Face Emancipation and the Freedmen: An Analysis of the Role of Religion During Presidential Reconstruction, 1865-1867." *University of Dayton Review* 9 (Winter 1972): 47-65. Alexander examines the response of the Presbyterian, Baptist, Methodist, and Episcopalian churches in North Carolina to emancipation. The general theme of the responses was both sectional and racial, and they show how the churches contributed to postwar tensions. Southern white supremacy and racial control within the churches encouraged segregation and helped to drive black members to establish separate churches, usually as African Methodist Episcopal and A.M.E. Zion. The Episcopal Church encouraged blacks to stay within the Episcopal faith, and it cultivated black leaders and congregations.

2284.   Alexander, Roberta Sue. *North Carolina Faces the Freedmen: Race Relations During Presidential Reconstruction, 1865-1867.* Durham: Duke University Press, 1985. 238p. Bibl. Maps. Tbls.   Alexander focuses on statewide social, economic, and cultural developments in the state prior to Radical Reconstruction that were not well covered by earlier studies. The environment in North Carolina seemed different from most other Southern states due to its relatively small number of slaves and slaveowners and its liberal image toward race compared with other states. Alexander concludes that the period of Reconstruction up to the spring of 1967 showed that whites sought to dominate and control the lives of the freedmen and to restrict their freedoms as much as possible. Race relations deteriorated when blacks demanded civil rights and constructed their own institutions. (See also Alexander's Ph.D. dissertation with the same title from University of Chicago, 1974.)

2285.   Anderson, Mr. John H. "The University of North Carolina, Part 3: In the Reconstruction Era." *Confederate Veteran* 37 (March 1930): 91-94.   Anderson describes how the university experienced very difficult times after the Civil War, particularly regarding its lack of funding, the resignation of faculty in 1867, the closing of the university from 1871 to 1875, and its revival since it reopened in September, 1875. She refers to the important leadership of President David L. Swain until his death in 1868, and Kemp P. Battle, who helped revive the school from its low state.

2286.   Beck, Scott A. L.   "Freedmen, Friends, Common Schools and Reconstruction." *Southern Friend* 17, 1 (1995): 5-31.   The approach of Philadelphia and Baltimore Quaker organizations was to establish common schools for freedmen for practical, political, and religious education. Beck focuses on efforts made in North Carolina in the 1860s when public schools became part of the long term legacy of aid given by the Friends. He also describes the difficulties encountered by Northern teachers from whites opposed to black education and Republican ideology. Beck believes that the contribution of the common school to the freedom of blacks has been exaggerated, particularly in comparison with the need for economic opportunities recognized by Yardley Warner who experimented with combining education and land ownership near Greensboro. Quaker sympathy with abolitionism did not include incorporating racial equality into the Quaker community.

2287.   Bell, John L., Jr.   "Baptists and the Negro in North Carolina During Reconstruction." *North Carolina Historical Review* 42 (Autumn 1965): 391-409. The relationship between the freedmen and the Calvary Baptists in postwar years show a pattern of racial discrimination and black independence. The Baptists believed in the inferiority of blacks and would not allow equality of membership within the Church. Whites supported the establishment of black Sunday Schools, and decided that total separation of the races was best for the future. Black Baptists agreed with them, and as the number of black ministers increased, so too did black churches. Whites often gave physical and material assistance in the construction of black churches.

2288.   Bell, John L., Jr.   "The Presbyterian Church and the Negro in North Carolina During Reconstruction." *North Carolina Historical Review* 40 (Winter 1963): 15-36. Ports.   Before emancipation Southern Presbyterians sought black participation under white direction. After emancipation the Church enthusiastically offered to serve the spiritual welfare of blacks, but white church leaders practiced racial discrimination and contributed to the segregation of white and black Presbyterian churches. The Southern Presbyterian Church attempted to control black churches, but it gave up the policy in 1874.

2289. Bell, John L., Jr. "Samuel Stanford Ashley, Carpetbagger and Educator. *North Carolina Historical Review* 72 (October 1995): 456-483. Ills. Map. Ports. Ashley arrived in North Carolina in 1865 as the Freedmen's Bureau's superintendent of education for the Southern district of the state. He went on to make many contributions to education as an administrator for the American Missionary Association, state superintendent of public instruction, and organizer of a statewide system of tax supported public schools. Ashley fits the mold of carpetbaggers who supportered civil rights and property confisction, but he did not insist on integrated schools.

2290. Bogue, Jesse Parker. "Violence and Oppression in North Carolina During Reconstruction 1865-1873." Ph.D. University of Maryland, 1973. 304p.

2291. Bynum, Victoria. "Reshaping the Bonds of Womanhood: Divorce in Reconstruction North Carolina." In *Divided Houses: Gender and the Civil War*. Edited by Catherine Clinton and Nina Silber. New York: Oxford University Press, 1992. Pp. 320-333. Bynum compares divorce laws and petitions in prewar and postwar North Carolina to define the changing relationship between the state and the family within the context of traditional male domination. Prewar laws emphasized the preservation of family, but in the midst of postwar social and political disruptions, greater emphasis was placed on the rights of males as individuals while defining women only in the context of the family. Both white and black men could reject divorce instigated by wives, despite their own infidelity, as long as they did not abandon their wives. Women could be divorced merely for infidelity.

2292. Chaffin, Nora C. "A Southern Advocate of Methodist Unification in 1865." *North Carolina Historical Review* 18 (January 1941): 38-47. Braxton Craven, a Methodist Episcopal pastor in Raleigh, strongly advocated the reunification of the Northern and Southern branches of the Methodist Episcopal Church after the Civil War. He emphasized national unity over sectional differences that originally split the Church. On July 24, 1865 Craven wrote a letter to Rev. Bishop Edward R. Ames who was a national leader of the Northern Methodist Episcopal Church and a proponent of extending Church activities in the South. In the letter Craven outlines a proposal for reunification, including accepting only loyal members who have taken the oath of loyalty, and defends the character and culture of the South against Northern stereotypes.

2293. Chamberlain, Hope Summerell. *Old Days in Chapel Hill: Being the Life and Letters of Cornelia Phillips Spencer*. Chapel Hill: University of North Carolina Press, 1926. 325p. Ills. Ports. Chamberlain weaves Spencer's letters into her own description of Chapel Hill from the midninteenth century until the early twentieth century. Spencer's writings offer a perspective on the Civil War and Reconstruction, particularly with respect to the University of North Carolina with which she and her family were associated for many years.

2294. Cilly, Paul O. "Clinton A. Cilley, Yankee War Hero in the Postwar South: A Study on the Compatibility of Regional Values." *North Carolina Historical*

Review 68 (October 1991): 404-426. Ills. Ports.   Cilley established successful
relations with his neighbors in North Carolina. He administered the Freedmen's
Bureau in the western counties for several months in 1866 and continued to live in
the area until his death in 1900. Like many other Northern transplants, Cilly shared
many values with white Southerners that belie the stereotype of carpetbaggers in
Reconstruction.

2295.   Clement, Rufus Early. "A History of Negro Education in North Carolina,
1865-1928." Ph.D. Northwestern University, 1930.

2296.   Conner, R. D. W. "Rehabilitation of a Rural Commonwealth." *American
Historical Review* 36 (October 1930): 44-62.   Connor views Reconstruction as a
destructive period in North Carolina, but it brought unity to the white people of the
state as never before, and when it ended, a period of economic expansion and stable
race relations began.   Benevolent white rule in North Carolina created the best
environment of racial harmony in the South.

2297.   Coon, Charles L. "The Beginnings of the North Carolina City Schools,
1867-1887." *South Atlantic Quarterly* 12 (July 1913): 235-247.   Educational
reformers in the North Carolina constitutional convention of 1868 provided for poll
tax revenue to help support local schools. It was not until February, 1873 that
Wilmington and other towns sought local tax measures to support education, but
they met defeat and negative court rulings based on the unconstitutionality of a local
school tax. Only after Reconstruction were local tax measures widely approved.
White resistance centered on a reluctance to support educational facilities for blacks.

2298.   Edwards, Laura F. *Gendered Strife and Confusion: The Political Culture
of Reconstruction.* Urbana: University of Illinois Press, 1997. 378p. Bibl. Ills.
Edwards defines the intersection of gender, class, and race in relation to power and
aspirations of blacks and whites in postwar Granville County, North Carolina and
the South in general. She discusses family life, labor, and civil rights of elite and
poor whites and blacks. She finds that power in Southern society was not defined in
the context of only race but also elite versus poor. She focuses on sexual relations,
particularly black on white rape, ownership of wives and children, wage contracts,
tenant farming, male domination of political power, and the forces seeking to
suppress female expressions of power. (See also Edwards' "The Politics of
Manhood and Womanhood: Reconstruction in Granville County, North Carolina."
Ph.D. University of North Carolina, Chapel Hill, 1991. 389p.)

2299.   Edwards, Laura F. "'The Marriage Covenant is the Foundation of All Our
Rights': The Politics of Slave Marriages in North Carolina After Emancipation."
Law and History Review 14 (Spring 1996): 81-124.   In 1866 the state legislature
recognized slave marriages and cohabitations of men and women as legitimate
marriages. Edwards examines the legal and political implications of these and future
marriages in the black community in the context of civil rights. Marriage carried
certain rights and privileges that allowed blacks to extend their civil rights beyond
the severe limitations of the North Carolina black code.   Congressional

Reconstruction bolstered and enhanced their rights until Republican power in the state declined and was replaced by Democrats intent on reversing the reforms. Edwards links blacks and poor whites in the struggle for civil rights and cites various representative court decisions that define the postwar interaction of race, gender, and class. (See also Peter W. Bardaglio, *Reconstructing the Household: Families, Sex, and Law in the Nineteenth Century South*, University of North Carolina, 1995.)

2300.   Edwards, Laura F.   "Sexual Violence, Gender, Reconstruction, and the Extension of Patriarchy in Granville County, North Carolina." *North Carolina Historical Review* 68 (July 1991): 237-260. Facim. Ills.   Race and class played a role in male violence against women.   Edwards is particularly concerned with the sexual violence of lower class white males against black women.   During Reconstruction sexual violence against blacks represented the intentional degradation of blacks and women and the lack of female power.   She cites various law suits.

2301.   Farris, James J.   "The Lowrie Gang: An Episode in the History of Robeson County, N. C. 1864-1874." *Historical Papers of the Trinity College Society* Ser 15 (1925): 55-93.   The Lowrie Gang was a family of murderers and thieves that terrorized Robeson County throughout the years of Reconstruction. Farris explains that they were "half-breed Indians" (p. 57) from the Croatan tribe who were partly influenced by the social and economic depredations of the postwar period. He suggests that they were not brought to justice early in the postwar years because Republican regimes in North Carolina refused to vigorously pursue them due to the Republican sympathies of the Indians.

2302.   Fleming, John Emory.   "Out of Bondage: The Adjustment of Burke County Negroes After the Civil War, 1865-1890." Ph.D. Howard University, 1974. 234p.

2303.   Gross, Theodore L.   "The Fools Errand of Albion W. Tourgée." *Phylon* 24 (Fall 19630: 240-254.   Tourgée, a native of Ohio, moved his family to North Carolina in 1865 and lived there until 1879. He became perhaps the most hated carpetbagger in the state for his persistent criticism of white Conservatives. He also criticized local Republicans, such as Gov. William H. Holden, for their moderation and ability to compromise with the Conservatives. Despite his failures, he was praised for his honesty and fairness as Judge of the Superior Court   (1868-1974), and with his persistent radical agenda, he was admired for his courage and impact on the state constitution and laws.

2304.   Hamilton, J. G. de Roulhac.   "The Freedmen's Bureau in North Carolina." *South Atlantic Quarterly* 8 (January 1909): 53-67; 8 (April 1909): 154-163. Tbls. The bureau's positive contributions have been overlooked because it became "the most radical political agency in the South" (p. 53). Its work in relief and education were overshadowed by its corruption, political involvement, and promotion of false hopes to freedmen. The bureau was hurt by the ignorance and inefficiency of its local and national leadership.

2305.   Hickey, Damon D.   "Pioneers of the New South: The Baltimore Association and North Carolina Friends in Reconstruction." *Southern Friend* 11 (1989): 38-48.   The Baltimore Association of Friends to Advise and Assist Friends in the South in its effort to strengthen the Quaker community in North Carolina following the emigration of large numbers of brethren to other regions of the U.S. Francis T. King led the movement to establish common schools and a new mentality of education, progress, and reform that helped the redevelopment of the Quaker community and the organization of the association.

2306.   Hoffman, Carolyn Frances.   "The Development of Town and Country: Charlotte and Mecklenburg County, North Carolina, 1850-1880." Ph.D. University of Maryland, College Park, 1988. 253p.

2307.   Jones, Maxine D.   "The American Missionary Association and the Beaufort, North Carolina, School Controversy, 1866-1867." *Phylon* 48 (June 1987): 103-111.   The A.M.A. established a school for freedmen in Beaufort during November, 1863.   When it established a separate school for whites in December, 1866, but local blacks immediately protested as soon as it was clear that they were not welcome.   The incident seemed to indicate that the A.M.A. could be just as racist as most Southern whites, and it magnified several problems in communication and understanding between the Northern missionaries and Beaufort's black community.

2308.   Jones, Maxine D.   "'A Glorious Work':   The American Missionary Association and Black North Carolina, 1863-1880." Ph.D. Florida State University, 1982. 341p.

2309.   Jones, Maxine D.   "'They are My People': Black American Missionary Association Teachers in North Carolina During the Civil War and Reconstruction." *Negro Educational Review* 36 (April 1985): 78-89.   Jones describes the experiences of several black teachers in A.M.A. schools as a way to illustrate the significant contributions of blacks to education in Reconstruction.   She also points out the inconsistencies in the A.M.A.'s approach to race relations.

2310.   Jones, Maxine D.   "'They Too are Jesus' Poor': The American Missionary Association and the White Community in North Carolina." *Southern Studies* 23 (Winter 1984): 386-396.   A.M.A. workers in North Carolina sought to help destitute whites as well as the freedmen.   They helped whites by organizing schools and distributing clothing and food. In general, poor whites did not respond in a positive manner, because for them the A.M.A. represented Yankee intrusion, and whites who attended A.M.A. schools with blacks were ridiculed by other whites.

2311.   Keith, Alice B.   "White Relief in North Carolina, 1865-1867." *Social Forces* 17 (1938-1939): 337-355.   Keith uses newspapers and manuscripts as the basis for this discussion of mostly border state and Northern relief assistance to

North Carolina whites. The aid was mainly from private organizations that raised money and supplies for the destitute, but Keith also includes contributions from the Freedmen's Bureau. Local aid was often directed to poor and disabled Confederate soldiers.

2312.   Knight, Edgar W. "The Influence of the Civil War on Education in North Carolina." *Proceedings of the 18th Annual Session of the State Literary and Historical Association of North Carolina, Raleigh, November 20-21, 1917*. Raleigh: Edwards and Broughton, 1919. Pp. 52-60.   Knight believes that the post-bellum reforms in public education in North Carolina would have advanced more quickly and beneficially had it not been for the corruption of Radical Republicans and indiscretions of the Freedmen's Bureau that provoked the white population into opposition.

2313.   Magdol, Edward. "Against the Gentry: An Inquiry into a Southern Lower-Class Community and Culture, 1865-1870." In *The Southern Common People: Studies in Nineteenth-Century Social History*. Edited by E. Magdol and Jon L. Wakelyn. Westport: Greenwood Press, 1980. Pp. 191-210. (Rpt. from *Journal of Social History* 6 (Spring 1973): 259-283.)   Historical writing on Reconstruction does not cover the developing cultures of Southern lower classes. Magdol examines the lower class subculture in Robeson County where there was a community of blacks and Anglo-Indians. Both groups exhibited resistance to white upper class rule, and it was on this point that they showed the most cohesiveness as members of the same class.   The experiences of both groups in the competitive class environment of Reconstruction helped them to flourish and to recognize their own distinctiveness.

2314.   Miller, Robert D. "Of Freedom and Freedmen: Racial Attitudes of White Elites in North Carolina During Reconstruction, 1865-1877." Ph.D. University of North Carolina, 1976. 376p.

2315.   Mobley, Joe A. "In the Shadow of White Society: Princeville, a Black Town in North Carolina, 1865-1915." *North Carolina Historical Review* 63 (1986): 340-384. Ill. Ports. Tbls.   (Rpt. in *Church and Community Among Black Southerners 1865-1900*. Edited by Donald Nieman. New York: Garland, 1994. Pp. 28-72)   Princeville, located in Edgecombe County, was called Freedom Hill prior to 1885 and was part of a plantation where former slaves established a community of squatters. After the Civil War the town developed a cohesive community where black residents felt secure and had an opportunity to progress. Much of the article is about Princeville in the late 19th and early 20th centuries.

2316.   O'Brien, Roberta Gail. "War and Social Change: An Analysis of Community Power Structure, Guilford County, North Carolina, 1848-1882." Ph.D. University of North Carolina, 1975. 280p.

2317.   Padgett, James Absalom.   "From Slavery to Prominence in North Carolina." *Journal of Negro History* 22 (October 1937): 433-487.   Padgett discusses the social, economic, and educational progress from Reconstruction to the 1930s.

2318.   Piehl, Charles. "White Society in the Black Belt, 1870-1920: A Study of Four North Carolina Counties."   Ph.D.   Washington University, 1979.   430p. (Edgecombe County, Franklin County, Nash County, Wilson County)

2319.   Price, Charles L.   "John C. Barnett, Freedmen's Bureau Agent in North Carolina." *East Carolina University Publications in History* 5 (1981): 51-74.   Ills. After serving in the Northern Army Barnett became a Freedmen's Bureau agent near Charlotte.   His evenhanded and efficient service for freedmen and landowners belies the stereotype of bureau agents accepted by historians in the late 19th century.   Price describes Barnett as a conservative, sensitive agent who sought to ensure justice and civil rights for freedmen while also looking out for the labor concerns of plantation owners.

2320.   Reilly, Stephen Edward.   "Reconstruction Through Regeneration: Horace James' Work With the Blacks For Social Reform in North Carolina, 1862-1867." Ph.D. Duke University, 1983.

2321.   Scott, Rebecca. "The Battle Over the Child: Child Apprenticeship and the Freedmen's Bureau in North Carolina." *Prologue* 10 (Summer 1978): 101-113.   Ill. The issue of consensual and nonconsensual apprenticeships was complicated by the undefined nature of marriages that carried over from slavery and the legal status of their children.   Agents of the bureau were charged with resolving disputes over child indentureship, but their application of state and local laws was arbitrary until January, 1867 when the state Supreme Court ruled that parents or close relatives had to be given notice prior to the indentureship of their children.   Blacks resisted indentureship because it represented a new type of slavery.

2322.   Sutherland, Daniel E.   "Charles Force Deems and *The Watchman*: An Early Attempt at Post-Civil War Sectional Reconciliation."   *North Carolina Historical Review* 57 (October 1980): 410-426. Ills. Ports.   Deems, a Methodist clergyman, moved his family from North Carolina to New York City after the war. He established *The Watchman* (1865-1867), a newspaper dedicated to national reconciliation with a Southern tone.   Deems attempted to explain the Southern cause to Northerners with the hope of changing their attitudes toward the South, but his conservative tone depressed subscribers, and his occasional moderation turned away Southern readers.   Deems contributed to national reconciliation, although his newspaper was ahead of its time.

2323.   Thorpe, Margaret Newbold.   "A 'Yankee Teacher' in North Carolina." *North Carolina Historical Review* 30 (October 1953): 564-582.   Thorpe was a Quaker who went to Warrenton, North Carolina to teach in the freedmen school organized by the Friends' Association of Philadelphia and Its Vicinity for the Relief of Colored Freedmen.   Portions of her diary are printed from September, 1869 until April, 1871.   She describes her experiences as a 'Yankee teacher' in the

Reconstruction South. Richard L. Morton edited the diary entries and wrote an introduction.

2324. Walker, Jacqueline Baldwin. "Blacks in North Carolina During Reconstruction." Ph.D. Duke University, 1979. 222p.

2325. Westin, Richard B. "The State and Segregated Schools: Negro Public Education in North Carolina, 1863-1923." Ph.D. Duke University, 1966. 512p.

2326. Whitener, Daniel J. "Public Education in North Carolina During Reconstruction, 1865-1876." In *Essays in Southern History*. Edited by Fletcher Melvin Green. Chapel Hill: University of North Carolina Press, 1949. Pp. 67-90. (*James Sprunt Studies in History and Political Science*, 31) The North Carolina Constitution of 1868 established a structure for legalized racial integration in schools and financing public schools through taxation. In 1869 the state supreme court struck down the financing mechanism in the constitution and the School Law of 1869. Conservatives further disabled the law after they recaptured the legislature in 1871, but the basic concept remained.

2327. Whitener, Daniel J. The Republican Party and Public Education, 1867-1900." *North Carolina Historical Review* 37 (July 1960): 382-396. Although school legislation in North Carolina existed prior to Reconstruction, it was only during Reconstruction that the constitution authorized the General Assembly to establish a uniform system of public education supported by taxation. Whitener believes that the system of education was an important success that had a long term impact. The only error was not legislating against integrated schools which most Republicans opposed anyway. When the Democrats took control of the state in 1871, they restructured school financing and deemphasized public education.

South Carolina

General History

2328. Bellardo, Lewis Joseph, Jr. "A Social and Economic History of Fairfield County, South Carolina, 1865-1871." Ph.D. University of Kentucky, 1979. 515p.

2329. Burton, Orville V. "Ungrateful Servants? Edgefield's Black Reconstruction: Part 1 of the Total History of Edgefield County, South Carolina." Ph.D. Princeton University, 1976. 428p.

2330. Edgar, Walter. "The Civil War: Part II, 1865-1877." In *South Carolina: A History*. Columbia: University of South Carolina Press, 1998. 377-406. Edgar describes Reconstruction in the state as a white insurgency in the nature of a war intent on the rejection of Republican rule and equal rights for blacks. His main focus is politics and separating myth from reality.

2331.   Hollis, John Porter.   "The Early Period of Reconstruction in South Carolina." Ph.D. Johns Hopkins University, 1904. 129p. (See also *Johns Hopkins University Studies in Historical and Political Sciences*, vol. 23, no. 1-2, 1905; Rpt. by Johnson Reprint Co., 1973)

2332.   Macaulay, Neill W.   "South Carolina Reconstruction Historiography." *South Carolina Historical Magazine* 65 (January 1964): 20-32.   Macaulay describes and comments on the major works on Reconstruction in South Carolina published between the 1870s and the early 1960s. He includes general state histories, key articles, and monographs. No conclusions are drawn.

2333.   Reynolds, John S.   *Reconstruction in South Carolina, 1865-1877*. Columbia: The State Co., 1905. 522p. Port.   Reynolds characterizes the Reconstruction government in South Carolina as a completely corrupt, unjust, and oppressive regime dominated by blacks and their carpetbagger manipulators. He believes that the postwar state government formed in 1865 should have been given an opportunity to succeed. Instead, congressional Republicans sought vengeance and domination by oppressing the local, white population.

2334.   Simkins, Francis Butler and Robert Hilliard Woody.   *South Carolina During Reconstruction*. Chapel Hill: University of North Carolina Press, 1932. 610p. App. Bibl. Ills. Ports.   This book covers political, social, economic, educational, and religious life in South Carolina after the Civil War. It is considered a revisionist work for its recognition of positive results from Reconstruction and its greater objectivity toward the Republican governments and the participation of black citizens.

2335.   Taylor, Alrutheus A.   "The Negro in South Carolina During the Reconstruction." *Journal of Negro History* 9 (July 1924): 241-364; 9 (October 1924): 381-569. (Published as monograph by Washington, DC: The Association for the Study of Negro Life and History, 1924; New York: Russell and Russell, 1969; New York: AMS, 1971)   Taylor's study is an early revision of the widely accepted Reconstruction interpretations of William Dunning. He believes that Dunning's use of selected sources and interpretations was a deliberate attempt to justify personal prejudices. Taylor explains the freedmen's true contributions and activities during the period, and he argues against negative stereotypes about the freedmen, blames most of the political corruption on Northern and local opportunists, including some blacks, and discusses the intimidation and fraud perpetrated by Democrats against Republicans that corroded the rights of the freedmen. Taylor also writes about economic, social, and religious adjustments for blacks in the state.

2336.   Williamson, Joel.   *After Slavery: The Negro in South Carolina During Reconstruction, 1865-1867*. Chapel Hill: University of North Carolina, 1965. 442p. Bibl.   Williamson states that his work is a generational update to the work of Simkins and Woody (see # 2334). Their work was considered revisionist in its perspective towards Reconstruction. This book delivers a markedly upbeat message about blacks in South Carolina after the Civil War. In his coverage of reactions to freedom and the rise of a new order in economic, labor and race relations, Williamson recognizes the difficulties that the freedmen had to endure, but he projects an optimistic tone about their progress during the entire period of Reconstruction, particularly related to education, political rights, and the organization of black communities. (See also Williamson's "The Negro in South Carolina During Reconstruction, 1861-1877." Ph.D. University of California, Berkeley, 1964. 608p.; and Williamson's examination of the postwar mulatto elite in South Carolina *in New People: Miscegenation and Mulattoes in the United States*. Baton Rouge: Louisiana State University Press, 1995. Pp.77-93.)

2337.   Woody, Robert Hilliard.   "Studies in the Economic and Political Reconstruction of South Carolina." Ph.D. Duke University, 1930. 387p.

Politics and Law

2338.   Abbott, Martin. "County Officers in South Carolina in 1868." *South Carolina Historical Magazine* 60 (January 1959): 30-40.   Abbott prints a report delivered to Robert K. Scott shortly after his election as governor. The report, dated June 22, 1868, lists the current county officials in 16 counties with information about each person's post, political affiliation, ability to take the test oath of 1862, and whether they were black. Of the 119 officeholders in the 16 counties, 18 were black.

2339.   Abbott, Martin. "Freedom's Cry: Negroes and Their Meetings in South Carolina, 1865-1869." *Phylon* 20 (1950): 263-272.   During the early years of Reconstruction blacks took the initiative to organize themselves in celebration of their freedom and to discuss approaches and resolutions related to equal rights, voting, labor, and politics. The records of these meetings illustrate that blacks understood their freedom and could articulate their needs.

2340.   Abbott, Martin (ed.). "James L. Orr on Congressional Reconstruction." *South Carolina Historical Magazine* 54 (July 1953): 141-142.   Governor Orr wrote to U.S. Attorney General Henry Stanberry nine days after the passage of the Reconstruction Act of March 2, 1867 to express exasperation with the expected political, social, and economic consequences of the changes spelled out in the act. Orr expected the complete takeover of state government by the freedmen, and he predicted long term disaffection with the national government by white Southerners.

2341.   Abbott, Richard H. "A Yankee Views the Organization of the Republican Party in South Carolina, July 1867." *South Carolina Historical Magazine* 85 (July 1984): 244-250.   Abbott reprints a letter from Elbridge Gerry Dudley, a native of Massachusetts living in Beaufort, to John A. Andrew, wartime governor of the state.

The letter of July 31, 1867 describes the South Carolina Republican party organizing convention in Columbia. Dudley, a delegate at the convention, notes the high caliber of many of the black delegates. He was a supporter of emancipation and equal rights for blacks.

2342.   Allen, Walter.   *Governor Chamberlain's Administration in South Carolina: A Chapter of Reconstruction in the Southern States*. New York: G. P. Putnam's Sons, 1888. Port. 544p. (Rpt. in Negro Universities Press, 1969) Allen's book is a sympathetic account of Daniel Henry Chamberlain's period as Republican governor.   He quotes extensively from letters, newspapers, and government documents.   Chamberlain was elected in 1874 and reelected in 1876, but he was forced out of office by deals made in the national, disputed election of that year. Allen argues that if Chamberlain's Republican opponents had not worked against him, the Democrats would not have been successful.   He is particularly critical of the opposition of Robert B. Elliott, Speaker of the state House of Representatives, who opposed Chamberlain's conservative policies and his appeal to moderates in the state Democratic Party.

2343.   Aptheker, Herbert. "South Carolina Negro Conventions, 1865." *Journal of Negro History* 31 (January 1936): 91-97.   In the fall of 1865 conventions were held by freedmen in St. Helena Island and Charleston to petition the state constitutional convention and the legislature to demand equal civil rights as free men under the Declaration of Independence and the U.S. constitution.

2344.   Bell, John L., Jr. "Andrew Johnson, National Politics, and Presidential Reconstruction in South Carolina." *South Carolina Historical Magazine* 82 (October 1981): 354-366.   Bell examines Johnson's activities to organize a new, loyal government in South Carolina and concludes that the president's Reconstruction policy was not aimed at the organization of a new national political party as suggested by John and LaWanda Cox (see # 220). Johnson's appointment of Benjamin F. Perry as provisional governor on June 30, 1865 and his subsequent conversations with Perry do not seem to support the Cox's theory.

2345.   Bryant, Lawrence C.   (ed.).   *Negro Lawmakers in the South Carolina Legislature, 1868-1872*.   School of Graduate Studies, S.C. State College, 1968. 142p.   Brief information was compiled on each legislator.   The entries are arranged by county, and each includes information on land holdings and footnotes to sources used.

2346.   Bryant, Lawrence C.   *South Carolina Legislators: A Glorious Success, State and Local Officeholders, Biographies of Negro Representatives, 1868-1902. Commemorating South Carolina Tricentennial, 1970*. Orangeburg: South Carolina State College, L. C. Bryant Publ., 1974. 119p. App.   Provides information on a wide range of black officeholders, including postmasters, county commissioners, school commissioners, magistrates, officers of the state national guard, and national and state legislators.   The appendixes list blacks who served in the state House of

Representatives and Senate with their dates of service, county represented, and occupation.

2347.   Burton, Vernon.   "Edgefield Reconstruction Political Black Leaders." *Proceedings of the South Carolina Historical Association* (1988): 27-38.   Burton traces the development of local black political leaders in Edgefield. They sought and won leadership positions based on the support of the black community including close family ties and church. Most of the leaders were from the black social and economic elite, but upward mobility broadened as Reconstruction continued. Burton emphasizes that most black leaders were from the Edgefield area and many were ex-slaves.

2348.   Candelaro, Dominic.   "Louis Post as a Carpetbagger in South Carolina: Reconstruction as a Forerunner of the Progressive Movement." *American Journal of Economics and Sociology* 34 (October 1975): 423-432.   Condelaro argues that the experiences of Louis Post in Reconstruction influenced his later career as a progressive politician and publisher. Post believed in Radical rule in the South and maintained support for racial justice throughout his life. He published the Chicago *Public* from 1908 to 1913.

2349.   Carson, Mrs. J. R.   "The Great Triumvirate of the Reconstruction Period in South Carolina." *United Daughters of the Confederacy Magazine* 11 (September 1948): 6-8.   Carson describes the redemption of South Carolina from black carpetbagger misrule by white Democrats in 1876-77. The red shirt movement against the Republican government was led by Wade Hampton, Matthew Butler, and Martin Witherspoon Gary who are considered heroes of their state and democratic government.

2350.   Chamberlain, Daniel H.   "Reconstruction and the Negro." *North American Review* 128 (February 1879): 161-173.   The last Reconstruction governor of South Carolina presents a strong defense of black suffrage and their full, equal participation in the civil and political life of the nation. He views equal rights as a moral imperative, and criticizes people who reject universal manhood suffrage. Also, Chamberlain defends black contributions to Reconstruction governments and depicts white Southerners as racist, elitist, and perpetrators of caste and oppression.

2351.   Chamberlain, Daniel H.   "Reconstruction in South Carolina." *Atlantic Monthly* 87 (April 1901): 473-484.   Chamberlain, a Republican from Massachusetts, became increasingly conservative during his tenure as governor from 1874 to 1876.   In retrospect, Chamberlain believes that Congressional Reconstruction was a great error brought on by a vindictive minority in Congress, the South's harsh treatment of the freedmen, and President Johnson's foolish behavior. He describes Reconstruction as a struggle by whites to regain their rightful power taken by mostly ignorant blacks and unscrupulous white opportunists.   Chamberlain separates himself from Republicans who sought the continuation of black domination and corrupt rule.

2352.   Clark, E. Culpepper. *Francis Warrington Dawson and the Politics of Restoration: South Carolina, 1874-1889.* University, Ala.: University of Alabama Press, 1980. 251p. Bibl. Ills. Ports.   The first three chapters offer an examination of the politics involved in achieving a Democratic victory in the election of 1876. Dawson, who founded and edited the Charleston *News and Courier* beginning in April, 1873, supported cooperation between Democrats and Gov. Daniel Chamberlain's conservative Republican government. The "straight out" faction that spurned cooperation won over the state Democratic Party and controlled both the restoration government and the future position of the *News and Courier.*

2353.   Coleman, Caroline S.   "Origin of the 'Red Shirts' and Adoption of Uniform." *United Daughters of the Confederacy Magazine* 11 (July 1948): 12-13. Coleman describes in heroic terms the successful struggle of the red shirts - those men who were foot soldiers for Wade Hampton in the overthrow of Republican rule in 1876-77.

2354.   Cauthen, Charles Edward. *Family Letters of the Three Wade Hamptons 1782-1901.* Columbia: University of South Carolina, 1953. Pp. 117-154. App. Part 4 of this book includes letters written by Wade Hampton III to his sister referring to black laborers and one long letter written to President Johnson complaining about the course of Reconstruction in August, 1866.

2355.   Cummings, Charles M.   "The Scott Papers: An Inside View of Reconstruction." *Ohio History* 79 (Spring 1970): 112-118. Port.   Robert K. Scott served as head of the Freedmen's Bureau in South Carolina before his victories in the gubernatorial elections of 1868 and 1870. Although most impressions of Scott focus on negative aspects of his political career and his shady financial dealings, Cummings suggests that a group of Scott's private papers acquired by the Ohio Historical Society in 1969 provide a broader and clearer view of Scott's political career. The collection covers the years during and after Reconstruction.

2356.   Durden, Robert Franklin. *"The Prostrate State* Revisited: James S. Pike and South Carolina Reconstruction." *Journal of Negro History* 39 (April 1954): 87-110.   Pike, a Northern Republican journalist for the *New York Tribune*, expressed antislavery and anti-Southern sentiments in his writings. After the war he supported the Radicals and President Grant, but in 1872 Pike jumped to the Liberal Republicans led by his employer, Horace Greeley.   In his travel journal Pike describes conditions in South Carolina in a positive way, but his book, *The Prostrate State*   (New York: Appleton, 1873), was a political diatribe against Grant's Reconstruction policies and revealed Pike's racism that Durden traces back to antebellum days. (See also # 577)

2357.   Hall, Kermit L. and Lou Falkner Williams.   "Constitutional Tradition Amid Social Change: Hugh Lennox Bond and the Ku Klux Klan in South Carolina." *Maryland Historian* 16 (Fall-Winter 1985): 43-58.   Bond was one of the two federal judges who presided at the South Carolina Ku Klux Klan trials in 1871 and 1872. The authors describe Bond's judicial career and the famous trial.

Bond and Judge George S. Bryan took differing approaches toward the trial, with Bond seeking to enforce civil rights laws and Bryan emphasizing states' rights and Southern values. Bond is depicted as a moderate figure who symbolized the basic conservative nature of the judicial system. The authors explain that laws alone could not bring about reform, despite the theories of neorevisionist historians, such as McKitrick (see # 478), Franklin (see # 91), Stampp (see # 151), and Cox (see # 220).

2358.   Hennessey, Melinda Meek. "Racial Violence During Reconstruction: The 1876 Riots in Charleston and Cainhoy." *South Carolina Historical Magazine* 86 (April 1985): 100-112.   Hennessey counted 33 major riots in towns and cities throughout the South during Reconstruction. These racial incidents frequently shared characteristics, such as proximity to elections, black political meetings, and the ultimate victory of white rioters over black opponents. The Charleston County riots in 1876 illustrate the unique environment in Charleston compared with other Southern cities. Blacks were the majority population, and they had a tradition of resisting violence and oppression. This was evident in the 1876 riots.

2359.   Hine, William C. "Black Politicians in Reconstruction Charleston, South Carolina: A Collective Study." *Journal of Southern History* 49 (November 1983): 555-584. Tbls.   Hine compiled background information on 234 black men in Charleston from the period 1865 to 1875. His article is similar to the work of David Rankin (see # 1915) who studied characteristics of black leaders in New Orleans. Both Hine and Rankin seek to reveal the true nature of black politicians during Reconstruction that has not emerged in most of the existing studies of the period. At least half of the Charleston group were free prior to the war, literate, and either skilled laborers, professionals, or businessmen. Hine provides a list of names and characteristics.

2360.   Hine, William C. "Dr. Benjamin A. Boseman, Jr.: Charleston's Black Physician - Politician." In *Southern Black Leaders of the Reconstruction Era.* Edited by Howard N. Rabinowitz. Urbana: University of Illinois Press, 1982. Pp. 334-362.   Boseman, a native of New York, came to South Carolina in 1864 as a contract surgeon for the Union Army, and in the fall of 1865 established a medical practice in Charleston. As a state legislator for five years he supported social and health reform. Even though observers often identified him with white, conservative interests and his investments in railroads and phosphate mining, he stands out as a noteworthy black politician.

2361.   Hine, William C. "The 1867 Charleston Streetcar Sit-ins: A Case of Successful Black Protest." *South Carolina Historical Magazine* 77 (April 1976): 110-114.   When the Charleston City Railway Company commenced streetcar service in late 1866 no blacks were allowed to ride inside the cars. After the passage of the Reconstruction Act of March 2, 1867, blacks began to contest the policy by boarding street cars.   Local police and Union troops made many arrests. Congressional legislation raised black expectations for the enforcement of greater civil rights that could only be ensured through federal government force.

2362.   Hine, William C.   "Frustration, Factionalism and Failure: Black Political Leadership and the Republican Party in Reconstruction Charleston, 1865-1877." Ph.D. Kent State University, 1979. 519p..

2363.   Holt, Thomas. *Black Over White: Negro Political Leadership in South Carolina During Reconstruction.* Urbana: University of Illinois Press, 1977. 269p. App. Bibl. Graphs. Tbls.   Holt writes about the social background, recruitment, political role, ideology, and behavior of black leaders in South Carolina. He finds that the large middle class leadership contributed to the downfall of the state Republican Party. They possessed real power, but it was squandered by factional disputes and their failure to meet the needs of the state. Black leaders emphasized the socioeconomic and cultural differences in the black community. They failed to serve the interests of black peasants. The appendixes give detailed information on the background of black legislators and their roll call votes on various issues. The data is used, in part, to examine voting alignments and Republican dominance at the 1868 constitutional convention and in the state House of Representatives. (See also Holt's "The Emergence of Negro Political Leadership in South Carolina During Reconstruction." Ph.D. Yale University, 1974. 433p.)

2364.   Holt, Thomas.   "Negro Legislators in South Carolina During Reconstruction." In *Southern Black Leaders of the Reconstruction Era.* Edited by Howard N. Rabinowitz. Urbana: University of Illinois Press, 1982. Pp. 223-246. Tbls.   Holt disputes the idea that the failure of Reconstruction was due to the ignorance, inexperience, and corruption of blacks. Using South Carolina as an example, he explains that a major problem with Reconstruction was Republican disunity in state and local government between blacks and whites and also among blacks. Black legislators were literate, property owners, and experienced in various professional and skilled work. Even common ex-slaves demonstrated the ability to act collectively and with specific goals.

2365.   Jarrell, Hampton M. *Wade Hampton and the Negro: The Road Not Taken.* Columbia: University of South Carolina Press, 1950. 209p. App. Bibl. Port. Jarrell's account of Reconstruction and the two decades that followed is consistent with the traditional interpretation of a tragic era espoused by William Dunning. Hampton is depicted as a moderate figure during Reconstruction and his terms as governor from 1877 to 1879 and U.S. senator from 1879 to 1891. He fought the extremist whites and sought a gradualist approach toward settling race relations. The appendix includes correspondence between Hampton and G. L. Parks, President Rutherford B. Hayes, and a letter published in *Nation* (June 14, 1877) regarding events in Edgefield County on election day in 1876.

2366.   Jordan, Laylon Wayne. "'The New Regime': Race, Politics, and Police in Reconstruction Charleston, 1865-1875." *Proceedings of the South Carolina Historical Association* (1994): 45-53.   Jordan describes Charleston as a city making progress towards equal justice for black residence. This was symbolized by the participation of blacks in city government and the organization of a modern police department. But the forces seeking to turn back the clock in race relations and the influence of a difficult transition from Republican to Democratic regimes in 1876-1877 led to racial conflict.

2367. Kibler, Lillian Adele. *Benjamin F. Perry: South Carolina Unionist.* Durham, N.C.: Duke University Press, 1946. 562p. Bibl. Ill. Ports. Perry was a Unionist who stayed loyal to his state throughout the war. As the provisional governor in 1865, he sought a quick return of order, partly by the passage of black codes to force freedmen back to work and reestablish the traditional power structure in a unionist context. Kibler describes Perry as a progressive, independent Democrat, and expresses sympathy for him and the struggle of white South Carolinians against the Radicals during Reconstruction. (See also Kibler's Ph.D. dissertation with the same title from Columbia University, 1943.)

2368. Lawson, Peggy. *The Glorious Failure: Black Congressman Robert Brown Elliott and the Reconstruction in South Carolina.* New York: W. W. Norton, 1973. 330p. Bibl. Ill. Elliott, a black man known for his excellent education and articulate oratory, edited the *South Carolina Leader* in 1867, practiced law, and served in the state House of Representatives from 1868 to 1870 and 1874 to 1876, and the U.S. Congress from 1871 to 1874. Lawson emphasizes his work for equal rights for all citizens. Elliott's career illustrates that Reconstruction was a promising time for black Americans, but it failed due to racial prejudice. Included is a list of state political figures from 1868 to 1877.

2369. Leland, John A. *A Voice From South Carolina.* Charleston: Walker, Evans, and Cogswell, 1879. 231p. App. (*Black Culture Collection From Atlanta University*, Microfilm Roll 332, no. 7) Leland wrote this book between 1874 and 1876. He writes with complete sympathy for the Confederacy and the plight of the white South during Reconstruction. He provides a brief impressionistic view of the period with particular focus on Laurens County and his own period in jail due to accusations that he participated in violent activities. The narrative extends to the victory of Wade Hampton in 1876 and is followed by letters and other documents.

2370. Logue, Cal M. "Racist Reporting During Reconstruction." *Journal of Black Studies* 9 (March 1979): 335-349. Logue examines the reports and editorials in the Charleston *Daily Courier* and the Charleston *Mercury* regarding the state constitutional convention of 1867-1868. The editors ridiculed the proceedings and paid more attention to the physical characteristics of the black delegates and the maintenance of the slave/master relationship than to the actual content of the convention.

2371. Louthan, Maj. Henry T. "General Wade Hampton: Planter, Soldier, Statesman." *Confederate Veteran* 40 (February 1932): 64-69. Louthan provides biographical background on Hampton and discusses his role in the Democratic victory in the 1876 election. Hampton had influence with many blacks, but he used intimidation against them to gain victory.

2372.   Mann, Kenneth Eugene. "Richard Harvey Cain, Congressman, Minister and Champion of Civil Rights." *Negro History Review* 35 (March 1972): 64-66. Born a free black in Virginia and educated in Ohio, Cain became a Methodist Episcopal minister. He organized a church in South Carolina that drew thousands of members because of his charismatic leadership. His leadership would bring him political success as well, with electoral victories for the state senate (1868-1872) and for Congress (1973-1875, 1877-1879). Cain was a consistent supporter of civil rights and land for freedmen.

2373.   Melton, Maurice. "The Gentle Carpetbagger Daniel H. Chamberlain." *American History Illustrated* 7 (January 1973): 28-37. Ills. Ports.   Melton describes the contrast in style and substance between Gov. Chamberlain (1875-1877) and his predecessors, Robert K. Scott and Franklin J. Moses, both of whom he criticizes for contributing to the corruption and chaos in South Carolina during Reconstruction.

2374.   "Men of Distinction in South Carolina." *Negro History Bulletin* 5 (March 1940): 127-128. Ports.   Brief biographical capsules cover the contributions of five black Congressmen - Joseph H. Rainey, Robert Brown Elliott, Robert Smalls, George Washington Murray, and Thomas E. Miller. Murray and Miller served after Reconstruction.

2375.   Miller, Edward A., Jr. *Gullah Statesman: Robert Smalls From Slavery to Congress, 1839-1915.* Columbia: University of South Carolina Press, 1995. 285p. Bibl. Ills. Ports.   In this biography of Smalls, a South Carolina slave who escaped during the Civil War and served in the Union Army, Miller praises his ability to rise to influential political positions in state government including the U.S. House of Representatives and the Senate. Smalls accomplished this without formal education, but he demonstrated his desire to fight injustice and to improve the life of South Carolina blacks.

2376.   Miller, M. Sammy. "Robert Brown Elliott: Reconstruction Leader." *Crisis* 80, 8 (1973): 267-268. Port.   Miller offers a brief sketch of Elliott's life, including his work in politics and law in South Carolina and in Congress.

2377.   Moore, Robert J. "Governor Chamberlain and the End of Reconstruction." *Proceedings of the South Carolina Historical Association* (1977): 17-27. Moore's explanation of the failure of the Chamberlain's Republican administration and Reconstruction focuses on the inevitability of failure and the forces working inexorably against the continuation of Republican rule. Chamberlain later wrote about the impossibility of success. (See # 2351)

2378.   Morris, Thomas D. "Equality, 'Extraordinary Law,' and Criminal Justice: The South Carolina Experience, 1865-1866." *South Carolina Historical Magazine* 83 (January 1982): 15-33.   Morris analyses how the provost courts and the Freedmen's Bureau courts treated whites and blacks prior to Congressional Reconstruction.   The provost courts were military courts appointed by federal authorities for the purpose of offering "impartial authority" to the criminal justice system. The bureau courts were charged with following state law, but in a racially impartial way. In his examination of cases from both courts Morris concludes that impartiality was not accomplished. White defendants usually received more lenient treatment, and decisions on labor contracts weakened the concept of free labor and equality for blacks.

2379.   Osthaus, Carl R. "Francis Warrington Dawson and South Carolina's Spirit of 1876: A Case Study of the Perils of Journalistic Heresy." *Hayes Historical Journal* 1 (Fall 1977): 270-282. Ills. Ports.   Dawson, a native of New England who fought with the Confederacy, became a journalist after the war and, in 1873, owned and edited the Charleston *News and Courier*. He and his paper became a powerful voice in Charleston that overwhelmed other newspapers.   By 1876 Dawson's conservatism had moderated as he befriended conservative Republican Gov. Daniel H. Chamberlain and favored him for the gubernatorial race in 1876. He also defended blacks after the Hamburg massacre. As the *News and Courier* lost popularity, Dawson decided that only a switch back to favoring the Democratic Party and Wade Hampton could save his business.

2380.   Painter, Nell Irvin. "Martin R. Delany: Elitism and Black Nationalism." In *Black Leaders of the Nineteenth Century*. Edited by Leon Litwack and August Meier. Urbana: University of Illinois Press, 1988. Pp. 149-171. Port.   Delaney promoted black nationalism with an emphasis on the emigration of American blacks to Africa. After serving as a Union officer in the war, he became a representative of the Freedmen's Bureau in South Carolina and a popular speaker who sought to motivate blacks to the rewards of hard work. Delaney's efforts led to his identification with white planters and moderate and conservative Republicans. The freedmen eventually rejected his leadership. By the 1880s he would again push for emigration to Africa where he believed American blacks could build an independent nation.

2381.   Porcher, F. A. "The Last Chapter in the History of Reconstruction in South Carolina-Administration of D. H. Chamberlain." *Southern Historical Society Papers* 12 (1884): 173-181, 193-205, 241-253, 309-321, 554-558; 13 (1885): 47-87.   Porcher, president of the South Carolina Historical Society in 1884, reviews the period when Daniel H. Chamberlain, a carpetbagger from Massachusetts, was governor from 1875 to 1877. Most of his paper stresses the wrongdoings of the Republicans, the misguided and crooked behavior of black leaders and voters in general, and the bad days of Chamberlain's leadership. A significant portion of Porcher's paper is devoted to describing examples of riots, violence, and misconduct. Porcher views Reconstruction as the darkest period in the history of the state.

2382.   Post, Louis F. "A 'Carpetbagger' in South Carolina." *Journal of Negro History* 10 (January 1925): 10-79.   Post migrated from New York to Columbia in January, 1871. He describes his experiences and provides background information on Reconstruction based on John S. Reynolds' *Reconstruction in South Carolina* (see # 2333). He gives extensive information about the Ku Klux Klan and politics. Although he left the state in March, 1872 because of unfriendly treatment that he received as a carpetbagger, he concludes that the white reaction to Reconstruction was simply human nature.

2383.   Russ, William A., Jr. "Radical Disfranchisement in South Carolina (1867-1868)." *Susquehanna University Studies* 1 (1930): 148-159.   Russ is severely critical of Radical Reconstruction in South Carolina, particularly the disenfranchisement and disqualification from public office of many whites in accordance with the 14th Amendment. He describes the impact of Section 3 of the amendment as disastrous because it removed the vast majority of persons qualified to be public officials and left open the government to a corrupt and incompetent black-carpetbagger regime.

2384.   Shapiro, Herbert. "The Ku Klux Klan During Reconstruction: The South Carolina Episode." *Journal of Negro History* 49 (January 1964): 34-55.   Shapiro surveys the activities and influence of the Klan and compares his evidence with the conclusions of historian Francis B. Simkins (see # 2387).   Contrary to Simkins' conclusions, Shapiro believes that the Klan had a significant impact through its violent intimidation of potential black voters, the direct or tacit support from a cross section of the white community, and the feeling among at least some whites that the Klan made their communities safer and quieter.   The Klan helped create an environment for Northern compromise and the return to power of the Democratic Party.

2385.   Sheppard, William Arthur. *Red Shirts Remembered: Southern Brigadiers of the Reconstruction Period.* Atlanta: Printed by Ruralist Press, Inc., 1940. 339p. Bibl. Ills. Port.   Martin Witherspoon Gary helped lead the Democratic Party to victory in the 1876 gubernatorial election.   Gary devised the "Plan of Campaign, 1876" that set forth the tactics that Democrats would follow, including manipulation of black voters, threats of violence, and the organization of secret clubs in which members would wear red shirts.   After the Democratic victory, the red shirts found themselves in opposition to the liberal policies of the new governor, Wade Hampton.

2386.   Simkins, Francis Butler. "The Election of 1876 in South Carolina." *South Atlantic Quarterly* 21 (July 1922): 225-240; (October 1922): 335-351.   Simkins covers political events in the state from the beginning of Daniel H. Chamberlain's term as governor on December 1, 1874 until the resolution of the 1876 election. He writes with sympathy towards Chamberlain's goals of reforming state government and eliminating corruption left from the administration of Franklin J. Moses, Jr. and the Republican dominated legislature.   A divided Republican Party in South Carolina and increasing pressure from whites to overthrow the Republicans assisted the "straight-out" policy of Wade Hampton and the Democratics. Hampton used rhetorical persuasion, electoral fraud, and intimidation of black voters to ensure a Democratic victory.

2387.   Simkins, Francis Butler. "The Ku Klux Klan in South Carolina, 1868-1871." *Journal of Negro History* 12 (October 1927): 606-647.   The Klan played a role in intimidating the freedmen from the 1868 election to the fall elections of 1871, but it was not a monolithic movement throughout the state. The organization consisted of a small number of mainly lower class whites in locally controlled groups.   Simkins concludes that while Klan violence during the period did not overthrow Republican rule, but it taught the white population that it could be an effective tool in the future.

2388.   Simkins, Francis Butler. "Race Legislation in South Carolina Since 1865." (Part I: 1865-1869) *South Atlantic Quarterly* 20 (January 1921): 61-71; (Part II: 1869 and after) 20 (April 1921): 165-177.   Simkins criticizes black codes and generally applauds the 1867 constitution and the founding of tax supported public schools for all people, but he is harshly critical of Radical Reconstruction from 1868 to 1877 due to its corruption and ineffectiveness. A classless, race-blind society could be legislated on paper, but it could not change the attitudes of the dominant white class.

2389.   Smith, Mark M. "'All is Not Quiet in Our Hellish County': Facts, Fiction, Politics, and Race -- The Ellenton Riot of 1876." *South Carolina Historical Magazine* 95 (April 1994): 142-155.   The facts of the Ellenton riot in Aiken County have been in dispute. Smith places the riot in mid-September, 1876 and believes that it was rooted in the political and racial tensions leading up to the gubernatorial election of that year. The determination of white Democrats to intimidate black voters contributed to an environment conducive to violent confrontation.

2390.   South Carolinian. "The Political Condition of South Carolina." *Atlantic Monthly* 39 (February 1877): 177-194.   The author provides the Southern white perspective on the wrongs done to the state by the incompetence and theft of state resources by carpetbaggers and blacks. Blacks were completely unprepared for equal civil and political rights. (Other articles by the same pen name discuss racial differences in South Carolina morality and society. See also *Atlantic Monthly* 39 (April 1877): 467-475; and (June 1977): 670-684.)

2391.   Sweat, Edward F. "Francis L. Cardozo - Profile of Integrity in Reconstruction." *Journal of Negro History* 46 (October 1961): 217-232.   Sweat argues that corruption occurred among white and black Republicans, but writers have tended to focus solely on the negative aspects of Republican rule and avoided examples of honest, unselfish government. Cardozo, born a free black in Charleston, exemplifies the honest Republican politician in his service to in state government. His criminal conviction by Democrats was a political payback after their return to power.

2392.   Sweat, Edward F. "The Union Leagues and the South Carolina Election of 1870." *Journal of Negro History* 61 (April, 1976): 200-214.   On July 27, 1870 Secretary of State Francis L. Cardozo addressed the Grand Council of the Union

Leagues in the midst of a statewide election campaign. Cardozo's speech is printed. He offers a justification for Union leagues and how they differ from the Democratic Union Reform League organized by conservative whites. He defends the state government and the improved state finances compared with antebellum governments, and he calls for support for the Republican Party.

2393.   Thompson, Henry T. *Ousting the Carpetbagger From South Carolina.* New York: Negro Universities Press, 1969. 182p. App. Ills. (Rpt. of Columbia, S.C.: R. L. Bryan Co., 1926)   Reconstruction in South Carolina is depicted as a futile means to install black domination over white people. Violence and scandals are blamed on Radical Republican in Congress, corrupt carpetbaggers and blacks, a group almost totally unprepared for full and equal participation in society. Wade Hampton, elected governor in 1876, symbolizes for Thompson the restoration of good government and racial fairness. The lesson of Reconstruction is that blacks should never again gain ascendancy in politics.

2394.   Thompson, Michael Edwin. "Blacks, Carpetbaggers, and Scalawags: A Study of the Membership of the South Carolina Legislature, 1868-1870." Ph.D. Washington State University, 1975. 280p.

2395.   Trescott, William Henry.   "Letter of William Henry Trescott on Reconstruction in South Carolina, 1867." *American Historical Review* 15 (April 1910): 574-582.   Trescott's letter to Massachusetts Republican Senator Henry Wilson, dated September 8, 1867, provides a detailed critique of Congressional Reconstruction with emphasis on the suffering of Southern whites in the face of black rule, disenfranchisement, and federal domination.

2396.   Uya, Okon Edet. *From Slavery to Public Service: Robert Smalls 1839-1915.* New York: Oxford University Press, 1971. 178p. Bibl. Port. In this biography Uya emphasizes that Smalls was an outstanding political representative of the black community in the state, specifically the Beaufort area. As state senator and U.S. congressman, Smalls sought to establish equal rights for black citizens, represent Black racial pride, and seek the integration of the races in American society. Uya denies that Smalls was corrupt in any way. Despite the problems of Reconstruction, Smalls' contributions indicate that labeling black politics in South Carolina as totally corrupt and inept cannot stand up to the truth. (See also Uya's "From Servitude to Service: Robert Smalls, 1839-1915." Ph.D. University of Wisconsin, 1969; and a related book by Dorothy Sterling, *Captain of the 'Planter': The Story of Robert Smalls*, Garden City: Doubleday, 1958.)

2397.   Wells, Edward L. *Hampton and Reconstruction.* Columbia, S.C.: State Company, 1907. 238p. Port.   Wells writes a strongly white supremacist account of Reconstruction and the place of blacks in American history. He does not relate Wade Hampton to Reconstruction but simply provides a brief narrative of Hampton in the Civil War, a description of Reconstruction in general, particularly in South Carolina, and Hampton's contributions in restoring conservative, constitutional government after he was elected governor in 1876.

2398.   Wickham, Mrs. Julia Porter.   "Wade Hampton, the Calvary Leader, and His Time." *Confederate Veteran* 36 (December 1928): 448-445.   In addition to describing Hampton's heroic exploits in the Civil War, Wickham explains Hampton's role in South Carolina gubernatorial election of 1876 and conditions in the state.   She uses extensive quotations from Col. James Morgan's *Recollections of a Rebel Reefer* (Houghton Mifflin, 1917).

2399.   Williams, Alfred B.   *Hampton and His Red Shirts: South Carolina's Deliverance in 1876.*   Charleston, S.C.:   Walker, Evans and Cogswell Co., 1935. 460p.   Williams was a young journalist in 1876 who was assigned by the *Charleston Journal of Commerce* to cover Wade Hampton's campaign for governor. In 1926 he wrote a narrative of the election based on his memories and South Carolina newspapers at the Library of Congress.   The book was serialized in the Charleston *Evening Post* and Columbia *State* in the same year.   This book is the first edition of the entire narrative in one publication.   Williams' account of the tumultuous year in which Republican rule was overthrown by Hampton's Democratic Party strongly favors the return of white conservative rule.   He supports the aggressive action by Hampton and his supporters to thwart the corrupt carpetbaggers and blacks.

2400.   Williams, Lou Falkner.   "The Constitution and the Ku Klux Klan on Trial: Federal Enforcement and Local Resistance in South Carolina, 1871-1872." *Georgia Journal of Southern Legal History* 2 (Spring/Summer 1993): 41-70.   Map. Ports. Williams focuses on the Klan's activities in the up-country region of the state and how federal authorities sought to enforce the Enforcement Acts of 1870 and 1871. The trials turned out to be a success for opponents of federal jurisdiction over local violent acts, and the court decision weakened the intended federal authority proscribed in the 14th Amendment.   Constitutional principles of dual federalism prevailed in courts of law and had the support of many people throughout the nation.

2401.   Williams, Lou Falkner.   *The Great South Carolina Ku Klux Klan Trials, 1871-1872.*   Athens: University of Georgia Press, 1996.   197p.   Bibl.   Gov. Robert Scott appealed to President Grant to help stop the incessant violence and intimidation of blacks and white Republicans.   Federal troops captured hundreds of klansmen and put them on trial, but the leaders got away, leaving mainly the poor, upcountry followers to take the brunt of federal prosecution.   The trials tested, inconclusively, the constitutionality of legislated federal power to protect individual rights and the nationalization of the Bill of Rights.   The near total resistance of whites and the inability to change traditional ideas about race relations and federal-state power finally wore down the federal government and local Republican efforts to bring about the reform of Southern society.   (See also Williams' Ph.D. dissertation with the same title from University of Florida, 1991)

2402.   Williams, Lou Falkner.   "The South Carolina Ku Klux Klan and Enforcement of Federal Rights, 1871-1872." *Civil War History* 39 (March 1993): 47-66.   Federal District Attorney David T. Corbin, a carpetbag Republican, vigorously pursued cases against Klan members by attempting to demonstrate that the federal government had the power to guarantee the rights of citizens against public or private denial of rights when states could not or refused to do so. The Klan trials ended with the government's failure to establish national authority over the rights of citizens reserved by constitutional amendments. The negative phraseology of the Reconstruction amendments made them essentially conservative documents, and federal judges could not overcome the tradition of federalism that reserved rights to the states.

2403.   Wolfe, John Harold. "The South Carolina Constitution of 1865 as a Democratic Document." *Proceedings of the South Carolina Historical Association* (1942): 18-42.   The 1865 state constitution resulted in greater democracy in government based on an evolutionary rather than a radical process. It is more conservative than the radical changes in the 1868 constitution, but changes that were made in the earlier document should be recognized.

2404.   Woody, Robert H. (ed.).   "Behind the Scenes in the Reconstruction Legislature of South Carolina: Diary of Joseph Woodruff." *Journal of Southern History* 2 (February 1936): 78-102; (May 1936): 233-259.   Woodruff's diary, provides his perspective on the corruption within the administration of Gov. Franklin J. Moses, Jr., the election in 1874 of Daniel H. Chamberlain, state politics in Columbia and Charleston, and the preservation of both his job as Clerk of the State Senate and the business relationship that existed between the state and the Republican Printing Co. in which he had an interest. Excerpts from the diary cover the period from July 21 to October 21, 1874 and August 9 to December 31, 1875.

2405.   Woody, Robert H. "Franklin J. Moses, Jr., Scalawag Governor of South Carolina, 1872-1874." *North Carolina Historical Review* 10 (April 1933): 111-133. Moses was a native South Carolinian who supported the conservative cause until his transformation to Republicanism while editor of the Sumter *News* from June 1, 1866 until September 21, 1867. Woody describes Moses as the quintessential scalawag based on his low morality and high ambitions. His career as a Radical brought him influence in the Republican Party, participation in the constitutional convention of 1868, 2 terms as Speaker of the House from 1868 to 1872, and one term as governor from 1872 to 1874. Moses' term as governor was the nadir of Reconstruction in South Carolina.

2406.   Woody, Robert H. "Jonathan Jasper Wright, Associate Justice of the Supreme Court of South Carolina, 1870-1877." *Journal of Negro History* 18 (April 1933): 114-131.   Wright, a native of Pennsylvania, arrived in South Carolina in 1866 as a Freedmen's Bureau legal advisor for refugees and freedmen. He served in the state constitutional convention in 1868 and was elected to the state senate from Beaufort. During his years on the state supreme court, he built an admirable record, but his career was marred by charges of illegalities that Woody believes were based on political and racial animosities during 1876.

2407.   Woody, Robert H. *Republican Newspapers of South Carolina.* Charlottesville: Historical Publishing Co., 1936. 60p. (*Southern Sketches*, No. 10,

First Series)   Woody explains that the advent of Republican newspapers in South Carolina coincided with the establishment of military rule following the Civil War. The growth of these propaganda sheets did not pick up until after the beginning of Republican rule in 1868 and only then because of state government financial support with advertising and printing.   When the Republicans lost power, Republican newspapers withered. Most Republicans in the state were blacks, and most of them could not read. Woody accuses the Republican governments with corruption in their support for the Republican Printing Co. He also provides information about many of the newspapers throughout the state.

2408.   Woody, Robert H. "The South Carolina Election of 1870." *North Carolina Historical Review* 8 (April 1931): 168-186.   In the 1870 gubernatorial election, the Radical Republicans, led by incumbent Gov. Robert K. Scott, opposed the newly formed Union Reform Party, a moderately conservative group that nominated Republican Richard B. Carpenter.   Woody highlights the role of the conservative press in demonizing Scott's Republican administration and the attempts of the Reform Party to persuade blacks to support the conservatives. Another factor in the election was Ku Klux Klan violence, a phenomena that was born out of frustration with the black militias in the state. The Republican victory led to the dissolution of the Reform Party but conservatives continued to search for Republicans who would gain the confidence of both whites and blacks.

2409.   Workman, C. E. "Reconstruction Days in South Carolina." *Confederate Veteran* 29 (July 1921): 256-258.   The author describes the terrible state of political affairs for white South Carolinians after the government was taken over by blacks, carpetbaggers, and scalawags. He relates his own experiences, particularly confrontations with groups of blacks, the elections of 1876 and 1878, and the eventual disenfranchisement of blacks after Reconstruction.

2410.   Zuczek, Richard. "The Last Campaign of the Civil War: South Carolina and the Revolution of 1876." *Civil War History* 42 (March 1996): 18-31.   Zuczek views Reconstruction as an extension of the Civil War with South Carolina's state election campaign of 1876 as the last engagement. The Democrats, led by gubernatorial candidate Wade Hampton and supported by highly organized paramilitary rifle clubs, led a determined campaign of intimidation, violence, and voting fraud to take the state government away from the Republicans.   Gov. Chamberlain had little power to stop the rebellion, and President Grant would not commit adequate forces to stem the tide of "red shirts."

2411.   Zuczek, Richard. *State of Rebellion: Reconstruction in South Carolina.* Columbia: University of South Carolina Press, 1996. 250p. Bibl. Ills. Ports. Tbls. Zuczek focuses on the response of white South Carolinians to Radical Reconstruction, a topic that he believes has not been adequately explored. Conservative whites organized themselves for political campaigning in the Democratic Party and for intimidation and violence in the Ku Klux Klan. Their efforts were successful with the assistance of Republican disunity and corruption, and the weakening of federal commitments to reform and coercion in the South.

Zuczek emphasizes that Reconstruction was a continuation of the Civil War by means other than formal war and that Southern whites ultimately won a type of autonomy within the Union. (See also Zuczek's "State of Rebellion: People's War in Reconstruction South Carolina, 1865-1877." Ph.D. Ohio State University, 1993.)

Agriculture, Labor, and Business

2412.   Billington, Ray Allen. "A Social Experiment: The Port Royal Journal of Charlotte L. Forten, 1862-1863." *Journal of Negro History* 35 (July 1950): 233-264.   Forten, born to free black parents in Philadelphia, participated in the abolitionist movement prior to the Civil War. In 1862 the Philadelphia Port Royal Relief Association sent her to Port Royal as a teacher. In extracts from her journal, written from October 28, 1862 until February 7, 1863, she describes her initial impressions and experiences with ex-slaves who were taking part in an experiment in education and economic independence. (See also Charotte L. Forten's *The Journal of Charlotte L. Forten: A Free Negro in the Slave Era*. Edited with an introduction by Ray Allen Billington. London: Collier Books, 1953. 286p.)

2413.   Bleser, Carol Rothrock. *The Promised Land: The History of the South Carolina Land Commission, 1869-1890*. Columbia: University of South Carolina Press for the South Carolina Tricentennial Commission, 1969. 189p. App. Bibl. Maps.   On March 27, 1869 the Republican legislature created the Land Commission charged with purchasing land that would be sold with long term payment plans to former slaves. The program was designed to assist the landless freedmen to begin a new life as landowners and farmers. Perhaps as many as 14,000 families benefited from the program, but corruption was discovered and Democratic governments placed restrictions on its operation. Bleser concludes that most of the black landowners lost their holdings because racial prejudice and inequality would not allow the program to flourish. (See also Bleser's "The South Carolina Land Commission: A Study of a Reconstruction Institution." Ph.D. Columbia University, 1966.)

2414.   Burton, Orville V. "The Development of Tenantry and the Post-Bellum Afro-American Social Structure in Edgefield County, South Carolina."   In *Prestations Paysannes Dîmes, Rente Foncière/et Mouvement De La Productin Agricole à L'Epoque Préindustrielle. Acts du Colloque Préparatoire (30 Juin-ler et 2 Juillet 1977) au VIIe Congrès International d'Histoire Économique. Section A 3. Edinbourg 13-19 Août 1978*. Paris: Editions de L'École des Hautes Études en Sciences Sociales, 1982. Pp. 763-778. Tbls.   The 1870 and 1880 manuscript census returns are the main sources for this statistical study of black economic and social structure in Edgefield County. Burton emphasizes that grouping the freedmen together as if they were all at the same low level during this period is incorrect because such a perspective does not show, as the census does, that blacks were involved in a variety of occupations and some were landowners and renters. Many freedmen rejected wage labor for sharecropping and other work, their economic status actually improved, but their social status within the general community declined rapidly when Democrats regained political power.

2415.   Ford, Lacy K. "Labor and Ideology in the South Carolina Up-Country: The Transition to Free-Labor Agriculture." In *The Southern Enigma: Essays on Race, Class, and Folk Culture.* Edited by Walter J. Fraser and Winfred B. Moore, Jr. Westport: Greenwood Press, 1983. Pp. 25-41. Tbls.   Agricultural labor in upcountry South Carolina was virtually set in 1868 with sharecroppers and tenants working in association with planters. Ford discusses the development of black labor and interpretations of free labor for both blacks and whites. The differences among laborers, the racism and violence of the Reconstruction period, and the rise of a merchant class that helped finance agriculture and production, set the tone for upcountry agriculture until World War II.

2416.   Ford, Lacy K. "Rednecks and Merchants: Economic Development and Social Tensions in the South Carolina Upcountry, 1865-1900." *Journal of American History* 71 (September 1984): 294-318. Tbls.   The deminishing economic domination of large landowners in upcountry counties began during Reconstruction with the advent of land tenantry and sharecropping among the freedmen and increasing numbers of white yeomen.   The rise of a town merchant class that controlled credit, marketing, investment capital, and industrialization, actually began in the 1850s, but after the Civil War the merchants made the piedmont a region of vibrant economic activity. These developments changed the economy of the upcountry region and created class tensions that gave rise to populism among the white yeomen.

2417.   Fraser, Jessie Melville (ed.). "A Free Labor Contract, 1867." *Journal of Southern History* 6 (November 1940): 546-548.   Fraser prints the text of a contract between D. T. Crosby and five freedmen. The contract refers to provision of supplies and tools and the regulation of labor. The address on the contract is Fairfield District, South Carolina.

2418.   Graham, Glennon.   "From Slavery to Freedom: Rural Black Agriculturalists in South Carolina, 1865-1900." Ph.D. Northwestern University, 1982.

2419.   Hine, William C. "Black Organized Labor in Reconstruction Charleston." *Labor History* 25 (1984): 504-517. (Rpt. in *The Civil War and Reconstruction Era, 1861-1877*, New York: Garland, 1991: 96-109.)   The labor strikes among black longshoremen in Charleston during 1867-1869 brought limited but real success because of their solidarity and the refusal of white workers to perform this important heavy labor job. In 1868 the Longshoremen's Protective Union Association formed, but by 1870 the black labor movement had weakened because it was strongly opposed by local Republicans, whites, and some blacks.

2420.   Moore, John Hammond.   "Getting Uncle Sam's Dollars: South Carolinians and the Southern Claims Commission, 1871-1880." *South Carolina*

Historical Magazine 82 (July 1981): 248-262.   Congress approved the Southern Claims Commission on March 3, 1871 as a way to reimburse loyal Southerners who lost certain types of property as a result of the Civil War.   Moore briefly describes several cases and lists the names of the South Carolinians who made claims to the commission.   The list is arranged by county and includes case numbers, amount claimed and received, and an indication of which cases were disallowed.

2421.   Morris-Crowthers, Jayne.   "An Economic Study of the Substantial Slaveholders of Orangeburg County, 1860-1880.   *South Carolina Historical Magazine* 86 (October 1985): 296-314. Tbls.   The economic conditions of the elite planter class in Orangeburg during the Civil War and Reconstruction are compared with the same class in the Black Belt counties of Alabama as revealed in a study by Jonathan Wiener (see # 1451).   The author finds that the planter class studied by Wiener became wealthier and increased their land holdings after the war, but such was not the case in Orangeburg where planters struggled under the changes brought about by emancipation and changes to the credit system.   Orangeburg planters combined cotton farming and business to maintain a good income. Statistical tables illustrate planter landholdings and wealth.

2422.   Nielsen, J. V., Jr. "Post-Confederate Finance in South Carolina." *South Carolina Historical Magazine* 56 (April 1955): 85-91.   Nielsen briefly discusses the finances of the major South Carolina banks prior to and during the years following the Civil War.   His main sources are the *Charleston Courier* and the *News and Courier.*

2423.   Pease, William H   "Three Years Among the Freedmen: William C. Gannett and the Port Royal Experiment." *Journal of Negro History* 42 (October 1957): 98-117.   Gannett became a teacher of freedmen at Port Royal, S.C. in March, 1862.   Later he served as a superintendent of several plantations on St. Helena Island where freedmen worked the land as free people.   He believed that the experiment in black labor to be successful.   Gannett strongly supported the sale of land to freedmen, because it would engender self reliance and independence.   Work opportunities and education would lead to the integration of blacks into the mainstream of American society

2424.   Saville, Julie. *The Work of Reconstruction: From Slave to Wage Laborer in South Carolina, 1860-1870.*   New York: Cambridge University Press, 1994. 221p. Bibl. Ills.   Saville examines the impact of emancipation on the ex-slaves of rural South Carolina during the first few years of postwar Reconstruction.   In particular, she focuses on their adjustment to the concept of free labor and how it effected the social and political relationships among freedmen and the larger society. The freedmen vigorously responded individually and collectively to the attempt of white employers and renters to proscribe their lives within the bounds of a restricted freedom.   The freedmen's sense of themselves as free people, their ability to control and define their labor, and their participation in politics through voting and Republican Party activities contributed to the construction of a new social order.

(See also Saville's "A Measure of Freedom: From Slave to Wage Laborer in South
Carolina, 1860-1868." Ph.D. Yale University, 1986. 306p.)

2425.   Shick, Tom W. and Don H. Doyle. "The South Carolina Phosphate Boom
and the Stillbirth of the New South, 1867-1920." *South Carolina Historical
Magazine* 86 (January 1985): 1-31.   Business opportunities in postwar South
Carolina seemed limited because of the destruction from the war, the lack of capital,
and the conservatism of the old planter class that sought to maintain its power and
culture. The story of phosphate mining in the decades after the war illustrates the
resistance of coastal plantation owners to economic change effecting their way of
life and the challenges faced by employers in labor relations with the freedmen.

2426.   Simkins, Francis B. "The Solution of Post-Bellum Agricultural Problems
in South Carolina." *North Carolina Historical Review* 7 (April 1930): 192-219.
Tbls.   South Carolina agriculture rebounded quickly from the war because the
Freedmen's Bureau persuaded the freedmen to return to work and planters adjusted
to economic and social changes. Simkins views sharecropping and tenancy as
successful. The continuation of the cotton crop and the rise of creditors in towns
were instrumental in solving postwar agricultural problems.

2427.   Stagg, J. C. A. "The Problem of Klan Violence: The South Carolina Up-
Country, 1868-1871." *Journal of American Studies* 8 (December 1974): 303-318.
Stagg believes that an examination of violence in counties located in the South
Carolina upcountry, historians should not focus only on population relationships,
political intimidation, and white supremacy. Other important factors to consider are
conflicts over land tenantry promoted by Freedmen's Bureau agents and the
persistent disagreements between planters and freedmen over labor contracts. The
land and labor issues had a direct impact on the economic outlook for the planters.
Economic issues in the upcountry combined with the political strength of black
voters, the presence of armed black militias, and the influence of politics on
agriculture to generate resentment and violence from a cross section of whites.

2428.   Stickland, John Scott. "'No More Mud Work': The Struggle For the
Control of Labor and Production in Low Country South Carolina, 1863-1880." In
The Southern Enigma: Essays on Race, Class, and Folk Culture. Edited by Walter
J. Fraser, Jr. and Winfred B. Moore, Jr. Westport: Greenwood Press, 1983. Pp. 43-
62.   The attempts of white planters and Freedmen's Bureau agents to control black
labor in the coastal counties south of Charleston were only partially successful.
Planters were frustrated by the independence of black workers who frequently
refused contracts, desired subsistence farming, and would not work beyond task
oriented assignments related directly to planting and harvesting crops. Planters
usually resorted to pressure from government officials rather than violence to
influence laborers, but drought and starvation also played a role in lessening black
resistance.

2429.   Woody, Robert H. "The Labor and Immigration Problem of South
Carolina During Reconstruction." *Mississippi Valley Historical Review*   18

(September 1931): 195-212.   South Carolina newspapers frequently mentioned the need for foreign labor to replace the blacks who left plantations or who were no longer trusted as free laborers. Planters were not enthusiastic about using foreign labor, and Republicans were generally reluctant to promote a plan to displace black laborers who supported the party. A few Europeans, mostly Germans, did come to South Carolina to work, but most of them stayed only a short time due to low pay, poor food, maltreatment, and the inhospitable climate.

2430.   Woody, Robert H. "Some Aspects of the Economic Conditions of South Carolina After the Civil War." *North Carolina Historical Review* 7 (July 1930): 346-364.   Woody illustrates how far the economy of the state had fallen since 1860. Property values decreased, interest rates increased, the financial system was depressed, agriculture suffered, and famine seemed to be a real possibility.

Society, Education, and Religion

2431.   Abbott, Martin. "The Freedmen's Bureau and its Carolina Critics." *Proceedings of the South Carolina Historical Association* (1962): 15-23.   Local white Carolinians despised the Freedmen's Bureau from its beginnings because they believed it not only represented a Northern intrusion into their lives, but the institution and some of its agents were corrupt and encouraged freedmen to misbehave. Abbott emphasizes that much of the criticism is unjust. Whites generally got along well with most bureau agents, but their perspective was colored by a general abhorrence of the entire Radical Reconstruction experience.

2432.   Abbott, Martin. "The Freedmen's Bureau and Negro Schooling in South Carolina." *South Carolina Historical Magazine* 57 (April 1956): 65-81.   The Freedmen's Bureau brought organizational ability, government authority, and funding to the educational efforts in South Carolina. Northern religious and benevolent societies continued to provide teachers while the bureau coordinated efforts and insured adequate facilities. Despite their efforts, when the bureau stopped its operation in 1870, the vast majority of school age blacks had never attended school. The successes that occurred were due mainly to the dedication of individual teachers and bureau agents, such as Reuben Tomlinson, who was appointed state superintendent of education in the summer of 1865.

2433.   Abbott, Martin. *The Freedmen's Bureau in South Carolina, 1865-1872.* Chapel Hill: University of North Carolina Press, 1967. 167p. App. Bibl.   Abbott believes that the bureau was a "qualified failure" because the nation as a whole lacked the courage and conviction to carry out a long term program of economic, social, and educational assistance to the freedmen. He also emphasizes the mixed attitude of the local white population that both resented Northern intrusion into local race relations but also admired individual bureau agents. The bureau was directed by Robert K. Scott (1866-1868), John R. Edie (1868-1869), and Maj. Edward L. Deane (1869-1870). The appendix includes various documents, including the text of a typical labor contract. (See also Abbott's Ph.D. disseration with the same title from Emory University, 1954.)

2434. Ames, Mary. *From a New England Woman's Diary in Dixie in 1865.* New York: Negro Universities Press, 1969. 125p. (Rpt. from Plimpton Press, 1906) Describes the experiences of Ames and her friend, Emily Bliss, who lived among and taught the freedmen as part of a program established by the Freedmen's Bureau. They stayed in South Carolina from May 4, 1865 until the last week of September, 1866.

2435. Burton, Orville V. "Race and Reconstruction: Edgefield County, South Carolina." In *The Southern Common People: Studies in Nineteenth-Century Social History.* Edited by Edward Magdol and Jon L. Wakelyn. Westport: Greenwood Press, 1980. Pp. 211-237. (Rpt. of *Journal of Social History* 12 (Fall 1978): 31-56.) Burton describes race relations in Edgefield County to demonstrate the inadequacy of the theories on postwar race relations proposed by C. Van Woodward and Eugene Genovese who emphasize white paternalism and black accommodation. Experiences in Edgefield show that race relations were very competitive during Reconstruction with regard to politics, labor, land, religion, and the maintenance of order with black militias. Only after Reconstruction, with the power of the national Republican regimes withdrawn, did whites implement a paternalistic and oppressive society that blacks responded to with both accommodation and competitiveness. (See also Burton's *In My Father's House Are Many Mansions: Family and Community in Edgefield, South Carolina.* Chapel Hill: University of North Carolina Press, 1985.)

2436. Burton, Orville V. "The Rise and Fall of Afro-American Town Life: Town and Country in Reconstruction Edgefield, South Carolina." In *Toward a New South? Studies in Post-Civil War Southern Communities.* Edited by Orville V. Burton and Robert C. McGrath, Jr. Westport: Greenwood Press, 1982. Pp. 152-192. Census data supports this study of the economic and social life in Edgefield during and after Reconstruction. Blacks found town life to be safer and provided more opportunities than rural areas, but with the return of conservative white rule, towns seemed to offer whites greater means of controlling blacks.

2437. Childs, Arney Robinson (ed.). *The Private Journal of Henry William Ravenel 1859-1887.* Columbia: University of South Carolina Press, 1947. 428p. Bibl. Port. Ravenel was a well known botanist who supported his home state of South Carolina and the South during the Civil War. His journal reveals his activities and opinions regarding the war and Reconstruction. He clearly sided with the Democratic Party which he believed could restore order and integrity to state government and return prosperity to the state. Ravenel's journal also illustrates the condition of his family and the resumption of his scientific work after the war.

2438. Clark, E. Culpepper. "Sarah Morgan and Francis Dawson: Raising the Woman Question in Reconstruction South Carolina." *South Carolina Historical Magazine* 81 (January 1980): 8-23. Morgan wrote a series of editorials in 1873 in the Charleston *News and Courier* supporting equality among men and women and pointed out the hypocrisies in Southern attitudes toward women. Dawson, the editor of the newspaper, supported her, and they developed a relationship that resulted in marriage in 1874. Her active feminism made her the exception among Southern women.

2439.   DeForest, John William. *A Union Officer in the Reconstruction.* Edited with an introduction and notes by James H. Croushore and David Morris Potter. New Haven: Yale University Press, 1948. 211p. (Rpt. in Hamden, Conn.: Archon Books, 1968.)   DeForest, a native of Connecticut, was a professional writer of both fiction and nonfiction. The editors praise his writing style and unbiased account of his experiences as a Freedmen's Bureau agent in Greenville from October, 1866 until December, 1867. The book is comprised of ten chapters individually published in periodicals during 1868 and 1869. They are written in a clear, entertaining style with frequent use of dialogue representing actual conversations or events. DeForest comments on the social structure of Southern society as well as his work with black and white South Carolinians.

2440.   Eudell, Demetrius Lynn. "The Mind of Emancipation: Toward a Comparative History of Post-Slavery Thought in the Anglo-Americas."   Ph.D. Stanford University, 1997. 260p. (Jamaica and South Carolina)

2441.   Fowler, Wilton B. "A Carpetbagger's Conversion to White Supremacy." *North Carolina Historical Review*   43 (Summer 1966): 286-304.   Daniel Chamberlain, the moderate Republican governor of South Carolina from 1874 to 1877, supported civil rights and security for blacks against white terrorists. In the decades that followed his writings on racial equality reflected a change. By the early 20th century he decided that blacks had not progressed to the point that they should continue to hold political powers provided by Reconstruction. (See also # 2350, 2351)

2442.   Gatewood, Williard B., Jr. "'The Remarkable Misses Rollin': Black Women in Reconstruction South Carolina." *South Carolina Historical Magazine* 92 (July 1991): 172-188.   The five Rollin sisters of Columbia were well known for their influence within Republican Party circles. When reporters from *The Sun* and the *New York Herald* were surprised to find such highly educated black women who spoke strongly and eloquently in support of both black civil rights and women's rights. The women contradicted the Northern stereotype of Southern blacks. Not only were they outspoken, but they participated in the struggle for civil rights.

2443.   Gordon, Asa H. "The Negro's Part in the Reconstruction of South Carolina." In *Sketches of Negro Life and History in South Carolina.* 2nd Ed. By Asa H. Gordon. Columbia: University of South Carolina Press, 1971. Pp. 59-79. (Rpt. of Industrial College, Ga., 1929)   In an early revisionist work, Gordon, a black historian at South Carolina State A & M College at Orangeburg, tells of the accomplishments of the freedmen in his state during Reconstruction. As with more contemporary accounts, he criticizes the popular view of Reconstruction as a tragic period of black domination.

2444.   Hollis, Daniel Walker. "Robert W. Barnwell." *South Carolina Historical Magazine* 56 (July 1955): 131-137.   The life of Barnwell (1801-1882) is surveyed with particular emphasis on his contributions to South Carolina College and its successor, the University of South Carolina.   During Reconstruction the former Confederate senator worked as chairman of the faculty.   He defied pressure to resign when a Republican government arrived in 1868 and was eventually dismissed in 1873 when Republicans integrated the university and replaced all of the teachers from prewar days.

2445.   Hope, W. Martin and Jason H. Silverman. *Relief and Recovery in Post-Civil War South Carolina: A Death by Inches.* Lewiston: Edward Mellen Press, 1997. 336p. Bibl.   The authors describe the efforts made by many individuals and groups to provide assistance to the people of South Carolina from 1865 to 1869. Help came from Northern and local organizations and individuals, the Freedmen's Bureau, and through the expansion of public education and public entertainment. But health care was woefully insufficient, food was in short supply, agricultural development occurred slowly, and some Northerners were reluctant to give monetary help out of distrust of the South.   Also, President Johnson worked hard to undermine government assistance.

2446.   Jackson, L. P. "The Educational Efforts of the Freedmen's Bureau and Freedmen's Aid Societies in South Carolina, 1862-1872." *Journal of Negro History* 8 (January 1923): 1-40.   This article is Jackson's 1922 M.A. thesis completed at Columbia University.   He emphasizes the positive activities of the bureau and voluntary organizations in the development of public schools and colleges for black children and teacher training.

2447.   Jaquette, Henrietta Stratton (ed.).   *South After Gettysburg: Letters of Comelia Hancock 1863-1868.* New York: Thomas Y. Crowell, 1956. 288p.   This edition of Hancock's letters include descriptions of her experiences as a teacher in Mount Pleasant during the early years after the Civil War.   She was a Quaker from New Jersey who went to South Carolina under the sponsorship of the Philadelphia Yearly Meeting of the Society of Friends.   Most of the letters were written while she worked as a nurse in the Union Army.

2448.   Jenkins, Wilbert Lee.   "Chaos, Conflict and Control: The Responses of the Newly-Freed Slaves in Charleston, South Carolina to Emancipation and Reconstruction, 1865-1877."   2 Vols.   Ph.D.   Michigan State University, 1991. 410p.

2449.   Johnson, Clifton H. "Francis Cardozo: Black Carpetbagger." *Crisis* 78, 7 (1971): 226-228.   Johnson focuses mainly on Cardozo's life as a pastor for the American Missionary Association, an educator, and a politician in the state Republican government from 1868 to 1877.

2450.   Johnson, Elliott McClintock.   "The Influence of Blacks on the Development and Implementation of the Public Education System in South Carolina, 1863-1876." Ph.D. American University, 1978. 203p.

2451.   Jones, Newton B.   "Social Consciousness in South Carolina During Reconstruction: Imported or Indigenous." *Proceedings of the South Carolina Historical Association* (1962): 24-31.   Jones reevaluates the concept among historians that social humanitarianism was brought to the South by the Freedmen's Bureau and Northern religious and charitable organizations. He finds that local South Carolinians recognized the need to care for orphans, and they acted to provide for them. Orphanages were established and funded by local, private organizations, as the state government reduced its financial commitment.

2452.   Juhl (Julius J. Fleming).   *The Juhl Letters to the Charleston Courier: A View of the South, 1865-1871.*   Edited by John Hammond Moore.   Athens: University of Georgia Press, 1974. 391p.   Juhl, or Julius Fleming, was a Charleston born, college educated minister and teacher prior to the Civil War. Beginning in the summer of 1865, he began to write for the *Courier* while residing in Sumter and serving as a magistrate. The letters describe life in the upland region of the state and show Fleming's moderate and sympathetic views toward the freedmen. He also describes life in Florida (February, 1868) and Georgia (August, 1869) during periods of travel, and comments about state and national politics.

2453.   Knight, Edgar W. "The Reconstruction and Education in South Carolina." *South Atlantic Quarterly* 18 (October 1919): 350-364; 19 (January 1920): 55-66. Knight provides a narrative of how the Radical government reformed public education and brought constitutional sanction and state supervision to an existing, but limited, system of public education. Knight includes the debate over integrated schools, and he reviews the financial and organizational issues faced during the first few years of operation. Despite the progress in providing public education, schools in South Carolina suffered the same inefficiencies and corruption experienced by the Republican government.

2454.   McCandless, Peter. "'The Right Man in the Right Place': J. F. Ensor and the South Carolina Lunatic Asylum, 1870-1877." *South Carolina Historical Magazine* 90 (July 1989): 216-236.   Joshua F. Ensor was appointed superintendent of the insane asylum in 1870 by Republican Governor Robert K. Scott.   Ensor struggled to get adequate funding to rebuild and maintain a deteriorating facility, and he expressed exasperation with the corruption in state government. His desire to provide quality care led to his cultivation of support from both Republicans and Democrats.

2455.   McConaghy, Mary Delaney.   "Ordinary White Folk in a Lowcountry Community: The Structure and Dynamics of St. Bartholomew's Parish, South Carolina, 1850-1870." Ph.D. University of Pennsylvania, 1996. 805p.

2456. McCully, Robert S. "Letter From a Reconstruction Renegade." *South Carolina Historical Magazine* 77 (January 1976): 34-40.   Manson Sherrill Jolly of Anderson County organized a guerrilla band in 1865 to attack Yankee soldiers after the Civil War. Jolly's violent activities illustrate the difficult period in South Carolina following the war. He escaped to Texas in 1867

2457. McKivigan, John R. "James Redpath in South Carolina: An Abolitionist's Odyssey in the Reconstruction Era South." In *The Moment of Decision: Biographical Essays on American Character and Identity.* Westport: Greenwood Press, 1994. Edited by Randall M. Miller and John R. McKivigan. Pp. 188-210. Redpath was a Scotsman who emigrated to the U.S. in 1849 and became a journalist, entrepreneur, and strong abolitionist.   He supported equal rights and land redistribution for the freedmen, and his interest in black education was so great that the military occupation authorities asked him to supervise the creation of freedmens' schools in Charleston in the spring of 1865.   Redpath believed that the South deserved a stern Reconstruction, and by 1877 he lashed out at fellow Republicans as compromisers in the cause of civil rights for blacks.

2458. Pearson, Elizabeth Ware (ed.). *Letters From Port Royal Written at the Time of the Civil War.* Boston: W. B. Clarke Co., 1906. 345p. (Rpt in New York: Arno Press and the New York Times, 1969)   Included are letters written to and from Northern teachers and plantation administrators in Port Royal from February 10, 1862 to May 21, 1868. Except for identifying plantation administrators, Edward S. Philbrick and Reuben Tomlinson, and a teacher, Richard Soule, Jr., all other correspondents are identified with their initials. All writers were New England abolitionists who wrote about their experiences, particularly regarding the education of freedmen, labor, and adjustment to a new life. The letters show a puritanical, paternalistic attitude toward the ex-slaves, but they also show sympathy and agreement that the development from slavery to freedom must be based on equal opportunity for all. The letters reveal information about Maj. Gen. Rufus Saxton who organized the Port Royal experiment.

2459. Powers, Bernard E., Jr. *Black Charlestonians: A Social History, 1822-1885.* Fayetteville: University of Arkansas Press, 1994. 377p. Ills. Tbls.   The main focus of this book is the period of Reconstruction. Powers examines the impact of emancipation on freed and previously free blacks in the city and the transformation of their lives with particular emphasis on their vigorous attempts to secure real freedom and access to education, the work of their choice, the establishment of black churches, and the creation of better relations with whites. Reconstruction brought great improvements to the lives of the freedmen, but the lives of prewar free blacks became more complicated and reflected their desire to gain political power while also separating themselves from the lower classes who migrated to the city after the war. Powers recognizes that Reconstruction failed to secure true black freedom, but he emphasizes the efforts and seccesses of blacks in Charleston to develop a vital community.

2460.   Powers, Bernard E., Jr.   "Community Evolution and Race Relations in Reconstruction Charleston, South Carolina." *South Carolina Historical Magazine* 95 (January 1994): 27-46. Ills.   Powers describes the changing race relations in Charleston as black citizens actually sought to exercise their new civil rights after emancipation. Although black freedom generally met with white resistance, a rigid racial caste structure did not exist during Reconstruction. Charleston was a place of changing race relations in public places, employment, education, and political participation. The return of the Democrats in 1877 led to the reversal of black progress in custom and in law.

2461.   Rachey, John R.   "Gideonites and Freedmen: Adult Literacy Education at Port Royal 1862-1865." *Journal of Negro Education* 55 (Fall 1986): 453-469. The Gideonites were teachers and plantation supervisors from the Educational Commission (Boston) and the New York National Freedmen's Relief Association. Rachey focuses on religious education of the freedmen at Port Royal as a way to improve adult literacy.

2462.   Radford, John P.   "Social Structure and Urban Form: Charleston, 1860-1880." In *From the Old South to the New: Essays on the Transitional South*. Edited by Walter J. Fraser, Jr. and Winfred B. Moore, Jr. Westport: Greenwood Press, 1981. Pp. 81-91.   Radford focuses on urban spatial relationships in his examination of Charleston during the year prior to and after the Civil War. The transition from slavery to a nonslave based economy and from war to peace was based on continuity not change. Radford cites the local value structure and the power of the old elite as important contributors to this phenomenon and points out the lack of social, commercial, and environmental modernization after the war.

2463.   Rice, Elizabeth G. "A Yankee Teacher in the South: An Experience in the Early Days of Reconstruction." *Century Magazine* 62 (1901): 151-154.   Rice describes her experiences in Charleston beginning six weeks after Union forces occupied the city in February, 1865 until July. She mentions visits from Henry Ward Beecher and William Lloyd Garrison, and the general reaction to the assasination of President Lincoln.

2464.   Richardson, Joe M.   "Francis L. Cardozo: Black Educator During Reconstruction." *Journal of Negro Education* 48 (Winter 1979): 73-83.   Cardozo, a British educated, Congregationalist minister, established a teacher training school in Charleston as an employee of the American Missionary Association in October, 1865. His contributions at the Saxton School (Avery Institute in 1868) made it the premier black teacher training school in South Carolina. Cardozo's success in education led to his involvement in state politics for which he is better known.

2465.   Roper, John Herbert.   "A Reconsideration: The University of South Carolina During Reconstruction." *Proceedings of the South Carolina Historical Association* (1974): 46-57.   Roper refers to the University of South Carolina from 1873 to 1877 as "Radical University." The former South Carolina College was transformed into an institution that included black students and reform-minded faculty. He suggests that the university failed but offered a glimmer of what could develop in the future.

2466.   Rose, Willie Lee.   *Rehearsal For Reconstruction*:   *The Port Royal Experiment*. New York: Vintage Books, 1964. 442p. Bibl.   Rose provides an account of the federal occupation of the South Carolina sea islands during the Civil War and Reconstruction. After federal troops occupied the area in November, 1861, Northern missionary teachers followed within months to establish schools for the freedmen. Beginning in the spring of 1862 Rufus Saxton, Chief Quartermaster for Gen. Sherman's forces commenced the organization of abandoned plantations for cultivation by the slaves in the area. Thus began an experiment in black self reliance, labor and education that would have an impact on national politics and the hopes and dreams of freed slaves. Rose illustrates the relations between blacks and the Yankee invaders and the ways that life changed in the area. (See also Rose's Ph.D. disseration with the same title from Johns Hopkins University, 1962.)

2467.   Schwalm, Leslie A.   *A Hard Fight For We: Women's Transition From Slavery to Freedom in South Carolina*. Urbana: University of Illinois Press, 1997. 394p. Bibl.   Schwalm emphasizes that the transition to freedom black women in the South Carolina low country played a key role that extends beyond what most historians have described. She focuses on the environment of rice plantations where women continued to work and shape the meaning of freedom rather than withdraw from labor. Schwalm also examines the relationships of race and gender within the black family and how freedom influenced dependency on family and government agencies, such as the Freedman's Bureau. (See also Schwalm's "The Meaning of Freedom: African-American Women and Their Transformation From Slavery to Freedom in Lowcountry South Carolina." Ph.D. University of Wisconsin, 1991. 387p.)

2468.   Simkins, Francis Butler.   "White Methodism in South Carolina During Reconstruction."   *North Carolina Historical Review* 5 (January 1928): 35-64. Simkins writes that historians typically picture Reconstruction in South Carolina as nothing but a period of gloom and darkness. He asserts that these historians do not mention the many positive things that happened, such as the role of Methodism in making life a happier experience for thousands of whites. The Southern Methodists struggled against efforts of the Northern branch of the Church to reform the South and reunite both factions. Southerners also sought to halt the departure of most blacks who sought their own churches. Southern Methodists in South Carolina focused their efforts on the spiritual and moral welfare of the community, partly through the continued evangelical influence of prewar days and the influence of the Church in education and social organization.

2469.   Smedley, Katherine.   *Martha Schofield and the Re-education of the South, 1839-1916*. Lewiston: Edwin Mellen Press, 1987. 320p. Bibl. Port.   Schofield, born to an abolitionist Quaker family in Pennyslvania, dedicated her life to the academic and moral education of the freedmen in the South. She worked first in the Sea Islands of South Carolina in 1865 and later in Aiken where she remained for many years until her death. She faced up to the struggles encountered by Northern teachers in the South and eventually organized Schofield Normal and Industrial School, in Aiken in 1870. Schofield, who never married, also worked for women's right to vote. Her life illustrates the way women could break away from the traditional female role in American society.

2470.   Smith, Daniel E. Huger et. al. (eds.). *Mason Smith Family Letters 1860-1868*. Columbia: University of South Carolina Press, 1950. 292p. Genealogical Data. Ports.   The majority of these letters were written by or to Mrs. William Mason Smith of Charleston. Smith owned a plantation on the Combahee River near Beaufort when she and her children fled the Union Army in 1863. The letters from the spring of 1865 until the fall of 1868 reveal the way that she and her family coped with the problems of postwar South Carolina. Smith successfully sought the return of her plantation and Charleston property, and she offered contracts to her former slaves, most of whom had returned to the plantation and were waiting for her when she returned.

2471.   Sweat, Edward F.   "Some Notes on the Role of Negroes in the Establishment of Public Schools in South Carolina." *Phylon* 22 (Summer 1961): 160-166.   A lasting benefit of Reconstruction in South Carolina was the foundation laid for tax supported public schools by local blacks, particularly Francis Louis Cardozo, at the state constitutional convention of 1868. Many years after Reconstruction blacks continue to strive for equal access to public education and to take full advantage of a system that they did so much to establish.

2472.   Towne, Laura M. *Letters and Diary of Laura M. Towne: Written From the Sea Islands of South Carolina, 1862-1884*. Edited by Rupert Sargent Holland. New York: Negro Universities Press, 1969. 310p. Ills. (Rpt. from Cambridge: Riverside Press, 1912.)   Towne's writings illustrate her dedicated and unceasing work among the freedmen in the Sea Islands from April, 1862 until May, 1884, a period far longer than most of the other Northern aid workers. The abolitionist from Philadelphia provided relief aid, nursing care, and a school for the blacks.

2473.   Webster, Laura. "The Operation of the Freedmen's Bureau in South Carolina." *Smith College Studies in History* 1 (January 1916): 65-118; (April 1916): 119-163. App. Bibl. Maps. Tbls. (Rpt. by Russell and Russell, 1970.) Webster's detailed account offers a generally positive viewpoint of the bureau in South Carolina, particularly regarding contributions to relief, education, justice for freedmen, and the maintenance of order in labor relations.

2474.   Weiner, Marli Frances.   "Plantation Mistresses and Female Slaves: Gender, Race, and South Carolina Women, 1830-1880." Ph.D. University of Rochester, 1986. 430p.

2475.   Westwood, Howard. "The First Taste of Freedom, A Portfolio. The Port Royal Experiment: South Carolina Leaves Slavery Behind." *Civil War Times Illustrated* 25 (May 1986): 24-27. Ills.   Westwood offers a very brief description and photographs illustrating the wartime project that proved that blacks could be independent farmers on land confiscated from plantation owners. The Port Royal experiment existed from April, 1862 until 1865.

Tennessee

General History

2476.   Alexander, Thomas B.   *Reconstruction in Tennessee*. Ph.D. Vanderbilt University, 1947. 413p.

2477.   Fertig, James W. "Secession and Reconstruction of Tennessee." Ph.D. University of Chicago, 1898. 108p. (Rpt. by Chicago: University of Chicago Press, 1898; New York: AMS Press, 1972)

2478.   Neal, John Randolph. "Disunion and Restoration in Tennessee." Ph.D. Columbia University, 1899. 79p (Rpt. by Knickerbocker Press, 1899; Books for Libraries Press, 1971)

2479.   Taylor, Alrutheus Ambush.   *The Negro in Tennessee, 1865-1880*. Spartanburg, S.C.:   Reprint Co., Publishers, 1974.   306p.   Bibl.   (Repr. of Washington, D.C.: Associate Publishers, 1941)   Taylor's focuses on black politics, emigration, labor, economic progress, the development of education and religious institutions, and society in Tennessee. The book represents a contribution to the early revisionist trend with particularly with his emphasis on blacks in Reconstruction historiography.

Politics and Law

2480.   Alexander, Thomas B.   "Ku Klux Klan in Tennessee, 1865-1869." *Tennessee Historical Quarterly* 8 (September 1949): 195-219. Tbl.   Alexander expalins that the rule of a small Radical minority led by Gov. William G. Brownlow caused the rise of the Klan in Tennessee. The enfranchisement of blacks and the disenfranchisement of whites went far beyond the desires of the white majority. Alexander believes that complaints against Klan violence were exaggerated. Only after DeWitt C. Senter became governor in 1869 did many whites regain the vote and the need for the Klan disappeared.

2481.   Alexander, Thomas B. *Political Reconstruction in Tennessee*. Nashville: Vanderbilt University Press, 1950. 292p. App. Bibl. Tbls.   Alexander characterizes Reconstruction in Tennessee as the clash of extreme radical and conservative ideologies, even though the state included a large number of Unionists, particularly in eastern counties, and was able to avoid Congressional Reconstruction. Gov. William Brownlow became increasingly radical, and his allies abandoned him when he supported black suffrage and political participation. Unionists in eastern counties responded to his call for equal civil rights with more violence than the more conservative factions. Brownlow's policies of heavy railroad subsidies and tax increases, and his financial mismanagement, led to the fall of the Radical Republicans in the state. Moderation was totally absent from the political leadership of Tennessee.

2482.   Alexander, Thomas B. "Political Reconstruction in Tennessee, 1865-1870." In *Radicalism, Racism, and Party Realignment, the Border States During Reconstruction*. Edited by R. O. Curry. Baltimore: Johns Hopkins Press, 1969. Pp. 37-79. Maps.   Alexander's essay is an abridgement of his book *Political Reconstruction in Tennessee* (see # 2481).   He emphasizes the influences of geography, traditional party politics, civil rights for the blacks, and the influence of the Ku Klux Klan with the direction of Reconstruction in the state. Alexander downplays any lasting impact from Reconstruction related to civil rights, education, and economics.   He emphasizes that racism among all whites, including the Radicals, was a theme that ran through the period.

2483.   Alexander, Thomas B. "Strange Bedfellows: The Interlocking Careers of T. A. R. Nelson, Andrew Johnson, and W. G. (Parson) Brownlow." *East Tennessee Historical Society's Publications* 24 (1952): 68-91.   Alexander discusses the relationship of three Eastern Tennessee politicians who were united on the eve of secession in their support for the Union and dislike of abolitionism. By the end of the war and the beginning of Reconstruction their unity was crumbling. Nelson was a conservative Democrat, while Johnson and Brownlow were Republicans, but the latter two split over Reconstruction policies and the treatment of former Confederates.

2484.   Alexander, Thomas B. "Whiggery and Reconstruction in Tennessee." *Journal of Southern History* 16 (August 19500: 291-305.   Followers of the old Whig Party in Tennessee opposed Democrats and became Unionists during the Civil War. They emerged as the leaders of the early postwar government, and they combined with blacks and Northern whites in the Republican Party. When the government of William G. Brownlow sponsored Radical policies, conservative Whigs abandoned him by the summer of 1867 for a "liberal" alternative. Even though Whigs usually despised Democratic ideology, they gradually migrated to the Democratic Party in the 1870s in response to Republican race policies.

2485.   Argersinger, Peter H. "The Conservative as Radical: A Reconstructive Dilemma." *Tennessee Historical Quarterly* 34 (Summer 1975): 168-187.   William Alfred Peffer fought in the Union Army and settled his family in Clarksville after the war. His support for Republican Party ideals was tempered by his consistent opposition to the disenfranchisement of thousands of whites who were considered disloyal. He supported equal rights for blacks and whites as a conservative principle of the American system of government, but Peffer's conservatism led to his being labeled a carpetbagger and a Radical.

2486.   Binning, F. Wayne. "The Tennessee Republicans in Decline, 1869-1876. Pt. I." *Tennessee Historical Quarterly* 39 (Winter 1980): 471-484; "Pt. II." 40 (Spring 1981): 68-84. Tbls.   Between 1865 and 1868 Republican power in Tennessee centered in eastern counties and reached its height under the harsh and opportunistic leadership of Gov. William G. Brownlow.   Brownlow helped to disenfranchise thousands of white Democrats and to give the vote to freedmen. Once his hand picked successor, DeWitt Clinton Senter, became governor, the Republican Party began its decline.   In the elections of 1872 and 1876 Republicans could not overcome their lack of leadership, Brownlow's negative legacy, and the severe internal dispute over civil rights for blacks.   Part II includes a table of presidential and gubernatorial election returns from 1867 to 1876.

2487.   Cimprich, John.   "The Beginning of the Black Suffrage Movement in Tennessee, 1864-1865." *Journal of Negro History* 65 (Summer 1980): 185-195. Freedmen in Tennessee took an active part in demanding civil rights as early as 1863.   Blacks held conventions to plan their strategy, requested help from the Unionist Party, and petitioned state and federal legislatures to act on the suffrage issue.   But blacks in Tennessee had to wait until 1867 to vote in elections when the Unionist Party needed the votes of the freedmen to maintain control of state government.   Cimprich emphasizes that blacks were the major initiators in the struggle for black suffrage in Tennessee.   The appendix includes information about 30 black leaders during 1864 and 1865.

2488.   Cooper, Constance J.   "Tennessee Returns to Congress."   *Tennessee Historical Quarterly* 37 (Spring 1978): 49-62.   Cooper reviews the backgrounds of the 10 men who joined the U.S. House (8) and Senate (2) on December 3, 1866 as representatives of the first reconstructed Southern state.   The group was split between radical and conservative supporters, but in general, they remained quiet and not very influential during their terms.   Profiled are Senators David Patterson and Joseph Fowler, and Congressmen Nathaniel G. Taylor, Horace Maynard, William B. Stokes, Edmund Cooper, William G. Campbell, Samuel M. Arnell, Isaac R. Hawkins, and John W. Leftwich.

2489.   Coulter, E. Merton.   *William G. Brownlow: Fighting Parson of the Southern Highlands.* Chapel Hill: University of North Carolina Press, 1937. 432p. Bibl. Ills. Map. Ports.   Brownlow was a native of East Tennessee and a strong Unionist.   His Unionist credentials helped him win the gubernatorial election of 1865 and a seat in the U.S. Senate in 1869 as a Republican.   Coulter criticizes Brownlow for his vindictiveness against former Confederates, his Radical policies in favor of black suffrage, and his ruthless methods used to put down violence in the state.   He was a thoroughly political person who sought the support of poor citizens and led a corrupt, destructive regime.

2490.   Crofts, Daniel W.   "Reconstruction in Tennessee: An Assessment for Thaddeus Stevens."   *West Tennessee Historical Society Papers* 43 (December 1989): 13-27.   Crofts examines and prints a letter to Stevens from William M. Connelly, a Memphis Republican and former newspaper publisher.   The letter, written in February, 1868, provides a full and insightful assessment of the strengths, weaknesses and prospects of William G. Brownlow's Republican Party.   Connelly refers to the lack of quality leaders in the state and the huge postwar problems that face the government.   He asks Stevens to strengthen the party.

2491.   Feistman, Eugene G.   "Radical Disfranchisement and the Restoration of Tennessee, 1865-1866." *Tennessee Historical Quarterly* 12 (June 1956): 135-151. Gov. William G. Brownlow is credited with leading the state back into the Union in the spring of 1866 and avoiding Congressional Reconstruction, but Feistman criticizes the governor's vindictiveness against former confederates and his dishonesty in becoming a Radical leader who supported black suffrage, the disenfranchisement of white leaders, and the acceptance of the 14th Amendment.

2492.   Fisher, Noel C.   "'War at Every Man's Door':   The Struggle for East Tennessee, 1860-1869." Ph.D. Ohio State University, 1993. 500p.

2493.   Fowler, Russell.   "Chancellor William Macon Smith and Judicial Reconstruction: A Study of Tyranny and Integrity." *West Tennessee Historical Society Papers* 48 (1994): 35-59.   Fowler explains court reform directed by Military Governor Andrew Johnson during the federal occupation of Memphis and other parts of Tennessee.   Smith began as Chancellor of the Common Law and Chancery Court in February, 1865.   His service until November, 1869 illustrates how Smith's court functioned during the harsh period of Governor William G. Brownlow's Radical Republican administration.   Fowler describes Smith's later career in law and politics.

2494.   Fraser, Walter J., Jr.   "Barbour Lewis: A Carpetbagger Reconsidered." *Tennessee Historical Quarterly* 32 (Summer 1973): 148-168.   Lewis arrived in Memphis in January, 1863 with this U.S. Army unit, and he stayed on in the city after the war.   Fraser reviews Lewis' career as a Republican leader and congressman, and one who worked for the civil rights of freedmen.   His aggressiveness earned him the label "carpetbagger", but Fraser concludes that he does not deserve to be vilified. Lewis was disliked because of his enthusiastism for radical Republicanism.

2495.   Fraser, Walter J., Jr.   "Black Reconstruction in Tennessee." *Tennessee Historical Quarterly* 34 (Winter 1975): 362-382.   Fraser focuses on Western Tennessee counties around Memphis in his examination of black political leaders and the local Radical political machine.   Barbour Lewis and John Eaton maintained a Republican organization that actively sought the support of black voters.   Blacks, such as Hannibal C. Carter and Edward Shaw, gave their support but expected political appointments and support for elective offices for themselves.   Rivalries split the Republican Party, and Democrats competed to secure black votes for their candidates. Both parties used blacks to perpetuate white rule and deny black leaders an important role in government.

2496.   Going, Allen J.   "A Shooting Affray in Knoxville With Interstate Repercussions: The Killing of James H. Clanton by David N. Nelson, 1871." *East Tennessee Historical Society's Publications* 27 (1955): 39-48.   Going describes the shoot out in Knoxville as at least partially due to the continuing animosity and tension between former Confederates and Unionists. The case was complicated by the fact that the victim was visiting from Alabama on railroad business.

2497.   Graf, LeRoy P.   "'Parson' Brownlow's Fears: A Letter About the Dangerous,   Desparate   Democrats."   *East   Tennessee   Historical   Society's Publications* 25 (1953): 111-114.   Graf provides the text of a letter dated September 14, 1871 from Sen. William Brownlow to U.S. Commissioner of Education John Eaton, Jr. Brownlow warned Republicans that Southern Democrats would use fraud and intimidation to win the national election of 1872. If those tactics did not succeed in defeating the Republicans, he predicted that they would turn to assassination.

2498.   Green, John W.   "Judges of the Reconstruction Era   (1865-1870)." *Tennessee Law Review* 17 (1942): 413-422. Ports.   Between 1865 and 1870 seven different men served on the 3 man state supreme court. Green provides biographical sketches of 4 of them: Sam Milligan, Alvin Hawskins, George Andrews, and Henry G. Smith.

2499.   Green, John W.   "Some Judges of the Supreme Court of Tennessee 1865-1878." *Tennessee Law Review* 17 (1943): 789-804. Ports.   Green provides biograpical sketches of Horace H. Harrison, James O. Schackelford, Andrew McClain, Thomas A. R. Nelson, A. O. P. Nicholson, and John L. T. Sneed.

2500.   Groce, William Todd.   "Mountain Rebels: East Tennessee Confederates and the Civil War, 1860-1870." Ph.D. University of Tennessee, 1992. 251p.

2501.   Guild, George B.   "Reconstruction Times in Sumner County." *American Historical Magazine and Tennessee Historical Society Quarterly* 8 (October 1903): 355-368.   Guild tells stories of racial and political tension when Tennessee was oppressed by Republican rule.

2502.   Henry, Milton.   "What Became of the Tennessee Whigs?" *Tennessee Historical Quarterly* 11 (March 1952): 57-62. Tbls.   Henry follows voting trends (1848-1876), farm values, and per capita wealth (1860-1870) in seven dispersed Whig counties to assess the political home of Whigs in 1870. The counties were Carter, Knox, Davidson, Montgomery, Shelby, Carroll, and Gibson.

2503.   Hollingsworth, Harold M. "George Andrews - Carpetbagger." *Tennessee Historical Quarterly* 28 (Fall 1969): 310-323.   Andrews moved from Detroit to Knoxville shortly after the war. He served as U.S. Attorney for the eastern district of the state and a trustee of the University of Tennessee. Gov. Brownlow appointed him a justice of the state Supreme Court. Although he was a supporter of Radical Republicanism, his career does not follow the stereotype of the pernicious carpetbagger.

2504.   Jordon, Weymouth T.   "Negro Enfranchisement in Reconstruction Tennessee: An Interpretation." *Florida State University Studies* 10 (1953): 63-69. Jordon supports the idea that the vote was given to the freedmen of Tennessee mainly because the Republicans simply wanted to retain power, and enfranchising blacks was the way to retain their votes. When the Republicans no longer needed the black vote, they turned their backs on them.

2505.   Kelly, James C.   "William Gannaway Brownlow, Part II." *Tennessee Historical Quarterly* 43 (Summer 1984): 155-172. Ills. Port.   Part II of this two part article on Brownlow's career focuses mainly on the period when he was governor of Tennessee from 1865 until his death in 1877.   Kelly describes Brownlow's strengths and weaknesses, and believes that the virtues have been overlooked, particularly his courage and principled stand. Brownlow forced change in Tennessee when most Unionists hoped for a return to prewar conditions. While he acted as a politician without regard to proper procedures and in ways that would enhance his power, he accomplished the state's return to the Union expeditiously. (See also Part I in *T.H.Q.* 43 (Spring 1984): 25-43)

2506.   Kornell, Gary L.   "Reconstruction in Nashville, 1867-1869." *Tennessee Historical Quarterly* 30 (Fall 1971): 277-287.   Republicans controlled the city government of Nashville from September, 1867 to mid-1869. Traditionally this period, when A. E. Alden was mayor, has been remembered for corruption and squandering public tax money. Kornell explains that while the Alden administration was not perfect, the criticism has been exaggerated. Programs were intended to aid the poor and the blacks, improve medical facilities, and provide freedmen with civil rights.

2507.   Maness, Lonnie E.   "Henry Emerson Etheridge and the Gubernatorial Election of 1867: A Study in Futility." *West Tennessee Historical Society Papers* 47 (December 1993): 37-49.   By 1865 Unionists in Tennessee had split into factions - the Radicals led by Gov. William G. Brownlow and the Conservative Unionists who opposed disenfranchising whites, amnesty oaths, and full civil rights for blacks. Maness emphasizes that Brownlow's minority party depended on the disenfranchisement of whites and the enfranchisement of blacks to maintain power. In the gubernatorial election of 1867 Henry Etheridge, the Conservative Unionist candidate, sought the black vote, but there was little chance that he would win. Maness sympathizes with Etheridge.

2508.   Maslowski, Peter.   "From Reconciliation to Reconstruction: Lincoln, Johnson, and Tennessee, Part I." *Tennessee Historical Quarterly* 42 (Fall, 1983): 281-298; Pt. II (Winter 1983): 343-361. Ills. Ports.   Maslowski explains that Lincoln's approach toward wartime Reconstruction in Tennessee focused on gaining the support of East Tennessee Unionists. Lincoln's efforts were stymied by the disagreements among the Unionists about what a reconstructed Tennessee should be and the lack of loyal support in middle and western counties. By the time that Andrew Johnson became president in April, 1865 Tennessee had experienced a more successful government transformation than in other states where wartime Reconstruction was attempted. This was largely due to the efforts of Andrew Johnson as military governor.

2509.   Maslowski, Peter. *Treason Must Be Made Odious: Military Occupation and Wartime Reconstruction in Nashville, Tennessee, 1862-1865.* Millwood, N.Y.: KTO Press, 1978. 173p. Bibl.   Maslowski argues that Reconstruction began during the Civil War at the local level as the Union Army occupied portions of the South and established military governments and new local civil governments. Using Nashville as a case study, he reviews the Army's participation in government formation, city maintenance, and assistance to black refugees. These activities represent an attempt to reconstruct the city and the state. Andrew Johnson, as military governor, was unsuccessful at forming both a loyal, popular government and a plan to bring the freedmen into society as equal citizens. The Army's work was part of the evolving process of Reconstruction. (See also Maslowski's Ph.D. dissertation with the same title from Ohio State University, 1972.)

2510.   McBride, Robert M.   "Northern, Military, Corrupt, and Transitory: Augustus E. Alden, Nashville's Carpetbagger Mayor." *Tennessee Historical Quarterly* 37 (Spring 1978): 63-67.   Alden, formerly of Maine and the Midwest, was a Radical Republican mayor from 1867 until 1869 when he was forced out of office. His regime has been vilified for corruption, but McBride explains that corruption was never proven and Alden's positive contributions to education and assisting local blacks should be recognized.

2511.   McBride, William Gillespie. "Blacks and the Race Issue in Tennessee Politics, 1865-1876." Ph.D. Vanderbilt University, 1989. 420p.

2512.   M'Donnold, R. L. "The Reconstruction Period in Tennessee." *American Historical Magazine* 1 (October 1896): 307-328.   This article includes a brief survey of the Federal occupation from 1862 until redemption in 1870. M'Donnold emphasizes the special privileges granted to Tennessee when Andrew Johnson was military governor, the harsh policies of Governor William G. Brownlow, the positive contributions of the Ku Klux Klan, criticism of Union Leagues, and the disenfranchisement of former rebels.

2513.   Miscamble, Wilson D. "Andrew Johnson and the Election of William G. ('Parson') Brownlow As Governor of Tennessee." *Tennessee Historical Quarterly* 37 (Fall 1978): 308-320.   Johnson and Brownlow were bitter enemies before the Civil War, but they worked together as Unionists during the war. Miscamble explains that the two men continued to work together in the organization of the state constitutional convention in 1865 and Brownlow's nomination for governor. Only when Johnson softened his approach toward the South did the two men return to a bitter relationship.

2514.   M'Neilly, James H., Rev. "Reconstruction in Tennessee." *Confederate Veteran* 28 (September 1920): 340-342; (October 1920): 369-371. Ports.   Rev. M'Neilly of Tennessee describes experiences and stories of Reconstruction in western Tennessee and Nashville. He comments on Union troops, the state militia, and politics during the oppressive regime of Gov. William G. Brownlow.

2515.   Parker, James C. "Tennessee Gubernatorial Elections, I. 1869-The Victory of the Conservative." *Tennessee Historical Quarterly* 33 (Summer 1974): 34-48. In the Tennessee election of August, 1869 two Republicans competed, incumbent DeWitt C. Senter and U.S. Congressman William B. Stokes. Senter won the election by appealing to white voters after the state Supreme Court ruled that restrictions against them were unconstitutional. Senter's victory quickly led to the end of Radical rule and a new, conservative constitution within a year.

2516.   Patton, James Welch. *Unionism and Reconstruction in Tennessee 1860-1869.* Chapel Hill: University of North Carolina Press, 1934. 267p. Bibl. Ill. Patton devotes most of his attention to the politics under the leadership of Unionist William G. Brownlow, who was governor from 1865 until he resigned in February, 1869 to take a seat in the U.S. Senate. The Methodist minister and former Whig is depicted as a reluctant reformer who accepted Radical policies to build support in Congress for the quickest path toward political normalization of the state. White citizens generally did not support Brownlow's Radical policies, Northern Methodist faith, involvement with the state militia, and the rise of the state debt due to poor leadership and scandal. Patton also discusses the activities of the Freedmen's Bureau and the Ku Klux Klan. (See also Patton's "The Brownlow Regime in Tennessee." Ph.D. University of North Carolina, 1929.)

2517.   Queener, Verton M. "A Decade of East Tennessee Republicanism, 1867-1876." *East Tennessee Historical Society's Publications*, no. 14 (1942): 59-85. Queener attributes the state Republican victory in 1867 to the enfranchisement of the freedmen and the disenfranchisement of thousands of conservative whites. Despite the Republican advantage, they split over race issues, political scandals, and corruption. Elections were mismanaged and the Ku Klux Klan undermined active support. When disenfranchised whites regained a vote 1868, they helped elect a moderate Republican governor, DeWitt C. Senter, and a conservative legislature. Republican power gradually declined until conservative Republicans revolted against black civil rights and the Democrats took over East Tennessee.

2518.   Queener, Verton M. "The East Tennessee Republicans as a Minority Party, 1870-1896." *East Tennessee Historical Society's Publications*, no. 15 (1953): 49-73.   Queener focuses on how the Republicans responded to state issues, such as railroads, state debt and taxation, immigration, public education, and industrialization beginning in 1870, the year when the Republicans became a minority party. During the next 30 years Republicans had to ally with other minority parties, including Greenbacks, the Grange, the Farmers' Alliance, and Populists.

2519.   Queener, Verton M.   "A History of the Republican Party in Eastern Tennessee." Ph.D. Indiana University, 1940. 272p.

2520.   Queener, Verton M.   "The Origin of the Republican Party in East Tennessee." *East Tennessee Historical Society's Publications*, no. 13 (1941): 66-90. Ills. Tbls.   Queener analyses the voting patterns of Tennessee counties to demonstrate that support for the Republican Party in postwar years concentrated mostly in eastern counties, a region where Unionist Whigs predominated prior to and during the Civil War.   The Unionist Whigs were themselves divided over conservative and radical approaches toward Reconstruction, and many were not in favor of the emancipation of the slaves.   Tennessee's Republican strength came from the eastern counties, and they supported the reelection of Governor William G. Brownlow in 1867.   After 1867 Republicans controlled state politics, but Radical policies drove many supporters into conservative ranks.

2521.   Tannant, James G.   "Political Readjustment in Tennessee, 1869-1870." Ph.D. George Peabody College, 1943.

2522.   Temple, Oliver Perry.   *Notable Men in Tennessee From 1833 to 1875: Their Times and Their Contemporaries*.   New York: Cosmopolitan Press, 1912. 467p.   Port.   This volume includes biographies of William G. Brownlow and Andrew Johnson.   Brownlow, a Unionist and Republican govenor, is depicted sympathetically while Johnson receives criticism for his handling of Reconstruction and his inability to tame his ambition for power.   Brief biographies also appear on DeWitt Senter, Thomas A. R. Nelson, Sam Mulligan, Horace Maynard, and Andrew Fletcher.

2523.   Thurston, Gen. G. P.   "A Relic of the Reconstruction Period in Tennessee." *American Historical Magazine* 6 (July 1901): 243-250.   The author recalls his experiences and the bitter treatment of the South from congressional Republicans.

2524.   Tucker, David.   "Black Politics in Memphis, 1865-1875." *West Tennessee Historical Society Papers* 26 (1972): 13-19.   Black insistence on exercising their political rights in Memphis is symbolized by Ed Shaw, who sought public office despite opposition from white Republicans.   Shaw and others succeeded in 1872 and 1874, but their disillusionment with the National Republican Party led them to compromise with Southern whites.

2525.   Zebley, Kathleen R.   "Unconditional Unionist: Samuel Mayes Arnell and Reconstruction in Tennessee." *Tennessee Historical Quarterly* 53 (Winter 1994): 246-259. Ills. Ports.   Arnell was a Whig Unionist who turned Republican after the war.   As a member of the General Assembly, Arnell supported Brownlow and voted in favor of restricting suffrage for former rebels and enfranchising blacks.   In 1866 he became a congressman and continued supporting Republican Unionists and

Congressional Reconstruction.   He attempted to have Congress apply military Reconstruction to Tennessee after the Democrats regained power in the legislature in the election of 1869.

Agriculture, Labor, and Business

2526.   Beaver, R. Pierce.   "An Ohio Farmer in Middle Tennessee in 1865." *Tennessee Historical Magazine*, Series II, 1 (October 1930): 29-39.   The presence of Northern farmers in the South generated resentment among some local residents. Beaver cites the case of Colonel George F. Elliott of the Union Army, who leased a farm near Franklin in February, 1865.   Several letters are printed from the period between February and July that illustrate Elliott's problems, including threats on his life and theft of farm animals.

2527.   Belissary, C. G.   "Tennessee and Immigration, 1865-1880." *Tennessee Historical Quarterly* 7 (September 1948): 229-248.   The Republican Party actively sought new settlers to improve the stock of skilled labor and to provide needed capital for new businesses and industries.   A campaign began in December, 1867 with the creation of a board of immigration, and it lasted until well after the Democrats regained power in 1869.   The efforts failed due to local instability, the lack of industry, and the attractiveness of the Great Plains for prospective farmers and miners.

2528.   Campbell, James B.   "East Tennessee During the Radical Regime, 1865-1869."   *East Tennessee Historical Society's Publications* 20 (1948): 84-102. Campbell focuses on the daily lives of the people of East Tennessee, a region that was heavily Unionist and the source of postwar leadership.   He discusses urban conditions in Knoxville and Chattanooga, agriculture, and industrial development.

2529.   Davis, Dernoral.   "Against the Odds: Postbellum Growth and Development in a Southern Black Urban Community, 1865-1900." Ph.D.   State University of New York at Binghamton, 1987. 315p. (Memphis, Tn.)

2530.   Davis, Dernoral.   "Hope Versus Reality: The Emancipation Era Labor Struggle of Memphis Area Freedmen, 1863-1870." In *Race, Class, and Community in Southern Labor History*.   Edited by Gary M. Fink and Merl E. Reed.   Tuscaloosa: University of Alabama Press, 1994.   Pp. 97-120.   Freedmen expressed their new freedom by flocking to the city and many hoped to acquire their own land, but the U.S. Army and the Freedmen's Bureau coerced them to return to work on plantations.   The failure of the federal government to pursue a policy that would lead the freedmen toward economic independence guaranteed slow progress under the domination of distrustful whites.

2531.   Jones, Robert Brinkley, III.   "The State Debt Controversy in Tennessee, 1865-1883." Vanderbilt University, 1972. 382p.

2532.   Kenzer, Robert C.   "Black Businessmen in Post-Civil War Tennessee." *Journal of East Tennessee History* 86 (1994): 59-80. Port. Tbls.   Kenzer uses the R. G. Dun and Co. credit ratings, U.S. Census, and local records to analyze the 96 black businesses in Tennessee from 1865 to 1880. The sources offer characteristics of the black business community, including business distribution, success, and values. Information about the number of black businesses by county is provided in an appendix. Kenser compares entrepreneurs in Tennessee with businessmen in other states.

2533.   McGehee, C. Stuart.   "Military Origins of the New South: The Army of the Cumberland and Chattanooga's Freedmen." *Civil War History* 34 (December 1988): 322-343. Tbls.   The working relationship between U.S. Colored Troops in Tennessee and their white officers carried over into peacetime. The first few years of Reconstruction in the Chattanooga Valley were marked by opportunities for blacks to find work in urban industries and in politics. Among the white Union veterans who stayed in Chattanooga were John T. Wilder, who founded Roane Iron Company, and John C. Stanton, a major investor in the Alabama and Chattanooga Railroad. Both companies were major employers of blacks. Despite racial problems the local black population made economic progress that was unique to the Chattanooga valley.

2534.   McKenzie, Robert Tracy.   "Civil War and Socioeconomic Change in the Upper South: The Survival of Local Agricultural Elites in Tennessee, 1850-1870." *Tennessee Historical Quarterly* 52 (Fall 1993): 170-184. Ills. Map. Ports. Tbls. McKenzie analyses the impact of the war on the survival of elites in eight counties in various parts of the state. He concludes that the wealth of agricultural elite shrunk because of emancipation and debt, but they maintained their domination throughout the state between 1850 and 1870. There was turnover within the elite class, but when land exchanged hands, it was usually received by an established member of the community.   The counties studied include Haywood, Fayette, Robertson, Wilson, Lincoln, Grainger, Johnson, and Greene.

2535.   McKenzie, Robert Tracy.   "Freedmen and the Soil in the Upper South: The Reorganization of Tennessee Agriculture, 1865-1880." *Journal of Southern History* 59 (February 1993): 63-84.   In this statistical study of labor and farm ownership in Tennessee, McKenzie concludes that the standard historical account of the freedmen involved in agriculture glosses over a complicated, fluid environment in which the shift of the freedmen in Tennessee from laborer to sharecropper occurred more slowly than originally thought. The fact that blacks owned land was significant enough to note, although many landowners lost their land by 1880 and were more likely laborers than sharecroppers or tenant farmers.

2536.   McKenzie, Robert Tracy.   *One South or Many? Plantation Belt and Upcountry in Civil War-Era Tennessee*. Cambridge: Cambridge University Press, 1994. 213p. App. Bibl. Map. Tbl.   In McKenzie's case study of eight counties in the 3 large regions of Tennessee he examines the socioeconomic diversity of rural areas of the state from 1850 to 1889. He also studies the difficulties of poor white farmers and the adjustment and treatment of black laborers and farmers. In this statistical study McKenzie emphasizes that there were similarities in the ways that plantation and non-plantation (i.e. black belt v. upcountry) regions adjusted to the changes following the Civil War. But there were also broad differences that belie traditional generalizations and extending the experiences of the black belt plantation regions to the entire South. The counties studied are Haywood and Fayette in the west; Robertson, Wilson, and Lincoln in the middle region, and Johnson, Greene, and Grainger in the east. (See also McKenzie's "From Old South to New South in the Volunteer State: The Economy and Society of Rural Tennessee, 1850-1880." Ph.D. Vanderbilt University, 1988. 312p.)

2537.   Winters, Donald L. "Postbellum Reorganization of Southern Agriculture: The Economics of Sharecropping in Tennessee." *Agricultural History* 62   (Fall 188): 1-19.   Winters examines contracts between landowners and tenants or sharecroppers to reveal the varied nature of the relationship and the pressures placed on both parties. Sharecropping contracts were supposed to guarantee the rights of landowner and tenant, but they frequently revealed landowners' attempts to maintain racial dominance over blacks and possibly bind them to the land with crop liens. Liens were important to the tenants as a form of badly needed credit, and due to the the economic and labor environment, it was often in the landowners best interest to avoid taking advantage of tenants.

Society, Education, and Religion

2538.   Alexander, Thomas B. "Neither Peace Nor War: Conditions in Tennessee in 1865." *East Tennessee Historical Society's Publications* 21 (1949): 33-51. Alexander focuses primarily on the widespread violence caused by guerrilla bands and criminals, and the continuing fueds between Unionists and former Confederates. Blacks were also a problem as they left the countryside without sufficient labor and flocked to urban areas.   The presence of thousands of new black residences contributed to racial unrest in the cities.

2539.   Ash, Stephen V. "Middle Tennessee Society in Transition, 1860-1870." *Maryland Historian* 13 (Spring-Summer 1982): 19-38. Tbls.   Ash analyses the broad impact of war and Reconstruction on thirteen counties in Middle Tennessee. Using the census he traces various factors, including wealth and occupation. He finds that while class and wealth differences existed between white elites and the lower classes, they were overshadowed by their collective opposition to the equality of blacks in society. Whites sought an unchanged society, but blacks wanted change. Black society proved to be dynamic in Reconstruction, including migration and experimentation with work.

2540.   Ash, Stephen V. *Middle Tennessee Society Transformed 1860-1870: War and Peace in the Upper South*. Baton Rouge: Louisiana State University Press, 1988. 299p. App. Bibl. Maps. Tbls.   The counties of Middle Tennessee are viewed as a distinct region in the South that responded to war, emancipation, and Reconstruction in its own way. A biracial community was torn apart by white resentment over emancipation and the aggressive way that blacks asserted their new freedom. Violence and intimidation by the Ku Klux Klan and the victory of the Redeemers in the state elections of August, 1869 made it clear to the black community that a long, difficult struggle for equality lay ahead. Ash also discusses the unity among planters and white yeomen, economic and educational progress made by freedmen prior to 1870, and the armed resistance of blacks against white intimidators. (See also Ash's "Civil War, Black Freedom, and Social Change in the Upper South: Middle Tennessee, 1860-1870." 2 Vols. Ph.D. University of Tennessee, 1983. 802p)

2541. Ash, Stephen V. "Postwar Recovery: Montgomery County, 1865-1970." *Tennessee Historical Quarterly* 36 (Summer 1977): 207-221. Montgomery County experienced extensive damage to its economic, social, and cultural structures during the Civil War. Ash reviews how the people of the county responded to peace and worked to rebuild their lives. He cites the slow adjustment to emancipation and economic change, but the community eventually became more open to change and more willing to see the world beyond the boundaries of the county.

2542. Berkeley, Kathleen C. "Ethnicity and Its Implications for Southern Urban History: The Saga of Memphis, Tennessee, 1850-1880." *Tennessee Historical Quarterly* 50 (Winter 1991): 193-202. Ills. Port. A portion of this article deals with Republican reaction to the support of Memphis Jews for the Democratic Party in 1868. The "defection" (p. 195) of Jews to the Democrats occurred because they did not trust presidential candidate Ulysses S. Grant who issued General Order No. 11 that banned Jews as a class from the Department of Tennessee. The defection also encouraged Republican city officials to accuse Jews of dishonesty in commerce because of the misdeeds of a few merchants.

2543. Berkeley, Kathleen Christine. *"Like a Plague of Locusts": Immigration and Social Change in Memphis, Tennessee, 1850-1880.* Ph.D. University of California, Los Angeles, 1980. 420p.

2544. Bratcher, James T. "An 1866 Letter on the War and Reconstruction." *Tennessee Historical Quarterly* 22 (March 1963): 83-86. The impact of the Civil War is reflected in this single letter written by Tennesseans living in Kansas in May, 1866.

2545. Cimprich, John. "Slavery's End in East Tennessee." *East Tennessee Historical Society's Publications* 52-53 (1980-1981): 78-88. In Unionist counties of East Tennessee slaves represented only 9% of the population, but emancipation proved just as traumatic as in other regions with many more slaves. For political reasons Unionists voted in favor of emancipation on February 12, 1865, but their lack of real concern for the freedmen led to social and economic problems. Cimprich describes how the freedmen began to adjust to freedom in 1865 with the assistance of the Freedmen's Bureau.

2546.   Corlew, Robert Ewing. "The Negro in Tennessee, 1870-1900." Ph.D. University of Alabama, 1954. 408p.

2547.   DeLozier, Mary Jean. "The Civil War and Its Aftermath in Putnam County." *Tennessee Historical Quarterly* 38 (Winter 1979): 436-461.   DeLozier emphasizes the destruction of the war and Reconstruction in Putnam County and the Cumberland Plateau of Tennessee. The area was politically split over secession, and this caused internicine warfare, including guerilla raids during and after the war. The general prejudice and intimidation shown against black residents led to the departure of many of them to other counties.

2548.   Eaton, John. *Grant, Lincoln, and the Freedmen: Reminiscences of the Civil War With Special Reference to the Work For the Contrabands and Freedmen of the Mississippi Valley.* New York: Longmans, Green, and Co., 1907. 331p. App., Bibl. Facim. Ills. Port.   Eaton was a Union Army officer who was the wartime General Superintendent of Freedmen in the Department of Tennessee under Grant's command and later an assistant commissioner in the Freedmen's Bureau. He led freedmen away from Union lines for productive work and education. In his memoirs he discusses his activities, encounters, and impressions of President Lincoln and Gen. Grant. Eaton also discusses his postwar activities as editor of the *Memphis Post* and as an educator in Tennessee and the federal government.

2549.   Ezzell, Timothy Paul. "Yankees in Dixie: The Story of Chattanooga, 1870-1898." Ph.D. University of Tennessee, 1996. 329p.

2550.   Fleming, Cynthia Griggs. "The Development of Black Education in Tennessee, 1865-1920." Ph.D. Duke University, 1977. 226p.

2551.   Fleming, Cynthia Griggs. "A Survey of the Beginning of Tennessee's Black Colleges and Universities, 1865-1920." *Tennessee Historical Quarterly* 39 (Summer 1980): 195-207.   Missionary organizations provided the resources for the development of the first colleges for blacks in Tennessee, including Fisk University (1866), Central Tennessee College (1865), Roger Williams University (1867), and Meharry Medical College (1876). Fleming emphasizes the problems these schools encountered, including student financial aid, the moral and paternal approach of the schools, and the importance placed on manual arts and agriculture instead of a broad liberal education.

2552.   Hardwick, Kevin R. "'Your Old Father Abe Lincoln is Dead and Damned': Black Soldiers and the Memphis Race Riot of 1866." *Journal of Social History* 27 (Fall 1993): 109-128.   The Memphis riots of May 1-3, 1866 resulted from various causes, but mainly the frustration of white residents with the presence of black Union soldiers exhibiting their new freedom and their authority as soldiers. Labor problems between blacks and Irish residents also generated tension. The riot symbolized the attempted subjugation of the black community to the will of the whites.

2553.   Hesseltine, William B.   "Methodism and Reconstruction in East Tennessee." *East Tennessee Historical Society's Publications* no. 3 (January 1931): 42-61.   The Methodist Episcopal Church opposed slavery well before the Civil War, and the Church split in 1844 over the issue.   The M.E.C. South generally supported Southern institutions and gave its backing to the Confederacy.   Parson William G. Brownlow spoke against succession and slavery, and as governor beginning in March, 1865, he worked with Northern leaders to reunited the Church. Political differences made their efforts unsuccessful.

2554.   Hesseltine, William B. "Tennessee's Invitation to Carpet-Baggers." *East Tennessee Historical Society's Publications*   no. 4 (January 1932): 102-115. Governor William G. Brownlow, a Whig and Unionist, got Republican and Conservative support for encouraging the migration of Northern capital and labor so that Tennessee could rise above its impoverished state.   The State Board of Immigration commenced in 1867 and began to market the eastern part of the state as a destination for Northern and European immigrants and capital.   The campaign did not generate much interest in the region.

2555.   Hodgson, Frank M. "Northern Missionary Aid Societies, The Freedmen's Bureau and Their Effect on Education in Montgomery County, Tennessee, 1862- 1870." *West Tennessee Historical Society Papers* 43 (December 1989): 28-43. The Western Freedmen's Aid Committee and the American Missionary Association worked during the Civil War to establish schools for black refugees in Clarksville. After the war their efforts were assisted by the Freedmen's Bureau that brought added funds and organization to the efforts.   They achieved some success despite violence against them and general opposition from both poor and well-to-do whites. The Freedmen's Bureau put the county on the road to a permanent state supported education system.

2556.   Holmes, Jack D. L.   "The Effects of the Memphis Race Riot of 1866." *West Tennessee Historical Society Papers* 12 (1958): 58-79.   The bloody and destructive riot against the black community on May 1-3, 1866 had an immediate impact on race relations, police organization, and black migration in Memphis.   It also played into the political rivalry between eastern and western Tennessee, and after national newspaper coverage and congressional investigations, the riot became a Republican symbol for the failure of President Johnson's Reconstruction policy prior to the congressional elections of 1866.

2557.   Holmes, Jack D. L. "The Underlying Causes of the Memphis Race Riot of 1866." *Tennessee Historical Quarterly* 17 (September 1956): 195-221.   Holmes identifies an array of social, economic, and political issues that led to the riot. Among the underlying causes were the influx of blacks and immigrants, the presence of black soldiers, economic hardship, an aggressive conservative press, and white resentment against the Freedmen's Bureau and Northern teachers.   Holmes believes that historians have misunderstood the riot.

2558.   Horn, Stanley F.   "The Papers of Major Alonzo Wainright."   *Tennessee Historical Quarterly* 12 (June 1953): 182-184.   Wainright was a Union officer stationed in Knoxville in the spring of 1866.   Horn prints Wainright's description of how a mob murdered an Army officer and a black man, and threatened Wainright's life.

2559.   Jordon, Weymouth T.   "The Freedmen's Bureau in Tennessee."   *East Tennessee Historical Society's Publications* no. 11 (1939): 47-61.   Jordon provides a brief survey of the bureau's activities from 1865 to 1869.   The assistant commissioners of the bureau in Tennessee were Brig. Gen. Clinton B. Fisk and Gen. John R. Lewis.

2560.   Lester, Deegee.   "The Memphis Riots of 1866."   *Eire-Ireland* 30 (Fall, 1995): 59-66.   Lester focuses on the clash of Irish and black power in an environment of racial and political tension in Memphis.   As the influx of blacks increased after emancipation, the two groups clashed over economic and ethnic issues.   After the riot the black presence continued to increase and the Irish gradually left the city.

2561.   Lovett, Bobby L.   "Memphis Riots: White Reaction to Blacks in Memphis, May 1865-July 1966."   *Tennessee Historical Quarterly* 38 (Spring 1979): 9-33. The influx of rural freedmen into Memphis combined with the arrogance of black soldiers to produce a tender box that exploded with white riots against the black community.   Lovett emphasizes the behavior of blacks in his explanation of how and why the riots occurred on May 1 and 2, 1866.   Blacks did not understand the depth of white fear and disgust with their ostentatious display of power and freedom.

2562.   Lovett, Bobby L.   "The Negro in Tennessee, 1861-1866: A Socio-Military History of the Civil War Era."   Ph.D. University of Arkansas, 1978. 339p.

2563.   M'Neilly, James H.   "In the Days of Reconstruction."   *Confederate Veteran* 28 (July 1920): 253-256.   M'Neilly defends the South's secession and describes Reconstruction as a humiliating time for the white people of the region. He describes life in Nashville with particular focus on the black character and Presbyterian churches.

2564.   McGehee, C. Stuart.   "E. O. Tade, Freedman's Education, and the Failure of Reconstruction in Tennessee."   *Tennessee Historical Quarterly* 43 (Winter 1984): 376-389.   From 1866 until 1875 Rev. Ewing O. Tade served as a representative of the American Missionary Association in Chattanooga where he organized schools, provided relief, and founded the city's first Freedmen's Savings and Trust Bank.   Despite his successes he encountered a steady stream of problems that withered his attempts to transform the black community and Southern society. His Republican ideology and religious morality was rejected by Southern whites as intrusive and eventually by Northerners as passé.

2565.   O'Donnell, James H. III (ed.). "A Freedman Thanks His Patrons: Letters of Taylor Thistle, 1872-1873." *Journal of Southern History* 33 (February 1967): 68-84.   Thistle, an ex-slave from Missouri, enrolled as a student at the Nashville Normal and Theological Institute in October, 1871. The school began in 1866 with the help of the Home Mission Society of the American Baptist Church. Printed are copies of letters that he wrote to Olive Cushing of Massachusetts, a spinster who gave Thistle financial support while he attended school. A couple of letters were written by the principal of the school, Rev. Daniel W. Phillips, to Cushing. The letters offer thanks and insight into the life and goals of a freedmen.

2566.   Phillips, Paul David.   "Education of Blacks in Tennessee During Reconstruction, 1865-1870." *Tennessee Historical Quarterly*   46 (Summer 1987): 98-109. Ills. Ports.   As general superintendent of contrabands from 1862 to 1865 and then commissioner of public instruction for Tennessee, John Eaton administered the instruction of freedmen. He received assistance from the Freedmen's Bureau, his assistant Gen. Clinton Fisk, and benevolent organizations. Despite the lack of funding for black education, the paternalistic approach of instruction, and the scarcity of qualified teachers, an important beginning was made.

2567.   Phillips, Paul David. "A History of the Freedmen's Bureau of Tennessee." Ph.D. Vanderbilt, 1964. 539p.

2568.   Phillips, Paul David.   "White Reaction to the Freedmen's Bureau in Tennessee." *Tennessee Historical Quarterly* 25 (Spring 1966): 50-62.   Phillips describes the widespread rejection of the bureau in Tennessee and explains that this reaction was understandable in light of the attempt of bureau agents to ensure civil rights for the freedmen and the disenfranchisement of whites. The negative response to the bureau was moderated by the presence of local whites in the agency and its attempt to put the freedmen back to work on plantations.

2569.   Richardson, Joe M. "Fisk University: The First Critical Years." *Tennessee Historical Quarterly* 29 (Spring 1970): 24-41.   Fisk School opened its doors on January 9, 1866 for the purpose of providing a Christian based, private school education for future black teachers and for the general education of blacks. It was founded by Northerners John Ogden, Erastus M. Cravath, and Edward P. Smith with the financial and teaching assistance from voluntary organizations. Richardson discusses the initial successes and difficulties encountered by the school from 1866 until 1874.

2570.   Richardson, Joe M. "The Memphis Race Riot and its Aftermath: Report by a Northern Missionary." *Tennessee Historical Quarterly* 24 (Spring 1965): 63-69.   Rev. Ewing O. Tate, a representative of the American Missionary Association, wrote to a colleague in New York describing the riot. Richardson emphasizes Tate's bias in favor of the blacks and Congressional Reconstruction.

2571.   Richardson, Joe M. "The Negro in Post Civil War Tennessee: A Report by a Northern Missionary." *Journal of Negro Education* 34 (Fall 1965): 419-424.

Richardson introduces a letter dated May 1, 1866 from Mrs. Caroline S. Crosby, an American Missionary Association representative in Nashville, to Rev. Michael E. Strieby, secretary of the A.M.A.. Crosby wrote about her observations of black religion, education, poverty, and family life.

2572.   Ridley, May Alice Harris. "The Black Community of Nashville and Davidson County [Tn.], 1860-1870." Ph.D. University of Pittsburgh, 1982. 224p.

2573.   Robinson, Armstead. "Plans Dat Comed From God: Institution Building and the Emergence of Black Leadership in Reconstruction Memphis." In *Toward a New South? Studies in Post-Civil War Southern Communities*. Edited By Orville V. Burton and Robert C. McMath, Jr.. Westport: Greenwood Press, 1982. Pp 71-102.   Robinson explores how the black leadership formed in the religious, business, and cultural life of the black community in Memphis. He recognizes the complex nature of institutional formation among the freedmen in the urban South, but he focuses on the pressures of a capitalist society and the working class experience of most blacks.

2574.   Ryan, James Gilbert. "The Memphis Riots of 1866: Terror in a Black Community During Reconstruction." *Journal of Negro History* 62 (July 1977): 243-257.   The riots of May 1-3 took a heavy toll in human life and property in the black community. Ryan believes that both blacks and whites share the blame for the violence; that white political leaders aggravated tense race relations and took part in the riots; and that the refusal of Gen. George Stoneman to declare martial law prior to May 3 allowed white mobs to operate. The riots have never been adequately explained.

2575.   Stonehouse, Merlin. *John Wesley North and the Reform Frontier*. Minneapolis: University of Minnesota Press, 1965. 272p. Chron. Ill.   North, a lawyer and judge from Nevada, settled in Knoxville to establish a foundary in February, 1866. Until he moved to California in 1869, he found that his image as a carpetbagger and his sympathy for the freedmen led to his failure in business. He tried to promote Northern immigration to Eastern Tennessee in an attempt to organize a New England community, but when conservative politics predominated by the late 1860s, he admitted defeat. See pages 178-210.

2576.   Swint, Henry Lee   (ed.). "Reports From Educational Agents of the Freedmen's Bureau in Tennessee, 1865-1870." *Tennessee Historical Quarterly* 1 (March 1942): 52-80; 1 (June 1942): 152-170.   Swint provides a selection of correspondence and reports from various Freedmen's Bureau officials regarding the organization, construction, financing and administration of schools for the freedmen. Many of the reports were written by assistant commissioners Brig. Gen. Clinton Fisk and Brvt. Lt. James Thompson, and also the superintendent of education for the bureau in Tennessee, Brvt. Lt. C. E. Compton and his assitant, J. A. Barnum.

2577.   Taylor, Alrutheus Ambush. "Fisk University and the Nashville Community, 1866-1900." *Journal of Negro History* 39 (April 1954): 111-126.

Fisk School was founded in Nashville on January 9, 1866 under the direction of Rev. E. M. Cravath. The college program began in 1871. During Reconstruction the school was warned to keep a low profile in order to avoid trouble with whites.

2578. Waller, Altina L. "Community, Class, and Race in the Memphis Riot of 1866." *Journal of Social History* 18 (Winter 1984): 233-246. The riot of May 1-3 is examined in the context of collective protest during a time of political and economic conflict and the process of urban modernization. Waller reviews the course of the riot and the congressional investigation and suggests that while race was certainly an issue, historians should also recognize the sociological forces that my have had a larger role in causing the riots.

2579. Williams, Frank B. "John Eaton, Jr., Editor, Politician, and School Administrator, 1865-1870." *Tennessee Historical Quarterly* 10 (December 1951): 291-319. Eaton, a native of New Hampshire, lived in Memphis from 1865 to 1870 following service with the Freedmen's Bureau. He edited the Republican *Morning Post* newspaper that was a propaganda tool for Radicalism. As state superintendent of public instruction beginning in 1867, Easton tried to institute a system of tax supported public education, but he was unsuccessful because the white population opposed his inclusion of blacks. He held strong links to the Radical power structure in Memphis until his exodus from the state in 1870.

Texas

General History

2580. Crouch, Barry D. "'Unmasking' Texas Reconstruction: A Twenty-Year Perspective." *Southwestern Historical Quarterly* 93 (January 1990): 274-302. Crouch finds that historical interpretations of Reconstruction in Texas have changed slowly, but since 1969 increasing numbers of studies have excluded myths and traditions in favor of seeking the truth about Reconstruction history. He identifies and describes research in four areas still needing reassessment - the U.S. Army and the Freedmen Bureau, Republican politics, life in black and white communities, and county and urban studies.

2581. Dugas, Vera L. "A Social and Economic History of Texas in the Civil War and Reconstruction Periods." Ph.D. University of Texas, 1963. 718p.

2582. Nunn, William C. *Texas Under the Carpetbaggers*. Austin: University of Texas Press, 1962. 304p. Bibl. Ills. Port. Nunn writes a general history of Texas during the years of Republican Governor Edmund J. Davis from 1870 to 1874. The focus is not on carpetbaggers and mentions the freedmen only briefly. Mainly Nunn surveys the political, economic, and social activities in the state. Significant space is given to the decline of Radicalism, advances in farming and transportation, the build up of state debt by Davis, Indian policy, law enforcement, and immigration. Nunn criticizes Davis's attempt to maintain order, the state debt, and the air of confusion in his government. (See also Nunn's "Texas During the Administration of E. J. Davis." Ph.D. University of Texas, 1938.)

2583.   Ramsdell, Charles W. "Reconstruction in Texas." Ph.D. Columbia, University, 1910. (Rpt. in *Columbia University Studies in the Social Sciences*, 95 *Studies in History, Economics, and Public Law*, 36; Gloucester: Peter Smith, 1964)

2584.   Sneed, Edgar P. "A Historiography of Reconstruction in Texas: Some Myths and Problems." *Southwestern Historical Quarterly* 72 (April 1969): 435-48. Sneed calls for a total reexamination of Reconstruction in Texas because past historians have been biased to the point of obscuring the truth. He focuses on new studies of Ku Klux Klan violence, black codes, the nature and influence of carpetbaggers, legal and state constitutional issues, the Freedmen's Bureau, and economic development.

2585.   Wooster, Ralph A. "The Civil War and Reconstruction in Texas." In *A Guide to the History of Texas*. Edited By Light Townsend Cummins and Alvin R. Bailey, Jr. New York: Greenwood Press, 1988. Pp. 37-50.   Includes a very selective list of books, articles, and theses.

Politics and Law

2586.   Ashcroft, Allan C. "Texas in Defeat: The Early Phases of A. J. Hamilton's Provisional Governorship of Texas, June 17, 1865 to February 7, 1866." *Texas Military History* 8 (1970): 199-219.   Ashcroft praises Andrew Jackson Hamilton's efforts during his term as provisional governor through the election of the state legislature in February, 1866. He describes Hamilton's leadership and decision-making regarding the enhancement of Unionism in Texas, amnesty, state finances, emancipation, changes in race relations, Indian affairs, and the occupation of the state by Union troops.

2587.   Avillo, Philip J., Jr. "Phantom Radicals: Texas Republicans in Congress 1873-1878." *Southwestern Historical Quarterly* 72 (1974): 431-444.   Avillo examines just how radical the state Republican delegates to Congress were during their service in the 41st and 42nd Congresses. The congressmen included Edward Degener, a German immigrant; William T. Clark, a former Union soldier; and George W. Whitmore, a Tennessee native. The senators who were Texas natives were James W. Flanagan and Morgan C. Hamilton. The conservative press complained bitterly about Radical control, but Avillo finds that the delegation acted much more conservatively than expected.

2588.   Baensinger, Ann Patton. "The Texas State Police During Reconstruction." *Southwestern Historical Quarterly* 72 (April 1969): 470-491.   Gov. Edmund J.

Davis organized the state police to help restore and maintain law and order in the violent, postwar years, but conservatives criticized the force as a Republican tool, and because it included blacks. Baenzinger concludes that the criticism was unwarranted and reflects more on political and racial conflict than on the true nature of the police.

2589. Baggett, James Alex. "Birth of the Texas Republican Party." *Southwestern Historical Quarterly* 78 (July 1974): 1-20. Baggert seeks to revise traditional ideas about Texas Republicans by examining the party from 1865 to 1868. The party, comprised of Unionists, carpetbaggers, and blacks, was divided between moderates, led by Andrew Jackson Hamilton and Elisha Pease, and Radicals, led by Edmund J. Davis. They quarreled over the extent of liberalization of black civil rights and the exclusion of whites from politics. But even when the Radicals prevailed in 1869 and the factions generally agreed about policies, the chance of success was slim because the Radicals had to rely on the suppression of conservative power and the full support of the Grant administration. (See also Baggett's "Origins of Early Texas Republican Party Leadership." *Journal of Southern History* 40 (August 1974): 441-454 in which he argues that the party was not dominated by carpetbaggers and blacks; also see first two chapters of Paul D. Casdorph, *A History of the Republican Party in Texas 1865-1965.* Pemberton Press, 1965.)

2590. Baggett, James Alex. *The Rise and Fall of the Texas Radicals, 1867-1883.* Ph.D. North Texas State University, 1972. 249p.

2591. Barr, Alwyn. "Black Legislators of Reconstruction Texas." *Civil War History* 32 (December 1986): 340-352. Barr describes the background of fourteen black legislators and senators who served in the 12th Legislature in Texas in 1870. Most of them were literatte, formerly slaves from other states, and relatively young. They supported the black community in Texas, but their interests were much broader, and they frequently voted differently on various issues.

2592. Barr, John. "If Lincoln Had Lived: Texans Reconsider Lincoln's Assassination." *Lincoln Herald* 91 (Winter 1989): 151-155. Barr discusses how Texans viewed Lincoln at the time of his assassination and how that view changed during the next several decades. Many Texans rejoiced at hearing of Lincoln's death, because he was blamed for bringing on the war. Opinions eventually became much more conciliatory as Texans believed that Reconstruction might have been easier for them had Lincoln lived. Barr also discusses the transition in historical interpretation of Reconstruction in Texas and speculation on Lincoln's role.

2593. Baum, Dale. *The Shattering of Texas Unionism: Politics in the Lone Star State During the Civil War Era.* Baton Rouge: Louisiana State University, 1998. 283p. App. Bibl. Maps. Ports. Tbls. Baum analyzes the course of Unionism or dissent in Texas from the gubernatorial election of Sam Houston in 1859 to the victory of Republican Edmund J. Davis in 1869. Unionists fragmented over the course of the war and early years of Reconstruction. The forces of secession, black freedom and civil rights, and local politics eroded Unionist dissension against the Democrats. Baum studies voting patterns and participation in statewide elections from 1859 to 1869 that help explain how antebellum politics in the state persisted during and after the war and reveal the fundamental weakness of Republicanism as a viable political force.

2594.   Brewer, J. Mason. *Negro Legislation of Texas and Their Descendants.* Austin: Jenkins Publishing Co., 1970.   154p.   Bibl.   (Rpt. of 1935 edition) Brewer's book is an account of black participation in state legislatures in Texas from the constitutional convention of 1868 to the 24th legislature that began in 1895. Approximately half of the text is devoted to the period prior to 1876 when the largest number of blacks were in the state legislature. After a brief discussion of emancipation, Congressional Reconstruction, and black suffrage, Brewer describes the backgrounds of black legislators and the contributions that they made. He includes a list of all black legislators and the county or district that they represented in chronological order.

2595.   Brockman, John Martin. "Railroads, Radicals, and Democrats: A Study in Texas Politics, 1865-1900," Ph.D. University of Texas, 1975. 329p.

2596.   Brockman, John Martin. "Railroads, Radicals, and the Militia Bill: A New Interpretation of the Quorum-Breaking Incident of 1870." *Southwestern Historical Quarterly* 88 (October 1979): 105-123. Tbls.   Texas railroad lobbyists persuaded 10 state senators to thwart the legislature's ability to vote on the Radical Republican's Militia Bill of 1870 by leaving the Senate floor to create less than a quorum required for a vote. The arrest of the 10 and their forced return to the Senate led conservatives and historians to refer to the senators as heroes attempting to defeat the Radicals. Brockman shows that political principles were less important than their opposition to railroad subsidies attached to the Militia Bill. He lists the names of senators and legislators and their votes by party on key issues in the 12th legislature.

2597.   Brown, Arthur Z. "The Participation of Negroes in the Reconstruction Legislatures of Texas." *Negro History Bulletin* 20 (January 1957): 87-88.   Black legislators served in the 19th century from 1871 to 1895. Brown emphasizes their work for the general welfare of their districts and the state. Among the legislators mentioned were Rep. Richard Allen and Senators G. T. Ruby, Matt Gaines, and W. M. Burton.

2598.   Campbell, Randolph B. "Carpetbagger Rule in Reconstruction Texas: An Enduring Myth." *Southwestern Historical Quarterly* 97 (April 1994): 587-596. Tbl.   Many historians of Reconstruction in Texas have perpetuated the myth that the state was dominated by carpetbaggers.   Campbell demonstrates that carpetbaggers were only a small minority of public officeholders, and the local power heavily favored the scalawags or local white Republicans. The carpetbaggers have been a convenient scapegoat for all perceived Reconstruction ills, mainly because they were Northerners.

2599.   Campbell, Randolph B. "The District Judges of Texas in 1866-1867: An Episode in the Failure of Presidential Reconstruction." *Southwestern Historical Quarterly* 93 (January 1993): 357-377. Maps.   The district judges in Texas carried much power. Campbell reviews the identity of the judges elected on June 25, 1866 and how they reveal important information about the early years of Reconstruction in Texas. Most of the judges were former Confederates who sympathized with postwar obstructionists and persons who defied federal authority effecting states' rights and race relations. Their legal decisions on issues, such as jury selection and their habit of following the lead of local leaders, generated protests from Unionists and contributed to Northern perceptions of politics and society in Texas and the South.

2600.   Campbell, Randolph B. "The End of Slavery in Texas: A Research Note." *Southwestern Historical Quarterly* 88 (July 1984): 73-80. Ports.   A review of several court decisions in Texas courts illustrates that the traditional date of emancipation in Texas, June 19, 1865, was also the legal date as well. The issue of the date was important to slaveholders who were concerned about contracts related to the sale or rent of slaves.

2601.   Campbell, Randolph B. "George W. Whitmore: East Texas Unionist." *East Texas Historical Journal* 28 (1990): 17-28.   Whitmore, a former Whig from Harrison County, serves as an example of Southerners who adamantly opposed secession and courageously accepted political and racial changes brought about by the Union victory. His wartime Unionism and postwar participation in the Republican Party made him a pariah among most of his fellow white Texans and effected his personal and political future. He served in the U.S. Congress from 1870 to 1871.

2602.   Campbell, Randolph B. *Grass-Roots Reconstruction in Texas, 1865-1880.* Baton Rouge: Louisiana State University, 1997. 251p. Bibl. Maps.   Campbell offers case studies of 6 counties located in the eastern two-fifths of Texas - Colorado, Dallas, Harrison, Jefferson, McLennan, and Nueces. He illustrates the wide differences in the way various parts of Texas experienced the postwar years. Conditions and experiences in each county were so different that few generalizations about Reconstruction in Texas can be made. Campbell does highlight, however, the impact of federal authorities, such as the Freedmen's Bureau, the domination of scalawags in the Republican Party, economic expansion, the persistence of economic elites, the effect of racial distribution on race relations, and the determination of many freedmen to exercise their rights and improve their lives.

2603.   Campbell, Randolph B. "Grassroots Reconstruction: The Personnel of County Government in Texas, 1865-1876." *Journal of Southern History* 58 (February 1992): 99-116. Tbls. Map.   Campbell presents a statistical study measuring several characteristics of county officeholders in eastern Texas. He notes that in the fall of 1867 Gen. Joseph J. Reynolds, commander of the Department of Texas, replaced more than 500 county officers who were not deemed to be loyal to the U.S. Reynolds put reformers in local offices who would have an impact on politics from 1867 to 1869. Beginning in 1870 the trend was for more conservatives to gain office. Campbell emphasizes the importance of county politics in Reconstruction, a topic that has been overlooked by historians.

2604.   Campbell, Randolph B.   "Reconstruction in McLennan County, Texas 1865-1876." *Prologue* 27 (Spring 1995): 17-35. Ills. Ports.   Focusing mainly on sources in the National Archives, Campbell describes the political and social developments in McLennan County and the town of Waco. He reveals the turmoil that emancipation and Radical Reconstruction provoked between white Texans, freedmen, Unionists, and Northerners.   The Freedmen's Bureau and the U.S. Army played a prominent role in attempting to resolve disputes and put down the pervasive violence in the county. The ultimate success of white conservatives could not reverse permanent and positive change for the black community.

2605.   Campbell, Randolph B.   "Reconstruction in Nueces County, 1865-1876." *Houston Review* 16, 1 (1994): 3-26.   At the close of the Civil War Nueces County, which includes Corpus Christi, had a small population, almost no cotton, and very few slaves. Campbell describes a region that did not experience political problems and violence compared with other parts of Texas.   There were very few freedmen and the government consisted of either moderate Unionists or a mix of Republicans and Democrats. Reconstruction controversies were directed more towards state and national government issues instead of local issues. Black residents held no political offices but were making progress after just a few years of freedom.

2606.   Campbell, Randolph B.   "Scalawag District Judges: The E. J. Davis Appointees, 1870-1873." *Houston Review* 14, 2 (1992): 75-88. Map. Tbl.   The traditional idea that Texas was ruled by carpetbaggers is a myth that continues to persist in popular and scholarly literature. Campbell tests the myth in his study of district judges appointed by Gov. Edmund J. Davis. He concludes that fully two-thirds were scalawags and one-fifth were Northerners who settled in Texas prior to the Civil War.   Scalawags dominated the Republican regime.

2607.   Campbell, Randolph B.   *A Southern Community in Crisis: Harrison County, Texas, 1850-1880.*   Austin: Texas State Historical Association, 1983. 443p. App. Bibl. Map. Tbls.   Harrison County, located in northeastern Texas, was a site of prosperous cotton plantations and a large number of slaves before the war. After the war whites resisted change, and dramatic changes did not occur until after 1870 when Texas reentered the Union controlled by Republicans.   Black votes maintained a Republican majority and local white Republican leadership. Even after Democrats returned to power in state government in 1874, Harrison did not lose Republican control until 1878.

2608.   Cantrell, Gregg.   "Racial Violence and Reconstruction Politics in Texas, 1867-1868." *Southwestern Historical Quarterly* 93 (January 1990): 333-355. Ill. Tbl.   There were many reasons for racial violence in Texas after the Civil War, but Cantrell finds that politics was the basis for violence in 1867 and 1868.   Even though it is difficult to prove that individual acts had a political basis, statistics show a relationship between proximity to important political events, such as elections, and the level of violence perpetrated by whites against blacks. He suggests that political changes brought on during Radical Reconstruction raised frustration about the future of white supremacy, the only type of relationship acceptable to most white Texans.

2609.   Carrier, John Pressley.   "A Political History of Texas During Reconstruction, 1865-1874." Ph.D. Vanderbilt University, 1971. 558p.

2610.   Chapin, Walter Tribble.   "Presidential Reconstruction in Texas, 1865-1867." Ph.D. University of North Texas, 1979. 157p.

2611.   Crouch, Barry A.   "'All the Vile Passions': The Texas Black Code of 1866." *Southwestern Historical Quarterly* 97 (July 1993): 12-34. Port.   Crouch argues that the Texas black code has been misrepresented by historians as an example of discretion and moderation compared with codes in other Southern states. In his examination of the codes and the social and economic conditions in 1865-1866, he concludes that the legislature intended harsh restrictions on the freedoms of blacks and to force them into a situation of virtual slavery. The idea that the black codes duplicated actions already taken by the Northern occupation Army and the Freedmen's Bureau is a gross exaggeration.

2612.   Crouch, Barry A. "Black Dreams and White Justice." *Prologue* 6 (Winter 1974): 255-265. Illus.   Did the experience of slavery prepare the freedmen for freedom? Crouch argues that the complex slave society and its exposure to white society created an understanding of citizenship and rights that was put into practice immediately after emancipation came. He provides various examples from Texas where freedmen aggressively used the Freedmen's Bureau courts and occasionally local civil courts to press their grievances.

2613.   Crouch, Barry D. "Self Determination and Local Black Leaders in Texas." *Phylon* 39 (December 1978): 344-355.   Crouch explains how key black leaders in Texas actively sought to organize freedmen to demand civil rights and real freedom, and how this activity led to violence and intimidation of blacks from the Ku Klux Klan. Politics played a role in the participation of blacks in defining their freedom. There were differences between black political activities and white responses in urban and rural areas.

2614.   Dobbs, Ricky Floyd.   "Defying Davis: The Walker County Rebellion, 1871." *East Texas Historical Journal* 32, 2 (1993): 34-47.   Dobbs explains that Governor Edmund J. Davis's response to violence and lawlessness against his Republican government and racial reforms was reasonable and certainly did not reach the level of irresponsibility claimed by most historians of Reconstruction in Texas in the 20th century. He provides a detailed description of Davis' use of the state police to put down violence in Walker County after a group of white men were accused of murdering a freedman.

2615.   Elliott, Claude. *Leathercoat: The Life History of a Texas Patriot.* San Antonio: Standard Printing Co., 1938. 315p. Bibl.   James Throckmorton opposed secession but supported the Confederacy when Texas withdrew from the Union. He won the gubernatorial election in 1866 as a moderate Democrat. Elliott defends Throckmorton's opposition to military rule and Radical Republicans that eventually led to the governor's removal from office in July, 1867 by Gen. Philip Sheridan. Throckmorton supported railroad expansion and was elected to the U.S. Congress more than once beginning in 1874. Elliott believes that Throckmorton made important contributions for the benefit of Texas and the South during his political career from the 1850s until the 1890s. (See also Elliott's "The Life of James W. Throckmorton." Ph.D. University of Texas, 1934.)

2616.   Gray, Ronald N.   "Edmund J. Davis: Radical Republican and Reconstruction Governor of Texas." Ph.D. Texas Tech University, 1976. 481p.

2617.   Greene, A. C. "The Durable Society: Austin in the Reconstruction." *Southwestern Historical Quarterly* 72 (April 1969): 492-518. Ills.   Greene writes a brief account of life in Austin from the end of the war until the election of Democratic governor Richard Coke in 1873. In general, the city was politically cautious and moderate compared with rural Texas, and it experienced significant economic development during the period.

2618.   Horton, Louise   (ed.).   "Samuel Bell Maxey on the Coke-David Controversy." *Southwestern Historical Quarterly* 72 (April 1969): 519-525. Horton prints 2 letters written in January, 1874 from Maxey to his wife describing the election controversy between Republican Edmund J. Davis and Democrat Richard Coke after the decision of the state Supreme Court that gave an advantage to Davis. Maxey was an officer in the Confederate Army.

2619.   Ledbetter, Billy D.   "White Texans' Attitudes Toward the Political Equality of Negroes, 1865-1870." *Phylon* 40 (September 1979): 253-263.   White Texans were nearly unanimous in their rejection of political equality for blacks. They objected to giving freedmen the vote, and they assumed that granting any sort of equal status with whites would lead to demands for social equality as well. It was not until 1870, with a Republican governor, Edmund J. Davis, and a Republican majority in the legislature, that the state government agreed to the 13th, 14th, and 15th amendments.

2620.   Lovett, Leslie A. "Biracial Politics and Community Development: The Reconstruction Experience in Ft. Bend County, Texas 1869-1889." *Houston Review* 16, 1 (1994): 27-39.   In Ft. Bend County blacks outnumbered whites and became important participants in local government.   Lovett explains that biracial, Republican government existed from 1869 to 1889 and produced prosperity and racial cooperation. White resistance to black influence led to violence against the black majority during the Jaybird-Woodpecker War. Black power decreased after 1870, but the county serves as an example of how biracial government can work.

2621.   Lowry, Sharon K.   "Portrait of an Age: The Political Career of Stephen W. Dorsey, 1868-1869." Ph.D. University of North Texas, 1980. 460p

2622.   Malone, Ann Patton. "Matt Gaines: Reconstruction Politician." In *Black Leaders: Texans For Their Times*. Edited by Alwyn Barr and Robert A. Calvert. Texas State Historical Association, 1981. Pp. 49-82. Port.   Gaines, born a slave in Louisiana, was elected in 1870 and 1874 to the Texas senate. Malone emphasizes Gaines' outspoken and sometimes inflammatory style that upset fellow Republicans. He was a stalwart supporter of black civil rights and block voting, integrated education, and black immigration to Texas.

2623.   Marten, James. "Drawing the Line: Dissent and Disloyalty in Texas, 1856-1874." Ph.D. University of Texas, Austin, 1986. 386p.

2624.   Marten, James. "John L. Haynes: A Southern Dissenter in Texas." *Southern Studies*, New Series 1 (Fall 1990): 257-279.   Haynes was a dissenter against the elitist and racist Anglo Texans throughout his career as a south Texas legislator, Union soldier, and Republican during Reconstruction. After the Civil War he helped organize the Republican Party in 1867. After the part split into radical and moderate factions, he supported the moderates, but favored civil rights for the freedmen. He exemplified the persistence of Jacksonian idealism among some Southerners.

2625.   Miller, E. T.   "Repudiation of State Debt in Texas Since 1861." *Southwestern Historical Quarterly* 16 (October 1912): 169-183.   Miller explains that the only state debt that was repudiated was the debt incurred to aid the war effort.   All other debts, even debts incurred during the war to pay prewar obligations, were the responsibility of the postwar governments.

2626.   Miller, E. T. "The State Finances of Texas During the Reconstruction." *Quarterly of the Texas State Historical Association* 14 (October 1910): 87-112. Tbls.   Miller delineates two periods of postwar financial administration, the period of military government followed by the conservative administration of Gov. James Throckmorton prior to July, 1867, and the subsequent period of Radical Republican rule and the handling of the state's large debt by a responsible Democratic government beginning in 1874. Under the Radical government of Gov. Edmund J. Davis taxation, spending, and debt rose dramatically. Financial abuses occurred under the Radicals, but not to the extent that happened in other Southern states. Three statistical tables illustrate state finances.

2627.   Moneyhon, Carl H. "George T. Ruby and the Politics of Expediency in Texas." In *Southern Black Leaders of the Reconstruction Era*. Edited by Howard N. Rabinowitz. Urbana: University of Illinois Press, 1982. Pp. 363-392. Port. Moneyhon describes Ruby as "the most important black politician in Texas during Reconstruction in terms of power and ability" (p. 389). He won elective office and worked to bring moderate whites and blacks together within the Republican Party. His moderate tendency led him to support the Edmund J. Davis faction in the party and lost him support in the black community. His influence remained high until the Democratic electoral victory in 1872.

2628.   Moneyhon, Carl H. *Republicanism in Reconstruction Texas.* Austin: University of Texas Press, 1980. 319p. App. Bibl. Ports.   After the Republicans took control of the governor's office and the legislature, they remained weak throughout the state. They tried to establish public schools and expand the railroads, but they could not overcome factional disagreements over civil rights for blacks and economic policies. Democrats used these issues to regain the legislature in the 1872 election and the governor's office in the election of 1873. The appendix includes detailed gubernatorial election results (1853-1873), biographical information on delegates to the 1866 constitutional convention, and information about statistical analysis. (See also Moneyhon's "The Republican Party in Texas Politics, 1865-1874." Ph.D. University of Chicago, 1973. 432p.)

2629.   Nieman, Donald G. "African Americans and the Meaning of Freedom. Washington County, Texas as a Case Study, 1865-1886." *Chicago-Kent Law Review* 70, 2 (1994): 541-582. Tbls.   In this case study of a wealthy, mid-state county during Reconstruction, Nieman puts greater emphasis on the positive developments in political and social life of blacks than on the fact that the reforms did not last very long. Black citizens took the initiative to organize and participate in politics, to serve on juries, and to vote in elections. Black political power in a multiracial democracy was real and had a long range impact on the black community even after their rights were curtailed.

2630.   Nieman, Donald G.   "Black Political Power and Criminal Justice: Washington County, Texas, 1868-1884." *Journal of Southern History* 55 (August 1989): 391-420.   Washington County was a rich growing area between Houston and Austin.   Beginning in 1868 the black majority combined with German immigrants and a few white Unionists to make the county a bastion of Republicanism long after the Democrats won the gubernatorial election of 1872. Black residents played a significant part in the political and criminal justice system by working as sheriff's deputies, jurors, and voters. This had a positive impact on how blacks were treated by the justice system. Washington County was one of the many regions in the South where black political participation remained high after 1876.

2631.   Norvell, James R. "Oren M. Roberts and the Semicolon Court." *Texas Law Review* 37 (February 1959): 279-302.   Roberts was the chief justice of the Texas Supreme Court beginning in 1874 when the Democrats retook the state government from the Republicans.   Norvell describes how the Roberts court interpreted pending cases during the last three Reconstruction courts from 1866 to 1873. His main focus is not the Semicolon Court, the last and least reputable court. Its decisions were long disregarded because it consisted of Republicans, and it sought to reverse a Democratic victory in the election of 1873 in *Ex parte* Rodriguez (39 Tex 706, 1873). Norvell offers an annotated list of Roberts' court decisions on cases left from the "Semicolon Court."

2632.   Norvell, James R. "The Reconstruction Courts of Texas." *Southwestern Historical Quarterly* 62 (October 1958): 141-163.   Norvell describes Radical Reconstruction in Texas very critically, but his main focus is on the three state supreme courts between 1866 and 1873.   He briefly examines the rulings and membership of the immediate post-Reconstruction court organized according to the 1866 constitution, the military court appointed in 1867 after the passage of the Reconstruction Acts, and the "Semicolon Court" appointed after the passage of the 1868 constitution. Norvell examines the details of the court's decision in *Ex parte Rodriguez* (39 Tex 706, 1873) which involved the power of the legislature to control elections and the court's power to rule elections invalid based on interpretations of the state constitution. Democrats believed that the case was fabricated to void a Democatic victory.

2633.   Owens, Nora Estelle. "Presidential Reconstruction in Texas: A Case Study." Ph.D. Auburn University, 1983. 551p.

2634.   Pitre, Merline. "The Evolution of Black Political Participation in Reconstruction Texas." *East Texas Historical Journal* 16, 1 (1988): 36-45.   Pitre focuses on the background and activities of black delegates to the state constitutional convention that commenced in Austin on June 11, 1868. Despite the experience gained in the convention, most of the delegates did not run for election to the legislature.   The social and economic characteristics of this group was not consist with negative stereotypes of black politicians.   The black delegates were George T. Ruby, James McWashington, Charles W. Bryant, Benjamin Franklin Williams, Sheppard Mullins, Benjamin O. Watrous, Mitchell Kendall, Ralph Long, Stephen Curtis, and Wiley Johnson.

2635.   Pitre, Merline. "A Note on the Historiography of Blacks in the Reconstruction of Texas." *Journal of Negro History* 66 (Winter 1981-82): 340-348. The lack of research on blacks in Texas has led to the acceptance of several myths about the role of the freedmen in the state. Pitre explains that Texas never really experienced Radical rule and that the Republican leaders were actually moderates at best. Blacks never ruled the state and did not dominate the state police. The rights of freedmen were constantly under attack and segregation was a common practice.

2636.   Pitre, Merline. "Richard Allen: The Chequered Career of Houston's First Black State Legislator." *Houston Review* 8, 2 (1986): 79-88.   Allen represents the complex nature of politics in Reconstruction. He was a former slave and expert carpenter who used his oratorical skills and true concern for helping people to build a political career in the Texas Republican Party that began in 1866 and ended with his death in 1911. But Allen's ambition and opportunism got the best of him, and his relationship with Republican leader, James G. Tracy, compromised his ability to improve conditions for blacks even as his own career improved.

2637.   Pitre, Merline. *Through Many Dangers, Toils, and Snares: The Black Leadership of Texas, 1868-1900.* Austin: Eakin Press, 1985. 260p. App. Bibl. Maps. Ports.   Pitre explores the background of black leaders and their contributions to securing and maintaining civil rights during and after Reconstruction. The blacks who served in the constitutional convention of 1868-1869 and the state legislature during the 12th and later sessions illustrate the political successes and failures that produced reforms and the political divisions among white and black Republicans. Pitre reviews the careers of Matthew Gaines, George T. Ruby, Richard Allen, Robert L. Smith and Norris W. Cuney. Three appendixes list black legislators and their committee assignments from 1868 to 1899 and those who were delegates to the Republican national conventions from 1868 to 1896.

2638.   Platt, Harold L. "The Stillbirth of Urban Politics in the Reconstruction South: Houston, Texas as a Test Case." *Houston Review* 4 (Summer 1982): 54-74. Ill. Tbls.   Platt explores Armstead Robinson's themes (e.g. see # 992) of class and ethnic alliances in the post-Civil War Southern states by looking at the case of a growing urban center.   He finds that biracial politics involving blacks and German immigrants in Houston held promise for the local Republican Party, but by 1874 the Democrats had won both the state legislature and the governor's office, and the Republican-held city government quickly lost power to Democratic manipulation. Racial supremacy destroyed biracial politics.

2639.   Ramsdell, Charles W. "Presidential Reconstruction in Texas." *Quarterly of the Texas State Historical Association* 11 (April 1908): 277-317; 12 (January 1909): 204-230.   Ramsdell provides a narrative of Reconstruction from 1865 to end of the Conservative administration of Gov. James Throckmorton in July, 1867. He examines the proceedings of the 1866 constitutional convention, the election of a governor, and the achievements of Throckmorton and the Eleventh Texas Legislature.   In general Ramsdell gives a positive assessment, except for the black code and the lack of flexibility in the legislature.   He emphasizes the work of the Freedmen's Bureau to maintain order, particularly to keep black laborers on the plantations.   Congress upset the progress made by conservatives with its own Reconstruction policies.

2640.   Ramsdell, Charles W. "Texas From the Fall of the Confederacy to the Beginning of Reconstruction." *Quarterly of the Texas State Historical Association* 11 (January 1908): 199-219.   There was a state of confusion and disorder in the civil administration of government after the war.   Ramsdell describes the difficult transition from war to peace under military and provisional governments in a state that was spared significant destruction during the war.   He also examines economic and labor issues related to cotton sales and the status of the slaves.

2641.   Richter, William L. *The Army in Texas During Reconstruction, 1865-1870.* College Station: Texas A&M University Press, 1987.   165p.   Bibl. Richter divides the Army's role in Texas into three chronological periods: Presidential Reconstruction under Gen. Philip Sheridan (May, 1865 to December, 1866); and two periods of Military Reconstruction under Gen. Charles Griffin (December, 1866 to September, 1867) and Gen. Joseph J. Reynolds (September, 1867 to April, 1870).   The personalities of these men greatly influenced the Army's approach to the maintenance of order, the organization of the state government, and the public response to the Army. Richter concludes that the Army interfered excessively in local and state government and elections. The resistance of the conservative, white majority to Republican power and reforms, particularly black civil rights, combined with the disinclination of Texans to follow centralized authority, to make the Army a dispersed and transitional force during Reconstruction. (See also Richter's Ph.D. dissertation with the same title from Louisiana State University, 1970.)

2642.   Richter, William L. "'Better Time is in Store For Us': An Analysis of the Reconstruction Attitudes of George Armstong Custer." *Military History of Texas and the Southwest* 11, 1 (1973): 31-50.   The flamboyant, ambitious Custer commanded a division of cavalry in the occupation of Texas in June, 1865. He testified before Congress in October about conditions in Texas and became increasingly involved in politics on the side of President Johnson. Although he told the Republican Congress what it wanted to here about the continued need for the occupation and the Freedmen's Bureau, his correspondence reveals that he wanted a lenient Reconstruction that would mend the Union without getting bogged down in the affairs of the freedmen. Custer supported emancipation, but he believed that the war had really been to restore the Union.

2643.   Richter, William L. "The Brenham Fire of 1866: A Texas Reconstruction Atrocity." *Louisiana Studies* 14 (Fall 1975): 287-314.   On September 7, 1866 marauding, drunken soldiers burned a section of Brenham and threatened further conflagrations. The fire was brought on by the poor relations between the U.S. Army and defiant white Texans. The Army lacked consistent local leadership and it could not get the cooperation of Gov. James W. Throckmorton. Adding to the Army's challenge was the Republican approach to race relations and the virulent response of the local press.

2644.   Richter, William L. "'Devil Take Them All': Military Rule in Texas, 1862-1870." *Louisiana Studies* 25 (Spring 1986): 5-30. Tbls.   Richter focuses on military rule as the weakest approach that the federal government could have taken to control events in Texas. Texans, who disliked the power of the Confederate military, responded negatively to the attempt to centralize power in federal authorities. The emphasis on arbitrary, military authority, commanded by Maj. Gen. Philip H. Sheridan, led to defeat of military government in Texas.

2645.   Richter, William L.   "General Phil Sheridan, the Historians, and Reconstruction." *Civil War History* 33 (June 1987): 131-154.   Richter reviews Sheridan's postwar career as an Army commander principally in Texas and Louisiana from 1865 until President Johnson removed him in September, 1867. He also discusses Sheridan's reputation among his contemporaries and post-Reconstruction historians. Sheridan found the transition from commander in war to commander in peace to be difficult, and his impatient, fiery temperament, as well as his hatred for Southern intransigence, made him particularly unpopular with the local white population. Richter believes that Sheridan's dismissal of Texas governor

James W. Throckmorton exemplified his lack of political sense and want of moderation.

2646.   Richter, William L.   "'It is Best to Go in Strong Handed': Army Occupation of Texas, 1865-1866." *Arizona and the West* 27, 2 (1985): 113-142. Ills. Ports.   The U.S. Army's occupation of Texas beginning in June, 1865 was a huge undertaking that encountered more problems within the Army ranks than with stubborn, rebellious Texans.   Richter describes how the Army moved into the state and Army commanders' response to rebellious troops that wanted only to be discharged and to return home.   Even with a large force in Texas, the regional commander, Major Gen. Philip H. Sheridan, faced a difficult task fulfilling his mission to protect freedmen and safeguard their civil rights, secure the U.S./Mexican border, and guard against Indian attacks from the north and west.

2647.   Richter, William L.   "Outside...My Profession: The Army and Civil Affairs in Texas Reconstruction." *Military History of Texas and the Southwest* 9, 1 (1971): 5-21.   Richter describes the many nonmilitary tasks handled by the occupying U.S. Army during the first few years after the war.   Such tasks included political organization, tax collection, newspaper censorship, mail service, sanitation management, and regulation of commerce.   Texans resented the U.S. Army's interference in self government, and many officers within the Army hated nonmilitary assignments.

2648.   Richter, William L.   "Texas Politics and the United States Army." *Military History of Texas and the Southwest* 10 (1972): 159-198.   The military occupation of Texas after the Civil War had little impact on the political loyalties of Texans who were overwhelming conservative.   They elected moderate Unionist James Throckmorton as governor in June, 1866 along with former rebels who won seats in the state legislature.   The legislature's defiance of reform and its passage of the black code increased U.S. military involvement in politics, and the Reconstruction Acts in March, 1867 led to widespread Army involvement in replacing disloyal public officials, including Throckmorton.   But Gen. Sheridan's delay in beginning removals contributed to the weakness of Reconstruction in the state.   Beginning in the summer of 1867 the Army, under Major Gen. Charles Griffin and later Major Gen. Joseph Reynolds, led the campaign for Republican reforms.

2649.   Richter, William L.   "Tyrant and Reformer: General Griffin Reconstructs Texas, 1865-1866." *Prologue* 10 (Winter 1978): 225-241. Ports.   During the military occupation of the South commanding officers had to balance political and security issues with the reactions of Washington and the local population.   In the case of Texas Bvt. Maj. Gen. Charles Griffin was determined to rid the state of disloyal authorities and bring about reforms following Republican principles.   He took up his command in December, 1865, a time when Texas was the scene of much violence against blacks and the Army.   Richter believes that the harshness of his methods have been overstated and that his early death from yellow fever in September, 1867 cut short the path toward unified Republican rule in Texas.

2650.   Richter, William L. "'We Must Rubb Out and Begin Anew': The Army and the Republican Party in Texas Reconstruction, 1867-1870." *Civil War History* 19 (December 1973): 334-352.   In Texas the Army and the Republican Party became allies in an effort to overcome the influence of President Johnson and conservative Republicans and Democrats.   The most influential person in the Radical's election victory in 1869 was Brev. Major Joseph J. Reynolds, commander of the District of Texas since September 17, 1867.   He used his power to help Provisional Gov. Elisha Pease replace disloyal officeholders and to help President Grant provide patronage jobs to maintain Republican victories in elections. Reynolds was talented but he misused his military power for political purposes.

2651.   Russ, William A., Jr.   "Radical Disfranchisement in Texas, 1867-70." *Southwestern Historical Quarterly* 38 (July 1934): 40-52.   Russ describes how Federal Army officers applied the laws of the Reconstruction Acts and the 14th Amendment to disenfranchise former state and local officeholders and a host of other officials and potential voters who could not swear an oath that they had never aided and abetted rebellion. Widespread complaints were voiced about the actions of Gen. Philip Sheridan, commander of the 5th District, and his local commanders, Gen. Charles Griffen and later Gen. E. R. S. Canby and Major Gen. Joseph Reynolds. Russ suggests that military rule in Texas was characterized by Sheridan's arbitrary style.

2652.   Sandlin, Betty J. "The Texas Reconstruction Convention 1868-1869." Ph.D. Texas Tech University, 1970. 267p.

2653.   Scarborough, Jane Lynn.   "George W. Paschal, Texas Unionist and Scalawag Jurisprudent." Ph.D. Rice University, 1972. 193p.

2654.   Shelley, George E.   "The Semicolon Court of Texas." *Southwestern Historical Quarterly* 48 (April 1945): 449-468.   The wartime members of the Texas Supreme Court were dismissed after the Civil War and replaced in 1867 with appointments made by Gen. Phil Sheridan, military commander of Texas. The new court became derisively known as the semicolon court because it was a Republican appointed court of strong Unionists, even though the label actually applied to three judges who made up the entire court in 1873 during the *Ex parte* Rodriguez (39 Tex 706, 1873) case. The court has been denied respect by legal authorities in Texas.

2655.   Shook, Robert W. "The Federal Military in Texas, 1865-1870." *Texas Military History* 6 (Spring 1967): 3-53. Maps. Tbls.   Shook provides a narrative of the U.S. Army occupation with emphasis on the Army's administration of the state until civil government took control in 1870. He recognizes the biased accounts of the Army written by past historians and believes that the evidence warrants more objective accounts of the Army's role in implementing reforms and maintaining order in a violent society.   He doubts whether the Army commanders were appropriate for their political assignment.

2656.   Shook, Robert W.   "Federal Occupation and Administration of Texas, 1865-1870." Ph.D. North Texas State University, 1970. 542p.

2657.   Shook, Robert W.   "Military Activities in Victoria 1865-1866." *Texana* 3 (1965): 347-352.   The federal military occupation around Victoria resulted in several confrontations between members of the U.S. Army and the local population, but in general, the problems have been exaggerated in traditional histories of the period.

2658.   Singletary, Otis A.   "The Texas Militia During Reconstruction." *Southwestern Historical Quarterly* 60 (July 1956): 23-35.   In 1870 the new Republican administration of Gov. Edmund J. Davis sought a militia as a security force because Congress had disbanded militias in the southern states in 1867.   The Texas militia included both white and black member and officers, but the presence of armed blacks in a position of authority generated great criticism and violence against the force.   The militia contributed to Davis' defeat in the gubernatorial election of November, 1872 against Democratic Judge Richard Coke, but a nearly violent dispute over the validity of the election put off Davis' acceptance of the vote until January, 1874.

2659.   Smallwood, James.   "When the Klan Rode: White Terror in Reconstruction Texas." *Journal of the West* 25 (October 1986): 4-13.   Violent Ku Klux Klan activities were widespread in Texas from 1867 to 1872.   Only through the concerted efforts of state officials and some private individuals did the worst Klan activities subside.   Past attempts by historians to justify Klan activities on the basis of black rule or claim that the organization did not exist in Texas are clearly wrong.   A great deal of evidence exists to show that Klan violence was pervasive, and that there was no justification for it.

2660.   Somers, Dale A.   "James P. Newcombe: The Making of a Radical." *Southwestern Historical Quarterly* 72 (April 1969): 449-469.   Newcombe was hounded out of Texas for his Unionist views during the war, but he returned as a Radical Republican.   Texans criticized him as a selfish, corrupt scalawag seeking career success, but Somers explains that Newcombe was sincerely dedicated to Unionism.   He worked with the Union League of Texas and Radical election campaigns, served as secretary of state for Gov. Edmund J. Davis, and edited the Austin *State Journal*.

2661.   Wallace, Ernest.   *The Howling of the Coyotes: Reconstruction Efforts to Divide Texas*.   College Station: Texas A&M Press, 1979. 217p. Bibl. Ills. Maps. Ports   Since Texas became a state in 1845, various proposals were discussed to divide the state into two or more states.   Residents of western Texas have been particularly persistent, so much so that supporters were derisively labeled "howling coyotes."   In 1868 and 1869 efforts to create the state of West Texas failed because of historical traditions.   Local supporters of the new state were viewed as Reconstruction Radicals who used undemocratic means and supported the enfranchisement of freedmen. Included is the text of a constitution for the proposed state.

2662.   Waller, John L. *Colossal Hamilton of Texas: A Biography of Andrew Jackson Hamilton, Militant Unionist and Reconstruction Governor.* El Paso: Texas Western Press, 1968. 152p. Ports. Ill.   Waller writes a sympathetic biography of Hamilton, a devoted Texas Unionist who became a general in the Union Army. In March, 1865 Hamilton was appointed Provisional Governor of Texas, a post he held until August, 1866. Although he supported black suffrage, his support for Radical ideology was tempered by his objection to disenfranchisement of all former rebels at the 1868-1869 state constitutional convention. In 1868 he strongly supported Ulysses Grant for president, but his moderate Republicanism, dislike of radical policies of Governor Edmund J. Davis, and increasing friendship with Horace Greeley, led to Grant's rejection of him. Waller admires Hamilton for his patriotism and courage.

2663.   Williams, Patrick George. "Redeemer Democrats and the Roots of Modern Texas, 1872-1884." Ph.D. Columbia University, 1996. 494p.

2664.   Winkler, E. W. (ed.). "The Bryan-Hayes Correspondence." *Southwestern Historical Quarterly*, Pt. III 25 (April 1922): 274-299; Pt. IV 26 (July 1922): 58-70; Pt. V 26 (October 1922): 149-162; Pt. VI 26 (January 1923): 234-241; 26 (April 1923): 280-316; 27 (July 1923): 52-73.   A portion of the correspondence published in S.H.Q. between Texas Democrat and former Confederate soldier Guy M. Bryan and Rutherford B. Hayes includes their thoughts on Reconstruction politics and elections at the national and state levels. The correspondence actually covers the years 1843 to 1892, but cited above are only the portions covering 1865 to 1877. Bryan's perspective is clear regarding Reconstruction issues in Texas, and he pleads with Hayes to help the South by resisting the most radical of the Republicans. Hayes seems to give Bryan the impression that he is a conservative Republican.

2665.   Wood, W. D. "The Ku Klux Klan." *Quarterly of the Texas State Historical Association* 9 (April 1906): 262-268.   Wood depicts the Klan as a savior from Radical rule under the domination of blacks, carpetbaggers and scalawags. He places particular emphasis on the impact of black rule as the basis for Klan activities. The activities were intended to scare blacks into submission based on their superstitious nature. Wood believes that violence was not an important tool of the Klan.

Agriculture, Labor, and Business

2666.   Adams, Larry Earl.   "Economic Development in Texas During Reconstruction, 1865-1875." Ph.D. University of North Texas, 1980. 238p.

2667.   Ellis, L. Tuffly. "The Revolutionizing of the Texas Cotton Trade, 1865-1885." *Southwestern Historical Quarterly* 73 (April 1970): 478-508.   The postwar revolution in cotton trade relied on rail transportation overland to Houston, Galveston, New Orleans, and St. Louis. Galveston was the key local site for Texas cotton distribution to foreign and domestic markets, but Northern an Eastern competitors offered distribution and manufacturing centers connected to rail lines that extended to Texas.

2668.   Reese, James V. "The Early History of Labor Organization in Texas, 1838-1876." *Southwestern Historical Quarterly* 72 (July 1968): 1-22.   Reese stresses the importance of postwar industrial growth on labor. Until the 1870s labor organization was weak and unsuccessful in building a labor movement, but the growth of railroads in Texas offered opportunities for labor that reached a key point when laborers went on strike in 1877. During Reconstruction development occurred in organizations for printing telegraphers, black longshoremen, and railway builders, and the introduction of national and international unions, such as the International Workingmen's Association and the National Labor Union.

2669.   Rogers, William Warren. "From Planter to Farmer: A Georgia Man in Reconstruction Texas." *Southwestern Historical Quarterly* 72 (April 1969): 526-529.   Printed is a letter from plantation owner Thomas E. Blackshear to Lucius C. Bryan, editor of the Thomasville *Southern Enterprise*, describing how he was getting along with free, black laborers in Grimes County, Texas in early 1867. He complained about their work habits and considered getting workers from Georgia. Blackshear died of yellow fever in 1867.

2670.   Smallwood, James M. "Perpetuation of Caste: Black Agricultural Workers in Reconstruction Texas." *Mid-America* 61 (January 1979): 5-23.   The lack of capital forced the freedmen to either agree to labor constracts with white landowners or migrate to urban areas with the hope of finding employment. Despite the efforts of Freedmen's Bureau agents to regulate labor contracts and ensure basic freedoms for blacks, they could not stop white Texans from creating a caste system to keep blacks under control.   Black codes, wage contracts, sharecropping, apprenticeships and vagrancy laws, convict lease programs, threats of violence and the disregard for federal laws were all designed to keep blacks from progressing toward an equal place with whites in Texas society.

2671.   Wooster, Ralph A. "Wealthy Texans, 1870." *Southwestern Historical Quarterly* 74 (July 1970): 24-35. Tbls.   Wooster examines the characteristics of wealthy Texans both before and after the Civil War. During both periods farming, merchandising, and banking were the professions that led to wealth. Wealth was effected by the rapid postwar economic development in cotton, milling and cattle ranching. Most of the postwar wealthy families lived in the state prior to the war. (For a related article see Wooster's "Wealthy Texans, 1860," *Southwestern Historical Quarterly* 71 (October 1967): 163-180.)

Society, Education, and Religion

2672.   Campbell, Randolph B. "The Burden of Local Black Leadership During Reconstruction: A Research Note." *Civil War History* 39 (June 1993): 5-23. Campbell emphasizes the problems and commitments of black political leaders by publishing a letter from Plato Thompson to Gen. Joseph J. Reynolds, commander of the District of Texas. Thompson turned down a job offer in San Augustine county in late 1867 due to the demands of a large family, his work as a minister to a Methodist Episcopal church, and the opposition of whites to blacks in public offices.

2673.   Campbell, Randolph B. "Population, Persistence and Social Change in Nineteenth-Century Texas: Harrison County, 1850-1880." *Journal of Southern History* 48 (May 1982): 185-204.   Census records and tax rolls are used to document whether white residents in a rural county were so effected by the Civil War and Reconstruction that they moved to other places. Campbell finds that 52.8% of the planter elite in Harrison County remained on their land between 1860 and 1870 and even by 1880 the number had slipped to only 30.2%. The planters seemed to be less effected by recent traumatic events compared with white yoeman farmers and laborers.

2674.   Cohen-Lack, Nancy. "A Struggle for Sovereignty: National Consolidation, Emancipation, and Free Labor in Texas, 1865." *Journal of Southern History* 58 (February 1992): 57-98.   The Union Army occupied Texas in June, 1865 primarily to intimidate recalcitrant Confederates, protect the border with Mexico from a French Army on the border, and generally to extend U.S. national authority to the entire former Confederacy. After the Army emancipated the slaves, they strongly encouraged freedmen to sign labor contracts during the period of transition. The Army, as well as the Freedmen's Bureau, considered the contract labor system as an expression of the Republican ideology of free labor, but the freedmen resisted contract labor as just short of slavery. The Army and the bureau worked for equal rights and justice for the freedmen, but these rights would not secure the economic freedom and personal autonomy.

2675.   Colby, Ira Christopher. "The Freedmen's Bureau in Texas and its Impact on the Emerging Social Welfare System and Black-White Social Relations, 1865-1885." D.S.W. University of Pennsylvania, 1984.

2676.   Crouch, Barry D. and L. J. Schultz. "Crisis of Color: Racial Separation in Texas During Reconstruction." *Civil War History* 16 (March 1970): 37-49.   The authors discuss the historical and ingrained racism of white America, particularly in the South, and that racial separation in education and discrimination in society that was the norm in Texas during Reconstruction. Whites frequently used violence to emphasize the separation and degradation of blacks. The authors reject C. Van Woodward's explanation of the origins of racial segregation in *Strange Career of Jim Crow* (New York: Oxford Unversity Press, 1955; 3rd ed., 1974).

2677.   Crouch, Barry, D. and Donaly E. Brice.   *Cullen Montgomery Baker: Reconstruction Desperado.*   Baton Rouge: Louisiana State University Press, 1997. 190p. Bibl. Maps.   Historians and contemporary writers have vilified Baker as a ruthless murderer of blacks and any whites who opposed him in Texas, Arkansas, and Louisiana. The authors believe that Baker's violent activities between 1865 and his murder in 1869 cannot be explained by describing him as a klansman or independent redeemer of the "lost cause." Instead, Baker had a personal history of violence and antisocial activities going back to prewar days, and his actions during the war and afterwards were consistent. He was part of the violent environment of the postwar years.

2678.   Crouch, Barry D.   *The Freedmen's Bureau and Black Texans.*   Austin: University of Texas Press, 1992. 187p. Ills. Essay on Sources.   In this comprehensive account of the bureau in Texas, Crouch emphasizes what historians have written and the sources they used, how the bureau operated at the local level, and how the local agents dealt with the issues of labor, politics, and race relations. Crouch looks closely at the 13th subdistrict and its agents, particularly the work of William G. Kirkman who was assassinated, and difficult conditions in Brazos County. He believes that the bureau accomplished all that it could given the tremendous problems it faced. (See also Crouch's "Guardian of the Freedpeople: Texas Freedmen's Bureau Agents and the Black Community." *Southern Studies* N.S. 3 (Fall 1992): 185-201.)

2679.   Crouch, Barry D. "The Freedmen's Bureau and the 30th Sub-District in Texas: Smith County and its Environs during Reconstruction." *Chronicles of Smith County, Texas* 9 (Spring 1972): 15-30.   Tyler was the headquarters of the bureau subdistrict that included Smith, Henderson, Wood, Van Zandt, and Cherokee Counties in northeast Texas. Crouch examines the varied responsibilities of the bureau agents in the district, including relief, labor relations, acting as justice of the peace, organizing schools, and protecting freedmen from random and organized violence and intimidation. He describes the work of the 4 agents, Capt. David L. Montgomery, Maj. Levi C. Bootes, 1st lt. Gregory Barrett, Jr. and Capt. Horace Jewett.

2680.   Crouch, Barry D. and Larry Madaras. "Reconstructing Black Families: Perspectives From the Texas Freedmen's Bureau Records." *Prologue* 18 (Summer 1986): 109-122.   Using Texas as a case study, the authors illustrate the usefulness of the Freedmen's Bureau records at the National Archives. The most valuable records are those from local bureau agents who worked directly with freedmen. The emphasis is on the struggle of black parents to control their rights as parents and the freedom of their children. The authors reject the idea that the bureau was a political tool of Radical Republicans, whether the Radicals were corrupt or honest, and they believe that the agency was not allowed to achieve its potential. (See also Crouch's "Hidden Sources of Black History: The Texas Freedmen's Bureau Records as a Case Study." *Southwestern Historical Quarterly* 83 (January 1980): 211-226.)

2681.   Crouch, Barry D.   "A Spirit of Lawlessness: White Violence, Texas Blacks, 1865-1868." *Journal of Social History* 18 (Winter 1984): 217-232. Tbls. Couch examines the violence perpetrated by whites against the freedmen during the first three years following the Civil War. The level of violence in Texas was quite high and was caused by resentment against emancipation and attempts by blacks to exercise their freedom on an equal basis with whites. Violence was also the result of the labor and economic disruptions of emancipation and the violations of antebellum social mores that the freedmen were expected to follow. Texas was a particularly violent state where law enforcement to protect blacks was lax.

2682.   Dorsett, Jesse.   "Blacks in Reconstruction Texas, 1865-1877."   Ph.D. Texas Christian University, 1981. 236p.

2683.   Edwards, John Austin. "Social and Cultural Activities of Texans During Civil War and Reconstruction, 1861-1873." Ph.D. Texas Tech University, 1985. 358p.

2684.   Elliott, Claude. "The Freedmen's Bureau in Texas." *Southwestern Historical Quarterly* 56 (July 1952): 1-24.   Elliot surveys the history of the bureau in Texas with emphasis on the development of schools for the freedmen and the general, unceasing, resistance of white Texans against black education and military authority.   The press was particularly strong in its condemnation of the bureau. If the Freedmen's Bureau had any accomplished in Texas, it was related to commencing a system of black education.

2685.   Hornsby, Alton Jr.   "The Freedmen's Bureau Schools in Texas." *Southwestern Historical Quarterly* 76 (April 1973): 397-417.   Hornsby discusses the active participation of black workers in funding the start up of schools, the violence encountered by Northern teachers, and the devastation of the yellow fever epidemic as well as crop failures and natural disasters. By the time the bureau left Texas in 1870, it had made solid contributions to building a foundation for state supported public education for black Texans.

2686.   Neal, Diane and Thomas W. Kremm. "'What Shall We Do With the Negro?': The Freedmen's Bureau in Texas." *East Texas Historical Journal* 27, 2 (1989): 23-34.   The authors provide a narrative of bureau operations in Texas from its commencement on June 19, 1865 until June 30, 1870 when the bureau withdrew. The bureau was faced with difficulty in labor relations, racial tension, insufficient resources, and internal disagreements about how to bring the ex-slaves into society as free people. It achieved only limited success, but it still managed to provide important help to the freedmen.

2687.   Richter, William L. *Overreached on All Sides: The Freedman's Bureau Administration in Texas, 1865-1868.* College Station: Texas A&M University Press, 1991. 436p. Bibl. Maps.   Richter analyses the bureau administrations of four assistant commissioners - Brigadier Gen. Edgar M. Gregory (Sept., 1865-May, 1866), Major Gen. Joseph B. Kiddoo (May, 1866-Jan., 1867), Major Gen. Charles

Griffin (Jan.-Sept., 1867), and Major Gen. Joseph Jones Reynolds (Sept., 1867-Dec., 1868). Each man had a virtually impossible task to accomplish as originally conceived. None could reconcile the needs of the freedmen with the obstructionist white community. Not only were the roadblocks to success based in Washington, where the bureau was ineffectively administered and inadequately funded, but the rapid decrease in the Army's manpower following the war meant that the establishment of control over the state could not happen. The bureau's successes in education and helping the freedmen make the transition to freedom were overshadowed by its failures.

2688.   Richter, William L. "'The Revolver Rules the Day!': Colonel DeWitt C. Brown and the Freedmen's Bureau in Paris, Texas, 1867-1868." *Southwestern Historical Quarterly* 93 (January 1990): 303-332.   Brown served as subassistant commissioner for the Freedmen's Bureau in northeastern Texas from October, 1867 to 1869. His territory covered Fannin, Lamar, and Red River Counties. Richter discusses the violence in the region from criminals, gangs, and the Ku Klux Klan, and Brown's feeble attempts to stop it. Brown did not have the military support needed from the Army or the Freedmen's Bureau, but Richter also notes the influence of white racism and the difficulty of protecting people from crimes committed in rural areas.

2689.   Richter, William L. "Spread-Eagle Eccentricities: Military-Civilian Relations in Reconstruction Texas." *Texana* 8, 4 (1970): 311-327.   Relations between the U.S. Army and white Texas civilians were usually quite bad during Reconstruction. Richter blames both sides for the violence and resentment that prevailed. Texans resented the presence of the Yankee soldiers, particularly if they were blacks, and they responded sharply to the Army's attempts to protect freedmen and bring criminals to justice. The soldiers' behavior, such as drunkenness, theft, and insensitivity reinforced Texans' negative feelings.

2690.   Richter, William L. "'This Blood-Thirsty Hole': The Freedmen's Bureau Agency at Clarkesville, Texas, 1867-1868." *Civil War History* 38 (March 1992): 51-77.   The white population of Northeastern Texas responded to Reconstruction with defiance and violence. Clarksville in Red River County was the scene of constant intimidation of freedmen, loyal whites, and Freedmen's Bureau agents by gangs of criminals and Ku Klux Klan members. U.S. Army assistance to protect the bureau and the freedmen came late, and the weak leadership of Army commander Major Gen. Jospeh Reynolds symbolized the federal government's lack of strong support for Reconstruction.

2691.   Richter, William L. "Who Was the Real Head of the Texas Freedmen's Bureau?: The Role of Brevet Col. William H. Sinclair as Acting Assistant Inspector General." *Military History of the Southwest* 2, 2 (1990): 121-156.   Sinclair worked with the Texas bureau from 1866 until the end of field inspections in 1868. During his service he had a crucial role in inspecting bureau agents and conditions throughout East Texas and ensuring that the state organization was properly administered. Sinclair's administrative efforts were necessary in light of the varied interests and priorities of the Assistant Commissioners - Gens. Edgar M. Gregory, Joseph B. Kiddoo, Charles Griffin, and Joseph J. Reynolds. His long period of service provided continuity in an environment of constant staff turnover.

2692.   Roberts-Jackson, Lavonne. "'Freedom and Family': The Freedman's Bureau and African-American Women in Texas in the Reconstruction Era, 1865-1872." Ph.D. Howard University, 1996. 226p.

2693.   Smallwood, James M. "The Black Community in Reconstruction Texas: Readjustments in Religion and the Evolution of the Negro Church." *East Texas Historical Journal* 16 (Fall 1978): 16-28.   Smallwood briefly describes the development of separate black churches in Texas. The separation from whites was nearly total by 1870 as blacks sought to express their freedom and escape from racial discrimination in religion. Blacks received assistance from their own communities and from the Freedmen's Bureau, the American Missionary Association, and some local whites. Most blacks chose Baptist or Methodist churches because of their style of worship.

2694.   Smallwood, James M. "Black Freedwomen After Emancipation: The Texas Experience." *Prologue* 27 (Winter 1995): 303-317. Ills.   Freedwomen faced the same racial discrimination and injustices as black men, but they also had their own perspective on freedom and relations with family and the white community. Smallwood's case study of Texas emphasizes freedwomen's struggle to define their own role in society as mothers, wives, employees for whites, teachers, and volunteers in their communities. In addition, they had to cope with physical and sexual abuse, while successfully maintaining their self worth.

2695.   Smallwood, James M. "Charles E. Culver, A Reconstruction Agent in Texas: The Work of Local Freedmen's Bureau Agents and the Black Community." *Civil War History* 32 (December 1981): 350-361.   Bureau agents, such as Culver, belie the stereotype of the corrupt agent who sought to subjugate the South to the will of the North. Culver's career was marked by dedicated service to the freedmen in Freestone, Navarro, and Limestone Counties. His efforts to maintain order and uphold justice and basic rights for freedmen were largely unsuccessful due to white resistance to change and to his image as a federal official.

2696.   Smallwood, James M. "Early 'Freedom Schools': Black Self-Help and Education in Reconstruction - Texas, A Case Study." *Negro History Bulletin* 41 (January/February 1978): 790-793. Ill.   Smallwood emphasizes the organizational efforts of the freedmen to establish schools. Before the Freedmen's Bureau arrived, blacks raised money, selected teachers, and received cooperation from black churches. They were not passively waiting for the government or white organizations to begin organizing for education.

2697.   Smallwood, James M. "Emancipation and the Black Family: A Case Study in Texas." *Social Science Quarterly* 57 (March 1977): 849-857. Tbls.   In this statistical comparison of black and white families in Matagorda, Smith, and

Grayson Counties in Texas, Smallwood finds that the traditional view of black families is a myth. While there was great instability forced on black families under slavery, this quickly changed between 1865 and 1870. The level of stability and the characteristics of black families largely parallel those of whites. The heritage of slavery cannot be used to explain the problems among black families in the mid-20th century.

2698.   Smallwood, James M.   "The Freedmen's Bureau Reconsidered: Local Agents and the Black Community." *Texana* 11 (Spring 1973): 300-324.   William S. Kirkland served as a Freedmen's Bureau agent in Bowie County in northeast Texas from 1867 until his murder in October, 1869. Smallwood's research shows that Kirkland was a shining example of a hardworking, dedicated bureau agent who sought to be fair to freedmen and their employers, to help freedmen establish social institutions, and to protect them from widespread violence from the Ku Klux Klan and outlaws, such as Cullen Baker.

2699.   Smallwood, James M.   "G. T. Ruby: Galveston's Black Carpetbagger in Reconstruction Texas." *Houston Review* 5 (Winter 1983): 193-315.   Ruby, a mulatto born in New York City and educated in Maine, serves as a good example of a carpetbagger who does not fit the stereotype of the corrupt, self serving invader from the North. Smallwood describes Ruby's career in postwar Louisiana and Texas where he served as a teacher, Freedmen's Bureau agent, journalist, and Republican politician. He worked to help the black community and to make Reconstruction a time of progress for freedmen.

2700.   Smallwood, James M. *Time of Hope, Time of Despair: Black Texans During Reconstruction.*   Port Washington: Kennikat Press, 1981.   202p. Smallwood explains that black Texans showed great resilience in their response to emancipation and citizenship. Most freedmen had not internalized the master-slave relationship but were ready and eager for independence and freedom. During Reconstruction blacks organized themselves to improve their families and black society by building schools and creating black churches. Most white Texas insisted on stifling black equality either through legal or extralegal means.   U.S. governmental assistance to freedmen in the form of the Freedmen's Bureau was not very effective and local white Republican leaders were not inclined or could do little to ensure the safety and rights of black citizens and forestall a return to white supremacy. (See also Smallwood's "Black Texans During Reconstruction, 1865-1874." Ph.D. Texas Tech University, 1974. 461p.)

2701.   Smallwood, James M.   "The Woodward Thesis Revisited: Race Relations and the Development of Social Segregation in Reconstruction Texas, A Brief Essay." *Negro History Bulletin* 47 (July-December 1984): 6-9.   Ill.   Smallwood suggests that C. Vann Woodward's research on the origins of segregation (see annotation of # 2676) does not apply to Texas. Racial segregation did not begin in the 1890s but was practiced immediately after the Civil War and became part of life by the end of Reconstruction.

2702. Stripling, Paul Wayne. "The Negro Excision From Baptist Churches in Texas, 1861-1870." Th.D. Southwestern Baptist Theological Seminary, 1967.

2703. Walker, Donald R. "Penology for Profit: A History of the Texas Prison System, 1867-1912." Ph.D. Texas Tech University, 1983. 407p.

Virginia

General History

2704. Smith, James Douglas. "Virginia During Reconstruction, 1865-1870 - A Political, Economic, and Social Study." Ph.D. University of Virginia, 1960. 494p.

2705. Squires, W. H. T. *Unleashing at Long Last: Reconstruction in Virginia April 9, 1865-January 26, 1870.* New York: Negro Universities Press, 1970. 486p. Ills. Ports. (Rpt. of Printcraft Press, 1939) Squires offers a sentimental review of Virginia's experience during the last days of war and the years of Reconstruction. He criticizes Radical Reconstruction for its oppressive and provocative nature.

2706. Taylor, Alrutheus A. "The Negro in the Reconstruction of Virginia." *Journal of Negro History* 11 (April 1926): 243-415; (July 1926): 425-537. (Published as monograph by Washington, D.C.: The Association for the Study of Negro Life and History, 1926; New York: Russell and Russell, 1969.) Taylor criticizes the standard histories of Reconstruction Virginia because they depict blacks, if they are depicted at all, as lazy vagabonds or political enthusiast seeking power in government. Taylor uses a broader range of source materials than the conservative, white historians and seeks to give a clearer picture of black life at the time. His book covers postwar migration of blacks, their willingness and effectiveness as laborers, the development of black education, religion, and political participation. He emphasizes that blacks were never in control of Virginia politics and that black laborers generally worked very well as freedmen in factories and plantations. (See also Taylor's Ph.D. dissertation with the same title from Harvard University, 1936.)

2707. Works Project Administration. *The Negro in Virginia.* New York: Hastings House, 1940. 380p. Bibl. Ills. This book was written by many writers associated with the African-American section of the Federal Writers' Project of the Works Project Administration. The history of blacks in Virginia is told based on print sources and interviews with former slaves. Several chapters either focus on or mention blacks in postwar Reconstruction in the state, including chapters on emancipation, churches, schools, and labor.

Politics and Law

2708.   Bear, James A. (ed.). "Henry A. Wise and the Campaign of 1873: Some Letters From the Papers of James Lawson Kemper." *Virginia Magazine of History and Biography* 62 (July 1954): 320-342.   In the 1873 election between Democrat James Lawson Kemper and Republican Robert W. Hughes, attorney and Confederate veteran John Sargeant Wise supported the election of Kemper. Some of his letters to and from Kemper are printed, as well as a long letter from Wise's father, former governor Henry A. Wise, to the candidate. The elder Wise expressed anger at those who would compromise with the Republicans instead of opposing everything they stood for.

2709.   Blair, William A. "Justice Versus Law and Order: The Battles Over the Reconstruction of Virginia's Minor Judiciary, 1865-1870." *Virginia Magazine of History and Biography* 103 (April 1995): 157-180. Ills. Ports.   Freedmen in Virginia took advantage of the lower courts to obtain fair justice for a variety of claims and complaints, but the white establishment sought to implement their idea of postwar law and order. Whites sought to keep blacks in their place of subordination and under tight control. Blair explains the tensions that surrounded the freedmen's vigorous use of the courts and their protests against injustice. Black activism in pursuing justice represents a measure of success for blacks, despite the general appearance of failure in Reconstruction.

2710.   Boney, F. N. "John Letcher and Reconstruction in Virginia." *Mississippi Quarterly* 19 (Spring 1966): 53-66.   Letcher, governor of Virginia from 1860 to 1863, originally opposed secession, but he became a strong supporter of the Confederacy.   Boney describes Letcher's loyalty to Virginia and his postwar experiences, including his arrest, imprisonment, and parole after intervention by Northern friends. Eventually he returned to politics and public life by 1866 and strongly campaigned against Radical Reconstruction. Letcher worked for the organization of a new conservative political party in 1867-1868.

2711.   Bromberg, Alan B. "The Virginia Congressional Elections of 1865: A Test of Southern Loyalty." *Virginia Magazine of History and Biography* 84 (January 1976): 75-98.   Bromberg focuses on the significance of the Virginia congressional election because of its departure from the accepted image of Southern voters electing former Confederates to the House of Representatives. In 1865 political candidates generally agreed on their opposition to black suffrage and President Johnson's test oath. The oath, as well as warnings from congressional Republicans, caused many candidates to withdraw from the race, resulting in an election between Unionists, most of whom were former Whigs. But even with a Whig-Unionist delegation, the Republican Congress doubted their loyalty and acceptance of change.

2712.   Campbell, J. A. "Efforts For Reconstruction in April, 1865." *Southern Historical Society Papers* 36 (1908): 250-260.   Printed is a letter from Judge Campbell to Attorney General James Speed while Campbell was in prison at Ft.

Pulaski, Georgia on August 31, 1865. The letter describes his attempt to work out an armistice and the return of Virginia to the Union. The conversations that he had with Union officials included a meeting with President Lincoln, but his efforts led to his arrest because he was considered to be dishonest and disloyal in his negotiations.

2713.   Campbell, Otho Carlino.   "John Sergeant Wise: A Case Study in Conservative-Readjuster Politics in Virginia, 1869-1889. Ph.D.   University of Virginia, 1979. 240p.

2714.   Chesson, Michael B.   *Richmond After the War 1865-1890*.   Richmond: Virginia State Library, 1981. 255p.   Ills. Notes. Ports.   A substantial part of this book focuses on Reconstruction, a period Chesson defines as extending to 1902 when a new constitution disenfranchised blacks.   In his discussion of political and economic issues in Richmond, he emphasizes that the nightmare of black power and Republican domination was a myth.   Richmond recovered from the destruction of the war, but its earlier strength as a distribution center did not return.   (See also Chesson's Ph.D. dissertation with the same title from Harvard University, 1979.)

2715.   Chesson, Michael B.   "Richmond's Black Councilmen, 1871-1896."   In *Southern Black Leaders of the Reconstruction Era*.   Edited by Howard N. Rabinowitz.   Urbana: University of Illinois Press, 1982.   Pp. 191-222. Port. Tbl. In January 1870 Virginia reentered the Union and white conservatives took control of Richmond city government.   Technically Reconstruction was at an end in the state, but Chesson illustrates that it was at that point that blacks became very active in city politics.   In 1871 the conservatives formed a city ward composed mainly of blacks, and over the next 35 years 33 blacks were elected from that ward to the city council.   Their accomplishments as councilmen were not great, but their presence, and the willingness of whites to work with them, is noteworthy.   Chesson refers to this period as "shadow reconstruction."   He discusses the background of the black councilmen and includes a table of their terms of service, occupations, dates of birth, and year that their names appeared in the U.S. Census.

2716.   Eckenrode, Hamilton James.   *The Political History of Virginia During the Reconstruction*.   Ph.D. Johns Hopkins University, 1905. 128p. (See also *Studies in Historical and Political Science*. Series 22, 6-8.   Pp. 287-414.)

2717.   "The First Integrated Jury Impanelled in the United States, May, 1967." *Negro History Bulletin* 33 (October 1970):134.   Ill.   This jury, referred to as "half and half", was selected for the trial of Jefferson Davis in Richmond before the U.S. Circuit Court. The names of the black jurors are given.

2718.   Fraser, Walter J., Jr.   "William Henry Ruffner: A Liberal in the Old and New South."   Ph.D. University of Tennessee, 1970. 549p.

2719.   Fraser, Walter J., Jr.   "William Henry Ruffner and the Establishment of Virginia's Public School System, 1870-1874."   *Virginia Magazine of History and Biography*   79 (July 1971): 259-279.   Ruffner opposed slavery and supported

Whig political policies before the Civil War. He became the first Virginia superintendent of public schools as devised by the new state constitution of 1868. His work to gain the support of the legislature for public schools stalled because there was no tradition for mass education, and legislators favored fiscal conservatism and denying education to freedmen. Ruffner sought federal funding to help educate both blacks and whites, and he succeeded in establishing a free school system for both races.

2720.   Harahan, Joseph Patrick.   "Politics, Political Parties, and Voter Participation in Tidewater Virginia During Reconstruction, 1865-1900." Michigan State University, 1973. 331p.

2721.   Hartzell, Lawrence L. "The Exploration of Freedom in Black Petersburg, Virginia, 1865-1902." In *Edge of the South: Life in Nineteenth Century Virginia.* Edited by Edward L. Ayers and John C. Willis. Charlottesville: University Press of Virginia, 1991. Pp. 134-156.   Reconstruction seemed to end in Virginia in 1870 when conservative rule returned, but it continued in Petersburg where black voters held a majority over white voters. The prewar free black population formed the basis for black participation in government and the progress made in establishing black institutions.   The economic devastation of the war and the economic depression in 1873 worked against black power in Petersburg and generated a white conservative backlash that brought the conservatives back into power in 1874 and the gradual decline of black civil rights.

2722.   Henderson, William D.   *The Unredeemed City: Reconstruction in Petersburg, Virginia: 1865-1874.* Washington D.C.: University Press of America, 1977. 379p. Bibl. Ills.   After the Reconstruction Acts of 1867 power in Petersburg transferred from the traditional business and professional oligarchy to Republicans who were mostly conservative. Henderson's history of the city during the period reveals both the mild nature of the reforms in Petersburg and the white reaction. The end of Reconstruction in in the city in 1874 was caused by local Republican electoral losses and the fading national interest and fatigue with Reconstruction. In 1874 the business elite were back in power with business development as their main goal.

2723.   Hucles, Michael. "Many Voices, Similar Concerns: Traditional Methods of African-American Political Activity in Norfolk, Virginia, 1865-1875." *Virginia Magazine of History and Biography* 100 (October 1992): 543-566. Ills.   Black citizens in Norfolk took an active part in trying to guarantee their political and economic equality and access to education. They were noted for their political activism that established a foundation for the future. Their success was limited by the political victories of Conservatives and the factions among the Radical Republicans.

2724.   Hume, Richard.   "The Membership of the Virginia Constitutional Convention of 1867-1868:   A Study of the Beginnings of Congressional Reconstruction in the Upper South." *Virginia Magazine of History and Biography*

86 (October 1978): 4610484. Tbl.   Hume compiles data about the members of the Virginia constitutional convention to provide information for a new assessment of Southern state constitutional conventions following the Reconstruction Acts of 1867. He uses various primary sources to describe the demographic composition of the membership and their votes on key Reconstruction issues. Although Virginia did not experience a Radical Republican government after the convention, black and enough white delegates cooperated to vote down conservative proposals.

2725.   Jackson, Luther Porter. *Negro Office-Holders in Virginia 1865-1895*. Norfolk, Va.: Guide Quality Press, 1945. Ports.   Most of this book consists of brief biographical information on the elected members of the Virginia Constitutional Convention (1867-1868), General Assembly (1869-1890), and the Virginia representatives in the U.S. Congress (1889-1891).   There is also very brief information on members of city and county governments until 1885. Portraits of many of the men are included.

2726.   Jones, Robert R. "Conservative Virginian: The Post-War Career of Governor James Lawson Kemper." Ph.D. University of Virginia, 1964. 415p.

2727.   Lowe, Richard. "Another Look at Reconstruction in Virginia." *Civil War History* 32 (March 1986): 56-76.   Lowe provides a general survey of politics in Virginia from the wartime organization of West Virginia and a Unionist government under Francis H. Pierpont to the readmission of the state into the Union on January 24, 1870. He stresses the lack of unity within the Republican Party as the reason that it could not retain power longer than the three years from 1867 to 1870. Lowe believes that the Republican reform of the state constitution, a document that lasted for 30 years, and the introduction of blacks into state politics are the positive legacies of the Reconstruction.

2728.   Lowe, Richard. "The Freedmen's Bureau and Local Black Leadership." *Journal of American History* 80 (December 1993): 989-998. The Freedmen's Bureau collected information on local black leaders in most of the counties of Virginia. Most of the men named were free prior to the war, and compared with most other blacks, they were wealthier, more literate, and more likely to be of mixed race. When this group is compared with blacks in state constitutional conventions and leaders in New Orleans, they trail in every category.

2729.   Lowe, Richard. "The Freedmen's Bureau and Local White Leaders in Virginia." *Journal of Southern History* 64 (August 1998): 455-472. Tbls.   Lowe emphasizes that white Southerners have not been the focus of many studies since revisionism became the predominant interpretation of Reconstruction in the 1960s and 1970s. He adds to studies on the adjustment of whites to postwar change by examining lists of prominent whites in Virginia who were chosen by Freedmen's Bureau officers as potential political leaders. Lowe concludes that this group of whites were chosen for their potential to bring about change, not return the state to the past.

2730.   Lowe, Richard. "Local Black Leaders During Reconstruction in Virginia."
Virginia Magazine of History and Biography 103 (April 1995): 181-206. Ills. Ports.
Tbls.   Lowe uses Freedmen's Bureau records to examine the characteristics of 621
local black leaders and to compare them with better known urban and statewide
black leaders. He finds that local leaders held a middle ground between the general
black population and the other leaders in terms of their literacy, wealth, education,
skills, racial mix, and the number who were free prior to the war.

2731.   Lowe, Richard. *Republicans and Reconstruction in Virginia, 1856-1870.*
Charlottesville: University Press of Virginia, 1991. 261p. App. Bibl. Maps.
Republicans had a base of support among Unionists in Virginia, but the party's
support for black suffrage and the Underwood constitution scared away moderate
conservatives and led to a victory in the election of 1869 for Gilbert C. Walker's
moderate Republicans and the conservatives in the legislature. Despite their
weakness, state Republicans succeeded in bringing the freedmen into the political
process, instituting a new constitution, introducing free public schools and
democratic government, and maintaining an organization that remained a significant
force in state politics for decades. An appendix includes a list of members of the
constitutional convention of 1867-1868. (See also Lowe's "Republicans, Rebellion,
and Reconstruction: The Republican Party in Virginia, 1856-1870." Ph.D.
University of Virginia, 1968. 388p.)

2732.   Lowe, Richard.   "Virginia's Reconstruction Convention: General
Schofield Rates the Delegates." *Virginia Magazine of History and Biography* 80
(July 1972): 341-360.   In October, 1867 Virginia voters elected delegates to the
state constitutional convention.   A combination of blacks, scalawags, and
carpetbaggers teamed up to elect convention strongly partial to the Republican
Party. The military commander for the state, Gen. John M. Schofield, rated each
delegate as to their ethnic or racial group, profession, and political leanings. The
entire list is arranged by city or county. Lowe includes extensive notes clarifying or
elaborating on Schofield's remarks.

2733.   Maddex, Jack P., Jr. *The Virginia Conservatives 1867-1879: A Study in
Reconstruction Politics.* Chapel Hill: University of North Carolina Press, 1970.
328p. Bibl.   Virginia politics in the postwar period tended to follow a new path
from antebellum days. The Conservatives, consisting mainly of former Whigs and
some Democrats, dominated state politics, but they did not represent a return of the
prewar Bourbon ideology. The new group was dedicated to a new South that
followed the nationalism, industrial capitalism, and reformism of the North within
the context of Virginia. This included civil rights reforms without racial equality.
Success would elude them for many years. Maddex notes that his assessment is
consistent with C. Vann Woodward's thesis in *Origins of the New South* (Baton
Rouge: Louisiana State University, 1951) of a postwar revolutionary process of
industrial capitalism in the South. (See also Maddex's *The Virginia Conservatives:
A Study in 'Bourbon' Redemption, 1869-1879."* Ph.D. University of North
Carolina, 1966. 873p.)

2734.   Maddex, Jack P., Jr. "Virginia-The Persistence of Centrist Hegemony." In *Reconstruction and Redemption in the South*. Edited by Otto Olsen. Baton Rouge: Louisiana State University Press, 1980.   Pp 113-155.   Bibl.   During Reconstruction Virginia never elected a Republican governor despite the fact that Republicans wrote the new state constitution. Centrist elements of the Conservative Party controlled both the executive and the legislature after the 1869 election. They were a mix of former Whigs and reformed Democrats. Their interest in black civil rights was minimal as they focused instead on state business and economic issues. The Republicans split between radicals and moderates and were unable to gain substantial support from poor rural whites.

2735.   Majeske, Penelope Aspasia Kantgias. "Your Obedient Servant: The United States Army in Virginia During Reconstruction, 1865-1867." Ph.D. Wayne State University, 1980. 135p.

2736.   McDonough, James L.   "John Schofield as Military Director of Reconstruction Virginia." *Civil War History* 15 (September 1969): 237-256.   Gen. Schofield commanded the Department of the Potomac beginning in August, 1866. Until his appointment as Secretary of War on June 1, 1868 he followed a moderate course in politics and race relations by softening what he believed were harsh Reconstruction laws to avoid further inflaming the white population.   Schofield supported justice for freedmen, but clearly opposed the 14th Amendment and black suffrage. McDonough suggests that the general's actions were appropriate and reasonable.

2737.   McGrady, Joseph P. "Immigrants and the Politics of Reconstruction in Richmond, Virginia." *Records of the Columbia Historical Society* 83 (June 1972): 87-101.   O'Grady uses the census and newspapers as resources to show that the white immigrant population of specific regions of Virginia might have had more political influence in Reconstruction than was previously believed.

2738.   Moore, John Hammond. "Richmond Area Residents and the Southern Claims Commission, 1871-1880." *Virginia Magazine of History and Biography* 91 (July 1981): 285-295.   Moore briefly reviews the background, purpose, and procedures of the commission, and then focuses on claims made from Henrico County, Virginia. Several cases are described for information regarding the daily lives of people during the war. Moore includes cases of both blacks and whites, and he lists names and information about their claims.

2739.   Moore, Louis. "The Elusive Center: Virginia Politics and the General Assembly, 1869-1871." *Virginia Magazine of History and Biography* 103 (April 1995): 207-236. Ill.   Moore criticizes historical interpretations of Reconstruction politics that stress the importance of the New Departure among conservative white politicians. Moore points to the actions of the Virginia legislature to demonstrate that the New Departure was a facade that crumbled when words of compromise could not be translated into legislation. What was so successful for Virginia conservatives in 1869 did not exist by 1871 because they refused to implement moderate reforms.

2740.   Morton, Richard L.   "The Negro in Virginia Politics, 1865-1902."   Ph.D. University of Virginia, 1918.   199p.

2741.   O'Brien, John T., Jr.   "Reconstruction in Richmond: White Restoration and Black Protest, April-June 1865."   *Virginia Magazine of History and Biography* 89 (July 1981): 259-281.   Under the command of Gen. Edward O. C. Ord, the U.S. Army acted harshly toward the freedmen in Richmond and disregarded their complaints about local rules that restricted their freedoms.   Richmond blacks organized effectively to publicize their problems and convince the Johnson administration to reverse the injustices inflicted by the Army and local white authorities.   The show of political prowess reinforced the desire of freedmen to participate in the political process as their only hope of realizing true freedom.

2742.   Ours, Robert Maurice.   "Virginia's Funding Legislation, 1869-1875:   Its Background, Principle Features, Related Measures, and Effects."   Ph.D.   College of William and Mary, 1974.   296p.

2743.   Pincus, Samuel Norman.   "The Virginia Supreme Court, Blacks, and the Law, 1870-1902."   Ph.D. University of Virginia, 1978.   476p.

2744.   Rachal, William M. E.   (ed.).   "The Capital Disaster, April 27, 1870:   A Letter of Judge Joseph Christian to His Wife."   *Virginia Magazine of History and Biography* 68 (April 1960): 193-197.   The excitement and controversy surrounding the dispute over who was mayor of Richmond, Virginia in the spring of 1870 led to an overflow crowd in a second floor court room at the state capital.   The large crowd caused the second floor to collapse resulting in the killing or maiming of a large number of people.   A letter from Judge Joseph Christian describes the scene.

2745.   Russ, William A., Jr.   "Disfranchisement in Virginia Under Radical Reconstruction."   *Tyler's Quarterly Historical and Genealogical Magazine* 17 (July 1935): 25-41.   Russ summarizes the response of conservative whites in Virginia to the disenfranchisement of former Confederates and the election and work of the constitutional convention of 1867-1868.   He cites the outrage of the conservative press to the new constitution and a convention dominated by ignorant blacks. Voters accepted the constitution only after the removal of disenfranchisement clauses, and at the same time, they elected moderate Republican Gilbert Walker. Through persistence and persuasion, intelligence won over ignorance.

2746.   Shibley, Ronald Edward.   "Election Laws and Electoral Practices in Virginia, 1867-1902:   An Administrative and Political History."   Ph.D.   University of Virginia, 1972.   292p.

2747.   Simpson, Craig H. *A Good Southerner: The Life of Henry A. Wise of Virginia.* Chapel Hill: University of North Carolina Press, 1985. 450p. Bibl. Map. Ports.   Wise, former governor of Virginia (1856-1860), owner of a plantation and slaves, and strong supporter of the Confederacy, had been a reluctant supporter of secession in 1861.   After the war he found himself in opposition to the Conservatives.   Wise supported the Republican Party as the political leadership of the future, but his support for the rights of freedmen was tempered by his resistance to anything that would promote racial integration.

2748.   Stuart, Alex H. H. *A Narrative of the Leading Incidents of the Organization of the First Popular Movement in Virginia in 1865 to Re-establish Peaceful Relations Between the Northern and Southern States, and of the Subsequent Efforts of the 'Committee of Nine,' in 1869, to Secure the Restoration of Virginia to the Union.* Richmond: Wm. Ellis Jones, 1888. 72p. (Rpt. by AMS Press, 1973)   Stuart, a major participant in reuniting Virginia with the Union, describes his perspective on the political events from 1868 until July, 1869 when the Underwood Constitution was approved by voters. He includes letters written by himself and correspondents in Virginia and the U.S. government.

2749.   Teamoh, George. *God Made Man, Man Made the Slave: The Autobiography of George Teamoh.* Edited by Nash Boney, Rafia Zafor, and Richard L. Hume. Macon, Ga.: Mercer University Press, 1990. 219p. Notes, Ills. Ports.   Teamoh was born a slave in Norfolk and escaped to the northeast U.S. in 1853 where he remained until returning to Virginia after the war. He eventually became active in Republican politics, and served in the state constitutional convention in 1867 and the senate from 1869 to 1871. A large portion of this book covers Teamoh's experiences with Republican politics in Richmond.

2750.   Wicker, J. Tivis. "Virginia's Legitimization Act of 1866." *Virginia Magazine of History and Biography* 86 (July 1978): 339-344.   The act reversed the practice of disallowing legitimate marriage contracts among slaves by making legal the "marriage" of blacks who lived together as husband and wife. It also made legitimate those children born prior to February 27, 1866. The law had an impact on future court cases related to domestic relations.

2751.   Younger, Edward. *The Governors of Virginia, 1860-1878.* Charlottesville: University Press of Virginia, 1982. 428p.   Includes brief biographies of Reconstruction governors: "Francis Harrison Pierpont: Wartime Unionist, Reconstruction Moderate," by Richard G. Lowe (pp. 33-46); "Henry Horatio Wells: The Rise and Fall of a Carpetbagger," by Patricia Hickin (p. 47-56); and Gilbert Carlton Walker: Carpetbag Conservative," by Crandall A. Shifflett (p. 57-68). Pierpont (1865-1868), the Unionist father of West Virginia, is described as an excellent politician during the war, but he could not meet the challenges of the immediate postwar years. Wells (1868-1869), a Republican from New York and Michigan, also failed because of his lack of political acumen in a divisive environment. It was left to Walker (1869-1874), also from New York, to bring

Republican conservatism and compromise to play in order to return Virginia to the Union and assuage Southern whites.

Agriculture, Labor, and Business

2752.   Blake, Nelson Morehouse. *William Mahone of Virginia: Soldier and Political Insurgent.* Richmond: Garrett and Massie, 1935. 323p. Bibl. Ills. Maps. Port.   A portion of this biography of Mahone deals with his railroad interests in southern Virginia during Reconstruction. After returning home to Petersburg from service in the Confederate Army, Mahone reassumed the presidency of the Norfolk and Petersburg Railroad and set out to expand his business by consolidating other rail lines with his own. This resulted in the Atlantic, Mississippi and Ohio Railroad in June, 1870 after the consolidation was made lawful by an act of the General Assembly. Mahone supported conservative, Republican governor Gilbert C. Walker in 1869, became a leader of the Readjuster Party, lost a bid for governor in 1877, and won election to the U.S. Senate in 1879.

2753.   Burdick, John. "From Virtue to Fitness: The Accommodation of a Planter Family to Postbellum Virginia." *Virginia Magazine of History and Biography* 93 (January 1985): 14-35. Ills.   Burdick agrees with historian Jonathan Wiener that many Southern planters were able to keep their plantations in the family following the war, but he disagrees with Wiener's assertion that plantation owners represented a "semi-feudal class" that rejected capitalism. By using the family of Robert Hubard as an example, Burdick explains that the postwar planters who retained their prewar lands adjusted to the new market situation in the South by combining farming, industry, and the professions. They accepted at least the social Darwinist rhetoric of the rising Southern bourgeoisie while trying to maintain their ideal of the gentleman's life.

2754.   Hucles, Michael Edward.   "Postbellum Urban Black Economic Development: The Case of Norfolk, Virginia, 1860-1890."   Ph.D. Purdue University, 1990. 281p.

2755.   Kerr-Ritchie, Jeff. "Free Labor in the Virginia Tobacco Piedmont, 1865-1900." Ph.D. University of Pennsylvania, 1993. 334p.

2756.   Medford, Edna Greene. "The Quest for Black Economic Independence on Virginia's Lower Peninsula, 1865-1880." *Virginia Magazine of History and Biography* 100 (October 1992): 567-582. Ills. Tbls.   The Lower Peninsula counties included Elizabeth City, Warwick, York, James City, Charles City, and New Kent. Blacks in the region took advantage of the diversified economy that created alternative employment in nonagricultural jobs, such as fishing, oystering, forestry and railroads. The accumulation of income allowed them to purchase land and assume greater independence.

2757.   Medford, Edna Greene. "The Transition From Slavery to Freedom in a Diversified Economy: Virginia's Lower Peninsula, 1860-1900." Ph.D. University of Maryland, 1987. 224p.

2758.   Michel, Gregg L. "From Slavery to Freedom: Hickory Hill, 1850-1880." In *The Edge of the South: Life in Nineteenth Century Virginia.* Edited by Edward l. Ayers and John C. Willis. Charlottesville: University Press of Virginia, 1991. Pp. 109-133.   Hickory Hill was mainly a wheat plantation in Hanover County. Michel explains how war and emancipation effected the work of the plantation owned by William Carter Wickam.   While most Southern plantations began a wage labor system and then switched to sharecropping, Hickory Hill maintained wage labor throughout the postwar decades.   Wickham maintained his wage system because he had cash reserves from financial investments that he used to pay regular, quarterly wages and to purchase new farm implements.

2759.   Morgan, Lynda. *Emancipation in Virginia's Tobacco Belt, 1850-1870.* Athens: University of Georgia Press, 1992. 329p.   Bibl.   In the tobacco growing belt of Virginia, emancipation brought a thorough transformation of labor, economic, and social relationships.   While planters maintained much of their land and sought to dominate the state, Virginia turned toward industrial capitalism for future development. The freedmen's long experience in Virginia taught them about the nature of the society so that when emancipation came, they were prepared to act independently in developing free labor, family relations, education, land ownership, and churches.   Even when the conservatives became the center of power in 1869-1870, they could not turn back the tide of change or black persistence in managing their own freedom.   (See also Morgan's Ph.D. dissertation with the same title from University of Virginia, 1986.)

2760.   Rachleff, Peter J. *Black Labor in the South: Richmond, Virginia, 1865-1890.* Philadelphia: Temple University Press, 1984. 249p. Bibl. Tbls.   Black labor in Richmond is examined from the perspective of the "new labor history." The decades after the Civil War are viewed as a time of economic and social development within the black community and a period when black and white labor struggled to work out a satisfactory relationship that would offer a foundation for economic and political power.   In the first four chapters of this book, Rachleff explains the early adjustments of black laborers to freedom, Republican politics, and social and political activism.

2761.   Schweninger, Loren. "The Roots of Enterprise: Black Owned Businesses in Virginia, 1830-1880." *Virginia Magazine of History and Biography* 100 (October 1992): 315-342. Tbls.   The number of black entrepreneurs in Virginia increased between 1860 and 1880 despite racial prejudice and economic hardship during the period.   Many were free blacks prior to the war, and they established a precedent for freedmen who also established businesses as farmers, barbers, artisans, and other trades. Schweninger includes a discussion of his sources.

2762.   Shifflett, Crandall A.   *Patronage and Poverty in the Tobacco South: Louisa County, Virginia, 1860-1900.* Knoxville: University of Tennessee Press, 1982. 159p. App. Bibl.   The postwar period was full of promise for freedmen in Louisa County, but planters fixed the social and economic power structure to ensure that blacks would be bound in poverty and racism. Shifflet's work provides an analysis of planter-tenant relationships that illustrate the white resistance to change and the meaning of free black labor.

2763.   Thomas, Percial Moses. "Plantations in Transition: A Study of Four Virginia Plantations, 1860-1870." Ph.D. University of Virginia, 1979. 577p

2764.   Townes, A. Jane. "The Effect of Emancipation on Large Landholdings, Nelson and Goochland Counties, Virginia." *Journal of Southern History* 45 (August 1979): 403-412. Tbls.   Townes examines land tenure of large parcels of land, 500 acres or more, in two black belt counties of Virginia where slave populations were high in 1860 and the predominant crop was tobacco. By using agricultural statistics from the census and county land tax books, Townes finds that the revolution in labor conditions did not change the pattern of land tenure for large landholdings. The number of large plantations decreased, but not so much that would validate earlier claims of a dramatic breakup of large landownership.

2765.   Weis, Tracey M. "Negotiating Freedom: Domestic Service and the Landscape of Labor and Household Relations in Richmond, Virginia, 1850-1880." Ph.D. Rutgers, 1994. 334p.

Society, Education, and Religion

2766.   Alderson, William T. "The Freedmen's Bureau and Negro Education in Virginia." *North Carolina Historical Review* 29 (January 1952): 64-90. Alderson describes the contributions of the Freedmen's Bureau to education in Virginia from the spring of 1865 until mid-1870. He views the program as largely successful in working with benevolent associations to provide primary and teacher training education. The bureau funded land and buildings while the associations organized the curriculum and paid teachers. The free public education system persisted beyond Reconstruction.

2767.   Alderson, William T. "The Influence of Military Rule and the Freedmen's Bureau on Reconstruction in Virginia 1865-1870." Ph.D. Vanderbilt University, 1952. 318p.

2768.   Beales, Ross W., Jr. "An Incident at the Freedmen's School, Lexington, Virginia, 1867." *Prologue* 6 (Winter 1974): 252-254. Ills.   Beales describes an incident in which a few students of Washington College harassed Northern teachers and the black students. He includes a letter from one of the teachers, Zilpha R.

Harper, to a Freedmen's Bureau official describing the incident.   The story is intended to illustrate the hardships of teachers from the North.

2769.   Brown, Elsa Barkley.   "Uncle Ned's Children: Negotiating Community and Freedom in Postemancipation Richmond, Virginia."   Ph.D.   Kent State University, 1994. 624p.

2770.   Daniel, W. Harrison.   "Virginia Baptists and the Negro, 1865-1902." *Virginia Magazine of History and Biography* 76 (July 1968): 340-363.   After the war white Baptists in Virginia continued to believe that slavery was a lawful institution as expressed in the bible.   They rejected any idea of black equality and insisted on complete racial segregation.   Black Baptists were not removed from white churches, but their treatment by whites and a desire for independence led to the establishment of black Baptist churches and organizations by the early 1870s. Whites talked about the importance of helping their coreligionists, but their help was mostly token and offered in a paternalistic manner.   Race relations worsened as the century progressed.   (See also Daniel's "Virginia Baptists and the Myth of the Southern Mind, 1865-1900," *South Atlantic Quarterly* 73 (Winter 1974): 85-98.)

2771.   Engs, Robert Francis.   *Freedom's First Generation: Black Hampton, Virginia, 1861-1890.* Philadelphia: University of Pennsylvania Press, 1979. 236p. Bibl. Ills. Maps. Ports. Tbls.   Engs focuses on Hampton because of its unique characteristics for the study of postwar race relations and the development of the black community in freedom.   The lack of a repressive slave environment, the presence of free blacks, and the varied talents of black workers provided the black community with the ability and inclination to take advantage of resources given them by Northerners, such as the American Missionary Association and the Freedmen's Bureau.   The black community of Hampton actively sought quick integration into society.   They worked with Northern whites to bring about black success in labor, education, and politics that symbolized what might have been possible throughout the South and what was repressed in the 1890s when white racism set back black progress.

2772.   Greenwalt, Bruce S.   (ed.).   "Virginians Face Reconstruction: Correspondence From the James Dorman Davidson Papers, 1865-1880. *Virginia Magazine of History and Biography* 78 (October 1978): 447-463.   This selection of letters from the Davidson Papers were written by Davidson and various correspondents.   They give an idea of the observations and feelings of white Southerners during the first two years following war except for one poem written in 1880. Davidson was a lawyer, political counselor, antisecessionist who remained loyal to the Confederacy.

2773.   Haulman, Clyde A. "Changes in Wealth Holding in Richmond, Virginia." *Journal of Urban History* 13 (November 1986): 54-71. Tbl.   Haulman provides a brief analysis of wealth in Richmond to illustrate that despite the changes wrought by the Civil War, the distribution of wealth in Richmond from 1860 to 1870 remained very consistent. He measures the number and make up of the top 5% of wealth holders in the city. Except for a significant turnover among the wealthy group, the number of families and the basis for their wealth showed continuity throughout the period. The findings appear consistent with that of other southern cities.

2774.   Hayden, John Carleton. "Reading, Religion, and Racism: The Mission of the Episcopal Church to Blacks in Virginia, 1865-1877." Ph.D. Howard University, 1972.

2775.   Horst, Samuel L. "Education for Manhood: The Education of Blacks in Virginia During the Civil War." Ph.D. University of Virginia, 1977. 361p.

2776.   Horst, Samuel L. (ed.). *The Fire of Liberty in Their Hearts: The Diary of Jacob E. Yoder of the Freedmen's Bureau School, Lynchburg, Virginia.* Richmond: Liberty of Virginia, 1996. 192p. Ills.   Yoder, a Pennsylvania Mennonite, taught at or administered several schools for freedmen the Lynchburg area as part of the Pennsylvania Freedmen's Relief Association's program to assist black education in the South.   Yoder's diary provides information about his experiences and impressions of the freedmen and whites in postwar Virginia.   He remained in Lynchburg to devote his life to the administration of black education in the community. Horst provides an informative introduction to Yoder's life.

2777.   Jackson, Luther P. "The Origin of Hampton Institute." *Journal of Negro History* 10 (April 1925): 131-149.   Hampton Institute was originally called the Hampton Normal and Agricultural Institute when it was founded in 1867 and opened its doors to students in April, 1868.   The school was organized through the efforts of the Freedmen's Bureau, the American Missionary Association, and various other sources of funding.   Hampton was intended to serve as an institution of higher education for future black teachers and leaders in society.   (For more on the Hampton Institute see also Donald Spivey, *Schooling For the New Slavery: Black Industrial Education, 1868-1915.* Westport: Greenwood Press, 1978.)

2778.   Jones, Wilbur Devereux (ed.). "A British Report on Postwar Virginia." *Virginia Magazine of History and Biography* 69 (July 1961): 346-352.   Jones provides the text of a report written in January, 1866 by Sir Frederick W. A. Bruce, British representative in Washington, to the Fourth Earl of Clarendon, Foreign Secretary to Prime Minister Lord John Russell. Bruce's report is based partly on interviews with several people, including Robert E. Lee's son, Fitzhugh, about their feelings regarding the Confederacy, the Northern victory, and British relations with both the North and the South. Bruce's report reveals continuing distrust and hatred for the North along with an abiding allegiance for Virginia and a desire for a separate Southern nation.

2779.   Knight, Edgar W. "Reconstruction and Education in Virginia." *South Atlantic Quarterly* 15 (January 1916): 25-40; (April 1916): 157-174.   Knight's two part article offers a history of educational reform during Reconstruction. The new constitution of 1869 made public schools for all people an obligation of the state that would be funded by public taxation. Knight discusses at length the issue of racial integration in the schools, an idea that was totally rejected by a large majority of whites. Despite the urging of black delegates at the constitutional convention and later in the state legislature, schools were legally segregated. Knight believes that there was no inclination to discriminate against black students, and that race relations in education would have improved more quickly had it not been for the exploitation of the freedmen from the outside forces.

2780.   Lee, Leslie Winston. "Richmond During Reconstruction, 1865-1867." Ph.D. University of Virginia, 1974. 482p.

2781.   Majeske, Penelope K. "Virginia After Appomattox: The United States Army and the Formation of Presidential Reconstruction Policy." *West Virginia History* 43 (Winter 1982): 95-117. Ills.   The U.S. Army worked with President Johnson and local residents to restore order and normalcy to the devastated state of Virginia. They provided food, repaired roads and bridges, and worked to return productive agriculture. Despite the interpretations of most historians, Johnson's Reconstruction decisions were confirmations of changes already in motion. Majeske sympathizes with Johnson's policies.

2782.   Mansfield, Betty. "That Fateful Class: Black Teachers of Virginia's Freedmen, 1861-1882." Ph.D. Catholic University of America, 1980. 391p.

2783.   McConnell, John Preston. *Negroes and Their Treatment in Virginia From 1865 to 1867*. Pulaski, Va.: B. D. Smith and Bro., 1910. 126p. Bibl.   McConnell seeks to correct false impressions about the condition of blacks in Virginia. He concludes that between 1865 and 1867 race relations gradually improved as blacks learned the reality of freedom and whites altered or repealed harsh black codes. He blames Freedmen's Bureau agents, Northern teachers, scalawags, and carpetbaggers for creating unnecessary difficulties that upset the transition to freedom for the former slaves and peace for all. Congressional Reconstruction destroyed the progress made prior to 1867 and led to bitterness and unrest. (See also McConnell's Ph.D. dissertation with the same title from University of Virginia, 1904.)

2784.   Moore, John Hammond. "The Norfolk Riot: 16 April 1866." *Virginia Magazine of History and Biography* 90 (April 1982): 155-164.   The riot resulted from accumulated tensions since Union troops first occupied the city on January 2, 1862. The white population reacted defiantly to four years of occupation, defeat, and the demands of freedmen for civil rights. The riot added to the violence throughout the South, and helped to strengthen the Radicals in Congress.

2785.   Morton, Richard L. "'Contrabands' and Quakers in the Virginia Peninsula, 1862-1869." *Virginia Magazine of History and Biography* 61 (October 1953): 419-429.   The Friends' Association of Philadelphia and Its Vicinity for the Relief of Colored Freedmen was founded on November 5, 1863 to assist with the education and general assistance of the freedmen. Morton tells the story of the association's activities in the peninsula region where agents were already hard at work prior to the arrival of the Freedmen's Bureau in March, 1865.   Jacob H. Vining from the Friends' Association and Samuel Chapman Armstrong from the Freedmen's Bureau worked together to establish schools.

2786.   Morton, Richard L.   "Life in Virginia by a 'Yankee Teacher', Margaret Newbold Thorpe.*"   Virginia Magazine of History and Biography* 64 (April 1965): 180-207.   Thorpe traveled from Philadelphia to Fort Magruder near Williamsburg, Virginia to teach the freedmen in schools established by the Freedmen's Bureau and the Friends Association of Philadelphia and Its Vicinity for the Relief of the Colored Freedmen.   She arrived in February, 1866 and stayed until the spring of 1869. During this time Thorpe kept a notebook of her experiences.   The text of the notebook is printed.   It illustrates her perspective on the life of freedmen.

2787.   Muggleston, William F.   (ed.).   "The Freedmen's Bureau and Reconstruction in Virginia: The Diary of Marcus Sterling Hopkins, a Union Officer."   *Virginia Magazine of History and Biography* 86 (January 1978): 45-102. Hopkins, an Ohio native, served as a bureau agent in Prince William City and in Orange and Louisa Counties following the war until December, 1868.   His diary reveals how the bureau functioned in rural Virginia.   Muggleston notes that compared with his official reports, Hopkin's diary is more pessimistic and reveals greater skepticism about the capabilities of blacks.   The diary covers January 1 until December 8, 1868.

2788.   O'Brien, John T., Jr.   "From Bondage to Citizenship: The Richmond Black Community, 1865-1867."   Ph.D. University of Rochester, 1975. 522p.

2789.   Pearson, C. Chilton.   "William Henry Ruffner: Reconstruction Statesman of Virginia."   *South Atlantic Quarterly* 20 (January 1921): 25-32; (April 1921): 137-151.   Ruffner, a Virginia native, served as superintendent of education from 1870 until 1882.   Through his diligent, creative efforts in the organization and finance of local schools for both white and black students, he is remembered as a true statesman.   Ruffner was strongly favorable towards black education and believed in their "improvability", but he rejected racial integration. He tried to avoid politics, but it was the political movement of the "readjusters" that eventually forced his retirement.

2790.   Reidy, Joseph P.   "'Coming From the Shadow of the Past': Transition from Slavery to Freedom at Freedom's Village, 1863-1900."   *Virginia Magazine of History and Biography* 95 (October 1987): 403-428.   Freedom's Village was a sanctuary for freed slaves during the Civil War on land abandoned by Gen. Robert E. Lee and his wife Mary Curtis Lee near Washington, D.C. Established in 1863 by the American Missionary Association and the Union Army, it was intended to relieve congestion in Washington and provide work for freedmen.   Reidy describes the postwar conflicts between the Freedmen's Bureau and the residents involving rents, work, and attempts to evict the residents.

2791.   Stennette, Janice Schmid.   "Teaching for the Freedmen's Bureau: Lynchburg, Virginia, 1865-1871." Ph.D. University of Virginia, 1996. 127p.

2792.   Tripp, Steve Elliott.   "Restive Days: Race and Class Relations in Lychburg, Virginia 1858-1872." Ph.D. Carnegie Mellon University, 1990. 298p.

2793.   Vance, Joseph C.   "Freedmen's Schools in Albemarle County During Reconstruction." *Virginia Magazine of History and Biography* 61 (October 1953): 430-438.   Vance describes the experiences of abolitionist Anna Gardner of Massachusetts who began teaching in Charlottesville in the fall of 1865.   Her suspicion of white Southerners and her emphasis on teaching political and social equality to the freedmen caused local dislike for her.   Despite the problems, Gardner's approach to training blacks to become teachers of their own people became well established.

2794.   Vance, Joseph C. "Race Relations in Albemarle During Reconstruction." *Magazine of Albemarle County History* 13 (1953): 28-45. Map.   Life for freedmen in Albemarle County, including Charlottesville, did not dramatically change after the war until the beginning of Congressional Reconstruction in the spring of 1867. At that time, particularly when the Underwood Constitution was completed, race relations deteriorated. Vance examines relations from 1865 until the conservatives returned to power in 1869. Blacks are depicted as generally confused about politics and freedom. Whites who responded violently were concentrated within the lower classes.

2795.   Whitman, James P. "Incidents in Reconstruction." *Confederate Veteran* 32 (June 1924): 220-222.   Whitman describes his own run-in with abusive U.S. Army troops in October, 1865 in southwestern Virginia.

Washington, D. C.

2796.   Corrigan, Mary Elizabeth.   "A Social Union of Heart and Effort: The African-American Family in the District of Columbia on the Eve of Emancipation." Ph.D. University of Marlyand, College Park, 1996. 418p.

2797.   Everly, Elaine Cutler. "The Freedmen's Bureau in the National Capitol." Ph.D. George Washington University, 1972. 170p.

2798.   Horton, Lois E. and James Oliver Horton.   "Race, Occupation, and Literacy in Reconstruction Washington, D. C." In *Toward a New South? Studies in Post-Civil War Southern Communities*. Edited by Orville V. Burton and Robert C. McMath, Jr.   Westport: Greenwood Press, 1982.   Pp. 135-151.   Tbls.   By examining occupational and literacy rates the authors explain that education alone made little difference in the ability of blacks in the capital city to overcome social and economic barriers. They were not provided with the tools necessary, and racism proved too strong to defeat.   Most Republicans believed that only through an evolutionary process would education uplift the freedmen.

2799.   Indritz, Phineas.   "Post Civil War Ordinances Prohibiting Racial Discrimination in the District of Columbia." *Georgetown Law Journal* 42 (January 1954): 179-209.   Indritz discusses how Reconstruction legislation in the District of Columbia survived later court and legislative changes to play a role in desegregating city restaurants, public accommodations, and other public facilities in 1953.

2800.   Johnson, Thomas R.   "Reconstruction Politics in Washington: 'An Experimental Garden of Radical Politics.'"   *Records of the Columbia Historical Society, Washington, D.C.* 50 (1980): 180-190.   Jackson explains that the politics of the District of Columbia from 1865 to 1876 serves as a model for Reconstruction throughout the South.   The city, under control of the Republican Congress, seemed to be a place that Radical reforms could be thoroughly put into practice.   Apathy among white conservatives led to Republican control of city government, greater black involvement in politics, and the expansion of black education and public improvements.   But corruption, fading concern for civil rights, and growing opposition to black suffrage led Congress to eliminate voting rights in the District.

2801.   Johnston, Allan John.   "Surviving Freedom: The Black Community of Washington, D. C., 1860-1880." Ph.D.   Duke University, 1980.   371p.

2802.   Powell, Frances Lajune Johnson.   "A Study of the Structure of the Freed Black Family in Washington, D.C., 1850-1880."   D.A.   Catholic University of America, 1980.   122p.

2803.   Roach, Brett R.   "Prejudice Against Blacks Freed in Post-Civil War Washington." *Negro History Bulletin* 47 (January-March 1985): 3-6.   The black population of Washington expanded by more than 300% from 1860 (14,316) to 1880 (59,596).   The influx led to racial strife, but it also generated tension within the black community based on prewar status (ie. free v. slave), social and economic differences, and shade of skin.   Both whites and well-to-do blacks wanted the rough, uncultured blacks to leave.

2804.   Williams, Melvin R.   "Blacks in Washington, D.C., 1860-1870."   Ph.D. Johns Hopkins University, 1976.   265p.

2805.   Williams, Melvin R.   "Blueprint For Change: The Black Community in Washington D.C., 1860-1870." *Records of the Columbia Historical Society of Washington, D.C.* 48 (1971-1972): 359-393. Map. Tbls.   Williams examines demographic characteristics of the black population in Washington, D.C. followed by a review of racial reforms including emancipation, public education, and political participation.   He emphasizes the work of black residents and Radicals in Congress to bring about reforms.   Much of the progress dissipated in 1871 when Congress eliminated voting in the district and took control over the district.   Williams believes that Congress sought to disenfranchise blacks and that it generally disapproved of civil rights reforms in the district.

2806.   Williams, William H.   *The Negro in the District of Columbia During Reconstruction.*   Howard University, Department of History, June, 1924.   52p. *(Howard University Studies in History, 5)*   Williams surveys the political, economic, and social advancement of blacks in the capital city.

2807.   Whyte, James H.   *Uncivil War: Washington During Reconstruction, 1865-1878.* New York: Twayne, 1958. 316p. Bibl. Ills. Ports.   Whyte provides a colorful narrative about Washington, D. C. society, culture, and politics during the postwar years. It was a time of changes in the political relationship between the city and the federal government.   Despite the economic and political burdens of thousands of former slaves, Washington experienced good race relations and the future of black participation in representative government looked promising. The elimination of local suffrage by Congress in 1871 was a setback to local democratic government.

West Virginia

2808.   Casdorph, Paul D.   "The 1872 Liberal Republican Campaign in West Virginia."   *West Virginia History* 29 (July 1968): 292-302.   By 1870 a conservative, Democratic backlash to Reconstruction reforms had emerged, illustrated by the election of Democrat John J. Jacob as Governor. The backlash continued in the spring of 1872 when the Liberal Republican movement began in West Virginia brought together disaffected Democrats and anti-Grant Republicans, but Grant carried West Virginia. Horace Greeley had supporters mainly in the southern and eastern panhandle counties where there were large numbers of slaves prior to emancipation.

2809.   Curry, Richard O.   "Crisis Politics in West Virginia, 1861-1870."   In *Radicalism, Racism, and Party Realignment, the Border States During Reconstruction.* Edited by R. O. Curry. Baltimore: Johns Hopkins Press, 1969. Pp. 80-114. Map.   Reconstruction in West Virginia was mainly a struggle over identifying citizens who were loyal and would be eligible to vote. The liberal Republicans sought a vindictive policy of denying voting rights to former rebels or persons suspected of former loyalty to the Confederacy so that Republicans could continue in power. The confrontational politics of Reconstruction in the state was substantially determined by geography, because the state included a large minority of secessionist counties. West Virginia, a region of rugged individualism and strong racism, refused to do much more for blacks than to eliminate slavery. Curry characterizes Republican party policies as "the politics of negative reform" (p. 103). The weakness of Republicanism led to its defeat in 1870.

2810.   Curry, Richard Orr. "The Virginia Background for the History of the Civil War and Reconstruction Era in West Virginia: An Analytical Commentary." *West Virginia History* 20 (July 1959): 215-246.   Curry's main concern is that the final shape of West Virginia included counties which contained many slaveholders. The inclusion of these counties, located along the eastern border with Virginia, led to a traumatic period of Reconstruction. He writes that the postwar experience would have been much different had the state included the core of counties that actually participated in the separation from Virginia. Most of Curry's article deals with historical developments prior to the war that shaped the relationship between Virginia and it's northwestern counties.

2811.   Gerofsky, Milton. "Reconstruction in West Virginia." *West Virginia History* 6 (July 1945): 295-360; 7 (October 1945): 5-39. Tbls.   This two part article is Gerofsky's M.A. thesis from West Virginia University in 1942. He focuses mainly on legislative and judicial activities, from the beginning of the state in 1863 until 1872 when voters accepted a new constitution. The main issues were loyalty oaths, the disenfranchisement of disloyal citizens, and the passage of the 14th and 15th Amendments. Gerofsky criticizes Republicans for their vindictiveness toward former Confederates and lack of real concern for the freedmen. Reconstruction came to an end after Democrats won the state election of 1870 and the passage of the Flick amendment to the state constitution in 1871.

2812.   Gooden, Randall Scott. "The Completion of a Revolution: West Virginia From Statehood Through Reconstruction." Ph.D. West Virginia University, 1995. 374p.

2813.   Lewis, Virgil A. "How West Virginia Became A Member of the Federal Union." *West Virginia History* 30 (July 1969): 598-606.   Lewis provides a chronological description of how the state was formed from April 22, 1861, when the first meeting of Unionists organized, to the commencement of statehood on June 20, 1863.

2814.   Moore, George Ellis. "Slavery As a Factor in the Formation of West Virginia." *West Virginia History* 18 (October 1956): 5-89.   Two-thirds of this article deals with slavery in West Virginia prior to the Civil War. Slavery was one of the key issues that generated the statehood and union movement in the western counties of Virginia, but when a constitution was proposed to the U.S. Congress in May, 1862, slavery remained. Moore explains that for many persons from the area the formation of a new state within the Union was the focus of their efforts, and slavery was thought to be necessary for economic and social well being. The inconsistency was partially eliminated with pressure from Congress and key state founders, particularly Gordon Battelle. West Virginia did not free its slaves until February 3, 1865, three days after Congress approved the 13th Amendment.

2815.   Riggs, Joseph Howard. "A Study of the Rhetorical Events in the West Virginia Statehood Movement." *West Virginia History* 17 (April 1956): 191-251. This article is a narrative of the creation of the state as illustrated in the speeches given at important events. Meetings, conventions, and resolutions are described with frequent quotations to show how they form a thread from the beginning to the end of the path toward state creation. Although calls for a new state date back to the eighteenth century, Rigg focuses on the period following the presidential election in November, 1860 until West Virginia joined the Union on April 20, 1863. Two sections focus on the two Wheeling Conventions. The appendix lists speeches recorded in the *Wheeling Intelligencer* by date and location.

2816.   Shaffer, Dallas S. "Lincoln and the 'Vast Question of West Virginia.'" *West Virginia History* 32 (October 1970): 86-100.   Lincoln approved the statehood bill for West Virginia based on the necessities of the war effort to preserve the Union even if it ran counter to his Reconstruction plans and the Emancipation Proclamation. He was personally in favor of bringing the whole of Virginia back into the Union, and he recognized the inconsistencies of freeing slaves outside of federal control but agreeing to the demands of West Virginia leaders to bring the new state into the Union with slavery. Politics, expediency and difficulties on the battlefield played a large role in Lincoln's decision making.

2817.   Stealey, John Edmund III. "The Freedmen's Bureau in West Virginia." *West Virginia History* 39 (January-April 1978): 99-142.   A large part of the bureau's work took place in Jefferson and Berkeley Counties where there was a concentration of freedmen. The bureau had a presence from late 1865 until Autumn, 1868. Its main accomplishment was the help it gave to establish public schools that benefited both whites and blacks. Stealey cites the establishment of Storer College (1868) as the bureau's most important achievement. The bureau failed in its efforts to protect the rights of freedmen.

2818.   Stealey, John Edmund III (ed.). "Reports of the Freedmen's Bureau District Officers on Tours and Surveys in West Virginia." *West Virginia History* 42 (Winter 1982): 145-155. Ill.   Printed are letters written by bureau agents John Kimball and G. N. Clark who report on the general conditions of the freedmen, race relations, and the availability of education to the freedmen in 1867.

2819.   Stealey, John Edmund III (ed.). "Reports of the Freedmen's Bureau Operations in West Virginia: Agents in the Eastern Panhandle." *West Virginia History* 42 (Fall 1980-Winter 1981): 94-129.   Printed are reports from Freedmen's Bureau agents J. H. McKenzie (January-March, 1866), George H. Wells (April-May, 1866), A. F. Higgs (June, 1866-May, 1867), and J. C. Brubaker (September, 1867-September, 1868). The agents offer evaluative comments regarding public assistance to the needy, the establishment of public schools, Republican politics, Confederate sympathies, and the progress of the freedmen.

2820.   Talbott, Forrest. "Some Legislative and Legal Aspects of the Negro Question in West Virginia During the Civil War and Reconstruction." [Part I] *West Virginia History* 24 (October 1962): 1-31; [Part II] 24 (January 1963): 110-133; [Part III] 24 (April 1963): 211-247.   In this three part article Talbott describes the long process of achieving emancipation and civil rights for blacks in West Virginia between 1863, when the state was formed, and 1872, when voters rejected a state constitutional amendment that would have required public officeholders to be white. The issue of race was forced on the state from the beginning of statehood, and while a majority of conservative Unionists cared little for the slave and later the freedmen. The state gradually accepted reforms setting up segregated free public educational institutions for blacks, and black suffrage, office holding, and jury service. The last two reforms did not come until 1872 with the passage of the new constitution of 1872. Only then was the "Negro question" considered a "dead issue."

2821.   Winston, Sheldon. "Statehood for West Virginia: An Illegal Act?" *West Virginia History* 30 (April 1969): 530-534.   The act of statehood by a gathering of Unionist West Virginians may have been illegal, and it is still not recognized by present day Virginia.

2822.   Woodson, Carter G. "Early Negro Education in West Virginia." *Journal of Negro History* 7 (January 1922): 23-63.   This survey of school development extends from Reconstruction to the beginning of the 20th century. The legislature enacted laws in 1866 and 1867 for the establishment of public schools for blacks, but the lack of enthusiasm among whites throughout the state hindered the development of black education. Progress came with the help of the Freedmen's Bureau, and missionary and freedmen's aid societies. In 1872 the state mandated segregated schools. Woodson highlights the opening of black schools, including Storer College, a teacher training school.

2823.   Woodward, Isaiah A. "Arthur Ingraham Boreman: A Biography." *West Virginia History* 31 (July 1970): 206-269;   32 (October 1970): 10-48.   Port. Boreman was a leader of the movement to restore Virginia to the Union that ultimately led to the formation of West Virginia. He was governor from 1863 until 1869 and then U.S. senator from 1869 to 1875. Woodward depicts his subject as a conservative Republican who believed in civil rights and education for the freedmen, but he objected to racial equality and black suffrage. His career illustrates how Reconstruction in West Virginia was mainly a struggle between white Unionists and ex-Confederates over political control of the state.

2824.   Woodward, Isaiah A. "Opinions of President Lincoln and His Cabinet on Statehood for Western Virginia 1862-1863." *West Virginia History* 21 (April 1960): 157-185. Ports. Facim.   Eight letters between Lincoln and his cabinet in December, 1862 are printed that relate to the constitutionality of West Virginia's request for statehood.   Included are communications from Postmaster General Montgomery Blair, Secretary of State William H. Seward, Attorney Geneal Edward Bates, Secretary of War Edwin M. Stanton, Secretary of Treasury Salmon P. Chase, and Secretary of the Navy Giddeon Welles. Also included are one letter from Lincoln to his cabinet and one statement of opinion by Lincoln. The cabinet reasoned that there was not a problem with statehood, but Lincoln made sure that the new state constitution provided for the gradual emancipation of the slaves residing in the state.

Reconstruction in Northern and Western States

2825. Abbott, Richard H. *Cotton and Capital: Boston Businessmen and Antislavery Reform, 1854-1868.* Amherst: University of Massachusetts Press, 1991. 294p. Bibl. Abbott discusses the contributions of several Bostonians to the organized efforts to eliminate slavery and encourage the spread of Republican principles of free labor for blacks and whites. He focuses primarily on the New England Emigrant Aid Society and the leadership of businessmen Amos A. Lawrence, Edward Atkinson, John Murray Forbes, George Luther Stearns, Eli Thayer, and Unitarian Minister Edward Everett Hale. The group lacked ideological unity, but they favored freedom for the slaves for practical reasons, particularly because blacks would be Republican voters and as free laborers who could contribute to economic prosperity, particularly in the production of the all important cotton crop. For this reason the Bostonians supported Congressional Reconstruction, the protection of the freedmen, and, in varying strength, black civil rights. By 1868 interest began to wane among Boston businessmen with the apparent success of the 15th Amendment and their disillusionment with Southern blacks as laborers and farmers.

2826. Ahern, Wilbert H. "The Cox Plan of Reconstruction: A Case Study in Ideology and Race Relations." *Civil War History* 16 (December 1970): 293-308. In his campaign for governor of Ohio during the summer of 1865, Jacob D. Cox proposed a plan to transfer all black Americans to one region of the South where they would enjoy complete freedom. He believed that the races were not compatible and that blacks would never have a fair chance in white society. Ahern criticizes Cox's plan as racist and unworkable. It was a reflection of the *laissez faire* social ideology that strengthened racism.

2827. Angle, Paul M. "The Illinois Black Laws." *Chicago History* 8(Summer 1967): 65-75. Ill. On February 4, 1865 the Illinois legislature voted to repeal the state's "Black Laws" that originated with a code adapted by the state on March 30, 1819. The repeal followed a strong campaign by John Jones, a black from Chicago.

The Emancipation Proclamation eventually made the change acceptable to the public.

2828.   Baum, Dale. "Woman Suffrage and the 'Chinese Question': The Limits of Radical Republicanism in Massachusetts, 1865-1876." *New England Quarterly* 56 (March 1983): 60-77.   After the Civil War Radical Republicans in Massachusetts showed the most radical of attitudes toward issues of equality and civil rights for all citizens. Baum illustrates that there were cracks in their unity for radical reforms. There was general support for ensuring that women were first class citizens, but support for women's suffrage was weak due to politics and social conservatism. The issue of Chinese laborers also raised difficult problems because state Republicans increasingly feared the impact on American culture and politics of mass immigration of Chinese. Baum explains both press opinions and attitudes of public figures.

2829.   Berrier, G. Galis. "The Negro Suffrage Issue in Iowa-1865-1868." *Annals of Iowa*, 3rd Series 39 (Spring 1968): 241-260. Ports.   Berrier credits Edward Russell for initiating and maintaining pressure for changing the Iowa state constitution so that black citizens could vote. Using mainly Iowa newspapers, he describes Republican efforts to generate support for black suffrage throughout the state.   Republicans explained that suffrage did not mean social equality, but Democrats used racial animosity in an effort to scare Iowans into rejecting reform. The differing approaches helped lead to the Republican election victory in 1865, but it was not until 1868 that black suffrage was approved by the voters. Reforms in Iowa helped lead to the 15th Amendment and set an example for other Northern states.

2830.   Berwanger, Eugene H. "Reconstruction on the Frontier: The Equal Rights Struggle in Colorado, 1865-1867." *Pacific Historical Review* 44 (August 1975): 313-329.   The struggle and the rhetoric regarding equality of rights for blacks in the South extended to the Colorado territory. Between 1864 and 1867 white Coloradans sought statehood but with a restriction denying black citizens to vote. William J. Hardin, a black barber in Denver, and other black leaders, fought to eliminate the restriction or to push Congress to vote against statehood. The white citizens of the territory voted overwhelmingly against black suffrage. Congress did not object, but President Johnson vetoed the statehood bill. Berwanger argues that through the persistent efforts of black leaders like Hardin, they influenced Congress to pass legislation in January 1867 that eliminated racial discrimination in voting in U.S. territories. Colorado blacks next turned to access to public education, but they did not soon succeed.

2831.   Berwanger, Eugene H. "Three Against Johnson: Colorado Republican Editors React to Reconstruction." *Social Science Journal* 12-13 (October-January 1975-76): 149-158.   Coloradans closely followed postwar Reconstruction politics in Washington and the South. Berwanger traces the opinions of three newspapers in the territory - *The Rocky Mountain News* (Denver), the *Miner's Register* (Central City), and the Black Hawk *Mining Journal*. Opinions varied but all three supported

Johnson's Reconstruction policy until the spring and summer of 1866 when he vetoed the Civil Rights Bill and riots in the South indicated the rejection of reform among white Southerners. There was mixed opinion on impeachment. All three papers were particularly critical of Johnson's veto of statehood for Colorado, a key issue that contributed to anti-Johnson sentiment.

2832.   Berwanger, Eugene H. *The West and Reconstruction.* Urbana: University of Illinois Press, 1981. 294p. App. Bibl.   Berwanger believes that contrary to traditional scholarship, the citizens of western territories and states were very concerned about Reconstruction issues in the South and the way those issues would effect them.   He surveys the impact of Reconstruction on the West and discovers that newspaper editors, politicians, and private citizens had much to say about black suffrage, civil rights, states' rights, and the impeachment of President Johnson. Western Republicans originally supported Presidential Reconstruction, but the struggle between Congress and Johnson turned them toward the Radical perspective on reforming the South.   In their own states black suffrage became a divisive issue, even in states where the black population was quite low.   Westerners sought the quick resolution of post Civil War problems, and their spirit of reform and attention to civil rights following 1867 waned quickly as the Democratic Party gained more power in the South.

2833.   Berwanger, Eugene H.   "William J. Hardin: Colorado Spokesman for Racial Justice, 1863-1873." *Colorado Magazine* 52 (Winter 1975): 52-65. Ports. Hardin has been a forgotten leader of racial justice in Colorado. Berwanger weeks to lift him from obscurity by emphasizing his contributions to achieving black suffrage and integration. His aggressive style and personal problems weakened his political influence, but he was undoubtedly the main force behind reforms during Reconstruction.

2834.   Bonadio, Felice. *North of Reconstruction: Ohio Politics, 1865-1870.* New York: New York University Press, 1970. 204p.   Ohio politicians did not respond to Reconstruction from a principled, ideological perspective. Their main concern, explains Bonadio, was political advantage, locally and nationally. Southern Reconstruction and black rights dominated the political landscape, but the main battles were among Republican factions that had been fighting for years, third party organizations, and and Democrats. Both the Reconstruction Acts of 1867 and black suffrage were used as tools that had little to do with justice for the freedmen. They had everything to do with beating political opponents, even if denying suffrage would accomplish this. (See also Bonadio's "Ohio Politics During Reconstruction, 1865-1868." Ph.D. Yale University, 1964. 320p.)

2835.   Bonadio, Felice. "Ohio: A 'Perfect Contempt of All Unity.'" In *Radical Republicans in the North: State Politics During Reconstruction.* Edited by James C. Mohr. Baltimore: Johns Hopkins University Press, 1976. Pp. 82-103.   By the end of the Civil War the Republican Party in Ohio was badly split over black suffrage and the pace of Reconstruction. Most Ohio Republicans supported the concept of black suffrage for the Southern states in order to develop the Republican

Party in the South, but convincing Ohioans that blacks should vote in Ohio was difficult and may have led to Democratic gains in local elections in 1866. Most Republicans wanted to eliminate suffrage as a political issue by encouraging its acceptance, but it was not until 1870, when the Ohio legislature passed the 15th Amendment, that the issue finally disappeared from state politics. By that time various differences among state Republicans had badly split the party.

2836.   Bowersox, LaVerne K. "The Reconstruction of the Republican Party in the West, 1865-1870." Ph.D. Ohio State University, 1931. 328p.

2837.   Bradley, Erwin S. *Post-Bellum Politics in Pennsylvania, 1866-1872.* Ph.D. Pennsylvania State University, 1952. 441p.

2838.   Bridges, Roger D. "Equality Deferred: Civil Rights for Illinois Blacks, 1865-1885." *Journal of Illinois State Historical Society* 74 (Summer 1981): 83-108. Facim. Ills. Ports.   It was not until early February, 1865 that the Illinois legislature approved a bill to repeal the state's "Black Laws" that restricted civil rights and prohibited Black immigration to the state. Bridges explains that from that time until the mid-1880s Illinois moved slowly and reluctantly towards providing equality of civil rights for black citizens.   The state was drawn into the reforms by Reconstruction in the South and by black citizens in the state. Politics played a leading role in local Republican concessions on the race issue.

2839.   Brown, Ira V. "Pennsylvania and the Rights of the Negroes, 1865-1867." *Pennsylvania History* 28 (January 1961): 45-57.   Pennsylvania's history was marked by discrimination against black citizens of the state. The actions of the Republican Congress after the Civil War to bring about equality of civil rights in the South had a clear impact in Pennsylvania. In every instance, whether the issue was suffrage or the integration of streetcars, the state was forced to follow the lead of the federal government. Segregated schools continued until 1881.

2840.   Caldwell, Martha Belle. "The Attitude of Kansas Toward Reconstruction of the South." Ph.D. University of Kansas, 1933. 134p.

2841.   Cochrane, William Ghromley. "Freedom Without Equality: A Study of Northern Opinion and the Negro Issue, 1861-1870." Ph.D. University of Minnesota, 1957. 464p.

2842.   Cohen, Roger Alan. "The Lost Jubilee: New York Republicans and the Politics of Reconstruction and Reform, 1867-1878." Ph.D. Columbia University, 1976. 866p.

2843.   Cowden, Joanna Dunlap. "Civil War and Reconstruction Politics in Connecticut, 1863-1868." Ph.D. University of Connecticut, 1975. 337p.

2844.   Current, Richard N. "The Politics of Reconstruction in Wisconsin, 1865-1873." *Wisconsin Magazine of History* 60 (Winter 1976-1977): 83-108. Ills. Ports.

Current explains that Reconstruction in Wisconsin was a period of continued enmity between Republicans and Democrats. The Republican governor, Lucius Fairchild, used the issues of patriotism, internal improvements, and opposition to the treason of the Democratic copperheads to gain political advantage. Wisconsin Republicans supported Congressional Reconstruction, but support for black civil rights could not overcome overwhelming opposition to black suffrage in the state. Blacks gained suffrage in 1866 after a successful lawsuit. Although the Liberal Republicans lost Wisconsin in the 1872 presidential election, the passions of Reconstruction politics gave way to various ethnic, economic, and social issues that eventually swept Republicans out of office in 1873.

2845.   Dallinger, Frederick W. "Massachusetts in Reconstruction 1865-1871." In *Commonwealth History of Massachusetts.   Vol. 4:   Nineteenth Century Massachusetts.* Edited by Albert Bushnell Hart. New York: States History Co., 1930. Pp. 552-587. Bibl. Ills. Ports.   Dallinger outlines the major events of Reconstruction and explains the role of Massachusetts representatives in Congress and the response of the state in general. The state had a tradition of conservatism that was altered by a minority of abolitionists before and after the Civil War. The citizens of the state did not seek a harsh Reconstruction, and their racial prejudice was quite strong, but by the end of the war state laws made blacks equal citizens under the law. The dedicated efforts of federal statesmen from Massachusetts, particularly Charles Sumner, led the state towards greater democracy for all citizens.

2846.   Dante, Harris L. "Reconstruction Politics in Illinois, 1860-1872." Ph.D. University of Chicago, 1951. 358p.

2847.   Dante, Harris L.   "Western Attitudes and Reconstruction Politics in Illinois, 1865-1872." *Journal of the Illinois State Historical Society* 49 (Summer 1956): 149-162.   Illinois was strongly Republican following the war, but the approach of most Republicans toward Reconstruction in the South was moderation. Even though the state congressional delegation went along with Congressional Reconstruction and the impeachment of President Johnson, they sought stability and an end to experimentation in the South. They also sought the wrestle power away from the Northeastern faction in the party to help their state's agricultural interests in its opposition to tariff increases and tight currency. Their economic policy was clearly similar to Westerners and Southerners. With the leadership of men such as U.S. Senator Lyman Trumbull and *Chicago Tribune* editor Horace White, many prominent Illinois Republicans contributed to the Liberal Republicans in 1872.

2848.   Doyle, Don. "Slavery, Secession, and Reconstruction as American Problems." In *The South as an American Problem.* Edited by Larry J. Griffin and Don H. Doyle. Athens: University of Georgia Press, 1995. Pp. 102-125.   Doyle briefly analyses the Northern tradition of reform that led from abolitionism to emancipation and attempts to change Southern society.

2849.   Dykstra, Robert R. "Iowa: 'Bright Radical Star.'" In *Radical Republicans in the North: State Politics During Reconstruction.* Edited by James C. Mohr.

Baltimore: Johns Hopkins University Press, 1976. Pp. 167-193.   Iowa was the first and only state where a grassroots movement in favor of black political equality was successful in a public vote on November 3, 1868. The movement succeeded because Iowa had a core of dedicated Republicans who stuck by the issue. Using quantitative methods, Dykstra compares several variables to weigh public support for black suffrage. The genuine support given for equality did not translate into solid, progressive reforms on other issues in Iowa, but state Republicans maintained strong support for President Grant and the Reconstruction of the South.

2850.   Dykstra, Robert R. and Harlan Hahn.   "Northern Voters and Negro Suffrage: The Case of Iowa, 1868." *Public Opinion Quarterly* 32 (Summer 1968): 202-215.   This is a statistical study of Iowa's referendum on black suffrage in 1868. The authors focus on the votes from small towns and townships, the characteristics of the voters, and how they voted for party candidates. The socioeconomic status of voters was revealed as a key factor. The Democratic appeal to the fears of immigrants and farmers was generally successful, but the measure passed along party lines.

2851.   Farley, Ena L.   "The Issue of Black Equality in New York State, 1865-1873." Ph.D. University of Wisconsin 1973. 287p.

2852.   Farley, Ena L.   "Methodists and Baptists on the Issue of Black Equality in New York, 1865-1868." *Journal of Negro History* 61 (October 1976): 374-392. Farley explains that Methodist and Baptist church leaders in New York believed that the 13th Amendment decided the important moral issues in relations between blacks and whites. Apart from efforts by laity to educate the freedmen, church leaders did not see any reason to get involved in political matters. The talk of merging black and white churches failed due to the lack of strong interest by either race. White Methodists, in particular, wanted nothing to do with racial equality in the church. The Christian Church accepted the separation of the races and then directed more attention to other problems, such as temperance and converting European immigrants.

2853.   Field, Phyllis F.   *The Politics of Race in New York: The Struggle for Black Suffrage in the Civil War Era.* Ithaca: Cornell University Press, 1982. 264p. App. Bibl. Maps. Tbls.   White New Yorkers consistently rejected black suffrage in 1846, 1860, and 1869 because racism and ethnicity were entangled in party politics and the struggle for popular support. The state Republican Party supported the issue but refused to push too hard in public lest voters reject them in elections. Party unity and the maintenance of power were far more important than suffrage in their state, but they strongly pushed for black suffrage in the South. Reconstruction encouraged the promotion of black voting rights in New York on the basis of morality and justice, but only the 15th Amendment decided the issue. (See also Field's "The Struggle For Black Suffrage in New York State, 1846-1869," Ph.D. Cornell University, 1974.   419p.; and "Republicans and Black Suffrage in New York State: The Grass Roots Response," *Civil War History* 21 (June 1975): 136-147 in which she examines the failed attempts to eliminate property qualifications.)

2854.   Fishel, Leslie H. "The North and the Negro, 1865-1900: A Study in Race Discrimination." 2 Volumes. Ph.D. Harvard University, 1954. 516p.

2855.   Fishel, Leslie H. "Northern Prejudice and Negro Suffrage, 1865-1870." *Journal of Negro History* 39 (January 1954): 8-26.   Fishel argues that Northern racial prejudice was strong after the Civil War, and it delayed the general acceptance of black suffrage. Only when the 15th Amendment became part of the constitution did the Northern states finally accept it, despite the prejudice that existed. Ironically, the suffrage that the freedmen fought so hard for was clearly not enough to overcome many other racial barriers.

2856.   Fishel, Leslie H. "Repercussions of Reconstruction: The Northern Negro, 1870-1883." *Civil War History* 14 (December 1968): 325-345.   Fishel explains that the traditional interdependence of blacks in the North and the South hurt Northern black leaders after 1870 when they struggled to claim civil rights while also attempting to maintain a national focus on problems of their race in the South. Their lack of clear goals, their traditional reliance on white Republicans, and the internecine quarrels over school integration typified the fragmentation of the Northern black community and reduced the influence of their leadership for many years.

2857.   Foner, Philip S. "The Battle to End Discrimination Against Negroes on Philadelphia Streetcars: Part I: Background and Beginning of the Battle." *Pennsylvania History* 40 (1973): 261-290; "Part II: The Victory." 40 (1973): 355-379. (Rpt. in *The Civil War and Reconstruction Era, 1861-1877*, New York: Garland, 1991: 96-109.)   Foner clarifies that while the long struggle against discrimination on streetcars in Philadelphia ended with success in March, 1867, the black community viewed it as only partially successful, because it required an act of the Pennsylvania state legislature and the signature of the governor, rather than local action. Philadelphia was infamous for its entrenched racism.

2858.   Foulke, William Dudley. *Life of Oliver P. Morton, Including His Important Speeches*.   Indianapolis: Bower-Merrill, 1899. 2 Vols. 1080p. Morton, a Republican governor of Indiana from 1861 to 1866 and U.S. senator from 1867 to 1877, supported the war effort with emphasis on saving the Union not eliminating slavery. He tolerated slavery, believed in the supremacy of the white race, and supported a quick Reconstruction. His views gradually shifted towards the Radicals regarding civil rights and reform in the South. He originally opposed black suffrage but became a strong supporter of the 15th Amendment and the anti-Ku Klux Klan Enforcement Acts of 1870 and 1871. As an Indiana politician Morton had to tread carefully in a conservative state where the Republican Party's power was not great. Foulke emphasizes Morton's pragmatic politics, and the lengthy quotations from Morton's speeches illustrate his strong, convincing style that earned him the respect of his Republican colleagues.

2859.   Grossman, Lawrence. "The Democratic Party and the Negro: A Study in Northern and National Politics, 1868-1892." Ph.D. City University of New York, 1973. 504p.

2860.   Harrison, John M. "David Ross Locke and the Fight on Reconstruction." *Northwest Ohio Quarterly* 35 (Winter 1962-63): 18-31. Port.   Locke was editor of the Toledo *Blade* during 1865 and 1866. He wrote editorials under his own name and a pseudonym, Petroleum Vesuvius Nasby.   Harrison examines Locke's editorials in the context of his reputation as a Radical Republican sympathizer. Locke's writings reveal that he was actually a moderate who supported conciliation between mainstream Republicans and Johnson so that the Radicals would not gain so much power that the president would be pushed into the Democratic camp.

2861.   Huff, Carolyn B. "The Politics of Idealism: The Political Abolitionists of Ohio in Congress, 1840-1866." Ph.D. University of North Carolina, 1969. 185p.

2862.   Hyman, Harold Melvin. *Era of the Oath: Northern Loyalty Tests During the Civil War and Reconstruction.* Philadelphia: University of Pennsylvania Press, 1954. 229p. App. Bibl. Ills. Tbl. of Cases.   In Hyman's examination of oaths, he concludes that they were not successful at separating the loyal from the disloyal or even defining who the disloyal were. In practice, the taking of an oath had little relation to an individual's thoughts, interpretations, or future behavior. Also, the Republican Party used the oath laws to try to ensure Republican loyalty and strengthen their political future. The federal courts took on many legal challenges to the test oaths and contributed to striking down or weakening the oath laws until the wartime oaths were eliminated in May, 1883 by an act of Congress signed by President Chester Arthur. The appendix includes the text of loyalty oath acts of Congress from 1861, 1862, and 1865. (See also Hyman's Ph.D. dissertation with the same title from Columbia University, 1952.)

2863.   Johannsen, Robert W.   "The Oregon Legislature of 1868 and the Fourteenth Amendment." *Oregon Historical Quarterly* 51 (March 1950): 3-12. Johannsen describes the efforts of the Democratic legislature in Oregon to rescind the earlier adoption of the 14th Amendment. Democrats, who won a majority in the legislature in the election of June, 1868, opposed the amendment and considered the methods used to pass it to be highly unusual.

2864.   Knapp, Charles Merriam. *New Jersey Politics During the Period of the Civil War and Reconstruction.* Geneva, N.Y.: W. F. Humphrey, 1924. 212p. App. Bibl. Map.   A small portion of the text (162-185) refers to Reconstruction in New Jersey. The state resisted constitutional reforms, including the 13th Amendment and black suffrage, based on support for states' rights and a desire for a quick period of Reconstruction in the South. These issues led to a Democratic victory in state elections in 1868 and the subsequent revolt against legislative approval of the 14th Amendment and black suffrage proposals.

2865.   Lake, James A. and Richard Hansen.   "Negro Segregation in Nebraska Schools 1860-1870."   *Nebraska Law Review* 33 (November 1953): 44-53. Nebraska became a state on March 1, 1867 only after it agreed to congressional demands that it eliminate restrictions related to suffrage or any other right to citizens based on race or color.   The state passed the 14th Amendment on June 14, 1867. The authors could find no contemporary comments about the proposed amendment, and they also found a lack of documents regarding the change of school laws in 1867 that eliminated segregation.   Nebraskans must have been responding to the "temper of the time" (p. 53).

2866.   Loewenberg, Ted.   "The *Blade* and the Black Man: 1867."   *Northwest Ohio Quarterly* 44 (1972): 40-50.   The Toledo *Blade* newspaper enthusiastically supported amending the Ohio constitution to allow black citizens to vote if they could pass a literacy test.   The test would apply to whites as well.   Their support was based on fairness, justice, and the ability of blacks to protect themselves, but Ohio voters resoundingly defeated the measure, because they believed that the black voter would symbolize racial equality in society.

2867.   Masel-Walter, Lynne.   "Their Rights and Nothing More: A History of *The Revolution*, 1868-1870."   *Journalism Quarterly* 53 (Summer 1976): 242-251.   *The Revolution* was a newspaper dedicated to pushing for women's suffrage and civil rights during the reform environment of Reconstruction.   Elizabeth Cady Stanton, Susan B. Anthony, and Parker Pillsbury founded the paper on January 8, 1868.   It was the first such periodical to make the case for women's rights, but it failed financially by the early 1870s.

2868.   McAfee, Ward M.   "Reconstruction Revisited: The Republican Public Education Crusade of the 1870s."   *Civil War History* 42 (June 1996): 133-153. The Republican program for public education in the South became a national effort based on the ideology of reforming the South in the image of the North and broader attempts to stifle the expanding influence of the Catholic Church in Northern public education.   Catholic baiting in the 1870s was political phenomena conducted by Protestant politicians and clergy, but Democrats saw it as a smoke screen for racial reforms that they believed would result in integrated schools.   The anti-Catholic "crusade" was extended to attempts by Congress to fund public education, but the effort died in the 1880s.

2869.   McLaughlin, Tom L.   "Grass-Roots Toward Black Rights in Twelve Nonslave-holding States, 1846-1869."   *Mid-America* 56 (July 1974): 175-181. McLaughlin studies referendum in New York, Connecticut, Ohio, Indiana, Illinois, Michigan, Wisconsin, Minnesota, Iowa, Kansas, Colorado, and Oregon regarding black suffrage and immigration.   The evidence from the study could be useful in measuring Northern support for black suffrage during Reconstruction.   He finds that prior to the Civil War public opinion was generally against the blacks, but Democrats were strongly against reform compared with Whigs and Republicans.   By 1860 the consensus was shifting closer to support for reform, particularly among Whigs and Republicans.

2870.   Mirak, Robert. "John Quincy Adams, Jr. and the Reconstruction Crisis." *New England Quarterly* 35 (June 1962): 187-202.   Adams, the grandson of President John Quincy Adams, won election to the Massachusetts House of Representatives in 1866 as a moderate Republican.   His opposition to Radical policies and his sympathy for President Johnson's interpretation of the constitution led to his move to the Unionists in the fall, 1866 election and eventually to the Democratic Party.   Adams second place showing in the gubernatorial election of 1867 made him a prominent, respected figure in his state and one who upheld his principles against political expediency.

2871.   Mohr, James C. "New York State's Free School Law of 1867: A Chapter in the Reconstruction of the North." *New York Historical Society Quarterly* 53 (July 1969): 230-249. Ills.   Mohr implies a connection between reform of public education finances in New York and the education reforms being implemented in the South and North. Until 1867 the state expected users of public schools to pay a portion of the cost of education. The Free School Law of 1867 eliminated the "rate bill system" under pressure from growing urban areas and replaced it with total state funding paid for with an expanded state income tax that represented the commitment of all citizens to education.

2872.   Mohr, James C. *Radical Republicans and Reform in New York During Reconstruction.* Ithaca: Cornell University Press, 1973. 300p. Bibl.   Mohr views various social, educational, and municipal reforms in New York as illustrative of Reconstruction in the state. Among the reform issues pursued by the Radicals was black suffrage. While suffrage was allowed for blacks who owned at least $250 of property, such a qualification was not applied to whites. In July, 1867 the Radicals proposed an amendment to the state constitution to eliminate such discrimination and to make other reforms, but political maneuvering led to the public's rejection of nondiscriminatory suffrage, and later the legislature also rejected the 15th Amendment. The suffrage issue severely wounded the general reform efforts of the state Radical Republicans. After losses in the 1867 election, state Republican Party leaders changed the party's course toward a more traditional, Whig image in succeeding years. (See also Mohr's "Civil and Institutional Reform in New York State, 1864-1868: A Radical Reconstruction at Home." Ph.D. Stanford University, 1969. 362p.)

2873.   Mohr, James C. (ed.). *Radical Republicans in the North: State Politics During Reconstruction.* Baltimore: Johns Hopkins University, 1976. 200p. Bibl. Articles by different authors cover Massachusetts, Pennsylvania, New York, Ohio, Illinois, Michigan, Wisconsin, and Iowa. Only the articles on Iowa, Ohio, and Illinois focus primarily on the impact of the Reconstruction of the South on those states. (See # 2835, 2849, 2895).

2874.   Montgomery, David. "Radical Republicanism in Pennsylvania, 1866-1873." *Pennsylvania Magazine of History and Biography* 85 (October 1961): 439-457.   Montgomery disagrees with the Beale theory that Radical Republicans were hypocritical about applying Reconstruction reforms to the North because of the influence of Northeastern business interests (see # 176, 439). Using Pennsylvania Radicals as a case study, he explains that the Radicals supported civil rights reforms at home to enhance democracy, and they were allied ideologically and economically with entrepreneurs, farmers, laborers, and small manufacturers. Radical influence began to crumble in the 1870s with the influence of Liberal Republicans and the depression of 1873.

2875. Moody, William P. "The Civil War and Reconstruction in California Politics." Ph.D. University of California at Los Angeles, 1950. 421p.

2876. Murphy, Lawrence R. "Reconstruction in New Mexico." *New Mexico Historical Review* 43 (April 1968): 99-115. Murphy examines the impact of the Reconstruction legislation in the territory of New Mexico. The U.S. Army was called on to eliminate Indian slavery and debt peonage, but local opposition and lack of command and coordination between Army officials and the government in Washington stymied reforms.

2877. Mushkat, Jerome. *The Reconstruction of the New York Democracy, 1861-1874.* Rutherford: Fairleigh Dickinson University Press, 1981. 328p. Bibl. Mushkat believes that the major themes of Democratic Party politics during the Civil War and Reconstruction were not obstructionism, racism, expediency, and ultra-conservatism. These characteristics existed, but the party should be viewed more clearly as one that maintained its traditional ideology of governmental and individual rights to emerge "reconstructed" in the mid-1870s with a vision for the future. Mushkat recognizes that Democratic ideology did not include equality of civil rights for blacks and that this revealed the inconsistency of its ideals versus political expediency. The New York Democratic Party serves as a good example of what happened to the Democratic Party in other Northern states. New York state politics, with its dichotomy between New York City and the rest of the state, is the context in which Democrats decided political action regarding wartime and postwar issues.

2878. Nelsen, Anne Kusener. "The North, the South, and the Republican Ideology: The Northeastern Republican Press, 1865-1869." Ph.D. Vanderbilt University, 1977. 285p.

2879. Oder, Broeck N. "Andrew Johnson and the 1866 Illinois Election." *Journal of the Illinois State Historical Society* 73 (Autumn 1980): 189-200. Ports. Ills. Tbls. The Illinois counties that President Johnson visited during his campaign tour prior to the 1866 congressional elections tended to have an increase in voter turnout compared with the 1864 elections, but the Republicans outvoted the Democrats in most cases. Oder attributes this to a poor turnout among Democratic voters who were disappointed with the President's policies. Also, an important factor for the Republicans was the candidacy of war hero John A. Logan. In general, Johnson did not have a great impact on the election in Illinois.

2880.   Peterson, Kent Allan. "New Jersey Politics and National Policy-Making, 1865-1868." Ph.D. Princeton University, 1970. 373p.

2881.   Poole, William Joseph, Jr. "Race and the Chicago Press, 1850-1877." Ph.D. University of Chicago, 1980. 526p.

2882.   Potts, James B. "Nebraska Statehood and Reconstruction." *Nebraska History* 69 (Summer 1978): 73-83. Ills. Map. Ports.   Radical Republicans in Congress agreed to Nebraska's proposal for statehood in 1867 only after the state legislature changed the constitution to eliminate restrictions on civil rights based on race or color. The "Edmunds Amendment," proposed by George Edmunds of Vermont, made this requirement and established a precedent for the Southern states and national Reconstruction. The events leading to Nebraska statehood also represent the growing solidification of Republican congressional power over frontier regions under federal jurisdiction.

2883.   Quigley, David Vincent. "Reconstructing Democracy: Politics and Ideas in New York City, 1865-1880." Ph.D. New York University, 1997. 352p.

2884.   Quill, James Michael. "Northern Public Opinion and Reconstruction, April to December, 1865." Ph.D. University of Notre Dame, 1973. 272p.

2885.   Rawley, James A. "Senator Morgan and Reconstruction." *New York History* 34 (January 1939): 27-53.   Sen. Edwin Morgan was a wealthy businessman and former governor who became a Republican U.S. senator from New York in 1863. His support for Lincoln and Johnson led to his reputation as a conservative, but after sustaining Johnson's veto of the Freedmen's Bureau Bill in 1866, his position shifted towards the Radicals. He decided that his political survival depended on his support for his party's Reconstruction program, thus leading to his positive votes for the Civil Rights Bill of 1866, the 14th Amendment, and Johnson's conviction at the impeachment trial in 1868.

2886.   Russ, William A., Jr. "The Influence of the Methodist Press Upon Radical Reconstruction (1865-1868)." *Susquehanna University Studies* (1937): 51-62. The Methodist press served as the voice of the Methodist Church in the North in its complete support for Radical policies. Editors of newspapers, such as the *Western Christian Advocate* and the *Central Christian Advocate*, explained the Methodist position in favor of a just and righteous peace that included equality for blacks. The press consistently criticized President Johnson and belligerent Southern whites. It contributed to Church aid to freedmen and the content of pulpit sermons to build religious institutional pressure for change.

2887.   Sanelli, Thomas A. "The Struggle for Black Suffrage in Pennsylvania, 1838-1870." Ph.D. Temple University, 1978. 336p.

2888.   Sawrey, Robert D. *Dubious Victory: The Reconstruction Debate in Ohio.* Lexington: University of Kentucky Press, 1992. 194p. Bibl. Ills. Map. Ports. Tbls.

From 1865 until about 1870 the Republicans in Ohio held the political advantage in the state, because they focused their competition with Democrats on Reconstruction issues. Only when Ohio politicians and voters believed that it was time to turn toward other issues by the end of the 1860s did the Democrats find growing support in state elections. Important Ohio Republicans during the period included U.S. Senators John A. Bingham, John Sherman, and Benjamin Franklin Wade, Congressman James A. Garfield, and Gov. Jacob D. Cox.

2889.   Sawrey, Robert D.   "'Give Him the Hot End of the Poker':   Ohio Republicans Reject Johnson's Leadership of Reconstruction." *Civil War History* 33 (June 1987): 155-172.   Ohio Republicans stood by Johnson's Reconstruction policy until they were convinced that his policy was detrimental to national security and fairness to the freedmen. Gov. Jacob D. Cox, a conservative Republican, tried to convince the President to compromise, but Johnson's rejection of key Republican legislation eventually eroded his support in Ohio. In general, Ohio Republicans were less concerned with political and social equality for blacks than with allowing former Confederates to return to political office and the denial of basic civil rights to Southern blacks.

2890.   Sawrey, Robert D.   "Ohio and Reconstruction: The Search for Future Security, 1865-1868." Ph.D. University of Cincinnati, 1979. 271p.

2891.   Sawrey, Robert D.   "Ohioans and the Fourteenth Amendment: Initial Perceptions and Expectations." *Old Northwest* 10 (Winter 1984-1985): 389-407. The election of 1866 in Ohio was strongly influenced by the proposed 14th Amendment. Sawrey reviews the election campaign and concludes that although most Ohioans supported the Republican Party and the amendment, they assumed that the constitutional reform would bring an end to Reconstruction. If the public had perceived the amendment as extending rights to blacks and other minorities, they would have rejected it.   The strength of white supremacy in Ohio was illustrated by the rejection of black suffrage in 1867 and the attempt by Democrats to rescind ratification of the 14th Amendment.

2892.   Silcox, Harry C.   "Nineteenth Century Philadelphia Black Militant: Octavius V. Catto (1839-1871)." *Pensylvania History* 44 (January 1977): 52-76. Port.   Silcox describes Catto's life and work as a teacher and leader for black civil rights in Philadelphia. His murder, and the murder of other blacks, during a riot on October 21, 1871 proved to be a major setback to activities in favor of equal rights in the city.

2893.   Stanley, Amy Dru. "Conjugal Bonds and Wage Labor: Rights of Contract in the Age of Emancipation." *Journal of American History* 75 (September 1988): 471-500. Ills.   Reconstruction was a time of expanding civil rights for blacks and Americans in general, but these rights and the protection of them did not break the traditional marriage bonds that made wives dependent on their husbands. Stanley examines the deficiencies that Northern women endured regarding control of their own labor and the wages that they earned.

2894.   Sutherland, Daniel E.   *The Confederate Carpetbaggers*.   Baton Rouge: Louisiana State University Press, 1988.   360p.   App. Bibl. Ports. Tbls. Confederate carpetbaggers were Southerners who left their homes after the Civil War for a new life in the North. Sutherland analyzes the reasons for this migration and how this group adjusted to the new environment while continuing to maintain an identity with their Southern roots. In general this group provided the North with a link to understanding the South, and their influence quickened national reconciliation through their friendships, business contacts, literary output, and organized ties to their former homeland. Sutherland disputes the notion that white migration ultimately lengthened Reconstruction. The appendix provides a statistical survey of the personal characteristics of Confederate carpetbaggers.

2895.   Swenson, Philip D. "Illinois: Disillusionment with State Activism." In *Radical Republicans in the North: State Politics During Reconstruction.* Edited by James C. Mohr. Baltimore: Johns Hopkins University Press, 1976. Pp. 104-118. Illinois was clearly influenced by the emancipation of the slaves and the movement to provide equal civil rights for all blacks. The state repealed its black code in February, 1865, but it was not until 1870, when the 15th Amendment became law and a new state constitution was written, that race was eliminated as an issue for voting. Reconstruction in Illinois was a time of lost opportunities for state reform, partly because the Republican Party could not reconcile local and national goals.

2896.   Swenson, Philip David. "The Midwest and the Abandonment of Radical Reconstruction, 1864-1877." Ph.D. University of Washington, 1971. 143p.

2897.   Thelen, David P. and Leslie H. Fishel, Jr. "Reconstruction in the North: The *World* Looks at New York's Negroes, March 16, 1867." *New York History* 49 (October 1868): 409-440. Ills.   The authors reprint the results of a survey conducted by the *New York World* that illustrates black society in the city of New York. During the Civil War the *World*, owned by Manton Marable since 1862, expressed only criticism of Radical Republicans and never showed much interest in blacks. Some Republican newspapers interpreted the story as a political move to gain black votes for the Democratic Party. Thelen and Fishel suggest that it was Marable's attempt to show that the condition of blacks in New York was satisfactory and that they did not need extraordinary political support.

2898.   Thornbrough, Emma Lou. *Indiana in the Civil War Era, 1850-1880*. Indianapolis: Indiana Historical Bureau and Indiana Historical Society, 1965. 758p. Bibl. Ills.   Chapter 6 shows how state Democrats were demoralized by the Republican success at branding them as disloyalists and capturing the support of soldiers returning from duty. They also suffered from their support for President Johnson in his struggle with Congress over Reconstruction. The issue of black suffrage dominated state politics with most white citizens rejecting black suffrage and equality, but Republican reluctance on the issue changed as national Reconstruction politics became more heated and Governor Oliver Morton changed his stance to take the side of the Radicals.

2899.   Toppin, Edgar A.   "Negro Emancipation in Historic Retrospect: Ohio. The Negro Suffrage Issue in Postbellum Ohio Politics."   *Journal of Human Relations* 11 (Winter 1963): 232-246.   Toppin emphasizes the importance of the immediate postwar period as a crucial time for the black citizens of Ohio.   The Union victory and the elimination of slavery encouraged proposals for enfranchisement, but Republican timidity in an environment of partisan state politics caused politicians to put off consideration of the issue.   Only after the 15th amendment was assured did the legislature give its grudging approval.

2900.   Ulrich, William John.   "The Northern Military Mind in Regard to Reconstruction, 1865-1872:   The Attitudes of Ten Leading Union Generals." Ph.D. Ohio State University, 1959. 369p.

2901.   Voegeli, V. Jacque.   *Free But Not Equal: The Midwest and the Negro During the Civil War.*   Chicago: University of Chicago Press, 1970, c1967.   215p. Bibl.   Voegli provides background to race relations in Ohio, Indiana, Illinois, Iowa, Michigan, Wisconsin, and Minnesota.   He examines the responses of midwestern U.S. senators and congressmen in the national debates about emancipation, black emigration, treatment of runaway slaves by the U.S. Army, and Reconstruction plans.   Republicans held a wide variety of sympathies toward reform.   By the end of the war Midwesterners had broadly accepted emancipation but retained feelings of white supremacy and a strong reluctance to grant equal civil rights to blacks.

2902.   Ware, Edith Ellen.   "Political Opinion in Massachusetts during Civil War and Reconstruction."   Ph.D.   Columbia University, 1916.   215p.   (*Columbia University Studies* 74, no. 2)

2903.   Williams, Helen J. and Harry Williams.   "Wisconsin Republicans and Reconstruction, 1865-1870."   *Wisconsin Magazine of History* 23 (1939): 17-39. Wisconsin Republicans and voters in general were only mildly interested in the South after the Civil War, but they adhered to the national party policies in Reconstruction and supported the Republican Party.   Support for Republicans in elections and Republican policies maintained antislavery sentiment, abhorrence for the stigma of copperheadism, and most of all, the willingness of Republicans in Congress to fund state internal improvements that were considered important for development.

2904.   Wubbens, Hubert H.   "The Uncertain Trumpet: Iowa Republicans and Black Suffrage, 1860-1868."   *Annals of Iowa* 47 (1984): 409-429.   Wubbens traces the background of Iowa's acceptance of black suffrage with emphasis on political activities and public opinion as expressed in newspapers.   Iowa consistently rejected black suffrage until state Republicans formally supported it at their convention in June, 1865.   During the three years required to change the Iowa constitution, Democrats attempted unsuccessfully to turn the issue against the Republicans, but the Republican victories in the 1865 and 1866 state elections and their subdued support for suffrage led to voter acceptance of reform in 1868.

Wubbens concludes that for many Republicans the principle of justice for black citizens was important.

Appendix: Federal Constitutional Amendments, Acts and Cases Cited

Federal Constitutional Amendments

Thirteenth Amendment
Passed by Congress January 31, 1865; ratified December 18, 1865

Section 1.
Neither slavery nor involuntary servitude, except as a punishment for crime whereof the party shall have been duly convicted, shall exist within the United States, or any place subject to their jurisdiction.

Section 2.
Congress shall have power to enforce this article by appropriate legislation.

Fourteenth Amendment
Passed by Congress June 13, 1866; ratified July 28, 1868

Section 1.
All persons born or naturalized in the United States, and subject to the jurisdiction thereof, are citizens of the United States and of the State wherein they reside. No State shall make or enforce any law which shall abridge the privileges or immunities of citizens of the United States; nor shall any State deprive any person of life, liberty, or property, without due process of law; nor to deny to any person within its jurisdiction the equal protection of the laws.

Section 2.
Representatives shall be apportioned among the several States according to their respective numbers, counting the whole number of persons in each State, excluding Indians not taxed. But when the right to vote at any election for the

choice of Electors for President and Vice-President of the United States, Representatives in Congress, the executive and judicial officers of a State, or the members of the Legislature thereof, is denied to any of the male inhabitants of such State, being twenty-one years of age, and citizens of the United States, or in any way abridged, except for participation in rebellion, or other crime, the basis of representation therein shall be reduced in the proportion which the number of such male citizens shall bear to the whole number of male citizens twenty-one years of age in such State.

Section 3.

No person shall be a Senator or Representative in Congress, or Elector of President and Vice-President, or hold any office, civil or military, under the United States, or under any State, who, having previously taken an oath, as a member of Congress, or as an officer of the United States, or as a member of any State Legislature, or as an executive or judicial officer of any State, to support the Constitution of the United States, shall have engaged in insurrection or rebellion against the same, or given aid or comfort to the enemies thereof. But Congress may by a vote of two-thirds of each House, remove such disability.

Section 4.

The validity of the public debt of the United States, authorized by law, including debts incurred for payment of pensions and bounties for services in suppressing insurrection or rebellion, shall not be questioned. But neither the United States nor any State shall assume or pay any debt or obligation incurred in aid of insurrection or rebellion against the United States, or any claim for the loss or emancipation of any slave; but all such debts, obligations and claims shall be held illegal and void.

Section 5.

The Congress shall have the power to enforce, by appropriate legislation, the provisions of this article.

Fifteenth Amendment

Passed by Congress February 26, 1869; ratified March 30, 1870

Section 1.

The right of citizens of the United States to vote shall not be denied or abridged by the United States or by any State on account of race, color, or previous condition of servitude.

Section 2.

The Congress shall have the power to enforce this article by appropriate legislation.

Congressional Acts

Note: All citations to "Stat." refer to the volume and first page of the act in
   United States Statutes at Large.

Amnesty Act of 1872
   May 22, 1872, 17 Stat. 142
   (*Related acts*: December 8, 1863, 13 Stat. 737; May 29, 1865, 13 Stat. 758; April
   4, 1868, 15 Stat. 702; December 25, 1868, 15 Stat. 711)
Attorney's Test Oath Act
   January 24, 1865, 13 Stat. 424
Bankruptcy Act of 1867
   March 3, 1867, 14 Stat. 517
Captured and Abandoned Property Act
   March 3, 1863, 12 Stat. 820
Civil Rights Acts
   April 9, 1866, 14 Stat. 27
   March 1, 1875, 18 Stat. 335
Confiscation Acts
   August 6, 1861, 12 Stat. 319
   July 17, 1862, 12 Stat. 589
Electoral Commission Act
   January 29, 1877, 19 Stat. 227
   (*Related act*: March 3, 1877 19 Stat. 402)
Enforcement Acts
   May 31, 1870, 16 Stat. 140
   February 28, 1871, 16 Stat. 433
   April 20, 1871, 17 Stat. 13 (*Ku Klux Klan Act*)
Freedmen's Bureau Acts
   March 3, 1865, 13 Stat. 507
   July 25, 1868, 15 Stat. 193
Habeas Corpus Act of 1867
   May 5, 1867, 14 Stat. 385
Judiciary Acts
   July 23, 1866, 14 Stat. 209 (*Judicial Reform Act*)
   March 27, 1868, 15 Stat. 44
   March 3, 1875, 18 Stat. 470 (*Jurisdiction Act*)
Morrill Act
   July 2, 1862, 12 Stat. 503
Reconstruction Acts
   March 2, 1867, 14 Stat. 428
   March 23, 1867, 15 Stat. 2
   July 9, 1867, 15 Stat. 14
   (*Related acts*: March 11, 1868, 15 Stat. 41; December 11, 1869, 16 Stat. 59)

Southern Homestead Act
    June 21, 1866, 14 Stat. 66
Tenure of Office Act
    March 2, 1867, 14 Stat. 430
    April 5, 1869, 16 Stat. 6

Federal Court Cases

Note: Case citations to "U.S." refer to the volume and first page of court decisions in *United State Reports* (Washington, D.C.: G.P.O, 1884-) for cases decided since 1875. References to "Wallace" refer to the volume and first page of court decisions in an earlier, differently numbered edition of the reports compiled by John William Wallace (v. 68-90 using U.S. volume scheme for the years 1863-1874). Some cases include both citations, but both refer to the same physical item. The reference sources consulted for brief case descriptions were *The Oxford Guide to United States Supreme Court Decisions*, edited by Kermit L. Hall et.al., New York: Oxford University Press, 1999; *The Oxford Companion to the Supreme Court of the United States*, edited by Kermit L. Hall, New York: Oxford University Press, 1992; and *History of the Supreme Court of the United States, Vol. 6-7, Reconstruction and Reunion 1864-1888, Part 1-2*, by Charles Fairman, New York: Macmillan, 1971, 1987.

Blyew v. U.S.
    Decided April 1, 1872, 13 Wallace 583; 80 U.S. 583: The Court ruled that it did not have jurisdiction according to the Civil Rights Act of 1866 in the case of murders committed by 2 white men against a black family. The ruling called into question federal power to protect the rights of black citizens. Congress responded to such cases with additional legislation, including the Enforcement Acts of 1870-1871 and the Civil Rights Act of 1875. A parallel case on this point was Kennard v. U.S. (80 U.S. 590-600).
Brown v. Board of Education
    Decided May 17, 1954, 347 U.S. 483; April 11, 1955; 349 U.S. 294: Court ruled that the "separate but equal" doctrine decided in Plessy v. Ferguson in 1896 was unconstitutional
Civil Rights Cases
    Decided October 15, 1883, 109 U.S. 3: Court found unconstitutional key provisions of the Civil Rights Act of 1875 and weakened congressional efforts to legislate civil rights protection for blacks.
Cummings v. Georgia (Richland County Board of Education)
    Decided December 18, 1899, 175 U.S. 528: Court refused to enforce equal rights in the "separate but equal" doctrine it decided in Plessy v. Ferguson in 1896
Cummings v. Missouri
    Decided January 14, 1867, 4 Wallace 277; 71 U.S. 277: Court ruled in this case, and in the related *Ex parte* Garland (71 U.S. 333), against retroactive loyalty oaths established during the Civil War.
Ex parte Garland   *See under Cummings v. Missouri*

Ex parte McCardle
   Decided April 12, 1869, 74 U.S. 506: Called into question congressional authority over federal court jurisdiction; the Court dismissed the case after Congress, fearing a court ruling against the Reconstruction Acts, repealed the section of the *Habeas Corpus* Act (1867) that allowed appeals to the Supreme Court. The court thus accepted congressional power to regulate court jurisdiction. The Court ruled in U.S. v. Klein in 1872 (4 Wallace 382; 80 U.S. 128) against congressional authority to restrict the Court's jurisdiction in a case involving a claimant's right to property based on a presidential pardon.

Ex parte Merryman 17 Fed Cases 44 (case #9487)
   Decided in Maryland circuit by Justice Roger B. Taney on May 28, 1861. Taney ruled that Lincoln did not have the power to carry out arrests and deny *habeas corpus* to citizens deemed disloyal because only Congress had the authority to declare and wage war, but Lincoln disregarded the ruling as an intrusion into executive power.

Ex parte Milligan
   Decided April 3, 1866, 4 Wallace 2; 71 U.S. 2: Court ruled that civil liberties protected by the constitution were not suspended during wartime; trial of civilians by military courts unconstitutional when civilian courts remained open.

Ex parte Virginia   *See under Straughter v. West Virginia*

Ex parte Yarbrough
   Decided March 3, 1884, 110 U.S. 651: Court ruled in favor of federal authority to protect a person's voting rights against obstruction by a private individual

Ex parte Yerger
   Decided October 25, 1869, 8 Wallace 85; 75 U.S. 85: The court upheld its appellate jurisdiction in the case of a citizen's right to a writ of *habeas corpus*.

Georgia v. Grant, Mead, et. al.   *See under Mississippi v. Johnson*

Georgia v. Stanton   *See under Mississippi v. Johnson*

Hepburn v. Griswold
   Decided February 7, 1870; 8 Wallace 603; 75 U.S. 603: One of the Legal Tender Cases that refer to the federal government's authority to force creditors to accept paper money as payment for debt as stipulated in the Legal Tender Act of 1862. The court ruled that the act was unconstitutional, but the Hepburn ruling was overruled in 1871 in Knox v. Lee and Parker v. Davis (79 U.S. 457) in a case influenced by politics, thus confirming congressional power over the currency.

In Re Turner
   24 Fed.Case 337 (1867): In the Maryland circuit, Justice Chase ruled that the Civil Rights Act of 1866 and the Thirteenth Amendment protected citizens from unlawful private contracts that subjected them to involuntary servitude.

Kennard v. U.S.   *See under Blyew v. U.S.*

Mississippi v. Johnson
   Decided on April 15, 1867, 4 Wallace 475; 71 U.S. 475: The court ruled against an attempt to halt presidential enforcement of the Reconstruction Acts. In a similar case, Georgia v. Stanton (6 Wallace 50, 1867), the court ruled that it had no jurisdiction over political matters raised by Georgia's attempt to stop enforcement of the Reconstruction Acts. Georgia v. Grant, Meade et al. (6

Wallace 241, 1868) was another attack on the constitutionality of the Reconstruction Acts involving the legal mandate requiring the state to fund a new constitutional convention.

Plessy v. Ferguson

Decided May 18, 1896, 163 U.S. 537: The court upheld the constitutionality of separate but equal accommodations for blacks and whites. The court upheld a Louisiana law regarding segregated but equal facilities in the use of railroad cars.

Slaughter-House Cases

Decided April 14, 1873, 16 Wallace 36; 83 U.S. 36: The court weakened the privileges and immunities clause in section 1 of the Fourteenth Amendment when it ruled in favor of Louisiana's efforts to regulate the slaughter-house business in New Orleans. Slaughter-house owners opposed the regulations as a violation of their rights under the due process clause in section 2 of the 14th Amendment. The court decided that a corporate entity could be a "person" as described in the amendment.

Strauder v. West Virginia

Decided March 1, 1880, 100 U.S. 303: The court decided that a West Virginia law that excluded blacks from eligibility for jury selection was unconstitutional under the equal protection clause of the 14th Amendment. The court came to similar conclusions in other cases, including *Ex parte* Virginia, 100 U.S. 39 (1879).

Texas v. White

Decided April 12, 1869, 7 Wallace 700; 74 U.S. 700: The court decided that the suit by the government of Texas to recover securities sold by the state's Confederate government was valid because the Confederate government was illegal and its acts were null and void. The ruling strengthened the Republican Party position that secession was illegal and that the states had never left the Union.

U.S. v. Cruikshank

Decided March 27, 1876, 92 U.S. 542: The court decided that the federal government lacked the power to indict when there was no clear violation of federal rights. Acts of violence cited in this case - massacre of blacks in Louisiana seeking to vote - are not offenses indictable under the Enforcement Acts and the 14th Amendment. The court ruled that amendment limited states, not individuals, and that the states could prosecute the case to punish offenders. In a similar case in 1883, U.S. v. Harris (106 U.S. 629), the Court struck down the Enforcement Act (Ku Klux Klan Act) of 1871 on the grounds that it could only apply to acts committed by states, not acts done by individuals, who were subject to state prosecution.

U.S. v. Harris   *See under U.S. v. Cruikshank*

U.S. v. Klein   *See under Ex parte McCardle*

U.S. v. Reese

Decided March 27, 1876, (92 U.S. 214): The court ruled that the Enforcement Acts could not be used to enforce voting rights denied on grounds other than those explicitly stated in the 15th Amendment. This ruling made possible future voting rights restrictions not based on race, such as literacy tests.

Author Index

Subject Index

A

A.M.E. Christian Recorder, 1193

Abbott, Lyman, 1036

Abolitionists, 71, 124, 127, 312, 313, 361, 394, 581, 584, 753, 770, 790, 793, 825, 905, 1048, 1774, 2412, 2458, 2472, 2825, 2848, 2861; Anna Elizabeth Dickenson, 910; Southern, 1851

Adams, Charles Francis, 355

Adams, John Quincy, Jr., 2870

Advertiser (Boston, Ma.), 825

Advertiser and Register (Mobile, Al.) 1381

Advertiser and Tribune (Detroit, Mi.), 203

Affirmative Action, 775

Africa, 1702, 2380

African Civilization Society, 1089

African Colonization Movement, 1107

African Methodist Episcopal Church, 1141, 1165, 1181, 1193; Concept of freedom, 1150; Education of freedmen, 1187; Florida, 1577, 1638, 1639; Georgia, 1669, 1702; Mississippi, 2162; North Carolina, 2283; Mission of, 1188; Social services, 1125

African Methodist Episcopal Zion Church, 1141, 1181, 1187; Concept of freedom, 1150; North Carolina, 2283

Agriculture, 106, 831, 840, 944, 1198, 1217, 1253; Alabama, 1351, 1396, 1434; Capitalist development, 1269; Cotton (*See* Cotton); Crop Liens, 1208, 1309, 2537; Development problems, 1243, 1266, 1268, 1273, 1275, 1290, 1293; Economic issues, 830; Education, 1434, 1745; Federal assistance, 1272; Florida, 1976; Georgia, 1728, 1730, 1733, 1749, 1843, 1960, 1966; Grange, 1274; Historiography, 1306; Impact of emancipation, 1265, 1297; Impact of poor health, 1201; Legal issues, 1309, 1313; Louisiana, 1965, 1966, 1971, 1972, 1975, 1976; Mississippi, 2050, 2154; Missouri, 2197; North Carolina, 2210, 2277; Northern investment, 1260; Rice, 1206, 1728, 2226; River levees, 2098; South Carolina, 2415, 2416, 2418, 2421, 2426, 2445; Sugar, 1279, 1965, 1971, 1972, 1976, 1977; Tennessee, 2528, 2537; Texas, 1976, 2582, 2667;

Aiken, S.C., 2469

C

Territories, 1809-1820; International comparisons, 843, 873, 907, 953, 1209, 1217, 1222, 2440; Jamaica, 2440; Kentucky, 1822, 1825, 1846, 1849; Labor issues, 1238; Louisiana, 1982, 2007; Maryland, 2016, 2023, 2028, 2034; Mississippi, 2051, 2079, 2098, 2124, 2128, 2159, 2161, 2171; Missouri, 2179, 2199, 2202; National debate, 898; Northern response to, 903; North Carolina, 2283, 2284; Slave marriages, 2299; South Carolina, 2335, 2336, 2424, 2440, 2448; Southern response to, 857, 858, 890, 891, 903, 907, 1472; Tennessee, 2530, 2536, 2538, 2539, 2540, 2541, 2545; Texas, 2586, 2593, 2600, 2604, 2607, 2619, 2670, 2674, 2681, 2697, 2700; Virginia, 2707, 2757-2759, 2764, 2765, 2769, 2771, 2788, 2790; Washington, D.C., 2796, 2805; West Virginia, 2820
Emancipation Proclamation, 375
Emigration of Confederates, 834, 854, 895, 896, 2544, 2894; from La., 2012; from Ms., 2120
Enforcement Acts (1870-71), p. 559; 387, 655, 666, 679, 692, 698, 699, 709, 720, 788, 789, 1378, 1405, 1534, 2858; Failure of, 948; Federal powers, 813; Florida, 1595, 1598; Lyman Trumbull, 292; Mississippi, 2077, 2109; Relation to Civil Rights Act (1866), 727; South Carolina, 2357, 2400, 2401, 2402; Voting rights, 994
Ensor, Joshua F., 2454
Episcopal Church, 1145, 1160, 1178, 1460; Black rejection of, 1452; North Carolina, 2283; Virginia, 2774; Racism, 2774
Equal Protection. *See* 14th Amendment
Erskine, John, 943
Etheridge, Henry Emerson, 2507
Eutaw *Whig and Observer*, 1417
Evangelical Christians, 1065

Evarts, William M., 234, 323
Ex parte Garland, p. 560; 663, 734, 774, 2181
Ex parte McCardle, p. 561; 190, 657, 675, 676, 679, 729, 730, 734, 1539, 2078
Ex parte Merryman, p. 561; 276
Ex parte Milligan, p. 561; 190, 657, 663, 679, 690, 726, 730, 734, 752
Ex parte Rodriguez, 2631, 2632, 2654
Ex parte Virginia, p. 561; 739, 745
Ex parte Yarbrough, p. 561; 745
Ex parte Yerger, p. 561; 679, 729, 730
Exeter Plantation (S.C.), 1284

F

Fain, Eliza Rhea Anderson, 1180
Fairchild, Lucius, 2844
Fairman, Charles, 632, 678, 708
Families, *See* Black Family and Social Life
Farmers. *See* White Farmers; White Yeomen; Planters; Black Farmers
Farrar, George Daniel, 2131
Fast, Howard, 1330
Faunsdale Plantation, 1452
Federalism, 184, 635, 637, 641, 645
Fee, John G., 1849, 1851, 1852
Felton, William H., 1679
Fessenden, William Pitt, 212, 238, 273, 713
Ficklen, John Rose, 1913
Field, Stephen J., 663
Fifteenth Amendment, (text, p. 558), 151, 644, 656, 692, 733, 738, 746, 757, 802, 809, 812, 2829; Black activism, 684; Conservative support, 1703; Constitutionality, 759, 768; Court decisions, 929; Enforcement of, 666, 788, 789, 948, 994; Historiography, 693, 769; Holding public office, 628; Literacy tests, 622, 625; Maryland, 2017; New York, 2872; Northern states, 2855; Ohio, 2835, 2899; Origin of, 400, 401, 654,

1138; Educational activities, 1023, 1026, 1029, 1041, 1044, 1050, 1059, 1069, 1077, 1090, 1097, 1099, 1110, 1114, 1376, 1453, 1471, 1475, 1483, 1558, 1561, 1562, 1642, 1644, 1759, 1762, 1773, 1774, 1803, 1848, 1983, 1987, 2001, 2015, 2030, 2031, 2036, 2164, 2185, 2200, 2282, 2432, 2446, 2473, 2555, 2566, 2576, 2679, 2684, 2766, 2777, 2785, 2791, 2817, 2819, 2822; Failure of, 1408; Federal power, 722; Florida, 1570, 1582, 1589, 1602, 1606, 1613, 1617, 1622, 1626, 1642-1645; Georgia, 1669, 1677, 1692, 1731, 1749, 1754, 1757-1762, 1773, 1774, 1788, 1792, 1797, 1801, 1803; Health services, 1054, 1463, 1549, 1792, 1850, 1996, 2015, 2165; Historiography, 1043, 1062, 1089, 1797; Kentucky, 1077, 1823, 1825, 1838, 1848, 1850, 1854; Labor activities, 1062, 1079, 1196, 1207, 1211, 1228, 1238, 1250, 1376, 1445, 1453, 1543, 1570, 1622, 1626, 1749, 1754, 1758, 2015, 2153, 2320, 2473, 2530, 2639, 2674, 2678, 2679; Land distribution, 1196, 1220, 1235, 1254, 1731, 1758, 2015, 2152; Legal services, 1788, 2028; Louisiana, 1861, 1869, 1932, 1983, 1987, 1988, 1994, 1996, 2001, 2015; Maryland, 2030, 2031, 2035, 2036; Mississippi, 2041, 2042, 2047, 2053, 2060, 2062, 2106, 2110, 2114, 2143, 2145, 2152, 2153, 2160, 2164, 2165; Missouri, 1077, 2185, 2200; North Carolina, 2282, 2289, 2294, 2304, 2311, 2312, 2319, 2320, 2321; Political activities, 1376, 1387, 1433, 1606, 1613, 1861, 2304, 2678; Race relations, 1082; Racism, 2153; Relief aid, 1096, 1453, 1472, 2311, 2473, 2679; Reports of violence, 824; Segregation, 874; Social welfare, 1041, 1060, 1557, 1564, 2451, 2675, 2819; South

Carolina, 2355, 2378, 2380, 2406, 2426-2428, 243-2434, 2439, 2445, 2446, 2451, 2467, 2473; Tennessee, 2516, 2530, 2545, 2548, 2555, 2557, 2559, 2566-2568, 2576, 2579; Texas, 2580, 2602, 2604, 2612, 2639, 2642, 2670, 2674, 2675, 2678, 2679, 2680, 2684-2688, 2690-2693, 2695, 2696, 2698, 2700; Virginia, 1077, 2728-2730, 2766-2768, 2771, 2776, 2777, 2783, 2785-2787, 2790, 2791; Washington, D.C., 2797; West Virginia, 1077, 2817, 2818, 2819, 2822; White southern response, 926, 2431

Freedmen's Bureau Act (1865), p. 559; 178; Bill passage, 221, 292
Freedmen's Bureau Act (1866): Bill passage, 220, 494, 767, 2885; Johnson's veto, 455
Freedmen's Savings Bank, 14, 15, 1221, 1227, 1252, 1443; Arkansas, 1542; Documents, 1300; Tennessee, 2564
Freedmen's Union Commission in New York, 1642
Friends. *See* Quakers
Friends' Association of Philadelphia and Its Vicinity for the Relief of Colored Freedmen, 1115, 2323, 2785, 2786
Futch, Robert W., 1893
Fyall, F. H., 1723

G

Gaines, Matthew, 2597, 2622, 2637
Gainesville, Fl., 1058, 1632, 1642
Galaxy, 404
Gale, Thomas, 2154
Galveston, Tx., 2667
Gamble, Hamilton R., 2179
Gannett, William C., 2423
Gardner, Anna, 1108, 2793
Gardner, Samuel, 1387
Garfield, James A., 2888; Correspondence from N.C., 2262
Garland, Augustus Hill, 1489, 1502

Higbee, Edwin, 1724
Higby, Lewis J., 1255
Higgs, A. F., 2819
Hill, Benjamin H., 216, 839, 1283, 1699, 1703, 1763; Critique of reconstruction, 1685
Hill, Joseph B. F., 1399
Hill, Joshua, 1693, 1707
Historiography, 20, 35, 36, 37, 46, 48, 51, 54, 64, 69, 72, 74-78, 85, 88, 90, 93, 95, 101, 129, 131, 163, 166, 219, 283, 347, 348, 494, 847; 1960s-1980s, 154; 19th Century-1930s, 153; 20th Century, 49, 122; Biases of historians, 148, 149, 151, 159, 161, 2048; Prior to 1960, 148; Role of Blacks, 97; Since 1860s, 86; *See also historiography under topics*
Hoag, J. Murray, 1773
Holden, William W., 2215, 2223, 2228, 2229, 2235-2237, 2240, 2251, 2253, 2265, 2281, 2303
Holden-Kirk War. *See* Holden, William W.
Holmes, G. W., 1618
Holmes, Mary Jane, 1315
Holsey, Lucius Henry, 1180, 1799
Home Mission Society of the Baptist Church, 1080, 2565
Homer, Winslow, 904
Homestead Act (1866), 1443
Hopkins, J., 1509
Hopkins, J. H., 1160
Hopkins, Johns, 207
Hopkins, Marcus Sterling, 2787
Horton, Gustavus, 1355
Hough, Warwick, 2203
Houston, George Smith, 1427
Houston, Tx., 2638; Black leadership, 2636
Houzeau de la Haie, Jean Charles, 1986
Howard University, 1026, 1068
Howard, Jacob, 648
Howard, James H., 1494

Howard, Oliver O., 41, 1066, 1083, 1091; Depictions of, 1043
Hubbs, Isaac G., 1983
Huckleberry Finn, 1331
Hughes, Robert W., 2708
Humphreys, Benjamin Grubb, 2119, 2136
Hunnicutt, John L., 1388
Huntington, C. P., 1295
Hyman, John Adams, 311, 2267

I

Illinois, 2846, 2827, 2869, 2873, 2895, 2901; 14th Amendment, 650; Election of 1866, 2879; Newspapers, 2881
Illinois Central Railroad, 1287
Impeachment of Andrew Johnson, 63, 306, 342, 500, 512-551; Benjamin F. Butler, 318, 387, 405; Benjamin F. Wade, 389; Civil rights, 551; Constitutional issues, 523, 541; Edwin Morgan, 2885; Foreign observation, 544; George Boutwell, 192, 522; Historiography, 72, 540, 545; Indiana, 279; Iowa delegation, 547; James A. Ashby, 264; John Sherman, 519; Liberal view, 374; Michigan opinions, 531; Military influence, 466, 475; Press opinion, 513, 531, 538, 542; Prosecution, 514; Republican failure, 549; Republican reluctance, 516; Republicans against, 238, 273, 512, 513, 517, 526, 527, 530; Salmon P. Chase, 190, 539; Thaddeus Stevens, 328b, William M. Evarts, 234
Imperialism, 1330
In Re Turner, p. 561; 711
Independent Monitor (Tuscaloosa, Al.), 1419, 1422
Indiana, 2869, 2898, 2901; Response to Reconstruction, 279
Indians of North America: North Carolina, 2227; New Mexico, 2876; Texas, 2582, 2586; *See also* Cherokee Nation, Chickasaw Nation,

Choctaw Nation, Creek Nation, Five Nations, Lumbee Indians, Seminole Nation
Industrialists, Northern, 64, 89, 91, 221, 224; Relations with Republicans, 290
Industrialization, 830, 831, 840, 1294; Mississippi, 2147; North Carolina, 2211; Racial issues, 1216; Tennessee, 2518, 2528; Texas, 2668;
Ingrahm, James H., 1940
International Workingmen's Association, 2668
The Invisible Empire, 1335, 1342
Iowa, 2829, 2849, 2850, 2869, 2873, 2901, 2904
Iron Manufacturing, 1430, 1440, 1441, 1447, 2533
Isbelle, Robert H., 1940

J

Jackson, Ms., 2172
Jacksonianism, 451, 457
Jacksonville, Fl., 1644
Jacob, John J., 2808
Jacobs, Harriet, 1168
Jacobs, Louisa, 1168
James, Horace, 2320
Jay, John, 207
Jenkins, Charles Jones, 1667
Jenks, Jeremiah W., 1336
Jenks, Lorenzo B., 1893
Jewell, Edwin, 1893
Jewell, Frederick, 1893
Jewett, Horace, 2679
Jews, 2542
Jim Crow. *See* Segregation
John F. Slater Fund, 1044, 1069
Johnson, Andrew, 152, 171, 317, 386; Amnesty and Pardon, 230, 1517; Annual message (1865), 457; Assessment of, 58, 67, 98, 144, 156, 445, 446, 451, 460, 463, 464, 467, 468, 471, 473, 478, 479, 480, 492, 493, 495, 496, 506, 511, 1528, 2081, 2522; Bibliography, 477; Cabinet,

175, 190, 193, 208, 234, 251, 265, 353, 358, 384, 398, 403, 474, 1836; Carl Schurz, 354, 355; Civil rights, 453, 1091; Compared with Lincoln, 413, 421, 423, 428, 429, 432, 437, 446, 497; Confiscated land, 1605; Constitutional stand, 459; Democratic support, 244; Documents, 5, 10, 461, 503; Election campaign (1866), 449, 454, 469, 488-491, 498, 2879; Encouraging southern conservatives, 1368; Historiography, 450, 451, 465, 478, 482, 485; Impeachment (*See* Impeachment of Andrew Johnson); Tennessee, 2483, 2493, 2508, 2509, 2512, 2513; Jefferson Davis, 172; Letter from Wade Hampton, 2354; Mexican views, 498; Military and politics, 936; Military governor, 453; National Unionists, 509, 510; Nationalism, 484; North Carolina correspondence, 2245; Opinion of Colorado, 2831; Press Opinion, 435, 436, 2831; Protestant clergy, 448; Racial attitudes, 118, 220, 444, 551; Reconstruction Plan, 118, 265, 331, 336, , 367, 404, 432, 437, 443, 447, 462, 464, 481, 486, 501, 508, 832, 1868, 2128, 2344; Rejection Ohio, 2889; Relations with Britain, 458; Relations with Congress, 135, 170, 187, 192, 220, 438, 439, 452, 459, 462, 470, 475, 476, 481, 483, 486, 494, 500, 502, 505, 507, 2885; Relations with Grant, 570; Relations with military, 474, 475, 570; Rhetorical style, 491; Salmon P. Chase, 190, 356; Suffrage, 499; Veto messages, 455, 487; View of Southern elite, 505; View of the South, 484; *See also* Impeachment of Andrew Johnson
Johnson, Herschel V., 1686
Johnson, James, 1667, 1712
Johnson, James M., 1504
Johnson, Reverdy, 378

O

R

Race Relations. *See* Civil Rights and Equality

Racial Equality. *See* Civil Rights and Equality

Railroads, 679, 830; Alabama, 1349, 1386, 1432, 1436, 1442; Arkansas, 1205; Cotton transport, 1298; Expansion of, 1205, 1249; Federal assistance, 1204; Florida, 1620, 1623, 2276; Georgia, 1732, 1739, 1744, 1746, 1747, 1804; Kansas., 1205; Kentucky, 1841; Local support of, 1289, 1432, 1841; Louisiana, 1205, 1251; Merchant development, 1439; Missouri, 1205, 2191, 2192; North Carolina, 2276, 2280, 2281; Northern investment in, 1286, 1288, 1295; Panic of 1873, 1288; Postwar conditions, 893; Restoration and expansion, 1219, 1251, 1287, 1289, 1386, 1436, 1442; State assistance, 1230; Tennessee, 2518; Texas, 1205, 2582, 2595, 2596, 2628, 2667, 2668; Virginia, 2752;

Rainey, Joseph H., 210, 311, 2374

Raleigh, N.C., 876, 984, 1102

Raleigh Standard (Raleigh, N.C.), 2229, 2236

Randall, John, 1893

Randall, Samuel J., 266

Randolf, William M., 1952

Randolph, Ryland, 1367, 1419

Ransier, Alonzo J., 210, 311

Rape, 1129, 1175, 2298, 2300

Rapier, James T., 311, 1354, 1372, 1373, 1402, 1403, 1404, 1446

Ravenel, Henry William, 2437

Ray, John, 1893

Raymond, Henry J., 227, 470

Reagan, John H., 879, 938

Reconciliation, 235, 292, 365, 581, 1837, 2322, 2894; Fiction, 1315

Reconstruction, 114, 141, 158, 842; Abandonment of, 2896; Assessment

of, 492; Black activism, 1241; Business interests, 214; Collapse of, 81; Collected articles, 866; Compromise, 180; Conservative Reform, 123, 634, 636, 638, 668, 710, 743, 790, 812; Constitutional issues, 671; Continuity, 110, 142; Counterfactual study, 832; Economic exploitation of South, 1233; Economic factors, 214; Enforcement of, 136, 137, 1378; Failure of, 112, 113, 134, 136, 137, 152, 165, 167, 191, 250, 314, 508, 553, 568, 638, 831, 853, 869, 889, 905, 979, 980, 1152, 1860, 1927; Federal court expansion, 700; Federal power, 672, 677, 684, 709, 710, 718, 722, 745; Fiction, 1315; Germany and U.S. compared, 82; Historiography, 833, 862, 905; Illustrated history, 132; Impact of, 853, 865, 870; International comparisons, 165; Legacy, 809; Moral tone, 1163; Myths, 1316, 1321; National movement, 61; Nationalism, 128, 141, 164, 988, 1021; Northern opinion, 200, 290, 336, 2884; Progress, 77, 78, 149, 151, 840, 917; Reform, 109, 139, 142, 635; Resistance to, 808; Revolution, 50, 54, 62, 77, 89, 110, 126, 164, 167, 309, 361, 634, 652, 672, 718, 883, 1271; Social consensus, 992; Southern politics (1865), 924; Southern rejection, 931; Southern response to, 827, 828, 855, 878, 988, 998; Tragedy of, 58, 80, 102, 103, 104, 105, 155, 156, 511, 1194, 1328, 1351; Wade-Davis Bill, 179; War, 494

Reconstruction Acts (1867), p. 559; 180, 229, 644; Black activism, 1401; Disenfranchisement, 431; Enforcement of, 758, 1608; Impact on free blacks (prewar), 2011; Louisiana, 1877; Military influence, 474; Ohio,

V

W

About the Compiler

DAVID A. LINCOVE is Associate Professor and Librarian for history, political science, and philosophy at Ohio State University Libraries in Columbus. His previous publications include *The Anglo-American Relationship: An Annotated Bibliography of Scholarship, 1945–1985* (Greenwood, 1988), which was selected as a *Choice* Outstanding Academic Book.

ISBN 0-313-29199-3

90000>

EAN

9 780313 291999

HARDCOVER BAR CODE